"As a stimulating overview of the multidimensional present state of the field, the *Companion* has no peer."
CHOICE

"If you want to understand how cultures come into being, endure, and change, [the editors] imply, then you need to come to terms with the rich and often surprising history of the book . . . . Eliot and Rose have done a fine job. Their volume can be heartily recommended as the best available starting point for any historian interested in learning about this enterprise . . . the *Companion* does not restrict itself to chronicling the development of the book itself. It also devotes attention to regimes of regulation and jurisdiction – censorship, intellectual property, and the like – and to systems of storage and taxonomy-libraries and bibliography."
Adrian Johns, Technology and Culture

"A valuable resource. Academic libraries with any kind of interest in the history of the book or the history of publishing will want this *Companion* on their shelves."
Publishing Research Quarterly

"An exceptional resource for anyone working in fields such as literature, history, cultural studies or media studies – to name a few. Drawing on a large group of experts, Simon Eliot and Jonathan Rose have compiled a selection of essays that guide readers through many episodes in the long history of books, both inside and outside the Western tradition . . . *A Companion to the History of the Book* is just that – a companion . . . an essential text for students and scholars from a wide variety of disciplines who are led to ask questions about the commissioning, publication, distribution and consumption of books. This book is a milestone in the history of the book for it makes the first attempt to map the field like no other book before it."
Script and Print

"This book serves as a coherent guide to the study of the history of the book. The experts bring the latest research to their work."
Umbrella Magazine

"*A Companion to the History of the Book* provides a wealth of information to readers of all levels in a well laid out and written volume . . . a very solid foundation to the history of the book."
The Bonefolder

Blackwell Companions to Literature and Culture

This series offers comprehensive, newly written surveys of key periods and movements and certain major authors, in English literary culture and history. Extensive volumes provide new perspectives and positions on contexts and on canonical and post-canonical texts, orientating the beginning student in new fields of study and providing the experienced undergraduate and new graduate with current and new directions, as pioneered and developed by leading scholars in the field.

Published

A COMPANION TO

THE HISTORY OF THE BOOK

EDITED BY

SIMON ELIOT AND JONATHAN ROSE

WILEY-BLACKWELL

A John Wiley & Sons, Ltd., Publication

This paperback edition first published 2009
© 2009 Blackwell Publishing Ltd except for editorial material and organization © 2007 by Simon Eliot and Jonathan Rose

Edition history: Blackwell Publishing Ltd (hardback, 2007)

Blackwell Publishing was acquired by John Wiley & Sons in February 2007. Blackwell's publishing program has been merged with Wiley's global Scientific, Technical, and Medical business to form Wiley-Blackwell.

Registered Office
John Wiley & Sons Ltd, The Atrium, Southern Gate, Chichester, West Sussex, PO19 8SQ, United Kingdom

Editorial Offices
350 Main Street, Malden, MA 02148-5020, USA
9600 Garsington Road, Oxford, OX4 2DQ, UK
The Atrium, Southern Gate, Chichester, West Sussex, PO19 8SQ, UK

For details of our global editorial offices, for customer services, and for information about how to apply for permission to reuse the copyright material in this book please see our website at www.wiley.com/wiley-blackwell.

The right of Simon Eliot and Jonathan Rose to be identified as the author of the editorial material in this work has been asserted in accordance with the Copyright, Designs and Patents Act 1988.

Library of Congress Cataloging-in-Publication Data

A companion to the history of the book / edited by Simon Eliot and Jonathan Rose.
      p. cm.—(Blackwell companions to literature and culture ; 48)
   Includes bibliographical references and index.
   ISBN 978-1-4051-9278-1 (pbk. : alk. paper)—ISBN 978-1-4051-2765-3 (hardback : alk. paper)
   1. Books—History.   2. Printing—History.   3. Book industries and trade—History.   I. Eliot,
Simon.   II. Rose, Jonathan, 1952–
   Z4.C73 2007
   002.09—dc22

                                            2006102104

A catalogue record for this book is available from the British Library.

Set in 11 on 13pt Garamond
By SNP Best-set Typesetter Ltd., Hong Kong
Printed in Singapore

03   2010

Contents

Illustrations

Notes on Contributors

Michael Albin was an acquisition specialist for Islamic books, most recently as Director of the Library of Congress office in Cairo, Egypt. He is now an independent scholar and teacher of Arabic.

Martin Andrews is a senior lecturer in the Department of Typography and Graphic Communication at the University of Reading, where he teaches the history of printing. He is Deputy Director of the Centre for Ephemera Studies at the university and curator of the department's extensive lettering and printing collections. He is also the author of *The Life and Work of Robert Gibbings* (2003).

Rob Banham is a lecturer in the Department of Typography and Graphic Communication at the University of Reading, where he teaches the history of graphic communication and practical design. He is Chairman of the Friends of St. Bride Library, and edits and designs *The Ephemerist*, the journal of the Ephemera Society.

Megan L. Benton is a fellow of the Humanities Faculty at Pacific Lutheran University. She is the author of *Beauty and the Book: Fine Editions and Cultural Distinction in America* (2000), and co-editor of *Illuminating Letters: Typography and Literary Interpretation* (2001).

Michelle P. Brown, formerly Curator of Illuminated Manuscripts at the British Library, is Professor of Medieval Manuscript Studies at the Institute of English Studies in the School of Advanced Studies, University of London. She is also a lay canon and member of the chapter of St. Paul's Cathedral, London. Her publications include *A Guide to Western Historical Scripts from Antiquity to 1600* (1990), *The Lindisfarne Gospels: Society, Spirituality and the Scribe* (2003), *Painted Labyrinth: The World of the Lindisfarne Gospels* (2004), and *The World of the Luttrell Psalter* (2006).

Marie-Françoise Cachin is Professor Emerita of British Literature and Literary Translation at the University of Paris VII. Her current research and publications concern British publishing in the Victorian period, and she is in charge of a research group working on various aspects of book history in the English-speaking world. She has recently co-edited a special issue of the *Cahiers Charles V* entitled *Histoire(s) de livres* with a preface by Roger Chartier.

Hortensia Calvo has a PhD in Spanish from Yale University (1990) and is currently Doris Stone Director of the Latin American Library at Tulane University. She has published essays on sixteenth- and seventeenth-century Spanish-American chronicles and on the historiography of the early Spanish-American book.

Charles Chadwyck-Healey received an honors degree from Oxford University. In 1973, he founded the Chadwyck-Healey publishing group, which published reprints, microforms, CD-ROMs, and online via the Internet in the humanities and social sciences for libraries all over the world. There were Chadwyck-Healey companies in the United Kingdom, the United States, France, and Spain, and the company was the largest publisher of German literature in electronic form. Now retired, he is a director of openDemocracy.net, writes and takes photographs, and invests in start-up companies, mainly in IT and biotech.

M. T. Clanchy is Professor Emeritus of Medieval History at the Institute of Historical Research, University of London. He is the author of *From Memory to Written Record: England 1066–1307* (2nd edn., 1993) and *Abelard: A Medieval Life* (1997).

Stephen Colclough is a lecturer in nineteenth- and twentieth-century literature at the School of English, University of Wales, Bangor. He has published widely on the history of reading and text dissemination and is currently completing a monograph entitled *Consuming Texts: Readers and Reading Communities, 1695–1870*.

Patricia Crain is Associate Professor of English at New York University. She is the author of *The Story of A: The Alphabetization of America from The New England Primer to The Scarlet Letter* (2000).

J. S. Edgren received his PhD in Sinology from the University of Stockholm. After employment at the Royal Library (National Library of Sweden) in Stockholm, he was active in the antiquarian book trade. Since 1991, he has served as Editorial Director of the Chinese Rare Books Project, an online international union catalogue of Chinese rare books, based at Princeton University. He is writing a book on the history of the book in China.

Simon Eliot is Professor of the History of the Book in the Institute of English Studies, part of the School of Advanced Study in the University of London, and Deputy Director of the Centre for Manuscript and Print Studies. He is General Editor of the new multivolume *History of Oxford University Press* and editor of the journal *Publishing History*. His publications include *Some Patterns and Trends in British Publishing, 1800–1919* (1994) and *Literary Cultures and the Material Book* (2007). He was president of the Society for the History of Authorship, Reading and Publishing between 1997 and 2001.

John Feather has been Professor of Library and Information Studies at Loughborough University since 1987. He was educated at Oxford, and was the first Munby Fellow in Bibliography at Cambridge. His writings on book history include *The Provincial Book Trade in Eighteenth-century England* (1985), *Publishing, Piracy and Politics: An Historical Study of Copyright in Britain* (1994), and *A History of British Publishing* (rev. edn., 2006), as well as many articles in *Publishing History* and other journals.

David Finkelstein is Research Professor of Media and Print Culture at Queen Margaret University College in Edinburgh. His publications include *The House of Blackwood: Author–Publisher Relations in the Victorian Era* (2002), and the co-authored *An Introduction to Book History* (2005). He has co-edited *The Nineteenth-century Media and the Construction of Identities* (2000), *The Book History Reader* (rev. edn., 2006), and *The Edinburgh History of the Book in Scotland, 1880–2000* (2007).

David Greetham is Distinguished Professor of English, Interactive Technology and Pedagogy, and Medieval Studies at the City University of New York Graduate Center. He was founder and past president of the interdisciplinary Society for Textual Scholarship and co-editor of its journal, *Text*. He is the author of *Textual Scholarship: An Introduction* (1994), *Textual Transgressions* (1998), *Theories of the Text* (1999), and other works, and wrote the most recent essay on "Textual Scholarship" for the MLA's *Introduction to Scholarship in Modern Literatures and Languages*. He is currently working on copyright theory and practice as it affects textual studies.

Robert A. Gross holds the James L. and Shirley A. Draper Chair of Early American History at the University of Connecticut. A social and cultural historian focusing on eighteenth- and nineteenth-century America, he is the author of *Books and Libraries in Thoreau's Concord* (1988) and *The Minutemen and their World* (25th anniversary edn. 2001). He is a member of the general editorial board of *A History of the Book in America*, sponsored by the American Antiquarian Society, and co-editor with Mary Kelley of the second volume in the series, *An Extensive Republic: Books, Culture, and Society in the New Nation, 1790–1840* (forthcoming).

Deana Heath is a lecturer in South Asian and World History at Trinity College Dublin. She has published a number of articles on censorship, sexuality, and governmentality in India, Australia, and Britain, and is currently working on a book on the governmentalization of the obscene in all three contexts.

Lotte Hellinga was until 1995 a deputy keeper at the British Library. Her publications include *The Fifteenth-century Printing Types of the Low Countries* (1966, jointly with her late husband Wytze Hellinga), *Caxton in Focus* (1982), and, most recently, the "England" volume of the *Catalogue of Books Printed in the XVth Century now in the British Museum* (2007). She edited jointly with J. B. Trapp, *The Cambridge History of the Book in Britain*, volume 3 (1999).

T. H. Howard-Hill, who is editor of the *Papers of the Bibliographical Society of America*, has published nine volumes of the *Index to British Literary Bibliography* (1969–99) and contributed to the forthcoming Edinburgh *History of the Book in Scotland*. His multi-volume *The British Book Trade, 1475–1890: A Bibliography* is expected to be published by the British Library in 2007.

Peter Kornicki is Professor of Japanese History and Bibliography at the University of Cambridge. He is the author of *The Book in Japan: A Cultural History from the Beginnings to the Nineteenth Century* (1998), *Catalogue of the Early Japanese Books in the Russian State Library*, 2 vols. (1999, 2004), and *The Iwakura Embassy, 1871–3*, vol. 4 (2002). He set up and maintains the bilingual Union Catalogue of Early Japanese Books in Europe website, and is currently working on vernacularization and publishing for women in seventeenth-century Japan.

Beth Luey is Director Emerita of the Scholarly Publishing Program at Arizona State University, and an editorial consultant in Fairhaven, Massachusetts. She is the author of several books, including *Handbook for Academic Authors* (4th edn., 2002) and *Revising your Dissertation* (2004). She has served as president of the Association for Documentary Editing and of the Society for the History of Authorship, Reading and Publishing.

Paul Luna is Professor of Typography and Graphic Communication at the University of Reading, where he teaches the practice, theory, and history of the subject. His research centers on the design of complex texts such as dictionaries. While design manager for Oxford University Press, he designed the second edition of the *Oxford English Dictionary*, the *Revised English Bible*, and many trade series. He has recently designed the sixth edition of the *Shorter Oxford English Dictionary*, and published the first serious appraisal of the typographic design of Samuel Johnson's *Dictionary*.

Russell L. Martin III is Director of the DeGolyer Library at Southern Methodist University. He contributed to volume 1 of *A History of the Book in America* (2000) and has published other articles and reviews on bibliographical matters. He is at work on an edition of the poems of Jacob Taylor, compiler of almanacs in eighteenth-century Philadelphia.

Jean-Yves Mollier is Professor of Contemporary History and Director of the Doctoral Program in Cultures, Organizations and Laws at the University of Versailles Saint-

Quentin-en-Yvelines, where he also helped found the Centre d'Histoire Culturelle des Sociétés Contemporaines, which he directed from 1998 to 2005. He specializes in nineteenth-century subjects on which he has published numerous books, including *Louis Hachette (1800–1864), le fondateur d'un empire* (1999) and *La Lecture et ses publics à l'époque contemporaine* (2002).

Angus Phillips is Director of the Oxford International Centre for Publishing Studies and Head of the Publishing Department at Oxford Brookes University. He is a member of the International Advisory Committee for the International Conference on the Book and a member of the editorial advisory board for the *International Journal of the Book*. He has written articles on the Internet, book covers, and the role of the publishing editor. He is the editor, with Bill Cope, of *The Future of the Book in the Digital Age* (2006), and the author, with Giles Clark, of *Inside Book Publishing* (2008).

Eleanor Robson is a university lecturer in the Department of History and Philosophy of Science at the University of Cambridge, and a Fellow of All Souls College, Oxford. A major focus of her research is the social history of literacy and numeracy in ancient Iraq and its neighbors. She is the author of *Mesopotamian Mathematics, 2100–1600 BC* (1999) and co-author, with Jeremy Black, Graham Cunningham, and Gábor Zólyomi, of *The Literature of Ancient Sumer* (2004).

Cornelia Roemer is Director of the Vienna Papyrus Collection and Papyrus Museum in the Austrian National Library. Before joining the team in the library, she was the curator of the Cologne Papyrus Collection and had taught for several years at University College London. Her main interests in papyrology are literary texts and the uses of writing in Greco-Roman Egypt.

Jonathan Rose is Professor of History at Drew University. He was the founding president of the Society for the History of Authorship, Reading and Publishing, and is co-editor of the journal *Book History*. His publications include *British Literary Publishing Houses, 1820–1965* (1991), *The Holocaust and the Book: Destruction and Preservation* (2001), and *The Intellectual Life of the British Working Classes* (2001).

Emile G. L. Schrijver is curator of the Bibliotheca Rosenthaliana, the Hebraica and Judaica special collection at Amsterdam University Library. He is editor-in-chief of the yearbook *Studia Rosenthaliana* and serves on the boards of related national and international institutions. He has published on the history of the Hebrew book in general, and on Hebrew manuscripts in particular. He has catalogued for auctioneers, book dealers, and private collectors, and has contributed to numerous international exhibitions.

David J. Shaw is Secretary of the Consortium of European Research Libraries (CERL) and previously taught French at the University of Kent at Canterbury. He is a former president of the Bibliographical Society and writes particularly on the history of the book in France in the fifteenth and sixteenth centuries.

Graham Shaw is Head of Asia, Pacific and Africa Collections at the British Library. His particular field of research is the history of printing and publishing in South Asia. Apart from many articles on the subject, he has published *Printing in Calcutta to 1800* (1981) and *The South Asia and Burma Retrospective Bibliography (SABREB): Stage 1: 1556–1800* (1987), and was co-compiler of *Publications Proscribed by the Government of India* (1985). Most recently, he has completed a study of censorship in India and its circumvention under the British Raj from the 1920s to the 1940s.

Claire Squires is Senior Lecturer in Publishing in the Oxford International Centre for Publishing Studies at Oxford Brookes University, and Programme Leader for the MA in Publishing. Her publications include *Philip Pullman, Master Storyteller: A Guide to the Worlds of His Dark Materials* (2006) and *Marketing Literature: The Making of Contemporary Writing in Britain* (2007).

Rietje van Vliet writes as a freelance research journalist for various media about higher education in the Netherlands. In 2005, she took her PhD at the University of Leiden for her dissertation "Elie Luzac (1721–1796): Boekverkoper van de Verlichting." She has, among other subjects, published about Dutch hacks, propaganda in the Dutch revolution of 1783–99, and Dutch–German book-trade relations. She is currently working on a research project about the eighteenth-century Amsterdam bookseller Marc-Michel Rey.

James Wald is Associate Professor of History at Hampshire College, where he directs the Center for the Book. He is also a member of the board of the Massachusetts Center for the Book and treasurer of the Society for the History of Authorship, Reading and Publishing.

Rowan Watson is a curator in the National Art Library, part of the Word and Image Department of the Victoria and Albert Museum. He has published works on illuminated manuscripts, and on illustrated and artists' books of the nineteenth and twentieth centuries. He teaches in the History of the Book program at the Institute of English Studies, University of London.

Alexis Weedon is the author of *Victorian Publishing: Book Publishing for the Mass Market 1836–1916* (2003) and co-editor of *Convergence: The International Journal of Research into New Media Technologies*. She is Professor of Publishing Studies and Director of the Research Institute for Media Art and Design at the University of Bedfordshire. Her research interests include the economics of nineteenth- and twentieth-century publishing, the publishing industry and cross-media integration, and online bookselling.

Adriaan van der Weel is Bohn Professor of Recent Dutch Book History at the University of Leiden. His research interests include Anglo-Dutch relations in the field of the book; the production, distribution, and consumption of popular and trivial literature; and digital textual transmission. He edits the yearbook of the Dutch Book Historical Society.

Wayne A. Wiegand is F. William Summers Professor of Library and Information Studies and Professor of American Studies at Florida State University. He is the author of *"An Active Instrument for Propaganda": American Public Libraries during World War I* (1988) and *Irrepressible Reformer: A Biography of Melvil Dewey* (1996). He is co-editor with James P. Danky of *Print Culture in a Diverse America* (1998), with Thomas Augst of *Libraries as Agencies of Culture* (2001), and with Anne Lundin of *Defining Print Culture for Youth: The Cultural Work of Children's Literature* (2003).

Eva Hemmungs Wirtén is an Associate Professor in Comparative Literature at Uppsala University, Sweden, where she held a Swedish Research Council Postdoctoral Research Fellowship between 2002 and 2006. Her most recent book is *No Trespassing: Authorship, Intellectual Property Rights, and the Boundaries of Globalization* (2004).

Introduction

Simon Eliot and Jonathan Rose

The history of the book is a new scholarly adventure, still in its pioneering phase, which offers an innovative approach to studying both history and literature. It is based on two apparently simple premises, which have inspired some strikingly original work in the humanities. The first is that books make history. In *The Printing Press as an Agent of Change* (1979), Elizabeth Eisenstein argued that the invention of print technology made possible the scientific revolution, mobilized the Protestant Reformation, and broadcast the achievements of the Italian Renaissance. Meanwhile, Robert Darnton was making the case that scurrilous underground literature undermined France's *ancien régime* to the point where it collapsed in 1789. They inspired other scholars to pose similar questions about books and historical causation. Did escalating press rhetoric precipitate the French Reign of Terror and the American Civil War? Did *samizdat* literature contribute to the implosion of Soviet communism? Can the arrested development of Middle Eastern print culture, hemmed in by censorship, help to explain problems of modernization in that part of the world? Book historians do not claim that books explain everything, but they do recognize that books are the primary tools that people use to transmit ideas, record memories, create narratives, exercise power, and distribute wealth. (That remained true even in the twentieth century, when cinematic, broadcast, sound recording, and digital media became increasingly pervasive.) Therefore, when we study any literate human society, we must ask what books it produced, where they were distributed, which libraries held them, how they were censored (or smuggled past the censors), where and how they were translated, and who was reading them. We should also be aware that readers can read the same book in a variety of ways, with important consequences: after all, wars have been fought over differing interpretations of scriptures and treaties.

Conversely, books are made by history: that is, they are shaped by economic, political, social, and cultural forces. No book is created solely by its author: printers, publishers, literary agents, editors, designers, and lawyers all play a role in molding the final product. Critics, booksellers, and educational bureaucrats can proclaim a book a classic or consign it to oblivion. And every writer must take into account the demands of the reading public and the laws of literary property.

These issues have engaged a growing body of scholars working in a range of fields: history, literature, librarianship, art, sociology, religion, anthropology. Recently, these scholars have come together to build the apparatus of a new academic discipline of their own, including undergraduate and graduate courses, monographs, textbooks, bibliographies, conferences, and journals. In 1991, they organized the Society for the History of Authorship, Reading and Publishing (SHARP), whose website (www.sharpweb.org) is the most comprehensive and up-to-the-minute source of information about the world of book historians. Academics have worked collectively on multivolume national histories of the book in France, Britain, the United States, Scotland, Ireland, Canada, and Australia. What has been lacking is a wider, more comparative history of the book, surveying all historical periods, distilling the best of recent scholarship. We have designed this volume to fill that gap. Our intended audience includes specialists, students, and lay readers alike – in fact, anyone who needs a broad, general introduction to the whole field of book history and the questions that it addresses.

Book history uses the word "book" in its widest sense, covering virtually any piece of written or printed text that has been multiplied, distributed, or in some way made public. This means that a book historian is interested in graffiti on a wall in Pompeii as well as in a letter by Cicero, in an eighteenth-century German chapbook as well as in Diderot and d'Alembert's *Encyclopédie*, in a catalogue of the Great Exhibition of 1851 as well as in a first edition of *David Copperfield*. Given the discipline's breadth and depth, and in order to make this very rich subject fully accessible, we offer a number of different but complementary ways of approaching it.

Part I, "Methods and Approaches," introduces the reader to a number of techniques used by book historians and allied specialists, ranging from the long-established disciplines of bibliography and textual scholarship to newer, frequently IT-based, approaches such as bibliometrics.

Part II, "The History of the Material Text," offers a chronological survey of the forms and content of books from the third millennium BC to the third millennium AD. It is too easy for us to think of the "book" as always having looked like the volume that we today take off a library shelf or buy in an airport lounge: a "codex" to use the jargon. However, for roughly the first three thousand years of its existence, the "book" would most usually have taken the form of a clay tablet or a roll of papyrus. The section "The World before the Codex" therefore begins with two chapters that study this long and important stage in the evolution of the material text, too often overlooked by those of us brought up on the Western codex. Similarly, and all too frequently, book historians in the West (and by this we mean mostly Europe, North America, and Australasia) devote themselves exclusively to their relatively small part of the world. However, we forget the book beyond these narrow confines at our intellectual peril. The section "The Book beyond the West" therefore has chapters devoted to China, to Japan, Korea, and Vietnam, to South Asia, and to Latin America, which, though it became an extension of Western print culture after the arrival of Europeans in the sixteenth century, had a long and separate textual culture before that event. This section also focuses on two important religious and linguistic traditions of the book that mainly employ non-Roman alphabets: the Hebraic and the Islamic book. The section "The Codex in the West 400–2000" returns to more familiar territory to study the evolution of the codex from the early centuries of the first millennium to the present day.

Part III, "Beyond the Book," moves us away from conventional forms to look at other types of text that are less traditional but no less important: the development of periodicals and periodical publishing; the significance of all sorts of ephemeral printing, and the emergence of new textual technologies from the microform revolution through CD-ROMs to the World Wide Web.

Finally, Part IV, "Issues," discusses broader themes, including the concept of literary property, the relationship between obscenity and censorship, the book as an aesthetic and ritual object, and the nature and function of the library. The *Companion* concludes with an exploration of what the book might become in the future.

A common theme runs through every chapter in this volume: that is, the book has always been inextricably embedded in the material world. Though literary critics and theorists feel able to talk about a text as though it were some disembodied entity, for the book historian the text always takes an embodied form. In entering the world of things, a text becomes an object created out of certain materials and taking characteristic forms (a clay tablet, a papyrus roll, a parchment codex, a printed book on paper, an image on a screen). The manufacturing of a book using these materials is a process through which the nature and cost of the materials, and the strengths and weaknesses of the human beings using them, will influence the product, sometimes to the extent of modifying or significantly changing the original text and thus its meaning.

Embodying the text has two contrary effects. It becomes fixed, unlike most oral performances. It can also be copied, though copying opens up the possibility of variations, intended or accidental. But once written down, even those variations seem to claim an authority through permanence that orality cannot (and probably would not wish to) match. Some texts remain pretty firmly fixed: quite often those that are copied only a very few times or exist in few places, such as the early texts of the Book of the Dead carved in the walls of Egyptian tombs or the Chinese texts inscribed in stone which could be copied by means of a rubbing. Some cultures in India have preserved, through a tradition of very careful copying, a culture of limited textual variation, as have the Jewish and Islamic traditions of meticulous scribal reproduction. But in most other cultures, the more copies, the more variations; the more generations through which a text passes, the more errors, as though book production were some epic game of Chinese whispers (or "telephone" as it is sometimes known) conducted over time and through space.

Distribution is another aspect of the inescapable materiality of books. Until the coming of the railways in the nineteenth century, transport, particularly of vulnerable and often bulky merchandise such as books, was usually slow, difficult, and consequently expensive. Until the arrival of mass literacy and mass production in the nineteenth and twentieth centuries, the number of people who could afford to buy books within a modest ride of the place of production was often too small to represent a profitable market, so books had to travel great distances to sell sufficient copies. It is quite possible, for instance, that the first book printed on movable type in the West, Gutenberg's forty-two-line Bible, would not have sold so well without the easy transport route to other parts of Europe offered by the Rhine. Getting books to their markets, how they are sold when they get there, their place of sale, their price, and the other goods that are sold with them are all material factors that concern our contributors.

For much of the past, many books, unless they were single sheets or small rolls or pamphlets, were relatively expensive. As an alternative to outright purchase, readers often borrowed, rented, or perused reading matter in (for example) bookshops, libraries, and coffee houses. Such different physical circumstances of reading would have influenced to a significant extent what the reader derived from it. In fact, readers, even in the best and most comfortable circumstances, often read and use books in ways unintended by their makers: reading inevitably generates difference, diversity, and dissension. No wonder books, unless their production and distribution are under strict control, have often been regarded as potentially dangerous and in need of control or censorship for religious, political, or moral reasons – or for a mix of the three.

As books spread out, a counter-movement becomes evident. This is the desire to bring copies together: to collect, to compare, to preserve, to edit, to control, to censor. If not quite as early as the earliest books, libraries, in the form of archives that contained mainly bureaucratic records but also preserved versions of myth-based literature, can be found as early as 2250 BC (Casson 2001: 3). But even the grandest and the oldest collections, such as the Alexandrian Library, faltered, declined, and had their collections dispersed. And so the distribution of their books began again.

As we can see from the contents of early Sumerian collections, texts in the past were, as they still are today, overwhelmingly practical and functional. "Literature" tends to come later and always occupies a smaller part of most collections. Indeed, even in nineteenth-century Europe and North America, when literature in general and fiction in particular became so commercially significant, no more than a fraction of all titles was devoted to it. This *Companion* gives due attention to non-fiction publishing, ranging from textbooks to timetables.

Access to books has always been a pressing and difficult matter, and this is why institutional collections in royal palaces, schools, monasteries, great men's houses, universities, and local public libraries have always been so important. But it also explains why, at various stages in history, attempts have been made to make texts cheaper. The introduction of printing in mid-fifteenth-century Europe, and particularly the application of steam power to printing and papermaking in the early nineteenth century, made real mass production possible. There is, however, much earlier evidence for cheap books: the text of a play in classical Athens, a cheap leaf or two from the Book of the Dead in Ptolemaic Egypt, a collection of Martial's poems in imperial Rome. However, much of what was cheapest and most readily available has not survived: as with most historical evidence, it is the best and most valuable that has tended to be preserved. But, by good luck, just occasionally one can perceive – in the dust heaps of Oxyrhynchus, in a poorly copied student text of the late medieval period, in a seventeenth-century news-paper, or a Victorian advertising poster – the remarkable world of cheap and accessible texts that we have mostly lost.

Most forms of text (very special forms, such as Buddhist scriptures, excepted) have a value in history because of their potential to be read or used in some way or other. However important the author, the manufacturer, the distributor, the seller, or the librarian, books would mean little without readers or users of books. Thinking about readers in history raises the difficult problem of how one determines literacy rates in cultures and times remote from our own: what proportion of the population could read or (a very different question) write? Still more challenging is the recovery of the actual experience of past readers: how did they interpret and respond to *The Waste Land*, dime novels, *The Social Contract*, the Qur'ān? In what sources can we find evidence of some-thing so internal and non-material as reading? This may be one of the most intriguing questions that book historians confront, and this *Companion* reports some fascinating answers.

Yet reading is only one of many ways of accessing a text. We should not underesti-mate oral and aural traditions, which did not cease when writing was invented. Right up to the present day, many people have had their first and sometimes only experience of a text by hearing it. The oral delivery of text has a lively history even in the most literate of societies: monks of the Benedictine order listening to readings as they worked, a newspaper being read out in a pub by the most literate member of a group of working men, the enormous success in the past few decades of audio books on cassettes and CDs. Just as writing complemented rather than replaced orality, so too manuscript culture did not vanish when printing arrived. Many collections of high-status verse were circulated in Italy in the sixteenth century and in England in the seventeenth century in manuscript rather than be subject to the vulgar and commercial process of printing. Eighteenth- and nineteenth-century readers often compiled handwritten com-monplace books in which favorite verse and prose would be laboriously copied out to create an individualized anthology of texts. Writing is vital in that frequent dialogue between a published author and a reader (sometimes an exasperated one) which often takes the form of handwritten notes or marks in the margin of a printed text. In addi-tion, such dialogues often provide an invaluable form of evidence for reading experience in the past. This *Companion* recognizes that book history involves a continuous interplay of orality, writing, and print.

The book is a survivor. Over its more than five thousand years of history it has moved from one material form to another and spread to almost all cultures and climes. It has taken on roles and then relinquished them. It has recorded, informed, entertained, provoked, inspired, and outraged. In the past couple of centuries it has been threatened with extinction by the telegraph, by the cinema, by radio, by television, and by com-puters and the Internet. It rarely meets these challenges head on but, like the endlessly protean form that it is, it adapts and reconfigures and comes back in new forms offering new services. The computer may be the book's latest challenger, but go into any book-shop and look at the rows of books devoted to getting the best out of your computer, or its software, or its peripherals. Go to any newsagent and count the number of magazines devoted to the use of that very electronic hardware that was supposed to replace the book. As virtually every book historian who has given a public lecture will attest, the question of whether or not the book as we know it has a future is almost always the first and most pressing question asked. Given the book's adaptability and its ability to migrate from one material form to another, one might be inclined to be optimistic. However, whatever the future of the book may be, we hope that you, the reader, having perused this volume, will agree that the book has had quite a past.

REFERENCES

Casson, Lionel (2001) *Libraries in the Ancient World.* New Haven: Yale University Press.

Eisenstein, Elizabeth L. (1979) *The Printing Press as an Agent of Change: Communications and Cultural Transformations in Early Modern Europe.* Cambridge: Cambridge University Press.

PART I
Methods and Approaches

1
Why Bibliography Matters

T. H. Howard-Hill

Year by year millions of copies of books are published and distributed to all the countries of the world. Books are printed on paper, on vellum or parchment, on wood, and on metal: any surface capable of bearing ink can carry text. The common codex – a collection of leaves hinged at the left – is given paper covers, or none, or covers of cloth, pasteboard, plastic, leather, or even human skin. Books are disseminated to institutions, warehouses, bookshops, libraries, private collections, and households so that they are omnipresent: it is unusual for anyone to be far from books. Books are among the most widely dispersed artifacts in world culture, and the book is still the commonest form of transmitting information and knowledge.

It is primarily the task of bibliographers to deal with the flood of books that issues from the world's presses. Bibliographers are the good housekeepers of the world of books. Even though most books declare their origin and auspices on the title page or its verso, bibliographers must determine a host of crucial details that many people would think transparently obvious. There are books with title pages in unexpected places and books without title pages at all. Many books do not have clear author statements. Many official publications, for instance, credit the contributions of so many committees, commissions, departments, and offices that it is difficult to decide which of them gives the books their author-ness or authority. A significant portion of popular modern books such as novels are published pseudonymously; unless authors' real names are discovered, such authors will be deprived of part of their work and their literary biographies will be inadequate. This is only one area in which potential obscurities in the identification of a book must be resolved.

In order to put books – or at least bibliographical records – in their right places, at the very least bibliographers must establish who wrote a book or at least assumed intellectual responsibility for its content; its title (if it is a translation, the title in the original language); the edition (whether the book has been published before and where the edition stands in relation to the title's previous publishing history); the place of publication and the name of the publisher (that is, the issuing body); and the date of publication, possibly the most crucial datum of all, about which more will be said.

The process of putting books into their right places and of recording where they are is *bibliographical control*. Without such fundamental instruments of bibliographical control as bibliographies (lists of books) and catalogues (libraries', booksellers', publishers'), and their modern extensions into cyberspace, particularly as databases and OPACs (online publicly accessible catalogues), the complex modern literary culture that we take for granted would scarcely exist. Without these tools, which the Internet is making more widely and usefully accessible, the information explosion of the past decade or so could not have occurred. Modern students are more familiar with electronic databases (for instance, the MLA International Bibliography or the English Short Title Catalogue [ESTC]) than catalogues and bibliographies, but in most cases they depend on print. Historians of the book particularly should not neglect the printed works that lie behind the electronic records, or the artifacts that underlie the printed records.

Bibliographical control probably began when an individual or an institution had too many books to recall their titles or their position in the collection. To classify or even to arrange books on a shelf in alphabetical order of authors' names or titles is a form of bibliographical control whether or not the arrangement is accompanied by a written list. However, early librarians found that it was not efficient to arrange all their books, ranging from huge elephant folios to miniature books like thumbnail Bibles, in a single sequence on the shelves. It was better to classify the books by size or form (as maps are in most large libraries). Alternative forms of classification could be considered, from which arose the considerable physical complexity of modern libraries, where catalogues must reveal not only which books are in the collection but where they might be found. Librarians are the foremost of the bibliographers who exert control over the multifarious products of the world's presses.

So the merest neophyte in book history studies is already the beneficiary of three or more thousand years of bibliographical activity: the discipline of bibliography has a long history and an extensive literature. Its essence is taxonomy (classification), which bibliography shares with such studies as botany, paleontology, and astronomy, and therefore depends on logical principles common to most sciences. Of this kind is *enumerative* (or systematic) bibliography, *analytical* (or critical) bibliography, and *descriptive* bibliography, to employ common distinctions (Stokes 1969). The greatest English bibliographer of the first part of the twentieth century enlarged the simple definition of bibliography to "the science of the transmission of literary documents" (Greg 1966: 241, see also 75–88, 207–25, 239–66). Therefore, often regarded as a further division of bibliography is *textual* bibliography, in which bibliographers or textual critics study the taxonomy of the texts that are transmitted through documents that may have a different taxonomy. Finally, there is *historical* bibliography, which in itself is basically not taxonomic. (This chapter and the illustrative examples it cites necessarily depend on my experience with British books and bibliography.)

Enumerative Bibliography

Bibliographers, particularly enumerative bibliographers – those who make lists or catalogues of books – consider books from several viewpoints. Titles can be selected for inclusion in a bibliography on the basis of their *period* of publication: hence the well-known printed short title catalogues of English books printed 1475–1640 (Pollard and Redgrave 1976–91) and 1641–1700 (Wing 1972–88) and lists of *incunables* (books printed before 1500). There are lists of books written or printed in particular *languages* (for instance, Lloyd 1948), or printed or published in particular *places* (Cordeaux and Merry 1981), or produced by particular *printers* or *publishers* or *binders* (Isaac 1989), or printed in particular *types* (Carter 1967), or – too common to require illustration – books written by individual *authors* or classes of authors like women or children. And, of course, innumerable bibliographies gather together records of books on particular *subjects*. Of paramount importance to historians of the book are the bibliographies that take bibliography and book history as their subjects. A principal example for English bibliography is Howard-Hill (1969–99); for American bibliography, Tanselle (1971). These bibliographies are readily approached through such general reference guides as Harner (2002).

All of these bibliographical attributes can exist in different combinations in a single bibliography. However, in every instance, the compilation of a list depends on the bibliographical (analytical) examination of copies of books. The longest bibliography starts with the first copy. Not even book historians appreciate the extent to which their work depends on the products of enumerative bibliography: that is, lists of books. Enumerative bibliographies and library catalogues are constructed from descriptions of copies of individual books that are taken to represent, more or less faithfully, individual works that contain distinct texts. Incorporating the products of analytical and descriptive bibliography, it is enumerative bibliography that provides the basic material for the history of books. If books incorporate the collective memory of humankind – that is, preserve what is worth preserving – then without enumerative bibliographies access to the record of civilization would be random: civilization itself would experience a kind of Alzheimer's disease. Enumerative bibliographers and library cataloguers bind together the elements of civilization and society, providing access that magnifies the power of each element. The increasing sophistication of libraries and the development of bibliographical method exactly parallel the progress of civilization as we know it, not merely as a consequence but as an essential enabling factor. More narrowly, as book historians participate in the extension of knowledge, they build on foundations erected by bibliographers.

I will elaborate more specifically. Usually, bibliographical description for any purpose starts with a single copy of a document. (I will use "bibliographer" for "cataloguer" mostly hereafter.) Identification of the copy to hand is the first concern of the bibliographer. When the cataloguing is "original" (that is, when the bibliographer is not simply matching the copy to hand against a description written by someone else), identification may not be easy, particularly if the work itself was hitherto unknown to bibliographical history. Information sufficient to identify the work or book may be lacking or be false, or the bibliographer may not have the means to make a correct identification. To illustrate this, there are records of twenty-five Hookham and Company Circulating Library catalogues, scattered amongst eleven libraries in my database. For all but three of the catalogues, the dates are conjectural, in some instances pro forma. For instance, the Bodleian Library conjectures "[1829]" for a volume (Bodleian Library 2590 e.Lond.186.1) that consists of a catalogue that contains "Addenda 1821" and a separate 1829 supplement with its own pagination, register, and printer. The Bodleian cataloguer apparently dated the book 1829 as the year in which the three parts were issued together, but that obscures the fact that the volume was produced in three different years.

Further, the extent of anonymous and pseudonymous books in the early period is considerable and the bibliographer may have great difficulty in determining what the authority of such a book is (Griffin 1999). Many books lack much of the information that may allow a bibliographer readily to put them into their historical context exactly. Of 10,904 monographs recorded in my database in June 2002, 1,058 (roughly 10 percent) did not identify the author on the title page, 129 were pseudonymous, 1,407 were anonymous, 2,672 did not supply the place of publication, 2,587 did not give the name of the publisher or printer, 2,293 did not give the date of publication, and in 1,087 records the date of publication is doubtful. Identifying such books is essentially an historical enterprise because the author of an anonymous or pseudonymous book can rarely be identified without recourse to *external* biographical or literary information. Sometimes also the bibliographer must interpret the text of the document, as in the case of *Proposals by the Drapers and Stationers, for the Raising and Improving the Woollen Manufacture, and Making of Paper in England* (1677), a broadside signed "H. 1000000", that is, Henry Million (Wing 1972–83: no. P3715D).

A glance at the *National Union Catalog* (NUC), in which square brackets are employed to denote information not supplied by the title page, illustrates the extent to which the fundamental basis of authority in intellectual discourse is the creation of bibliographers operating within and on book culture. In an age in which accountability is a prevalent social concern, the bibliographer's attribution of authority and therefore responsibility for the contents of books has larger than bibliographical relevance. In earlier times, when the press was often under state control, the consequences of a bibliographer's attribution of responsibility for works were generally more serious. Bibliographers interpret the individual written responses to the common (human) condition and, by interpreting and classifying them, enable readers to participate fully in the world's business. Further, a work may survive in only a few copies, but the record of its existence is disseminated in a multitude of bibliographical descriptions that may even sometimes be more numerous than the number of copies of the work originally printed: such dissemination enlarges immeasurably the work's possible intellectual influence. Enumerative bibliographies amplify the effects of books in all communities.

A catalogue or bibliography is fundamentally a work of historical interpretation, as can be seen even more clearly when we consider the bibliographer's paramount obligation to place a book in its correct place in history. Just as many early books are anonymous, so were many issued without a statement of the date of issue. A date may not have been perceived to be necessary at the time for purchasers, for the publishers knew when it was published and the readers knew when they read it as a contemporary document. This is particularly true of early library catalogues, in which modern book historians naturally have an interest. Very often catalogues of subscription and circulating libraries bear no dates: this should not be surprising. The recipient of such catalogues knew what year it was, and unreflectingly discarded them whenever an updated edition appeared.

This points to another interesting characteristic of undated literature. Some printed documents (sometimes called "ephemeral") may be so fully dependent on their intellectual or social contexts that they may not even contain information that allows them to be placed chronologically with any precision or confidence. Apparently, readers were expected to insert the text into their existing knowledge of the circumstances and discourse surrounding the ostensible subject of the pamphlet. Nevertheless, bibliographers must accept the task of identification as at least a guide to scholars who might want to include the work in their intellectual investigations.

Analytical Bibliography

Analytical bibliography is predicated on the simple principle that even mechanized or repetitive tasks, especially if human beings are involved, are often performed incorrectly. For instance, compositors may misread authors' handwriting and introduce errors into the text; in early works an ink ball can lift a type which may be replaced incorrectly; the work may be imperfectly imposed so that the sheets when folded show the pages of the text in the wrong reading order; or the binder might stamp an incorrect title on the binding. Whatever can go wrong will sooner or later go wrong, even in modern books. On the other hand, there are variations amongst copies of books that may be intentional; for instance, an issue of a title might be given a different colored binding, or be printed on large paper, or be trimmed to a different size. Any such physical variation raises the question of identity and requires resolution.

The bibliographer's next task after identifying the book is to ascertain if it is perfect; that is, if it embodies the proper intentions of all the agents in its production correctly. Some errors are obvious; some will only be detected from comparison of many copies of the same title, often by optical collation of the text. When the Hinman Collator (developed to compare copies of the Shakespeare First Folio) was applied to the works of Elizabeth Barrett Browning, the result was "the discovery of 'a variant state or concealed impression' . . . for every one of the first English editions collated" (Howard-Hill 1992: 124). From analysis of variations in copies in relation to their understanding of the physical processes that made the book, bibliographers move toward writing a description of the book based on the concept of the "ideal copy," that is, the intended form of the book against which particular copies can be measured. (Hence such notes on copies of books in catalogues as "Lacks leaf [A4]".)

Analytical bibliography of the material object is fundamentally historical. To understand the production of the book at a certain period in history, employing the characteristic means of production of the age within the social practices that influenced both labor and capital, involves bibliographers' knowledge of those processes and social

conditions and the ability to apply them to the material object at hand. Not all bibliographical analyses may lead to formal descriptions of books, but as an historical science
analytical bibliography needs no further object.

Descriptive Bibliography

Descriptive bibliography, which Tanselle (1992a: 25) characterized as "history, as a genre
of historical writing," seeks to establish a description of the book beyond the simplest
level used in basic enumerative bibliographies in relation to various levels of potential
use. Its primary function is "to present all the evidence about a book which can be
determined by analytical bibliography applied to a material object" (Bowers 1949: 34).
Descriptive bibliographies differ from enumerative "in respect of the quantity and kind
of detail which is included" (Stokes 1969: 96). To illustrate this point, Stokes compares
the one-line entry for the Shakespeare First Folio in the *New Cambridge Bibliography of
English Literature*, adequate for its simple purpose; the twelve- (now nine-) line entry
with additional bibliographical information in Pollard and Redgrave (1976–91: no.
22273); the more detailed four-page description in Greg's *A Bibliography of the English
Printed Drama to the Restoration* (1957: 1109–12); and the 468 pages of his *The Shakespeare
First Folio: Its Bibliographical and Textual History* (1955). Now, following Hinman's mag-
isterial analysis of copies of the Folio in the Folger Shakespeare Library (1963), Anthony
James West (2003) has been able to extend the description of the Folio to details of the
surviving copies, in a volume of 438 pages. These last works show how strenuous analytical and descriptive bibliography may be, especially when, as in the preparation of a
descriptive bibliography of the works of a prolific author, a bibliographer must travel
widely to obtain access to multiple copies of the author's work. This and the formal
requirements of bibliographical description (Bowers 1949), elaborated in recent years
by Tanselle (see Howard-Hill 1992: 129), render the preparation of a descriptive bibliography a most demanding scholarly task.

　　Historians of the book do not always need to be able to undertake bibliographical
analysis or description themselves: they may have other concerns. However, they should
be able to read bibliographical literature with a modicum of understanding, and certainly be able to read bibliographical descriptions of books for the historical and cultural
information they contain. Many recent bibliographies devoted to individual authors are
essentially biographical (Laurence 1983), presenting descriptions of their works in
chronological order of publication. They usually include documentary information
about the gestation and composition of these works, the authors' relations with publishers, their publishing history, and notices of textual variations. Such bibliographies go
far beyond the provision of what has been traditionally considered "bibliographical"
information into wider realms of culture, economics, and textual transmission and
reception. In so doing, they underscore the importance of bibliography for the history
of the book.

Textual Bibliography

The interest of literary students in the works of authors contributed to the growth of textual bibliography in the previous century. Textual bibliography (or textual analysis) is essentially the bibliographical study of text in relation to the material processes of its transmission. Editing is the application of the findings of textual analysis to the production of different kinds of editions for different kinds of readers, under the aegis of one or another theory of editing. Although "[t]he chief purpose of bibliography is to serve the production and distribution of correct texts" (Gaskell 1972: 1), not all bibliography is subordinated to text, and not all textual bibliography is promulgated in the form of editions. Later twentieth-century bibliotextual theory, as developed by Jerome McGann, treated a published text as the result of a collaboration between the author and all those (amanuenses, proof-correctors, editors, publishers) who had an opportunity to alter that text (McGann 1983). This trend was propelled by an egalitarian devaluation of authorial intentionality, combined with a growing interest in popular forms of literature and their dissemination amongst lower-income readerships, often in adaptations and abridgements. (For a fuller discussion of this approach to the book, see chapter 2.)

Historical Bibliography

Historical bibliography focuses on the physical processes that contribute to the production of books, such as copy-editing, composing, proofreading, printing, binding, and illustrating. Historical bibliographers have compiled biographical dictionaries of printers, booksellers, and publishers, as well as individual biographies of prominent members of the book trade. They have also produced studies of the history of type-founding, papermaking, composition, printing, binding, publishing, bookselling, and the personnel and organization of the book trade. The history of libraries and book-collecting, both personal and institutional, is also an interest shared by book historians and historical bibliographers.

Book historians learn from historical bibliographers that the literary contents of a book at any time may have been modified for non-literary reasons. For instance, when Benjamin Franklin undertook to publish Samuel Richardson's novel, *Pamela*, he was obliged to commit a large amount of his capital to purchase paper for it, usually the main cost of a book. Despite setting the text in small type in order to condense its three volumes into one, he used seventeen sheets of paper for each copy, instead of the up-to-four sheets normally required for his other publications. Later eighteenth-century American printers found that it was possible to compete with British imports only by abridging the novel: Franklin's was the only full text among thirty-eight editions published in America in the century (Stallybrass 2004: 1348), where *Pamela* was usually read in shortened form.

Bibliography and Modern Book History

Now, after the naming of parts, we can consider more specifically how bibliographers support book history in exploring authorship, reading, and publishing. The benefit to book historians of familiarity with bibliographical scholarship is incontestable; its neglect, as the president of the Bibliographical Society of America illustrated in her annual address (Mayo 2004: 15), can be debilitating. Historical bibliography makes a definitive contribution to book history through the history of libraries. Analytical bibliography plays its part by defining the contents of libraries or collections, which necessarily must be identified before any library history can be written. For the study of early British or American libraries, for example, book historians and bibliographers both use a variety of manuscript materials: diaries, minutes of library societies, and lists of books in national and county archives; advertisements and references to libraries in newspapers, histories, and memoirs; and, of course, the surviving printed catalogues, regulations, and transactions of libraries. And bibliographers are essential for overcoming the two main problems for the study of libraries: chronology and access.

Chronology (needless to say) is crucial to history. But even when one narrows attention from the comprehensive history of libraries to simply the history of their catalogues (bearing in mind that to a great extent their catalogues *are* their histories) chronological problems are rife. Bibliographers discover that many library catalogues consist of an initial edition to which was added any number of additional lists, appendices, or supplements. These may have concurrent page numbers, extending the pagination of the original catalogue. Sometimes the register of gatherings will be continuous, or the supplement may begin at signature A or B. Sometimes the supplement will start a new register but continue the pagination – or the converse. The supplements or appendices may have title pages or merely caption- or head-titles. A printer's colophon may give an indication of the place of publication, but dates in colophons are quite rare. Most catalogues survive only in single or a very few copies, widely dispersed, making it difficult for bibliographers to determine by comparison of copies whether to catalogue a volume as a single bibliographical item or many separately datable items. Most often, they will not be able to determine whether a particular volume was reissued with the supplements or whether they were bound-in subsequently.

The style of the book entries in early library catalogues designed for general use is remarkably succinct, often merely an abbreviated name and truncated title. Dates are usually not given for monographs, but they may appear when the library lists its holdings of a serial such as the *Annual Register* or *Gentleman's Magazine*. In the absence of any explicit dating, bibliographers must attempt to locate each item in history themselves. They follow the rough working principle that supplementary catalogues usually appear in chronological order, after the initial dated or datable catalogue that establishes the base date for the supplements. The appendices can be dated from entries that bear dates in the catalogue (for example, *"Annual Register.* 1794") or from entries that appear to relate to recently published novels that are datable from other bibliographical sources, such as the British Library catalogue (BLC). In the first instance, bibliographers do not know whether *un*dated items later than the noted dated items occur in the catalogue. In the second, they cannot be sure that the items that they have selected to look up in BLC or NUC truly provide a *terminus ad quem* for the publication of the catalogue: had bibliographers selected different entries to check in bibliographies or catalogues, they might have reached different conclusions about the conjectural date of publication. Eventually, any such dates that bibliographers assign to undated catalogues, without unimpeachable external evidence, are merely more- or less-informed guesses, indicated in modern catalogues and bibliographical databases by the use of square brackets and/or question marks with the date.

It is clear that the chroniclers of these library catalogues are themselves creating a history of the book. The history of libraries in Britain and America during the eighteenth and nineteenth centuries depends to a substantial extent on the interplay of the datable information supplied by the document and the bibliographer's knowledge of the existing historical literature related to the works being catalogued. Insofar as the historicity of the book is concerned, therefore, bibliographers make a crucial and indispensable contribution.

Access to this material is another matter. The United Kingdom deposit libraries, notably the British and Bodleian libraries and the National Library of Scotland, may possess no more than a fraction of the catalogues of provincial libraries: calculations made from my records suggest about 30 percent. Many catalogues can be found only in the libraries or archives of the regions where they originated, but even such well-documented extant libraries as the Leeds Library or the Newcastle-upon-Tyne Literary and Philosophical Society do not hold complete runs of their own catalogues. Often access to these catalogues cannot be sought in such tools as the ESTC (English Short Title Catalogue), NSTC (*Nineteenth Century Short Title Catalogue*), COPAC (the University Research Libraries' Catalogue), UK Public Libraries on the Web, or OBI (OPACs in Britain and Ireland) that give access to British public libraries and their OPACs, simply because many small libraries do not have home pages on the Internet, and many more do not have OPACs. Also, most OPACs are not retrospective and do not include older material.

There are other aspects of bibliographical description vital to historians of the book. The localization of the products of presses and publishers is almost as important as authority and dating to book historians: if they are to understand the conditions and character of local book trades correctly, they must have the information that bibliographers have made available in printed catalogues and bibliographies (with indexes) or in on-line databases like the ESTC, which can facilitate searches by places of origin and the names of the makers and distributors of books. The ESTC, which is available on-line, "assisted, if it did not actually encourage, the transformation of bibliographical studies to Book History" (Williams 2003: 219).

However, as essential as short title catalogues are to constructing a full understanding of the place of books in society, they do not provide all the information that might have been expected from them. In particular, efforts to write the histories of local book production or of individual members of the book trade are frustrated by the variability of information supplied in catalogues. It is difficult to reconstruct the publishing activities of stationers whose names in imprints or colophons have been omitted by modern bibliographers to save space in databases. Also, the omission in the STCs of a record of printers' colophons as well as publisher's imprints similarly affects the possibility of understanding the relationship between publishers and the country printers who often worked for them, and fails to provide a direct way of identifying printers' output. The recognition that existing enumerative bibliographical resources do not supply the whole range of information that book historians require in order fully to sociologize "the book" points to the contribution that other forms of descriptive or even analytical bibliography may make to the history of the book.

D. F. McKenzie famously advocated a movement from the conception of bibliography as the study of books as material objects to the history of the book in society, i.e., "to what their production, dissemination, and reception reveal about past human life and thought" (McKenzie 1992: 298). He urged that the study of all forms of symbolic communication should be seen not as a new and competing area of study, still less as a rejection of bibliography, but rather as a natural expansion of bibliography's scope and function into a wider sphere. His central position was that, historically, the historiography of the book in Anglophone countries has been a development of Anglo-American bibliography. Even the most apparently straightforward bibliographical approach to books through the preparation of a checklist or catalogue is inherently historical and interpretive. As such, book historians cannot neglect, despite its contingency, the basic bibliographical foundation that affords the starting-point of their wide-ranging investigations.

Bibliographies supply an immediate overview of the world of books that is all the more commanding because it depends on the hands-on experience of countless copies of books. No one has done more to make the modern world aware of the significance of books than the bibliographers who have devoted their lives to studying them. It may be, as Peter Stallybrass (2004: 1351) protests, "one of the hidden scandals of the literary profession" that literary historians turn so infrequently to librarians: certainly the latter should be consulted more often. And it is worth noting that the sensibility toward books that the "history of the book" invokes in its more florid moments is not new. In 1830, Sir Henry Parnell wrote: "Books carry the productions of the human mind over the whole world, and may be truly called the raw materials of every kind of science and art, and of all social improvement" (Dagnall 1998: 347). These words remind us that without books there is no history, and without bibliography there is no history of books.

REFERENCES AND FURTHER READING

Adams, Thomas B. and Barker, Nicolas (1993) "A New Model for the Study of the Book." In N. Barker (ed.), *A Potencie of Life: Books in Society*, pp. 5–43. London: British Library.

Bowers, Fredson (1949) *The Principles of Bibliographical Description*. Princeton: Princeton University Press.

Carter, H. G. (1967) "Books in Fell Type Published by the University of Oxford from 1902 to 1927." In Stanley A. Morison and H. G. Carter, *John Fell, the University Press, and the Fell Types . . .* , p. 253. Oxford: Clarendon Press.

Cordeaux, Edward H. and Merry, D. H. (1981) *A Bibliography of Printed Works relating to Oxfordshire . . .* , 2nd edn. Oxford: Clarendon Press.

Dagnall, H. (1998) "The Taxes on Knowledge: Excise Duty on Paper." *The Library*, 6th ser., 20: 347–63.

Darnton, Robert (1982) "What is the History of Books?" *Daedalus*, 111: 65–83.

Ehrman, Albert and Pollard, H. G. (1965) *The Distribution of Books by Catalogue from the Invention of Printing to AD 1800*. Cambridge: Printed for Presentation to Members of the Roxburghe Club.

Gaskell, Philip (1972) *A New Introduction to Bibliography*. Oxford: Clarendon Press.

Greg, W. W. (1955) *The Shakespeare First Folio: Its Bibliographical and Textual History*. Oxford: Clarendon Press.

— (1957) *A Bibliography of the English Printed Drama to the Restoration*, vol. 3: *Collections, Appendix, Reference Lists*. London: Bibliographical Society.

— (1966) *Collected Papers*, ed. J. C. Maxwell. Oxford: Clarendon Press.

Griffin, Robert J. (1999) "Authority and Authorship." *New Literary History*, 30: 877–96.

Harner, James L. (2002) *Literary Research Guide: An Annotated Listing of Reference Sources in English Literary Studies*, 4th edn. New York: Modern Language Association of America.

Hinman, Charlton (1963) *The Printing and Proofreading of the First Folio of Shakespeare*, 2 vols. Oxford: Clarendon Press.

Howard-Hill, T. H. (1969–99) *Index to British Literary Bibliography*, 8 vols. Oxford: Clarendon Press.

— (1992) "Enumerative and Descriptive Bibliography." In Peter Davison (ed.), *The Book Encompassed: Studies in Twentieth-century Bibliography*, pp. 122–9. Cambridge: Cambridge University Press.

— (1998) *British Book Trade Dissertations to 1980*. Signal Mountain, TN: Summertown.

Isaac, Peter C. G. (1989) *A Tentative List of Bensley Printing*. Wylam: Allenholme.

Laurence, Dan H. (1983) *A Portrait of the Author as a Bibliography*. Washington: Library of Congress.

Lloyd, D. Myrrdin (1948) "Llfryddiaeth Gymraeg [Welsh Eighteenth-century Literature]." *Welsh Bibliographical Society Journal*, 6: 225–41.

McGann, Jerome J. (1983) *A Critique of Modern Textual Criticism*. Chicago: University of Chicago Press.

McKenzie, D. F. (1992) "History of the Book." In Peter Davison (ed.), *The Book Encompassed: Studies in Twentieth-century Bibliography*, pp. 290–301. Cambridge: Cambridge University Press.

McKerrow, Ronald B. (1994) *An Introduction to Bibliography for Literary Students* (with introduction by David McKitterick). Winchester: St. Paul's Bibliographies.

Mayo, Hope (2004) "The Bibliographical Society of America at 100: Past and Future." *Papers of the Bibliographical Society of America*, 98: 425–48.

Pollard, A. W. and Redgrave, G. R. (1976–91) *A Short-title Catalogue of Books Printed in England, Scotland, & Ireland and of English Books Printed Abroad, 1475–1640*, 2nd edn. London: Bibliographical Society.

Stallybrass, Peter (2004) "The Library and Material Texts." *Proceedings of the Modern Language Association of America*, 119: 1347–52.

Stokes, Roy (1969) *The Function of Bibliography*. London: André Deutsch.

Tanselle, G. Thomas (1971) *Guide to the Study of United States Imprints*, 2 vols. Cambridge, MA: Belknap Press of Harvard University Press.

— (1981) *The History of Books as a Field of Study*. Chapel Hill: Hanes Foundation, Rare Book Collection, Academic Affairs Library, University of North Carolina.

— (1992a) "A Description of Descriptive Bibliography." *Studies in Bibliography*, 45: 1–30.

— (1992b) "Issues in Bibliographical Studies since 1942." In Peter Davison (ed.), *The Book Encompassed: Studies in Twentieth-century Bibliography*, pp. 24–36. Cambridge: Cambridge University Press.

West, Anthony James (2003) *The Shakespeare First Folio: The History of the Book*, vol. II: *A New Worldwide Census of First Folios*. Oxford: Oxford University Press.

Williams, W. P. (2003) "The History of the Book." *Review*, 25: 211–29.

Wing, Donald (1972–88) *Short-title Catalogue of Books Printed in England, Scotland, Ireland, Wales, and British America, and of English Books Printed in Other Countries, 1641–1700*, 2nd edn. New York: Index Committee of the Modern Language Association of America.

2

What is Textual Scholarship?

David Greetham

The basic problem in producing an unambiguous and singular response to the question posed in the title of this chapter is that the phrase "textual scholarship" is itself not singular and, as we shall see, is full of ambiguities. Clearly, "textual scholarship" must in some way focus on a "text," but that term can be particularly fraught and contentious. Similarly, "scholarship" may at first look fairly innocuous and straightforward: is it not just the serious, "scholarly" study of, and research into, a particular body of knowledge or information? Yes, it is certainly all of this; but, especially as it relates to "texts," how is "scholarship" different from, or similar to, such possibly related activities as criticism, or interpretation, or editing, or commentary, or annotation?

That was a question addressed by A. E. Housman, lyrical poet and fierce textual polemicist. Reacting against what he saw as the over-reliance on positivist system and "scientific" philology, Housman significantly used the label "textual criticism" to emphasize the human, the critical, and the personal in the approach to texts.

> Textual criticism is not a branch of mathematics, nor indeed an exact science at all. It deals with a matter not rigid and constant, like lines and numbers, but fluid and variable; namely the frailties and aberrations of the human mind, and of its insubordinate servants, the human fingers. It is therefore not susceptible of hard-and-fast rules. It would be much easier if it were; and that is why people try to pretend that it is, or at least behave as if they thought so. Of course you can have hard-and-fast rules if you like, but then you will have false rules, and they will lead you wrong; because their simplicity will render them inapplicable in problems which are not simple, but complicated by the play of personality. (Housman 1921: 132)

Housman's promotion of the human over the scientific, and of the particular and aberrational over the general and the normative, was a necessary corrective to a late nineteenth- and early twentieth-century desire for codification, system, and demonstrable proof. And what it suggested was that, in dealing with texts produced and transmitted by imperfect humanity, the critical and the evaluative attributes of the discerning scholar of texts were not just desirable but absolutely necessary. Information, historical research, and an intellectual familiarity with the bibliographical features of the text were all valuable assets in the scholarly armory of the reader/editor of ancient texts, but without a critical sensibility they would not yield a true understanding of the potential meaning of the text.

This emphasis on critical understanding and intervention may seem obvious enough in a contemporary culture that has thrust the reader (even perhaps more than the author) into the forefront of all negotiations with texts, but the lure of the scientific, the positivist, and the perfectly demonstrable has continued to exert a powerful attraction, not just on those charged with constructing texts but on publishers and consumers of literature (see Tanselle 1974, who takes a position similar to Housman in rejecting a correlation between scientific principle and critical judgment). The practices of some adherents of so-called "strict and pure" bibliography in the mid-twentieth century, who somehow felt that, given enough positive data, any textual problem could be solved, represent just one of many attempts to arrive at the surety that Housman derided. For example, during his hegemony as the arbiter of Anglo-American bibliography, Fredson Bowers often made some very doctrinaire statements about the role of scientific method, such as "I do not see how one can escape the conviction that the 'scientific' is basic in true descriptive bibliography" (Bowers 1949: 34n, quoted in Thorpe 1972: 64–5).

From Quentin (1926) to Greg (1927) to Maas (1927) to Hrubý (1965) and Dearing (1974), there have been frequent attempts to reassert a scientific security based on algebraic or statistical or systematic logical principles, or (more recently) on electronic retrieval and demonstration. Even a publisher's desire to claim that an edition is "definitive" (with the implication that it somehow stands outside its cultural moment of production, and will never have to be done again) confirms this wish for the perfected, the complete, and the unassailable. I have claimed (Greetham 1999: 86) that this textual positivism "aimed for the same objective standards of demonstration appropriate to all the empirical sciences," and Donald H. Reiman designates this period of apparent historical surety as a "brazen" age of editing "because of the too-sanguine hopes they, at least for a time, entertained about the results obtainable through systematic application of fixed principles to a wide variety of texts" (1984: 242).

However, this concentration on the determinate (and the determined), and the confidence in scientific logic over Housman's "play of personality," has lately fallen into disfavor both within academic circles and among the reading public at large. Even in "scholarly" journals, the response of literary critics to the retreat of textual scholars into small-scale certainties in the bibliographical features of texts has all too often been dismissive, if not downright hostile. In reviewing an edition of Pound for the *Times Literary Supplement*, C. H. Sisson (1979: 616) pronounced that "the prestige of fiddling with minute variants and bibliographical details should be low. It is, intellectually, the equivalent of what is done by clerks everywhere, labouring to pay wages and to feed computers. Such things hold the world together." And Gerald Graff (1992: 354) has claimed that the "declining status of textual editing" (once "the staple of doctoral dissertations") is symptomatic of a general decline in positivist and "detailed" scholarship.

While it would be difficult to contradict Graff's analysis of the symptoms, I believe that he is mistaken in his prognosis that only by making "an alliance with theory" can textual scholars "reverse the downward fortunes of editing," just as I believe that Paul de Man is wrong in characterizing Reuben Brower's concentration on "the text itself" as a "return to philology, to an examination of the structure of language prior to the meaning it produces" (1986: 24). I have claimed (Greetham 1997: 10–11), following Housman, that it is a mischaracterization to regard the textual operations on a text (no matter how seemingly "minute") as somehow "prehermeneutic" (i.e., "prior to . . . meaning"); for all such operations, from a decision to use old or modern spelling to the selection and evaluation of variants to the question of when and how to annotate (and for what sort of reader) are already deeply hermeneutic, already "critical" as well as "scholarly."

The "critical" and the "scholarly" were brought together in the Society for Textual Scholarship (STS, founded 1979), a cross-disciplinary, extra-national, and theoretically inclined organization. We had art historians talking to musicologists talking to historians talking to epigraphers talking to literary theorists, in a very deliberate attempt to find common problems, questions, and even resolutions that would emphasize the community of "scholarship" as it related to "texts," whatever their medium, ontology, or historical period. We were consciously confronting the tendency of specialists to stay within their self-defining limitations; and this promotion of boundary-crossing clearly made some people uncomfortable, while it illuminated the work of others (see Reiman 2006).

In his inaugural address as the first president of the STS, G. Thomas Tanselle noted that the term "textual *criticism*" has a very long tradition, principally associated with the study of biblical and classical texts. Tanselle quite properly recognized that the "criticism" element in the term "suggests the important role that individual judgment plays in the process of evaluating authority" (Tanselle 1984: 2), a role that unfortunately has not always been recognized, especially by those wishing to emphasize the "scientific" aspects of the field. Tanselle then declared that "[t]his Society has chosen the term 'textual scholarship' rather than 'textual criticism' not in any sense as a rejection of the latter term but only because the former is the more encompassing term. The great tradition of classical and biblical criticism forms but one branch of textual scholarship as a whole" (Tanselle 1984: 2). So "textual scholarship" inherits "textual criticism" but then enfolds it into a more comprehensive enterprise.

Finally, Tanselle pointed to the *necessity* for this newly defined enterprise by sadly noting that scholars in different fields not only do not "have much knowledge of one another's editorial rationale" but,

> [w]hat is worse, they may even think there is no reason why they should, assuming that the materials and objectives to be so different that there is no significant overlapping between the two fields. This attitude results from a failure to think through the basic

questions that textual work involves and from a tendency simply to follow procedures that seem to be well established within a given field. (Tanselle 1984: 2)

So textual scholarship begins (in its current formulation) in potential conflict; it begins in challenging the definitions of fields; it begins in a cooption of a related area of critical discourse; it begins in interrogating the validity of disciplinary and period (and even genre) self-portraits. In other words, it begins as a series of questions, and thus it may be perfectly appropriate that my consideration of the term itself should be as a question. And because the scholarship of "texts" (still contained within the ambiguity of quotation marks) in a sense begs the question of what is a "text," the interrogative may be the appropriate mode for another reason. I take my cue for "text" from Gerald Graff's having found (1987: 257, 258) that the proper or most productive *position* for "theory" is in the interstices, the boundaries, and the margins of discourse: "The pedagogical implication of dialogics seems to be that the unit of study should cease to be the isolated text (or author) and become the virtual space or cultural conversation that the text presupposes . . . How do we institutionalize the conflict of interpretations and overviews?" For just as "theory" is best located in this medial position of conflict, so "text" is a weaving, a network, a tapestry; in other words, a *textile*, as its etymology displays.

But while this "woven" sense of text is historically quite accurate – and is certainly the one that has been adopted by poststructuralists from Barthes (1977) onwards – there is another, competing sense that has become familiar (and enters the language at roughly the same time as the "textile" meaning). From the Latin *textus*, often, perhaps usually, referring to the validity and definitiveness of the biblical text, we have also come to look on "text" as something fixed, something carrying the weight of authority: "the *text* for today's sermon is. . . ." And so we have scholarship devoted to a strange mixture of the immutable and the ever-changing, the fixed and the indeterminate. It is this pull between two opposing conditions of *textuality* (the concept and state of a text) that textual scholarship confronts, and has done for many centuries, without yet showing any sign of the resolution of this conflict.

What is a text, then? In 1991, I determinedly offered a broad definition:

> While literary texts (or, at least, texts composed of words) are the most familiar objects of textual scholarship, the textual scholar may study any means of textual communication – a painting, a sculpture, a novel, a poem, a film, a symphony, a gesture. All these media have meaning or form, and it is in part the textual scholar's aim to preserve (or, if necessary, to re-create) this meaning or form in the face of the laws of physical decay. (Greetham 1991: 103–4)

Of course, that was then, and we are now in a new century and perhaps a new dispensation. As far as the range of media is concerned, I now think that the 1991 list is, if anything, too constrained, for its genres are all (more or less) the "conventional" ones for textual study. But in the interim, the edges of textual scholarship (charted in the

STS conferences and in journals like *Text*) have become more expansive. One obvious area of new practice and theory has been the proliferation of texts and criticism of electronic media (a definition that strains the edges of the "book"; see Chernaik et al. 1996). This is too large a topic to be covered here, but several discussions of the new medium have been particularly challenging: Heim (1993, 1998); Turkle (1995); Finneran (1996); Landow (1997); Levinson (1997); Masten et al. (1997); Sutherland (1997); Levy (2001). As a parallel movement, there have been a number of recent collections that interrogate the basic concepts of text and scholarship, usually with a pronounced inter-disciplinary range: Shillingsburg (1997); Gurr and Hardman (1999); Loizeaux and Fraistat (2002); Dane (2003); Modiano et al. (2004). The major issue would seem to be whether the shift from the printed book to hypertext is of a different order from previous shifts in medium (for example, from manuscript to print, from roll to codex, from oral transmission to the written word). Duguid (1996) claims that what he deri-sively calls the "liberation technology" of some enthusiasts for electronic media is over-stated. For a more measured view of the epistemological changes brought about by hypertextual reconfiguration of "the book," see McGann (1997).

The extension of that 1991 list of genres can be shown in some illuminating recent research in such nontraditional fields as the design and implementation of the Olmstead "greensward" plan for Central Park, the cultural meaning and impact of the British and US composition of early Beatles albums, or the graphical and design variants in Edison's technological plans. At the 2005 STS conference, it was even suggested that textual scholars ought to move beyond the merely human, and (for example) begin to study phrasal and intonational variants in birdsong, just as D. F. McKenzie (1986) had earlier claimed that a textualized topography in Maori culture was a significant object of study. Perhaps "communication" (bibliographical, environmental, geographical, bio-logical) still holds as a central concern, at least as far as the receiver of the communica-tion is concerned.

But there is at least one assumption underlying my 1991 prescription that does need some modification, and that is the acceptance of the inevitable "decay" in the media. I think it is now well recognized that casting physical change as "decay" too easily plays into a Platonist view of the ideality of an irrecoverable originary form, from which all subsequent physical manifestations or embodiments are but shadows, lacking their own authenticity. If the enormously influential work of Jerome McGann (1983/1992, 1985, 1991, 1997, 2001) during the past two decades has done anything, it is to insist that all of these supposedly derivative and second-order states of text are integral to its total-ity of cultural expression, and that this ineffable "originary" form is but one (albeit an important one) of the various guises in which a text negotiates its way in history and society. In fact, in some cases, it is these very "belated" or "corrupt" states that have achieved the status of cultural icons, as witness the seventy-five-year reign of the "cen-sored" version of Dreiser's *Sister Carrie* (1900, 1912, before the manuscript-based Penn-sylvania edition was published in 1981) or the similarly "cut" version of Lawrence's *Sons and Lovers* (1913, before the Cambridge edition, similarly based on manuscript, of 1992, 2002). As is well known, there are some media (a good deal of opera, the plays of

Shakespeare) in which the performance history – and thus general public awareness – is most frequently characterized by sizable cuts, judicious or otherwise, the Gielgud performance of the "full" text of *Hamlet* (whatever that is) being an anomaly.

None of this should surprise historians of the book, who typically study exactly this *Nachleben* (or "afterlife") of the artifact. The "original" publication (or, beyond that, the author's prepublication intention) is usually seen in book history as just one of a series of motivating forces that together create the "culture" of the book. But for textual scholars (and before them, for textual critics, even those with Housman's sophistication), the attractions of this presumptive, presocial stage of textual production have had a long run in inspiring the efforts of textuists to "cleanse" or to "purge" the received text of its inevitable corruptions and to present an ideality of text fresh to current readers, a text that, in some almost beatified state, stood outside the history of its own production.

The shift I am acknowledging can be illustrated by a couple of examples from my own textual experience. In the first case, when I participated in the collaborative editing of Trevisa's Middle English translation of the *De Proprietatibus Rerum* (*On the Properties of Things*), under the general editorship of M. C. Seymour (Trevisa 1975), there was an unquestioned assumption that what we were aiming to produce was a text as close as possible either to what Trevisa had actually written or at least to what he must have intended to write. The fact that our author had almost certainly made his "fair copy" of that text in the muniments room of Berkeley Castle in Gloucestershire (one of the few remaining privately held castles in England) and that the current owners had refused the editors access to the room was a great hindrance but, at the same time, it ironically conferred enormous editorial license upon us as textual scholars. Lacking any possibility of an authorial original intention, we were free to construct this intention out of the inevitably "corrupt" scribal copies. In the mid-1970s, that meant arranging the extant manuscripts into a "family tree" (*stemma*) of relationships based on the charting of "error," with the most erroneous at the bottom of the tree and those least affected by scribal intervention at the top. And we went even further than this. Since Trevisa's Middle English was a translation from the Latin of Bartholomaeus Anglicus (for whom there was similarly no authorial autograph text), and since we assumed that Trevisa (a) was a good Latinist and (b) wanted to represent Bartholomaeus' Latin accurately, we were presumptuous enough to use two Latin texts of the *Proprietatibus* as arbiters when a "crux" (or otherwise unresolvable ambiguity) occurred in the English witnesses. In other words, we were so intent upon this reach for origins that we were prepared to go beyond the actual English transmission to construct a text that Trevisa *ought* to have written, whether he did or not.

The basic ideology behind this arrangement and use of witnesses was for the most part thought unexceptionable at that time (though we did come in for a bit of flak for the over-reliance on the Latin). We were simply "doing what comes naturally"; for textual scholarship, just like any other intellectual or artistic endeavor, is always firmly embedded in its own culture and the basic assumptions about creation, aesthetics, and reception. Indeed, in a justifiably influential essay, and working under the "originalist" principles I have described for traditional textual criticism, Lee Patterson (1985) claimed that the Kane–Donaldson edition of the B Text of *Piers Plowman* (Langland 1975) was a "modernist" (and specifically a "New Critical") edition, produced under the auspices of the late formalism of the mid-1970s, the same period as our production of Trevisa.

> In claiming to be able to discover an original text from the fragments and vestiges that history has left us, textual criticism subscribes to this general idealism . . . textual criticism . . . deploys its erudition in a struggle to wrest from the past an originality that time threatens to efface, an originality it designates as the text. In this effort, then, textual criticism aligns itself more closely than might be expected with New Criticism. Just as New Criticism proclaims the text's autonomy from historical forces, so does textual criticism reconstitute the text from the context of scribalisms in which it is submerged. (Patterson 1985: 86)

At this remove, the single most startling (and now embarrassing) sin of editorial *omission* that we made in the Trevisa edition was our very deliberate dismissal of the evidence contained in what at the time seemed to us an irrelevant, idiosyncratic, and almost perversely variant manuscript: Cambridge University Library MS Ii.v.41. This manuscript, unlike the other, more formally produced witnesses, was on paper not vellum, was written in a careless, casual, amateur hand, and was full of erasures, second thoughts, interlinear comments, and other marks of a highly "personal" take on the text. (Where the other witnesses read "loued," the Cambridge preferred "desirid" and so on: variance for variance sake.) To our editorial purposes, it was simply unusable to help establish textual authenticity: we considered it a manuscript put together in a slapdash way, probably for the scribe/reader's own use rather than as part of the professional production of the work. We thus placed it way off to the side in our *stemma*, in a graphically marginal position, with no obvious descendants.

That was then. What if I (or any other textual scholar attuned to the shifts of the early twenty-first century) were now confronted with the same set of witnesses? The irony is that the dismissed and unusable manuscript would probably have acquired a very different cultural status. It might not contribute much to a reconstruction of a putative original, but it would show the text in social negotiation, being worked on by an intelligent *user*, someone who was more concerned with making the *Properties* a part of his own culture than with reaching after a lost and unrecoverable authorial intention. If I were to edit the *Properties* now, in this period of the "socialization" of text, this aberrant witness would be the most fascinating, if still the least "authentic."

The second example illustrates a similar shift but on a much larger scale. While by no means an expert on ninth-century Irish philosophy or theology, I was asked to contribute an essay on a recent edition of Eriugena's *Periphyseon* to a commemorative issue of the *American Catholic Philosophical Quarterly* (Greetham 2005). The terms of this invitation were very specific, ideologically and methodologically: I was to examine the weighty, five-volume edition of the *Periphyseon* – produced under the auspices of the Corpus Christianorvm Continuatio Mediaeualis (CCCM) by a learned Jesuit, Édouard

Jeaneau – "like the postmodernist you really are" (as the journal editor put it). What could this mean? Could there be such a thing as a "postmodernist" edition of an early medieval work in the same way that Patterson had posited "modernism" as the guiding principle for the Kane–Donaldson *Piers* of thirty years earlier?

As I began to do research into the history of the editing of Eriugena, I began to see what the journal editor had meant. I discovered that the precedent edition of *Periphyseon*, produced from the mid-1960s by Sheldon-Williams, was guided by the twin tropes of "satisfaction" and "fullness." The editor had claimed that "*[t]he present edition* attempts to present the text with which the author finally came to be satisfied, and at the same time to exhibit the stages of its development" (1968: 1.27, italics in original), a teleo-logical/processional relation that, as I was soon to discover, is inverted in the Jeaneau edition. Then, Sheldon-Williams had articulated his rationale for the critical apparatus by observing that "[i]n view of the fact that MSS R B P represent three successive recensions of the text it has been decided to give a full 'positive' apparatus criticus, and to do so, for the sake of consistency, even where a manuscript variant is merely a scribal blunder" (1.34).

These desires for "satisfaction" (the "making complete" of a work as it progresses toward that most thorny of contemporary textual states, "authorial final intention") and for "positive" evidence (again, for the sake of "fullness," and in a confidence that the "scribal blunder" can be effectively distinguished from authorial idiosyncrasy) move the Sheldon-Williams edition in an epistemological direction that I saw as the almost total reverse of the Jeaneau. Where Sheldon-Williams aims for teleology and completion, authorial and transmissional, the proliferation of textuality in the Jeaneau edition sets out the "critical" edition as only one state in the presentation of textual variance, and allows the "synoptic apparatus" to become the "fullest" part of the editorial enterprise. Furthermore, what Sheldon-Williams hopefully enlists as a " 'positive' apparatus criti-cus" is nonetheless presented in his edition in a conventional "inferior" textual space, in reduced type at the *bottom* of the page, so that its positivism is in fact a mark of its degenerative status, again a conventional assumption. In the massive Jeaneau edition, in contrast, the synoptically presented variant versions are no longer confined to this "inferior" position but are given a visual and spatial equality with one another (and, by implication, with the "critical" edition that sets the whole procedure in motion). In Jeaneau, the reader's eye is forcibly moved to accept variance as a normative condition. The current edition thus holds the earlier editorial aims of "satisfaction" and "fullness" in abeyance, if they are accorded any value at all, in the face of textual fragmentation and proliferation. The editorial rationale now emphasizes not a "*produit fini*," but "*une matière en fusion, non point d'un texte établi et fixé de façon canonique, mais d'un texte en per-pétuel devenir*" (Eriugena 1968–95: 1.xix). A "perpetual becoming" indeed. In these postmodernist days, we are a long way from "satisfaction," preferring process and demonstrable incompletion (or "becoming") over fulfillment (and "being").

What do these two examples suggest about the current state of textual scholarship, especially as it differs from the model of just thirty years ago? And in what way is my present response to the question in the title of this chapter different from what it would have been in the earlier period? The most general response is that textual scholarship is not a discipline or a practice somehow immune from the ideological and philosophical pressures of its times. Just as Patterson (1985) remarked of the "modernist" *Piers*, any act of textual scholarship is going to be the product of a sometimes unacknowledged negotiation with what is literally "thinkable" in a particular cultural moment. During the hegemony of the organicism, completion, and unitary consciousness of the New Critical period in Anglo-American studies, it became just "natural" (or unquestionable) that the aim of textual scholarship should be to resuscitate and to make manifest this unitary consciousness as it was applicable to the recovery and construction of authorial texts. One of the mantras of this period was "the text that never was," that ideal state not representable in any given historical documents but immanent in their collation and conflation. The "eclectic" text, as it became known, was like that of the 1970s' Trevisa or the 1960s' Eriugena: something lying behind or above the so-called "veil of print" and requiring the intervention of an editor convinced of the ethical requirement that full justice to authoriality could be achieved only by reaching for a romantic organicism beyond the raw and corrupt phenomena of the textual *remaniements*. In a word, textual modernism was (like that of modernism in music, in architecture, in painting, and so on) Platonist and essentialist. Modernism sought the "essence" of the specific medium, and in textual scholarship this essence was the purified, cleansed, and unmediated text of the author, usually presented in "clear text" editions, with all sign of editorial handiwork removed so that the reader was confronted with "the text itself," shorn of both historical accretions and of the evidence of the editorial intervention that had recreated this text.

If this period of textual activity could be called Platonist, then the postmodernist descriptive mode might be seen as Aristotelian, in a reflection of the famous Raphael painting of the philosophical school of Athens, in which Plato is pointing upwards toward the ineffable empyrean and Aristotle is gesturing downwards toward the hard, phenomenological, untidy world of the here and now. The idiosyncratic and personal *Properties* manuscript and the proliferation of *"matière en fusion"* and the *"texte en perpétuel devenir"* in the Jeaneau *Periphyseon* are both representative of this concrete reality. They are not resolvable or organicist texts, and there is a sense in which they will be forever incomplete. That is their condition.

And I believe that this Aristotelian condition in current textual scholarship ties in quite appropriately with the growth of the history of the book as a very successful discipline. As I have charted that growth (Greetham 1999) in its relation to the theory and practice of textual scholarship, *l'histoire du livre* is the textual working through of the *annaliste* view of history as *mentalité* or the cumulative effect of *histoire totale* rather than just of traditional "great-figure" historiography. I have noted that *l'histoire du livre* can thus be seen as a "postmodernist dispersal of the subject as an originary figure and its replacement by materiality, economics, and power, just as New Historicism treats of not the creator himself but what we may call the negotiations between the creator and the institutions of society" (1999: 101). It is, I believe, no accident that during the hegemony of modernist textual scholarship, there was a concentration on the canonical major-figure authors (especially of nineteenth-century American literature: Melville, Hawthorne, Whitman, and so on). And it is similarly no accident that the most influential proponents of a more "socialized" view of textuality (like McGann or McKenzie) have insisted on placing the author and the production of texts into a shifting matrix of such material "negotiations." In fact, even when "major-figure" editions are concerned, these social "negotiations" are made the *raison d'être* of an edition. As the editors of the Oxford Shakespeare insist, their texts represent the socially adjudicated "play as it appeared when performed" rather than what "Shakespeare originally wrote" (1986: xxxiii). In a major break from "textual" tradition, "the Oxford edition has admitted into the *Works* the theatrical interpolations that would have formerly been considered non-authorial playhouse documents" (De Grazia 1993: 203).

And as one of the most culturally powerful of such "negotiations," the book has emerged as an extremely productive site for showing how the means of production and consumption affect and inform our concepts of literature, of genre, of meaning, and of authoriality itself. For example, Alan Dooley's study (1992) of such Victorian authors as Browning, Arnold, Tennyson, and Eliot shows very persuasively how the technology of book production (for example, from standing type to stereotypes) is inextricably linked to the market value and canonical status of an author's work. Simply put, a book that is set in inexpensive stereotypes is a publisher's recognition (or, at least, anticipation) that future reprints will be called for, and that the author is a "bankable" commodity. The physical form of the book is a direct representation of the book as a proprietary investment.

The impressive academic and intellectual success of the "history of the book" can thus be linked to a general shift away from formalism and from the "master narratives" (*grand récits*) of modernism toward an emphasis on social context. The efforts of the "social" textual scholars like McGann and McKenzie to place all texts within these cultural "negotiations" should therefore be seen as part of this general shift and thus sharing many of the same objectives and methods as historians of the book. Housman's "play of personality" is still with us, but its scope is now wider, moving beyond just the author to all of those other agents (scribes, printers, publishers, booksellers, readers) who participate in the single great enterprise of a reformulated textual scholarship.

References and Further Reading

Barthes, Roland (1977) "From Work to Text." In *Image, Music, Text*, trans. Stephen Heath, pp. 155–64. New York: Hill and Wang.

Bowers, Fredson (1949) *The Principles of Bibliographical Description*. Princeton: Princeton University Press (reprinted New Castle, DE: Oak Knoll, 2005).

— (1970) "Textual Criticism." In James Thorpe (ed.), *The Aims and Methods of Scholarship in Modern Languages and Literatures*, 2nd edn,

pp. 29–54. New York: Modern Language Association of America (originally published 1963).

Chernaik, Warren, Deegan, Marilyn, and Gibson, Andrew (eds.) (1996) *Beyond the Book: Theory, Culture, and the Politics of Cyberspace*. Oxford: Office for Humanities Communications.

Dane, Joseph A. (2003) *The Myth of Print Culture: Essays on Evidence, Textuality, and Bibliographical Method*. Toronto: University of Toronto Press.

De Grazia, Margreta (1993) "What is a Work? What is a Document?" In W. Speed Hill (ed.), *New Ways of Looking at Old Texts*, pp. 199–207. Binghamton, NY: Renaissance English Text Society/Medieval and Renaissance Texts and Studies.

De Man, Paul (1986) "The Return to Philology." In Paul De Man, *The Resistance to Theory*, pp. 21–6. Minneapolis: University of Minnesota Press.

Dearing, Vinton A. (1974) *Principles and Practice of Textual Analysis.* Berkeley: University of California Press.

Dooley, Allan C. (1992) *Author and Printer in Victorian England.* Charlottesville: University Press of Virginia.

Dreiser, Theodore (1900) *Sister Carrie.* New York: Doubleday (1981 edn, ed. James L. W. West, III. Philadelphia: University of Pennsylvania Press).

Duguid, Paul (1996) "Material Matters: The Past and Futurology of the Book." In Geoffrey Nunberg (ed.), *The Future of the Book*, pp. 63–101. Berkeley: University of California Press.

Eriugena (1968–95) *Iohannis Scotti Eriugenae, Periphyseon (De Diusione Naturae).* Scriptores Latini Hiberniae, ed. I. P. Sheldon-Williams, Ludwig Bieler, and Édouard Jeaneau. Dublin: Institute for Advanced Studies.

— (1996–2003) *Johannis Scotti seu Erivgenae, Periphyseon*, ed. Edvardvs A. Jeaneau, 5 vols. Corpus Christianorvm Continuatio Mediaevalis CLXI. Tvrnholti: Typographi Brepols Editores Pontifici.

Finneran, Richard (ed.) (1996) *The Literary Text in the Digital Age.* Ann Arbor: University of Michigan Press.

Foucault, Michel (1979) "What is an Author?" In *Textual Strategies: Perspectives in Post-structuralist Criticism*, ed. and trans. Josué V. Harari. Ithaca: Cornell University Press.

Graff, Gerald (1987) *Professing Literature: An Institutional History.* Chicago: University of Chicago Press.

— (1992) "The Scholar in Society." In Joseph Gibaldi (ed.), *Introduction to Scholarship in Modern Languages and Literatures.* New York: Modern Language Association of America.

Greetham, D. C. (1991) "Textual Scholarship." In Joseph Gibaldi (ed.), *Introduction to Scholarship in* *Modern Languages and Literatures*, pp. 101–37. New York: Modern Language Association of America.

— (1997) "The Resistance to Philology." In D. C. Greetham (ed.), *The Margins of the Text*, pp. 9–24. Ann Arbor: University of Michigan Press.

— (1999) *Theories of the Text.* Oxford: Oxford University Press.

— (2005) "Édouard Jeaneau's Edition of Eriugena's *Periphyseon* in the Light of Contemporary Textual Theory." *American Catholic Philosophical Quarterly*, 79 (4): 527–48.

Greg, W. W. (1927) *A Calculus of Variants: An Essay on Textual Criticism.* Oxford: Clarendon Press.

Gurr, Andrew and Hardman, Philippa (eds.) (1999) *The Text as Evidence: Revising Editorial Principles (A Hermeneutics of External Evidence).* Special Issue of *Yearbook of English Studies* 29.

Heim, Michael (1993) *The Metaphysics of Virtual Reality.* New York: Oxford University Press.

— (1998) *Virtual Realism.* New York: Oxford University Press.

Housman, A. E. (1921) "The Application of Thought to Textual Criticism." In John Carter (ed.), *Selected Prose*, pp. 131–50. Cambridge: Cambridge University Press, 1961.

Hrubý, Antonín (1965) "A Quantitative Solution to the Ambiguity of Three Texts." *Studies in Bibliography*, 18: 147–55.

Landow, George (1997) *Hypertext: The Convergence of Contemporary Critical Theory and Technology*, 2nd edn. Baltimore: Johns Hopkins University Press.

Langland, William (1975) *Piers Plowman: The B Version*, ed. George Kane and E. Talbot Donaldson. London: Athlone.

Lawrence, D. H. (1913) *Sons and Lovers.* London: Heinemann.

— (2002) *The Cambridge Edition of the Works of D. H. Lawrence*, 2 vols, rev. edn, ed. Helen Baron and Carl Baron. Cambridge: Cambridge University Press.

Levinson, Paul (1997) *The Soft Edge: A Natural History and Future of the Information Revolution.* New York: Routledge.

Levy, David M. (2001) *Scrolling Forward: Making Sense of Documents in the Digital Age.* New York: Arcade.

Loizeaux, Elizabeth Bergmann and Fraistat, Neil (eds.) (2002) *Reimagining Textuality: Textual*

Studies in the Late Age of Print. Madison: University of Wisconsin Press.

Maas, Paul (1927) *Textkritik*. Leipzig: Teubner; vol. 1, pt. 7 of *Einleitung in die Altertumswissenschaft*, ed. A. Gercke and E. Norden, 3rd edn (rev. edn, Leipzig: Teubner, 1950; 3rd edn, 1956; trans. Barbara Flower, Oxford: Clarendon Press, 1958).

McGann, Jerome J. (1983) *A Critique of Modern Textual Criticism*. Chicago: University of Chicago Press (revised edn, Charlottesville: University Press of Virginia, 1992).

— (ed.) (1985) *Textual Criticism and Literary Interpretation*. Chicago: University of Chicago Press.

— (1991) *The Textual Condition*. Princeton: Princeton University Press.

— (1997) "The Rationale of Hypertext." In Kathryn Sutherland (ed.), *Electronic Text: Investigations in Method and Theory*, pp. 19–46. Oxford: Clarendon Press.

— (2001) *Radiant Textuality: Literature after the World Wide Web*. New York: Palgrave/St. Martin's.

McKenzie, D. F. (1986) *Bibliography and the Sociology of Texts*. The Panizzi Lectures. London: British Library.

Masten, Jeffrey, Stallybrass, Peter, and Vickers, Nancy J. (eds.) (1997) *Language Machines: Technologies of Literary and Cultural Production*. New York: Routledge.

Modiano, Raimonda, Searle, Leroy, and Shillingsburg, Peter L. (eds.) (2004) *Voice, Text, and Hypertext at the Millennium*. Seattle: University of Washington Press.

Nunberg, Geoffrey (ed.) (1996) *The Future of the Book*. Berkeley: University of California Press.

Patterson, Lee (1985) "The Logic of Textual Criticism and the Way of Genius: The Kane–Donaldson *Piers Plowman* in Historical Perspective." In Jerome J. McGann (ed.), *Textual Criticism and Literary Interpretation*, pp. 55–91. Chicago: University of Chicago Press.

Quentin, Dom Henri (1926) *Essai de critique textuelle*. Paris: Picard.

Reiman, Donald H. (1984) "The Four Ages of Editing and the English Romantics." *Text*, 1: 231–55.

— (2006) "A Great Society." *Textual Cultures: Texts, Contexts, Interpretation*, 1 (1): 75–87.

Shakespeare, William (1986) *The Complete Works*, ed. Stanley Wells and Gary Taylor. Oxford: Clarendon Press.

Shillingsburg, Peter L. (1997) *Resisting Texts: Authority and Submission in Constructions of Meaning*. Ann Arbor: University of Michigan Press.

Sisson, C. H. (1979) "Pound among the Pedants." *Times Literary Supplement*, May 20.

Sutherland, Kathryn (ed.) (1997) *Electronic Text: Investigations in Method and Theory*. Oxford: Clarendon Press.

Tanselle, G. Thomas (1974) "Bibliography and Science." *Studies in Bibliography*, 27: 55–89 (reprinted in *Selected Studies in Bibliography*, pp. 1–35. Charlottesville: University Press of Virginia, 1979).

— (1984) "Presidential Address: Society for Textual Scholarship." *Text*, 1: 1–10.

Thorpe, James (ed.) (1970) *The Aims and Methods of Scholarship in Modern Languages and Literatures*, 2nd edn. New York: Modern Language Association of America (originally published 1963).

— (1972) *Principles of Textual Criticism*. San Marino, CA: Huntington Library.

Trevisa, John (1975) *Trevisa's Translation of Bartholomaeus Anglicus De Proprietatibus Rerum*, ed. M. C. Seymour et al. Oxford: Clarendon Press.

Turkle, Sherry (1995) *Life on the Screen: Identity in the Age of the Internet*. New York: Simon and Schuster.

3

The Uses of Quantification

Alexis Weedon

Because text production – in the past and now – frequently aimed at multiplying and spreading its product as much as possible, and because those texts commonly became subject to markets and market forces, historical records of books and the book trade sometimes take the form of lists of quantities. Particularly since the invention of printing, we sometimes have information about the fee paid to an author, the cost of paper, the cost of composition, print runs, the cost and rate of binding, the costs of advertising and distribution, and sales figures. In addition, there are sources that go back beyond the 1450s, such as lists of library acquisitions and catalogues of royal, state, church, and private collections. This historical information is usually patchy, the way it was recorded varied a great deal, and much more has been lost than survives, but, even so, the data available are rich enough and important enough to be treated seriously. This is where the quantitative history of the book, or *bibliometrics*, comes in. It does not answer all the questions, and often its answers need careful interpretation, but it does give us access to parts of book history that would otherwise be wholly inaccessible.

The historical data come from three main sources: from members of the book and allied trades who needed to account for their income and expenditure; from scholars, librarians, and bibliophiles who have described and listed their books; and from those who governed and wanted to legislate for the book trade, whether through copyright laws or taxation. As the motives for the collection of information vary for each source, so does the way in which it was collected. For these reasons there is little consistency between different sets of data available from the historical record. Unsurprisingly, more statistics are available for the later periods – the nineteenth and twentieth centuries in particular – and the following discussion does have a bias toward these centuries. Even so, quantitative analysis of existing data has provided some insights on subjects as various as the origin of the codex, the decline of the English Stock, and the distribution of books in eighteenth-century North America, as we shall see.

Common Sources for the Quantitative Study of the Book Trade

Members of the book and allied trades kept various kinds of record. Perhaps the most accessible are the trade publications. In Britain, *The Publishers' Circular* for the nineteenth and earlier twentieth centuries, and *The Bookseller* (Whitaker Information Services) for the later nineteenth and twentieth centuries contain statistics on the number of series published, a count of titles, and reviews of different sectors of the industry. Eliot and Sutherland's (1988) guide to the microfilm edition of *The Publishers' Circular* has an appendix referencing some of the statistical information published in the journal. Eliot's (1994) study of the trade journals, the British Library legal deposit ledgers, and Spicer's paper figures draws on a number of sources to compare trends between paper manufacture, the periodical trade, and book production in Britain from 1800 to 1919. The book contains a large number of tables containing the original data. National bibliographies can also be useful as they record new titles, with author, publisher, price, and date of publication. For the nineteenth century, such lists as *The English Catalogue* and *The Reference Catalogue to Current Literature* can prove useful.

The records of guilds, associations, and societies can often tell us a lot about book production. The Stationers' Company archive in Britain holds a wealth of information, some of which can be used for quantitative purposes, such as the list of works registered at Stationers' Hall, sales of English Stock, Bibles and almanacs, the number of apprentices bound, and so on. Robin Myers's (1990) guide is essential to understanding its contents and possibilities. Typographical societies published lists of members, recorded wages, and published their own descriptions of the working practices of the period. In Britain, in the nineteenth and twentieth centuries, trade associations (for example, the Publishers' Association, the Booksellers' Association, the Libraries' Association, and the Society of Authors) were established and they recorded legal cases, data on membership, and gathered statistics on matters of interest to their members.

Some bookselling, publishing, and printing firms also preserved their own records which include details of publications, costs for plant and different types of work, correspondence, and names of employees and shareholders. Robert Darnton's work in the archives of the Société typographique de Neuchâtel is a leading example (Darnton 1979). The society holds information which can be used for quantitative projects: Dominique Varry has extracted lists of book-trade workers in the eighteenth century for the French *Gens du livre* project, for example (Varry 1997, 1998). Similarly, in Britain, William St. Clair has gathered data from fifty publishing and printing archives in the Romantic period on prices, print runs, intellectual property, and readerships, and his work contains tables relating to these data (St. Clair 2004). In my own work on Victorian publishing, I have extracted production costs from publishers' and printers' ledgers and used them to quantify the growth by value of the industry and to estimate the size of the reading public, and I have drawn on official sources to compare this with the export trade in printed matter (tables containing these data are in the appendix to the book: Weedon 2003). Secondary sources are useful and point to what the archive contains and are a guide to its limitations. More general reference works, such as Basil Mitchell's (1988) collection of British historical statistics, also contain relevant data, such as wage indices for compositors, common economic indices for prices, production, and exports, and references to original sources which often offer more detailed data.

Moving from trade sources to the work of scholars, librarians, and bibliophiles, there is a range of possible resources. Bibliographers have examined books in terms of printing and techniques of illustration, binding, size, price, and number of sheets used. Book collectors tracing the provenance of a book have focused attention on ownership and the output of individual presses. Book historians have widened the view and used the firm's investment in plant, presses, foundry, machinery, and the range and quantity of a particular fount as an indicator of the firm's cultural capital and aesthetic contribution. Librarians and collectors have also compiled catalogues of book collections, listed and dated rare books – and estimated their value. All these have provided sources for bibliometrics. For example, Roberts and Skeat (1983) base their count of rolls and codices largely on Roger A. Pack's *The Greek and Latin Literary Texts from Greco-Roman Egypt* (1965) supplemented by more recent studies. They counted the number of surviving Greek texts in roll and codex form from the first to the fifth century and found that "it was only in the course of the third century that the codex obtained a significant share of book-production and it was not until about AD 300 that it achieved parity with the roll." However, by the fifth century, the codex had become the predominant form (Roberts and Skeat 1983: 37).

Particularly rich sources for bibliometrics are the union catalogues (International Federation of Library Associations and Institutions [IFLA] have a directory of National Union Catalogues). Much work was done during the past century on compiling a series of Short Title Catalogues, such as Pollard and Redgrave's *A Short Title Catalogue of Books Printed in England, Scotland and Ireland, and of English Books Printed Abroad, 1475–1640* (known as STC) or the *Eighteenth Century Short Title Catalogue* (known as ESTC). There is also the *Nineteenth Century Short Title Catalogue* which, although valuable, is less reliable, having been compiled on different principles and having not been updated for some time. The earlier STCs (many of which have now been combined to form the *English Short Title Catalogue* [also confusingly called the ESTC]) have formed the backbone for the quantitative statistics presented in *The Cambridge History of the Book in Britain*, the third volume of which, covering the period 1400–1557, contains STC statistical breakdown for the years 1547–58, and an overall survey of book production for the same period. The fourth volume, which covers the period from 1557 to 1695, contains statistical tables on annual book production from 1475 to 1700, subject classification of entries 1668–1709, translations into English 1560–1603, and numerous other tables. Similar work has been carried out for other national histories of the book. For example, in volume 1 of *The History of the Book in Canada*, Sandra Alston and Jessica Bowslaugh (2004) have drawn on the work of cataloguers for their statistical analysis of seven thousand Canadian imprints from 1760 to 1840. They sort and count the list by province and by subject to illustrate the increasing importance of Upper Canada after 1821; they also, by means of simple graph, demonstrate the increase in the number of titles after 1821. However, as the authors admit, only limited analysis has been done.

The third source of book-trade statistics are official records. Governments at all levels record and count. Official papers hold copyright records, customs records, records of parliamentary debates, inquiries, and commission reports, and so on. In these papers are quantitative data on the book trade derived from legal cases, investigations into the printing and allied trades, accounts of the quantities of books and stationery exported, and the duties payable on printed material. One instance is the Indian customs records of import duty on books and stationery in the nineteenth century from which the government produced an annual statement of trade. In Britain, national surveys of industrial production were carried out in 1907, 1924, 1930, and 1935 which quantified output and employment in, among many others, the printing and paper trades. The "Blue books," or parliamentary records, have statistics on the tax paid on advertising and paper, import and export duty paid at customs, and copyright dues. Many reports were hotly debated in parliament, recorded in *Hansard*, which then provoked public discussion in the press.

While many of these sources are well indexed and referenced, new discoveries are sometimes still made. In 1975, Michael Harris turned up a ledger in the Public Record Office among the State Papers Domestic. It was written by Charles Delafaye, then Secretary of State, and listed the names and quantities of newspapers he distributed in Queen Anne's reign, 1702–14 (Harris 1975).

Wills and bank records can also be useful sources: Lotte Hellinga and Margaret Lane Ford found wills useful in identifying books imported into Britain before 1550 (Hellinga and Trapp 1999). J. D. Fleeman drew on Samuel Johnson's diaries and the bank records of the account of the printer William Strahan in Gosling's bank to estimate Johnson's income. Fleeman calculated that over a twenty-one-year period Johnson's pension and earnings "would have produced £6,800, perhaps even £7,000." Yet Johnson, who was poor at accounting, died worth a little less than £3,000 (Fleeman 1975: 223).

Some sources have had more attention than others. Robert Darnton has commented:

> When book history began to establish itself in Western Europe, it relied heavily on quantification. The sources were always imperfect: the papers of the Stationers' Company and the library catalogues in the case of Britain; the registers for permission to publish and the depot legal in France; the catalogues of the Frankfurt and Leipzig book fairs in Germany. But however flawed or distorted, the statistics provided enough material for book historians to construct a general picture of literary culture . . . (Darnton 2002: 240)

Much of this work relies on simple counts of titles and quantities printed. There is still much more that can be done through the use of more sophisticated statistical methods.

Statistical Methods Used

Unlike social or economic history, book history does not have a long tradition of using quantitative methods. It must learn to borrow methods from economic and business historians, statisticians, and accountants to broaden the scope and definition of the subject. Each method, however, must be tailored to the peculiar needs of book-trade research.

The most common forms of quantitative analysis are those of the historian and the most common techniques of the historian are measures of central tendency and dispersion, trends, fluctuations, and correlation. Some projects require sampling of populations which can be difficult when the historical record is fragmentary. All these measurements must be balanced with measurements of error and statistical confidence which are essential in the interpretation of the data.

First, it is important to understand the form of the data before selecting a method of analysis. It may be nominal data giving numerical information on the number of surviving codices or rolls (Roberts and Skeat 1983). Or the data may be ordinal and therefore display a relationship between the categories; for example, readers of different occupations can be ordered by income and social status, as an extract from Richard Altick's list of new borrowers to a branch of Manchester Public Library in 1857–8 shows (1963: 236):

Clergymen, surgeons, other professions	11
Clerks, salesmen, commercial travellers	121
Labourers, porters etc.	29
Errand and office boys	74

Or, finally, the data could be interval data which contain information on the numerical increments. For example, signatures relate to imposition schemes, and must be divisible by four. Eli MacLaren used interval data from the collation formulas of Canadian, American, and British editions of Henryk Sienkiewicz's historical romance, *The Knights of the Cross* (1900) to prove that publishers affixed the title, imprint, copyright statement, and advertisements to the preprinted book blocks in order to produce and monopolize a bestseller in what was an intense international race to corner the market (MacLaren 2005).

Measures of central tendency are key to understanding what was usual practice and what was exceptional. They allow for comparison and evaluation of, for example, the average (or *mean*) print run of a Bible in 1647 and 1679, or the most frequently ordered print run (modal) by a publisher in the 1880s – which turned out to be a thousand (Weedon 2003). Once central measurements have been made, it is essential to record the level of deviation from them.

The most common statistical method used by book historians is frequency distribution. One example is the South African *Production Trends Database* established by the

Information Science Department at the University of Pretoria in 2001 using data from the *South African National Bibliography* (SANB), augmented and verified by other sources, such as records obtained from libraries, literary museums, and publishers' catalogues and price lists. They have also added data from publishers' archives and bibliographical information from the books themselves. The SANB is primarily a tool for librarians, which limits its usefulness as a source for book publishing statistics and production trends. Nevertheless, Francis Galloway (2005) has been able to analyze these data and produce tables of ISBN production by language from 1990 to 1998, concluding:

> There was a marked change in the language composition of title output in the 1990s. English grew from 48% of the annual production in 1990 to 58% of the annual production in 1998; Afrikaans declined from 28% to 21% of the annual production in these years; and the combined output in the nine African languages grew from 8% to 11%.

Trends and fluctuations require the data to be analyzed over a specified period of time: correlation requires the analysis of how different variables affected, for example, the geographical spread of books. Using bibliometric methods on the sequence of Short Title Catalogues from the *Incunable Short Title Catalogue* (ISTC) to the *Nineteenth Century Short Title Catalogue* (NSTC), book historians have been able to determine "the origins and nature of the printed books imported into England and Scotland in the late fifteenth and early sixteenth centuries, and of annual book production in England, Scotland and Ireland between 1475 and 1700" amongst other things (Eliot 2002: 284). For example, in 1992 Maureen Bell and John Barnard published their preliminary count of the titles in the STC from 1475 to 1640, vividly illustrating the increase in titles over the period with a frequency analysis exploring the fluctuations of continental books in the STC as well as the significance of British cities as centers of publication. This was done before the machine-readable version of the STC was available from the British Library. Revised statistics were later published in *The Cambridge History of the Book in Britain*, volume 4: *1557–1695* (Barnard and McKenzie 2002). Computers make statistical analysis easier and sometimes aid the gathering of the data, but rarely make the answers clearer. Bell and Barnard's work shows how a simple count can give us a clearer view of the topography of the publishing landscape.

Whatever method is employed it needs to be faithful to the original data and alert to the reasons for its original collection. Nevertheless, data collected for one purpose can often be used by the historian for quite a different one. Take, for example, the history of company records. Cyprian Blagden (1960) was able to illustrate how the Stationers' Company built up new capital during the eighteenth century by small increases in the number of shares and to demonstrate how this became an unsustainable business practice when, after 1796, the cash was used to pay tax. Half a century later, printing, newspaper, and publishing companies were forced to keep good accounts by law, and this makes it easier to examine the workings and profitability of their business. One good example from the United States is Michael Winship's (1995) account of the firm of Ticknor and Fields. His insights into the practices of mid-nineteenth-century American literary publishing are sharpened by statistics showing the firm's output, sales, and production costs extracted from the accounts of the time. Later still, the more sophisticated management systems in use in the latter half of the twentieth century make it appropriate for historians to seek to quantify the intellectual capital of a firm. Data on the length of product development, the extent of revisions and corrections, and the number and value of copyrights owned are also recorded in this period (*Bookseller* 1995; O'Donnell et al. 2006).

Common Limitations to Quantitative Analysis

The chief problem for the book historian wanting to use quantitative methods is the quality of the data. The sample is often small, selected for preservation or significance rather than at random, and the information on how the data were compiled or what they measured is sometimes lost. Primitive administration, book-keeping, and reporting procedures have created pseudo-statistics in the historical record; even published government figures are not necessarily clear or reliable. Nevertheless, they are all the book historian has and, though we may distrust them, we can also offer a guide to how they should be interpreted through stated degrees of uncertainty, ranges of confidence, and levels of significance. There are standard measures for error and deviation, correlation and confidence which give this information.

Where there is a wealth of historical data, quantitative descriptions seek to find trends and look for patterns. Categorization is a useful tool to group together similarities whether through the putting together of books by genre, authors by social background, or publishers by turnover. This aids the analysis of broader historical trends which could not be otherwise understood. However, statistical descriptions can retain evidence of the diversity in the data by measurements of variance and error. And unlike the consciously – or unconsciously – selective gathering of evidence in qualitative research, the means of gathering and interpreting patterns in quantitative data are made explicit with clear statements as to the levels of divergence from the patterns found.

Variance may not be recorded in the historical data series, though in some cases it can be partially retrieved. Take, for example, the average wage of a compositor in 1866 in Mitchell's (1988) statistics and in Howe and Waite's *The London Society of Compositors* (1948). Mitchell's figures are largely derived from Bowley's (1900) analysis of the *Reports* of the Scottish Typographical Society. Going back to his sources, the book historian can see that the figures for 1866 range from 18s 3d to 28s 3d per week. The London Society of Compositors' report in 1866 cited a range from 21s to 30s. The wages in their sample varied by region: yet the variation of 10s and 9s is comparable, and though there is not enough data to calculate standard deviation, this knowledge aids the interpretation of both authors' average wage figure.

Another frequent problem is comparability between two sets of figures. For example, it is tempting to compare Alex Hamilton's annual round-up of the top hundred British fastsellers with the Public Lending Right statistics on the most popularly borrowed books from libraries to see if there are related trends in borrowing and buying books (see Hamilton 2005). Hamilton lists books published in the calendar year with their country of origin, genre, recommended retail price, sales – home and export – and a simple calculation of their monetary value. The list ranks these in order, starting with the title with greatest sales. It offers quantitative information on the year's activity in the high-turnover fiction market. The Public Lending Right (PLR) issues statistics on the most borrowed authors from a sample of public libraries in the UK. Among other measures, their charts show the most popular genres, the top children's writers, and the most borrowed authors of classics. The statistics run from July to June, which makes direct comparison awkward but possible as both Hamilton's and the PLR's statistics have been published for more than two decades. The subject categories, however, are not compatible as they reflect the difference between the Dewey subject classification system and publishers' genre labels. What emerges from this study is not so much the presence of comparable trends as evidence for the influence of other media, particularly of film releases, on the borrowing and sale of specific titles.

Gaye Tuchman and Nina E. Fortin (1989), in their study of novelists, publishers, and social change, observed that "[s]ampling problems often tell researchers about the topic they are studying." They asked the question: were manuscripts by women authors as likely to be accepted as those by men in Victorian Britain? One of their sources was the record of the submission of manuscripts to the publisher Macmillan. In the appendix, Tuchman outlined two problems with the approach: first, the number of submissions per year increased over the period, and, secondly, the submission of manuscripts was seasonal, more manuscripts were received on some topics in some months:

> To draw quickly a sufficiently large sample, Tuchman would have had either to sample (1) every "xth" manuscript from November 1866 through 1917, (2) the first 350 manuscripts in systematically selected years, or (3) every manuscript in specified entire years enlarging the number of years sampled when in the chosen year Macmillan received relatively few submissions, as occurred in 1867 and 1877. The first method would have overrepresented the later decades; the second might have overrepresented some months. So Tuchman chose the third method. (Tuchman and Fortin 1989: 219)

The authors supported their thesis with quantitative evidence from numbers of submissions (percentage accepted, rejected, and published), and the qualitative judgments of reviewers on women's and men's fiction. They also used the nineteenth-century edition of *The Dictionary of National Biography* as a source of women writers. This is more problematical as the entries were selected by the editors, who applied their own criteria to determine what made a person distinguished enough to be included. Thus, any sample of these entries is already skewed by the editors' choice. Tuchman and Fortin wanted to examine the attitudes to women writers in comparison with their male counterparts, and this process of selection was one which, they concluded, reflected the "shift in gender concentration of novelists." In addition, coding the entries with a customized "fame index" introduced a further subjective element derived, in this case, from the research team who made efforts to ensure that this was consistently applied. Coding qualitative data for quantitative use is a recognized practice in statistics for social sciences and can be a useful tool. However, once qualitative values are brought into quantitative descriptions, readers have to judge the rigor of the researchers' methods – in this case the customized "fame index" and its application – for themselves. As with much statistical analysis, there is a tendency to discard things that do not fit the pattern. A clear statement of how the statistical exercise was conducted and monitored is vital. In this case, Tuchman and Fortin were concerned with the "edging out" of women novelists through the professionalization of the field, and they used their quantitative data to support their thesis, stating: "Before 1840 at least half of all novelists were women; by 1917 most high-culture novelists were men" (Tuchman and Fortin 1989: 7). Tuchman and Fortin's ideologically motivated work uses methods widely accepted in the social sciences, but care must be taken when applied to historical data.

Understanding Trends with Time Series

Most questions arising in book history contain an element of change though time. Where data are ordered chronologically, time-series analysis methods can be used. These methods are designed to help separate the different possible influences on the series so that we can estimate the importance of each. One simple way of showing year-by-year changes is to use ratios and indices. For instance, it might be useful to know how the number of titles published – as recorded in the STC – grew in the decades following the 1560s (see table 3.1). The raw figures show that between 1560 and 1600 the number of titles more than doubled. By using 1560 as the index figure, we can see that, in these forty years, the number of titles in fact increased by 133.2 percent. Plot the data and the increase looks linear. The rate of growth, should you want to calculate it, is 1.72 percent per year, but this is hardly necessary. However, a plot of the number of titles published in the nineteenth century has a curvilinear form indicating exponential growth (figure 3.1). When plotted on a logarithmic scale, the trend is apparent, and

Table 3.1   Growth in number of titles published 1560–1600, as recorded in the STC

Decade	Titles published	Percentage of 1560 total
1560	1,392	100.0
1570	1,908	137.1
1580	2,373	170.5
1590	2,549	183.1
1600	3,246	233.2

Source: Bell and Barnard (1992)

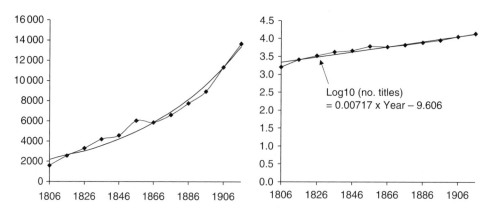

Figure 3.1   Number of titles published in nineteenth-century Britain. Data from A. Weedon, *Victorian Publishing: The Economics of Book Production for the Mass Market 1836–1916*, 2003.

we can show that the rate of growth published was 1.66 percent per year over the century.

However, if your time series shows fluctuations then other methods may be necessary to distinguish between different influences. Monthly figures for tonnage of paper can show the long-term *trend* in paper production. In addition, there may be *regular fluctuations* which indicate a seasonal variation. Lastly, there may be *irregular fluctuations*, such as the fall in paper production during civil war, or changes in tariffs and taxes. The book historian has to decide what the factors might be, then use the tool of time-series analysis to estimate the effect of short-term influences on the long-term trends. Another way of isolating trends from regular fluctuations is to plot four- or five-year moving averages, as Simon Eliot does to considerable effect in his essential source (Eliot 1994). However, it can have its limitations: if you do not know the frequency of the fluctuations, you can misrepresent the data by selecting the wrong length of time. (In my work on book-production costs, time-series data are affected by business cycles, which in the nineteenth century varied in length from five to ten years.)

To isolate the variations, you calculate the original data as a percentage of the trend, and then the deviation from the original data as a percentage of the trend. This result conflates regular cycles with irregular fluctuations which can make interpretation difficult; for example, showing seasonal variations in the cost of paper, the overall trend in the cost and the irregular variations caused by supply problems during blockades, wars, transport problems, and so on. You can isolate the regular cycles from the irregular fluctuations to separate the long-run trend, recurrent seasonal fluctuations, and residual fluctuations so that you can analyze each separately. Feinstein and Thomas give a clear account of how this is calculated on data on bankruptcies in England from 1780 to 1784 (2002: 28–30). Of course, this has to be used appropriately: applied to the STCs, the regular cycles of five and ten years may tell us more about cataloguers' habits of "rounding" the date of publication to the next half-decade, decade, or century than giving us insights into cycles of production. In this case, the seasonal and irregular fluctuations caused by other factors may be of more significance. In the end, the mode of presentation is the choice of the book historian who is, after all, simply offering an interpretation of the statistics.

Reading Variables

Many questions book historians want to ask are about the relationship between different factors. We want to know if there is a relationship, how strong it is, and, if possible, what form it takes and whether it is coincidental. I might be interested to know, for instance, if there is a relationship between the quantity of books manufactured and the average price, or perhaps the number of books written by an author and his or her wealth at death. As a comparison between two numerical variables, the task is largely a statistical one. However, when qualitative responses are coded for statistical analysis, some level of interpretation becomes integrated into the data. Social scientists familiar with the design of questionnaires have strict methodological procedures to reduce researcher bias and numerous statistical methods to interpret combinations of numerical and category variables.

Researchers in this field have employed techniques found in studies of contemporary society from questionnaires to content analysis of the media. One powerful tool is multivariate analysis, which is commonly used by media and marketing analysts today and requires large, robust datasets or survey data. Eiri Elvestad and Arild Blekesaune use data about newspaper-reading in twenty-two European countries from the European Social Survey (2002), demographic data from Eurostat, and data from World Press Trends 2005. Their multivariate analysis is used to describe national differences in newspaper-reading and to explain how these differences occur (Elvestad and Blekesaune 2006). Vincent Greaney (1980), on the other hand, uses data from a survey to explore the factors related to amount and type of leisure-time reading. Among the variables he examined were gender, level of reading attainment, leisure activities, socio-economic status, family size, choice of television programs, and location and type of primary school attended. Not all had a significant influence on the 5.4 percent of leisure time the pupils devoted to recreational reading. Using multiple regression analyses, Greaney deduced that "most of the explained variation (22.9 per cent) in time devoted to books was accounted for by a combination of the variables gender, reading attainment, school location, library membership, and birth order" (1980: 337). To improve our understanding of the book and its effect on society through history, it is important to adapt and extend these kinds of analysis so that we can use them on the historical record.

One project that seeks to record elusive information on changes in reading habits is the Reading Experience Database (RED). The project has a web-based public interface for researchers, who can input data to the project wherever they are connected. The online form prompts the researcher to input the details of who read what, where and when, in company or alone, silently or aloud. As the historical period is wide – from

1450 to 1945 – standard sociological groupings are not useful and categories have been designed for the purpose. The genre groupings are also specially designed to capture popular subjects through the period. Information is drawn from a range of sources, including autobiographies, diaries, letters, scrapbooks, and annotations in books, and thus obviously cannot be considered a random sample of historical reading practices. The sample is selective, representing as it does those who had the leisure and inclination to record their reading experience. It will also be biased by the sources read by the contributors – inevitably "rich" sources are preferred. Even within this group, however, it would be interesting to compare variables: what proportion of Bible readers in the first half of the sixteenth century read aloud to company? How did this change in the following centuries? What did agricultural laborers read at the time of the French Revolution and how had this changed by the fall of Napoleon Bonaparte?

The RED form was designed to investigate historical reading practice. But often historians have to use surveys or questionnaires created in the past. Researchers interested in mid-twentieth-century reading habits and library use in Britain have turned to the Mass Observation archive. Helpfully, interview subjects were coded according to sex, age group, class, and sometimes location, and the survey used standard sociological groupings. The numbers of respondents are known and this makes it far easier to analyze the findings and quantify the correlation. Joseph McAleer (1992), Alistair Black (2000), and Jonathan Rose (2001), amongst others, have made use of this valuable source of qualitative and quantitative information for the history of the book. Rose's investigation of the *Intellectual Life of the British Working Classes* (2001) quotes figures from a survey in 1944 which asked: "How many books were in your parents' home? And did your parents encourage reading?" The survey found "that nearly two-thirds of skilled workers and almost half of all unskilled workers grew up in homes with substantial collections of books and that working class parents of the previous generation had encouraged reading" (Rose 2001: 231). In this case, it may not be necessary to look for a statistical correlation between the factors; the link seems obvious. However, it might also be useful to calculate a correlation between the following question: "Do you think there are any changes in the way education is run which ought to be made after the war?" and the suggested changes ("Equal and greater opportunity" and "What do you feel about the school leaving age being raised?"). Of the two suggested changes, the stronger correlation turns out to be between low socio-economic class and the desire for equal and greater opportunity which supports the interpretation that this is the most desired change. Raising the school leaving age is not the reason as the correlation is low (at 0.54; see table 3.2).

There is a body of work on the phenomenon of book groups, which traces their history and resurgent popularity. Scholars in this field have used survey methods in their research. Elizabeth Long's (2003) ethnographic study takes an historical view of women's book groups from the Civil War in America to the present day, using questionnaires and observer-participation techniques to gather data from currently active groups. Jenny Hartley's (2001) survey of contemporary British book groups draws on a core of 350 groups which answered questionnaires designed to elicit qualitative information, which Hartley then followed up with e-mails and visits. Exploring their

Table 3.2   Correlating responses to questions asked in 1944 survey

	Middle class (%)	Upper working class (%)	Lower working class (%)
How many books were in your parents' home?			
Many books	87	63	42
Did your parents encourage reading?			
Yes	63	48	38
Do you think there are any changes [in education] which ought to be made after the war?			
Yes	90	85	79
If yes, what changes?			
Equal and greater opportunity	35	39	48
What do you feel about the school age being raised?			
Approve	61	72	50

Source: Rose (2001: tables 5.10 and 6.5A)

composition and processes, she presents the voices and attitudes of the various groups, supporting her commentary with an indication of their representativeness derived from a numerical analysis of the responses. Using the powerful reach of the Internet, DeNel Sedo's (2003) online survey of book clubs lends itself to statistical analysis of location, composition, age, genre preference, and so on. The self-selected sample supports Long's and Hartley's evidence that book groups appeal predominantly to women and are used largely as a place to reflect upon their life experience. Sedo compares members' views of the advantages and disadvantages of meeting as a group at a fixed time and place with the less constrained social interaction available online.

The Internet has been beneficial to many projects. Finding aids, census information, data sets, and a lot more besides are directly accessible. Creating a digital archive which can then be made available via the Internet is *de rigueur* for a new research project today. The Internet has made the tracking of books and dissemination of texts much easier for professionals and amateur enthusiasts alike. Information scientists analyze the information recorded about a book or article on a database or in a citation index such as the ISI Web of Knowledge[SM] (www.thomsonisi.com), Scientific Citation Index, Arts and Humanities Index, and so on. Applied to scientific publications, it is a way of determining the life-cycle of the literature on a specific subject. The analysis of the number of citations – in particular, their distribution and longevity – can be used to quantify "reputation," and this has been used to inform policy on scientific research and as an indicator of the spread of ideas and research findings. At the opposite end of the spectrum, a community site, bookcrossing.com, enables enthusiasts to track the life of a book as it passes though the hands of readers. Both measure the dissemination and usage of the printed text, but for very different purposes.

Geographical Distribution

Globalization, visionaries proclaim, changes our understanding of time and space, and this is perhaps particularly true in the case of the application of Geographical Information Software (GIS). Early studies of book distribution in Canada traced the westward spread of communication routes though the building of roads and railways and the rise of newsagent networks. Harold Innis and others working in the 1950s and 1960s showed the importance of geography in our conceptualization of the historical spread of print (Innis 1950, 1951; Carpenter and McLuhan 1960). However, the logistics of collating and plotting geographical data by hand meant that spatial analysis of historical data was limited. Now GIS can offer the opportunity of storing, mapping, and interrogating spatial data on an unprecedented scale. This has given rise to a number of fascinating historical atlases which show graphically, for instance, examples of agricultural land use, urbanization, or the transport infrastructure in the past. The correlation of spatial and temporal data gives insights into such things as the rise and decline of centers of print production within a country. Data from other historical sources can be included as variables within the analysis of print culture and help to confirm old theories (such as the links between the stage coach and sea routes and the spread of print distribution) and raise new and now potentially answerable questions such as "Do the demographics of printers and religious sects correlate?"

While the potential of GIS is considerable, two obstacles have slowed down its adoption in book history. First, the task of collating and combining databases to ensure the information is in a suitable form for analysis is a big one, particularly when many databases were originally constructed without reference to the needs of GIS software. Secondly, GIS software is better at exploring data spatially at a specific historical moment than tracking developments through time. Ian Gregory points out how it has been used effectively in historical research and then points to its limitations:

> A good example of this approach is taken by Kennedy *et al.* (1999) in their atlas of the Great Irish famine. The atlas uses census data to show demographic changes resulting from the famine. At its core are layers representing the different administrative geographies used to publish the censuses of 1841, 1851, 1861 and 1871. These layers are linked to a wide variety of census data from these dates. This allows sequences of maps to be produced showing, for example, how the spatial distribution of housing conditions and use of the Irish language change over time.
>
> While this approach is simple and effective, it is only suitable for a limited number of dates or where change occurs at clearly defined times between periods of relative stability. More complex situations are more problematic. (Gregory 2002)

Alternative approaches have been used to resolve this problem. The Great Britain Historical GIS has used a "date stamping" system where each feature has a date stamp attached which defines the time during which it was in existence, while Langran (1992) proposed a space–time composite approach which has been used by the Swedish

National Topographic Database, the Belgian Quantitative Databank, and others. Both have their limitations.

Nonetheless, the advantages of GIS are sufficiently great that book historians have begun to engage with it. Pioneers in this field, the Canadian scholars Fiona Black, Bertrum MacDonald, and J. Malcolm Black proposed "A New Research Method for Book History: Geographical Information Systems" in 1998. They observed that both the Great Britain Historical Database and the Data Library and UK Borders project "are examples of large historical GIS projects that have begun to seek researchers in a wide variety of fields, who may have databases that could be linked to already available historical map information" (Black et al. 1998: 23). Looking for international collaboration, they sought to combine available information from Scottish customs records, shipping manifests, and other book-trade and demographic databases. Seven years later, research completed for the second volume of *The History of the Book in Canada* (*Histoire du livre et de l'imprimé au Canada*) permits analysis and comparison, by region and by town, of the ethnicity, religion, and specific occupation of book-trade members compared with the general population for the same region in the later nineteenth century (Lamonde et al. 2005). Currently, Malcolm Black and Fiona Black are developing an interactive site where researchers will be able to use map-based queries to investigate aspects of book-trade and library development for selected periods, and to combine the responses with transportation information and with rich demographic data about potential readerships.

The strong heritage of history and bibliography has exerted a guiding hand over the emergence of book history as a separate field. As Michael Schudson points out, this has created a vibrant and thriving discipline, but he also sounds a note of warning:

> In no other area of communication history has there been such a systematic gathering of archival sources, piggybacking on the work of bibliographers and bibliophiles. In no other domain of communication history have the various workers in the field had enough common interaction to establish a critical community . . . For all these virtues the history of the book may become too successful as a "subdiscipline" of history proper and fail to exploit the bolder vision of communication history that comes from its more adventurous proponents in cultural and literary studies and anthropology. (Schudson 1991: 176)

The variety of methods being used in book history is broadening as researchers from different backgrounds and with different questions enter this fertile field. Web-based projects, GIS software, and the social analysis of reading, book clubs, and print circulation take researchers beyond the confines of a strictly historical methodology. Nevertheless, new methods should always be sought for the insights they give. Sources are always imperfect, yet the appropriate use of quantitative methods can carry great persuasive power. They can confirm or question an impression and, employed well, can offer greater degrees of certainty than many other forms of historical analysis.

References and Further Reading

Alston, S. and Bowslaugh, J. (2004) "A Statistical Analysis of Early Canadian Imprints." In P. L. Fleming, G. Gallichan, and Y. Lamonde (eds.), *The History of the Book in Canada*, vol. 1: *Beginnings to 1840*, pp. 88–93. Toronto: University of Toronto Press.

Altick, R. (1963) *The English Common Reader: A Social History of the Mass Reading Public 1800–1900*. Chicago: University of Chicago Press.

Barnard, J. and McKenzie, D., with Bell, M. (2002) *The Cambridge History of the Book in Britain*, vol. 4: *1557–1695*. Cambridge: Cambridge University Press.

Bell, M. and Barnard, J. (1992) "Provisional Count of STC Titles, 1475–1640." *Publishing History*, 31: 47–64.

Black, A. (2000) *The Public Library in Britain 1914–2000*. London: The British Library.

Black, F., MacDonald, B., and Black, J. M. (1998) "A New Research Method for Book History: Geographical Information Systems." *Book History*, 1: 11–31.

Blagden, C. (1960) *The Stationers' Company: A History 1403–1959*. Stanford: Stanford University Press.

Bookseller (1995) *Book Publishing in Britain*. London: J. Whitaker and Sons.

Bowley, A. L. (1900) *Wages in the United Kingdom in the Nineteenth Century*. Cambridge: Cambridge University Press.

Carpenter, E. and McLuhan, M. (eds.) (1960) *Explorations in Communication: An Anthology*. New York: Beacon.

Darnton, R. (1979) *The Business of Enlightenment: A Publishing History of the Encyclopédie, 1775–1800*. Cambridge, MA: Belknap Press of Harvard University Press.

— (2002) "Book Production in British India, 1850–1900". *Book History*, 5: 239–62.

Eliot, S. (1994) *Some Patterns and Trends in British Publishing 1800–1919*. Occasional Papers of the Bibliographical Society, 8. London: The Bibliographical Society.

— (2002) "Very Necessary but Not Quite Sufficient." *Book History*, 5: 283–93.

— and Sutherland, J. (1988) *The Publishers' Circular 1837–1900: Guide to the Microfiche Edition*. Cambridge: Chadwyck-Healey.

Elvestad, Eiri and Blekesaune, Alrid (2006) "Newspaper Reading and Reading about Politics and Current Affairs in Europe: A Comparative Study." Paper presented at the Conference on Media in the Enlarged Europe, University of Luton, May 5–6.

European Social Survey (2002) Available at http://ess.nsd.uib.no/index.jsp.

Feinstein, C. H. and Thomas, M. (2002) *Making History Count: A Primer in Quantitative Methods for Historians*. Cambridge: Cambridge University Press.

Fleeman, J. D. (1975) "The Revenue of a Writer." In R. W. Hunt, I. G. Philip, and R. J. Roberts (eds.), *Studies in The Book Trade in Honour of Graham Pollard*. Oxford: Oxford Bibliographical Society.

Floud, R. (1973) *An Introduction to Quantitative Research Methods for Historians*. London: Methuen.

Galloway, F. (2005) "Trends in the South African Book Publishing Industry since the 1990s" (available at www.nlsa.ac.za/bibliophilia8_2005/edgalloway.doc).

Greaney, V. (1980) "Factors Related to Amount and Type of Leisure Time Reading." *Reading Research Quarterly*, 15 (3): 337–57.

Gregory, I. (2002) "A Place in History: A Guide to Using GIS in Historical Research" (available at hds.essex.ac.uk/g2gp/gis/index.asp).

Hamilton, A. (2005) "The Winners Decoded." *Guardian* review section, January 1: 30–1.

Harris, M. (1975) "Newspaper Distribution during Queen Anne's Reign: Charles Delafaye and the Secretary of State's Office." In R. W. Hunt, I. G. Philip, and R. J. Roberts (eds.), *Studies in the Book Trade in Honour of Graham Pollard*. Oxford: Oxford Bibliographical Society.

Hartley, J. (2001) *Reading Groups*. Oxford: Oxford University Press.

Hellinga, L. and Trapp, J. B. (1999) *The Cambridge History of the Book in Britain*, vol. 3: *1400–1557*. Cambridge: Cambridge University Press.

Howe, E. and Waite, H. (1948) *The London Society of Compositors: A Centenary of History*. London: Cassell.

IFLA (International Federation of Library Associations and Institutions) *Directory of National*

Union Catalogues (available at www.ifla.org/VI/2/duc/index.htm).

Innis, H. A. (1950) *Empire and Communications*, ed. David Godfrey. Victoria, BC: Press Porcepic, 1986.

— (1951) *The Bias of Communication*, with an introduction by Marshall McLuhan. Toronto: University of Toronto Press, 1964.

Kennedy, L., Ell, P. S., Crawford, E. M., and Clarkson, L. A. (1999). *Mapping the Great Irish Famine: A Survey of the Famine Decades*. Portland: Four Courts.

Lamonde, Y., Fleming, P. L., and Black, F. A. (eds.) (2005) *History of the Book in Canada*, vol. 2: *1840–1918*. Toronto: University of Toronto Press (published in French as *Histoire du livre et de l'imprimé au Canada*, vol. 2: *1840–1918*. Montreal: Presses de Université de Montréal).

Langran, G. (1992) *Time in Geographical Information Systems*. London: Taylor Francis.

Long, E. (2003) *Book Clubs: Women and the Uses of Reading in Everyday Life*. Chicago: University of Chicago Press.

McAleer, J. (1992) *Popular Reading and Publishing in Britain 1914–1950*. Oxford: Oxford Historical Monographs.

MacLaren, E. (2005) "*The Knights of the Cross*: Bibliographic Evidence of Copyright Law in Early Twentieth-century Canada." Paper presented at the Annual Conference of the Society for the History of Authorship, Reading and Publishing, Halifax, July 14–17.

Mitchell, B. (1988) *British Historical Statistics*. Cambridge: Cambridge University Press.

Myers, R. (1990) *The Stationers' Company Archive: An Account of the Records 1554–1984*. Winchester: St. Paul's Bibliographies.

— (2001) *The Stationers' Company: A History of the Later Years 1800–2000*. London: The Worshipful Company of Stationers and Newspaper Makers.

O'Donnell, D., Henriksen, L. B., Sven, C., and Voelpel, S. C. (2006) "Intellectual Capital: Becoming Critical." *Journal of Intellectual Capital*, special issue, vol. 7, no. 1.

Pack, R. A. (1965) *The Greek and Latin Literary Texts from Greco-Roman Egypt*, 2nd edn. Ann Arbor: University of Michigan Press.

Reading Experience Database (available at www.open.ac.uk/Arts/RED).

Roberts, C. H. and Skeat, T. C. (1983) *The Birth of the Codex*. London: The British Academy/Oxford University Press.

Rose, J. (2001) *The Intellectual Life of the British Working Classes*. New Haven: Yale University Press.

St. Clair, W. (2004) *The Reading Nation in the Romantic Period*. Cambridge: Cambridge University Press.

Schudson, M. (1991) "Media Contexts: Historical Approaches to Media Studies." In K. B. Jensen and N. W. Janowski (eds.), *A Handbook of Qualitative Methodologies for Mass Communication Research*, pp. 175–89. London. Routledge.

Sedo, D. (2003) "Readers and Reading Groups: An Online Survey of Face-to-face and Virtual Book Clubs". *Convergence: The International Journal of Research into New Media Technologies*, 9 (1): 66–90.

Tuchman, G. and Fortin, N. E. (1989) *Edging Women Out: Victorian Women Novelists, Publishers and Social Change*. London: Routledge.

Varry. D. (1997) "Round about Rue Mercière: The People of the 18th-century Book Trade in Lyon" (available at histoire.enssib.fr/5outils/livre_lyonnais/rue_merciere.html#note2).

— (1998) "Women in the 18th-century Lyons Book Trade" (available at histoire.enssib.fr/5outils/livre_lyonnais/women18e.html#note1).

Weedon, A. (2003) *Victorian Publishing: The Economics of Book Production for the Mass Market 1836–1916*. Aldershot: Ashgate.

Winship, M. (1995) *American Literary Publishing in the Mid-nineteenth Century: The Business of Ticknor and Fields*. Cambridge: Cambridge University Press.

4
Readers: Books and Biography

Stephen Colclough

Some book historians are concerned to reveal what people actually read in the past, rather than what literary history suggests they should have read. By using the archival records of publishers, printers, and booksellers, it is possible to uncover vital information about print runs, prices, and purchasers and, through an accumulation of these data, to discover which books were most widely available. This work has already begun to alter the way in which we think about literary history. For example, William St. Clair's (2004) study of the period 1790–1840 dispels many of the myths associated with textual production and reception during the Romantic period. The publisher John Murray, St. Clair notes, "seems habitually to have claimed to have sold more editions of works by Byron than his ledgers show were manufactured" (2004: 25). He also demolishes Byron's oft-repeated claim that a bad review by Southey greatly encouraged sales of Shelley's *Revolt of Islam* by looking at the record of the actual number of copies sold, which was few (2004: 189).

It is, perhaps, not all that surprising to discover that Shelley's first audience was very small, but St. Clair's investigation of book prices reveals that even the most popular new books produced during this period sold in relatively small numbers. This was because they were often staggeringly expensive. In 1812, a bound quarto copy of Byron's *Childe Harold's Pilgrimage* cost "about half the weekly income of a gentleman" (St. Clair 2004: 195). Byron may have thought that he had become famous overnight, but only 500 copies of the first edition of this work were produced and it cost around £2 10s to buy. The size of Byron's audience grew as cheaper editions of his work became available, and some pirated editions were very cheap, but the majority of books bought during the Romantic period were cheap reprints of earlier works. Often issued in series, they sold for as little as 1s 6d per volume. This meant that the work of out-of-copyright authors, such as Oliver Goldsmith and James Thomson, had a much wider audience than most of the major authors that we associate with this period (St. Clair 2004: 207).

This is a very important revisionist argument, and St. Clair, like other book historians, is keen to demonstrate how book history as a discipline can throw new light on the way in which Enlightenment thought was communicated. Throughout his work, he notes the way in which "the censorship of price" restricted access to texts, but he is also able to dispel the myth that Thomas Paine's pamphlet *The Rights of Man* (1791) was one of the most widely available, and therefore most influential, texts of the 1790s simply because it was produced in a cheap edition. Paine's rejoinder to Edmund Burke's *Reflections on the Revolution in France* (1790) was initially published at the relatively cheap price of 3s 6d. There is some evidence to suggest that it was popular with middle-class reading clubs, but the government quickly suppressed a later 6d edition because it was worried about the pamphlet becoming available to working-class readers. Paine was convicted of seditious libel and a number of booksellers who continued to sell the pamphlet after the ban were imprisoned. Reading clubs removed the pamphlet from their stock, and by 1794 the book was no longer easy to obtain. As this account makes clear, *The Rights of Man* was less widely available than the *Reflections*, which after 1794 "was left triumphant in the field as the main political text of the time" (St. Clair 2004: 257). This is a brilliant reassessment of the cultural impact of a text, and of what was available to be read at a given moment, but it leaves the question of *how* these texts were interpreted almost completely unexplored.

As Robert Darnton has argued, "to pass from the *what* to the *how* of reading is an extremely difficult step" (Darnton 1984: 222). For most of us, reading is just one of our everyday activities, and because it is so comprehensible, so familiar, it is difficult to imagine that it has a history — that reading "now" is not the same as reading was "then." Darnton's own work on the history of reading in Enlightenment France often begins by defamiliarizing this everyday event. He asks his own reader to think about Ovid's account of a love letter inscribed upon the body of a Roman slave, or the way in which the recitation of texts at a Balinese funeral is thought to ward away evil demons, in order to suggest that the reading practices of the late eighteenth century can appear similarly alien to a modern consciousness (Darnton 1984: 206; 1990: 154–87). For example, he notes that during the 1780s French readers often commented upon the material quality of the books that they studied in order to suggest that "this typographical consciousness has disappeared now that books are mass produced for a mass audience" (Darnton 1984: 223).

Other scholars interested in the ways in which books were used and interpreted in the past have discovered similarly unfamiliar practices. For example, Michael Clanchy's work on texts produced between 1066 and 1307 reveals a vast range of reading practices. "Medieval texts," he argues "were designed to be read in a variety of ways – orally or silently, by one person or in a group – and at different levels of meaning, taking account of word and image and a variety of linguistic registers" (Clanchy 1993: 195). Even legal documents were embellished with seals and illustrations which needed interpretation. As this evidence suggests, medieval ideas about "literacy" were very different from our own. Readers such as Lady Eleanor De Quincy, for whom the Lambeth Apocalypse was produced, probably could not write, but their books demanded the ability to read in three languages (Latin, French, and English) and the skill of meditating upon the "book of imagery." The Lambeth Apocalypse contains many illustrations which show that keeping a holy image in the mind's eye was particularly important to medieval readers. As Clanchy argues, "the ultimate stage" for these readers "was contemplation, when the reader 'saw with his heart,' like St. John the author of the Apocalypse, the truth of hidden things." This "non-utilitarian approach to reading is," he concludes, "alien to modern western culture" (Clanchy 1993: 195).

Similarly, the books of the Renaissance scholar Gabriel Harvey reveal that he was paid to guide readers through classical texts in order that they might direct their reading toward political action. As Lisa Jardine and Anthony Grafton note, this discovery has important implications for the history of the book, as well as the history of reading: "If we use our own understanding of the salient features of the text of Livy (say) to identify the points of crucial importance to an Elizabethan reader we are very likely to miss or to confuse the methods and objects at which reading was directed" (Jardine and Grafton 1990: 30). Their work casts doubt upon the ability of descriptive bibliography to recover reading practices from a close study of typographical features or the protocols of reading embedded in texts. Our reading of Livy, they suggest, can never be the same as Harvey's even if we study exactly the same text.

Of course, all reading takes place in context, and to return to the example from St. Clair, it is possible that a reader examining a copy of Burke's *Reflections* borrowed from an ideologically conservative subscription library would have read the text in a recognizably conservative way. However, the history of reading needs to give at least some account of what it was possible to do with a text in any given period. As St. Clair's work makes clear, institutions of reading (such as subscription libraries) helped to shape individual reading practices by encouraging the public discussion of texts. Several readers who were members of such institutions left records of their reading. The diaries of one such reader, Joseph Hunter (1783–1861), reveal that it was possible for a member of such an institution to interpret texts in ways that were fundamentally opposed to the rules that governed their reading community.

During the late 1790s, Hunter was a member of the Surrey Street Library in Sheffield, Yorkshire. Surrey Street was a subscription library owned by its members. Members were charged an annual fee of one guinea, and both they and the books that they ordered had to pass the scrutiny of the library committee to be admitted. As Hunter records, he made frequent trips to the library to borrow a wide range of texts, including novels and magazines. The *Analytical Review* was a particular favorite, and he made notes on its contents and read texts, such as Robinson's *The Causes and Consequences of English Wars* (1798), reviewed in its pages. However, in the autumn of 1798 the committee decided to remove many of the texts associated with the contemporary radical movement from its shelves. As Hunter noted on October 31, 1798: "[I] brought the 2[n]d number of the Anti-Jacobin Review & Magazine, which is got into the Surry Street Library instead of the Analytical which they have turned out. It is a most virulent attack upon all the friends of liberty or *jacobins*, as they are pleased to stile them; it is ornamented with caricature prints" (Colclough 2000: 33).

Conservative writers viewed the *Analytical* as an important source of opposition to the war that Britain was fighting against France in the 1790s. James Gillray's cartoon, "The New Morality," which appeared in the inaugural issue of the *Anti-Jacobin*, depicts a number of texts (including Robinson's *Causes*) spilling forth from a "cornucopia of ignorance" inscribed with the titles of three reviews, the *Analytical*, the *Monthly*, and the *Critical*. The library committee may well have excluded the *Analytical* because it wanted to disassociate itself from opposition to the war against France, but the effect on Hunter was to make him aware of his own position as a member of an audience that was under attack. He is referring to himself as one of "the friends of liberty" in this passage from the diary, and it is from this position that he completed an oppositional, or resisting, reading of the contents of the *Anti-Jacobin*.

As this example suggests, Hunter's diaries provide an important account of both the range of his reading (which included everything from ephemera to novels) and of the variety of strategies that he used to make sense of texts. He even noted the presence of posters for political meetings in the streets and that he had seen men reading seditious periodicals at work (Colclough 2000: 44). Such autobiographical documents are an important source of information about how texts were used. They provide vital evidence about reading as an everyday practice (sometimes passive, sometimes, as in his reading of the *Anti-Jacobin*, resisting) that cannot be recovered from inert sources such as publishers' records. Hunter's diary records that he was exceptionally well read in contemporary texts, but he was also exposed to older texts which he borrowed from his guardian or bought second-hand.

Of course, it is possible to argue that most diarists are not "typical" or "common" readers. As a member of a library with an exclusive membership, Hunter certainly had much greater access to recently published texts than most of his contemporaries, but this does not mean that we should discount his evidence. Indeed, the concept of the "common" or typical reader has begun to appear increasingly anachronistic to scholars who are concerned with issues of difference and diversity. Hunter's experience was obviously very different from the majority of readers who could not afford to join a subscription library, but it was also very different from other members of the same reading community. As Kate Flint has argued, evidence of what "individual women were actually reading" complicates our view of "the woman reader" of the nineteenth century by "challenging many of the generalizations advanced by contemporary commentators." She goes on to suggest that such evidence "reminds us of the specificities of circumstance, the variables of parental occupation and family affluence, of urban and rural lives, of religious affiliations, enthusiastic relatives, and modes of education which militate against establishing neat patterns of generalization whether contemporaneous or retrospective" (Flint 1993: 187).

This argument suggests that the "typical" or "common reader," like the "woman reader," is something of a fantasy, and many historians of reading have begun to use the term "the historical reader" instead. This term takes into account the way in which the individual reader is situated within a personal history, of the kind referred to by Flint, as well as the broader historical contexts of gender, class, and race. As Margaret

Beetham has argued, historians who use this term pay attention to both the materiality of the source being investigated and the "historical specificity of the reader as a complex subject" (2000: 94). No source simply offers an unmediated insight into reading practices, and Beetham's own study of periodical readers pays attention to the way in which the genre or convention of the source (in this instance the newspaper correspondents' column) helps to define the historical reader that is uncovered.

By examining autobiographical sources to reveal the experience of historical readers, such as Hunter, it should be possible to recover something of what Anthony Grafton has called "the obstinate, irreducible individualism" of the reader (Grafton 1997: 141). And if we are able to locate enough archival material, it may also be possible to suggest something about the range of reading practices available in a given period. Hunter's account of willfully misreading the *Anti-Jacobin Review*, for example, suggests that he made sense of this text within the rules laid down by his own reading community. His reading was certainly "obstinate" and individual, but the quotidian experience of visiting the library to borrow books was one that he shared with many other readers during the 1790s.

What kind of archive material do we need to investigate in order to recover the historical reader? Much of the most compelling evidence for the history of reading recovered so far has come from studies of the ways in which readers annotated the books that they owned or borrowed. Indeed, it is possible to think of the history of reading as "a marginal enterprise," but many historians remain skeptical about using marginalia to reconstruct reading practices (Grafton 1997). As H. J. Jackson has noted, these historians tend to question whether annotations give any useful insight into the "mental processes of reading"; "doubts focus on the privacy of the experience and the typicality of the surviving records" (Jackson 2001: 255). Anyone making notes on their reading in the margin is, of course, restrained by the amount of room available at the edge of the text, and may well be conscious that their marks are going to be interpreted by a later reader, but Jackson's argument that annotations "stay about as close to the running mental discourse that accompanies reading as it is possible to be" (2001: 256) is convincing. As this study of marginalia also makes clear, however, the concern with "mental process" is something of a chimera. Annotations made during the Romantic period frequently reveal evidence of reading as a social process – they were indeed made with other readers in mind – and in order to work in this way they often reproduced typical patterns of reading. Jackson argues that Hester Piozzi's annotations reveal that "she read both as a particular reader under special circumstances and as a typical reader of her time, governed and constrained by deep structures common to all" (2001: 257).

Most of the studies of marginalia undertaken so far have tended to look at professional writers, such as Piozzi, or the reception of canonical texts, but it is possible to find collections of books that belonged to readers who did not have the easy access to texts enjoyed by many intellectuals. For example, much of the library compiled by an officer in the London excise, John Dawson (1692–1765), has survived because it was left to the local parish church in his will. A catalogue compiled by Dawson during the 1730s reveals that he owned over a hundred volumes. To possess this number of books was not that unusual for a Londoner of the "middling sort" during this period, but Dawson's library was particularly well stocked with histories and chronologies and he added more annotations to this genre than any of the other books that he owned. Dawson corrected printers' errors and added pagination where it was missing in order to make these books easier to use, but he also used them to store information. Many of his histories have additional manuscript pages containing chronological tables or lists of significant historical figures, and he added new indices and tables of contents in order to make the information that he had stored there easier to recover. Like a reader from before the age of print, Dawson treated the book as an object to be augmented and adapted.

There are few marginal comments in any of Dawson's books, but his copy of Thomas Salmon's *The Chronological Historian* (1733) is marked throughout with a strange code. Some passages are marked "R R" or "R R R," others "PM" and "PD." As a manuscript table of "The Signification of the marks in this book" added to the end pages makes clear, Dawson used these codes to compile a series of lists and tables that were later bound into the rear of the book. The use of "PM" and "PD" in the margins identified passages that recorded when "Parliament met" and when it was "dissolved." Dawson used this information to compile a table of the parliaments associated with each English monarch which was later bound into the book. All of this evidence suggests that when Dawson "read" history, he engaged in this practice of compiling lists and constructing tables, but his annotation practices – including the use of code – would have been familiar to many contemporary scholars. As an examination of the rare books collection of the British Library reveals, during the eighteenth century many books were used to store information on the same (or a similar) topic, and additional indices or tables were often added to works of history (Colclough 2004).

As Robert Darnton has argued, there is enough evidence to suggest that early-modern readers tended to concentrate on small chunks of text, which they picked out of the books that they were reading and placed in manuscript books, or, as in Dawson's case, rearranged into new lists that could be easily consulted (Darnton 2000). Dawson certainly imposed his own pattern on texts such as Salmon's *Chronological Historian*, but he also used his reading to construct a series of autobiographical writings that placed his own life within the context of contemporary European history. This context was mined from the large number of chronologies and contemporary histories that he owned, but he did not simply read for this purpose as his compilation of a chronology of the Anglo-Saxon period attests. Reading for Dawson was a process of reconfiguration that remade the text into a series of lists or tables.

It is not my intention to suggest here that *all* early-modern readers engaged in this process of annotation, list-making, and extraction, but the evidence from surviving texts indicates that reading with the pen in hand was a much more common practice during this period than it is today. Early-modern readers frequently marked the pages of the books that they owned and filled manuscript books with extracts from their reading. These readers understood reading as a process of taking the essence from a book. For example, between 1627 and the end of the 1650s, William Drake left extensive notes in the texts that he owned and filled thirty-seven commonplace books with extracts (Sharpe 2000). The term "commonplace book" needs some explaining as not all manuscript books followed the format developed during the Renaissance. The commonplace book proper encouraged the compiler to make notes on their reading under a series of predetermined headings that were then recorded in the book's index in order to allow the reader to retrieve information. The most influential model was that proposed by Erasmus in his *De Copia verborum* (1513). Peter Beal has argued that this form of the commonplace book was the "primary intellectual tool for organising knowledge" in the early-modern period. Such books certainly made readers look at texts in the context of pre-existing headings, and encouraged them to recognize *sententiae* in established authors (Beal 1993: 134).

John Locke's essay "A New Method of a Common-Place Book" (published posthumously in 1706) modified the form and helped to perpetuate the use of these books well into the eighteenth century and beyond. Gertrude Savile (1697–1758), a member of the gentry who spent much of her life in London, compiled a manuscript book during the 1720s (Savile n.d.). This book is divided into twenty-seven different subjects, including "Hope," "The Passions," and "Ruin." Under these headings, she transcribed short, apposite quotations from contemporary plays, such as John Sturmy's *Sesostris, Or, Royalty in Disguise* (1728), older dramatic works, including Shakespeare, and the poetry of Cowley and Young. Savile's commonplace book is thus a great source for recovering information about the kinds of texts that she read, but it also tells us something about *how* she read. In order to construct this volume, Savile must have kept her commonplace headings in mind as she read, and a close analysis of the extracts shows that she often needed to adjust or amend the text in order to make it fit these categories more easily.

As Darnton has noted, by studying commonplace books historians and literary scholars "have come closer to understanding reading both as a specific cultural practice and as a general way of construing the world," but moving from an analysis of "what they read to the problems of how they made sense of books" is fraught with difficulty (Darnton 2000: 82). Savile's commonplace book reveals that, like other early-modern readers, she tended to break texts into fragments in order to reassemble them into new configurations, but her contemporaneous journal also reveals that she employed a wide range of other reading strategies or techniques. She enjoyed reading aloud to friends and acquaintances, and was sometimes read to by her maid. This evidence suggests that manuscript books can only ever reveal one aspect of the reading life of the compiler. Savile did not always read with the pen in hand, but the methodology of cutting texts into digestible chunks associated with the commonplace-book tradition remained an important part of the way in which she made meaning from the various texts that she consumed (Saville 1997).

For early eighteenth-century readers such as Savile, the commonplace book remained an important but residual reading practice. Despite the continued production of printed commonplace books throughout the late eighteenth and early nineteenth centuries, readers rarely used their organizing principles, preferring instead to write across the page as though it were a blank notebook. Of course, some scholarly readers continued to keep traditional commonplace books, but in the nineteenth century it was much more common for readers to compile miscellanies of their favorite verse. Often called albums, these manuscript books provide important evidence about reading during this period. Although they sometimes belonged to an individual, during the 1820s and 1830s albums tended to be compiled by groups of friends or the members of a family. Each book thus provides an important record of the texts that these groups were sharing. Reading in the past was rarely a solitary activity and albums provide a record of the way in which small communities of readers appropriated and preserved texts in new contexts. There is some evidence to suggest that texts sometimes passed from album to album without the reader ever having seen the original printed text. This process of transmission allowed readers to share extracts from, or versions of, texts that were rare, or too expensive to buy.

The study of these books reveals the complex interweaving of manuscript and print culture in an age that we usually associate with the fixity of print. They suggest that, until at least the late 1830s, many readers continued to experience texts in quotation, that is, in forms dictated by the reader as scribe rather than by the printer. The transcription of a text allowed it to be rewritten, and such rewritings provide evidence of the transcriber's attitude toward the original text. For example, one group of friends who compiled an album in the 1820s chose to transcribe Letitia Landon's "The Improvisatrice" (1824) in its entirety, but the majority of readers tended to transform such long poems into short extracts (Colclough 1998). These extracts help to reveal what it was that Romantic readers most admired about authors such as Landon, Byron, and Scott, whose books were popular but expensive.

Joseph Hunter was inspired to keep a commonplace book after reading Locke's famous essay on the subject, and he used it to transcribe passages from the various texts that he borrowed from the Surrey Street Subscription Library. Unfortunately, Hunter's miscellany has not survived, but we know of its existence from the diaries and journals that he kept during the late 1790s. These journals provide a comprehensive record of *what* he was reading throughout this period. Recently published works borrowed from the Surrey Street Library dominated his reading at this time. He particularly enjoyed the novels of Ann Radcliffe, and his enthusiasm for the Gothic novel was shared by many of the other members of the library. In March 1797, he noted that Radcliffe's *The Italian* was in such "great call" that he was forced to wait for the second volume to be returned by another reader. It took ten days and many, often fruitless, visits to the library to complete the whole text. He also sometimes used a local circulating library to supply the novels that he could not find at Surrey Street (Colclough 2000: 33). Hunter was a library-goer, rather than a library owner, and as his reading of Radcliffe suggests, this meant that his reading was often dictated by the availability of texts at the library. Such was the demand for *The Italian* that a strict limit was placed upon the amount of time that he could spend reading the text.

Hunter recorded relatively little about *how* these texts were consumed, but his combination of elements of "extensive reading" (the ability to pass from text to text) with the practices associated with "intensive reading" (such as close study and transcription) suggests that he had much in common with other readers from the same period. The terms "intensive" and "extensive" come from one of the key debates in the history of reading. As Darnton has noted, historians of reading often look at the "interplay of binary opposites":

> Reading by turning the leaves of a codex as opposed to reading by unrolling a volumen, reading printed texts in contrast to reading manuscripts, silent reading as distinct from reading aloud, reading alone rather than reading in groups, reading extensively by racing through different kinds of material vs. reading intensively by perusing a few books many times. (Darnton 2000: 87)

Each of these oppositions marks a supposed paradigm shift in reading practices, and the movement from "intensive" to "extensive," usually associated with the eighteenth century, is sometimes referred to as "the reading revolution." This phrase was first used by Rolf Engelsing to describe changes in book ownership and consumption in urban Germany after 1750, but the term has been adopted to describe both eighteenth-century Europe and early nineteenth-century America (Engelsing 1974; Darnton 1984; Hall 1996). These studies suggest that as books became more widely available, readers moved from an "intensive" to an "extensive" style of reading. In the "intensive" mode, it is argued, readers had access to a limited number of books, often religious in character, or designed to be read regularly and frequently. This kind of reading was often practiced publicly and aloud, and recitation and learning by heart imbued the printed word with a strong sense of authority. By contrast, "extensive" readers had access to a much wider range of texts, and most of their reading took place privately and silently. This allowed them to pass rapidly from text to text and the written word was no longer imbued with the same power.

In order to test this model, we need sources that provide evidence of the kinds of text that an individual was reading and of the way in which they were read (silently, aloud, and so on). Diaries and letters provide the best evidence for these practices, and a number of recent studies have used these sources to test and challenge the "reading revolution" hypothesis. For example, Darnton has used the letters written by a "solidly middle-class" French reader of the 1780s to demonstrate that "extensive" readers did not simply pass from one book to the next. Jean Ranson, who was a significant figure in the merchant oligarchy of La Rochelle, read a wide range of texts, but he was also "an impassioned Rousseauist" who incorporated the philosopher's ideas "in the fabric of his life as he set up business, fell in love, married and raised his children" (Darnton 1984: 156).

A similar challenge to the model comes from John Brewer's survey of the diaries of an English middle-class reader, Anna Larpent. Between 1773 and 1783, Larpent read 440 titles from many different genres. She often read novels and plays aloud to her family, but also engaged in regular, repeated readings of sermons and the Bible while alone in her room. Like Darnton, Brewer discovers a reader engaged in a diversity of reading practices. He concludes that if a general theory of reading were to be constructed from this record it would be that "reading practices did not become more extensive but rather more diverse." Intensive and extensive modes "were complementary rather than incompatible" (Brewer 1996: 244). Other investigations of diaries have questioned the progressive optimism of the reading revolution theory. Arianne Baggerman's study of Otto Van Eck, a young boy from a Dutch gentry family who kept a diary in the early 1790s, discovers a reluctant reader, forced to study by parents who controlled his access to texts (Baggerman 1997). However, Brewer is reluctant to move toward a general theory using just the evidence from Larpent's diaries because she lived in a household where books were unusually common. Her husband was a professional reader and she had easy access to the bookshops and libraries of London, the center of the English book trade. Ranson, Van Eck, and Joseph Hunter all shared a similar easy access to texts, and it is important to note that any modification to the "reading revolution" theory put forward by these studies rests upon the testimony of only a handful of middle-class readers. In the late eighteenth century, extensive reading was a possibility for readers such as Larpent and Hunter, but the number of texts that they regularly acquired would have amazed many of their contemporaries. It is perhaps best to think of these readers as in the avant-garde of a new and emerging set of reading practices rather than as representing the norm.

This conclusion indicates that historians of reading need to be particularly sensitive to the biographical determinants of class, gender, and geographical location that helped to shape the individual's reading life. But it also suggests that in order to test theories, such as the "reading revolution" hypothesis, we need to compile as many case studies as possible. The Reading Experience Database, launched by the Open University and the British Library in the late 1990s, is designed to bring such case studies together in order to help determine how readers of earlier periods approached their books. As the various case studies referred to in this chapter reveal, the reading experience since 1750 cannot be described as uniform or monolithic. However, by bringing together enough of these case studies, it should be possible to replace the opposed terms "intensive" and "extensive" with a more nuanced account of the various practices available to readers in the eighteenth century. This is, in part, a question of deciding which kind of history we want. The broad, epochal sweep favored by those historians who contrast manuscript with print, or intensive with extensive, is important, but such models may, of necessity, neglect or ignore those individuals or groups who appear to be "atypical." These individual or local practices are important because they help us to recognize that many different forms of reading were taking place at a given historical moment. For example, in the same period that the middle-class Joseph Hunter was beginning to read extensively, many working-class readers still had access to only a very limited number of texts (Vincent 1983).

If reading extensively was increasingly the norm for middle-class readers during the early nineteenth century, what evidence do we have for those lower down the social scale? As Martyn Lyons has noted, "the lower-middle classes, aspiring artisans and white-collar workers" were amongst those who "swelled the clientele of lending libraries" throughout Europe during the Victorian period, but records of their borrowings tell us little about the way in which they actually read (Lyons 1999). By the 1870s, two-thirds of the British working class could read, but most studies of working-class reading are reliant upon the autobiographical writings of a small but eloquent artisan elite (Vincent 1982). When narrating the story of their life, members of this group "rarely failed to give a description of their reading, and many of them outlined the detailed reading programmes which had guided and improved them" (Lyons 1999: 331–2). For example, the Chartist poet and lecturer Thomas Cooper recalled how he had attempted to master several languages and memorize "the entire Paradise Lost, and 7 of the best plays of Shakespeare" by reading in the early hours of the morning before going to work (Lyons 1999: 337). Such texts confirm the importance of reading to the ideology of self-improvement and they demonstrate just how much effort some working-class readers were prepared to put into becoming well read.

As Kate Flint has noted, however, it is important to "exercise a certain amount of caution when using autobiographical material." All autobiography is a form of self-fashioning and involves the selection and arrangement of events (Flint 1993: 187). This is, of course, also true of other sources, such as letters and diaries, which involve the framing of events, but autobiography shares many of the literary techniques associated with fiction. Each author had different reasons for wishing to foreground the importance of reading in his or her intellectual or emotional development, but they often used established tropes or motifs to write about this experience. One such trope often found in working-class writing is the undertaking (or failure) of a detailed "programme of reading," such as that referred to by Cooper. Many working-class writers also describe an epiphanic moment in which they encountered a text that transformed their life. Flint notes that a scene of childhood reading becomes a recurrent motif in female autobiography where it is often used to reflect upon freedoms lost after marriage (Flint 1993: 208).

However, despite these limitations, autobiography provides vital information about the new readers of the nineteenth century. As Flint's work suggests, the recollection of adolescence provides a substantial body of evidence about the control exercised over young female readers during this period, as well as an important insight into the ways in which women surreptitiously acquired and enjoyed forbidden texts (Flint 1993: 209). Similarly, working-class autobiography provides evidence of the rules governing reading within specific families or communities. For example, in an autobiographical essay drafted shortly after he became famous as "the Northamptonshire Peasant Poet" in 1820, John Clare recalled how his skills in reading and writing made him different from his parents: "Both my parents was illiterate to the last degree. My mother knew not a single letter ... my father could read a little in the bible or testament and was very fond of the supersti[ti]ous tales that are hawked about a sheet for a penny" (Clare 1996: 2).

Clare uses the term "illiterate" here to refer to writing rather than reading, and it is clear that he was the only member of his family that could both read and write. Households in which various levels of literacy operated were common amongst working-class communities during this period, and it is important to note that the inability to read did not necessarily prevent people who were as "illiterate" as Clare's mother from participating in print culture. Both Clare and his father frequently read aloud and this form of text transmission remained important amongst groups where different levels of literacy coexisted well into the twentieth century. Clare also reveals that he began to hide his own fondness for "reading and scribbling" from his parents when it became apparent that he was not using these skills to acquire a better-paid job, and he makes several other references to concealing his reading from the rest of his community. His autobiography and others like it thus help to reveal the complex nature of working-class attitudes toward literacy and culture. A close study of these texts will allow historians of reading to avoid what Roger Chartier has described as a naïve identification of "the people" with the oral transmission of texts (Chartier 1994: 22). Clare's solitary, hidden reading is an important part of the history of working-class reading, but it would be equally naïve to assume that he is a typical working-class reader.

In order to understand better the activity of reading, book historians have begun to explore a wide range of sources, including representations in literary and pictorial texts, and the new physical forms taken by texts as they are reproduced. As Chartier has noted, such sources are of limited use because reading "cannot be deduced from the texts it makes use of," but he also argues that the reader is never entirely free to make meaning. Readers "obey rules, follow logical systems, imitate models" (Chartier 1994: 22–3). The best way in which to rediscover the systems that underpinned past reading practices is to explore the kinds of autobiographical materials that have been the subject of this chapter.

REFERENCES AND FURTHER READING

Baggerman, Arianne (1997) "The Cultural Universe of a Dutch Child." *Eighteenth Century Studies*, 31 (1): 129–34.

Beal, Peter (1993) "Notions in Garrison: The Seventeenth-century Commonplace Book." In W. Speed Hill (ed.), *New Ways of Looking at Old Texts*, pp. 131–47. New York: RETS.

Beetham, Margaret (2000) "In Search of the Historical Reader." *Siegener Periodicum zur internationalen empirischen Literaturwissenschaft [SPIEL]*, 19: 89–104.

Brewer, John (1996) "Reconstructing the Reader: Prescriptions, Texts and Strategies in Anna Larpent's Reading." In James Raven et al. (eds.), *The Practice and Representation of Reading in England*, pp. 226–45. Cambridge: Cambridge University Press.

Chartier, Roger (1994) *The Order of Books*. Cambridge: Polity.

Clanchy, M. T. (1993) *From Memory to Written Record: England 1066–1307*, 2nd edn. Oxford: Blackwell.

Clare, John (1996) *John Clare by Himself*, ed. Eric Robinson and David Powell. Ashington and Manchester: MidNag and Carcanet.

Colclough, Stephen (1998) "Recovering the Reader: Commonplace Books and Diaries as Sources of Reading Experience." *Publishing History*, 44: 5–37.

— (2000) "Procuring Books and Consuming Texts: The Reading Experience of a Sheffield Apprentice, 1/98." *Book History*, 3: 21–44.

— (2004) " 'R R, A Remarkable Thing or Action': John Dawson as Reader and Annotator." *Variants*, 2/3: 61–78.

Darnton, Robert (1984) *The Great Cat Massacre*. London: Allen Lane.

— (1990) *The Kiss of Lamourette: Reflections in Cultural History.* New York: Norton.

— (2000) "Extraordinary Commonplaces." *New York Review of Books,* December 21: 82–7.

Engelsing, Rolf (1974) *Der Burger als Leser: Lesergeschichte in Deutschland 1500–1800.* Stuttgart: Metzler.

Flint, Kate (1993) *The Woman Reader 1837–1914.* Oxford: Clarendon Press.

Grafton, Anthony (1997) "Is the History of Reading a Marginal Enterprise? Guillaume Bude and his Books." *Papers of the Bibliographical Society of America,* 91: 139–57.

Hall, David (1996) "The Uses of Literacy in New England, 1600–1850." In David Hall (ed.), *Cultures of Print: Essays in the History of the Book,* pp. 36–76. Amherst: University of Massachusetts Press.

Jackson, H. J. (2001) *Marginalia: Readers Writing in Books.* London: Yale University Press.

Jardine, Lisa and Grafton, Anthony (1990) "'Studied for Action': How Gabriel Harvey Read his Livy." *Past and Present,* 129: 30–78.

Lyons, Martyn (1999) "New Readers in the Nineteenth Century: Women, Children, Workers." In Guglielmo Cavallo and Roger Chartier (eds.), *A History of Reading in the West,* pp. 313–44. Amherst: University of Massachusetts Press.

Reading Experience Database at www.open.ac.uk/Arts/RED/

St. Clair, William (2004) *The Reading Nation in the Romantic Period.* Cambridge: Cambridge University Press.

Savile, Gertrude (n.d.) "The Commonplace Book of Gertrude Savile." Nottinghamshire Archives, Nottingham, DD512/212/12.

Saville, Alan (1997) *Secret Comment: The Diaries of Gertrude Savile.* Thoroton Society Record Series 41. Nottingham: Thoroton.

Sharpe, Kevin (2000) *Reading Revolutions: The Politics of Reading in Early Modern England.* London: Yale University Press.

Vincent, David (1982) *Bread, Knowledge and Freedom: A Study of Nineteenth-century Working-class Autobiography.* London: Methuen.

— (1983) "Reading in the Working-class Home." In John K. Watton and James Walvin (eds.), *Leisure in Britain 1780–1939,* pp. 207–26. Manchester: Manchester University Press.

PART II
The History of the Material Text

The World before the Codex

5

The Clay Tablet Book in Sumer, Assyria, and Babylonia

Eleanor Robson

If a book is a collection of pages bound together and sold on the open market, then there were no books in the ancient Middle East. If, on the other hand, a book is a means of recording and transmitting in writing a culture's intellectual traditions, then there were very many, and there is a rich and extraordinary history of the ancient Middle Eastern book to be explored and told. Although much has been written on the origins and development of early writing in the Middle East (Walker 1987; Nissen et al. 1993), and rather less on archives (Pedersén 1998; Brosius 2003) and libraries (Michalowski 2003; Black 2004), there has been no comprehensive study of writing media, still less on literate intellectual culture. This chapter is a first attempt at such a venture and, as such, I hope that book historians of other periods and places will read it with a certain indulgence. Equally, I write in the hope that colleagues of mine will take up the challenge of taking this project further, integrating the first half of recorded history more fully into the history of the book.

After a brief survey of the mechanics, media, and cultural context of cuneiform writing, I will take three case studies to try to determine whether – and, if so, when, where, and how – we can talk of books in the first three millennia of recorded human history in the Middle East (figure 5.1).

Books of Clay? Cuneiform Culture

Writing emerged in the context of temple bureaucracy in the cities of the southern Iraqi marshes some time in the late fourth millennium BC (Nissen et al. 1993). A tiny number of accountants used word signs (usually pictograms) and number signs to account for institutional assets – land, labor, animals – and their secondary products. They wrote on refined clay tablets, about the size of a credit card but around 1 cm thick, incising the signs for the objects they were recording with a pointed stylus and impressing the numbers with a cylindrical one. The front surface of the tablet was marked out

Figure 5.1 Map of ancient Iraq showing major cities.

into boxes, each one containing a single unit of accounting, logically ordered, with the results of calculations (total wages, predicted harvests, and so on) shown on the back. This writing was barely language-specific – it represented concrete nouns, numbers, and little else, with only occasional clues to pronunciation and none at all to word order – and was known only to a handful of expert users. Its functionality was as yet so limited that it was used only to keep accounts, or to practice writing the words, numbers, and calculations needed for accountancy.

In the course of the third millennium BC, scribes and accountants expanded writing's capabilities to record legal transactions and agreements, dedicatory inscriptions to gods, and, finally, narrative texts of many kinds, including letters, accounts of political events, hymns to deities, and incantations (Van De Mieroop 1997). Several innovations were needed to bring this about. Most important was that writing should represent the sounds of words rather than the appearance of objects. At this point, Sumerian becomes visible in the written record. Sumerian is an isolate language whose linguistic relatives, if it ever had any, all died out before they were written down. It is agglutinating: its nouns and verbs are composed of unchanging lexical stems with grammatical particles prefixed and suffixed to them to indicate their function in the sentence. For instance, the phrase *ka egalakshe ngenangune* ("On my arrival at the palace gate") is composed of the particles *ka* "gate"; *e* "house," *gal* "big," *ak* "of," and *she* "at"; *ngen* "go," *a* (nominalizer), *ngu* "my," and *ne* (verbal phrase marker). The earliest script had been capable only of writing the lexical stems in this phrase – *ka*, *egal*, and perhaps *ngen* – but now punning allowed grammatical particles to be written down for the first time. It thus became essential to write signs in a linear order, both to show which stem particles were attached to and to indicate the order of the words in the sentence.

Paradoxically, the tailoring of early writing to the grammatical particularities of Sumerian also freed it from the necessity of writing Sumerian alone. If signs represented sounds, they could represent the sounds of any language, with some adaptations if necessary. Sumerian's closest neighbor was the Semitic language Akkadian, an indirect ancestor of Hebrew and Arabic, which today we subdivide into Assyrian, the dialect of ancient northern Iraq, and Babylonian, the dialect of the south.

Not so essentially, but perhaps inevitably, as writing grew to be representational of sounds rather than objects, it became more abstract in appearance too. The scribes developed a new technique of sign formation which entailed pressing a length of reed stylus obliquely into the clay to create linear strokes or wedges; hence our name "cuneiform" from Latin *cuneus*, "wedge." The size and shape of the tablets themselves also became much more varied, with shape and layout becoming closely associated with function. Indeed, it is often possible to identify the genre of the text on a tablet simply by looking without reading, as, for instance, the five different types of school tablets from House F discussed below.

Cuneiform writing was fully functional by about 2400 BC but remained the preserve of the professionally literate and numerate who were employed by temples and palaces to uphold and manage institutional authority. Later in the millennium, prosperous families and individuals also began to use the services of scribes to record legal transfers of property on marriages, adoptions, and deaths, loans and sales, and the resolution of legal disputes. Cuneiform remained fearsomely complex with some 600 signs in its repertoire, many of which could take one of up to a dozen different syllabic or ideographic values depending on context. It was potentially susceptible to simplification, but in fact grew in complexity over the centuries, ensuring that its use remained almost exclusively in the hands (and the eyes) of highly trained scribes. When alphabetic Aramaic reached Assyria and Babylonia from the west at the turn of the first millennium BC, it was quickly adopted for an increasing range of everyday writings, almost always on perishable media like animal skins and papyrus. Whereas in early Mesopotamia cuneiform literacy had been primarily a tool for controlling the ownership and rights to assets and income (some 95 percent of extant tablets attest to this function), in the first millennium it increasingly became a prestige medium. With cuneiform, the scribes communicated with the gods, learned and created intellectual culture, and wrote certain sorts of legal documents. The last known datable cuneiform tablet is an astronomical almanac from AD 75 (Geller 1997).

For the most part, cuneiform scribes wrote on clay which had been prepared in much the same way as clay for fine pottery production. It had to be levigated, or sieved, to remove particles of stone and plant fiber, and puddled, or kneaded, to remove air bubbles and to increase its elasticity. Tablets could be as small as a postage stamp or (rarely) as large as a laptop computer, but scholarly tablets infrequently contained more than about 500 lines of text. Tablets were rarely baked in antiquity; more usually they were left to dry in the sun. They were filed in archives or libraries on shelves, in pigeonholes, or in labeled baskets. Clay basket tags and shelf records occasionally survive, as do a few acquisition lists from Ashurbanipal's Library (discussed below), but no complete inventories are known.

When the archival lives of the tablets were over they were recycled by soaking in specialist basins and reshaped. Whole archives and libraries *in situ* are thus found only in exceptional circumstances: the sudden abandonment of a building or city, or accidental conflagration (which, baking the tablets, paradoxically served to aid their preservation). Of the three case studies discussed below, the House F tablets were reused as building material; the tablets in Ashurbanipal's Library baked in the fires set during the Median sack of Nineveh in 612 BC; and the Rêsh temple's library was abandoned as the temple itself fell into disuse along with the entire cuneiform tradition.

Clay was not the only medium of cuneiform script. Monumental inscriptions were carved on stone, of course, but from the late third millennium onward there are also textual references to wooden boards with waxed writing surfaces. Almost all of those writing boards, and all of their surfaces, have long since perished along with other organic writing media, but clay tablets have survived in the archaeological record in many hundreds of thousands. Most cuneiform tablets known today are the yield of pre- and proto-archaeological digging in the late nineteenth century, or illicit excavations in the twentieth. Their original contexts can to some extent be recovered from internal evidence from the tablets themselves, in conjunction with the acquisition records of the museums and collections that house them. But controlled and documented archaeological excavation of textual objects *in situ* inevitably reveals far more than the historical record alone about the practices of creating, using, storing, and destroying cuneiform tablets. It enables us too to situate tablets in socio-intellectual contexts of production, communication, and preservation that allow them to be considered within the world history of the book.

School Books in Bronze Age Sumer?

When is it meaningful to talk of "clay tablet books," as in the title of this chapter? Cuneiformists have traditionally divided tablets into two discrete genres. Much the largest consists of archival tablets: utilitarian documents with limited shelf-life that together comprised complex administrative and/or legal systems. Memoranda, letters, accounts, receipts, rosters, court records, legal documents: they all have their counterparts in more recent literate cultures, and intuitively we can say that these records and documents are not in themselves books. More interesting for our purposes are those tablets that Leo Oppenheim famously described as transmitting the "stream of tradition," or the intellectual culture of ancient Mesopotamia. Their contents range from literature and poetry to magic and medicine, although on closer inspection these modern genre designations often prove inadequate to capture the intellectual content and social function of such texts. But what they have in common is the fact that they were memorized and/or copied from generation to generation, often over millennia, collected and edited and commented upon. Such tablets embody the production of knowledge in ancient Iraq and thus have first claim to being considered in the light of book history.

In the Bronze Age (c.3000–1200 BC in the Middle East) the production and transmission of literate knowledge was sited in scribal schools. No doubt temples, courts, and other places were also centers of intellectual and cultural exchange at this time, but they have not yet been identified and analyzed as such through the archaeological record. Second-millennium schools, on the other hand, have been carefully studied in recent years, enabling us to look at them in the light of book history. For instance, in the early 1950s over a thousand tablets, mostly in fragments, were excavated from "House F," a small urban house in Nippur near modern Najaf (Robson 2001). According to the datable household documents found in it, House F was used as a scribal school in the 1740s BC, immediately after the reign of Hammurabi (1792–1750 BC), most famous of the early Babylonian kings.

About half of the tablets in House F are the by-products of an elementary scribal education. They take the trainee from learning how to use a stylus to make horizontal, vertical, and diagonal wedges on the tablet to writing whole sentences in literary Sumerian. The students doubtless learned to make their own tablets too, because in the corner of the tiny courtyard was a bitumen-lined basin filled with a mixture of fresh tablet clay and crumpled up tablets waiting to be recycled. Both the elementary exercises and the tablets themselves were standardized, with format and content closely related to pedagogical function.

The tablets were made in just five shapes and sizes. Most interesting and useful for historians are those now called Type II tablets (figure 5.2), which are typically half the size of a hardback novel (Veldhuis 1997). They were designed to give the scribal student first exposure to a new exercise, through repeated viewing and copying of a 10–20-line extract on the obverse, and revision through recall and writing from memory of a longer section of an earlier exercise on the reverse, often explicitly joining the new onto the end of the old. No other tablet type is dual-function; but like the obverse of Type II tablets, Type III and Type IV tablets are witnesses to the early stages of students' learning a new piece of work. Type I tablets and Prisms (long four- or six-sided tablets), like the reverse of Type II tablets, were probably written as the student recalled and wrote out a whole piece of work, or a significant section of it, before moving on to acquire new knowledge.

The tablet format's functional dichotomy between memorization and recall is corroborated by the fact that the long extracts on Type I, reverse Type II, and Prism tablets

Figure 5.2   A Type II tablet from House F, showing the teacher's and student's copies of a school exercise on the obverse and the student's recall of a longer passage on the reverse (3N-T 393 = UM 55-21-318). Reproduced by kind permission of the University of Pennsylvania Museum of Archaeology and Anthropology.

are almost invariably from the first half or third of an elementary exercise, whereas the short extracts on Type II obverses and tablet Types III and IV are randomly distributed across the beginnings, middles, and ends of those exercises. Looking at the textual stability of the compositions, there is much more consensus between manuscripts attesting the start of a composition than those from the end. The situation is slightly complicated, however, by the fact that there is not an even preservation of tablet types in House F. Type II tablets account for fully two-thirds of the 366 elementary tablets with identifiable formats, perhaps because they were ideally suited to reuse as building materials (the circumstances in which they were found). Two-thirds of the 50 Type III tablets identified are multiplication tables, whereas half of the 70 Type Is and Prisms are either exercises in the more abstruse aspects of cuneiform or model legal contracts. There are only five Type IV tablets among the 500 elementary tablets in House F.

A further 500 tablets, the other half of the surviving school corpus from House F, contain works of Sumerian literature, or extracts from them (Black et al. 2004). About 80 different compositions are attested in the house, including epic stories of legendary heroes like Gilgamesh and Lugalbanda, myths about gods and their deeds, hymns to gods, kings, and temples, debates, dialogues, and humorous stories about scribal students. What were once thought of as ancient genre designations at the end of some literary works should probably be understood rather as indicators of performance style, at least in those cases where the labels are susceptible to translation. The physical typology of Sumerian literary tablets is still under-researched, but other kinds of evidence reveal how they were created and used. Extracts were not copied from a model on the same tablet as the elementary exercises were, and neither has direct copying from one tablet to another ever been proved. While there is often a lot of agreement between individual manuscripts, variation at the level of spelling, grammar, synonyms, line order, and even compositional length and structure are also well attested and point again to memorization within a fairly fluid oral tradition (Michalowski 1992).

On the other hand, catalogues of incipits, or first lines, and large tablets containing several literary works demonstrate that compositions could be grouped into more or less fixed sequences. Some of those sequences are clearly curricular: a group of ten literary works, now known as the Decad, is found at the start of several ancient catalogues from Nippur and other cities (Tinney 1999). In House F, whereas there was one or at most two copies of most literary works, there were typically twenty copies of each Decad composition. The Decad crosses modern generic boundaries – it includes hymns, myths, and humorous works – whereas other apparently curricular groupings are primarily thematic. Its widespread distribution also points to a shared pedagogical culture within southern Mesopotamia, with remarkable textual stability across time and space. The Decad is highly unusual in its coherence and stability, however: ancient catalogues and shelf lists point to locally meaningful thematic groupings of literary works but little wider curricular standardization.

There are still many unsolved – and unasked – questions about schooling in House F. Yet it is clear that the primary pedagogical tactics were copying and memorization in the form of piecemeal rote learning. There were no textbooks to copy from, but rather scribal teachers wrote out lessons from memory, according to the needs of the students, and often moved them on to new tasks before they had fully mastered and memorized their current exercises. Nor were the trainee scribes themselves creating books but writing in order to memorize an oral tradition of knowledge, which could be very fluid, at the same time as learning to be literate for more mundane purposes. Both elementary and literary tablets, despite their overwhelmingly non-utilitarian content, functioned to train future scribes for their administrative careers (Wilcke 2000). There is no early Mesopotamian evidence of reading for pleasure, or even creating or using tablets as reference works: the intellectual tradition was almost entirely composed of knowledge internalized through repeated copying, recitation, and memorization.

Books as Cultural Capital in Iron Age Assyria

The second case study comes from a much grander setting than a humble scribal school, over a thousand years after the demise of House F. In the early first millennium BC, the political heart of the Middle East was the city of Nineveh, on the opposite bank of the Tigris to modern-day Mosul in northern Iraq. The Assyrian kings had made their capital here in c.700 BC, on a settlement founded millennia earlier. It was strategically placed for easy riverine and overland access to a vast empire, stretching east into the Zagros Mountains of Iran, west to the Mediterranean coast and Egypt, and south to the Babylonian shores of the Gulf. The Assyrian empire depended on the annual extraction of tribute and taxation, as well as the regular influx of labor from the peripheries to the center, in order to develop and maintain a sophisticated complex of palaces and temples in which the daily ceremonial of empire was performed and its ideological support system upheld.

The magnificently monumental edifices of Nineveh were amongst the first Assyrian remains to be discovered by European scholars in the mid-nineteenth century, decades before the development of professional stratigraphic archaeology. Thus the 28,000-odd tablets found in the royal citadel of Nineveh, which are now housed in the British Museum, rarely have good archaeological context (although modern museum curators have gleaned much useful data from their Victorian predecessors' documentation and correspondence). Collectively, the Nineveh tablets are rather loosely known as Ashurbanipal's Library, after the monarch who ruled Nineveh in 668–c.630 BC and who had his mark of ownership inscribed on many of them (Lieberman 1990). Apart from letters, administrative documents, and legal records, the palace complex contained literary and historical works, religious rituals and prayers, medical collections, and long compilations of terrestrial and celestial omens, with complex commentaries on them.

The Assyrian kings surrounded themselves with large retinues of military, political, and scholarly advisers. The scholars' ultimate function was to guide the monarch's political decision-making according to divine will. An "inner circle" of about a dozen highly educated men posed strategic questions to the gods and interpreted their answers through divination, by close inspection of events in the skies and on the earth. They relayed their findings and advice in letters and reports to the king, often supporting their conclusions with citations from the scholarly collections housed in the royal library. The letters themselves, many hundreds of which survive, are in Assyrian dialect, while the scholarly quotations are invariably in Babylonian.

The scholarly library tablets of Nineveh have much greater claim to be considered as books than the schoolboys' writings of House F. They show unequivocal evidence for several levels of textual standardization, from spellings up to the categorization of texts into generic corpora associated with named scholarly disciplines (Rochberg-Halton 1984). For the Assyrian scholars, the textual stability of the literate tradition was enmeshed with the theological hermeneutics of cuneiform writing. Such works were considered to be the writings of gods or divinely inspired sages, with multiple layers of meanings embedded within the multiple possible interpretations of every sign and word. The scholars explicated this multivalency, and also collected textual and oral variants, in learned commentaries of various kinds.

Because very long compositions – collections of omens, for instance, or ritual series and their incantations – could not fit on a single tablet, they were divided into standard tablet-sized chapters. Colophons on the tablets themselves recorded their place in the sequence and the first line of the next tablet, while separate indices of long works and their subdivisions were another means of managing multi-tablet compositions. Colophons explicitly state that tablets were "written, copied, and checked" from older originals, both tablets and writing boards (figure 5.3). Colophons and the evidence of library

Figure 5.3 Scribes using writing boards and parchment depicted on a bas-relief from the royal palace of Nineveh. Reproduced by kind permission of the Trustees of the British Museum.

records reveal two types of tablet production and acquisition: writing and inheritance by indigenous scholars who were members of prestigious courtly families close to the king; and the forced transfer of both tablets and scholars from Babylonia.

Ashurbanipal was one of the few Assyrian kings to have been trained in the scribal arts – by one Balasî, a senior royal scholar. He systematically built up the palace library holdings through a variety of means, as attested, for instance, on the colophons of tablets from the great *Epic of Gilgamesh* found at Nineveh (George 2003). The oldest set of *Gilgamesh* tablets in the library was probably written several hundred years earlier; another was perhaps written for his grandfather Sennacherib and only later inscribed with Ashurbanipal's mark of ownership. A third set had belonged to the famous scholar Nabû-zuqup-kena, the grandfather of Ashurbanipal's senior scribe. The colophons of a fourth set claim them to be in Ashurbanipal's own hand, as do copies of many other scholarly works (figure 5.4). None of these four sets comprises the full sequence of twelve tablets that made up the *Epic*; it is unclear whether this is a consequence of partial preservation and recovery or reflects actual patterns of ownership.

The Assyrian *Gilgamesh* was a much longer and more standardized composition than the Sumerian literary works attested in schools like House F a thousand years earlier. Tradition had it that a Babylonian scholar by the name of Sîn-leqi-unninni had crafted the new work from various different sources some time in the late second millennium

Figure 5.4   A tablet from Nineveh recording the myth of the goddess Ishtar's descent to the Underworld. The colophon at the bottom reads: "Palace of Ashurbanipal, great king, king of the land of Ashur." Reproduced by kind permission of the Trustees of the British Museum.

BC. While a confident editorial hand is clearly discernible in the new *Epic*, almost no manuscript sources survive from the 500-year period during which the transformation was supposedly wrought that might allow further insight into the process.

Forced acquisition of cultural products had been an important part of the Assyrian strategy for the subjugation of Babylonia throughout the eighth and seventh centuries BC, but was particularly favored by Ashurbanipal (Frame and George 2005). Three long letters, known only from Babylonian apprentices' copies of several hundred years later, suggest that he ordered the temples of Babylonia to make copies of all scholarly works in their possession to send to Nineveh. One letter, supposedly from Ashurbanipal himself, commands the recipient to go to Borsippa near Babylon to "search out for me" a long list of named works, "and any texts that might be needed in the palace, as many as there are, and also rare tablets that are known to you but do not exist in Assyria, and send them to me." The other two purport to be responses from Babylonian scholars to a royal command for copies of similar material. They both quote the king's command directly, and are at pains to portray themselves as obediently responsive.

Ashurbanipal's younger brother Shamash-shumu-ukin had been designated prince regent of Babylonia by their father Esarhaddon. In 652 BC he rebelled against Assyria, claiming Babylonian independence. Ashurbanipal responded by declaring war, which ended four years later in Assyrian victory. Fragmentary library acquisition records from Nineveh, dated 647 BC, detail the contents of a large number of scholarly tablets and writing boards from various named towns and individuals in Babylonia (Parpola 1983), presumably booty or tribute, while a contemporary letter reports on the writing activities of several captive Babylonian scribes: "Ninurta-gimilli, the son of the governor of Nippur, has completed the Series [of celestial omens] and been put in irons. He is assigned to Banunu in the Succession Palace and there is no work for him at present. Kudurru and Kunaya have completed the incantation series 'Evil Demons.' They are at the command of Sasî."

Recent cataloguing in the British Museum has enumerated some 3,700 scholarly tablets from Ashurbanipal's Library written in Babylonian script and dialect – about 13 percent of the entire library (Fincke 2004). Ashurbanipal's obsession with Babylonian books did not, then, completely overwhelm indigenous production, but he did view them as highly valuable cultural capital: their forced removal to Nineveh undermined Babylonian claims to the intellectual heritage of the region and thus pretensions to political hegemony, while reinforcing Ashurbanipal's own self-image as guardian of Mesopotamian culture and power.

Books and Professional Identity in Hellenistic Babylonia

After the collapse of the Assyrian empire in 612 BC, Babylonia regained its independence for some seventy years, only to be conquered by the Persians (539 BC) and, much later, by Alexander the Great (330 BC) and his Seleucid successors. Despite losing political autonomy, Babylonia retained a large share of cultural, religious, and intellectual independence, particularly in the priestly and scholarly communities based around the urban temples. This last case study examines the scholarly tablets belonging to one Shamash-êtir of the Ekur-zâkir family, the chief priest of the great sky god Anu in the southern Babylonian city of Uruk in the 190s BC. The colophons of his tablets enable us to situate him in a kin-based professional context, within a five-generation continuous tradition of priesthood and book-learning (figure 5.5; Robson forthcoming).

Shamash-êtir is named on nine surviving tablets that he owned or wrote. At first sight, they are an eclectic mix. As might be expected, two contain instructions for the performance of rituals in Anu's temple Rêsh: for the four daily meals of the gods; and for the night-time rituals of the autumnal equinox. Both are part of the copied tradition. The latter is explicitly stated to have been "written and checked from an old

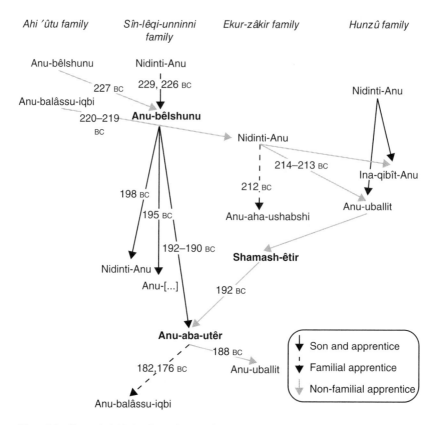

Figure 5.5   Shamash-êtir's intellectual network.

writing board," while the colophon of the food ritual tells a narrative of its capture in the mid-eighth century, followed by rescue in c.290 BC by one of Shamash-êtir's ancestors. But there are also six tablets of mathematical astronomy, containing complex instructions for the calculation of dates and positions of key events in the journeys of Mars, Jupiter, and the moon across the night sky, and tabulations of those data. None of the colophons suggest that they are copies of older works; the predictive tables certainly, and perhaps even the mathematical methods, are original compositions. Finally, Shamash-êtir was the scribe of at least one legal document, recording the purchase of shares in temple income by one Anu-bêlshunu, descendant of Sîn-lêqi-unninni (the legendary editor of *Gilgamesh*) and a lamentation priest of Anu, which was witnessed by nine named members of four different families.

    Shamash-êtir copied the equinoctial ritual for an older man named Anu-uballit of the Hunzû family, while four of the astronomical tables were written for him by Anu-aba-utêr of the Sîn-lêqi-unninni family. Both men wrote other surviving scholarly tablets too. The dates of the tablets, where known, suggest that younger men wrote tablets for older established scholars as part of the apprenticeship process (Gesche 2000). As far as we can tell, this was the only circumstance in which scholarly tablets were produced or reproduced in Hellenistic Uruk. Anu-uballit Hunzû was educated by two different men in the 210s BC. From his father he learned lots of alternative rules of thumb for the short-term prediction of ominously significant phenomena, such as the timing of lunar eclipses or the length of the following lunar month; from Nidinti-Anu Ekur-zâkir (and thus an older relative of Shamash-êtir) he learned the 70-chapter celestial omen series *Enûma Anu Ellil* ("When the gods Anu and Ellil") and the equally long standard sacrificial omen series *Bârûtu* ("Extispicy," divination from the configuration of sacrificed animals' entrails). The form and content of both series had been standardized by at least the seventh century BC, and are well known from Ashurbanipal's Library. Apart from the four astronomical tablets, Shamash-êtir's pupil Anu-aba-utêr Sîn-lêqi-unninni wrote seven surviving tablets for his father in the late 190s BC, just after he was writing for Shamash-êtir; five were written for him shortly afterwards by Anu-uballit Ekur-zâkir (presumably a young relative of Shamash-êtir's). He also owned or wrote five others, including two copied by a nephew in the 180s and 170s. Over two-thirds of his tablets contain computational astronomy; the remainder is made up of incantations, zodiacal calendars, and a collection of mathematical problems (figure 5.6).

The colophons thus enable us to situate Shamash-êtir within five generations of scholars over a forty-year period, c.215–175 BC. While it is perhaps dangerous to make too many inferences from such a small dataset (and it is but a subset of the known scholarly corpus from Hellenistic Uruk), some intriguingly suggestive patterns can be

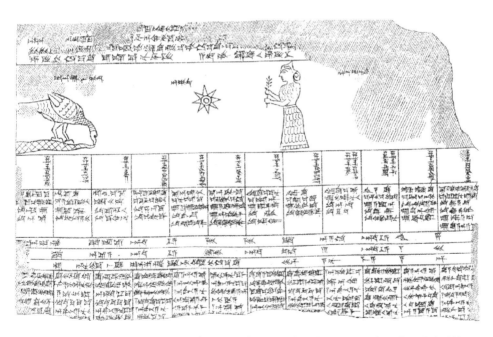

Figure 5.6 A tablet from Hellenistic Uruk, written by Shamash-êtir's apprentice Anu-aba-utêr in 192 BC, depicting constellations including Hydra and Virgo.

seen. First, there appears to be a striking shift in the type of astronomy transmitted (Rochberg 2004). While the second generation apparently learned only short-term prediction methods based on simple periodicities, the fifth generation was exclusively trained in sophisticated computational methods. The middle generations were involved in both approaches as well as horoscopy. And while traditional omen collections were copied only by the older men, there was a consistent preservation of the temple rituals and cult songs across the generations. The younger members of the Sîn-lêqi-unninni family added injunctions to the colophons of their astronomical tablets, such as "Whoever fears Anu and Antu shall not deliberately take it away." This suggests that the restricted circle of scholars that we infer from the colophons was strictly enforced in practice: a tiny number of men from a tiny social group were allowed access to this material.

In fact, just three families were involved in this intellectual network. Indeed, taking the entire Hellenistic scholarly corpus into account would at least double the number of individuals involved, but add only one further family: the descendants of Ahi'ûtu. Shamash-êtir's intellectual world was also embedded within his social circle. In the legal document he wrote, the buyer of the prebend was no other than the father of his apprentice Anu-aba-utêr, while seven of the nine witnesses were from the Ahi'ûtu and Hunzû families. The seller and remaining witnesses are from just two further families: the descendants of Kurî and Lushtammar-Adad. We also know of several intermarriages, between the Hunzûs and Ekur-zâkirs, and between the Lushtammar-Adads and Ahi'ûtus.

The colophons of their tablets reveal that all of Shamash-êtir's scholarly associates were priests of one kind or another: after their apprenticeships, the Hunzûs and Ekur-zâkirs all carried the title "incantation priest of Anu and Antu," while the Sîn-lêqi-unninnis were "lamentation priests of Anu and Antu" (McEwan 1981). The Rêsh temple was uncovered during the course of long-running German archaeological excavations at Uruk. It may date back to the seventh century BC, but the excavated building is all attributable to work in 202 BC. It was a truly monumental construction of baked and mud brick, towering over the city. Anu and his divine spouse Antu's shrines, which backed on to an enormous mud-brick ziggurat some 100 m square, were the focus of the complex, but the Rêsh also housed at least twenty further chapels and installments for divine statues. In one storeroom, which had already been subject to clandestine excavations, were found nearly 140 cuneiform tablets dated to 322–162 BC: hymns and rituals, as one might expect, but also horoscopes, collections of omens, and astronomical works, as well as a significant number of legal documents. Several of the scholarly tablets belonged to Shamash-êtir's apprentice Anu-aba-utêr, and it is widely agreed that many of the other tablets discussed in this section were illicitly dug from this area too.

Finally, there is the conundrum of the scholars' astronomical activity to solve. It is clear to see why, as priests, they would need to possess and understand the complex temple rituals (Linssen 2003). But as the primary object of their worship was Anu, the sky god, many of those rituals had to be performed at celestially significant times. Some of those were a regular part of the calendar, such as the equinoctial rituals. Others, such as the propitiatory rituals for placating the gods during the disruptive repair of their temples, had to be performed "on a propitious day, in a propitious month," when the sun, moon, and planets were in auspicious configurations in the sky. And, finally, on the occasion of particularly inauspicious celestial events, such as lunar eclipses, the priests were charged with soothing the angered gods through ritual public lamentation. All of these rituals were elaborate and costly, requiring much preparation and expenditure, such as in the ritual manufacture of kettle-drums. On one infamous occasion in 531 BC, the lamentation priests of Uruk, all from the Sîn-lêqi-unninni family, had been the subject of an official temple enquiry after a lunar eclipse they had lamented over had not taken place. That put an onus on succeeding generations dramatically to improve their predictive ability – and jealously to guard their knowledge as inherited professional secrets. Shamash-êtir and his colleagues, while upholding the age-old ritual traditions, were still improving their astronomical methods, generation by generation, so that they could be confident of fulfilling their priestly duties on time, every time without embarrassment to their professional and familial heritage or their temple. In the end, though, new beliefs won out and the Rêsh – and cuneiform scholarship itself – went into terminal decline.

Conclusions: Re-reading Tablets in the Light of Book History

I have attempted to avoid generalizing about the three thousand years of cuneiform culture by taking three very different case studies to shed light on the variety, individuality, and fluidity of scholarly literacy and numeracy in the ancient Middle East. The early intellectual tradition was predominantly one of oral transmission, with repeated copying for memorization, in which tablets functioned essentially as ephemera. By the beginning of the Iron Age in the later second millennium BC – unfortunately, a period badly understood archaeologically – cuneiform tablets (and presumably also perishable writing media) begin to reflect concerns with textual stability, genre, and editing, which might lead us to think about them as "books." In the first millennium BC, acquisition of such "books" is attested by inheritance, conquest, and copying. Costs of production were minimal: the easily available raw materials were presumably procured and prepared by junior apprentices, while the writing itself was carried out by captives (in the exceptional Assyrian case) or by apprentices as part of their training (as in Hellenistic Uruk). There was no sale market as far as we know, although sales of movable objects were not subject to written contracts, so it is equally fair to say that we have no evidence for the sale of food. Cuneiform literacy was by and large restricted to tiny handfuls of professionals   supported through royal patronage or by inherited positions in the independently wealthy temples – who were both consumers and producers of books. Yet the knowledge contained in books could have political power as well as professional import.

Modern text editions of the ancient scholarly literature have tended to aim for the (re)construction of "complete" works by drawing equally on Assyrian and Babylonian

manuscript sources from the eighth to the second centuries BC. This approach un-
avoidably emphasizes continuity, conservatism, and authorial anonymity over
novelty, variation, and individuality. But there was nothing inherently conservative in
the medium of the clay tablet itself. While continuity of tradition was valued and
upheld through preservation of ancient texts, innovation and intellectual development
through new composition remained a vital part of that tradition, right up until the
very end. But although cuneiform culture died out nearly two millennia ago, its
academic study is less than two centuries old: we are only just beginning to understand it.

References and Further Reading

Black, J. A. (2004) "Lost Libraries of Ancient Mes-
opotamia." In J. Raven (ed.), *Lost Libraries: The
Destruction of Great Book Collections since Antiq-
uity*, pp. 41–57. London: Palgrave Macmillan.
—, Cunningham, G., Robson, E., and Zólyomi, G.
(2004) *The Literature of Ancient Sumer*. Oxford:
Oxford University Press.
Brosius, M. (ed.) (2003) *Ancient Archives and Archi-
val Traditions: Concepts of Record-keeping in the
Ancient World*. Oxford: Oxford University
Press.
Fincke, J. C. (2004) "The British Museum's Ashur-
banipal Library Project." *Iraq*, 66: 55–60.
Frame, G. and George, A. R. (2005) "The Royal
Libraries of Nineveh: New Evidence for their
Formation." *Iraq*, 67: 265–84.
Geller, M. J. (1997) "The Last Wedge." *Zeitschrift
für Assyriologie*, 87: 43–95.
George, A. R. (2003) *The Babylonian Gilgamesh
Epic: Introduction, Critical Edition and Cuneiform
Texts*, 2 vols. Oxford: Oxford University Press.
Gesche, P. (2000) *Schulunterricht in Babylonien im
ersten Jahrtausend v. Chr.* [School-teaching in
Babylonia in the First Millennium BC]. Münster:
Ugarit-Verlag.
Lieberman, S. (1990) "Canonical and Official
Cuneiform Texts: Towards an Understanding of
Assurbanipal's Personal Tablet Collection." In
T. Abusch, J. Huehnergard, and P. Steinkeller
(eds.), *Lingering over Words: Studies in Ancient
Near Eastern Literature in Honor of William L.
Moran*, pp. 305–36. Atlanta: Scholar's Press.
Linssen, M. J. H. (2003) *The Cults of Uruk and
Babylon: The Temple Ritual Texts as Evidence for
Hellenistic Cult Practice*. Leiden: Brill.

McEwan, G. J. P. (1981) *Priest and Temple in Hellenistic Babylonia*. Wiesbaden: Steiner.
Michalowski, P. (1992) "Orality, Literacy and Early
Mesopotamian Literature." In M. E. Vogelzang
and H. L. J. Vanstiphout (eds.), *Mesopotamian
Epic Literature: Oral or Aural?*, pp. 227–45. Lam-
peter: Edwin Mellen.
— (2003) "The Libraries of Babel: Text, Authority,
and Tradition in Ancient Mesopotamia." In G.
J. Dorleijn and H. L. J. Vanstiphout (eds.), *Cul-
tural Repertories: Structure, Function and Dynamics*,
pp. 105–29. Leuven: Peeters.
Nissen, H. J., Damerow, P., and Englund, R. K.
(1993) *Archaic Bookkeeping: Writing and
Techniques of Economic Administration in the
Ancient Near East*, trans. P. Larsen. Chicago:
University of Chicago Press (originally pub-
lished 1990).
Parpola, S. (1983) "Assyrian Library Records."
Journal of Near Eastern Studies, 42: 1–29.
Pedersén, O. (1998) *Archives and Libraries in the
Ancient Near East*. Bethesda, MD: CDL Press.
Robson, E. (2001) "The Tablet House: A Scribal
School in Old Babylonian Nippur." *Revue
d'Assyriologie*, 95: 39–67.
— (forthcoming) "Secrets de famille: prêtre et
astronome à Uruk à l'époque hellénistique
[Family Secrets: Astronomy and Priesthood in
Hellenistic Uruk]." In C. Jacob (ed.), *Les Lieux
de savoir, I: Lieux et communautés*. Paris: Michel
Albin.
Rochberg, F. (2004) *The Heavenly Writing: Divina-
tion, Horoscopy, and Astronomy in Mesopotamian
Culture*. Cambridge: Cambridge University
Press.

Rochberg-Halton, F. (1984) "Canonicity in Cunei-form Texts." *Journal of Cuneiform Studies*, 36: 127–44.

Tinney, S. J. (1999) "On the Curricular Setting of Sumerian Literature." *Iraq*, 61: 159–72.

Van De Mieroop, M. (1997) "Why Did They Write on Clay?" *Klio*, 79: 7–18.

Veldhuis, N. C. (1997) "Elementary Education in Nippur." Unpublished PhD thesis, University of Gröningen.

Walker, C. B. F. (1987) *Cuneiform*. London: British Museum Press.

Wilcke, C. (2000) "Wer las und schrieb in Babylo-nien und Assyrien: Überlegungen zur Literalität im Alten Zweistromland [Who Could Read and Write in Babylonia and Assyria: Investigations into Literacy in Ancient Mesopotamia]." *Bayer-ische Akademie der Wissenschaften, Philosophisch-Historische Klasse, Sitzungsberichte*, 6. Munich: Bayerische Akademie der Wissenschaften.

6

The Papyrus Roll in Egypt, Greece, and Rome

Cornelia Roemer

For does a crop grow in any field to equal this [papyrus], on which the thoughts of the wise are preserved? . . . For it opens a field for the elegant with its white surface; its help is always plentiful; and it is so pliant that it can be rolled together, although it is unfolded to a great length. Its joints are seamless, its parts united; it is the snowy pith of a green plant, a writing surface which takes black ink for its ornament; on it, with letters exalted, the flourishing corn-field of words yields the sweetest of harvests to the mind, as often as it meets the reader's wish. It keeps a faithful witness of human deeds; it speaks of the past, and is the enemy of oblivion.

Cassiodorus, *Variae*, xi. 383–6

Books in Egypt, in classical Greece and Rome were made of papyrus. Sheets of this material are easy to roll, but break when they are folded; hence, it naturally favored the medium of the roll. The codex form, which resembled the modern book, was introduced later, and from the second century AD onwards it made papyrus increasingly redundant as a material for book production. After a time in which codices, too, were made from papyrus, parchment – easily folded and stitched together – became more common as a material for codices. The last extant examples of the type of papyrus roll predominant in the ancient world date from the eleventh century and come from the papal chancery in Rome (Lewis 1974: 92–4).

The ancient Egyptians had used rolls made of papyrus from the early days of the Old Kingdom. The oldest known papyrus roll was found in the tomb of Hemaka in Saqqara, and dates to the 1st dynasty, around 2900 BC (Emery 1938: 14). The hiero-glyph for "papyrus roll" existed already in inscriptions from this period. The 1st dynasty roll was blank; the oldest examples with writing date from the 4th and 5th dynasties (Černý 1952: 9–10).

Egypt was and remained essentially the only country in which papyrus was manufac-tured, and from where it was shipped to all places around the Mediterranean. It is not clear whether the production of papyrus sheets was a state monopoly in Egypt. There is no secure evidence for this assumption in any period, even if the meaning of the Egyptian word papyrus ("that of the king") may indicate a Pharaonic monopoly in that period.

Thucydides, Plato, and Cicero all wrote on papyrus; their works, both in classical and Hellenistic Athens and in the Roman Empire, were published in rolls. Other writing materials, such as wooden tablets coated in wax, were used for more ephemeral note-taking. The writing on such tablets could be removed easily, and they were therefore used for words and phrases not intended to be kept for long. Papyrus was the writing material *par excellence* for texts meant to be read time and again, and for those whose continuing preservation had a legal force. A fresco of the first century AD from Pompeii shows Terentius Nero and his wife both holding "books." It tells a story not only about different writing materials, but also about the respective social roles of these materials. While the husband holds a papyrus roll, thus showing his literacy and noble education, his wife holds a wax tablet, presenting herself as a good housewife who keeps her records carefully.

Papyrus is made from the plant from which it takes its name. Papyrus *cyperus* L. grew especially in the swamps of the Nile Delta, where it was manufactured into writing papyrus throughout the Pharaonic, Greek, and Roman periods. It became the heraldic plant of Lower Egypt, while Upper Egypt was represented by the lotus. The names used to describe different grades of quality of papyrus show its geographical home; one degree of quality was named "Saitic" after the town of Sais in the Delta (Pliny, *Naturalis historia* xiii. 69 and 76). The plant had already died out in Egypt when Napoleon entered it in 1798; it is not mentioned in the *Description d'Egypte*. These days, papyrus, produced by the same method as in antiquity, has become a popular tourist souvenir on the Nile.

The triangular stalks of the plant, which can grow to more than 4 meters in height, were cut into pieces of 25–35 cm, and their hard green sheaths peeled away. The pith was then sliced into strips as wide as possible. It looks as if the most common procedure would have been to cut the strips away from the stem slice by slice. But a different, more elaborate method seems also to have been used in which the stem was sliced by a needle that peeled the stalk from the outside to the inside, thus producing very wide single strips, whereas the strips cut by the simpler method could not have been wider than the diameter of the stalk. However they were produced, these strips were laid side by side in one layer, before a second layer was put on top at an angle of 90 degrees. Once it had been formed in this way, the papyrus sheet was pressed, the fluid from the stem being the only glue to hold the layers together. Pliny the Elder, our only source for the manufacturing of papyrus in antiquity (*Naturalis historia* xiii. 68–89), got it wrong when he claimed that it was the muddy water of the Nile that made the layers of the sheet cohere. The finished sheets were polished with shells or pumice-stone. The different qualities of writing-papyrus certainly depended on the methods of production – whether, for instance, the strips were peeled or cut – and perhaps on the parts of the stalk from which the strips were taken. Since all papyrus sheets consist of two layers, all have one side on which the fibers run horizontally (the "recto") and another on which they run vertically (the "verso").

The size of the sheet depended on the length of the pieces cut from the stalk; it seems that a height of between 25 and 33 cm was the most common for a roll, at least from the first century AD onwards. Also, the width of the sheets could vary according to their quality. Pliny lists measures of width from 16.7 to 29.6 cm, the widest forming rolls of the most expensive types (Pliny, *Naturalis historia* xiii. 78–80). Single sheets were glued to each other, and theoretically there was no limit to how many sheets could form a roll. The unit sold was not the single sheet but the roll, and pieces were cut from it as required for the length of text to be written.

From the Pharaonic period onward, we have book rolls which measure well over 30 meters, but these were found in tombs, and it is possible that they only served their "readers" in the underworld. The normal roll of the Pharaonic period contained twenty sheets glued together, and was no more than 6 meters in length (Černý 1952: 9). One of the most common texts in Egyptian culture was a collection of spells, ritual declarations, and hymns now known as *The Book of the Dead*. Selections from this anthology were originally inscribed on tomb walls and later painted on coffins; by 1550 BC they were appearing on papyrus. Some versions were extensive, beautifully written, and illustrated; others consisted of a few key texts on a scrap of papyrus. The length of the roll in classical antiquity was certainly dictated by the length of the book to be copied, within the limits of a format that could be handled with ease by the reader. Whether scribes and their clients could have agreed on a product which measured more than 15 meters in length, as has been calculated for a papyrus roll containing one book of the historian Thucydides, is more than questionable (so Johnson 2004: 146–52). A length of even 22.9 meters has been proposed for a roll containing one of the books of Herodotus. The diameter of such a roll would have amounted to more than 10 cm, and it seems rather unlikely that someone would have enjoyed handling such a book, which would not only have been difficult to hold while reading, but also hard to roll back for closing and storage. Since these roll lengths are only calculated from fragments written by the same scribe and in the same format, and no example of such a long roll has come down to us in one piece from the Greco-Roman period, it is possible that the rolls in question contained only excerpts, or that these long books were copied on two or more rolls by the same scribe and according to the same layout. To protect the roll as a book, the first sheet, the so-called *protokollon*, was glued to the rest at an angle of 90 degrees. To facilitate the handling of the roll, a wooden stick could be attached to the last sheet. This *umbelicus* (navel) made it easier to roll the book around its center and to hold it during the reading process.

To make the roll into a Greek or Latin book, a scribe copied a text from a master copy onto the new roll. He started from the left, distributing the text over the entire roll into columns of the same width and height. Little dots in the upper margin may have guided him in keeping the *intercolumnia*, the open spaces between columns, uniform (Johnson 2004: 93–7). The title was usually written at the end of the text. To see the content of the book without rolling it to its end, little pieces of papyrus or parchment, so-called *sillyboi*, were glued to the upper margin of the roll, hanging out and providing the title and the name of the author.

The ink used by the ancient scribes consisted of carbon, gum arabic, and water. This mixture, a black, shiny fluid, was waterproof to a high degree. Only from the third century AD did a new mixture of brown color, containing iron salt or iron-gall, become more popular. Pens were cut from reeds, forming a hard writing instrument with a thin, split nib. This instrument was quite different from the one the Egyptians were accustomed to use. Their script was better adapted to writing with a soft, brush-like pen. The different writing instruments must have influenced the posture in which scribes copied the texts. While the Egyptian scribe sat on his heels on the ground, holding the roll on his lap and writing, the harder writing instruments of the Greeks required a more solid surface on which to put the papyrus. They must have used wooden boards on their laps or sat at tables.

Papyrus rolls usually carried writing only on the inner side, where the fibers of the papyrus sheets ran in a horizontal direction, the so-called recto. But sometimes, for lack of a new roll or because of the destitution of the client, a scribe would copy a literary text on the back of a roll that had been already used for a different text. Often these first texts were tax lists or other official documents that had gone out of use. We may assume that these rolls were produced for very serious readers who did not intend to impress anyone with their ownership of the book, but who were very keen about its content.

The quality and value of a book were established by the quality of the hand, the layout, and the material used. Luxury copies were carefully written in even book hands that followed the handwriting styles fashionable at the time. These could be influenced by the forms of letters in inscriptions, but could also borrow from the contemporary styles of writing found in documents. The handwriting used in the chancery of the Ptolemaic kings in the third century BC in Alexandria, characterized by broad, cursive letters, the high, horizontal strokes of which are emphasized so that they seem to hang from an upper line, had a clearly visible influence on the book hands of the period. Handwriting styles are the main tool by which these books can be dated.

Most scholars agree that the survival of the two long, epic poems of Homer would have been unthinkable without a medium on which the forty-eight books could have been fixed in written form. This means that some sort of books must have existed already in the seventh century BC. How far they were diffused and how many people used them is another question. We hear more of books, and of people reading and using them, only toward the end of the fifth century. In Aristophanes' *Frogs* (produced in 405 BC; v. 1114) the chorus claims that "these days everybody has a book." This is certainly an exaggeration, and only intended to make fun of the intellectuals in the audience. There is no doubt, however, that the Sophists (intellectuals who showed that, with the art of speech, anyone could be persuaded about anything as long as the right words were used) increased the popularity of the written word and the book (Thomas 1989: 32–3). Only a written record could provide a pattern to follow that promised success to the orator, even if the delivery of the speeches themselves continued to be extempore. But the teaching of this *techne*, a term which became popular in this period, must have been based on written records, and therefore on the availability of books.

Direct evidence for the physical appearance of the book in classical antiquity is not extant before the fourth century BC. For the sixth and fifth centuries, we are dependent on vase paintings (Immerwahr 1964, 1973, with plates 31–3), two illustrative examples being a cup painted by Douris (Berlin 2385; dating to between 490 and 480 BC) and a hydria showing "Sappho reading" in the National Museum in Athens (no. 1260; dating to between 440 and 430 BC). The aim of these representations is not to show specific books: the interest of the painter is to show a person in the act of reading. In the case of the Douris cup, a man in a schoolroom is reading a text that recalls the *Iliad,* that being the noblest reading possible for an educated person. The book in the hands of the person reading thus conveys a certain idea (and ideal) of education, and dedication to that idea, the form of the book being a negligible part of the representation. The teacher in the school scene on the Douris cup holds the papyrus roll vertically, so that the viewer can read the opening line of the text more easily. Literary texts were never written in this way on book rolls in antiquity, but always horizontally from left to right.

In representations from the Greek and Roman worlds, we frequently see people reading, but we never see them writing. The act of reading was worthy of the artist's brush, whereas the act of copying was not. This attitude was completely different from that of the Egyptians, where scribes were held in high honor and numerous sculptures show the scribe in the act of doing his duty. The attitude of the Greeks and Romans toward the activity of writing was to change only in the early Christian period, when the act of copying the Holy Scriptures became a sacred act and therefore worthy of representation in art.

The earliest examples of surviving Greek books come from the fourth century BC. As in inscriptions, word division and accents and breathings on the Greek letters are unknown. The scribes wrote their majuscule letters one after another without any indication of where they saw the end of a word and the beginning of the next. All the signs that facilitate the reading of Greek texts for us, such as word division and accents, are, in the form in which we use them, inventions of the Byzantine period.

Two copies rival each other as the oldest extant Greek book. The Derveni papyrus, a roll discovered in carbonized state in a tomb in northern Greece, contains a difficult text which may be by the poet and sophist Diagoras of Melos (Janko 2002: 1–62). Another book roll, with the poem "The Persians" by Timotheus, was excavated near Saqqara in Egypt. Both the Derveni papyrus and the Timotheus papyrus are fragments; we do not know how long the rolls were in their original state. Nor do we know who copied them, or how they found their way to the people who owned them.

The forms of the letters used in these books, and the archaeological context of each, date both rolls clearly to the middle or the second half of the fourth century BC. Both carry a text distributed over columns, although the Timotheus papyrus does not distinguish the verses of the poem. The width of the columns was, it seems, dictated only by a sense for how wide a column should be. Both books show so-called *paragraphoi,* little strokes on the left edge of the column to indicate a new section of the text. The Timotheus papyrus also has a wonderful *koronis* ("crow"), a little bird-shaped mark to indicate the end of a main section of the poem. What we see here for the first time was to become standard in the following centuries; the *paragraphos* is also used to indicate a change of speaker in copies of the great tragedians.

From the period after the fourth century BC, we have a large number of papyrus rolls excavated in Egypt (good pictures of extensive examples can be found in Johnson 2004: plates 6–9 and 14–18). The dry climate of that country preserved organic material that would have decayed almost anywhere else in the Mediterranean. After Alexander the Great occupied Egypt in 332 BC, the language of the upper class and the administration was Greek.

The library in Alexandria (see below) housed copies of all the works of the Greek authors, and scholars were busy in that library and in the museum at Alexandria establishing the best texts, by which they meant the text closest to the author's original manuscript. The foundation of the library and the museum in Alexandria in the first half of the third century BC, and the work carried out there, had a visible impact on the texts that were copied onto rolls; that is, on the product we call "the book." From the third century BC onwards, poems are copied *kata stichon*, i.e. verse by verse, for the work of the scholars in Alexandria had made readers aware of metrical patterns. From the second century BC, basic systems of accentuation were tried out to facilitate the reading of difficult dialect words. For instance, signs for long and short syllables found their way into copies that were obviously produced for scholarly use.

Prose was written in shorter lines of between 4.5 and 6 cm, usually half a hexameter in length. The scribes adjusted the right margin, sometimes even inserting little line fillers if rules of syllable division did not allow a straight right margin. Scribes were paid according to the number of lines they had copied, a hexameter line becoming the standard pattern, a prose line counting half of the full line. Stichometric signs, little dots on the left margin, facilitated the calculation of the scribe's work.

The book market in antiquity was fundamentally different from our modern book trade in two aspects. First, because only a small percentage of the population was able to read and write, the market was restricted to an educated and elite few. Secondly, because the production of a book depended on the skill of a scribe who had to copy the text by hand, the copying process required a master copy from which the scribe could copy his text. This master copy could be provided by the person who wanted the text to be copied for his use or by someone who wanted the text to be copied for sale or at least for distribution. Master copies could come from the private library of a friend or, in the first century AD and after, from a public library.

In the Greek world, the tyrant Peisistratus of Athens (c.600–527 BC) is said to have been the first founder of a library, but whether his library had the status of a public library is questionable. The idea that a library should provide the opportunity for study of the texts and a means to discover the original words of the authors, even those who had lived long before, first became manifest in the library of Alexandria. This, the most famous library in antiquity, was the workplace of the scholars of the museum, with nearly half a million book rolls. The library at Alexandria was a development of the idea of a book collection that originated in the philosophical school of Aristotle at

Athens, the Peripatos. Here, the aim of study had been directed toward the universal knowledge of all the visible phenomena in the world. At Alexandria, alongside medicine and geography, the texts of the Greek authors, too, became a main subject of study.

All the texts of the Greek authors were collected, and the Ptolemaic kings were keen to acquire the best available copies. In the middle of the third century BC, Callimachus, the poet, was employed here, organizing the material and carrying on scholarly work at the same time. The knowledge Callimachus gained through his study of the works of the great poets offered him topics and phraseologies for a poetry, the characteristic feature of which is how it remodels the knowledge of the past into new forms. Callimachus' so-called _Pinakes_, in which the works of the authors were organized in alphabetical order, was the first ever library catalogue.

Yet another kind of library arose in the Hellenistic period, when they seem to have become the status symbols of monarchs. The foundation of the library at Pergamum in the second century BC can be understood as a conscious act of the king, who wished to found an institution which would rival the library at Alexandria. When Aemilius Paullus dragged the Macedonian king Perseus in triumph through the streets of Rome after defeating him at Pydna in 168 BC, the king's library was carried as one of the most precious items of booty. At the same time, gymnasia in the cities all around the Mediterranean installed book collections as places of cultural identification in towns and cities where the majority of inhabitants were not Greeks, but Syrians, Egyptians, or Carians. Like knowledge of the verses of Homer, a collection of books in the Greek language provided a means for cultural identification – and status. In the library of the gymnasium at Taormina in Sicily, a book catalogue has been found written on pieces of plaster which come most likely from a _stoa_ of the gymnasium. In most libraries of this period, niches and cupboards provided places for the book rolls. A relief from Neumagen on the Mosel (now lost) gives a vivid picture of a book case from the Roman period. The _sillyboi_ on these rolls had a triangular shape.

These libraries could be called public in the sense that all the members of the gymnasia certainly had access to the books housed there. Private individuals also became interested in using the foundation of a library as a monument of their generosity, offering to share their collections with other interested individuals. The first public library in Rome was planned by Julius Caesar, who wished to install the polymath Varro as the purchaser of books and organizer of the institution, a choice that meant Roman literature would have prevailed here. Celsus, a rich man in Ephesus, founded a library in which he also wanted to be buried. The library had become not only a public space but also a sacred place.

Antiquity had no publishers in our modern sense. T. Pomponius Atticus, who is sometimes called Cicero's "publisher," provided a wide distribution of the works of his friend Cicero in Greece by having his slaves copy it many times and passing the copies on to other friends, this being intended more as a gesture of friendship than as a form of commercial activity. There were bookshops whose owners had to provide copies to sell by keeping slaves who copied the texts onto new rolls. It is most likely that it was the booksellers who were the focus of the distribution of books, as well as private circles of interested scholars. This kind of publication caused no problems because of the lack of any copyright. Very specialized titles, however, were certainly not available in bookshops. Also, a man like Cicero collected books for his libraries (which contained both Greek and Latin works) from friends or through the mediation of friends as well as from bookshops, even if he deplored the low quality of the Latin texts offered in the bookshops of Rome (*Ad Quintum fratrem* iii. 5, 6). In the later first century AD, Martial advises the potential buyers of his books to go to the bookshop of Secundus, a freedman of an educated citizen, which was located behind the Temple of Peace.

It seems that booksellers also traveled to smaller places where they had clients. In a papyrus letter from the second century AD found in the Fayum, the great oasis southwest of modern Cairo, we hear from a certain Julius Placidus who writes to his father about the traveling bookseller Deius (*P. Petaus* 30): "Deius came to us and showed six parchments, of which I did not buy any. However, I collated eight other ones for which I have paid 100 Drachmai." Besides the fact that the mention of parchments is noteworthy at this early date, it is striking that Julius Placidus, without doubt a member of the upper class with a full Roman name, collated texts from the copies of a bookseller. This means that he compared the texts the bookseller provided with texts already in his possession. In this way, he tried to establish the best text in the tradition of the great scholars in Alexandria. The bookseller acted as a traveling library for scholars who did not have constant access to the main collections.

Another papyrus from the second century AD shows how scholars procured from their friends the copies they needed for their work. *P. Oxy.* 2192 is a private letter in which an obviously very literate person asks a friend in Alexandria to send him copies of a work on "Characters in comedy," of which there is a copy in the library of another mutual friend. The letter was returned with the answer that the bookseller Demetrius had the required copy, so that the book would not have to be copied anew. The names of the friends involved in this circle of highly educated readers and writers include some whose work was famous in antiquity, such as Harpokration who compiled a lexicon on the works of the ten great Attic orators. The papyrus letter was written at Oxyrhynchus, where members of this circle owned houses and land. As for Cicero, the procurement of books was a highly private matter, depending on the circles of friends and booksellers who were available.

Since our evidence of real books from the Greek or Roman areas is so limited, it is difficult to give a coherent picture of what was copied, sold, or exchanged and what was read around the Mediterranean. Egyptian papyri provide a welcome source for statistics. Naturally, this evidence depends largely on where excavations have taken place, and which layers of an abandoned settlement have been searched. But the overall evidence from excavated pieces is corroborated from what we know from literary sources that describe reading and educational practices. The author most frequently read was Homer. He was studied in schools, and to know parts of the Homeric epics by heart was considered essential to the education of a respectable man. Books and their contents were indications of belonging to the higher social and economic ranks in societies in which only a few could read and write. Homer was the greatest author, and the *Iliad* the noblest work of literature. The over one thousand fragments of papyrus rolls from Egypt with Homeric texts vary widely in quality. There are luxury copies in wonderful book hands with wide spaces between the columns on the one hand and, on the other, verses whose clumsy writing betrays the hand of an inexperienced scribe.

The texts read in schools determined the taste and reading habits of adults. After Homer, most literary papyri are fragments of books containing the tragedies of Euripides and the speeches of Demosthenes, both authors being part of the educational curriculum. For these authors, too, the quality of books varies greatly. The place in Egypt where most of these book fragments were excavated is Oxyrhynchus in Middle Egypt, about 220 kilometers south of modern Cairo. This provincial capital was not very important in the Ptolemaic period, but became a flourishing center of Hellenized life in the Roman period, counting numerous highly educated people among its inhabitants. It is the libraries of these people that were excavated from the end of the nineteenth century by the British scholars B. P. Grenfell and A. S. Hunt. So far, no public library has been identified in Oxyrhynchus, but we see that time and again it is the same scribes who copied the texts on papyrus rolls in Oxyrhynchus, most of whom copied prose texts as well as poetry (Johnson 2004: 16–37).

Oxyrhynchus may count as a typical Hellenized city where writing and reading was part of the daily life of a higher percentage of inhabitants than in rural areas and less Hellenized towns. What we find here may be comparable to the situation in cities like Ephesus, Pergamum, and Corinth in other parts of the Roman Empire, where public libraries existed and have been excavated, the most famous example being the library of Celsus in Ephesus. Here, inhabitants who regarded themselves as educated and aimed at belonging to a certain class, were reading Homer, the tragedians, and the orators. They were made acquainted with these texts while attending the gymnasium, and a thorough knowledge of them became a form of social distinction. The many representations of individuals holding papyrus rolls on tombstones and frescoes from around the Mediterranean show the importance of the book as a marker of education and class. In such contexts, the content of the book is not important; its outer form alone is enough to imply social status. Books had indeed become a status symbol.

The old concept inherited from classical Athens that a good person is a person who knows a lot is still at work here. It is in this light that the novel, a new literary form that came into being around the turn of the first century BC, can be considered as a form of text that gives even those who are less educated, and are unable to understand and enjoy the "great works," something to read. Those reading the novels who had a good education would enjoy identifying numerous allusions to the great works of the past, but others who were not able to do so could just enjoy them for the story.

The old curriculum of reading, based on a progression from Homer to the orators, lasted long into the Christian era. However, the canon was gradually reduced to fewer and fewer works. Of Homer, the *Iliad* was considered more fruitful for a moral education, and most examples we have on papyrus come from the first book of that epic. Of the comedies of Aristophanes, only eleven survived into the medieval period, and of

Menander's plays, none made it past the end of the sixth century, even though the so-called *Sententiae Menandri* had a splendid career long after. These short maxims applicable to the everyday lives of all sorts of people were more fitting for readers who sought moral help, rather than education, from literature. The Bible had, between the fourth and fifth centuries, become the main text for education. When St. Basil the Great tells his nephews about the ideal education, he still advises them to read classics like Homer and Hesiod, but adds that younger readers should be given only what is "useful" as long as they cannot fully appreciate the holy words of the Bible (*Oratio ad adolescentes* ii. 7).

For book production, these tendencies meant a steady narrowing of titles being copied. Texts not considered of value any more were not copied from the old form of the roll to the new form of the codex. Most of the Greek lyric poets, except Pindar, did not make it into codex form. The next barrier at which many authors disappeared occurred in the eighth century AD when texts began to be copied in the new form of minuscule writing. At that stage, Sappho too was left behind.

Codex-type books became increasingly popular after the second century AD. The reasons why readers now wanted to have books in this new form, and chose to abandon the old form of the roll, will have been manifold. First, practical reasons can be adduced: there is no doubt that a codex is less fragile than a roll. The pages of a book, lying flat on top of each other, form an item more solid than a fragile roll wound round and round itself. A codex also has greater capacity, since its pages are written on both sides. It can also be easily opened, closed, and opened again at the same page, whereas a roll has to be rolled back completely after use. Thus, the codex also provided random access to any part of the text required, as opposed to the linear access of the roll (in our age, the videocassette offers only linear access, while a DVD offers random access).

It is striking that the change from roll to codex goes hand in hand with the change from the pagan religions to Christianity. All early examples of New Testament texts from the second century AD are written in papyrus codices and not on rolls. Here, ideological motives may be important besides the practicality of the new form. The Old Testament, the holy book of the Jews, had always been written on rolls. Christians may have wanted their holy book to look different from the Torah. The notebooks that the Apostle Paul used and mentioned in his epistles, small booklets made of parchment, may have been considered the right form for the books of humble people, a status desirable to many Christians. Later, the Codex Sinaiticus and the Codex Alexandrinus, luxury copies of the Bible written on parchment in the fourth century, were to make a very different point. By the fourth century, the holy scriptures had become a book that was expected to reflect the holiness and value of its content.

There are only few examples of illustrated books from antiquity. It is obvious that the insertion of drawings into the text required a special skill that the scribe who copied the text may not have possessed. Indeed, a private letter from late antiquity shows clearly that the copying of the text and the illumination of the pages were carried out by different people. Illumination of the text in the sense of ornamentation of the pages did not exist in the Greco-Roman world before the Christian area. The only examples of drawings and pictures in books from the earlier periods are illustrations that help to explain the text or give a visual counterpart to the text, like personae who appear in plays or geometrical figures in scientific treatises. The idea of putting ornaments at the beginning of a chapter or in the margins of a page, which we find so often in medieval and later manuscripts, developed only when the text copied was seen as an object sacred in its own right, the value of which could be emphasized through orna- mentation. It is at this time that the scribe's work started to become more and more valued, as it came increasingly to be seen as a sacred task. Scribes now began to put their names under the text when they had finished copying it.

REFERENCES AND FURTHER READING

Basilius (1984) *Oratio ad adolescentes* (Greek, Latin, and Italian), ed. M. Naldini. Florence: Nardini.

Černý, J. (1952) *Paper and Books in Ancient Egypt.* London: H. K. Lewis.

Emery, W. B. (1938) *The Tomb of Hemaka, Excavations at Saqqara.* Cairo: Government Press.

Immerwahr, H. R. (1964) "Book Rolls on Attic Vases." In C. Henderson (ed.), *Classical, Medieval, and Renaissance Studies in Honor of B. L. Ullman*, vol. 1, pp. 17–48. Rome: Edizioni di Storia e Letteratura.

— (1973) "More Book Rolls on Attic Vases." *Antike Kunst*, 16: 143–7. Olten: Urs Graf Verlag.

Janko, R. (2002) "The Derveni Papyrus: An Interim Text." *Zeitschrift für Papyrologie und Epigraphik*, 141: 1–62. Bonn: Habelt.

Johnson, W. A. (2004) *Bookrolls and Scribes in Oxyrhynchus.* Toronto: University of Toronto Press.

Lewis, N. (1974) *Papyrus in Classical Antiquity.* Oxford: Clarendon Press.

P. *Oxy.* 2192 (1941) *The Oxyrhynchus Papyri XVIII*, ed. E. Lobel, C. H. Roberts, and E. P. Wegener. London: Egypt Exploration Society.

P. *Petaus* 30 (1969) *Das Archiv des Petaus*, ed. V. Hagedorn, D. Hagedorn, L. C. Youtie, and H. C. Youtie. Cologne: Westdeutscher Verlag.

Pliny the Elder (2000) *Naturalis historia.* Loeb Classical Library. Cambridge, MA: Harvard University Press.

Roberts, C. H. and Skeat, T. C. (1983) *The Birth of the Codex.* Oxford: Oxford University Press.

Thomas, R. (1989) *Oral Tradition and Written Record in Classical Athens.* Cambridge: Cambridge University Press.

Turner, E. G. (1980) *Greek Papyri: An Introduction.* Oxford: Clarendon Press.

— (1987) *Greek Manuscripts of the Ancient World*, 2nd edn., revised by P. J. Parsons. London: Institute of Classical Studies.

The Book beyond the West

7
China

J. S. Edgren

Script appeared in China more than four thousand years ago. China's distinctive non-alphabetical script has been found on many kinds of ancient objects that are not books: written on pottery, engraved on animal bones (especially bovine) and tortoise shells, and cast on bronze vessels, from the Shang dynasty (circa fourteenth to eleventh centuries BC) to the Western Zhou period (eleventh century to 771 BC). Other portable bronze objects that bear brief inscriptions include weapons, mirrors, coins, and seals. The use of seals began in the Eastern Zhou period (770–221 BC) and continued throughout the Han dynasty (206 BC–AD 220). Early seals were often made of iron or bronze as well as gold, even jade and other precious stones, and impressions were usually made in soft sealing clay. Other text-bearing objects include inscribed monuments, such as the "stone drums" (not later than fifth century BC), so called because of their shape, and various commemorative stelae from the Han period onward.

The *jiance* or *jiandu*, a roll of thin bamboo or wooden strips inscribed by brush with indelible ink and fastened in sequence by cords, may be considered the earliest true book form in China. These books came into existence no later than the sixth century BC, and extant specimens date from the late Warring States period (403–221 BC) through the Han. Archaeological discoveries of *jiance* hoards in recent decades have greatly enhanced early historical and textual studies. As early as the fifth century BC, books were commonly referred to as *zhubo* (bamboo and silk), which points to the use of silk as a writing material. Silk books were also in the form of scrolls. The *jiance* arrangement of text from right to left in narrow vertical columns further influenced early manuscript copying on silk and paper. Eventually, the custom left its mark on the layout of manuscript books and on the printed page (figure 7.1).

An important *jiance* book of wooden strips from Juyan from the end of the first century AD was found intact, and it can be noted that the text was written before the strips were fastened (i.e., bound) together, resulting in some characters being covered by the hemp cord. The Han dynasty cache of wooden and bamboo inscribed strips found at Wuwei in Gansu province in 1959 is particularly significant. The text of the classic *Yili* (Book of Etiquette and Ceremonial) has spaces between characters where the cord

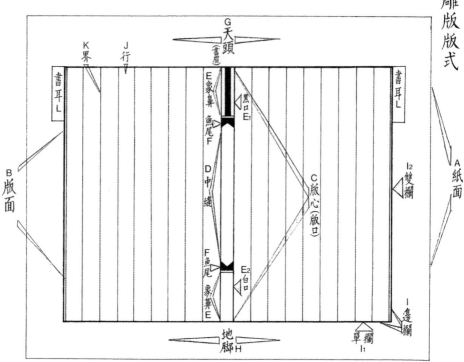

A *ZHIMIAN*, "paper face," the area of the sheet of paper.

B *BANMIAN*, "block face," the woodblock printed area.

C *BANXIN*, "block heart," the area of the center column of the page, also known as *bankou*, "block mouth."

D *ZHONGFENG*, "central seam," the middle part of the *banxin*.

E *XIANGBI*, "elephant trunk," the uppermost and lowermost segments of the *banxin*, which are divided into two types:

    E₁ *HEIKOU*, "black mouth," the name for the *xiangbi* area when it contains a black column of varying width.

    E₂ *BAIKOU*, "white mouth," the name for the *xiangbi* area when it is left blank.

F *YUWEI*, "fish tail," the appropriately shaped small

segments located below the upper *xiangbi* and above the lower *xiangbi*.

G *TIANTOU*, "heavenly head," the upper margin, also called *shumei*, or "book eyebrow."

H *DIJIAO*, "earthly foot," the lower margin.

I *BIANLAN*, "border lines," left, right, upper, and lower. When single they are called

    I₁ *DANLAN* or *DANBIAN*. When double they are referred to as

    I₂ *SHUANGLAN* or *SHUANGBIAN*.

J *HANG*, "row," the columnar spaces for text on the printed page.

K *JIE*, "boundary," the vertical dividing lines between columns.

L *SHU'ER*, "book ear," also called *erge*, is a narrow vertical box attached to the upper part of the right or left margin.

Figure 7.1 Standard format of traditional Chinese printed books and manuscripts (unfolded leaf). From S. Edgren (ed.), *Chinese Rare Books in American Collections*, New York, 1984. Reproduced by courtesy of the China Institute in America.

was tied, implying that the roll was constructed before the text was copied. Chapter number and name are indicated on the two outer strips of each roll, and a column number, somewhat akin to modern pagination, is written at the foot of each column. Compared to bamboo and wooden strips, silk was a more valuable material and appears to have been reserved for important texts and for illustrated works (Tsien 2004).

It is necessary to consider the possibility of the existence of *jiance* as early as the Western Zhou, or even the Shang. It so happens that the Chinese character *ce*, in *jiance*, is the common one for a volume or fascicle of a book, and its ancient graph is clearly a picture of three to five thin vertical strips intersected transversely by a circular thread-like line. The graph for *ce* as well as the one for *dian*, a related character showing *ce* as a presumed offering, occur in ancient bronze and oracle bone inscriptions, which has led to the assumption that books existed as early as this in China. Furthermore, the *Shangshu* (Book of Documents), an important ancient Chinese text, confirms that *ce* and *dian* existed in the Shang. If any archaeological evidence is forthcoming for the existence of bamboo or wooden strips with writing in the Shang, it is likely that the inscriptions will be limited to the sort of simple records we know from oracle bones and bronzes. After all, what surely contributed to the probable advent of the book in China around the sixth century BC was the rise of literary production in the Spring and Autumn period (722–481 BC) of the Eastern Zhou.

The earliest Chinese books of bamboo or wooden strips, however practical they may seem, became heavy and awkward when a complete text was assembled, and they were not conducive to the wide circulation of texts. The important silk books discovered in the early Han tomb at Mawangdui clearly were luxury products. It was not until after the invention and development of paper in China during the late Han period that the book could begin to rise above these limitations, and it took a few more centuries before books of paper replaced those of bamboo and silk. The invention of paper is usually associated with the Han eunuch Cai Lun (d. AD 114), who presented his method of paper manufacture to the emperor in AD 105, although we know that true paper existed at least two centuries prior to this date (Tsien 1985). According to Cai's biography in the *Hou Hanshu* (History of the Later Han, AD 25–220), he reported that, as writing materials, "Silk is dear and bamboo heavy, so they are not convenient to use. [Cai] Lun has the idea to use tree bark, hemp, rags, and fish nets to make a silk-like writing material" (Zhang 1989: 8). The significance of paper as the most important material for the evolution of book forms, in China and elsewhere, cannot be overstated.

The earliest manuscript books of paper were made by horizontally pasting sheets of paper on end in the form of *juanzizhuang* (scroll binding) or *juanzhouzhuang* (scroll and rod binding), clearly in imitation of the forms they were superseding. The scrolls opened on the right and rolled out to the left and, at the very end of the text, a wooden rod might be attached on which the scroll could be tightly rolled. Sometimes vertical lines, outlining columns for the text, were lightly traced on the surface. Coexisting with these early manuscript scrolls of paper were an ever-decreasing number of manuscript scrolls of silk.

Although paper itself was viewed as an inexpensive substitute for silk, the particular characteristics of paper, such as receptivity to folding, came to be recognized, and by the early Tang dynasty (618–907) the *jingzhezhuang* (sutra-folded binding, sometimes called accordion or concertina binding from its appearance) was in use in China. It was simply made by folding sections of a scroll at regular intervals to form a flat, vertically elongated rectangular volume. The chief advantage of the sutra-folded binding was that it afforded direct access to any section of the text. This style is believed to have been influenced by the Indian palm-leaf manuscript books (*pothî*) imported to China and adjacent central Asian territories by early Buddhist travelers. While it is altogether plausible that knowledge of palm-leaf books had some influence on the transition from rolled sheets of paper pasted on end to form a scroll to folded sheets of paper joined in the same manner, it is equally likely that the natural act of folding was intuitively understood directly through handling the paper. The sutra-folded binding represents the first codex form in China.

Once it was understood that the leaves of a book need not be attached continuously, the size and shape of books began to reflect the natural form of a sheet of handmade paper, limited as it was by the arm span of the papermaker. The next phase was represented by the *hudiezhuang*, or butterfly binding, which was achieved by folding each printed sheet in the center, text folded inward, and then pasting each sheet together at the fold to form the spine of the book. Each page thereby had three margins: upper, lower, and outer. Stiff paper covers were added with a band of paper or cloth covering the spine. This form was devised in response to the development of woodblock printing in the late Tang and early Song (960–1279). Partly from economic motives and partly from the use of a wider variety of raw materials, thinner and more absorbent papers began to be used for book printing, and these papers often were too limp to be rolled or folded. Moreover, xylographic printing did not employ a press, but instead applied pressure by rubbing the back of a sheet of paper that had been laid face down on an inked printing block. Rubbing the already-printed side to produce an impression on the other side of the paper would inevitably disturb the text, so one side of the sheet had to be left blank. In addition to the inconvenience of pairs of printed pages alternated with pairs of blank pages, the use of paste in the area of the spine of the book made butterfly binding attractive to insects. Furthermore, if leaves became detached through reading, the center column might be damaged and the leaves were not easily reattached.

The wrapped back binding, or *baobeizhuang*, simply reversed the process used for the butterfly form. By folding the sheet at the center column, but this time with the text facing outward, there were three margins left on the page: upper, lower, and inner. The text block was fastened by means of two or more twisted spills made from sturdy long-fibered paper, which were threaded through holes pierced along the inner margin. Thus the text extended out as far as the foredge of the book. A single sheet of durable paper or cloth, or a combination of separate cover sheets and a strip of material for the back, was used to form the covers and wrap the back: hence the name. The resulting volume could be shelved horizontally with the spine to the right and the foredge to the left, and it was popularly used in the Yuan dynasty (1279–1368) and the first half of the Ming dynasty (1368–1644). This book form was created to overcome the disadvantages of the butterfly form by strengthening the foredge and outer corners by folding the sheets there, by concealing the blank sides of the sheets inwardly, and by eliminating the potentially harmful paste used along the center column folds.

The next and final stage in the evolution of the traditional book in China was the familiar form of *xianzhuang* or thread binding. It evolved directly from the wrapped back binding during the Ming, and it simply resulted from removing the strip of paper or cloth covering the spine, piercing holes along the spine, and externally stitching the covers in place with silk thread. The advantages of thread binding were that it used virtually no paste and produced a lightweight, flexible fascicle that could be easily repaired or rebound without any loss or damage to the original form. This method predominated among new books published during the late Ming and throughout the Qing period (1644–1911), for more than four centuries. In fact, very few older books escaped being rebound in this manner, leaving us with a paucity of original early book bindings for study. There is an outstanding technique for rebinding *xianzhuang* volumes called *jinxiangyu* (jade inlaid with gold), which involves interleaving the entire book with intricately folded fine white paper in such a way as to produce new protective borders on all sides but the folded foredge.

The very characteristics described here that make Chinese books so desirable – that they consist of thin, lightweight fascicles whose parts are replaceable and whose production methods are reversible – also imply a degree of vulnerability. Chinese books must be handled with awareness of their special qualities and, unlike their Western counterparts, which have protective covers firmly attached to the text block, they are well served by a variety of detached protective coverings. As a general rule, in the earlier period books had durable or stiff covers and the fascicles were protected by soft coverings, such as wrapping cloths. Later, as the paper covers of bound fascicles became thinner and more vulnerable, especially after the introduction of thread binding, the covering materials became firmer and more protective. The most common means of protecting thread-bound fascicles is the *shutao*, generally called *hantao*, or folding book case. It is made of pasteboard, lined with paper, and covered with cloth, blue cotton for ordinary books and elaborate silk brocades for rare books. The *shutao* are less favored in the hot and humid climate of southern China, where mold is a serious threat to paper and cloth. Moreover, the paste used in the folding cases can attract insects and rodents. An alternative method for protecting thread-bound books and keeping them together are *jiaban* (clamping boards), which use no paste and expose the volumes to circulating air on four sides. An extremely effective means of protection can be provided by *muxia* (wooden boxes), ranging from plain and simple ones to superior ones made of rare and fragrant woods (Helliwell 1998).

The earliest books in China were not readily available throughout society. Chinese social and educational customs, habits of memorization and recitation of texts, traditions of discourse, and the cost and availability of materials all militated against the wide dissemination of books at first. Early manuscript libraries in China were chiefly institutional: they held official records, documents, and dispatches that appear to have been the exclusive property of archivists, teachers, and military or civil officials, or rather of the institutions that those persons served. From the time of Confucius (551–479 BC), however, the appearance of numerous schools of philosophy, as well as the study of military affairs, cartography, astronomy, and medicine, resulted in new categories of books. Diversified production of books eventually led to broader consumption, and finally to personal book collections.

The origin of classified book catalogues in China can be traced as far back as the Han dynasty. The *Hanshu yiwenzhi* (Bibliographical Section of the History of the Former

Han, 206 BC–AD 24) by Ban Gu (AD 32–92) was based on two earlier catalogues and is a reflection of the restoration of the Han imperial library in response to the infamous "book burning" by the emperor Shi Huang of the Qin dynasty (221–206 BC). Ban Gu's catalogue of some six hundred works provides a clear picture of the prevailing diversity of books. The ratio of bamboo and wooden strip books to silk rolls is about three to one. Despite evidence of increased private possession of books, beginning from the Warring States period, true democratization of the book awaited the greater availability of paper. From the Han period onward, the dynastic histories cite an increasing number of persons with collections of books.

By the Sui dynasty (581–618), after a few centuries of turmoil, manuscript book collecting had developed in China. The bibliographical section of the *Suishu* (History of the Sui Dynasty), completed in 656, is significant because it uses the four-part classification scheme (classics, history, philosophy, and literature) that continued to dominate book catalogues throughout the imperial era. Ink-squeeze rubbings from stone inscriptions, a form of proto-printing, are also included. An appendix contains books on Buddhism and Daoism. The steady introduction, translation, and compilation of Buddhist texts grew into a substantial canon. From the Tang and Five dynasties (907–960), Buddhist manuscript libraries grew rapidly. More than 30,000 manuscript scrolls were discovered in the Dunhuang grottoes at the turn of the twentieth century, the largest existing body of early manuscripts on paper, and the majority of them are Buddhist. They are dated from the fourth to the tenth century and provide a valuable source for the study of early Buddhist libraries (Drège 1991; Tsien 2004).

Despite the conspicuous advance of printing in the Song, collections of manuscripts were not suddenly eclipsed by printed books. For one thing, conservative scholars were skeptical of the textual quality of the impersonal printed products; for another, good-quality books were rather expensive. No matter the rapid growth of printing, many desirable titles were not in print and could only be obtained by making manuscript copies. By the end of the twelfth century, the imperial library in Hangzhou possessed several thousand titles, but it is estimated that only one-quarter were printed books. The social significance of calligraphy training, the practice of sutra copying by Buddhists, the belief that "the best way to read a book is to copy it," as well as traditions of handwritten annotation and textual collation, all contributed to the general prevalence of manuscript books in traditional China. The chief kinds were *gaoben* or *shou gaoben* (original manuscript or holograph), *qing gaoben* (clean copy of an original manuscript), *chaoben* or *xieben* (copied manuscript from a printed or handwritten source), and *ying chaoben* (facsimile manuscript). *Diben* was the source copy for a copied manuscript or facsimile manuscript, and *jiaoben* was a collated or annotated copy of a manuscript or printed book.

Imperially sponsored projects on a grand scale in the Ming and Qing periods further emphasized the importance of manuscripts. In 1403, the Yongle emperor (r. 1403–24) commissioned the voluminous classified encyclopedia of citations from known literature, the *Yongle dadian*. It comprised nearly 23,000 *juan* (chapter-like sections) of text bound in more than 11,000 folio-size volumes. It is reported that no less than 3,000 scholars and scribes consulted about 8,000 works covering many subjects and took several years to finish the task. Too vast to be printed, the manuscript compilation was stored in the imperial library.

In the eighteenth century, the Qianlong emperor (r. 1736–95) expanded the palace book collections, and he is best known for having created the *Siku quanshu* or Four Libraries collection. This manuscript repository comprises about 3,500 individual works in 36,000 volumes, stored in 6,000 individual boxes made of *nanmu* wood. It was edited and transcribed between 1773 and 1782 by a board of more than 350 eminent scholars and countless court scribes. Rare printed works and manuscripts were solicited from all over the country to serve as *diben*, and more than 10,000 works were reviewed for consideration. The resulting bibliographical descriptions for 10,254 titles were published in 1782 in 100 volumes as the *Qinding siku quanshu zongmu*, which still remains the most comprehensive Chinese descriptive bibliography. No matter that one of the emperor's undisclosed aims in soliciting all these titles was to compile a list of proscribed works to censor, the main thrust of the effort was to preserve an extensive body of literature.

Between 1782 and 1787, seven identical sets of the Four Libraries collection were produced in manuscript on the emperor's orders, to be deposited in seven library buildings erected between 1775 and 1784. The first four sets were designated for the imperial palace and three detached palaces in the north; the remaining three were to be placed in Zhenjiang, Yangzhou, and Hangzhou in the south. The magnitude of the project will be apparent if we realize that it produced a total of more than 250,000 uniformly written manuscript volumes. Three of the original buildings and manuscript collections wholly exist today, and a fourth survives thanks to considerable restoration.

That the invention of printing took place at all in China in the early Tang dynasty has to be seen as the direct result of the availability of paper, which existed as part of a widespread literate culture. Once high-quality paper was available for manuscript production, then impressions could be taken from inked seals and small wooden pictorial stamps, and ink-squeeze rubbings of text could be made from stone inscriptions. These simple means of duplicating word and image evolved into the use of carved wooden blocks (xylography) to print multiple copies of complete texts.

The enormous qualified labor force (especially block-cutters) available to the Chinese publishing industry insured a steady flow of books and printed matter over many centuries. The widespread locations of commercial publications are clearly recorded in the colophons of Southern Song (1127–1279) printed books. In addition to the well-known body of orthodox books produced for the educated elite, an abundance of popular publications circulated among the semiliterate: religious tracts, almanacs, storybooks, theatrical and musical texts, practical handbooks, artisan pattern books, and textbooks for children as well as for townsmen who needed to learn new skills, such as accounting, not to mention a wide variety of single-sheet posters, playbills, announcements, and new year and festival prints.

Most examples of pre-Song Chinese printing that we have today are from Dunhuang, where they were found together with the considerable storehouse of early manuscripts. That they are mostly regional products and Buddhist in content has prejudiced our view of early Chinese imprints. The most important specimen is the *Jin'gang jing*

Figure 7.2   Frontispiece woodcut and initial lines of text of the *Jin'gang jing* (Diamond Sutra), printed in 868 and bound in scroll book form. Reproduced by courtesy of the British Library (Or.8210/P.2).

(Diamond Sutra) of 868, a unique example in the British Library and renowned as the world's oldest complete printed book (figure 7.2). It is printed on six large sheets of hemp paper, pasted on end to form a scroll about 25 cm high and over 5 m long, with an impressive frontispiece woodcut, which shows Shakyamuni seated on a lotus throne behind an altar table, surrounded by disciples and heavenly figures, facing the aged Subhuti, who genuflects on a mat. In the printed colophon at the end of the text it is clearly stated that "On the fifteenth day of the fourth month of the ninth year of the Xiantong reign [11 May 868], Wang Jie, in honor of his parents, respectfully had this sutra printed for universal dissemination."

As printing matured in the tenth and eleventh centuries, innovations were introduced and some large-scale projects were carried out. The tenth century saw publication of the first woodblock edition of the canon of Confucian classics, followed by various dictionaries and other secular books. The *Kaibao tripitaka*, or Buddhist canon of the Kaibao reign (968–75), was printed at Chengdu, Sichuan, reputedly from a set of 130,000 woodblocks. It was bound in scroll form and consisted of more than 5,000 volumes, of which only a handful exist today.

The two voluminous *tripitaka* editions that were published in Fujian province in the south of China toward the end of the Northern Song (960–1127) have survived. The first was initiated at the Dongchansi Temple near Fuzhou around 1080, and the second one commenced publication at the Kaiyuansi Temple about three decades later. Each of these versions of the Buddhist canon consists of nearly 6,000 volumes in the sutra-folded binding form. They took many years to complete and obviously required a vast labor force of papermakers, block-cutters, printers, binders, scholars, and scribes. *Tripitaka* editions of equal magnitude were published in Zhejiang and Jiangsu provinces and elsewhere in the north before the close of the Song period. These huge sets were intended for important Buddhist temples and other institutions. Given the nature of xylography as a sort of "printing on demand," individual works from the vast *tripitaka* could be printed as required: thus parts of the whole came to circulate among the people.

At about the same time, in Hangzhou, a method of printing with movable type made of earthenware was invented. The Song polymath Shen Gua (1031–95) described it in a collection of essays entitled *Mengxi bitan*:

> During the Qingli reign (1041–1048) there was a commoner named Bi Sheng who made moveable type [printing]. His method was to use clay to carve characters as thin as coins, each character becoming a single type, which he fired to a [certain] degree of hardness. The surface of an iron tray was then prepared with [a layer of] pine resin, wax, and paper ashes. When he wished to print something he placed an iron frame upon the iron tray, and on the tray he set the type tightly in place, filling the frame, thus making a surface for printing. By warming the tray he could soften the wax, and using a flat board he leveled the surface of the type to be as flat as a finely ground whetstone. (Zhang 1989: 664)

Obviously this new technique owed much to traditional xylographic printing (Tsien 1984). Its chief disadvantage was the enormous number of characters (written graphs) required to express the Chinese language, thereby necessitating a sizable investment in very large founts of type.

At the end of the thirteenth century in the Yuan dynasty, Wang Zhen, in his *Nongshu* (Book of Agriculture), published a detailed description of a proposed printing project using carved wooden type, but it was never realized. Despite Bi Sheng's invention, significant typographic publications did not appear in China until the end of the fifteenth century, and the technique was used only sporadically after that. It should be remembered that the two major printing projects sponsored by the imperial court in the eighteenth century produced two founts, each of around 250,000 types, one of bronze and the other of wood.

Printing of this sort could not have been undertaken if profit were a motive, and it seems that the important and early development of commercial publishing in China influenced the dominant role of the more economically viable xylographic method of printing. According to abundant nineteenth-century data, it is clear that book production by woodblock printing in China was cheaper than any other method prior to the introduction of Western printing presses and electrotype type production in the second half of that century (Heijdra 2004a).

Xylography, of course, did not require type design in the usual sense. Nevertheless, calligraphers and copyists of texts for engraving played an important role in creating an aesthetic for the printed page. In addition to a uniform style for the main text, xylographic printing made it possible to produce prefaces in facsimile of the authors' actual handwriting. Books containing specimens of the calligraphy of celebrities possessed commercial appeal. In fact, xylographic facsimile editions of famous texts were conveniently produced in China long before the invention of photography.

Already in the Song dynasty, unauthorized editions were a problem, and attempts at employing a form of copyright to protect commercial publishers failed. Even official government editions published in the capital Hangzhou were reprinted without reprisal in the provinces. Book pirates were so bold as to copy printers' colophons and cover pages, including copyright warnings, so that buyers had no suspicion that they were acquiring a spurious edition. In the late Ming, the custom of printing veiled threats on the cover page (for example, *fanke bijiu*, "unauthorized reprints will be investigated") was widespread but utterly ineffectual. By then, with a highly stimulated economy, an increased demand for books, and a highly diversified publishing industry, book piracy had become endemic.

Commercially printed books in China have a long history, but because of different conditions they developed quite differently from the West. Earlier restrictions and a partial government monopoly over aspects of printing in the eleventh century did little more than impede its rate of growth, and by the next century the commercial implications of printing were full blown. More than twenty commercial publishers and booksellers are known to have been active in Hangzhou, the Southern Song capital, during much of the twelfth and thirteenth centuries. Classical, philosophical, religious, literary, educational, and geopolitical texts were sold to Japan, Korea, and other neighboring states throughout the Song. Attempts by Chinese authorities to control exports for political reasons failed to halt the flow of books: the smuggling was motivated by profit and seldom by politics (Tsien 1985; Zhang 1989).

From the twelfth century on, book collections began to show evidence of the impact of printing. For example, the private collection of about 1,500 titles of Chao Gongwu (d. 1171) contained both manuscript and printed editions. Chao's *Junzhai dushuzhi* (Bibliography of the Junzhai Collection), published shortly after his death, is the oldest extant descriptive catalogue in China: its printed edition of 1250 survives. As the Southern Song economy flourished and printed books became more plentiful, their prices decreased and their circulation increased. Nowhere was the impact more pronounced than in education, as reflected in the number of civil service examination candidates, which steadily swelled throughout the Song period (Zhang 1989).

Private book collections grew in the Yuan dynasty, and, after a period of economic depression in the first part of the Ming, they continued to expand. The Tianyige library in Ningbo, founded in 1561 by Fan Qin (1506–85) after a successful career as a government official, is the oldest existing private library in China. Fan not only collected books and passed them on to later generations, he also published several useful works. Tianyige was the acknowledged inspiration for the design of the seven libraries built to house the Qianlong emperor's *Siku quanshu* collections. Although the original Tianyige book collections have become depleted by calamity and attrition, they and their catalogues provide important material for the study of Ming libraries. Large book collections were also amassed by Ming booksellers and publishers, notably Mao Jin

(1599–1659) of Changshu in Jiangsu province. Jiguge was the name of his personal library as well as the most common hallmark for his commercial publications. The fact that, in this period, old books and manuscripts were increasingly being collected as artifacts greatly contributed to their preservation.

The growth of publishing activity in the late Ming led to the introduction of many new genres, especially those containing woodcut illustrations, as well as new methods of printing, such as polychrome printing (*caise taoyin*), which began by applying several colors to a single woodblock and developed into the "assembled-blocks" (*douban*) method, which uses separate woodblocks for different colors. The 1626 polychrome publication of *Luoxuan biangu jianpu* (Models of Letter Paper of the Wisteria Studio) by Wu Faxiang (b. 1578) in Nanjing apparently was the first to incorporate the *gonghua* technique, a form of blind printing in which subtle images are embossed on some blank pages. Hu Zhengyan (1582–1672) published *Shizhuzhai shuhuapu* (Ten Bamboo Studio Manual of Calligraphy and Painting) as a set sometime between 1633 and 1644, although parts may have been published as early as 1627, and *Shizhuzhai jianpu* (Models of Letter Paper of the Ten Bamboo Studio) in 1644. Both were published in Nanjing and printed in six or more colors, and the latter was the first to cite the *douban* technique. Two-color textual printing (*zhumo taoyin*) began in the Yuan, but it was first widely practiced by the Min and Ling lineages of Huzhou in the first decades of the seventeenth century. They also produced several editions with as many as four colors for commentaries in addition to the main text printed in black.

Private individuals, schools, governmental and religious institutions, as well as commercial publishers all contributed to the flourishing book culture in the Jiangnan region in the south of China at the time. In addition to standard texts, publications in demand included guidebooks to examinations, popular fiction, literary collections, local gazetteers, travel books, household encyclopedias, and reprint collections. The bookshops of Nanjing, Suzhou, and Hangzhou were renowned, as were the block-cutters of Huizhou. Book illustration prospered as never before, led by the Huizhou School and followed by other regional styles. The mobility of civil servants and of the literati class in general, as well as the itinerant nature of workers in the publishing industry (for example, editors and block-cutters), militated against narrow provincialism. Wang Tingna (1567–1612), for example, was a prominent Huizhou publisher who was active in the intellectual life of Nanjing.

Even the important commercial publishing center of Jianyang in Fujian province further south had close ties with Jiangnan. There is evidence of collaboration among publishers and booksellers in both places and even reports of the transfer of woodblocks for printing. Yu Xiangdou (c.1560–1637) was typical of successful publishers in Jianyang. Although unsuccessful as a candidate for civil service examinations, he seems to have considered himself better educated and a cut above many of his peers. In some of his publications, Yu takes the liberty of writing prefaces and adding textual commentaries. He also lists himself as editor or co-author of several works, and in a few he includes a woodcut portrait of himself assuming the role of a scholar (figure 7.3; Chia 2002).

Figure 7.3 Woodcut scene depicting the late Ming commercial publisher Yu Xiangdou. From *Shilin zhengzong* (Compendium of Literary Commentary), published by Yu in Jianyang in 1600. Private collection. Reproduced with permission.

Recognition of this surge of publishing activity beginning in the late sixteenth century has led to a scholarly debate about the "ascendance of the imprint." Did true print culture begin as early as late Song or as late as the end of Ming? The question posed is whether the Ming dynasty was the time when imprints finally dominated book culture and significantly outnumbered manuscript texts (McDermott 2005).

Xylographic publishing in the Qing period continued to expand, albeit without the flamboyance of late-Ming publications. Certain features of Chinese books, such as the use of thread binding and the inclusion of cover pages, became firmly established in the Qing. The cover page (*fengmianye*) can be traced back to the late Song or early Yuan period. Although it resembles a Western title page, the cover page was created for commercial advertising. In addition to the title of the book and the author's name, both usually expressed fancifully, it often included the publisher's name and the place and date of publication. Sometimes it reported forthcoming or recently published titles as well as the price. Use of the cover page became so widespread in the Qing that even noncommercial publications contained a simplified form of it. There is evidence that the cover page derived from the printer's colophon, in which respect it is also similar to the Western title page (Edgren 2004).

It has been suggested that the chief factor responsible for the failure of the traditional Chinese publishing industry to develop along Western lines was the absence of capitalism. Conditions began to change only after Japanese and Western merchants introduced lithography and Western lead type and printing presses into China, through Shanghai, in the late nineteenth century. The long history of traditional print culture in China and favorable conditions in Shanghai resulted in a unique response to the newly introduced technology (Reed 2004). Superficially, books gradually came to resemble their Western counterparts in the twentieth century. Western binding techniques and decorative styles were introduced, machine-made paper from wood pulp replaced traditional paper stock, and text began to be set horizontally rather than vertically. Due to historical circumstances and the particular characteristics of its language and script, the evolution of modern Chinese typography has followed an unusual course (Heijdra 2004b).

The most important modern Chinese publishers of the first half of the twentieth century were *Shangwu yinshuguan* (Commercial Press Ltd.), founded in 1897, and *Zhonghua shuju* (Chung Hwa Book Co.), founded in 1912, both located in Shanghai. Other influential publishers included *Kaiming shudian* (Kai Ming Book Co.) and *Shijie shuju* (World Book Co.), also of Shanghai. All kinds of publishing enterprises emerged in China during the turbulent decades before the end of the Second World War. After 1949, the major publishing houses were reorganized within China, and factious groups established new businesses under their old names on Taiwan. Newly founded publishers, such as *Wenwu chubanshe* (Cultural Relics Press) in Beijing, *Shanghai guji chubanshe* (Shanghai Ancient Books Publishing House) in Shanghai, and *Yiwen yinshuguan* (Yee Wen Book Co.) on Taiwan, appealed to the educated class of Chinese. University presses and specialty publishers were established to serve various segments of society.

The institution of public libraries, university libraries, and national libraries in the twentieth century in China has profoundly affected the availability of bibliographical resources. Leading libraries include the National Library of China (Beijing), the Peking University Library (Beijing), the National Central Library (Taiwan), and the Shanghai Library (Shanghai). Libraries have lately promoted automated cataloguing of books and digitization of texts.

By the end of the twentieth century, new electronic possibilities, especially for publishers, had leveled the proverbial playing field. The formerly clumsy hand-setting of Chinese characters from vast founts of type has been eliminated. Chinese text can now be entered by keyboard as efficiently as any other script in the world, while traditional reprints can be produced directly by "optical character recognition" scanning.

REFERENCES AND FURTHER READING

Brokaw, Cynthia (1996) "Commercial Publishing in Late Imperial China: The Zou and Ma Family Businesses of Sibao, Fujian." *Late Imperial China*, 17 (1): 49–92.

— (2005) "On the History of the Book in China." In Cynthia Brokaw and Kai-wing Chow (eds.), *Printing and Book Culture in Late Imperial China*, pp. 3–54. Berkeley: University of California Press.

Carter, Thomas (1955) *The Invention of Printing in China and its Spread Westward*, revised by L. Carrington Goodrich. New York: Ronald Press.

Chia, Lucile (2002) *Printing for Profit: The Commercial Publishers of Jianyang, Fujian (11th–17th Centuries)*. Cambridge, MA: Harvard University Asia Center.

Chow, Kai-wing (2004) *Publishing, Culture, and Power in Early Modern China*. Stanford: Stanford University Press.

Drège, Jean-Pierre (1991) *Les Bibliothèques en Chine au temps des manuscrits (jusqu'au Xe siècle)* [Libraries in China in the Age of Manuscripts to the Tenth Century]. Paris: École française d'Extrême-Orient.

Edgren, Sören (2004) "The *Fengmianye* (Cover Page) as a Source for Chinese Publishing History." In Akira Isobe (ed.), *Studies of Publishing Culture in East Asia*, pp. 261–7. Tokyo: Nigensha.

Heijdra, Martin (2004a) "Technology, Culture and Economics: Movable Type versus Woodblock Printing in East Asia." In Akira Isobe (ed.), *Studies of Publishing Culture in East Asia*, pp. 223–40. Tokyo: Nigensha.

— (2004b) "The Development of Modern Typography in East Asia, 1850–2000." *East Asian Library Journal*, 11 (2): 100–68.

Helliwell, David (1998) "The Repair and Binding of Old Chinese Books." *East Asian Library Journal*, 8 (1): 27–149.

Inoue, Susumu (2002) *Chūgoku shuppan bunka-shi* [Cultural History of Chinese Publishing]. Nagoya: Nagoya daigaku shuppankai.

McDermott, Joseph (2005) "The Ascendance of the Imprint in China." In Cynthia Brokaw and Kai-wing Chow (eds.), *Printing and Book Culture in Late Imperial China*, pp. 55–104. Berkeley: University of California Press.

Reed, Christopher (2004) *Gutenberg in Shanghai: Chinese Print Capitalism, 1876–1937*. Vancouver: UBC Press.

Tsien, Tsuen-hsuin (1984) "Technical Aspects of Chinese Printing." In Sören Edgren (ed.), *Chinese Rare Books in American Collections*, pp. 16–25. New York: China Institute in America.

— (1985) *Paper and Printing* (Science and Civilisation in China, ed. Joseph Needham, vol. 5: 1). Cambridge: Cambridge University Press.

— (2004) *Written on Bamboo and Silk*, 2nd edn. Chicago: University of Chicago Press.

Zhang, Xiumin (1989) *Zhongguo yinshua shi* [History of Chinese Printing]. Shanghai: Shanghai renmin chubanshe.

8

Japan, Korea, and Vietnam

Peter Kornicki

Japan

Like Korea and Vietnam, Japan had no writing system before the encounter with Chinese script in the sixth century, when Chinese Buddhist and Confucian texts were first brought to Japan. The earliest texts were therefore written in Chinese, which remained the language of learning until the nineteenth century. In the seventh and eighth centuries, vast quantities of Chinese Buddhist manuscripts were brought back to Japan by scholar monks and then copied for domestic use; the holdings of Japanese monastic libraries at the time often included thousands of titles from the Chinese Buddhist canon and easily exceeded the norms of medieval European monastic libraries. The basic texts of the Chinese Confucian tradition and the key literary works were also transmitted to Japan and they became the keystone of the education system for over a thousand years, exerting profound influence on ethical norms and social values. In the ninth century, a syllabic script known as *kana* was developed for writing Japanese, and it was used for court poetry and romances such as the *Tale of Genji* (early eleventh century). It was sometimes known as the "women's hand," but it was used by both men and women for writing poetry at least, while Chinese continued to be used by men for official documents, education, and diaries.

By the mid-eighth century, the technology of xylography, or woodblock printing, had also reached Japan from China, where it had been developed in the seventh century or earlier. The first evidence of printing in Japan comes from the years 764–70, when at least a hundred thousand, and possibly as many as a million, copies of a Buddhist invocation in Chinese were printed in Nara. These were then inserted into miniature wooden pagodas, and many thousands of these survive with their contents intact. Although indubitably the first instance of mass-production printing in the world, these invocations are evidence not of the printing of texts for the benefit of readers but of printing as a ritual act, for the point was simply the multiple production of copies of the text. They were not for reading or even distribution: the pagodas with their contents were stored in temples and not examined until the nineteenth century. Ritual printing of this sort was practiced in Japan occasionally over the ensuing centuries, while printing for reading in Japan can be dated to no earlier than the eleventh century, when Buddhist commentaries and doctrinal works in Chinese were first printed.

Over the next four centuries, printing was undertaken spasmodically, for the most part by the great monastic institutions. Almost all the works printed were Buddhist texts and in Chinese. A few secular works in Chinese, the Confucian canon and medical texts, were also printed, but by secular printers. However, the classic works of Japanese literature were not printed until the seventeenth century, probably because the court society which had produced and transmitted them remained hermetic; another factor was the close association between calligraphy and literature which printing would have threatened. In spite of the growing familiarity of printed books, both through domestic production and through imports from China, there is until the seventeenth century no trace of a book trade or of the kind of commercial printing that had already established itself in China.

At the end of the sixteenth century, typography reached Japan from two sources, almost simultaneously. In 1590, the Jesuits brought from Macao a printing press and established a missionary press which printed not only almanacs and devotional works in Latin, but also some Japanese works in specially cast Japanese type. Later, in the 1590s, Japanese troops who had participated in an invasion of Korea brought back a Korean printing press as booty. Within a decade, both the emperor and the shogun had experimented with this new technology to print secular books in Chinese, and this served to liberate printing from the monasteries. In the first years of the new century, the renowned calligrapher Honnami Kôetsu, with the financial backing of a wealthy entrepreneur, produced exquisite typographic editions of the *Tales of Ise* (tenth century?), Noh plays, and other Japanese works using ligatures to represent the flow of calligraphy and colored papers to enhance the aesthetic effect. By the 1620s, there were commercial printer–publishers in Kyoto producing books in Japanese as well as Chinese, and using both typography and woodblock printing technology. However, during the 1640s, typography went into a decline and woodblock printing predominated until the 1880s. The decline of typography was due to a number of factors: the large quantities of type needed for printing Japanese, amounting to thousands of different pieces given all the characters as well as the *kana*; the calligraphic possibilities of woodblock printing; the greater ease, in the case of woodblock-printed books, of including illustrations and textual glosses to make texts more accessible to less-sophisticated readers; and the ease of responding to slow markets with woodblocks, which could be used to print to demand.

With the seventeenth century, then, came the emergence and rapid growth of commercial publishing. It started in Kyoto, but rapidly spread to Edo (modern Tokyo) and Osaka, and by the end of the century to most of the larger castle-towns. By 1650, most of the canon of Japanese literature had been printed, mostly with monochrome woodblock illustrations, and new works were being written for print, from letter-writing manuals for women to guidebooks and popular fiction. Contemporaries wrote of a flood of publications, and in the 1660s the book trade began issuing classified catalogues of books in print. By that time, booksellers in Kyoto, Edo, and Osaka had already formed themselves into exclusive guilds to protect themselves against copyright disputes. It was at this time, too, that the first censorship edicts were promulgated; these were vague, but the import was to prevent the publication of erotic or sensational books, of any books that even mentioned Christianity (which was proscribed), and of any books which featured the shogun or his officials even if the intent was to praise. In the 1720s, these regulations were tightened up and the guilds were made responsible for their enforcement, but overall the hand of censorship was light in the Edo period (1600–1868) compared with more recent times.

Although reliable estimates of literacy rates are wanting, it is evident that the number of readers was growing rapidly in the seventeenth century. This applied to women, too, for male complaints about women wasting their time reading romantic fiction when they should be reading improving books were on the increase. By the 1660s, "women's books" had become a category in the booksellers' catalogues, and numerous books – moralistic, practical, or simply entertaining – were being published explicitly for women readers. There were no public libraries until the late nineteenth century, but booksellers began to undertake commercial book-lending, and colporteurs took books around rural villages offering them for sale or rent.

Although print dominated the production of books in the Edo period, it should not be supposed that manuscript traditions died out. There were three main reasons for the continued production of manuscripts: first, the demand for calligraphically and aesthetically pleasing copies of works of Japanese literature such as the *Tale of Genji* and the canonical poetry anthology *Kokinshû* (905), which were often prepared as wedding gifts; secondly, the desire not to publish commercially sensitive information such as medical advances or new techniques in flower arrangement, which were commonly recorded in manuscripts available only to followers of the teacher who had devised them; and, thirdly, the demand for books on proscribed topics, including political scandals. The last category was particularly large, and judging from the fact that a printed catalogue of them survives and that many extant copies bear the seals of book-rental merchants, they seem to have been popular and to have circulated widely.

With two exceptions, Japan was self-sufficient in books in the Edo period. The first exception was books imported from China via the only open port, Nagasaki. There was a constant supply, including canonical works and commentaries on them, but, increasingly, vernacular fiction too. In the mid-nineteenth century, there were accounts of the Opium Wars and Chinese translations of books on Western geography, which furnished crucial information in the years before 1858 when Japan signed its first trading treaties with the West. The other exception was Dutch books, which entered Japan through the outpost of the Dutch East India Company in Nagasaki, mostly from the beginning of the eighteenth century. Some Japanese became proficient in Dutch, and by the end of the eighteenth century were producing some important translations of Dutch editions of Western anatomical and medical works.

By the early nineteenth century, Japan had a sophisticated publishing industry that covered the entire country through networks of retail booksellers and commercial lending libraries. Publishers catered even to niche markets; for example, with books on games and pastimes like Go, chess, and flower arrangement, or volumes on anatomy and mathematics: all required extensive illustration, which woodblock printing rendered easy to produce (figure 8.1). The mainstay of the industry, however, was illustrated

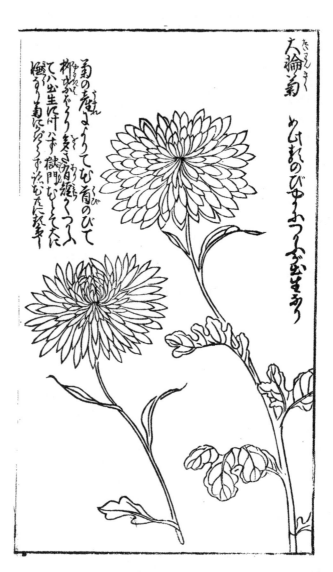

Figure 8.1   A page showing chrysanthemums from *Genji ikebana ki* (1765), a book of flower arrangements. Woodblock printing greatly facilitated the combination of illustrations and text on the same page, as here, and accounts for the very high proportion of illustrated books printed in Japan from the early seventeenth century onward.

fiction, which ranged from children's texts consisting mostly of pictures, with dialogue squeezed in around the edges, to demanding historical novels enhanced by elegant calligraphy and illustrations by Hokusai and other famous printmakers. Most of the well-known names of the "floating world" print tradition were also in the business of producing book illustration. In many cases, they also created *ehon*, books consisting of nothing but pictures, mostly in black and white but, from the late eighteenth century onward, sometimes in color. The arts of the book in Japan reached their apogee in the eighteenth and nineteenth centuries, when color printing using multiple blocks was combined with exquisite design sense to produce works like Utamaro's book of insects, *Ehon mushi erami* (1788).

Another kind of publication to make use of color was maps, which customarily included not only cartographic representations but also pictorial elements and substantial amounts of text. From the middle of the seventeenth century onward, Japanese consumers had a considerable appetite for maps. Commercial maps of the main cities of Kyoto, Osaka, and Edo were issued annually; and large maps were produced by using series of woodblocks. Colored maps of Japan published from the late eighteenth century onward contributed to a sense of national identity and, by including lines of latitude and longitude, to a consciousness of Japan's place in the larger world. By the 1850s, maps of Kobe and Yokohama were showing signs of a growing Western presence in Japan in the form of ships, consulates, and warehouses.

The economics of the book trade in the Edo period are obscure. Archival material is scarce and we have little information on print runs. It is usually estimated that, depending on the kind of wood used, no more than 8,000 to 10,000 copies could be printed from a set of printing blocks before the text became too poor in quality to be commercially marketable. At that point, the only option was to produce a new set of blocks: careful comparison of surviving copies indicates that this was not an uncommon practice by the nineteenth century, suggesting that some books were selling in tens of thousands of copies.

Authorship was now becoming a profession. *Ex gratia* payments to authors were sometimes made by grateful publishers even in the seventeenth century, but later writers became saleable commodities in their own right and publishers would trade on literary celebrities in publicity and advertising material. However, although a living could be made from writing fiction, copyright was held by publishers; authors enjoyed no intellectual property rights whatsoever.

A crucial financial consideration in the nineteenth century, when publishing larger and more expensive works of fiction, was the readiness of the commercial lending libraries to purchase copies. Commercial book-lending was practiced from the 1660s onward, but by the early nineteenth century there were more than five hundred commercial lending libraries in Edo alone, and many more scattered throughout the provinces, so that their purchasing power had an appreciable impact on profitability. Most of them specialized in current fiction, but many also stocked nonfiction, such as topographical works. The largest of them all, Daisô of Nagoya, had a stock in excess of 20,000 titles, ranging from sinology to light fiction.

Although commercial typography had come to an end in the 1650s, wooden movable type had been used occasionally by private printers thereafter. In 1848, however, a printing press and founts of Dutch type reached the Dutch East India Company outpost in Nagasaki, and they were purchased the same year by Motoki Shôzô, a government interpreter. In 1851–2 he used them, together with some *kana* type he had cast in Japan, to print a basic Dutch–Japanese dictionary. Under his direction, the government office in Nagasaki began printing some Dutch books for the benefit of Japanese scholars, and in the late 1850s and 1860s there were further experiments with imported presses to print books in Dutch, English, and Japanese. In 1854–5, the first treaties opening Japan to limited contact with Western countries had been signed and the number of resident foreigners began to grow, leading in 1861 to the *Nagasaki Shipping List and Advertiser,* the first newspaper published in Japan, albeit intended solely for the expatriate community. During the Edo period the thirst for news had been satisfied by occasional broadsheets known as *kawaraban,* which gave details of sensational events such as natural disasters, murders, and love suicides.

In 1868, the new Meiji government immediately began to put its stamp on the publishing industry. On the positive side, a government gazette was issued for the first time, giving the text of official decrees, but simultaneously the first steps were taken to impose a more effective system of prepublication censorship. In the 1870s, the regulations became ever more stringent in response to political opposition to the government's authoritarian tendencies, and in 1875 the Libel Law stipulated that matters that reflected badly on government ministers and officials could not be reported even if true. From this point up to 1945, censorship became increasingly severe in application and punitive efficacy.

Although private and commercial libraries had long existed in Japan, travelers such as Fukuzawa Yukichi, who visited the West in the 1860s, perceived Western libraries as something different, emphasizing that they were open to all free of charge. The first such institution established in Japan was the Shojakkan created by the Ministry of Education in 1872, but in 1885 it started charging fees, thus differing from earlier commercial lending libraries only in the fact that provision was made by the state. It was in 1872, too, that commercial lending libraries adapted their stocks to the new shibboleths of the day and undertook to provide newspapers and foreign books on professional or scientific subjects, but many of them continued to stock the fiction of the 1830s. The publication in the 1880s of typographic editions of old favorites indicates that reading tastes had not surrendered completely to the lure of the West.

For the first twenty years of the Meiji period (1868–1912) woodblock printing remained the dominant technology, but thereafter the tide turned irrevocably in favor of movable type. The government had early on committed itself to typography, establishing in the Ministry of Works a bureau charged with casting type for the presses of central and local government agencies and of the newly founded Imperial University in Tokyo. This official encouragement had the greatest impact at first on newspapers. The first daily, *Kankyo Yokohama Shinbun,* founded in 1870, was printed for the first few years with wooden type, but in 1873 it adopted metal type. In the late 1870s and

1880s, movable type was increasingly used for book publication too, especially translations of Western books and new works of fiction.

New publishers, such as Hakubunkan (1887–1947), now came to the fore. Hakubunkan made its name with innovative journals and magazines, such as *Nihon Taika Ronshû* (Essays by Great Writers of Japan, from 1887), which carried articles by well-known contemporaries on issues ranging from medicine and hygiene to literature and education; *Nisshin sensô jikki* (True Account of the Sino-Japanese War, from 1894), which was the first photo magazine and carried pictures of the war; and *Taiyô* (The Sun, from 1895), the most popular general magazine. At the same time, it was undertaking bold publishing projects, such as a multivolume encyclopedia in 1889, and from 1893 the hundred-volume series *Teikoku Bunko* (Imperial Library), which reprinted literary favorites of the Edo period that had hitherto circulated either as woodblock books or as manuscripts. By the 1890s, very few of the old publishing companies, some of which went back to the seventeenth century, were still in business. Their place had been taken by new companies like Hakubunkan, which relied on typography, steam-driven technology, and new business methods.

In the twentieth century, leaving aside technological developments that were by no means unique to Japan, the most striking features of the publishing business were the vigor of the periodicals market and the continuing appetite for new titles. Of the many new periodicals, the most influential were *Chûô Kôron* (Central Review) and *Bungei Shunjû* (Literary Times), while the launch in 1903 of *Katei no tomo* (The Family's Friend) and in 1917 of *Shufu no tomo* (The Housewife's Friend) inaugurated long-lasting, mass-market magazines aimed at women readers. From the outbreak of war with China in 1937 onward, stringent controls were applied to periodicals and many were forced to close down. Immediately after the end of World War II, a number of new magazines were launched which took advantage of the end of wartime censorship to adopt a more liberal stance or to look to the West for fashions and lifestyle information. In successive decades, new launches established *Shônen janpu* (1968), a comic magazine for boys which reached a circulation of 6.5 million in 1993; *an-an* (1970), a very successful fashion magazine; and *Focus* (1981), a photo magazine that often carried sensational news items. *Manga*, or comics, have in postwar Japan constituted a large proportion of both magazine and book consumption. They have sometimes been criticized for violence, racism, or sexism, but they remain a visibly popular form of entertainment that is now closely tied to *anime*, or the Japanese animation film.

Over the past ten years, sales of new books have been in decline both in terms of numbers of copies and of net value, and the number of bookshops has also been falling, although it is still above 8,000 for the whole of Japan. The number of new titles published each year defies the downward trend and continues to rise, reaching 74,000 in 2002. Although an overwhelming proportion of the books published in Japan were originally written in Japanese, publishing globalization is demonstrated by the fact that the first printing of the Japanese translation of J. K. Rowling's *Harry Potter and the Goblet of Fire* was 2.3 million copies. On the other hand, the globalization of Japanese books, as measured by the number of translations of Japanese books into foreign languages and by the number of copies of translations sold, remains at a low level, even in the English-speaking world. While the Japanese classics and the best of current fiction are now available in most European languages, it remains rare for academic, political, and other books to appear in English translation.

Korea

Korea is remarkable as the source both of what is considered by many to be the oldest datable printed item in the world (before 751) and of the oldest extant sample of typography, nearly a hundred years before Gutenberg. Both these texts are in Chinese, for, like Japan and Vietnam, Korea had no writing system before its encounter with Chinese characters and the written traditions of Buddhism and Confucianism. Hence Koreans, until the development in the fifteenth century of an alphabetic script for writing Korean, were constrained to write in Chinese. Their oldest surviving texts are Chinese translations of Buddhist sutras, which were copied in Korea in the eighth century. Chinese remained the written language of intellectual discourse until the twentieth century, but under King Sejong in the middle of the fifteenth century a phonetic alphabet was devised for writing the highly inflected Korean language; this script is now called *hangul*. Today, Korean is written exclusively with *hangul* in the Democratic People's Republic of Korea (DPRK) in the north, while in the Republic of Korea (ROK) in the south Chinese characters continue to be used for words of Chinese origin, although newspapers increasingly use *hangul* for them as well.

By the seventh century at least, woodblock printing was practiced in China, and the technology was transmitted, before the eighth century was over, to both Korea and Japan. In 1966, a printed Buddhist invocation in Chinese was discovered in a pagoda, constructed in 751, in the Bulguksa temple in Gyeongju; the date has been challenged and it has also been suggested that the invocation may have been printed in China. However, the paper is indubitably Korean and the consensus is that it was printed in Korea more than a dozen years before similar Buddhist invocations were printed in quantity in Japan. If printing was then practiced in Japan, it is *a priori* likely that it was also practiced in Korea, which was technologically ahead of Japan. In both countries, however, this was printing for ritual purposes, not for reading; the same was true of a sutra printed with illustrations in 1007, which was produced for inserting into a reliquary.

Thereafter, woodblock printing was put to more practical uses to produce Buddhist texts for study and devotion. The most ambitious undertaking was the production of a Korean edition of the vast Buddhist canon, inspired by the Chinese printed edition of 983, of which a copy reached Korea by royal request in 991. The carving of the blocks for the 6,000 volumes of the Korean edition began in 1010, but they were later destroyed during the Mongol invasion of 1232; no complete copy survives, but substantial parts are preserved in Japan. In 1236–51, however, the blocks for a second edition were cut, and more than 80,000 of these are preserved to this day in the Haeinsa temple in southern Korea. This edition of the canon, containing 1,516 texts in 6,815 volumes, was a more comprehensive collection of sutras and exegetical writings than anything previously produced in China or elsewhere, and was much sought after in Japan and the Ryûkyû kingdom.

The tradition of woodblock printing was joined in the twelfth century by typography. Movable type had been invented in China in the eleventh century, but it was put to much more extensive use in Korea. The oldest extant book in the world printed with metal movable type is a book written in Chinese by a Korean Buddhist monk, which was printed in Korea in 1377 and is preserved in the Bibliothèque Nationale in Paris. There is, however, reliable documentary evidence of typographic printing in the early thirteenth century, and a twelfth-century matrix for casting type has recently been unearthed, taking the origins of Korean typography back even further. In 1392, the Korean court established the Seojeogweon, a printing office for casting type and publishing books, but it was in 1403, after the foundation of the Yi dynasty (1392–1910), that King Taejong declared his intention of harnessing typography for the benefit of the state: "In order to govern the country well, it is essential that books be read widely . . . It is my desire to cast copper [bronze] type so that we can print as many books as possible and have them made available widely. This will truly bring infinite benefit to us" (Lee 1993: 537). In the course of the fifteenth century alone, new sets of type were cast at least twenty-one times to print mostly Chinese works but also, for example, *Dongguk jeong'un* (1448), a guide to the Korean pronunciation of Chinese characters. By this time, wooden type was being used as well as metal type, and after the Japanese invasions of the 1590s, which left Korea deprived of its founts of metal type, wooden type predominated for half a century.

Thus, until the early twentieth century, Korean printers made use of a wide range of technologies in parallel: typography utilizing bronze, ferrous, or wooden type; woodblock printing; and a hybrid technology whereby different elements on the same page were printed using typography or woodblocks. The best example of the last is the 1797 edition of *Chunchu jwa ssi jeon*, which is the Korean name of the Chinese text called *Zuo's Commentaries on the Spring and Autumn Annals*: on each page, the text of the *Annals* was printed in large size with woodblocks, while both the commentary in half size and notes by Korean editors in quarter size were printed with type cast in 1777 (figure 8.2).

These various technologies were used to produce five different types of book: Chinese volumes of Chinese authorship, such as the Confucian canon, which dominated education and intellectual life and which therefore constituted a high proportion of books printed; books written by Korean authors in Chinese, such as the *Samguk Sagi* (1145), a history of the three kingdoms of early Korea, the many works of the greatest Confucian scholar of Korea, Yi Toegye (1501–70), and even fictional works; books in Korean, which were fewer in quantity and often consisted of commercial editions of works of popular fiction; hybrid books, such as *Hyogyeong eonhae*, an early eighteenth-century Korean edition of the Chinese *Classic of Filial Piety*, which is furnished with *hangul* glosses and Korean translations; and maps. For maps obviously, and for books in Korean

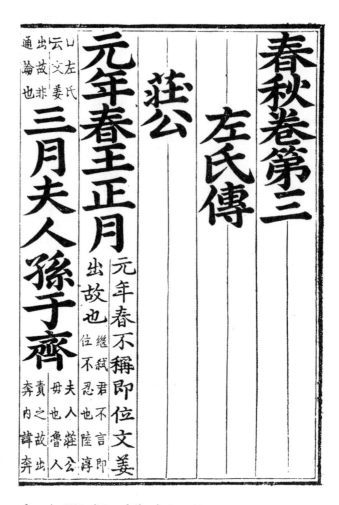

Figure 8.2   A page from the 1797 edition of *Chunchu jwa ssi jeon.*

and hybrid books, woodblocks were the customary technology, although it is true that *hangul* type was cast for printing Korean from 1447 onward. For books in Chinese, typography was as likely to be used as woodblocks. In spite of the association between typography and government printing, it is important to note that even as late as 1909 some official publications were produced from woodblocks.

The use of various printing technologies by no means spelled the end of manuscript traditions, however. Many works of Korean fiction circulated mainly in the form of manuscripts, such as the seventeenth-century *Nine Cloud Dream*, which survives in nineteenth-century woodblock editions and in numerous manuscripts. It was common also to make manuscript copies of printed books, for reasons of economy or sometimes because the original was scarce. Thus, the copy of an agricultural manual titled *Nongga chipsoeng* in the Asami Library was made in 1891 from the 1686 edition, even though in 1734 the king had ordered all provincial governments to print and distribute it; apparently that edition had become hard to find by the end of the nineteenth century.

Western-style typography was introduced to Korea in 1883 by Kim Okhyun, a pioneer of Westernization who brought back from Japan a Western press and an experienced Japanese printer. Together they printed Korea's first newspaper, the *Hanseong Sunbo* (Hanseong Ten-daily), which was printed in Chinese and appeared every ten days until late 1884. In 1885, American Methodist missionaries established a press in Seoul which printed in Korean, Chinese, and English, and it was joined in 1891 by the Anglican Mission Press. Western-style typography, however, did not replace existing technologies, even woodblock printing, until the twentieth century.

In 1910, Korea was annexed by Japan and remained a colony until 1945; during that time all publishing was under the control of the Japanese administration and prepublication censorship was introduced for Korean (but not Japanese) publications. At first, Korean publishing was suppressed, but after the anti-Japanese demonstrations of 1919 the rules were relaxed to allow the expression of moderate Korean nationalist sentiments, and the publication of books and newspapers in Korean flourished. Also, ways around the Japanese censors were found. As one of them complained in 1930, "The Koreans start the presses as soon as the sample copy is sent to the censor. They then keep the presses rolling until they get an order to stop" (Robinson 1984: 335).

Since 1945, publishing has followed very different trajectories in the DPRK in the north and in the ROK in the south. In the DPRK, all printed media are under the firm control of the ruling party, and it was reported as late as 1995 that "national newspapers are not sold on the streets; they are distributed to subscribers only, according to their political or professional affiliations" (Darewicz 2000: 141); however, the DPRK is in a state of flux and there has recently been some relaxation of earlier practices. In the ROK, meanwhile, freedom of expression was made a basic constitutional right in 1948, but this did not include the expression of views which contradicted the national ideals and policies of the government, one of which was anticommunism, and in practice repression was at times harsh. Consequently, in the 1970s, "the owner-publisher became the censor of his own publications" and the press "gradually became more concerned to protect its corporate interest as an enterprise than its freedom as a public trust" (Chang 1994: 258, 261). In 1987, the Basic Press Law was repealed and strict government censorship became a thing of the past.

Vietnam

Like Korea and Japan, Vietnam acquired from China not only a script but also Confucianism and Buddhism, both profoundly textual traditions. For around two millennia, an educated and bookish elite was brought up on Chinese texts. However, the melancholy fact is that, from the abortive Mongol invasion of the thirteenth century to the several wars of the twentieth century, the textual patrimony of Vietnam has suffered irreparable losses and wanton destruction. Laments for these losses have been repeated by many writers from the time of Lê Qui-Dôn (1726–84), who compiled the first bibliography of Vietnamese books.

Like Japanese and Korean, Vietnamese cannot readily be written in Chinese script, hence the invention of extra characters to facilitate writing in the vernacular. This script, a combination of Chinese characters and invented characters, is known as *nom*; it was being used by the end of the eleventh century and remained in use until the twentieth century. Meanwhile, European missionaries reached Vietnam in the seventeenth century, and in 1651 a French Jesuit published a romanization scheme for Vietnamese. The use of this script, now known as *quoc ngu*, was long confined to missionary circles, but after the southern part of Vietnam became a French colony in 1862, it was perceived as a tool to detach Vietnam from China and the Confucian tradition.

Buddhism was introduced into Vietnam in the second century. By the eleventh century it enjoyed state support, and a Vietnamese ambassador to China brought back with him a copy of the vast Buddhist canon which had been printed in China in 983. In 1031, there were nearly a thousand Buddhist temples in Vietnam, and in 1076 an imperial academy and a civil service college were established. It is evident, then, that Vietnamese must by this time have already been long acquainted both with the Buddhist textual tradition and the Chinese Confucian texts that were the cornerstone of education throughout East Asia. By this time, too, Chinese woodblock-printed books must have reached Vietnam, although when printing was first undertaken in Vietnam remains a mystery. There are persuasive accounts of a Vietnamese woodblock edition of the Buddhist canon and other works at the end of the thirteenth century, but no copies survive.

By the early fifteenth century, books had indisputably become familiar and accessible in Vietnam. Nguyen Trai (1380–1442), one of the greatest Vietnamese poets, refers often to books as a matter of course: in his Chinese poems he wrote "Beneath green trees, in silence you read books" and "Locked in your study, stay with books all day" (Huynh 1979: 73–4). Some at least of these must have been printed books, but the oldest surviving woodblock editions date from no earlier than 1697. It is from around that time, if not earlier, that printing began to add substantially to the body of texts circulated hitherto in manuscript, ranging from Chinese canonical texts and texts composed in Chinese by Vietnamese authors to Vietnamese works in *nom*. Government editions of the Chinese Confucian classics replaced Chinese imports, which were banned in 1731, and the *Dai Viet su ky toan thu*, a chronicle which covers the history of Vietnam from around 200 BC onwards, was printed in 1697. It has recently been established that some of the works written in Chinese by Vietnamese authors and printed in the eighteenth century betray the existence of earlier editions printed in Vietnam with wooden movable type, but it is not known if typography was practiced in Vietnam before the seventeenth century (Yamamoto 1999). Meanwhile, in 1668, and again in 1718 and 1760, edicts were issued banning the use of *nom* in print except for educational publications, which is a clear indication that woodblock printing in *nom* was already being practiced in the seventeenth century.

Under the Nguyen dynasty (1802–1945) Chinese continued to dominate education and learning. Scholars were repeatedly dispatched to China as envoys so that they could

Figure 8.3 A woodblock-printed school textbook printed in Vietnam in the late nineteenth century: the large characters are Chinese and the smaller glosses are in *nom*. The textbook was amongst the items brought back by Sir James George Scott (1851–1935), who, as war correspondent of the *Standard* newspaper, accompanied the French forces conquering Tongking in 1884 to complete the French colonization of Vietnam. Reproduced by courtesy of the Syndics of Cambridge University Library.

collect books, and in 1840 Emperor Minh-mang declared that what Vietnam needed from China was ginseng, medicines, and books (Woodside 1971: 114). Nevertheless, there was growing space for Vietnamese writing in *nom*, such as the celebrated verse novel *The Tale of Kieu* by Nguyen Du (1765–1820), and for translations of some of the Chinese classics into Vietnamese using *nom* script. The Nguyen strictly controlled printing, and most of it was undertaken in Chinese by the state or by Buddhist temples, so scribal traditions remained important for Vietnamese works in *nom*. Printing under the Nguyen continued to rely on woodblock technology, which remained the norm until the early twentieth century (figure 8.3).

Under the French colonial government from 1862 onward, typography made rapid progress and was used for both French and *quoc ngu* publications. The first publication in *quoc ngu* was the first Vietnamese newspaper, *Gia-dinh báo* (Daily Paper, 1865), a government publication which also carried articles on agriculture and Vietnamese culture. Vietnamese nationalists, however, used *nom* as the language of resistance and did so until 1907, when the Tonkin Free School, founded by reformers, advocated *quoc ngu* for its educational advantages. During World War I, the colonial administration encouraged *quoc ngu* journalism for propaganda purposes, and as a result journals such as *Nam Phong* (Breeze from the South, 1917–34) appeared to appeal to the Francophile community. But as use of *quoc ngu* became more widespread, it began to serve other purposes: in the 1930s, Marxist literature was published in *quoc ngu*, as well as large quantities of anti-French pamphlets and even popular Buddhist tracts. Typography was now the dominant technology and *quoc ngu* had become the language of print, and it remained so after 1945 in both North and South Vietnam.

Since the use of *quoc ngu* for education has rendered most Vietnamese now incapable of reading earlier Vietnamese writings in Chinese or *nom*, there has been, from the late twentieth century, an increasing commitment to the publication of translations from Chinese or of transcriptions from *nom* texts to render them accessible to *quoc ngu* readers. Most of the translations and transcriptions were published between 1956 and 1975, but since 1996 there have been renewed efforts to encourage publications of this type, for considerably less than half of the premodern literary and historical texts surviving are accessible to those who can only read *quoc ngu*.

References and Further Reading

Japan

Bauermeister, Junko (1980) *Entwicklung des modernen japanischen Verlagswesens: Fallstudie Iwanami Shoten*. Bochum: Studienverlag Dr. N. Brockmeyer.

Chibbett, David (1977) *The History of Japanese Printing and Book Illustration*. Tokyo: Kodansha International.

Forrer, Matthi (1979) *Eirakuya Tôshirô, Publisher at Nagoya*. Uithoorn: Gieben.

Hillier, Jack (1988) *The Art of the Japanese Book*. London: Philip Wilson.

Kornicki, Peter (1998) *The Book in Japan: A Cultural History from the Beginnings to the Nineteenth Century*. Leiden: Brill.

May, Ekkehard (1983) *Die Kommerzialisierung der japanischen Literatur in der späten Edo-Zeit.* Wiesbaden: Otto Harrassowitz.

Mitchell, Richard (1983) *Censorship in Imperial Japan.* Princeton: Princeton University Press.

Unno, Kazutaka (1994) "Cartography in Japan." In J. B. Harley and David Woodward (eds.), *The History of Cartography*, vol. 2, book 2, pp. 346–477. Chicago: University of Chicago Press.

Welch, Theodore F. (1976) *Toshokan: Libraries in Japanese Society.* London: Bingley.

Korea

Chang, Yunshik (1994) "From Ideology to Interest: Government and Press in South Korea, 1945–1979." In Suh Dae-Sook (ed.), *Korean Studies: New Pacific Currents*, pp. 249–62. Honolulu: Center for Korean Studies, University of Hawaii.

Darewicz, Krzystof (2000) "North Korea: A Black Chapter." In Louise Williams and Roland Rich (eds.), *Losing Control: Freedom of the Press in Asia*, pp. 138–46. Canberra: Asia Pacific Press.

Edgren, Sören and Rohstgrom, John (1974) *Koreanskt Boktryck 1420–1900* [Korean Printing 1420–1900]. Stockholm: Kungliga biblioteket.

Fang, Chaoying (1969) *The Asami Library: A Descriptive Catalogue.* Berkeley: University of California Press.

Kim, Hyo Gun (1973) *Printing in Korea and its Impact on her Culture.* Chicago: University of Chicago Press.

Lancaster, Lewis R., with Sung-bae Park (1979) *The Korean Buddhist Canon: A Descriptive Catalogue.* Berkeley: University of California Press.

Lee, Hee-Jae (1987) *La typographie coréenne au XVe siècle.* Paris: Editions du Centre National de la Recherche Scientifique.

Lee, Peter (1993) *Sourcebook of Korean Civilization*, vol. 1. New York: Columbia University Press.

McGovern, Melvin P. (1967) "Early Western Presses in Korea." *Korea Journal*, July 1: 21–3.

Robinson, Michael (1984) "Colonial Publication Policy and the Korean Nationalist Movement." In Ramon H. Myers and Mark R. Peattie (eds.), *The Japanese Colonial Empire, 1985–1945*, pp. 312–43. Princeton: Princeton University Press.

Sohn, Pow-key (1982) *Early Korean Typography.* Seoul: Po Chin Chai.

Vietnam

DeFrancis, John (1977) *Colonialism and Language Policy in Viet Nam.* The Hague: Mouton.

Huynh Sanh Thong (1979) *The Heritage of Vietnamese Poetry.* New Haven: Yale University Press.

McHale, Shawn F. (2003) *Print and Power: Buddhism, Confucianism and Communism in the Making of Modern Vietnam.* Honolulu: University of Hawai'i Press.

Pasquel-Rageau, Christiane (1984) "L'imprimerie au Vietnam: de l'impression xylographique traditionnelle à la révolution du quoc ngu." In Jean-Pierre Drège, Mitchiko Ishigami-Iagolnitzer, and Monique Cohen (eds.), *Le livre et l'imprimerie*

en Extrême-Orient et en Asie du Sud, pp. 249–62. Bordeaux: Société des Bibliophiles de Guyenne.

Tran Nghia (2002) "A Survey of Sino-nom Translations and Compilations in the 20th Century." *Vietnam Social Sciences*, 88: 57–66.

Woodside, Alexander B. (1971) *Vietnam and the Chinese Model.* Cambridge, MA: Harvard University Press.

Yamamoto, Tatsuro (1999) "Development of Movable Type Printing in Vietnam under the Lê Dynasty: A Study of the Comparative History between Vietnam and Japan." *Memoirs of the Research Department of the Toyo Bunko*, 57: 1–11.

9
South Asia

Graham Shaw

The book, in physical forms both familiar and unfamiliar to the West, has an extremely long, rich, and diverse history in South Asia. For two millennia, from the third century BC onward, that history primarily revolved around the widespread and large-scale commission, production, and dissemination of manuscripts – what has even been termed the "pre-print publishing industry" of South Asia (Pollock 2007). This sophisticated manuscript culture enjoyed a close and mutually influential relationship with the oral and performance culture that had preceded it but which continued to flourish in parallel. The cultivation of memory (often to a phenomenal degree) and oral transmission always remained central to Indian notions of cultural, religious, and literary authority and authenticity. The interaction of the oral and manuscript traditions has had a far deeper and longer-lasting impact on the Indian imagination than any attributable to print. By contrast, print culture is very much a latecomer to South Asia, a significant cultural carrier for only the past two hundred years from the early nineteenth century onward.

In fact, Indian culture seems to have shown a pronounced resistance to print technologies. On present evidence, the early East Asian tradition of woodblock printing (xylography) associated with Buddhism did not expand further south than Tibet and Nepal. This is despite the fact that northern Indians almost certainly knew of the technique from the Tibetans who had acquired it from the Chinese in the ninth century. Similarly, when printing with movable metal type was introduced from Europe by Portuguese Jesuits in the mid-sixteenth century, it did not replace traditional book-production methods at the Indian court or any other level. The Mughal emperor Akbar was presented with a copy of Plantin's famous polyglot printed Bible, but this did not result in an imperial printing press supplanting the well-established manuscript studio. The Islamic calligraphic tradition held in high regard by the Mughals was not suited to mechanical reproduction, and print could not match the visual splendor of contemporary illustrated manuscripts. Print's power of rapid duplication held no appeal when there was already a highly developed information network, underpinned by organized guilds of Muslim scribes (*katib* or *khush-navis*), with newsletters (*akhbar*) being regularly compiled and distributed by news-writers in every corner of the empire (Bayly 1996). The same held true for contemporary Hindu kingdoms where hereditary castes of professional scribes (*kayastha*) fulfilled the role of information providers and circulators.

The one printing technology that did strike a cultural chord, particularly with Muslim communities, was lithography, introduced to South Asia in the 1820s (Shaw 1998). This was precisely because it enabled the printed book to imitate the characteristics of the manuscript which still held cultural authority (Robinson 2000). Ironically, it was print that appeared strange and produced problems of legibility in South Asia. This was why as late as the 1830s Christian missionaries in Orissa paid scribes to copy biblical texts onto palm leaves, a practice begun by the Danish missionaries at Tranquebar in south India in the early eighteenth century – print yielding to the more familiar manuscript letter-forms. But lithography overcame this problem by realizing a paradox: the mass-produced manuscript.

South Asia's Manuscript Culture

The large-scale production of manuscripts in South Asia ceased only about 150 years ago, so that India's extant manuscript heritage is immense. Estimates range between five and thirty million manuscripts surviving in libraries, archives, temples, *madrasas*, monasteries, and, not least, private collections. And this must be a mere fraction of what was actually produced, given the perishability of the writing surfaces used. The choice of these was dictated by geography and flora, with different materials used in the Himalayan region and in the subcontinent proper. In western Himalayan areas such as Kashmir, birch bark was used, and aloe bark in eastern parts such as Assam. The earliest surviving South Asian manuscripts are Buddhist scrolls of birch bark from the ancient kingdom of Gandhara (which straddled modern Pakistan and Afghanistan) dating from the first century AD (Salomon 1999).

Below the Himalayas, the palm leaf was paramount. The usual writing palm of ancient India, the Talipat, was indigenous only to the far south of the peninsula. In the north, the leaves of other trees must have been used initially, such as plantain leaves traditionally written on in village schools. Only when the Mauryan empire expanded into the south in the third century BC would the northern Indians have become aware of the Talipat palm. The commercial cultivation of palm groves and a flourishing south–north trade in Talipat leaves ensued, as witnessed by the Chinese Buddhist pilgrim Hsuan Tsang during his seventh century AD visit. From about 1500, the Talipat palm was ousted by the Palmyra which offered more products (fruit and sap as well as leaves) and fared better in the northern Indian climate. But the Palmyra was an inferior writing surface. Whereas the Talipat palm was written on with a reed pen in ink, the Palmyra did not take ink at all well. Instead, the text was incised using an iron stylus, ink being smeared into the grooves afterwards. Once paper became widely available, palm cultivation became uneconomic, except in Sri Lanka where the leaves continued to be used for manuscript production until much later. The life expectancy of texts on palm leaf or bark was relatively short, given the heat and humidity of the Indian climate and the appetites of insects and rodents. The periodic re-copying of worn-out manuscripts was the tradition. Discarded copies were ritually buried in jars if Buddhist or if Hindu consigned to the waters of holy rivers – a "liquid *genizah.*"

Parchment and paper found no place in traditional Hindu, Buddhist, or Jain book culture. The Western use of parchment involving the slaughter of young animals for their skin (particularly the holy cow) would have been anathema to all. In 1931, a large cache of texts written on poor-quality paper was discovered at Gilgit in northern Pakistan, suggesting that papermaking was practiced there as early as the sixth century AD. But the widespread use of paper did not begin in northern India until the early thirteenth century, the Muslim world being the intermediary as for Europe. At first, paper must have been largely imported from Iran until local centers of manufacture developed, such as Daulatabad, Ahmedabad, and Lahore. Even when it was introduced, paper did not have the same impact in South Asia as it did in Europe, providing a cheap alternative to parchment and enabling the mass distribution of text. Although Islamic manuscripts were always written on paper in South Asia, non-Muslim scribes in many areas preferred to continue to use traditional writing surfaces. Birch bark continued in use in Kashmir up to the end of the seventeenth century, and in Nepal, where papermaking was well established by the twelfth century, the use of palm leaf far outstripped paper until the sixteenth century. When Hindus and Jains adopted paper, they imposed on it the traditional design parameters of the earlier palm leaf, paper sheets commonly having a height to width ratio of 1 : 3 at first and then 1 : 2 , the so-called *pothi* format (Losty 1982).

The Invention of Writing

Before the arrival of print, there were two key developments in the history of literary culture in South Asia. The first of these was the invention of the Indian writing system. That invention, it is now generally accepted, was made by the court administration of the Mauryan emperor Ashoka about 260 BC. Previously, the earliest written records from South Asia had been believed to be the inscriptions on clay and stone seals from the Indus Valley Civilization, the earliest urban culture in the subcontinent. This flourished between 2600 and 1900 BC, spreading over a vast area north to the Himalayas, south to Rajasthan and Gujarat, west to the Iranian border, and east as far as Delhi. The Indus Valley Script was initially variously interpreted as encoding some form of either Indo-Aryan or Dravidian, the major language families of South Asia. Recently, however, scholars have demonstrated convincingly that the signs do not encode speech at all but represent a nonlinguistic religious symbol system, for which ancient Near Eastern parallels exist. Their most likely function would have been to ensure social cohesion within the Civilization's large multilingual population, linking families, clans, cities, or whole regions with specific gods for ritual purposes (Farmer et al. 2004).

The earliest South Asian script invented at Ashoka's court was called Brahmi. Its invention was for political rather than literary purposes: the need to promulgate royal edicts throughout the Mauryan Buddhist empire which covered a vast swathe of the subcontinent from northern Afghanistan to southern Karnataka. In this way, Brahmi became the first "pan-Indian" script and the foundation of every regional script in South Asia and beyond in those parts of Central and Southeast Asia which came under Indian cultural influence. It must be emphasized that in South Asia, unlike other areas of the world, the adoption of writing did not eradicate the practices of orality. The collection of divinely revealed Hindu liturgical texts known as the Veda were transmitted from teacher to pupil for a thousand years without the use of writing but in remarkably stable form. For rituals to be effective depended critically upon recreating exactly the same sounds as the original divine revelation. Writing on transient palm leaf or birch bark was irrelevant in a tradition demanding such precise oral transmission. A Sanskrit couplet from the ancient Indian epic, the *Mahabharata*, translates as: "The sellers of the Vedas, the mis-pronouncers of the Vedas, and the writers of the Vedas, are all bound for Hell." The cultivation of memory was central to the Vedic tradition, and core cultural value continued to be placed on performance long after the arrival of literacy. Orality continued to play a major role in how a religious or secular literary text was actually experienced.

The very circumstances of the invention of writing in South Asia established a close relationship between the creation of text and political power. As the Mauryan empire expanded and united almost the entire subcontinent under a central government, so its literary culture grew into a trans-regional phenomenon – what has been dubbed the "cosmopolitan-vernacular revolution" (Pollock 2007: 83). Consequently, the primary written language, Sanskrit, attained a similar status in South Asia to that of Latin in Europe; that is, as the classical vehicle for literature, religion, and all forms of written knowledge. The primacy of this Sanskrit-based cosmopolitan culture under successor empires to the Mauryan was to last for some 1,200 years. Later, Persian under various Muslim dynasties and English under the Raj would create cosmopolitan cultures of their own across many regions of the subcontinent.

About AD 1000, the second momentous event in South Asian literary history took place. This was the so-called "vernacular revolution" when Sanskrit's monopolization of literary creation was at last challenged. This shift was associated with the fragmentation of centralized political power in South Asia and the consolidation of new regional power bases. A trans-regional mode of expression was no longer required; instead, the development of more local cultural identities became important. Accordingly, the various regional languages gradually emerged to replace Sanskrit as culturally respectable vehicles for literary creation. In most parts of India this "vernacularization" was promoted by the new regional royal courts, maintaining the close link between power and culture. Regional scripts developed and became more differentiated from each other. Other developments were also set in train to underpin the new local literatures, such as vernacular grammars, dictionaries, and orthographies. The regional languages were standardized in a way that runs counter to the Western orthodox view that such transformations only happened with the arrival of print. In South Asia, it was in the pre-print era that the process of standardization was in large measure achieved.

As has been stated, South Asia's manuscript culture was enormously productive and well organized. It was a cultural economy made up as much of professional scribes and patrons who paid for their services as of "amateurs" making copies for personal use or for family members or teachers. Manuscripts could be commissioned in various sociocultural contexts. An example of direct political motivation is represented by Hemachandra's famous twelfth-century Sanskrit grammar. This was commissioned by a king of Gujarat, Jayasimha Siddharaja, at the enormous cost of 300,000 coins. No less than 300 scribes were employed to make copies which were sent as far as Assam, Nepal, and Sri Lanka. As well as political patronage, religious patronage of manuscript production was also common to promote the interests of particular spiritual lineages. Krishnadasa Kaviraj's famous biography of the Vaishnava reformer Chaitanya, the *Chaitanyacharitamrita*, is a case in point. After the work was composed in the region of Braj (near Agra in modern Uttar Pradesh), one copy was sent back to Bengal (Chaitanya's homeland) where Srinivasa, the leader of the Chaitanya community, was also a professional scribe and, in effect, became a "manuscript publisher." Copies were made and distributed to every community group throughout Bengal, Orissa, and Braj. More than two thousand manuscript copies have survived and all are virtually identical, showing that in the South Asian context print was not a prerequisite for avoiding textual drift. Instances can even be found of works indicating that an early-modern intellectual economy was evolving. Around 1625, Annambhatta composed his *Tarkasamgraha* as an introductory textbook on logic and ontology. This seems to have been specifically compiled to meet the needs of a new educational market – a "precolonial set text" as it were. It was not produced under royal or religious patronage but initiated by professional scribes as a straightforward piece of commercial speculation (Pollock 2007). Whether such manuscript production was in fact truly on an "industrial" scale requires much further research and validation.

In the case of some religious texts, such as Tulsidas's immensely popular Hindi reworking of the *Ramayana* story, large-scale manuscript production went on alongside frequent oral performance, the relish in the work being heard feeding in turn the desire for the work to be read. The same is true of secular genres such as the *nautanki* folk theatrical tradition of northern India. Handwritten play-scripts circulated among troupes of actors helping them to memorize their parts for the stage, and from the 1860s onward cheap lithographed chapbooks of the plays performed the same function – an example of the interplay not only of orality and manuscript culture but of print also (Hansen 1992). Print and orality could also interact in a political context. In Hindu-ruled Kashmir in the early twentieth century, the movement for Kashmiri Muslim identity did not channel its views through newspapers, as might have been expected, because they were tightly controlled by state legislation. Instead, it channeled them through privately printed pamphlets, usually in the form of poetry familiar to the intended audience. These poems were then read aloud to pilgrims visiting shrines or at public recitations (*mushayras*; Zutshi 2004).

The Impact of Print

Although the existence of a widespread multipurpose manuscript culture in South Asia cannot be denied, this does not altogether negate the impact of print in the subcontinent. Rather, it puts that impact into a perspective unfamiliar to Western eyes. In the subcontinent, print did not enter a world of non-communication and fill the vacuum. It simply expanded the range of the modes of production and dissemination of texts available within existing cultural parameters, and accelerated the pace of communication within communities. It did not eliminate manuscript production altogether or completely erase oral traditions of learning and performance. Many of the genres which were in popular circulation in the era of the manuscript were simply continued in print – almanacs and astrological works, traditional ballads and stories, folk dramas, medical and religious pamphlets, and so on. There was, of course, one notable exception to this continuity of literary forms from the manuscript into the print era: South Asian writing in English. Its appearance was a direct consequence of British colonial rule and coincided closely with the formation of a modern print culture in the region. As a result, South Asia today stands both inside and outside the world of the English-language book.

The introduction of typographic printing from Europe in the mid-sixteenth century was very much a false dawn. The first two hundred and fifty years up to 1800 can almost be described as the "non-history" of printing in South Asia. Without any take-up by indigenous powers or communities, printing was very sporadic, confined to coastal enclaves, and entirely the preserve of Europeans – Christian missionaries and colonizers. The vast hinterland of South Asia and the overwhelming majority of its population were entirely unaffected by its arrival. Only nineteen works were produced in the sixteenth century, forty in the seventeenth, 454 in the first half of the eighteenth, and 1,258 in the second half (Shaw 1987). These figures show that the pace of publication was accelerating towards 1800, matching the development of an embryonic Indian book-trade infrastructure. But print was still catering only for the small expatriate European communities in Calcutta, Bombay, and Madras, or feeding their early attempts at conversion to Christianity. There were no Indian-owned presses at all, although many Indians provided the manual labor for the European-owned presses. Gangakishor Bhattacharya, for instance, who started the first Bengali-owned press in 1816, had previously worked in the famous Baptist Mission Press at Serampore. The only instance before 1800 of the press being used *by* Indians *for* Indians (without any direct European stimulus or involvement) was when two Parsee compositors working at the Courier Press in Bombay produced an edition of their Zoroastrian holy book, the *Khordeh Avesta*, in 1798 – truly a landmark in the history of South Asian publishing.

The trade in books from Britain to India is primarily thought of as a nineteenth-century phenomenon, as British publishers sought to take advantage of the vast potential of colonial markets for their books, particularly in the educational sphere. But up until the third quarter of the eighteenth century, the British in India were entirely dependent upon books published in Britain for their information and recreational reading needs. British books had been reaching India from the earliest decades of the seventeenth century, taken out in the baggage of East India Company employees. The Company itself also regularly exported batches of Christian literature to its trading settlements or "factories" in India, out of concern for the spiritual well-being of its employees, as well as works needed for military or administrative purposes. These initially small shipments formed the nuclei of the factory libraries which were placed in the care of the local Company chaplain. The 1729 catalogue of the library at Fort St. George (Madras) lists 1,235 works. These were mainly Christian texts, but there were editions of classical authors, travels, and utilitarian works, as well as plays and poetry for leisure-time reading. Next to the Company and its employees, the most prominent early exporters of books to India were missionary societies, primarily the Society for Promoting Christian Knowledge which supported missions in Madras and Bengal. The missionaries were responsible for the introduction of Western-style education through their charity schools, and books specifically for teaching purposes were first shipped out in 1717.

As well as books, Britain was also the source of materials and manpower for printing in South Asia. Types, presses, printers' tools, ink, and particularly paper (as local varieties were found unsuitable for printing) all had to be imported. Trained printers too began to chance a career in India, such as James Augustus Hicky who had been apprenticed to William Faden, and George Gordon, nephew of the King's printer, William Strachan. The commercial importation of British books began with the captains and officers of East Indiamen who could ship out freight-free a certain weight of speculative cargo, and some chose books. By the 1780s, when the first newspapers appeared in India, there were frequent advertisements for British books, magazines, and newspapers imported as speculative cargoes and bought up by local general merchants. The London newspapers were a common feature of Calcutta coffee-house life as the information available locally to the eighteenth-century British expatriate was otherwise very limited. Both newspapers and magazines were unashamedly plagiarized to provide content for the local weeklies.

One of the largest markets for imported British books were the circulating libraries which opened in the three British Presidency capitals, Calcutta in the 1770s and Madras and Bombay in the 1790s. These libraries were also the first local bookshops selling directly to the public. Thacker, Spink and Company, destined to become one of the Raj's leading booksellers, started this way in 1819. By the 1830s, the importation of books into India had become quite sophisticated. Compressed editions were especially desirable, as they reduced the costs of shipping and were more portable for the Company's peripatetic employees. The trade had also become more international, with cheap editions of English-language books imported from A. and W. Galignani in Paris and J. and J. Harper in New York. Book distribution within India was almost non-existent outside the three metropolitan centers (Shaw 2007).

Novels quickly became the most popular category of British books from the early nineteenth century onward. It was the more sensational novels, such as those issued by the Minerva Press, that sold best (Joshi 2002). Authors such as George W. M. Reynolds fared better than Charles Dickens, although an edition of *Pickwick Papers,* for instance, was published in Calcutta in the 1830s. Sir Walter Scott was also very popular, and many of his works were translated into regional languages such as Bengali and Gujarati. During the 1790s, over £150,000 worth of books were exported from Britain to India, doubling in the 1800s to over £340,000 and staying at that level for the next few decades. Once Thomas Macaulay's famous Minute on Indian Education of 1835 led to the widespread adoption of English as a medium of instruction and its adoption as the official language of government in 1844, the demand for English-learning among South Asians multiplied. This opened up a great new textbook market for British publishers who specialized in educational works, such as Macmillan, Blackie, Longman, and Oxford University Press. They were not slow to seize the opportunity, and on the back of that success they also launched fiction series aimed at the expatriate market, such as Macmillan's "Colonial Library" begun in 1886.

The key century during which print made its long-delayed impact upon the South Asian population as a whole was the nineteenth. This coincided with the development of religious revivals – Hindu, Muslim, and Buddhist – and cultural renaissances throughout the subcontinent, partly at least directly stimulated by the intrusiveness of colonial rule and the activities of Christian missionaries in particular. The presses of English, Scottish, American, and other missionary societies produced a welter of publications, biblical editions and scriptural tracts: in one decade alone, 1852–63, for instance, a total of nearly nine and a half million volumes. Missionaries often misread the eagerness with which these books were received by local communities. It was not the Word of God that was the attraction but the free source of paper, a valuable commodity widely used, for instance, for wrapping up spices and medicines in the bazaar. Large single sheets containing the Ten Commandments were used by boys to make kites (Shaw 2004).

What had taken Europe three centuries to achieve, the emergence of a fully fledged book culture, was in South Asia telescoped into less than one hundred years. At the beginning of the century all presses were still European-owned, so publishing even in the regional languages was under foreign direction. Few typefaces had been developed for the regional scripts (Bengali and Tamil being notable exceptions), which is another facet of lithography's importance in South Asia. It aided the "democratization" of print by extending the possibility of publication to any script and any language. The only prerequisite was trained scribes, of whom there was never any lack. This is why lithography entered the mainstream of publishing in South Asia, unlike Europe where it remained a marginal technology. By 1850, probably a thousand editions had been published in South Asia using this technology. Lucknow-Kanpur emerged as the lithographic capital of the subcontinent, and the Naval Kishore Press in Lucknow became the premier commercial publisher in the region. Perhaps most importantly, the relaxation of the press laws in 1835 paved the way for the widespread ownership and operation of presses by South Asians as well as Europeans.

The publishing of newspapers, books, and magazines of all kinds rapidly proliferated in all the major regional languages. Print served "low" culture as well as "high," epitomized in Bengal, for instance, by the chapbooks produced in the Battala suburb of

Calcutta satirizing the newly Westernized Bengali middle class (Ghosh 2006). Commercial, religious, institutional, and private presses gradually spread out from the metropolitan centers of Calcutta, Bombay, and Madras into the hinterland, along with a network of booksellers, bookbinders, type-foundries, libraries, and reading rooms. The Calcutta Public Library, for example, founded in 1835, would form the nucleus of the National Library of India. By the end of the century, virtually no region of the subcontinent was without a rudimentary book-trade infrastructure in place. In terms of book history, the modern geopolitical boundaries of the subcontinent are largely irrelevant. For instance, there was no printing press in Nepal until the 1860s but prior to that Nepalese books were published in Darjeeling, Varanasi, even as far away as Bombay. The Bengali book is as vibrant in Bangladesh as in the Indian state of West Bengal. Both Urdu and Panjabi publishing straddle Pakistan and India. All this enterprise was spurred on by the religious revivals (Hindu, Muslim, and Buddhist), the cultural renaissances, and the social reform movements that were springing up in different regions.

This print explosion in the regional languages inevitably raised concerns for the colonial government who sought to monitor its output and content. In 1867, the Government of British India passed an Indian Press and Registration of Books Act (later imitated by many of the Princely States and by Ceylon), but even before this, official surveys had been undertaken in each Presidency, such as James Long's three overviews of Bengali publishing during the 1850s. After the 1857 uprising against British rule, reports on regional-language newspapers throughout the subcontinent were compiled and printed on a regular fortnightly basis. Out of all this change came a heightened political consciousness which gave greater momentum to the independence movement, beginning with the first meeting of the Indian National Congress in 1885. In this struggle for freedom, publishing played an important role in rallying support and raising awareness of events. Revolutionary activity following the partition of Bengal in 1905 led to the passing of a draconian Indian Press Act in 1910, which attempted to prevent the publication and dissemination of seditious literature in all forms, whether home-grown or smuggled in from abroad. The Jallianwala Bagh atrocity in Amritsar of 1919 and the execution of the revolutionary Bhagat Singh in 1930 provoked great outpourings of anti-British pamphleteering, and the two non-cooperation campaigns led by Mahatma Gandhi in 1920–2 and 1930 were buoyed up by the mass circulation of nationalist poetry in hastily printed collections.

Publishing from Independence to Today

After independence, locally owned companies found it difficult to catch up and compete with British-owned companies with subsidiaries in the subcontinent, particularly in the lucrative field of educational publishing. The first Indian-owned publishing house to produce good-quality academic books in English along professional lines was the Asia Publishing House of Bombay, founded in 1943 just before independence. Throughout the 1950s and 1960s, it represented all that was best in Indian educational publishing, paving the way for later firms, such as the Vikas Publishing House, New Delhi, to emerge. Oxford University Press (OUP) was the largest of the British subsidiaries, with its Indian branch established in 1912 (Chatterjee 2006). It has now published over three thousand titles. OUP Pakistan began much later, in 1952, and is much smaller. Initially, it was mainly concerned with importing and promoting titles published in the UK, but more recently has started a local schools publishing program. Penguin India now claims to be the largest English-language publisher in the subcontinent. Founded in 1985 in New Delhi, it began publishing in 1987 and now releases over two hundred fiction and nonfiction titles per year. Interestingly, Penguin India has just moved into regional-language publishing, beginning with Hindi and Marathi, to be followed by Malayalam, Urdu, and Bengali by the end of 2006. A "phenomenal growth curve" in Indian regional-language publishing is predicted (Abraham 2005). HarperCollins, a subsidiary of News Corporation, has recently strengthened its position by entering into partnership with the India Today Group, which publishes India's largest-selling weekly news magazine, and gaining access to the Thomson Press, the largest commercial printing facilities in South Asia. Macmillan India, established in 1893, is diversifying into web-related services with its new division Emacmillan started in 2000. Macmillan has found its traditional educational business slowing down recently due to poor demand from Nepal (traditionally one of its largest market segments) and a ban on the use of private publishers' books by the State Government of Madhya Pradesh in India.

It is difficult to find up-to-date, reliable figures for total current book production in South Asia. This is partly due to the nature of publishing in the region itself. There are very few large publishing concerns (except in the English-language sector), but rather a plethora of medium- and small-scale enterprises scattered throughout the subcontinent. There are reputed to be over 15,000 publishers in India alone. In output terms, India dwarfs its neighbors, publishing probably well over 75,000 titles per year. Of these, roughly 80 percent are in the regional languages and 20 percent are in English. Among the regional languages, Hindi predominates (accounting for a quarter of India's total book production), with Tamil, Bengali, and Marathi also important. There are no statistics available for book production in either Pakistan or Nepal. According to official statistics, Sri Lanka produces 6,000 books annually, and Bangladesh about 500. But these are probably both underestimates. The legal deposit arrangements in all countries of South Asia (such as the 1954 Delivery of Books Act in India) are little known, inadequately complied with, and poorly enforced by government. This makes the role of the national libraries in collecting the national published archive and in compiling the national bibliography very difficult.

Distribution is still a major problem for South Asian publishers, both within and between the individual countries of the region. There are insufficient bookshops even in the metropolitan centers. In many rural areas it remains very difficult to obtain books except at special promotional fairs. In this respect the railway bookstalls throughout South Asia play a vital role. Those in northern India are still operated by A. H. Wheeler, who in the nineteenth century produced cheap editions of Kipling, and those in the south by Higginbothams, well-known booksellers of Madras. Book piracy between the countries of South Asia is extensive. Indian books are reprinted without permission on a large scale in both Pakistan and Bangladesh (and vice versa though to a much smaller extent). These pirated editions are transported back to India to damage the livelihoods of both Indian publishers and authors. But piracy is almost inevitable when free trade in books between India and Pakistan is not allowed by their respective governments. For several decades after independence, standards of South Asian book production were not high, due to the quality of the paper used, the methods of color printing employed, and the bindings produced. But production standards have risen more recently. Regional-language publishing in South Asia was slow in general to seize the wider market potential of the paperback. Hind Pocket Books from the mid-1950s onward was a notable exception (Malhotra 1998).

That South Asia is a region of book-lovers is shown by the huge crowds, for instance, attending the annual Book Fair in Calcutta, the largest retail book fair in the world, or the World Book Fair held in New Delhi biannually since 1972. South Asia's inhabitants are still avid newspaper readers, with sales having increased 17 percent in the four years up to 2002. Seven dailies enjoy a circulation of one million or more, the most popular being the Hindi *Dainik Jagran* of Kanpur with over 1.9 million readers. The power of the printed word to cause considerable controversy is illustrated by the case of the Bangladeshi novelist Taslima Nasreen whose works have been banned in her homeland for being anti-Islam and who has lived in exile since 1994 under the death threat of a *fatwa* (Jones 2001). Or take the case of Dwijendra Jha, a professor of history at Delhi University, and his book *The Myth of the Holy Cow*, documenting meat-eating by Hindus in the past. The original publisher suddenly withdrew during the final stages of printing under pressure from Hindu fundamentalists, and when it was published in 2001 by Matrix Books of New Delhi, a court order was obtained restricting its circulation and the author's life threatened. Authorial and academic independence also became a major issue when, in 2000, two further volumes of *Towards Freedom,* a documentary history of the independence movement 1937–47, being published by Oxford University Press, New Delhi, were unilaterally withdrawn from publication by the official sponsoring body, the Indian Council for Historical Research. Vigorous academic protests and press campaigns followed, seeing this as direct government interference in the writing of history (the Bharatiya Janata Party was then in power). Despite the ever-increasing importance of visual media – Bollywood and television – and the popularity of the Internet in South Asia, the region's appetite for the book, both in terms of production and consumption, remains undiminished.

References and Further Reading

Abraham, Thomas (2005) Quoted in *The Bookseller*, March 31.

Bayly, C. A. (1996) *Empire and Information: Intelligence Gathering and Social Communication in India, c.1780–1870.* Cambridge: Cambridge University Press.

Blackburn, S. and Dalmia, V. (eds.) (2004) *India's Literary History: Essays on the Nineteenth Century.* New Delhi: Permanent Black.

Chakravarty, S. and Gupta, A. (eds.) (2004) *Print Areas: Book History in India.* New Delhi: Permanent Black.

Chatterjee, R. (2001) "A Short Account of the Company's Trade with the Subcontinent." In E. James (ed.), *Macmillan: A Publishing Tradition, 1843–1970*, pp. 153–69. London: Macmillan.

— (2006) *Empires of the Mind: A History of Oxford University Press in India under the Raj.* New Delhi: Oxford University Press.

Darnton, R. (2001) "Literary Surveillance in the British Raj: The Contradictions of Liberal Imperialism." *Book History*, 4: 133–76.

— (2002) "Book Production in British India, 1850–1900." *Book History*, 5: 239–62.

Farmer, S., Sproat, R., and Witzel, M. (2004) "The Collapse of the Indus-script Thesis: The Myth of a Literate Harappan Civilization." *Electronic Journal of Vedic Studies*, 11: 19–57.

Ghosh, A. (2006) *Power in Print: Popular Publishing and the Politics of Language and Culture.* New Delhi: Oxford University Press.

Hansen, K. (1992) *Grounds for Play: The Nautanki Theatre of North India.* Berkeley: University of California Press.

Jeffrey, R. (2000) *India's Newspaper Revolution: Capitalism, Politics and the Indian-language Press, 1977–99.* London: Hurst and Co.

Jones, D. (2001) "Taslima Nasreen: Bangladeshi Novelist and Poet, 1961– ." In D. Jones (ed.), *Censorship: A World Encyclopedia*, vol. 3, pp. 1681–2. London: Fitzroy Dearborn.

Joshi, P. (2002) *In Another Country: Colonialism, Culture, and the English Novel in India.* New York: Columbia University Press.

Losty, J. P. (1982) *The Art of the Book in India.* London: British Library.

Malhotra, D. N. (ed.) (1998) *50 Years of Book Publishing in India since Independence.* New Delhi: Federation of Indian Publishers.

Pollock, S. (ed.) (2003) *Literary Cultures in History: Reconstructions from South Asia.* Berkeley: University of California Press.

— (2007) "Literary Culture and Manuscript Culture in Pre-colonial India." In S. Eliot, A. Nash, and I. Willison (eds.), *Literary Culture and the Material Book*, pp. 77–94. London: British Library.

Robinson, F. (2000) "Islam and the Impact of Print in South Asia." In *Islam and Muslim History in South Asia*, pp. 66–104. New Delhi: Oxford University Press.

Salomon, R. (1999) *Ancient Buddhist Scrolls from Gandhara: The British Library Kharosthi Fragments.* London: British Library.

Shaw, G. W. (1987) *The South Asia and Burma Retrospective Bibliography (SABREB) Stage 1: 1556–1800.* London: British Library.

— (1998) "Calcutta: Birthplace of the Indian Lithographed Book." *Journal of the Printing Historical Society*, 27: 89–111.

— (2004) "Communication between Cultures: Difficulties in the Design and Distribution of Christian Literature in Nineteenth-century India." In R. N. Swanson (ed.), *The Church and the Book*, pp. 339–56. Woodbridge: Boydell Press for the Ecclesiastical History Society.

— (2007) "The British Book in India 1695–1830." In M. Suarez and M. Turner (eds.), *The History of the Book in Britain*, vol. 5. Cambridge: Cambridge University Press.

Zutshi, C. (2004) *Languages of Belonging: Islam, Regional Identity, and the Making of Kashmir.* London: Hurst and Co.

10
Latin America

Hortensia Calvo

The study of books and printing in Latin America has followed a different path from that of Europe and the English-speaking world. Rather than stemming from the methods and concerns of the Annales School of social history in the 1950s and 1960s, modern approaches to the book in the region began in the 1910s, when research into the institutional context of the transatlantic book trade led to a reconsideration of cultural life in the Spanish colonies. Since then, most research on print culture has centered on the Spanish American colonial period (1498–1820s in most of the region, except Brazil and Cuba). Attention has concentrated mainly on Mexico and (to a lesser extent) Peru, the two countries with the longest typographical traditions. Since at least the 1980s, there has been an increased emphasis on the social and cultural aspects of print, and the initial focus on the colonial period has broadened to include subsequent centuries and other countries, such as Argentina and Brazil.

The printing press was brought first to Mexico City (1539) and then to Lima (1581), which remained the only two printing centers in the Spanish territories of the New World until the first presses were brought to Puebla (1640) and Guatemala (1660). The rest of the region did not have presses until much later. In the remote Jesuit missions of Paraguay, printing began in 1700, when a press was constructed with local materials by native Guaraní laborers who had converted to Christianity. The first Havana imprint is from 1707, and in Santafé de Bogotá printing did not start until 1736, exactly two hundred years after the city was founded. Most Spanish colonial cities, such as Quito (1759) and Buenos Aires (1780), did not have presses until the latter half of the eighteenth century. Printing began in Caracas in 1808, and a press functioned briefly in 1776 in Santiago de Chile. But in San José (1830), and most cities in what later became Central America, printing was not established permanently until after independence from Spain. The Portuguese crown prohibited printing altogether in colonial Brazil, and although a press may have operated briefly in 1747, the first permanent printing press arrived, along with the entire administrative entourage of King João VI, when he settled in Rio de Janeiro in 1808.

In the Spanish colonies, the printing press served the ideological, political, and administrative purposes of Spain. The first presses were brought to Mexico City and Lima for the explicit purpose of aiding missionaries in the Christianization of native populations. Multilingual catechisms, instructional religious tracts, and grammars and vocabularies of Amerindian languages were the first products of early colonial presses. In the course of the sixteenth century, the Crown's initial preoccupation with the moral and spiritual welfare of Amerindians shifted toward the education of increasing numbers of European settlers in the viceregal capitals. By the mid-seventeenth century, colonial printing primarily served the purposes of peninsular administrators and reflected the growing prosperity and intellectual needs of lettered urban *criollos*, Europeanized white or *mestizo* colonists. Both Mexico City and Lima produced printed sermons for funerals and religious celebrations, hagiographies, histories of religious orders, royal decrees, and other legal provisions, as well as officially sanctioned histories of the New World, chronicles of local events, and works on military topics.

Book production and the circulation of printed works in the Spanish colonies were circumscribed by a series of practical and legal restrictions, as well as by the nature of scholarly culture in the region. Paper was largely imported from Europe, and the high costs of imported machinery and other supplies, coupled with the Crown's monopoly on the book trade, constituted the main commercial obstacles to local publishing. Other restrictions arose from ideological concerns. The perceived threat of heresy stemming from the European Reformation during the sixteenth and seventeenth centuries and, in the eighteenth century, the fear of French and British sociopolitical philosophies resulted in a succession of laws and decrees designed to curtail the free flow of local presses and the circulation of books. Moreover, strict control of licenses and authors' rights, as well as the prohibitive costs of publishing, ensured that books were available for only a small fraction of the population. Despite these restrictions, European works were imported legally or illegally, supplying the bulk of reading material in the colonies.

Thus, in the first two centuries of Spanish rule, the printing press was not an agent of change. It served to consolidate the status quo rather than challenge established authority, in contrast to the situation in Europe. This was not primarily due to official censorship, but rather to the fact that the sociopolitical dynamics of viceregal societies inhibited the development of independent intellectual enclaves and literary circles outside the patronage of church and state. Centrally engaged in the civil and ecclesiastical bureaucracies of the colonies, and thus ultimately employed in the service of the metropolis, colonial lettered elites used the printing press to gain social ascendancy and wield power. Moreover, the Crown's control of local publishing kept colonial scholars heavily dependent on European presses for publication of original works, many of which circulated in America in manuscript form. For all of these reasons, until well into the eighteenth century, printed works were less a means for intellectuals to engage with local realities than vehicles that kept them connected to Spain and Europe.

The Western book in colonial Spanish America thus functioned as a powerful tool of European culture and domination. And the historiography of the book during this period has historically been shaped, either tacitly or explicitly, by polarized perspectives on the role of Spain in the Americas and the legacy of colonial institutions. The Spanish legacy was, in fact, one of the most passionately debated issues among nineteenth-century historians after independence was secured in most of the region (c.1820s). Throughout the century, efforts to reconstruct national cultural traditions produced a succession of bibliographical works documenting the intellectual production of the past. Largely compiled as part of the broader project of nation-building in the newly formed republics, these bibliographical catalogues played a key role in constructing a collective foundational history. Among liberal and positivist historians, there was a generalized indictment of Spain for keeping the colonies culturally isolated from Europe. By inventorying the limited output of printing presses in the colonies and uncovering records of legislation concerning metropolitan control of books and reading, nineteenth-century bibliographers seemed to provide solid documentary proof for the view that Spanish repression had stifled intellectual life in the colonies.

One major concern among scholars engaged in constructing national literary traditions was the meager presence of imaginative works, particularly novels, in colonial bibliographical inventories. In particular, two royal decrees (1531 and 1543) prohibiting the importation of fictional literature to the colonies were repeatedly invoked as evidence that Spain had effectively cut the colonies off from all but the most orthodox religious ideas from Europe. The work of the Chilean José Toribio Medina (1852–1930), the towering figure of Spanish-American bibliography, played a key role in cementing this vision of the region's cultural past. His monumental seven-volume *Biblioteca hispano-americana (1493–1810)* (1898–1907) and hundreds of works on colonial literary production, the Inquisition, and other topics set the foundations of modern critical studies of the book in the region. Medina also uncovered a wealth of previously unpublished legislation restricting the exportation of books to the New World, thus giving further credence to prevailing views of Spanish institutions as repressive mechanisms. This paradigm of cultural stagnation in the colonial period was reiterated by some scholars as late as the 1960s. However, starting in the 1910s, a shifting intellectual climate contributed to reconsidering the Spanish imperial enterprise as an essentially positive mission, in which the coming of the Western book was conceived as playing a civilizing role.

Two publications opened the door for subsequent research into the circulation of books in the colonies beyond the letter of the law. In 1911, Francisco Rodríguez Marín, a Spanish literary scholar, published documentary proof that several hundred copies of what was probably the *princeps* edition of *Don Quijote* had been registered for shipment to the colonies in 1605, only few months after publication. Three years later, the Mexican Francisco Fernández del Castillo's *Libros y libreros en el siglo XVI* appeared, containing a wealth of previously unpublished archival documents concerning the origins of printing and the diffusion of European books in New Spain.

The 1930s through the 1950s were watershed years, as new documentary evidence – such as ships' registers, bills of sale, Inquisitorial records, and other sources for inventories of books and private libraries – cast new light on the circulation of books in the colonies. In particular, two historians, the Argentine José Torre Revello and Irving Leonard from the United States, published a succession of books and articles revealing evidence of an extensive transatlantic book trade from Spain to the New World. Their investigations provided mounting and convincing evidence that, as in other areas of Spanish rule, a huge gap existed between legislation and actual practice. In 1940, Leonard was able to document the arrival and receipt of the same shipment of Cervantes' novel that Rodríguez Marín had confirmed registered in Seville, thus dispelling prevailing notions that even if books managed to leave Spain, they were systematically confiscated on arrival in the Indies. That same year, Torre Revello published his monumental history of printing and book circulation in Spanish America, *El libro, la imprenta y el periodismo en América durante la dominación española*, amply documenting the shipment of European books to the New World. By 1949, when Leonard published his now classic work, *Books of the Brave*, it was conclusively proved that whatever the official policy had been, major works of fiction such as *Don Quijote*, picaresque novels, even the popular chivalry novels expressly forbidden by royal decree, as well as secular dramatic works, classic Latin and Greek authors, and other nonreligious printed works not only arrived regularly in the New World but, in many cases, were shipped shortly after publication in Spain. Other scholars scoured archives for documentary evidence to disprove any notion that Spanish obscurantism had deprived colonial readers of the latest titles from Europe.

In the past four decades, most scholarship on the Western book in early Spanish America has remained largely within the thematic and methodological contours established by the modern founders of the discipline. Primary sources for documenting the book trade continue to be ships' registers, bills of sale, Inquisitorial and other official records of trials, book merchants' properties, and post mortem inventories. And the dominant goals have been either to document the establishment and development of printing in specific regions or to trace the dissemination of European ideas through print, whether through the transatlantic book trade or, to a much lesser degree, through colonial printing presses. Most studies are descriptive in nature and many, particularly those on regions beyond Mexico and Lima, are isolated findings, published in journals or as books that are not easily accessible.

Since at least the 1960s, early Spanish-American studies have undergone profound shifts in theoretical orientation and thematic focus that have generated strong critiques of the traditional methods and concerns of book historians. They have also created interest in the role of books and printed works in the processes of Europeanization and the cultural transformation of native societies. Rolena Adorno's re-examination of censorship and the role of chivalry novels in conquest scholarship is a prime example of this kind of approach. In her introduction to a new English edition of *Books of the Brave* (Leonard 1992), she critically re-evaluates Leonard's main tenets in the light of recent trends in early Spanish-American studies. Examining the publishing success of early works about native Americans within the epic genre, as opposed to narrative ethnohistories of the period on the same subject that never made it to print, Adorno reconsiders the role of the popular chivalry genre in this period. She concludes that, rather than firing the imagination of the conquistadors toward noble deeds, as Leonard suggested, the rigid conventions of epic forms of representation were promoted by the Crown toward political ends, as officially endorsed narrative frameworks to contain writings that dealt with the controversial topic of Amerindian customs and beliefs in Counter-Reformation Spain. So, too, recent reconsiderations of the relationship of literary expression to social institutions and networks of power have called into question the relevance of traditional debates concerning the perceived inadequacies of colonial literary production. Where Leonard and other book historians were perplexed by the scarcity of literary masterpieces in the Spanish colonies, Adorno argues that nineteenth-century definitions of literature are too narrow to encompass the richness and variety of colonial letters.

Likewise, Magdalena Chocano Mena (1997), a scholar focusing on elite Creole culture, highlights the circumscribed character of print culture in early Spanish America, where the primary ways of circulating ideas and information were probably either oral or by manuscript. Thus, she questions the relevance of "printing revolution" approaches to the study of the book in the region, at least for the first two centuries of Spanish rule. Some scholars are exploring scribal or notarial literature and practices, a key framework that shaped a wide array of written texts within the highly legalistic lettered culture of colonial Spanish America.

Book history in Latin America has largely been conceived as the study of the printed word produced by technologies imported from Europe. Native American "books" are often mentioned in surveys of the book as early autochthonous cultural products, but the study of native texts has remained separate from that of the Western book in the region. However, a number of contemporary studies by scholars working on pre-Hispanic and post-contact Amerindian texts and symbolic practices suggest fruitful insights and future directions for a broader conception of the "book," native and Western, including the tensions and intersections of print and non-print forms of communication among the peoples of the New World. Walter Mignolo (1998) situates early modern European conceptions of the book in the light of Renaissance philosophies of language and writing, which privileged European forms of recording (paper, book, writing instruments) as exclusive vehicles for knowledge, effectively excluding Amerindian ways of recording and knowing. Other scholars examine the role of printed works in cultural exchange, transformation, and indoctrination, including codices and pictorial representations that served as vehicles of Westernization among Mesoamerican populations.

Native traditions of recording in ancient Mesoamerican societies, as well as among Quechua-speaking inhabitants of Peru, are by no means a new concern in the historiography of early Spanish America. The earliest Spanish accounts of Peru mention the *quipus*, a system of color-coded knotted cords apparently used to document past events as well as for quantitative recordkeeping. In Mesoamerica, the Maya, Mixtec, Nahua (or Aztec), and other native cultures had developed writing traditions inscribed on various forms of paper, animal skin, tree bark, tombs, architectural structures, pottery, and other objects and materials. But those that made a deeper impression on the Spaniards because of their similarities to (and differences from) Western books were the painted manuscripts produced with a variety of materials, including native amate and agave paper, and in different formats. Initially, Amerindian painted books were viewed as curiosities by the Europeans, and descriptions appeared in a number of historical accounts of the time. However, once the process of evangelization was underway, they were construed as vehicles of idolatry and demonic beliefs. Most were burned or otherwise destroyed in wars of conquest or by zealous missionaries and administrators anxious to eradicate idolatry; some were destroyed by native leaders as a tactic of survival. Nevertheless, there are at least sixteen surviving pre-Hispanic painted manuscripts from the Mayan, Nahua, Cholultec, and Mixtec cultures.

A few decades after the conquest, it became clear that the Christianizing mission could best be carried out by learning the cultures and traditions of native peoples and teaching the faith using native languages. Thus, a process of alphabetization began, as priests worked with native scribes to develop conventions for writing Mesoamerican languages. Through this collaboration, native texts were produced throughout the sixteenth century by alphabetized Amerindian scribes, who transcribed traditional texts in Latin, Castilian, or their native languages or composed new ones on commission by local Spanish authorities. Since the nineteenth century, the entire corpus of native painted manuscripts has been known as the Mesoamerican codices.

During the eighteenth century, in response to European preconceptions of the supposed inferiority of America, a number of apologetic works written by patriotic *criollo* scholars exalted the ancient Amerindian writings as part of a common New World intellectual tradition. In the nineteenth century, Mexican bibliographers also included the codices in their inventories. Contemporary art historians, literary scholars, and anthropologists examine the ways in which the material aspects of native documents (whether they are painted screenfolds, rolls, or knotted cords) shape the production of meaning.

The rise of *gacetas* or newspapers during the late colonial and revolutionary periods is the main focus of book historians for this period. Colonial presses had sporadically produced broadsides featuring information about natural disasters and the arrival and departure of fleets since 1541, when the first such publication appeared in Mexico. The first Spanish-American periodical to be published regularly was the monthly *Gaceta de México y noticias de Nueva España* (1722), which lasted only six months; Lima's first newspaper, *Gaceta de Lima* (1743), was also of short duration. The *Gaceta de Guatemala* initially lasted two years (1729–31) and was subsequently revived (1794–1816). By the end of the eighteenth century, a number of specialized periodicals devoted to science, medicine, and literature were also being published, most of short duration.

Since at least the 1990s, a growing number of historians have sought to understand the role of the printing press and newspapers in broader social, cultural, and political transformations during the waning years of colonial rule, the revolutionary period, and the first two decades after independence (1780s–1850). To what extent did the printing press function as a catalyst of change, a vehicle for the dissemination of republican ideals that united the colonists in the cause of freedom against Spain? What role did the printed word play in the formation and consolidation of cohesive national identities in the fledgling republics? Recent research on the much-debated issue of the

Enlightenment in the region has tended to stress that it was the cultural, scientific, and economic aspects of Enlightenment thought that took hold in eighteenth-century Spanish America rather than the more politically subversive ideas, which were promoted retrospectively as a result (not a cause) of the independence movements.

A prime example of the intellectually progressive but politically conservative outlook that characterized earlier stages of the Spanish-American Enlightenment was the influential Peruvian newspaper *Mercurio peruano*, published in Lima from 1791 to 1794. While the publication was instrumental in forging a strong Creole patriotism by exalting all things Peruvian, it was nonetheless limited to an elite readership, including the Peruvian viceroy himself. So the *Mercurio* can hardly be regarded as a space for expressing politically subversive views. However, some scholars have pointed to a link between some late eighteenth-century *gacetas* and the independence movements. Such is the case of the community of readers that subscribed to the *Papel Periódico de Santafé de Bogotá* in the decade of the 1790s. While its readership was minute (150 subscribers among the estimated 1.8 million inhabitants in the Viceroyalty of New Granada), this publication nonetheless served as a forum of debate and progressive political opinion.

As for the role of the press in uniting the people in a common cause, it is increasingly clear that, initially, the movements for independence were not revolutions inspired by the French model, but rather political civil wars instigated by *criollo* elites, not by oppressed masses, in response to Napoleon's invasion of Spain in 1808 and the crisis of the Spanish Crown. These were revolutions "from the top," and did not substantially alter a centuries-long colonial legacy of social and racial hierarchies. The diverse ethnic and racial composition of the region, with a small, white, Europeanized minority, large Amerindian populations of widely different cultures and languages, slaves from numerous regions in Africa with their own distinct languages and religious practices, and growing numbers of *mestizos*, mulattos, and other racial mixtures, created deep divisions among the native born and hampered efforts to form cohesive national identities well into the nineteenth century. Moreover, urban centers that were peripheral during colonial rule, such as Santiago de Chile and most cities of Central America, did not have printing presses until after independence.

If printing presses did not serve to instigate the transition from an absolutist monarchy to representative government, they did play a role as vehicles in the formation of a public sphere for the first time in Spanish America, however uneven and circumscribed this process may have been. Several recent studies trace the emergence of new reading practices and communities centered around specific social spaces, such as cafés, print shops, bookstores, other commercial establishments, and *tertulias* (discussion groups). Perhaps the most marked trend toward modernization occurred in late colonial and early national Mexico, which experienced an exponential growth in print production. Bourbon educational reforms dramatically increased literacy in New Spain in the waning years of colonial rule. Based on school attendance figures, some scholars have estimated that one in six inhabitants in the Central Valley of Mexico received formal education in the decade of the 1780s, leading to a 62 percent literacy rate in Mexico City by 1820. Furthermore, there is evidence to suggest that between 1808 and 1814 printed works of a political nature increased dramatically, while religious and liturgical publications, which had predominated during the colonial period, decreased substantially. François-Xavier Guerra, one of the foremost scholars of the Spanish-American Enlightenment, has shown that the events of 1808 sparked a veritable explosion of writings, both printed and manuscript, as news of the crowning of Joseph Bonaparte as King of Spain reached the Viceroyalty of New Spain. Initial public outrage supporting the deposed rightful monarch soon gave way to heated debate regarding the need for representation for the colonies in the newly founded caretaker Spanish junta and, ultimately, to cries for independence. These ideas circulated in manuscript form in personal correspondence and orally in *tertulias*, but also in existing newspapers. They generated an outpouring of pamphlets, flyers, broadsides, anonymous letters, satirical verses, manifestos, and other ephemeral publications.

The revolutionary role of the Mexican press during this period is a subject of some debate and, in any event, seems to have been the exception. In Lima, for example, there was an equally dramatic shift in the proportions of religious and political works during the same period, but the latter largely advocated the royalist rather than the revolutionary cause. In the Viceroyalty of New Granada, where literacy was a mere 20 percent by some estimates in 1835, an increase in printed works occurred only after independence. In Venezuela and Chile, with no printing tradition before independence, oral and manuscript forms of communication were the norm. This has led Rebecca Earle (2004) to suggest that it is more likely that the Spanish-American wars of independence transformed print and not vice versa.

There is no comprehensive regional study to date of the development of print culture in post-independence nineteenth-century Spanish America, although there are a number of monographs and articles on each country, and a handful of publications with a regional scope that cover limited periods. The fragmented character of the literature is not surprising, given the widely divergent historical development of the individual countries of the region and the scarcity of information regarding print runs, book circulation and distribution, imports, and other data. Nonetheless, some general patterns can be discerned.

In the decades immediately following independence, Liberal political agendas largely prevailed, with the emphasis on curtailing the influence of the Catholic Church and secularizing education. The Liberal Spanish constitution of 1812 had declared limited freedom of the press, and among the first public acts of the newly formed republics was to expand this freedom by lifting censorship and eliminating tariffs on imported books. Most national governments established public education initiatives and programs to increase literacy, although they failed to fulfill these goals. The number of printing presses increased substantially due to state-sponsored and private initiatives, and their output reflected both the administrative demands of the new republics as well as public interest in the latest news and political and civic debates during those turbulent years.

Besides periodicals, the main products of local presses were instructional manuals, textbooks, ephemeral publications, such as pamphlets and flyers announcing civic events, and compendia of statutes and decrees. The bitter, violent, and protracted struggles between federalists and centralists that dominated the century led to a succession of short-lived governments, and it was not uncommon for printers and booksellers to face imposed or self-censorship in rhythm with the vicissitudes of political power. Despite this instability, printing presses were decidedly instruments of lively public debate on a wide variety of topics: morals, public education, literature and culture, scientific and medical knowledge, and news from abroad. Newspapers and printed material regularly provided a forum for dissension or acted as a mouthpiece for partisan politics, a far cry from the circumscribed role that printing presses had played during the centuries of Spanish rule.

Spanish-American presses produced few books but an extraordinary number and variety of periodicals: dailies, weeklies, and magazines devoted to poetry, literature, general culture, and the sciences. Nineteenth-century newspapers gradually diversified their formats to include special supplements and regular features and sections. Towards the latter part of the century, newspaper publishers occasionally embarked on book-publishing ventures as well. Educated Latin Americans received the latest titles from Britain, and later almost exclusively from France and Spain, via a European publishing industry that produced a variety of titles in Spanish translation. Early on, merchants regularly advertised titles for sale in newspapers, and these advertisements offer glimpses into the vitality of the book market and the reading habits of the Latin American public. Notices were placed for book raffles or to offer subscriptions for new publications; binders and translators also posted their services. In addition, books were sold not only in bookstores, but in a wide array of commercial establishments, such as shoe-shine salons, barber shops, bazaars, market stalls, clothing and sundry stores, or were peddled on the street. Readers could consult books or periodicals by buying, borrowing, or renting them from a reading salon or circulating library: by 1838 there were five such establishments in Buenos Aires.

An author from Havana, Bogotá, or Caracas who could afford to do so most likely would resort to self-publishing, an option open to a minority, or else seek a publisher in Paris, Madrid, New York, or Mexico City. Nonetheless, important Spanish-American historical and literary works of the nineteenth century were published locally as off-prints of specialized journals or as *folletines*: series published in newspapers, sometimes later reprinted locally in one volume. In Cuba, and perhaps in other places, authors would find their way into print through a subscription system, whereby the writer would approach a publisher with a list of friends, relatives, and other potential readers, each of whom had pledged to buy a certain number of copies. In this way, authors were connected to their reading public, and printers could publish without risk.

The publishing scene in Cuba, which remained a Spanish colony throughout the nineteenth century, was particularly fraught with obstacles. Along with its colonial status, slavery sustained the Cuban economy and structured society until the 1880s, when the practice was also abolished in Brazil. Contrary to trends elsewhere, as the century progressed, illiteracy grew. Nonetheless, Cuban presses produced an array of periodicals and books by national authors, including medical and scientific treatises, almanacs, poetry, and other literary works. But local production as well as the importation of foreign titles remained subject to the watchful eye of colonial authorities. Cuban *tertulias* acquired at times an extra-official character, a place where intellectuals and writers would gather semi-clandestinely to discuss prohibited imported works and circulate their own unpublished manuscripts. Ambrosio Fornet (2002), the foremost historian of nineteenth-century Cuban letters, provides important insights into the paradoxes of Cuban print culture, particularly during a brief but significant literary flourishing in Havana between the 1830s and 1840s. Publishing mechanisms remained largely unchanged through the mid-twentieth century until the Cuban Revolution in 1959.

Brazil, which became a monarchy in 1822 and a republic in 1889, remained in relative peace during the wars for independence in the rest of the region, and so the role of the printing press diverged in some respects from trends in other countries. Nonetheless, Brazil's road to independence (while preserving the monarchy) was not without turmoil. Major events of public interest – such as separatist movements in Pernambuco (1817 and 1824), the abdication of Prince Pedro I (1831), and the Regency years (1831–40) before the heir, Prince Pedro II, assumed the throne – produced an upsurge in political pamphleteering and periodical production, with rival newspapers espousing partisan views on the fate of the country. Laurence Hallewell (1982) reveals that, throughout the nineteenth century, the book trade was heavily dependent on exports from Lisbon and Paris, where there was a substantial Portuguese-language publishing industry. This was largely due to the prohibitive costs of domestic publishing as well as to cultural preferences for all things French. Rio de Janeiro (the imperial capital and main administrative, political, and cultural center until the emergence of São Paulo in the 1880s) was by far the leader in domestic publishing. Spurred by economic prosperity and increased literacy rates toward mid-century, literary and cultural works predominated over the political and administrative topics that had occupied presses earlier. As in other countries in the region, beginning in 1839, the main outlet for local authors was the *folhetim* or serialized novel that appeared in newspapers and was sometimes reprinted in book form.

Of particular note during this period is an increase in female readership that was substantial enough to influence the market, broadening the book trade to include topics geared to upper-class women and family-oriented issues. The first women's magazine in Brazil, *A mulher do Simplicio, ou a Fluminense exaltada*, ran from 1832 to 1846 and was quickly followed by others. Its publisher, Francisco de Paula Brito (1819–61), rose from humble origins to become a literary visionary, the first actively to cultivate aspiring Brazilian authors: he published Antônio Goncalves Texeira e Sousa and Joaquim Maria Machado de Assis not on commission (as was generally the custom) but for a salary. Another important publisher of fiction was the French émigré Baptiste Garnier (1823–93), of the Parisian firm Garnier Frères, who settled in Rio in 1844.

Between 1880 and 1930, a period of sustained economic prosperity brought about a modest expansion of the Spanish-American book industry. Book publishing in Rio suffered a temporary setback during the political turmoil of the newly formed republic during the decade of the 1890s. As the industrialized countries of the North Atlantic sought Argentine meat and grain, Brazilian and Colombian coffee, sugar from Cuba, silver from Mexico, bananas from Honduras and Costa Rica, nitrate and copper from Chile, foreign capital poured in, helping to build railroads, introduce new technologies, and fuel urbanization. Literacy rates increased, and a growing urban middle class could afford to purchase consumer goods, including reading material. Argentina, Chile, Uruguay, and southern Brazil attracted vast numbers of immigrants (largely Italian and Spanish, but also Irish, Eastern European Jewish, German, Austrian, French, and British) to work in agriculture-related industries and factories. The case of Argentina was particularly striking, with a population that ballooned from 1.7 million in 1869 to 7.9 million in 1914, when half the population of Buenos Aires was foreign-born. A number of recent studies trace the impact of this largely urban reading public (which now included the working class) on the book trade, local publishing, and print culture (Prieto 1988).

Although Mexico did not experience such massive foreign immigration, a cultural renaissance, emphasizing revisionist views of national history along with artistic and literary accomplishments, flourished after the Revolution of 1910–17 was consolidated. In the 1920s, spearheaded by José Vasconcelos and his successors in the newly created Secretaría de Educación Pública, the government implemented a successful national campaign to educate rural populations, founded public libraries, distributed free textbooks to schoolchildren, and launched a number of publishing ventures and other cultural initiatives fostering fresh perspectives on Mexican history, literature, and the arts.

As in Brazil, the Spanish-language book market in America was dominated by France, until Catalan firms began to take the lead around 1912, with the establishment of branches in major Latin American cities. However, by the 1920s a handful of local publishers – Porrúa and Bota in Mexico; Zig Zag and Ercilla in Chile; Claridad, Babel, and Minerva in Argentina; and Monteiro Lobato in Brazil – were beginning to make strides in the market, producing cheap editions of world classics in translation and actively cultivating national and regional authors. In Buenos Aires, there were publishers who had specialized niches, such as textbooks, musical scores, medical and scientific literature, telecommunications, jurisprudence, supremely popular detective and "pulp" fiction, Argentine avant-garde writers, or popular magazines and literary journals. There was a surge in local publishing in the wake of World War I, when Latin American firms stepped in to fill the wartime shortfall in European publications.

The two decades between 1930 and 1950 would be the "Golden Age" of Latin American publishing. This period was characterized by a substantial increase in domestic publishing output, a marked trend toward professionalization and specialization of labor (printing, editing, binding, distribution) in the book industries, and the internationalization of Latin American literature within the countries of the region and abroad. The Spanish Civil War (1936–9) and World War II (1939–45) both spurred this development. In the first few months of the peninsular conflict, Spanish publishing all but ceased, leaving 80 percent of the Latin American book market without supply, according to one estimate. The response was import substitution in those countries with larger domestic markets and/or a higher standard of living. Argentina, Mexico, and Chile expanded book production to fill the gap and satisfy the demand of increasingly literate masses at home as well as the Spanish-language market abroad.

Those three countries also received the largest proportion of exiles fleeing the Spanish Civil War. Most were educated, many were intellectuals sympathetic to the Republican cause, and they brought with them an intimate knowledge of the book trade as writers, publishers, printers, editors, or booksellers. Many settled in Buenos Aires, the largest publishing center in the region at the time, but the Mexican government implemented a concerted policy to offer asylum to Spaniards fleeing the conflict or certain retaliation by the victorious Franco regime. Nearly five thousand of those who emigrated to Mexico were academics, intellectuals, or book industry professionals. In all three countries, Spanish *republicanos* quickly established themselves by collaborating with existing publishers (such as the recently founded Fondo de Cultura Económica in México), founding their own firms (Emecé, Sudamericana, and Losada in Argentina), or working as translators or print technicians. The result, especially in Mexico and Argentina, was an invigorated domestic publishing scene that eventually placed Buenos Aires and Mexico City as industry leaders within the Spanish-speaking world, a position they hold to this day. Though the Chilean book industry also experienced a boom, the lack of official support, reflected in the imposition of taxes on printed material and bureaucratic obstacles to publishing, hampered further expansion after the 1950s. The increased activity of domestic publishing in Spanish America also broadened the catalogue of regional authors to include the works of Brazilian writers in translation for the first time.

The publishing industry received the benefit of government and professional institutional support during these years. In many countries, governments subsidized publishing ventures or established firms that disseminated the work of national and regional authors at affordable prices. In the wake of the petroleum boom in the 1940s, the Venezuelan government emerged on the publishing scene, spurring the domestic textbook industry in response to official educational promotion and, in later decades, founding Monte Avila Editores and Ediciones Ayacucho, which have produced important works with a regional focus and international distribution. Beginning in the 1940s, public and private sector participation in publishing also led to the founding of national and regional associations of book professionals to discuss intellectual property, translation rights, paper production, and other matters of common interest to the region, as well as to lobby for state regulation of the industry.

The spectacular growth of the Spanish-American book industry (Argentina grew from 823 registered titles published in 1935 to a peak of 5,323 in 1944) would prove to be short-lived with respect to its competitive edge with Spain. In the 1950s, peninsular publishing houses set out to regain their prewar status in the Spanish-language book market. The Franco regime, anxious to promote a transatlantic sentiment of *hispanidad* in this and other cultural arenas, provided subsidies to the industry and legal measures to facilitate production and exports, to the point where texts censored within Spain were allowed to be published and distributed abroad. While Spain successfully regained its predominance, the postwar years nonetheless altered the publishing land-scape in Latin America.

Expanded print production, along with increased national and international circula-tion, had an impact on newly literate and mass readerships and helped to consolidate national identities, for example in post-revolutionary Mexico or in Argentina during the first decades of the twentieth century. Many personal accounts, memoirs, and remi-niscences written by founders, publishers, and other individuals who participated in major editorial projects reveal that publishing houses were not just commercial estab-lishments but craft industries, cultural and often political ventures engaged with broader ideals. For the first time in Latin American history, cultural production was shared by wider audiences, not just elites, and those who worked in the major houses of this period convey a sense of contributing to this process, something that eludes quantitative analysis.

The Cuban Revolution (1959) merits particular attention in the history of print culture in the region for a number of reasons. Almost immediately, the Castro regime implemented a series of initiatives on the educational and cultural fronts designed to increase literacy, remove barriers to the circulation of printed material, and actively promote Cuban writers in all fields of intellectual and scientific activity. Other interven-tions by socialist and Marxist governments, such as the short-lived Allende regime in Chile (1971–3) and the Sandinistas' literacy campaign in Nicaragua in the 1980s, made print accessible for the first time to all sectors of society. Conversely, there were also episodes of repression and censorship of printed works, such as during military rule in Brazil (1964–85), the Pinochet regime (1973–90) in Chile, the dirty war carried out by the military in Argentina (1976–83), and the Cuban state in varying degrees since the late 1960s.

The expansion of literacy and publishing in Latin America set the stage for a "boom" of Latin American literature, when the work of Jorge Luis Borges, Gabriel García Márquez, Julio Cortázar, Carlos Fuentes, and Mario Vargas Llosa achieved international recognition. Both the Cuban Revolution and New York publishing houses played important parts in this phenomenon. Within months of taking power, the Castro regime implemented a cultural policy beyond its borders through the Instituto Casa de las Américas: it promoted the literature, arts, and social sciences of the region and attracted Latin American intellectuals by subsidizing publications, awarding prizes, founding journals, and sponsoring conferences. In response, the Ford Foundation, the Center for Inter-American Relations, and other US-based sources – many of them gov-ernmental or quasi-governmental entities – launched a concerted effort to promote Latin American literature through literary journals, prizes, and subsidizing translation series in major New York publishing houses and in Europe. The "boom" was thus as much the product of commercial interests and Cold War politics as a literary phenomenon.

Moreover, the intellectual repression exercised by the Cuban state in the late 1960s, and especially by the early 1970s, further polarized Latin American writers, critics, and artists, alienating some who had initially supported the regime. The result was that initial critical assessments of the Latin American "boom" that did not center on aesthetic or literary evaluations were largely driven by partisan political fervor from either the right or the left. By the 1970s and 1980s, several critics, most notably Angel Rama (1981), turned to sociological studies of book production and distribution, mass readership, and marketing techniques to ground their understanding of the "boom" on more solid foundations. Since then, the disciplinary shift away from text-based literary analysis to the role of cultural institutions and the material conditions of cultural production has produced a growing body of work on the intersections of print and literary production, including analyses of media beyond print.

In the last decades of the twentieth century, government engagement in publishing, either through joint ventures (for example, in Brazil and Venezuela) or outright ownership (as in Cuba), often countered the tendency of large presses to become part of transnational capitalist corporations. While the latter, particularly Spanish multinationals in Spanish America, grew to dominate certain fields by the early twenty-first century, the continuing tradition of successful small publishers in the region suggests that the role of print culture in nation-building remains recognized and appreciated by Latin Americans. Perhaps what characterizes publishing in Latin America is its exceptional capacity to survive different economic and political regimes, to cope with substantial national instability and still publish books recognized as important for worldwide consumption. Latin America is no longer dependent on foreign presses, as it was in the nineteenth century, when Brazil produced only one-quarter of the number of books it imported. Today Rio de Janeiro, São Paulo, Buenos Aires, Mexico City, Santiago de Chile, Caracas, and Santafé de Bogotá are all major publishing centers, though the challenge of uneven and inadequate distribution channels remains.

REFERENCES AND FURTHER READING

Adorno, Rolena (1986) "Literary Production and Suppression: Reading and Writing about Amerindians in Colonial Spanish America." *Dispositio*, 11: 1–25.

Calvo, Hortensia (2003) "The Politics of Print: The Historiography of the Book in Early Spanish America." *Book History*, 6: 277–301.

Castro-Klarén, Sara and Chasteen, John Charles (eds.) (2003) *Beyond Imagined Communities: Reading and Writing the Nation in Nineteenth-century Latin America*. Washington: Woodrow Wilson Center.

Chocano Mena, Magdalena (1997) "Colonial Printing and Metropolitan Books: Printed Texts and the Shaping of Scholarly Culture in New Spain, 1539–1700." *Colonial Latin American Historical Review*, 6 (1): 69–90.

Cobo Borda, Juan Gustavo (ed.) (2000) *Historia de las empresas editoriales de América Latina, siglo XX*. Santafé de Bogotá: CERLALC.

Earle, Rebecca (2004) "El papel de la imprenta en las guerras de independencia de Hispanoamérica." In A. Soto (ed.), *Entre tintas y plumas: historias de la prensa chilena del siglo XIX*. Santiago de Chile: Universidad de los Andes, Centro de Investigación de Medios Andes, Facultad de Comunicación.

Fornet, Ambrosio (2002) *El libro en Cuba, siglos XVIII y XIX*. Havana: Editorial Letras Cubanas.

Glass, John B. (1975) "A Survey of Native American Pictorial Manuscripts." In H. F. Cline (ed.), *The Handbook of Middle American Indians*, vol. 1, pp. 3–80. Austin: University of Texas Press.

Guerra, François-Xavier and Lempérière, Annick (eds.) (1998) *Los espacios públicos en Iberoamérica: ambigüedades y problemas, siglos XVIII y XIX*. Mexico: Centro Francés de Estudios Mexicanos y Centroamericanos and Fondo de Cultura Económica.

Guibovich Pérez, Pedro (2001) "The Printing Press in Colonial Peru: Production Process and Literary Categories in Lima, 1584–1699." *Colonial Latin American Historical Review*, 10 (2): 167–88.

Hallewell, Laurence (1982) *Books in Brazil: A History of the Publishing Trade.* Metuchen, NJ: Scarecrow (*O livro no Brasil: sua história*, 2nd rev. edn. São Paulo: Editora da Universidade de São Paulo, 2004).

Leonard, Irving (1992) *Books of the Brave: Being an Account of Books and of Men in the Spanish Conquest and Settlement of the Sixteenth-century New World* (intro. by R. Adorno). Berkeley: University of California Press (originally published 1949).

Martínez, José Luis (1986) *El libro en Hispanoamérica: orígen y desarrollo.* Madrid: Fundación Germán Sánchez Ruipérez and Ediciones Pirámide.

Medina, José Toribio, Feliú Cruz, Guillermo, and Zamudio Zamora, José (1958) *Historia de la imprenta en los antiguos dominios españoles de América y Oceanía.* Santiago de Chile: Fondo Histórico y Bibliográfico José Toribio Medina.

Mignolo, Walter (1998) *The Darker Side of the Renaissance: Literacy, Territoriality, and Colonization.* Durham: Duke University Press.

— and Boone, Elizabeth Hill (eds.) (1994) *Writing without Words: Alternative Literacies in Mesoamerica and the Andes.* Durham: Duke University Press.

Molina Jiménez, Iván (1995) *El que quiera divertirse: libros y sociedad en Costa Rica (1750–1914).* San José and Heredia, Costa Rica: Editorial de la Universidad de Costa Rica and Editorial de la Universidad Nacional.

Oudijk, Michel and Castañeda de la Paz, Maria (eds.) (forthcoming) *Supplement to the Handbook of Middle American Indians,* vol. 7: *A Census of Mesoamerican Pictographical Manuscripts* and vol. 8: *A Census of Indigenous Alphabetical Manuscripts.* Austin: University of Texas Press.

Prieto, Adolfo (1988) *El discurso criollista en la formación de la Argentina moderna.* Buenos Aires: Editorial Sudamericana.

Rama, Angel (1981) "El boom en perspectiva." In D. Viñas et al. (eds.), *Más allá del boom: literatura y mercado,* pp. 51–110. Mexico: Marcha Editores.

— (1996) *The Lettered City (Post-contemporary Interventions),* trans. John Charles Chasteen. Durham: Duke University Press (originally published as *La ciudad letrada.* Hanover, NH: Ediciones del Norte, 1984).

Rivera, Jorge B. (1998) *El escritor y la industria cultural.* Buenos Aires: Atuel.

Rostagno, Irene (1997) *Searching for Recognition: The Promotion of Latin American Literature in the United States.* Westport, CT: Greenwood.

Sagastizábal, Leandro de (1995) *La edición de libros en Argentina: una empresa de cultura.* Buenos Aires: Editorial Universitaria de Buenos Aires.

Subercaseaux, Bernardo (1993) *Historia del libro en Chile: alma y cuerpo.* Santiago de Chile: Editorial Andrés Bello.

Torre Revello, José (1940) *El libro, la imprenta y el periodismo en América durante la dominación española.* Buenos Aires: Jacobo Peuser.

Vázquez, Josefina (ed.) (1988) *Historia de la lectura en México.* Mexico City: El Colegio de México.

11

The Hebraic Book

Emile G. L. Schrijver

The term Hebraic book is considered here to refer to books, scrolls, and single sheets copied or printed in the Hebrew alphabet. Thus, a Hebrew book need not necessarily be in the Hebrew language. In the pre-medieval period, Aramaic had gradually become the second language of the Jews; all important Aramaic dialects used by the Jews were written in the Hebrew alphabet. Also, Jews in the Diaspora used to write their everyday language in Hebrew characters. Besides Hebrew, the most important "Jewish languages" are Yiddish, Ladino (so-called Judeo-Spanish), and Judeo-Arabic.

Jews have always displayed great interest in their literary heritage. Among the earliest handwritten Hebrew sources known are the Dead Sea Scrolls, found in eleven caves near Khirbet Qumran (south of Jericho) from 1947 onward. The scrolls, which were written between approximately 200 BC and AD 100, contain biblical texts, biblical interpretations, apocryphal and pseudepigraphical texts, hymns, and many other texts dealing with the organization of the community and with its specific customs and beliefs (Tov 1993; Parry and Tov 2004–5).

Medieval Hebrew Manuscripts

Later Hebrew manuscripts and thousands of fragments were found in the "Genizah" discovered toward the end of the nineteenth century in the Fostat synagogue in Cairo. As one is not allowed to destroy the divine name, religious books and other documents containing the divine name, and often simply all remnants of Hebrew books, are stored in a *genizah* (Hebrew: storage). Most important among the Genizah manuscripts are the greater part of the Hebrew text of the Book of Ben Sira, old manuscripts of classical rabbinical texts, thousands of known and unknown religious and secular poems, material relating to the history of Karaism, sources on the history of the Jews in the region, and autographs of great Sephardic scholars like Judah Halevi (before 1075–after 1140) and Moses Maimonides (1138–1204). One of the major methodological problems of the

Genizah sources is that the state of early medieval Hebrew paleography does not yet permit accurate dating; it is assumed that some of the manuscripts date back at least to the seventh century AD (Richler 1990: 112–34).

There are two important reasons for the absence of Hebrew manuscript sources from the period of the Dead Sea Scrolls to the seventh, eighth, or ninth centuries. Time and persecutions destroyed many Hebrew books, and there is reason to assume that during that period there still existed a genuine oral transmission of texts, which would mean that there were simply not as many books as one might perhaps expect. Compared with their non-Hebrew counterparts, Hebrew manuscripts appeared relatively late in the Middle Ages, but from approximately the tenth century onward there is firm ground on which to stand. By that time, the codex had definitively established its leading position as the most popular form of handwritten text. The use of papyrus had been abandoned, while the practice of writing on a scroll was continued for certain biblical texts only (Sirat 1985; Beit-Arié 1993a, c).

The earliest date mentioned in a colophon of a Hebrew manuscript is 895. The manuscript, known as the Moses ben Asher codex, was produced in Tiberias; it contains the text of the Prophets and is now housed in the Karaite Synagogue of Cairo. Codicological research by Mordecai Glatzer, however, has revealed that this manuscript, including the colophon, was copied at least a century later from an older (now lost) exemplar. Since Glatzer's refutation of the authenticity of the date mentioned in the colophon of the Ben Asher codex, a manuscript consisting of fragments of the text of Nehemia, kept in the Genizah Collection of Cambridge University Library and written in Da Gunbadan, Persia, in the year 904, is considered to be the earliest known dated Hebrew manuscript. The earliest dated Hebrew manuscript larger than a fragment is a codex of the Latter Prophets with Babylonian vocalization, finished in 916, which now reposes in St. Petersburg (Beit-Arié 1993c).

Whereas the earliest Hebrew manuscripts were produced in the Orient, in later centuries all regions of the Jewish Diaspora developed their own traditions. Hebrew manuscripts are therefore usually classified into geographical groups: Ashkenazic (England, Germany, northern and central France; later on, northwest Europe in general), Sephardic (Spain, Portugal, southern France, part of North Africa), Italian, Byzantine (Turkey, Greece, and the surrounding countries), and Oriental (the Middle East and beyond). Within the Oriental group, Yemen and Persia are sometimes considered as separate groups. (The word "Sephardic" is often incorrectly used to conflate Mediterranean and Oriental Jewries.) Hebrew books elucidate the varying circumstances under which the Jews of the Diaspora lived in the medieval period. Many Hebrew manuscripts ended up being burnt. Furthermore, professional Jewish scribes often had to change their place of residence under the pressure of anti-Jewish political developments. Their travels exposed scribes to new artistic influences and to new fellow practitioners (Beit-Arié 1981).

There is no proof that during the Middle Ages there existed anything approaching the institutionalization of the production of Hebrew manuscripts comparable to a Christian scriptorium. In the words of Malachi Beit-Arié (1993a: 11):

Colophons and random historical sources, including some documents found mainly in the Cairo Geniza, attest that Hebrew manuscripts were produced either by single professional scribes, or, more often, by learned men who copied the texts for their own use. Yet it is now clear that a considerable number of Hebrew manuscripts – about one tenth of the surviving dated medieval ones – were copied by more than one hand, usually by two, or three, but sometimes by more, up to ten hands. As the colophons of the manuscripts copied by several hands refer almost without exception to one scribe, who in most cases did indeed copy the major part or parts of the manuscript, one should assume that the additional hands were either sons or relatives of the main scribe, or students of a scholar, who assisted him in copying.

This demonstrates a fundamental difference between medieval Hebrew and Latin books. Latin works from the late seventh until the mid-thirteenth centuries were usually produced in multi-copyist scriptoria, while in a later period they were reproduced by university stationers according to the *pecia* system or in commercial workshops. Beit-Arié proves statistically that at least half the medieval Hebrew books were "personal user-produced books, copied by the scholars who were going to use them" and not by hired scribes. This fact sheds light on the transmission of Hebrew texts, as a hired scribe may be more vulnerable to mistakes caused by the copying mechanics, while an individual copyist is more likely to make deliberate changes to the text he is copying. These facts have certainly influenced the editions of many Hebrew texts (Beit-Arié 1993b; 1993c: 79–103, 119–24; more generally: Alexander and Samely 1993).

The Decoration of Medieval Hebrew Manuscripts

The decoration of medieval Hebrew manuscripts has drawn the attention of scholars since the late nineteenth century. Most studies concentrate on perhaps the most hackneyed theme in Jewish art history: namely, the question of whether Jewish art was allowed to exist during the Middle Ages. It is evident that the second commandment, "Thou shalt not make unto thee a graven image," did not result in a total rejection of art; it was forbidden to "bow unto them [and to] serve them," but it was generally permitted to produce them, especially two-dimensionally. Of course, a visual representation of God was strictly forbidden.

Hebrew decorated manuscripts from different regions share certain distinctive features. In Ashkenaz, *Haggadot* and prayer books were especially popular; in these manuscripts one often finds bird and animal heads instead of human heads, while in many other manuscripts people are depicted with their heads turned backward. This is not the place to discuss the backgrounds of these practices, but it is obvious that the artists were sensitive to the second commandment. In Sepharad, one encounters a multitude of exquisitely decorated manuscripts from the thirteenth century onward, and in most of these the artists were not concerned with the second commandment. The manuscripts produced in the so-called Lisbon School in the last third of the fifteenth century, of which more than thirty are extant, are an important, although not the only, exception; there, figural art is uncommon. Italian manuscripts, especially those from the fourteenth and fifteenth centuries, are the most abundantly decorated Hebrew manuscripts ever produced. Besides representational art, many manuscripts show a strong tendency toward elaborate multicolored floral decoration. In the Orient, abstract ornamentation of Hebrew manuscripts was most common; the artists usually refrained from a visual representation of human beings.

The text, which was copied by the scribe, was usually considered the most important part of the manuscript. There are examples of scribes who explicitly mention that they were themselves responsible for both the copying and the decorating of a codex; occasionally one may even find an artist's colophon, but in most cases the identity of the artist remains unknown. Artists were, of course, strongly influenced by the surrounding cultures. Although the actual background of the production of Hebrew illuminated manuscripts is not very clear, especially since contemporary documents are scarce, it is certain that both Jews and non-Jews were responsible for the decoration (Roth 1971; Metzger 1982; Narkiss 1984; Gold 1988; Melker et al. 1990; Richler 1990; Karp 1991).

Hebrew Scripts

There are many different types of Hebrew scripts. The most important modes were: the monumental square script, the somewhat less monumental semi-square script, the semi-cursive book hand, and the cursive script for everyday use. The geographical classification of Hebrew manuscripts mentioned earlier – distinguishing between Ashkenazic, Sephardic, Italian, Byzantine, and Oriental (with Yemen and Persia as separate groups) – is also used for Hebrew scripts. This means that there are dozens of different types of Hebrew script.

The widespread use of Hebrew scripts over a period of at least two millennia, and the fact that the traditional division into modes does not suit all types and periods, are the main reasons why a clear definition of all the different types and modes is still lacking. A further complication is the fact that the historical process behind the development of the shapes of Hebrew scripts, especially of the cursive mode, is often unclear due to the scarcity or lack of early book hands. It is evident, therefore, that the final word on the development of Hebrew script in the medieval and post-medieval periods has not been uttered yet, and may never be. All the same, the Hebrew Palaeography Project's new series of paleographical atlases may shed some new light on at least the medieval period (Beit-Arié et al. 1987; Beit-Arié 1993c; Beit-Arié and Engel 2002).

The Hebrew Printed Book

Hebrew printing started in Rome, with six books printed sometime between 1469 and 1473, most likely by "Obadiah, Manasseh, and Benjamin of Rome." Their first production was David ben Joseph Kimhi's dictionary *Sefer ha-shorashim*. It was followed by Solomon ben Abraham ibn Adret's collection of *Responsa*; Solomon ben Isaac (Rashi)'s, *Commentary on the Pentateuch*; Levi ben Gershom's *Commentary on the Book of Daniel*; Nathan ben Jehiel of Rome's Talmudic dictionary, *Arukh*; and Moses ben Nahman's *Commentary on the Pentateuch*. The first printed Hebrew book with an explicit mention of a date was Solomon ben Isaac's commentary on the Pentateuch, finished on February 17, 1475 in Reggio di Calabria. There are a total of 139 editions of Hebrew books that were almost certainly printed before January 1, 1501. These Hebrew *incunables* were printed on about forty presses, all active in the Mediterranean area: in Italy, Spain, Portugal, and one in Turkey (Offenberg 1990).

In the first half of the sixteenth century – that is, after the expulsion of the Jews from Spain and Portugal in 1492 and 1496 respectively – the most important Hebrew printing presses were situated in Venice, Mantua, Sabbioneta, Cremona, and (outside Italy) in Constantinople and Salonica. Ashkenazic centers of importance were Cracow, Augsburg, Basle, and Prague. After the Antwerp printer Daniel van Bomberghen, who had close contacts with Christopher Plantin's circles, established his printing press in Venice in 1516, Italy and particularly Venice determined the face of sixteenth-century Hebrew printing. During that century, close to nine hundred Hebrew books were published in Venice alone.

A particularly interesting aspect of the sixteenth- and seventeenth-century Italian Hebrew book is the near omnipresence of inquisitional censorship. From the second half of the sixteenth century onward, Christian censors (often converted Jews) would check all Hebrew books, would often sign them after checking, and expurgate passages that were considered negative toward Christianity. Apart from the obvious anti-Jewish stance of the Inquisition, one of the most prosaic explanations for this censorship may be financial: Jews, both printers and private owners of books, were expected to pay for the work of the censor. Among the most important censors were Dominico Irosolimitano, Camillo Jaghel, Hippolitus Ferrarensis, Giovanni Dominico Carretto, and Giovanno Domenico Vistorini. Christian censorship also led to active Jewish self-censorship. But Christian interest in Hebrew printing was not always negative. The humanist ideal of *eruditio trilinguis* gave rise to a large number of Hebrew books, mostly linguistic studies and Bible editions and commentaries, but also less obvious literary works, printed by Christian printers in important centers like Basle, Antwerp, Leiden, and Paris. These printers would usually hire Jewish typesetters and editors, who often maintained close intellectual contacts with the Christian authors.

In the course of the seventeenth century, Amsterdam took over Venice's leading role in Hebrew book production. The first Jew to print in Hebrew in Amsterdam was Menasseh ben Israel. His first Hebrew production, a daily prayer book, appeared on January 1, 1627. In this work Menasseh's corrector, Isaac Aboab da Fonseca, mentions the fact that the newly cut Hebrew types were based on letters written by the local Sephardic scribe Michael Judah Leon. Menasseh ben Israel printed a large number of books, not only for the newly established Portuguese Jewish community of Amsterdam, but also for the Western and Eastern European market. Other Amsterdam printers of importance were Immanoel Benveniste, Uri Fayvish ben Aaron Halevi, David de Castro Tartas, and the members of the printing dynasties of Athias and Proops.

The eighteenth century saw the development of a large number of smaller printing centers in the German lands and in Eastern Europe. An indication of the total number of printed books up to 1736 is provided by the collection of David ben Samuel Oppenheimer (1664–1736): after a life of collecting, he left more than five thousand printed Hebrew works, a collection purchased by Oxford's Bodleian Library in 1829. Although new printing centers, such as Metz and Paris in France, and especially Livorno in Italy, did continue to appear, by 1760 the center of Hebrew printing had really moved to Eastern Europe. The import of Hebrew books from abroad was effectively prevented there. Western Europe generally had become much more tolerant toward the Jewish book, but in Eastern Europe ecclesiastical and governmental censorship became more severe even than in sixteenth-century Italy.

The majority of printing presses in eighteenth- and nineteenth-century Eastern Europe were active in such well-known centers of the Hasidic movement as Vilnius, Shklov, and Zhytomir, as well as in a large number of smaller places. In the German-speaking countries, the presses of Anton Schmidt and Joseph Hraschansky in Vienna and of the Jüdische Freyschule in Berlin were most active. They mostly catered for the needs of a rapidly developing market of adherents of the Haskalah, the Jewish Enlightenment. The famous press of Wolf Heidenheim, who published a large number of critical editions of biblical and liturgical works in Rödelheim in the first half of the nineteenth century, was important as well. In North America, Christian printers had included isolated Hebrew words in theological studies as early as the seventeenth century. But in the course of the nineteenth century, as a result of the mass immigration from Eastern Europe to major North American cities, including Toronto, Hebrew presses were established by Jews.

The trends of the nineteenth century continued into the early twentieth, with Eastern Europe and its orthodox community becoming ever more important, and the traditional centers, such as Germany and the Netherlands, losing their importance entirely. Between the two world wars a short renaissance of artistic typography occurred in Europe. Artists such as El Lissitzky had art books published in Moscow, Kiev, Odessa, and Berlin. The Soncino Gesellschaft in Berlin fostered fine Hebrew printing and produced, among others, an important Pentateuch edition between 1931 and 1933. World War II destroyed Hebrew printing all over Europe. After the war, the State of Israel became the world center of Hebrew printing, with a few important exceptions only in orthodox circles in the United States. Nowadays, in spite of rapidly developing digital possibilities, there are very few printers outside Israel that may be considered capable of producing Hebrew books of any typographical value.

The two most important Jewish languages, other than Hebrew and Aramaic, are Yiddish and Ladino (Judeo-Spanish). Yiddish printing started in the sixteenth century. Through their Hebrew studies, humanist scholars became acquainted with Yiddish and, guided by their Jewish teachers, started to study it. This Germanic language with Semitic elements in Hebrew characters triggered their intellectual curiosity and at the same time helped them to learn to read Hebrew more easily, through the reading of Yiddish texts that were largely understandable to them. Important early centers of Yiddish printing were Constance, Isny, and Augsburg in southern Germany, where a specially developed "Yiddish type," an adaptation of the handwritten semi-cursive Ashkenazic book hand, was developed. Later on, during the seventeenth and eighteenth centuries, large numbers of Yiddish books were produced in Amsterdam and Germany. With the shift toward Eastern Europe in the late eighteenth century, Yiddish printing moved there as well. In the course of the nineteenth century Yiddish gradually became an object of study in the Yiddish language itself, stimulated by socialist, romantic, and nationalist ideologies. This development was accompanied by the appearances of numerous original literary works by Yiddish authors, as well as translations of famous non-Jewish authors. In late eighteenth-century Germany, the adherents of the Haskalah published a considerable number of works in grammatically sound German, printed in Hebrew characters. These texts are often mistaken for Yiddish. Nowadays, public interest in Yiddish literature is increasing rapidly: especially in Israel and North America, new editions of Yiddish literature have begun to appear.

It is noteworthy that the Western Sephardim of France, and later of northern Germany, Holland, and England, did not read their Spanish in Hebrew characters, but rather in Latin characters. It should be realized, therefore, that Ladino printing in Hebrew characters was done for, and mostly by, the Sephardic Jews of the Ottoman empire and not for the Western Sephardim. The history of printing of Ladino is generally divided into three periods. The first began with the publication in Constantinople in 1547 of a Polyglot Bible with a Ladino version, by members of the Soncino printing dynasty. Interestingly, this work was not followed by a larger number of Ladino publications. A limited number of books were published in the course of the sixteenth century in Constantinople, Salonika, and Venice, but during the entire seventeenth century, even into the first decades of the eighteenth century, only a few Ladino volumes were published. One reason may have been the strong objection to the use of the vernacular among Sephardic leaders in the Ottoman empire, which is a recurring theme in Ladino works, even as late as the nineteenth century.

The second period began in 1730 with the publication of the works of Abraham Assa and of Jacob Culi's (1665–1732) *Me-am Lo'ez*. This period saw the emergence of a completely new literature: the *Me-am Lo'ez* (an extremely popular commentary-like paraphrase of the Pentateuch), the first daily prayer book, the first complete Bible (with translations by Abraham Assa), the first book on Jewish history, and a number of books on Jewish law. The two most important publishers (and harsh competitors) in Constantinople were Jonah Ashkenazi (born in the Ukraine) and Benjamin Rossi.

The third phase began with the Vienna Ladino publications of 1811. The Gentile printer Anton Schmidt published a row of Ladino books for a market of Viennese Turkish Jews and their Sephardic co-religionists in the Balkans. In order to provide the Ladino market with the books they needed, Schmidt hired a Belgrade Jew, Israel ben Hayyim, who became his foremost translator and editor, and who also produced a new Ladino translation of the Old Testament, published by Schmidt in 1815.

Post-medieval Hebrew Manuscripts

The invention of printing did not bring an end to the production of Hebrew manuscripts, but it goes without saying that the Hebrew handwritten book lost a great deal
of its popularity. Toward the end of the fifteenth and in the course of the sixteenth
century, manual copying of Hebrew texts became a relatively marginal phenomenon,
especially in Europe. In the Orient the situation was different, as there, due to a general
scarcity of printed Hebrew books, many Hebrew manuscripts were produced well into
the twentieth century. The production of Hebrew manuscripts since the invention of
printing may be divided roughly into four overlapping categories.

First, there were certain liturgical texts that had to be written by hand according
to Jewish law, such as Torah scrolls, *tefilin*, and *mezuzot*. Descriptions of the rules
and practices connected with the copying of these texts may be found in a vast body
of medieval and post-medieval tracts on the topic, among which Moses Maimonides'
Hilkhot sifre torah in his halakhic code *Mishneh torah* is probably the best known. Many
of these texts were derived from the extra-canonical talmudic tractate *Soferim*.

The second category included single decorated sheets (for example, *ketubot*, Ten Commandments, Omer calendars), decorated scrolls (usually the Book of Esther, occasionally
Psalms and other smaller biblical books), and calligraphic art. One of the most important traditions that developed after the Middle Ages, both in the East and in the West,
was that of decorating the *ketubah*, the Jewish marriage contract. *Ketubah* decoration
was especially popular in Italy where, from the sixteenth century on, it became customary to read aloud the text of the marriage contract in front of the congregation. This
custom inspired well-to-do families to order beautifully decorated *ketubot*, as an appropriate present to the newlyweds, but certainly also just to show off. Italian *ketubah*
artists were inspired by both the rich contemporary Christian visual culture and the
immediate Jewish milieu. On account of their extensive use of Hebrew texts in the
decorative programs and their selection of specifically Jewish subject matter, the majority of the artists may be assumed to be Jewish. This is also true for the Italian artists
of the sixteenth century who initiated another artistic tradition: that of decorating
Hebrew scrolls of the Book of Esther. Since the divine name does not appear in the
Book of Esther, Esther scrolls, or *Megilot*, were manufactured with lavish illustration
and/or decoration, comparable to that of the aforementioned *ketubot*. Such scrolls were
used for the reading of Esther during the Purim festival in private households. Scrolls
for synagogue reading were never illustrated.

Thirdly, decorated books were written during the eighteenth century *be-otiyot Amsterdam* ("with Amsterdam letters") in central and northern Europe. Apart from several
dozen surviving decorated daily and festival prayer books, meant primarily for synagogue use, these manuscripts were usually deluxe Passover rituals, Books of Psalms,
prayer books for the Sabbath, and smaller collections of occasional prayers, such as
circumcision manuals. The manuscripts were commissioned by middle-class and
upper-class Jews, whose names appear on many title and dedication pages.

One of the most striking characteristics of what is often called the eighteenth-century school of Hebrew manuscript illumination is the fact that the manuscripts were modelled after contemporary printed Hebrew books, especially those of Amsterdam, which were esteemed highly for their typographical quality. Many European printers, from the beginning of the eighteenth century onward, even went so far as to print the word "Amsterdam" in large type at the bottom of the page, where one would expect the name of the place of printing. This indicated that the book was printed "with the letters of Amsterdam," not in the city of Amsterdam. The Hebrew scribes of the eighteenth century adopted this custom and many scribes indicated that their manuscripts were copied in the style of the Amsterdam imprints.

Today, a maximum of 450–500 decorated central and northern European Hebrew manuscripts of the eighteenth century survive. The earliest manuscript produced during this revival is almost certainly a magnificent daily prayer book, copied in Vienna between 1712 and 1714 by Aryeh ben Judah Leib of Trebitsch, Moravia, which is now in the Library of the Jewish Theological Seminary of America in New York. It is in itself puzzling why the new phenomenon would start off with such an elaborate daily prayer book, whereas the large majority of later manuscripts are smaller. Possibly the new fashion developed out of the existing custom of producing handwritten synagogue prayer books with occasional decoration, which were often donated to Jewish communities by the well-to-do. Once one scribe came up with the idea to write his manuscripts in accordance with the Amsterdam printed book tradition, perhaps others followed. In any case, most of the later, usually smaller, manuscripts were apparently prepared not for the upper-class but for the middle-class market.

At first, eighteenth-century artists copied directly from their printed models, and even tried to imitate in pen and ink their characteristic copper engravings. But soon the artists felt the urge to create their own illustrations. They usually maintained the most important elements of the Amsterdam compositions, but changed the costumes, furniture, and decor, in order to make the reader of the manuscript feel more at home with them. The two most important centers of this eighteenth-century decorated Hebrew manuscript production were northern Germany and the Bohemian/Moravian region, but there are examples of decorated Hebrew manuscripts written "*be-otiyot Amsterdam*" from practically all Western European countries, including Italy, France, the northern Netherlands, and even England.

The fourth important category of Western post-medieval Hebrew manuscripts are those that probably may be compared best to their non-Hebrew counterparts, such as autograph manuscripts, literary remains, bound correspondence, and archival material. Although these make up the majority of existing Hebrew manuscripts, modern systematic research on the topic from the point of view of book production is almost entirely lacking.

The post-medieval situation in the Oriental countries differed considerably from that in the Occident. Because printed books were usually scarce, there was often an almost "medieval" demand for handwritten books. Therefore, for Oriental manuscripts, a distinction between medieval and post-medieval is rather artificial. Little is known about the actual circumstances under which post-medieval Oriental manuscripts were produced, with the exception of perhaps the Yemenite community. The only systematic research done on the topic is Shalom Sabar's (1990) work on marriage contracts, which offers only limited insight into manuscript production in general. When studying Oriental Hebrew manuscripts in a more systematic way one would at least have to consider Moroccan, Palestinian, Yemenite, and Persian manuscripts as groups worthy of separate attention, while there may be reason to define even more subdivisions. Modern research on post-medieval Oriental manuscripts is therefore more than necessary, but it should be realized that it will be hampered considerably by the large quantities of available material.

In 1991, Alexander Samely published an important analysis of the various shapes that Hebrew manuscripts in general, but especially those of the post-medieval period, may take (Samely 1991: 13). He distinguishes:

(1)   The Codex Containing One Work;
(2)   The Homogeneous Codex Containing Several Works;
(3)   The Composite Codex Containing Several Works;
(4)   The Codex Defining One Work (the bibliographical identity of the texts contained in the manuscript is defined by the individual codex itself, and only by it).

Samely's is the first serious effort to classify a Hebrew manuscript collection, that of the John Rylands University Library in Manchester, England, according to other criteria than mere content or literary genre. In doing so, he also contributes to the discussion about Jewish literacy after the Middle Ages.

Book Trade and Bibliophilism

Little is known about the medieval Jewish book trade. There are book lists, deeds of sale, and similar legal documents that attest to a more or less free circulation of books. One can, however, only speak of a proper Jewish book trade since the invention of printing. Only then could larger numbers of Jews afford to gather larger collections of books. Early Hebrew books, for example those of Constantinople, were often printed and sold per finished quire, for example following a synagogue service, which may explain the rarity of complete editions. During the seventeenth century, the Frankfurt Book Fair was of importance to Hebrew publishers (who were mostly the printers as well), although it may be assumed that the large majority of books were sold and purchased through Jewish networks. In eighteenth-century Eastern Europe, itinerant Jewish book-dealers played an important role in the distribution of new and old books. As late as the nineteenth century there developed a clear distinction between printers, on the one side, and publishers and book dealers on the other, although especially in Eastern Europe printers were often their own publishers far into the twentieth century. Auctions of Jewish books have taken place ever since the seventeenth century. Today, Christie's, Sotheby's, and Kestenbaum in New York are the most important auctioneers of Hebrew books.

Little is known about the collecting of Hebrew books during the Middle Ages, although we know that some larger collections (dozens of books) did exist. One of the greatest Jewish bibliophiles of all times, David Oppenheimer (mentioned above), took a special interest in books printed on parchment and on tinted papers, notably blue. The abbot Giovanni Bernardo DeRossi (1742–1831) owned an equally important collection of Hebrew books, now in the Biblioteca Palatina in Parma. In Russia, the collections of David Guenzburg (1857–1910) and Abraham Firkovich (1786–1874) are worthy of mention, since they contain a large number of important early manuscripts. The private collection of Leeser Rosenthal (1794–1868) of Hanover, Germany is now the core of the Bibliotheca Rosenthaliana in Amsterdam University Library. Probably the most important private collection of the nineteenth and twentieth centuries was that of the Sassoon family of Bombay. The catalogue of its 1,153 manuscripts was published in 1932. The larger part of this collection was auctioned in the 1970s. Today, the needs of bibliophiles are catered for not only by specialized auctions of old books, but also by the appearance of the deluxe facsimile editions of splendid medieval and post-medieval manuscripts.

Conclusion

Alexander Samely's (1991) definitions of Hebrew manuscripts quoted above are especially significant as they underscore perhaps the most important aspect of Hebraic books in general, handwritten or printed – their variety. What binds the books is the Hebrew script and, in most instances, "Jewish culture." Otherwise, the variations are endless. Samely's analysis concentrates on the structure of codices, and consequently on the multifaceted history of their usage. But the variation is, of course, much greater than that. Many different languages were written and printed in Hebrew script: Hebrew, Aramaic, Yiddish, Arabic, Ladino, Italian, Greek, and German are the most frequent examples. Many centuries divide the Dead Sea Scrolls from modern Israeli literature, and the earliest biblical manuscripts from Syria from Yiddish literature in nineteenth-century Russia. Many miles divide the northern Netherlands from the Yemen, Constantinople (Istanbul) from Brooklyn, and Jerusalem from Poonah. Jewish culture can only on the most generic level accommodate the cultural and historical differences between the Jews of Spain in the Middle Ages, those of Italy in the sixteenth century, and those of India in the nineteenth century. It is only with this endless variation in mind that one can begin to appreciate the cultural-historical wealth of Hebrew book culture.

REFERENCES AND FURTHER READING

Alexander, Philip and Samely, Alexander (eds.) (1993) "Artefact and Text: The Re-creation of Jewish Literature in Medieval Hebrew Manuscripts." Proceedings of a Conference held at the University of Manchester, April 28–30, 1992. *Bulletin of the John Rylands University Library*, 75 (3).
Beit-Arié, Malachi (1981) *Hebrew Codicology: Tentative Typology of Technical Practices Employed in*

Hebrew Dated Medieval Manuscripts. Jerusalem: Israel Academy of Sciences and Humanities.

— (1993a) *The Makings of the Medieval Hebrew Book: Studies in Palaeography and Codicology.* Jerusalem: Magnes.

— (1993b) "Transmission of Texts by Scribes and Copyists: Unconscious and Critical Interferences." *Bulletin of the John Rylands University Library,* 75 (3): 33–51.

— (1993c) *Hebrew Manuscripts of East and West: Towards a Comparative Codicology.* The Panizzi Lectures 1992. London: British Library.

— and Engel, Edna (2002) *Specimens of Mediaeval Hebrew Scripts. 2: Sefardic Script.* Jerusalem: Israel Academy of Sciences and Humanities.

—, and Yardeni, Ada (1987) *Specimens of Mediaeval Hebrew Scripts. 1: Oriental and Yemenite Scripts.* Jerusalem: Israel Academy of Sciences and Humanities.

Brisman, Shimeon (1977) *A History and Guide to Judaic Bibliography.* Cincinnati: Hebrew Union College Press.

Gold, Leonard Singer (ed.) (1988) *A Sign and a Witness: 2,000 Years of Hebrew Books and Illuminated Manuscripts.* New York: New York Public Library.

Hill, Brad Sabin (1989) *Hebraica (Saec. X ad Saec. XVI) Manuscripts and Early Printed Books from the Library of the Valmadonna Trust: An Exhibition at the Pierpont Morgan Library, New York.* London: Valmadonna Trust Library.

Iakerson, S. M. (2005) *Catalogue of Hebrew Incunabula from the Collection of the Library of the Jewish Theological Seminary.* New York: Jewish Theological Seminary of America.

Karp, Abraham J. (1991) *From the Ends of the Earth: Judaic Treasures of the Library of Congress.* Washington: Library of Congress.

Melker, S. R. de, Schrijver, Emile G. L., and Van Voolen, Edward (eds.) (1990) *The Image of the Word: Jewish Tradition in Manuscripts and Printed Books. Catalogue of an Exhibition Held at the Jewish Historical Museum, Amsterdam (14 September–25 November 1990).* Amsterdam: Jewish Historical Museum.

Metzger, Thérèse and Metzger, Mendel (1982) *Jewish Life in the Middle Ages.* New York: Chartwell.

Narkiss, Bezalel (1984) *Hebrew Illuminated Manuscripts,* rev. Hebrew edn. Jerusalem: Keter.

Offenberg, A. K. (1990) *Hebrew Incunabula in Public Collections: A First International Census* (Bibliotheca humanistica & reformatorica 47). Nieuwkoop: De Graaf.

— (1992) *A Choice of Corals: Facets of Fifteenth-century Hebrew Printing* (Bibliotheca humanistica & reformatorica 52). Nieuwkoop: De Graaf.

— (2004) *Catalogue of Books Printed in the XVth Century Now in the British Library. BMC Part xiii: Hebraica.* 't Goy-Houten: HES & De Graaf.

Parry, Donald W. and Tov, Emanuel (eds.) (2004–5) *The Dead Sea Scrolls Reader.* Leiden: E. J. Brill.

Richler, Binyamin (1990) *Hebrew Manuscripts: A Treasured Legacy.* Cleveland: Ofeq Institute.

— (1994) *Guide to Hebrew Manuscript Collections.* Jerusalem: Israel Academy of Sciences and Humanities.

Roth, Cecil (ed.) (1971) *Jewish Art: An Illustrated History.* Greenwich, CT: New York Graphic Society.

Sabar, Shalom (1990) *Ketubbah: Jewish Marriage Contracts of the Hebrew Union College Skirball Museum and Klau Library.* Philadelphia: Jewish Publication Society.

Samely, Alexander (1991) "The Interpreted Text: Among the Hebrew Manuscripts of the John Rylands University Library." *Bulletin of the John Rylands University Library,* 73 (2): 1–20.

Sirat, Collette (1985) *Les papyrus en caractères hébraïques trouvés en Égypte.* Paris: Editions du Centre National de la Recherche Scientifique.

Steinschneider, Moritz (1852) *Catalogus librorum hebraeorum in Bibliotheca Bodleiana.* Berlin: Typis Ad. Friedlander.

Tov, Emanuel (ed.) (1993) *The Dead Sea Scrolls on Microfiche: A Comprehensive Facsimile Edition of the Texts from the Judean Desert.* Leiden: IDC.

Vinograd, Yeshayahu (1993) *Thesaurus of the Hebrew Book,* 2 vols. Jerusalem: Institute for Computerized Bibliography.

12

The Islamic Book

Michael Albin

The realm of the Islamic book includes the Arabic, Persian, and Turkish-speaking countries, as well as parts of South, Central, and Southeast Asia. There have been many differences among these regions in their approach to the book in the past as well as in modern times. But there are also some commonalities, including veneration of the Qur'ān, patronage of the book arts, periods of intolerance, and a three-hundred-year delay in introducing Gutenberg's invention.

There is no evidence that Arabs practiced the art of bookmaking before or during the lifetime of Muhammad the Prophet (d. 632). If the Arabs of Mecca and Medina possessed writing in the Arabic language, it was probably a primitive script adapted from elsewhere. Islamic tradition asserts that the Prophet was illiterate and that he occasionally dictated portions of the revelation to be written on materials such as bone, palm leaves, or animal hides. As it developed, Arabic script came to be formed of twenty-eight letters, graphemes indicating long vowels, and a number of diacritical markings indicating short vowels. Arabic is written from right to left and is cursive in appearance. It has no capital letters nor, in the classical form, punctuation. Although the earliest Muslims did not possess a script to represent their spoken language, they doubtless had knowledge of books in codex form, thanks to their contacts with Jews, Christians, Manicheans, and others whom they encountered in trade. The term *book* occurs frequently in the Qur'ān and may indicate (according to context) a book, anything written, or the Qur'ān itself. During Muhammad's life, the principal means of preserving the holy text was memorization. After his death, it was perceived that (for reasons including the death of Muhammad's contemporaries in battle and dialect differences) a standardization of the text was needed. According to Muslim tradition, this was begun under the first Caliph, Abu Bakr (d. 634), whose associates were commissioned to collect the various verses, written and oral. This work continued under the third Caliph, Uthman (d. 656), who directed that a universal text be established. At the time of Uthman, at least part of the scripture had been committed to writing. Some scholars have recently asserted that the text as we know it was not established until the eighth century.

With an accepted text thus established, the age of the Islamic manuscript can be said to have dawned. Muslims adopted the codex from the outset as the primary medium for copying the Qur'ān, using parchment in preference to papyrus. (Paper was introduced at a later date.) Muslims retained a high regard for the powers of memorization. In fact, to this day millions of Muslim schoolchildren learn to read and write by memorizing and copying the Qur'ān. The very meaning of "Qur'ān" is ambiguous in this regard, as it can be translated as a text to be read or, alternatively, recited. From the seventh century onward, there is evidence that copyists at the Umayyad court in Damascus and in certain important provincial towns such as Kufa in Iraq began to copy the Qur'ān in what is called Kufic script. This hand, angular and largely devoid of vowel indicators or other aids to reading, bears little resemblance to today's cursive Arabic *naskh* style of handwriting and typography. Early Qur'āns were copied on parchment, in Kufic script, in a horizontal codex format or as vertical *cahiers*.

In addition to the rapid development of the script in the century after Muhammad's death, the book arts (including binding, ink manufacture, and parchment preparation) advanced as well, stimulating a lively interest in books both religious and secular. Three elements contributed to this outpouring of books. First, the canon was expanded beyond the Qur'ān to include traditions of the Prophet and Islamic law. Secondly, history, biography, astronomy, astrology, medicine, philosophy, and literature were translated into Arabic. And demand was driven by book purchasers, from the lowly to the princely. The elite of the ruler's court and the wealthy merchant classes commissioned works to fill their libraries, which served scholars and were regarded as symbols of refinement. Scholars and laymen alike frequented booksellers' markets to read, copy, and discuss texts: vestiges of this trade can be found in many Islamic cities today.

Practitioners of the book arts and crafts from early Islam to the mid-nineteenth century (when modern methods of book production became firmly established in the major cultural centers) included calligraphers, copyists, painters, sketchers, gilders, cutters, and binders. The bookseller was often adept at some, if not all, of these crafts, and he was the essential middleman in this commerce.

The codex was introduced soon after the Prophet's death. The techniques and "feel" of Islamic binding differ from Coptic or Greek antecedents. Most characteristic of Islamic bindings is the foredge flap, which extends from the front cover to protect the entire foredge of the volume. This flap is usually made of two parts: a rectangular strip covers the foredge and is articulated to a triangular extension that tucks into the book. Thus only the top and bottom of the text block are left unprotected. Spines usually bore no title; instead, a brief title was written on the top or bottom edge. The book was usually shelved on its foredge. As is the case with Islamic arts and crafts generally, elite binding differed from more quotidian covers. Great sums were lavished on beautifully bound Qur'āns, adorned with elaborate tooling on leather covers. Little is known about early bookbinders, their styles or techniques. The earliest extant fragment of a book cover dates to ninth-century Egypt. Scholars have had to content themselves with citations in early works on the craft and the plentiful specimens available from the fourteenth century onward.

From earliest times, the manuscript took on a form that it did not relinquish until well after printing was established in the mid-nineteenth century. The text opens with the *basmallah*, the invocation of the name of God. After a few lines of introduction, which may include the titles, the text proper begins with the phrase *amma ba'd*: "and thus". Commentaries and super-commentaries are common. The original text might occupy the center of the page, with one or more commentaries written in the margins. Sometimes material is added to the end of the main work. An important feature of the manuscript, as well as early printed books, is the colophon, or tailpiece, providing the name of the author, the title of the work, the copyist, date, and place of copying. There is often reference to the regnant governor or patron.

Not all manuscripts were *chefs-d'oeuvre* such as we are accustomed to seeing in museums. The vast majority were workaday copies prepared for use by the author's students or other interested persons. Standards of transmission were fixed by tradition. In a typical scenario, the scholar would dictate his text to his students in the mosque. One or more of these would act as amanuensis. After the work was complete, the professor would review and correct what the scribe had written. Those who mastered the text would receive written permission (*ijazah*) to teach it.

No other aspect of book production has received more attention than manuscript ornamentation. Systematic scholarship in the field began in the early twentieth century and continues with Sheila Blair, Jonathan Bloom, and others. These scholars have produced valuable surveys of the history of paper, calligraphy, and miniature painting. Today, Ottoman book illustration receives much attention, perhaps because Turkish museums and libraries are generally accessible to scholars.

The layperson visiting an exhibit of Islamic book illustration or binding from Central Asia, Turkey, Iran, or Mogul India may be surprised to find that pictorial arts flourished in these Muslim territories. He or she may well ask what became of the well-known prohibition of animal or human images. Sir Thomas Arnold, writing in the 1920s, tackled this question squarely. He noted that because of religious strictures, book illustration enjoyed a lower status than calligraphy. While the Qur'ān is silent on the subject of figurative painting, the traditions of the Prophet (*hadith*) are unambiguously opposed to it. Arnold quoted an operative *hadith* from Bukhari (d. 870) to the effect that "the Prophet is reported to have said that those who will be most severely punished by God on the Day of Judgment will be the painters."

Underpinning this attitude toward representational painting is the idea that the painter blasphemes in "usurping the creative function of the Creator" (Arnold 1965: 6). Arnold argued simply that the monarchs and the wealthy, while flaunting the religious prohibition, took care to confine their appreciation and patronage of figurative art within the palace walls. This topic remains alive. In a 1996 report on the stance of modern theologians toward painting, Ahmad Issa concludes that the majority of modern religious authorities concur in the view of the ancients. In Issa's interpretation, however, painting is permissible as long as it does not lead to blasphemy. The traditionalists, and those who followed them through the centuries, found nothing wrong with non-representational art. Early Qur'āns featured geometric or vegetative ornamentation to mark the divisions of the text or adorn chapter headings. The arabesque has entered the English language from this source.

Few specimens of Islamic book illustration existed before 1200, although human forms appear in extant manuscripts produced in Baghdad in the years preceding the Mongol destruction of the city and its libraries. The successors of Genghis Khan formed dynasties of their own and patronized the book arts, including painting. Central Asian and Mogul courts in India achieved fame as much for their artistic books as for any other aspect of their culture. Later, in the sixteenth century, the Iranian court fostered similar interest in the high art of book illustration. The influence of both the Timurid and Persian painters was transmitted to the Ottoman court in Istanbul, where painting thrived from the seventeenth century to the end of the empire in 1924.

Beyond the problems of the anathema on painting, Blair and Bloom, in their important article "The Mirage of Islamic Art" (2003), list challenges in the field of Islamic arts in general, including book illustration. Among the points they raise are: the definition itself of the Islamic book; art history viewed through a colonial and postcolonial lens; the artificial dichotomy between architecture and other Islamic arts, such as calligraphy and painting; the cultural differences generated by geography and 1,400 years of history; the lack of biographical information about artists; the inaccessibility of art in museums and libraries; problems of authenticity, fakes, and revivals; and the illegibility of calligraphy to Western museum-goers and even scholars.

The most well-known miniaturists flourished from the early fifteenth century onward. Tamerlane (1336–1405) and his successors created great libraries and ateliers in what is now Iran, the Central Asian countries, Afghanistan, and India. The vast reach of the Mongol empire, extending from China westwards, led to the incorporation of Chinese motifs in Islamic painting. They are one of the distinct characteristics of what we call the Timurid style. As Blair and Bloom note (1994: 69):

> The Timurid visual vocabulary which had developed in Iran and Central Asia in the fifteenth century came to permeate the visual arts of other regions, notably Turkey and Muslim India, and there developed what has come to be called an International Timurid style characterized by chinoiserie floral motifs integrated into languid arabesques which became particularly important in the development of a distinct Ottoman style in the sixteenth century.

The apogee of Timurid miniature painting was reached with Kamal al-Din Behzad (d. c. 1536). Educated as a painter in a palace environment, he perfected his skill in the studios of Timurid Herat. When the Safavid Persians occupied the city, he moved to their capital, Tabriz, in western Iran, where he administered the Shah's library and scriptorium. He had many apt pupils and is credited with introducing a relaxed, humanistic style into the art form. Also associated with Herat was Crown Prince Baysungur (d. 1433), a patron who lavished attention and treasure on books and other arts. One report from Tabriz to Baysungur detailed the work done on twenty-two artistic projects, including manuscripts. Artisans included "painters, illuminators, calligraphers, binders, rulers and chest-makers, who worked individually and in teams"

(Blair and Bloom 2003: 59). Herat and Tabriz were joined by the central Iranian city of Shiraz as the chief centers of bookmaking artistry. However, artists dispersed eastward during the politically unsettled sixteenth century, fleeing the court of Tabriz to Central Asia and India.

Calligraphy was greatly admired by the Ottomans, practiced by many sultans, and remains a major art form in today's Turkey. Hafez Osman (d. 1698) is recognized as the master calligrapher of the Qur'ān. Blair and Bloom note that his style "remained the model for calligraphers of later generations; in the late nineteenth century manuscripts of the Koran penned by him were lithographed and circulated throughout the Islamic world" (2003: 248). Nevertheless, court painting continued, producing such high accomplishments as the *Shahnama-yi Al-I 'Uthman* (The Book of the Ottoman Dynasty).

The libraries of medieval Islam offer scholars useful ways of studying Muslim cultural life in general and the treatment of books in particular. For instance, Arnold Green (1988) uses the anthropological concept of diffusion to explain much about the nature of Islamic libraries. Diffusion involves the selective adoption of an activity or institution of one culture by another, often by reason of propinquity. In Green's view, Arabs, although conquerors in the Middle East, borrowed much from the conquered, including the institutionalization of book collections. In the seventh and eighth centuries, Arab Muslims used these collected religious writings, the Qur'ān, and *hadith*, for "introspective" purposes. Later, under the Umayyads, "extrospective" interest in the writings of the Greeks, Copts, and others led to translations into Arabic and thence to the building of libraries such as the Bayt al-Hikma in Damascus.

Large, well-endowed libraries containing universal learning were established in the Umayyid and Abbasid realms, notably Baghdad. Several factors underpinned the Abbasid florescence, including the substitution of paper for parchment and papyrus, and the encouragement of passing books and other property to pious foundations for the benefit of future generations. The famous translation movement of Harun al-Rashid and his son Ma'mun encouraged scholars of all faiths and nationalities, Christian, Jew, Manichean, and Zoroastrian. The fall of Baghdad to the Moguls in 1258 led to the destruction of its libraries.

The Fatimids of Cairo established significant libraries, the most well known of which is attached to al-Azhar Mosque. Founded in the tenth century, it is still in use. Another large library was founded by the Caliph al-Hakim in the early eleventh century in support of the study of secular sciences and the promotion of the dynasty's Shiite theology and law. These libraries were subject to the same vicissitudes as those of Baghdad and Damascus. They were sacked and their contents disbursed or destroyed. In Muslim Spain (Andalusia), al-Hakam II (d. 976) founded a library in Cordova that is said to have contained 400,000 volumes. The large Ottoman libraries of the fifteenth to nineteenth centuries were generally established for the study of Sunni orthodox theology and were housed in large mosques such as the Aya Sophia.

Chroniclers make much of the vast size of medieval libraries. Almeria in al-Andalusia boasted a collection of 400,000 volumes. Saladin's book booty from his Levantine campaigns is recorded at almost a million and a half volumes. One Fatimid library is said to have had collections of, variously, 120,000, 600,000, 1,000,000, and 2,600,000 volumes, depending on the account. The largest of all, a library in Lebanon, is reported to have contained three million books. These fantastical numbers are not trustworthy in themselves, but they may reflect the relative size of the collections and the passion for copying, collecting, and study.

Paper was the substrate of the Golden Age of Islamic civilization. According to Bloom (1999: 1), "papermaking between the eighth and fourteenth centuries wrought enormous change in such diverse realms as literature, mathematics, commerce and the arts, just as printing with movable type spurred the conceptual revolution whose effects are still being felt today." Accounts of the path of paper from China to the Middle East differ, but there is consensus that at some point Samarqand played a role in its transfer to the Muslim world. Central Asian paper factories exported to the central Islamic capitals. By the mid-eighth century, Baghdad had its own mills. Yemen followed, as did Egypt, which turned out paper of high quality for copyists. This new trade helped Egypt overcome the loss of its monopoly of papyrus that it had enjoyed for thousands of years.

Paper was cheaper to manufacture than rival materials, and thus made books available in unprecedented numbers. Religious authorities eventually approved it for the copying of the Qur'ān. Demand increased for scientific, literary, and theological works. Muslim jurists, compilers, and commentators used paper in works of *hadith*, Qur'ān interpretation, and legal rulings that helped spread and entrench the faith. Historians connect Fez in Morocco with the transfer of papermaking to southern Europe, whence it spread northward. Increasingly, European paper was imported into the Ottoman empire and Iran, a development attributed to production efficiencies adopted by European (primarily Italian) paper manufacturers, the high quality of the product, and disincentives to innovation and commerce imposed in Islamic realms. A contributing factor was the sensitivity of Italian merchants to the Islamic cultural milieu to which they were marketing. For instance, sizing and burnishing were accomplished to conform to local preferences, and watermarking displayed familiar Islamic devices, such as the crescent and stars.

As we move from consideration of manuscripts to printing, we shift from Baghdad and Cairo as political and cultural centers to Turkey, Iran, and India. The former two capitals were marginalized in the face of domination by the Ottomans or ambitious European powers: the central players were now in Istanbul, Iran, and Delhi. Printing with movable type was introduced into the Middle East by Jews, indigenous Christians, and Western missionaries. Jews working in Istanbul and Salonika issued the first printed books in the Ottoman empire in the 1490s. When Muslims eventually established presses of their own, they did so only in fitful bursts of production; manuscripts were produced in significant numbers well into the nineteenth century. The sultans had banned printed books as early as 1485, and in 1515 reissued the ban, which did not apply to religious minorities.

Scholars continue to speculate about the delayed adoption of printing in Muslim lands. One factor must have been the centrality of oral tradition and memorization of the Qur'ān. For centuries, literacy was acquired by reading and reciting the Qur'ān by heart. Even today, it is widely held that no other books are necessary. Secondly, illiteracy has been widespread throughout Islamic history. Only in the past half-century have literacy rates exceeded 50 percent in much of the region. Thirdly, the isolation of the Muslim world from the print-possessed culture of the West endured in many cases until the mid-nineteenth century. Ultimately, the advantages of the press were recognized by Islamic rulers, thanks to the travels of princes, educational missions sent to Europe, and the influence of colonial administrators and missionaries. Muhammad Ali in Egypt and the Ottoman sultans made printing a part of their modernization programs to gain advantages against other Muslim governors and the European powers. Finally, there is the argument from aesthetics. Early Arabic books printed in Europe and exported to the Middle East did not comport with Muslims' preference for the beauty of the manuscript. The handwritten book, while not always a work of art, was familiar in its script, paper, and binding.

It was not until 1727 that the sultan and religious authorities relented to grant a license to print to Ibrahim Muteferrika (d. 1745), who is recognized as the first Muslim to print anywhere in the Islamic world. He was born in Eastern Europe and converted to Islam when he came to Turkey. Muteferrika argued before the sultan and his jurists that the art of printing would make knowledge more accessible and strengthen the empire in the face of Europe. He received permission to publish, but with the proviso that books on Islam must not be printed. The ban was universal within the empire, extending to most Arab countries as well as southern Europe. Muteferrika's press issued seventeen titles in small print runs, including dictionaries and histories. He ceased printing because of ill health and the press fell into desuetude until it reopened in the 1790s when it was bought by the government. Though much honored today in Turkey, Muteferrika's success was modest. The land never caught fire with the passion to print.

The next noteworthy development occurred in Egypt under the modernizing rule of its governor, Muhammad Ali, the European-born warrior who seized power after Napoleon evacuated the country in 1801. Napoleon's press had printed public proclamations, a few books, and the first two periodicals to be printed in the Islamic world, *Courier d'Egypte* and *La Decade egyptienne.* The press made no discernible impact on either the general populace or the leading intellectuals of the city who were invited to watch it in operation. The machinery was destroyed during anti-French rioting in Cairo. After this brief introduction, twenty years passed before Muhammad Ali (r. 1805–49) made printing books and periodicals part of his program to modernize his army. He ordered a printing press to be set up in Bulaq, a suburb of the capital. This is the famous Bulaq Press that in the course of the next twenty years brought out approximately 250 titles in military science, popular literature such as the *One Thousand and One Nights,* and the Qur'ān. Machinery was acquired from Milan and Paris and workmen were dispatched to Europe to learn the printing trade, including type design and cutting. Books were published in Turkish (the official language), Arabic, and occasionally in Persian. During Muhammad Ali's rule, traditional objections to printing disappeared. Government employees were obliged to subscribe to the new official gazette, *al-Waqa'i' al-Misriyah*. Type designs were improved to suit local tastes. At the same time, a press had reopened in the Ottoman capital, and printing was being introduced into Iran and Muslim India.

Early nineteenth-century rulers and their religious confidants saw the advantages printing offered to *propagation fide*. Ottoman Sultan Mahmud II (r. 1808–39) ordered the printing of Islamic titles to encourage strictness in religious practice throughout his empire. Strengthening of orthodoxy stimulated private initiatives in Egypt, where printer–publishers issued pious works on spec for the government and for wealthy individuals who subsidized the printings as an act of devotion. But private secular publishing was slow to develop in the Muslim world. In Egypt, Turkey, and Iran, the main impetus for publishing came from the state printing houses, which issued periodicals that were sometimes recognizable as newspapers. These promulgated new regulations, keeping bureaucrats informed of the ruler's desires and sometimes printing news from abroad. Such "official gazettes" continue to be published today.

The Christian minority in Syria and Lebanon had been printing books for use by their sizable congregations from the first decade of the eighteenth century. The crucial figure in early Christian printing was Arab Catholic Abdallah al-Zahir (d. 1748). He established a printing operation in Aleppo for the Orthodox community, moving on to the mountain monastery at al-Shuayr in Lebanon after differences with the Orthodox authorities in Aleppo. The press did not print more than eight titles under al-Zahir. Another twenty-five titles were added in the second half of the eighteenth century. Al-Zahir's importance lay in his pioneering role in organizing the workshops, designing type, and training staff.

Missionary publishers made a significant contribution to the spread of education and culture among their communicants and, to a significant degree, to the larger public through training of personnel who went on to become not only printers but modern publishers, journalists, and intellectuals. Rome had been exporting books to its Arabic-speaking flock in the Middle East for centuries. Protestants, on the other hand, had no Arab brethren in the region and had to build their evangelical activities from the ground up. They chose Malta as the place to establish their press, and in 1825 the first products of the Church Missionary Society Mediterranean Mission were issued. These were spellers, primers, Bible extracts, and translations of English tracts badly translated into Arabic by William Jowett (d. 1855). Over time, the Arabic became more polished with the addition of Faris al-Shidiaq (d. 1887) and a staff of better-trained European missionaries. The type founts were also improved. The books, especially the primers in print runs of 8,000, were widely used in Middle Eastern schools.

American missionary efforts began at much the same time. The American Board of Commissioners for Foreign Missions, a Congregationalist enterprise from Boston, established presses in Izmir (Turkey) for printing in Armenian and Greek and in Beirut for Arabic, after first struggling to find roots in Malta. The American Press was at first hampered by lack of Arabic knowledge and poor-quality type. A breakthrough occurred in 1842 when Eli Smith (d. 1857) designed a new and attractive "American Arabic" fount that found acceptance throughout the region: it was even employed by French Catholic missionaries operating in Beirut. The willingness of the press to publish secular books attracted several writers and thinkers who would go on to become major figures in the "Arab Renaissance."

The 1990s were a particularly productive decade for research into the deeper implications of the Muslim print revolution in the second half of the nineteenth century. This research is well summarized and glossed by Juan Cole (2002), who gives full weight to the role of the press in the birth of Islamic modernity. Printed books gradually replaced manuscripts for the public display of ideas and ideologies, secular but also religious. He also credits the periodical press for promoting pan-Islamism, anti-colonial nationalism, women's emancipation, secular education, and increased political participation, if not mass mobilization among the illiterate and barely literate. Perhaps most important of all, print media broke forever the hold of the professional religious class on education, literacy, piety, and law, bringing the entire Islamic world into a discussion of its current condition and future.

In this period, Beirut became home to the first true, native, privately owned publishing industry. Leaders in the field were Butrus al-Bustani and Khalil Sarkis of the firms Matba'at al-Ma'arif and Matba'ah al-'Arabiyah. These men and their confrères were Christian, and largely interested in spreading modern secular knowledge. They included the Taqla brothers who, as refugees from Lebanon to Egypt, founded the famous *al-Ahram* newspaper. A Muslim effort was begun by 'Abd al-Qadir al-Qabbani (d. 1935) who published a newspaper, *Thamarat al-Funun,* as well as Arabic primers emphasizing Islamic themes. In Istanbul, al-Jawa'ib Press was founded in 1861, with the sultan's approval, by Faris al-Shidiaq, formerly of the Church Missionary Society. Al-Jawa'ib released many carefully redacted editions of the Arabic classics, which contributed to the Arabic literary revival. Its books look distinctively modern, with proper title pages, clear layout, and crisp founts: gone are the marginalia and cramped script.

Although a study has yet to be made of these private presses, a few generalizations are possible. In Lebanon, Egypt, and Iran, translation of European fiction, largely from the French, occurred at a rapid rate from the late nineteenth century until the end of the empire. In Istanbul, Cairo, Tabriz, and Teheran, works of natural science, European history, national histories, and politics were published. Among the most influential and controversial works was *Tahrir al-Mar'ah* by Egyptian journalist Ahmad Amin, a devout but free-thinking Muslim who advocated women's equality. Nationalism and different sorts of pan-Islamism were in the air in the late nineteenth century, exemplified best perhaps by the peripatetic Jamal al-Din al-Afghani. His charisma as a preacher and writer energized Muslims everywhere and caused much difficulty for the European occupiers and established monarchs. Al-Afghani's *Urwah al-Wuthqah* was printed in Cairo and reprinted throughout the region.

East of the Ottoman empire, in Iran and southern Asia, publishing took somewhat different paths. As far as we can tell, the first Iranian book set in type dates from 1817. As in the Ottoman capital and provinces, the establishment of the press was impelled by political competition from European powers. Tabriz was the center of early printing:

the governor of the province imported a press from Russia and sent workmen to England and Russia for training. A key printer, Miraz Zayn al-'Abidin, moved to Teheran where he printed about thirty works, many of them religious, over fourteen years. By 1844, his activities were taken over by his apprentices. It is safe to speculate that these early typographical presses were private businesses, although closely linked to high-ranking figures at court who commissioned the imprints.

Movable type in Iran and India was soon followed and eclipsed by lithographic printing. According to Ulrich Mazolph (2001), the first Iranian lithograph was a Qur'ān printed in Tabriz in 1832–3, followed by more works of piety and some Persian classics. Presses were set up in Teheran later in the decade. Lithographs supplanted typographically produced books during the middle decades of the nineteenth century, for aesthetic and economic reasons. Scribes were able to reproduce the flowing *nastaliq* script beloved of readers and calligraphers alike. Text was copied on special paper and transferred to the lithographic stones that were plentiful in Iran. Lithographic equipment was cheaper to acquire and operate than typographical presses, and lent itself to reproducing illustrations. If the basic intent of printing was to duplicate manuscripts, then lithography was the perfect technique. A list published in the early 1890s reveals the scope of lithographic books on the market: they include science, technology, history, linguistics, and even books for children. Lithographic printing did not pass from the Iranian scene until the 1950s. The technique is still preferred in Pakistan and among Muslims in India.

Iran's first newspaper, *Kaghaz-i Akhbar*, appeared in 1837. The first government newspaper was begun in 1851 and was followed by other long-lived official periodicals, some lithographed and some typeset. Their most noteworthy long-term impact was their influence on the development of a modernized Persian prose style and lexicon.

Ian Proudfoot (1997) has extended the detailed study of print culture beyond what are called the Central Islamic Lands (the Arab countries, Turkey, and Iran) to India and the European colonies of Southeast Asia. Each area has a distinct history that only occasionally parallels the Middle Eastern countries, but they share several common features. In India, a Catholic mission press was established in the mid-sixteenth century. Typography spread slowly, but at first not at all among the Muslim population. Protestant missionaries and East India Company personnel established presses, cut types, and experimented with printing books in the *nastaliq* style in Persian and other languages. The first Muslim-run press was not established until 1819, in the princely state of Oudh. "Then," writes Proudfoot, "suddenly everything changed" when the Company imported lithographic presses for its administrative regions and supplied textbooks in several languages including Urdu, the principal language of Muslims. The Muslim community adopted the technique as it own, to the extent that it has been called "a Muslim technology." Book production exploded in all parts of India, but especially in the north. Research by Proudfoot shows that "Lucknow alone had more than a dozen lithographic presses in 1848, all in Muslim hands. By that time the presses of Lucknow–Cawnpore alone had published about 700 titles, some in up to ten editions, mainly comprising students' books, polemics, and religious tracts" (Proudfoot 1997: 163). The reasons for the success of lithography were the same as in Iran.

Although starting later than Indian Muslims, Malaysian, Indonesian, and Singaporean Muslims were also smitten with lithography. Their first printed book was a Qur'ān issued in 1854. From then on, the lithographic press grew into a veritable cottage industry. Religious works as well as entertaining folk tales were published and distributed through sales networks that included traveling vendors, agents, and mail order.

Thus, the contrast between the print experience of the eastern and western Muslims is striking. First, the lithographic press came to dominate the early decades of printing in the east, while it was a minor factor further west. Secondly, printing in the east was quickly commercialized and became a thriving (if not lucrative) trade, while in the west it remained largely (if not entirely) in government hands or under government control. Thirdly, book content in the east was largely Islamic, while in the west it could be technical, historical, or literary as well as religious.

In the turbulent twentieth century, the Muslim press spread the call for independence from foreign rule imposed by force and ratified as mandates after World War I. Western-educated nationalists, radicals, and women opened newspapers in Egypt, Iran, India, and elsewhere. Largely illiterate, the majority of the population listened to the recitation of these ideas in coffee shops, mosques, and other public places. During the turmoil of Iran's Constitutional Revolution of 1906 the press had a major impact on the national movement and government reform. Ahmad Amin's call for women's rights cited earlier was translated in Iran and provoked rebuttals from religious leaders. Later, a tidal wave of Islamic discussion was generated by Sayyid Qutb, who was executed in 1966 for his extreme Islamist views, and whose books are read today throughout the Islamic world. In a more secular vein, the works of Egyptian scholar Taha Husayn (d. 1973) are widely reprinted, as are the novels of Nobel Laureate Najib Mahfuz (d. 2006).

Soon after private Muslim publishers emerged, governments became aware that they posed a threat to the established order, and imposed press laws. In Turkey, printers required a license from 1857. Iran had equivalent laws, which remained in force in one way or another until the fall of the Shah in 1979. Thereafter, the Islamic Republic was even charier of free press and media. Today, post-publication censorship is widespread throughout the region, imposed by ministries of culture or information. Even an Islamic classic such as *al-Futuhat al-Makkiyah* by the thirteenth-century mystic Muhi al-Din Ibn al-'Arabi, published by the Egyptian government publishing house, was pulled from the market after protests by conservative religious leaders. Al-Azhar Mosque, recognized by millions as the headquarters of Sunni orthodoxy, regularly reviews not only editions of the Qur'ān, but also other books published in or imported to Egypt. The Arab book trade is dominated by large, state-owned publishing houses, such as the General Egyptian Book Organization and Dar al-Ma'arif. Governments usually own the largest newspapers, publish the majority of books, organize the book fairs, and award prizes. Censorship is a sad fact of life and is a constant concern of authors and private publishers.

Numerous barriers and inconveniences confront private publishers and authors, including poorly administered copyright laws, custom and currency barriers, low rates of literacy (50 percent in Egypt), as well as political and religious censorship. Moreover, the industry is poorly integrated horizontally. Publishers generally market only their own publications, in effect keeping them in the condition of printer–publishers. General bookstores are rare, and adaptation to electronic commerce is slow. Book bazaars, such as those in Baghdad and Tunis, may be picturesque but are not models of efficiency. In Istanbul, the famous Sahaflar book market retains little of its former vitality. Yet publishers are relatively numerous and free in Lebanon and Turkey, and Egyptian publishers enjoy a wide market in the Arab world.

As may be expected in so vast a region, library service varies greatly. Most countries follow a Western pattern, with a flagship national library and more or less vital branch and provincial libraries. The expansion of higher education in recent decades has required new and better-equipped university libraries, though many countries have meager funds for adequate services and collection building. The situation is better in the oil-rich states of the Arabian peninsula, and at the American universities in Beirut and Cairo. The new Bibliotheca Alexandrina in Alexandria seeks to become a model of service in the electronic age as well as a center for researchers attracted by its collections and scholarly programs.

References and Further Reading

Arnold, Thomas (1965) *Painting in Islam*. New York: Dover.

Atiyeh, George N. (ed.) (1995) *The Book in the Islamic World*. Washington: Library of Congress.

Blair, Sheila and Bloom, Jonathan (1994) *The Art and Architecture of Islam 1250–1800*. New Haven: Yale University Press.

— and — (2003) "The Mirage of Islamic Art." *Art Bulletin*, 85 (1): 152–84.

Bloom, Jonathan (1999) "Revolution by the Ream." *Saudi Aramco World*, 50: 1–9.

Bosch, Gulnar, Carswell, John and Petherbridge, Guy (1981) *Islamic Bindings and Bookmaking*. Chicago: University of Chicago Press.

Cole, Juan (2002) "Printing and Urban Islam in the Mediterranean World, 1890–1920." In Leila Fawaz, et al. (eds.), *Modernity and Culture from the Mediterranean to the Indian Ocean*, pp. 344–64. New York: Columbia University Press.

Green, Arnold (1988) "The History of Libraries in the Arab World: A Diffusionist Model." *Libraries and Culture*, 25: 454–73.

Ibn al-Nadim (1970) *The Fihrist of al-Nadim*, trans. B. Dodge. New York: Columbia University Press.

Issa, Ahmad Mohammad (1965) *Painting in Islam*. New York: Dover.

Marzolph, Ulrich (2001) *Narrative Illustration in Persian Lithographed Books*. Leiden: Brill.

Pedersen, Johannes (1984) *The Arabic Book*. Princeton: Princeton University Press.

Proudfoot, Ian (1997) "Mass Producing Houri's Moles." In Peter G. Riddell and Tony Street (eds.), *Islam: Essays on Scripture, Thought and Society*, pp. 161–86. Leiden: Brill.

The Codex in the West
400–2000

13

The Triumph of the Codex: The Manuscript Book before 1100

Michelle P. Brown

The two major vehicles for writing in classical antiquity were the papyrus scroll (*rotulus* or *volumen*), used for formal literary texts, and sets of wooden or wax tablets (*tabulae* or *codex*) for informal and pragmatic uses. Tablets were not confined to antiquity; they continued alongside other media throughout succeeding centuries – an important "missing link" in the written record (Brown 1994). One of the earliest examples of writing from Ireland consists of extracts from the Psalms inscribed at the beginning of the seventh century upon thin, oblong, wax tablets (the Springmount Bog Tablets), probably by an aspirant priest who was memorizing them to become "psalteratus" (being able to recite the Psalms from memory). Other early medieval examples include decorated diptychs of bone or ivory covered with wax, upon which liturgical feasts were inscribed. Medieval accounting tablets survive, and tiny sets of tablets could be worn as girdle-books, as notebooks, devotional talismans, or love tokens.

The codex assumed respectability along with Christianity during the fourth century, when it became the state religion of the Roman empire. Books were no longer a cheap alternative favored by a persecuted underclass, but honored receptacles of sacred text within a powerful established religion. Leaves of wood were too cumbersome for lengthy texts and folded sheets of papyrus cracked, so techniques of book production developed featuring the use of parchment (sheep or goatskin) and vellum (calfskin). Emperor Constantine (who began to promote Christianity from 313) ordered Bibles for his foundations, for prestigious churches needed prestigious books – the chosen vehicle for Christian Scripture, as the scroll was for the Judaic Torah. Codex Sinaiticus (BL Add. MS 43725), the earliest extant full Bible, probably made in fourth-century Caesarea, features a four-column page layout resembling a section of unfurled scroll, indicating technological adaptation, but this soon gave way to a one- or two-column page (de Hamel 2001; Brown 2006b).

From the fifth century, Scripture began to be illustrated (such as the Byzantine Vienna Genesis, Vienna, ÖNB, Cod. Theol. Gr. 31, and the Syriac Rabbula Gospels, Florence, Bibl. Medicea-Laur., MS Plut. I.56; Weitzmann 1977; de Hamel 1986; Nordenfalk 1988; Brown 2006b) and penned in gold and silver on purple pages, opulent materials imparting symbolic stature to tomes such as the sixth-century Italian Codex Brixianus (Brescia, Bibl. Civica Queriniana) and the Canon Tables painted on gold-stained vellum in Constantinople around 600 (BL Add. MSS 5111–12). Pictures, not favored by classical bibliophiles, also appeared in old favorites such as the Italian fifth-century illustrated copies of works by Virgil, Terence, and Homer (Weitzmann 1977; Wright 1993).

In the sixth century, the flexible quill (*penna*) replaced the reed pen (*calamus*), completing the technological revolution. The codex has remained the primary means of publication ever since. The scroll endured for storing cumulative data, such as financial records, and display contexts, such as genealogical and heraldic rolls and Italian eleventh-century Exultet Rolls, which were unfurled over the lectern during the dedication of the Paschal Candle (their images upside down, so that they could be "read" by the congregation). The text no longer ran horizontally along the roll, but vertically, like the scrolling computer screen.

The fifth and sixth centuries witnessed the emergence of successor states and the evolution of the Byzantine empire from the old eastern Roman empire. Urbanized classical civilization gave way to new networks of power bases and intellectual centers. Many towns became bishoprics and were joined by rural manors, royal citadels, and monasteries. Monastic rules proliferated, most including study and scribal work, but the growing popularity of the Benedictine rule from the ninth century increasingly fostered organized copying within the scriptorium (writing office).

The Roman system of scripts had consisted of capitals, uncials, half-uncials, cursive half-uncials/quarter-uncials, and cursive minuscules. "Upper case" letters occupying the space between two lines, such as "D" and "Q," are considered "majuscule," and "lower case" letters with ascending and descending strokes, such as "d" and q," "minuscule." These, and other paleographical and codicological practices, were adapted or replaced by a plethora of local variations favored by individual monastic scriptoria or monastic federations, and by the chanceries established by the papacy, the Byzantine Exarch of Ravenna, and the Merovingian dynasty of Gaul (Brown 1990: 32–47).

Book production continued in the Middle East and North Africa, with distinctive codicological practices and styles of script and illumination developing in Caesarea, Armenia, Georgia, Syria, Coptic Egypt, Nubia, and Ethiopia (Badawry 1978; Nersessian 2001; Brown 2006b). The bibliographical traditions of their churches, and of Hebrew scribes, who eschewed figural representation in their Scriptures, continued despite the Islamic conquest of the "fertile crescent" of the eastern and southern Mediterranean from the seventh century onward (Avrin 1991; Déroche and Richard 1997). Islamic book production did not really get underway until the ninth century, avoiding "idolatrous" figural imagery and evolving sacred calligraphy to glorify the Word. Scholars such as Avicenna (d. 1037) and Averroës (d. 1198) did much to preserve and extend classical learning, including the works of Aristotle which were lost to the early medieval West and reintroduced through contact with Islam during the Crusades.

In the West, public literacy contracted; book production was no longer undertaken by secular scribes and publishers but was perpetuated by the Church. The pagan Celts and Germans had proto-writing systems of their own, ogam and runes, inspired by Roman writing, but used them only for commemorative or talismanic purposes, preferring to cultivate the memory and oral literacy (Brown 1998). Their conversion to full literacy accompanied their conversion to Christianity. As we shall see, faced with the challenges of learning Latin as a foreign language, and how to write, they made major contributions to book production. Their enthusiastic recognition of its potential, along with that of their eastern counterparts, gave the book much of its distinctive appearance and apparatus – the codex was here to stay.

Visigothic Spain fostered early Christian scholarship through the writings of scholars such as Isidore of Seville (whose works included encyclopedic classification of subjects such as natural history, building on Pliny's work), and poetry could help promote resistance to invasion: Orosius' *History Against the Pagans* and Prudentius' *Psychomachia* (an allegorical battle between the virtues and vices). Visigothic scribes developed a distinctive minuscule script, which survived into the twelfth century, signaling independence from Carolingian authority and the perpetuation of Christian identity under Islamic rule (Brown 1990: 32–3, 46–7; Walker 1998). In the 780s, Beatus of Liebana composed his influential commentary upon the Apocalypse, and the raw energy and Picasso-esque images in its tenth- to twelfth-century copies made in scriptoria such as San Salvador de Tavara and Silos, speak eloquently of Mozarabic culture.

In Italy, power passed to the Byzantine province of Ravenna, the papacy in Rome, the Ostrogoths and the Lombardic kingdoms of northern Italy and Benevento. The romanophile Ostrogothic kingdom did not survive, weakened by its espousal of the Arian heresy, but its disaffected Roman officials composed influential works: Boethius' *Consolation of Philosophy*, written in a prison cell, and the exegesis and *Institutiones* of Cassiodorus, who retired to found the monastery of Vivarium, devoted to studying and copying Scripture. Cassiodorus' injunctions to scribes proved influential, including "the scribe preaches with the pen" and "unleashes tongues with the fingers" and "each word written is a wound on Satan's body," asserting that the pen is mightier than the sword (Brown 2003). Such works span the transition from late antiquity to the early Middle Ages. The Lombards fostered their own Beneventan minuscule, which survived until 1300 and beyond (Brown 1990: 32–3, 116–19), along with a Germanic love of animal ornament, whilst the eighth-century Codex Beneventanus, a splendid Gospel-book, its canon tables set within classical marble columns, is a tribute to the more classicizing book production.

In Rome, arts and learning were given a boost under Pope Gregory the Great (d. 604). This great missionary, intent upon reviving Rome's western empire in Christian guise, was a gifted theologian whose letters, exegesis, and *Cura pastoralis* exerted a lasting impact. Books produced in his Rome displayed elegant uncial script, with initials featuring Christian symbols such as crosses and fish, and sometimes illustrations: portraits of the evangelists as classical authors and registers of biblical scenes, such as those preserved in the St. Augustine Gospels, traditionally thought to have accompanied Augustine on his mission to Anglo-Saxon England in 597 and still used at the installation of his successors as Archbishop of Canterbury (Ganz 2002).

Another force was Ireland, which received Christianity during the fifth century. Over the next three hundred years, Irish scribes significantly developed the book arts (although the earliest extant books date from c.600). They introduced word separation and systematic punctuation to clarify legibility – inspired by the injunctions of Isidore of Seville and Bede to engage in silent reading to facilitate meditation and comprehension, in addition to the classical emphasis upon oratorical reading out loud (Parkes 1992). They also began enlarging and decorating initials to mark text divisions and developed half-uncial script for Scripture and calligraphic minuscule for less formal purposes.

The Anglo-Saxons, whom the Irish helped to convert via monasteries such as Iona and Lindisfarne, further developed the range of scripts under renewed influence from Rome via centers such as Canterbury and Wearmouth/Jarrow, adding capitals and uncials, perfecting half-uncials and evolving several grades of minuscule. Within this system of scripts, termed "Insular" (i.e. of the islands of Britain and Ireland, c.550–850), form was suited to function: it was generally inappropriate to use the same script for a Gospel-book as for a letter (Brown 1990, 2007b; Bately et al. 1993). The role of the scribe was varied: Bede described himself as simultaneously "author, notary and scribe" as a manifestation of his monastic humility, and St. Columba and others achieved public acclaim as saintly hero-scribes (Brown 2003). For copying the Gospels was seen as the highest scribal calling, in accordance with the teachings of Cassiodorus, Cummian, and others, in which the scribe became an evangelist by contributing to the process of transmission and, by study and meditation upon the text (*ruminatio* and *meditatio*), became a living ark of Scripture and might glimpse the divine (*revelatio*). The Lindisfarne Gospels, one of the most elaborate books of its age, was accordingly the work of a single gifted artist-scribe (probably Eadfrith, bishop of Lindisfarne, 698–721), his work conducted not in the eremitic solitude of the eastern desert fathers, but in the context of an active communal monastic life (Brown 2003). Classical and medieval authors rarely penned their own works, but some of these monastic author–scribes were exceptions. Patterns of book production varied, however. The Book of Kells, probably made on Iona c.800, was the work of a team of at least eight (Alexander 1978).

The power of writing was reinforced by the iconic nature of the book in a religious context. Secular rulers were quick to employ it, enlisting the support of the Church in penning law codes, charters, and genealogies to legitimize their rule (Kelly 1990; Webster and Brown 1997). The earliest English seventh-century documents are written not in the cursive scripts of the late Roman bureaucracy, as elsewhere, but in uncials used for Scripture. In the early ninth century, Archbishop Wulfred of Canterbury could assert in court that his impressively penned charter contained the written proof of the matter, establishing the primacy of written evidence at law over age-old oral witness (Brown 2002). Forgeries soon flourished.

Fascination with the remnants of antiquity led monastic scribes to preserve what they could of classical learning, imported to northern Europe from Italy, Spain, Asia Minor, and North Africa, copying works by Pliny, Dioscorides, and the Grammarians, as well as writings by Christian poets and the Church Fathers (Bately et al. 1993). Such learning combined with their own imaginative cultures to produce new works of poetry, prayer, exegesis, science, and history (such as the great Irish epic the *Táin Bó Cuailgne*, the poetry and correspondence of Columbanus, and the Anglo-Saxon *Dream of the Rood*, Aldhelm's *Riddles* and Bede's *Historia ecclesiastica gentis Anglorum*). There was no inherent resistance to the learning of pagan antiquity on the part of such Christian authors (any constraints being due more to lack of availability) and there was little segregation between the sacred and the secular. Bede (d. 735), one of the leading post-Roman scholars, did not write biblical studies, history, or scientific works (such as his "On the Nature of Time") per se, but was engaged in a more integrated exploration of the divine plan, addressing the why as well as the how.

Copying past works led Insular scholars to apply the lessons learned to their own literary cultures, making Old Irish and Old English amongst the earliest written Western vernaculars. One of St. Augustine's first tasks was to write down the law code of King Ethelberht of Kent – inventing written Old English in the process by adding Germanic runic symbols to the Latin alphabet. On his deathbed, Bede was translating St. John's Gospel into English (Brown 2003), free of the persecution later directed at Wycliffe and Tyndale – everything possible was employed to share the Good News (Old English "Godspell").

The Middle Eastern churches also employed their own languages (Armenian, Syriac, Coptic, Ethiopic, Georgian), even for Scripture, but in the West the primacy of the "sacred languages" – Hebrew, Greek, and Latin (in effect, the Roman vernacular) – generally prevailed, although knowledge of Hebrew was rare amongst scholars and Greek patchy (Herren 1988; Brown 2005, 2006b). The reluctance of the East and West Franks and of Italy to promote the vernacular has been ascribed to the gradual evolution of the Romance languages from late Roman latinity and to Carolingian promotion of Latin, and caroline minuscule, as a means of cultural cohesion and control throughout the territories forged into the Carolingian empire (McKitterick 1989, 1990). In this way, German identity could not be unduly distinguished from that of Gaul, with its marked Roman legacy and mixed population (Brown 2005).

Insular vernacular writers followed in the steps of Ulfila, apostle to the Goths, who translated the Gospels into Gothic as part of his fourth-century mission to Moesia (Brown 2005, 2006b). His translation survives in the splendid Codex Argenteus (Uppsala UB, DG I), written in Ravenna for the Ostrogothic king, Theodoric, in the early sixth century (Webster and Brown 1997: 242–3). The adaptation of the Greek alphabet to produce those of Armenia and Georgia is similarly ascribed to the missionary St. Mesrob during the early fifth century (Brown 1998: 39). Cyrillic script, used for over sixty languages, is descended from the forty-character, Greek-based, Glagolitic alphabet, ascribed to St. Cyril (c.827–69), who was sent from Byzantium as a missionary to the Slavs at the request of King Ratislaw of Moravia (Brown 1998: 39). Other aspects of Greek influence can likewise be seen in the way in which books from these regions were constructed, written, and decorated.

The appearance of the Insular book was equally distinctive and indebted to varied cultural sources (Alexander 1978; Webster and Backhouse 1991; Brown 2006b, 2007b). The well-understood hierarchy of scripts, combined with pen-drawn initials and display lettering, enlivened even modest volumes, whilst the great Gospel-books (such as the Book of Durrow, Dublin, Trinity College Library, MS 57; the Lindisfarne Gospels, BL Cotton MS Nero D. iv; and the Book of Kells, Dublin, Trinity College Library, MS 58) blended influences from Celtic, Germanic, European, Byzantine, and North African art in decorated incipit pages in which the word exploded across the page as an iconic image in its own right, carpet-pages resembling prayer-mats (sometimes used in northern Europe as well as the Middle East), arcaded canon tables and evangelist miniatures in which the Gospel writers were depicted by author portraits and/or by their symbols (Henderson 1987; Brown 2003). The Insular "historiated" (storytelling) initial, in which the letter contained an illustration of the text, integrated text and image, and some full-page miniatures appeared, often containing layers of meaning. Hierarchies of initials marked chapters, lections, and the like, whilst decorative line-fillers and run-over symbols further articulated text layout.

Some works were consciously "romanizing," notably the three great Ceolfrith Bibles made in the Northumbrian twin monasteries of Wearmouth/Jarrow, one of which (Codex Amiatinus, Florence, Bibl. Medicea-Laurenziana, MS Amiatino 1) was taken by Abbot Ceolfrith as a present to the Pope in 716 and subsequently considered the work of Italo-Byzantine, rather than English, craftsmen (Webster and Brown 1997; Brown 2006b, 2007b). Yet it was no antiquarian facsimile but a dynamic feat of editorial scholarship, probably led by Bede. In eighth- and ninth-century Southumbria (Mercia), Insular features blended with Byzantine and nascent Carolingian classicism and near-eastern exoticism, reflecting the international aspirations of its rulers (as in the Barberini Gospels, Vatican, Bibl. Apost., MS barb. lat. 570, and the Royal Bible, BL Royal MS 1. E. vi; Brown 2002).

Insular nuns also made books. Two prayer-books (the Royal Prayerbook, BL Royal MS 2. A. xx, and the Book of Nunnaminster, BL Harl. MS 2965) made in Mercia in the early ninth century, show signs, from their language, devotional themes, and provenance, of being written by and for women. Abbess Eadburh and the nuns of Minster-in-Thanet supplied books to St. Boniface in the German mission fields during the early eighth century and may have helped furnish books to major English churches, just as the nuns of Jouarre, Chelles, and Faremoutiers-en-Brie had in Merovingian Gaul (Brown 2002, 2006b).

Merovingian and early Carolingian books featured colorful initials composed of fish, birds, and beasts and, from the late eighth century, human figures (as in the Sacramentary of Gellone, Paris, BNF, MS Lat. 12048). Scripts varied with scriptoria, influential local varieties including Luxeuil minuscule and Corbie "ab" minuscule (Brown 1990: 32–47). During the late eighth century, experiments to produce a more regular, standardized script occurred, initially at Corbie (with "Maurdramnus minuscule" under Abbot Maurdramnus, d. 781) and at Charlemagne's court at Aachen, which harbored scholars and craftsmen from as far afield as Ireland and Byzantium (Ganz 1990; McKitterick 1994). Amongst the earliest examples of the cultural renaissance they produced were the Godescalc Evangelistary of c.781–3 (Paris, BNF, MS Lat. 1203), which echoes Insular style, the works of the Palace School (such as the Coronation Gospels in

Vienna), illuminated by Italo-Byzantine artists, and the great Court School Gospelbooks made around the time of Charlemagne's imperial coronation in 800 (including the Soissons Gospels, Paris, BNF, MS Lat. 8850, and the Harley Golden Gospels, BL Harley MS 2788).

These sumptuous volumes, designed for display on the altar or as prestigious gifts (such as the Dagulf Psalter, made around 800 as a gift for the Pope, Vienna, ÖNB, Cad. 1861), ooze gold and purple, recalling imperial Rome and Byzantium. They fuse the figural and architectural styles of classical antiquity with the exoticism of the early Christian East and the symbolic pattern-making of "barbarian" northern Europe, building upon Insular tendencies introduced via Insular mission churches such as Echternach, Fulda, Salzburg, Luxeuil, St. Gall, and Bobbio, which in turn transmitted continental influence to Britain and Ireland (Bischoff 1979; Brown 2007b).

The Carolingians standardized script, the multipurpose caroline minuscule spreading throughout Carolingia as part of a campaign to disseminate approved versions of scriptural and liturgical texts, fostering cultural cohesion and common religious observance throughout its disparate territories (McKitterick 1989, 1990). The scriptorium of Tours, established by Alcuin of York, played a leading role, producing massive singlevolume Bibles (large teams producing three such tomes per year) which were circulated to other scriptoria (Kessler 1977; Ganz 1990). These include the Moutiers-Grandval Bible (BL Add. MS 10546) and the Vivian Bible (Paris, BNF, MS Lat. 1). The edition of the Bible produced by Alcuin (heavily indebted to Jerome's Vulgate and the Northumbrian Ceolfrith Bibles), along with that by Bishop Theodulf of Orléans, underpinned subsequent medieval biblical studies. The Tours (or Alcuin) Bibles made during the early ninth century also contained full-page miniatures, arranged in registers (like cartoon-strips), recalling early Christian art.

Nonetheless, the Carolingian stance on imagery was ambivalent. They used it to emphasize the interdependence of Church and state, but were uncomfortable about idolatry. In 787, the Byzantine Council of Nicaea restored the use of images after a period of iconoclasm that had endured since the 720s (and temporarily recurred during the early ninth century). The Carolingian *Libri Carolini*, composed soon after by Theodulf of Orléans, asserted the primacy of text over images, which were permitted in accordance with the teachings of Gregory the Great (who wrote, c.600, to Serenus, bishop of Marseilles, that "in images the illiterate read") but deemed to possess no inherent holiness or iconic value (Diebold 2000: 100–1, 117–18; Brown 2006b). Copies of Scripture produced from this time until around 810 are noticeably devoid of pictures of the divine, preferring biblical illustrations or evangelist portraits and paving the way for substitute royal iconography (Mütherich and Gaehde 1976).

The Carolingian expansion absorbed many fine monastic libraries and archives containing much classical learning which had languished undiscovered whilst book production focused on supplying religious texts. Some classics would not have survived had they not been copied at this time. Insular and Merovingian scribes had preserved such works, when available, but many more now came back into scholarly circulation, including Cicero's *Aratea* (his Latin translation of the Greek *Phenomena* of Aratus, dealing with the constellations and their mythology), Vitruvius on architecture, and medical texts by Dioscorides and Pseudo-Apuleius. Hrabanus Maurus' oeuvre included *carmina figurata*, word poems in which figural images were superimposed upon grids of letters, isolating some to form a poem within a poem – a genre popularized by Emperor Constantine's court poet, Porphyrius (McKitterick, 1994). Other classical works were preserved within Islamic territories; some survived only in fragmentary form in anthologies or lists compiled by scholars such as the Byzantine authors Stobaeus (fifth century) and Photius (ninth century); some were lost forever; others, such as Archimedes, are still being recovered through archaeology and digital image enhancement techniques.

Revived classical devices included Tironian *notae*, the shorthand system of Cicero's secretary, Tiro, some symbols of which were also used by Insular scribes. The Irish system of punctuation using *distinctiones* – a system in which either an escalating number of points (. .. ...) or the positioning of a point on the line (low, medial, or high) denoted a rising value of pause – was extended by the introduction of the *punctus versus* (;), the *punctus elevatus* (a point with a tick above), and the *punctus interrogativus* (?). Neumes were introduced by the Carolingians to record music, previously taught orally. Glossing (a technique used for language teaching in England and Ireland), and parallel texts alongside one another on the page, also enjoyed popularity in Carolingian schoolrooms and scriptoria, as did diagrams. Codicology (the way in which books were physically constructed) favored late Roman practices: thinly prepared membrane with a marked distinction in appearance between hair and flesh sides, necessitating care in the arrangement of quires (gatherings) to ensure that like faced like when the book was open (so that a bifolium with its flesh-side uppermost had to have the next bifolium placed on top of it with its flesh-side downwards, and so forth). Bifolia were pricked and ruled one at a time, before folding, although templates were sometimes used to speed up and standardize the ruling (Bischoff 1979; Brown 1991; Bately et al. 1993).

Insular scriptoria, conversely, used skins that had not been scraped down so far and exhibited little distinction between hair and flesh sides. Insular skins were therefore beiger, with a suede-like knap. Insular quires were usually arranged with four bifolia folded into gatherings of eight leaves, with hair-side outermost and with flesh facing hair throughout. Pricking and ruling were conducted after the quire was folded and ruled with a hard point, so that the impression penetrated through the quire. Such codicological variations can indicate whether an Insular scribe was working abroad or at home (Brown 1991; Bately et al. 1993), although Insular scribes sometimes experimented with late antique or continental codicological methods, usually in romanophile contexts, as at Wearmouth/Jarrow c.700, and Kent and Mercia c.800 under Carolingian influence. During the tenth century, Carolingian methods were more generally introduced into England.

Ninth-century Carolingian authors, such as the Irishmen Duns Scotus and John Eriugena, Walafrid Strabo, the Visigoth Theodulf, the Italian Paul the Deacon, and Einhard (Charlemagne's biographer), composed new works of scholarship, poetry, history, and theology. The Carolingian empire's impetus toward cultural renovation outlived its territorial reality. Frankish inheritance laws partitioned it between Char-lemagne's grandsons: Charles the Bald, Louis II, and Lothar. Competition split the empire and laid the foundations of France and Germany. Amongst the most opulent ninth-century books were the First Bible of Charles the Bald or Vivian Bible (made at Tours in 846 as a gift to Charles from Abbot Vivian) and the Lothar Gospels (Paris, BNF, MS Lat. 266), also made at Tours c.850 as a gift for its monastic community from Charles's rival, Lothar, to extend his influence. Such books depicted the ruler enthroned, like Christ in Majesty, his power acknowledged by supporting figures from Church and state or personifications of subject territories.

A particularly significant Carolingian book is the Utrecht Psalter (van der Horst et al. 1996), made nears Reims c.830, containing an extensive illustrative cycle of outline drawings. It inspired several Psalters made at Canterbury from the early eleventh century, when it was imported to England, through the twelfth century. These include the Harley Psalter, the Trinity Psalter, and the Eadwine Psalter. It is extremely rare for an exemplar and its "copies" to survive, enabling them to be compared – hence the Utrecht Psalter's fame. The first English version, the Harley Psalter (BL Harley MS 603) was made at Christ Church in the early eleventh century by a team of artists and scribes including Eadui Basan (Eadui the Fat), one of the foremost and most prolific Anglo-Saxon artist-scribes (Noel 1996; van der Horst et al. 1996). The images were adapted to emphasize different theological nuances, colored outline drawings replaced ink draw-ings, and details of Anglo-Saxon implements were introduced, situating the English within the biblical landscape. The words presented an even greater challenge, for the text used at Canterbury (Jerome's Romanum) differed from the prototype's Gallicanum – so the words were not the same. Utrecht was written in rustic capitals and Harley in English caroline minuscule – so the letter size differed. This complicated the planning of the "copy" to ensure that text and image marched in tandem. Usually scribes pre-pared layout, but in Harley it is possible to see the artists rebelling and seizing the initiative, thereby squeezing the script into inadequate spaces – at which point the scribes complained. Utrecht was disbound to enable the team to see "how it ticked," but 150 years later the scriptorium was still struggling with the project, although it had learned a lot about book production in the process.

Carolingia influenced England in earnest from the late ninth century. Viking raids disrupted northwestern Europe throughout the century, their first victim being the monastery of Lindisfarne which was raided in 793. Shock waves reverberated around Europe, and from Carolingia Alcuin wrote to one of the monks who survived, com-miserating but opining that it was divine retribution for relinquishing the ascetic life-style of its founder saints. This was a recurrent theme during the death throes of the Roman empire and was revived by King Alfred the Great when he embarked upon the unification of what remained of free England and the reconquest of the Danelaw. For Alfred and his scholarly English, Celtic, and Carolingian advisers, lax standards of morality, spirituality, and learning were to blame for England's woes and a program of religious and educational renewal presented the solution. Instrumental within this was the book (Lapidge 2006; Brown 2007b).

Alfred founded schools for his subjects' sons and acquired for himself a standard of literacy unusual amongst the laity of the day. Charlemagne attempted to learn in middle age but could not master the letters inscribed on the little wax tablet he kept hidden beneath his pillow. Old English played an important role in improving the nation's literacy, and Alfred himself translated Orosius' *History Against the Pagans* and Gregory the Great's *Pastoral Care*, copies of which he circulated to his bishops, along with an *aestel*, probably a pointer (the Alfred Jewel may be a surviving example) used when reading aloud from sacred texts, like the Jewish *yad*. Other translations came to include Bede's *Ecclesiastical History of the English People*. Latin works, such as Aldhelm's *In Praise of Virginity*, were revived or composed, including Asser's biography of Alfred. Also composed during Alfred's reign, perhaps at the behest of one of his ealdormen, was the *Anglo-Saxon Chronicle*, compiled from sets of annals (records of annual events originally annotated in the margins of Easter tables). During the Alfredian revival, script (Anglo-Saxon pointed minuscule) and decoration (zoomorphic initials of Mercian-style beasts, given clumps of Carolingian acanthus to munch upon) were largely indebted to earlier ninth-century Mercian practice, with Carolingian overtones introduced by recruits such as the historian Grimbald of St. Bertin.

Greater rapprochement with Carolingian styles and texts occurred under Alfred's grandson, King Athelstan, a renowned book collector who acquired Carolingian, English, and Celtic manuscripts – some as relics from the "age of the saints" (Temple 1976; Turner et al. 1984; Brown 2007b). An eighth-century Gospel-book (BL Royal MS 1. B. vii), made in Northumbria or Mercia, and presented by Athelstan to Canterbury Cathedral, had inscribed within an Old English manumission, freeing slaves at his accession. Such holy "books of the high altar" could serve as the sacred ground upon which legal transactions were enacted (we still swear oaths in court upon sacred texts) and recorded within them. Athelstan's books include his little Psalter, for personal devotions, made around Liège in the ninth century and modernized at Winchester, and a Carolingian Gospel-book from Lobbes, subsequently used at the coronation of Anglo-Saxon kings.

The symbolic role of the book, as well as its spiritual, educational, and scholarly value, was evidently also revived. Insular cultural collaboration was over, however, and henceforth Celtic regions protected their traditions in the face of English expansion, stimulating the compilation of such works as the *Historia Brittonum*, a collection of texts (some relating to "King Arthur") celebrating British identity copied c.830 by the Welsh priest Nennius. Irish script and decoration remained remarkably conservative: tenth- and eleventh-century Psalters and two Gospel-books written at Armagh in the early twelfth century all resemble earlier Insular books (Alexander 1978).

During the second half of the tenth century, the English Church was reformed along mainstream continental Benedictine lines by Saints Dunstan, Ethelwold, and Oswald, under the patronage of King Edgar. Church and state were closely aligned, as in Carolingia, and likewise opulent book commissions, such as the *Regularis Concordia* (the "Monastic Agreement of the English Church"), the New Minster Charter (the instrument by which Edgar reformed Winchester Cathedral), and the magnificent Benedictional of

St. Ethelwold contain images reinforcing that relationship (Brown 2007b). Illumination is characterized by a classicizing, stylized figure style with agitated flying drapery and frames of exuberant, fleshy acanthus. Although practiced elsewhere, this is known as the Winchester (or "First") style. It was also used for elegant tinted drawings. Around 1000, it was joined by the "Utrecht" (or "Second") style, stimulated by the importation of the lively Reimsian drawing style. These styles fused to form the monumental, mannerist style encountered in the mid-tenth-century Tiberius Psalter (BL Cotton MS Tiberius C. vi).

Caroline minuscule was adopted for Latin texts, often assuming a characteristic English rotund style probably influenced by Insular half-uncial. Anglo-Saxon minuscule continued to be used for Old English, often alongside caroline in bi-lingual parallel texts, such as the Anglo-Saxon Scientific Miscellany (BL Cotton MS Tiberius B. v) and the Old English Herbal (BL Cotton MS Vitellius C. iii). Carolingian learning also had an impact, stimulating Anglo-Saxon copies of texts by Cicero, Dioscorides, Pseudo-Apuleius, Vitruvius, Boethius, Prudentius, and others.

Around 1000, in the face of renewed Viking aggression, English monastic librarians and scribes codified their heritage, assembling compilations of scientific texts, exegesis, and poetry to preserve their identity. Famous compilations of vernacular poetry, such as the Exeter Book and the Vercelli Book (Exeter Cathedral Library, MS 3501; Vercelli, Bibioteca Capitolare, CXVII), were assembled and the great epic *Beowulf* was committed to writing (BL Cotton MS Vitellius A. xv, pt. ii; Brown 2007b). Some see it as the product of centuries of oral transmission, its cultural allusions recalling the early seventh-century ship burial at Sutton Hoo; whilst others see it as the composition of a Christian author c.1000, emphasizing the shared Germanic origins of the Anglo-Saxons and Vikings. Also of this period were rousing collections of sermons, designed to stiffen national resistance, by Aelfric and Wulfstan. Aelfric also produced an abbreviated Old English Pentateuch (or Hexateuch, as another book was added; BL Cotton MS Claudius B. iv), perhaps for a female audience, linking illustrations to vernacular summaries and prefiguring medieval picture Bibles, as does the Old English Genesis (Bodleian Library, Junius MS 11; Brown 2007b).

Late tenth- and eleventh-century Anglo-Saxon books continued to be influenced by, and to influence, those made on the continent under the Ottonians, successors to the Carolingians in the northern and eastern (German) part of their empire from c.962 to 1056. The imperial concept flourished, along with conscious allusion to the symbolism and scholarship of the Roman and Carolingian empires. But Ottonian scriptoria (such as Trier, Cologne, Echternach, Regensburg, and Reichenau) concentrated upon imposing illuminated volumes for use in public liturgy and the private devotions of wealthy patrons (Mayr-Harting 1991; Brown 2006b). Amongst them are the Gospels of Otto III, made at Reichenau c.996 (Aachen, Domschatzkammer), the Sacramentary of Henry II, made in Regensburg, 1002–14 (Munich, Bayerische Staatsbibliothek, Clm 4456), and the Gospels of Abbess Hitda of Cologne, c.1000 (Darmstadt, Hessische Landes- und Hochschulbibliothek, Hs. 1640). Like their Carolingian and Anglo-Saxon counterparts, they favored classically inspired, yet stylized, figures and lavish use of imperial purple, gold, and silver. As in the Gospel-books of Charlemagne's Court School, entire books might be written in gold ink (chrysography). Such trends received stimulus from renewed Byzantine influence following the marriage of Emperor Otto II to the Byzantine princess Theophanu (972).

Byzantine book production, focusing upon scriptural and liturgical volumes, patristic exegesis, and works of history and scholarship, flourished during the early Christian period (from which little survives) but hit a low during the Iconoclast Controversy (720s to 787 and 814–43) when imagery was largely outlawed – only the book and the cross being considered acceptable public manifestations of belief and art. Learning likewise stagnated. The Council of Nicaea (787) reinstated images, and book production stepped up, featuring Gospel-books containing decorative head-pieces and bearded portraits of evangelist-scribes and Psalters enlivened with marginal illustrations (such as the Theodore Psalter, written in Constantinople in 1066, BL Add. MS 19352; Lowden 1997; Safran 1998). Such images, and the writings of Eastern Church Fathers, such as Gregory Nazianzen, John Chrysostom, and Ephrem the Syrian, impacted upon the West.

Appreciation of the iconic status of the book as an object of veneration was also transmitted to the West, as was the practice of enshrining sacred texts within treasure bindings. Metalwork plates attached to wooden binding boards, sometimes adorned with gemstones, are encountered from Byzantine, Coptic, Armenian, Irish, Anglo-Saxon, Carolingian, and Ottonian contexts (particularly important examples include the Lindau Gospels, New York, PML, MSM 1, and the Codex Aureus of Charles the Bald, Munich, Bayerische Staatsbibliothek, Clm 14000). Coptic and Irish metalwork shrines occurred, such as the Soiscél Molaise (National Museum of Ireland; Brown 2003). Ivories also adorned books (such as the Lorsch Gospels cover in the Victoria and Albert Museum); late Roman consular diptychs and early Christian ivories were sometimes adapted to adorn early medieval bindings, or contemporary covers were carved from walrus ivory.

Gatherings were sewn together, either onto supports (leather bands) or unsupported with only the sewing thread linking them together. The latter technique is known as "Coptic sewing," although widely practiced throughout the eastern Mediterranean. Sewing on supports was the preferred Western technique, but the earliest Western binding to have survived, on the St. Cuthbert Gospel, a little copy of St. John's Gospel made in Wearmouth/Jarrow in Northumbria in the 690s and found inside St. Cuthbert's coffin in 1104, is made in unsupported Coptic fashion – tangible evidence of the links between these far-flung regions. Wooden boards were then laced on, often with thongs tying them together to keep the vellum flat. These might be covered with leather, sometimes tooled or molded, as on the St. Cuthbert Gospel (formerly the Stonyhurst Gospel, BL Loan MS 74; T. J. Brown 1969; Needham 1979; van Regemorter 1992). Some Coptic bindings resemble their books' carpet pages, and a late eighth-century Irish shrine (the Lough Kinale Shrine, National Museum of Ireland) likewise bears metalwork reminiscent of the Lindisfarne Gospels' carpet pages. It was tossed into an Irish lake during the ninth century when a disappointed Viking raider found that it contained only an old book (Brown 2003).

Vikings also threatened the Carolingian empire, Duke Rollo carving out the kingdom of Normandy in the ninth century. In the eleventh century, Normans impacted upon the European stage in earnest, when Duke William seized the English throne in 1066. Norman influence was apparent in England from c.1000, especially under King Edward the Confessor (whose mother, Emma, was Norman), with intermarriage and Normans holding plum positions in the English Church, such as Archbishop Robert of Jumièges. The influence flowed in both directions, and Norman books, such as the Jumièges Gospels and the Préaux Gospels (BL Add. MSS 17739 and 11850), were heavily indebted to Winchester-style illumination and English caroline script. The twelfth-century "Channel School" had its origins in a trans-manche cultural milieu of the tenth and eleventh centuries.

Women were amongst the leading book-owners. Edward the Confessor's mother, Emma, joined her second husband, the Danish King Cnut, in a policy of giving books to court leading subjects following his seizure of the English throne (1016). Impressive illuminated books abound, several by Eadui Basan, who also penned important royal charters and seems to have been given leave from the cloister to follow Cnut's court – a monk working in a secular context for lay patrons. Laity were also sometimes involved in making books. In the Pericope Book of Henry III, made at Echternach c.1039–43, is a miniature depicting a monk and a layman working together in the scriptorium (Bremen, Universitätsbibliothek, msb 0021, f. 124v; Diebold 2000: 132–3, pl. 61). We do not know how widespread lay participation was, but Charlemagne and Alfred established schools for boys, and they and their sisters might always obtain an education in monastic schoolrooms. There is some indication of laymen writing charters in early medieval Switzerland (McKitterick 1990), and it is likely that literate lay managers helped run estates.

Women could be scribes and authors; for example, the Anglo-Saxon missionary Leoba of Tauberbischofsheim was renowned for her literary style (Brown 2001) and female bibliophiles included the eleventh-century Anglo-Saxon noblewomen Countess Judith of Flanders and St. Margaret of Scotland, wife of King Malcolm Canmore who, although illiterate himself, commissioned books for her. She reformed the Scottish Church and her Gospel-book allegedly survived miraculously when lost in a river – a relic by association, as were cult-books associated with Saints Columba and Cuthbert.

Following the Norman Conquest, English scriptoria perpetuated their traditions, but as Church reform and the number of Norman personnel within the Church escalated in the late eleventh century, Norman scribes trained in scriptoria such as Mont St. Michel, Jumièges, and Bec can be detected working alongside their English counterparts in leading scriptoria such as Canterbury, Salisbury, and Durham (Alexander 1970; Kauffmann 1975; Webber 1992; Gameson 1999). Acquisition of advanced Anglo-Saxon administration aided the success of Norman rule, enabling the construction of the Angevin empire. An early manifestation of this new power was to be a book – Domesday Book of 1086 (National Archives), the first full census in the post-Roman world.

From such political and cultural fusion – along with the Norman espousal of reformed Cluniac monasticism and expansion into parts of France, Italy, Sicily,

Byzantium, and the Crusader kingdoms – came the international culture termed "Romanesque," which characterized the twelfth century. The book was one of its foremost vehicles, for the early Middle Ages had ensured the triumph of the codex as the primary means of conveying thought, of establishing and administering power, and of recording collective memory and individual achievement and aspiration.

References and Further Reading

Alexander, J. J. G. (1970) *Norman Illumination at Mont St. Michel, 966–1100*. Oxford: Clarendon Press.

— (1978) *Insular Manuscripts, 6th to the 9th Century*. London: Harvey Miller.

— (1992) *Medieval Illuminators and their Methods of Work*. New Haven: Yale University Press.

Avrin, L. (1991) *Scribes, Script and Books*. London: British Library.

Badawry, A. (1978) *Coptic Art and Archaeology*. Cambridge, MA: MIT Press.

Bately, J., Brown, M. P., and Roberts, J. (ed.) (1993) *A Palaeographer's View: Selected Papers of Julian Brown*. London: Harvey Miller.

Bischoff, B. (1979) *Paläographie des römischen Altertums und des abendlandischen Mittelalters*. Berlin: Schmidt (English edn.: *Latin Paleography*, trans. D. Ganz and D. Ó. Cróinín. Cambridge: Cambridge University Press, 1989).

Brown, M. P. (1990) *A Guide to Western Historical Scripts from Antiquity to 1600*. London: British Library (rev. eds: 1994, 1999).

— (1991) "Continental Symptoms in Insular Codicology: Historical Perspectives." In P. Rück (ed.), *Pergament*, pp. 57–62. Sigmaringen: Thorbecke.

— (1994) "The Role of the Wax Tablet in Medieval Literacy: A Reconsideration in Light of a Recent Find from York." *British Library Journal*, 20 (1): 1–15.

— (1998) *The British Library Guide to Writing and Scripts*. London: British Library.

— (2001) "Female Book-ownership and Production in Anglo-Saxon England: The Evidence of the Ninth-century Prayerbooks." In C. Kay and L. Sylvester (eds.), *Lexis and Texts in Early English: Papers in Honour of Jane Roberts*, pp. 45–68. Amsterdam: Editions Rodopi.

— (2002) "Mercian Manuscripts? The 'Tiberius' Group and its Historical Context." In M. P. Brown and C. Farr (eds.), *Mercia: An Anglo-Saxon Kingdom in Europe*, pp. 278–91. Leicester: Leicester University Press (rev. edn. 2005).

— (2003) *The Lindisfarne Gospels: Society, Spirituality and the Scribe*. London: British Library (facsimile and commentary volume, also published as a monograph).

— (2005) "The Tower of Babel: The Architecture of the Early Western Written Vernaculars." In A. J. Duggan, J. Greatrex, and B. Bolton (eds.), *Omnia Disce: Medieval Studies in Memory of Leonard Boyle, O.P.*, pp. 109–28. Aldershot: Ashgate.

— (2006a) *How Christianity Came to Britain and Ireland*. Oxford: Lion Hudson.

— (ed.) (2006b) *In the Beginning: Bibles before the Year 1000*. Washington: Smithsonian Institute.

— (2007a) "The Barberini Gospels: Context and Intertextuality." In Alastair Minnis and Jane Roberts (eds.), *Text, Image, Interpretation: Studies in Anglo-Saxon Literature and its Insular Context in Honour of Éamonn Ó Carragáin*. Turnhout: Brepols.

— (2007b) *Manuscripts from the Anglo-Saxon Age*. London: British Library.

Brown, T. J. (ed.) (1969) *The Stonyhurst Gospel of St. John*. Oxford: Roxburghe Club. (For the collected papers of T. J. Brown, see Bately et al. 1993.)

Déroche, F. and Richard, F. (1997) *Scribes et manuscrits du Moyen-Orient*. Paris: Bibliothèque Nationale de France.

Diebold, W. (2000) *Word and Image: A History of Early Medieval Art*. Boulder: Westview.

Gameson, R. (1999) *The Manuscripts of Early Norman England (c.1066–1130)*. Oxford: Oxford University Press.

— (ed.) (forthcoming) *The Cambridge History of the Book in Britain*, vol. 1. Cambridge: Cambridge University Press.

Ganz, D. (1990) *Corbie in the Carolingian Renaissance*. Sigmaringen: Thorbecke.

— (2002) "Roman Manuscripts in Francia and Anglo-Saxon England." In *Roma fra Oriente e Occidente*, vol. 49. Spoleto: Settimane di Studio del Centro Italiano di Studi sull'Alto Medioevo.

de Hamel, C. (1986) *A History of Illuminated Manuscripts*. London: Phaidon.

— (2001) *The Book: A History of the Bible*. London: Phaidon.

Henderson, G. (1987) *From Durrow to Kells: The Insular Gospel-books 650–800*. London: Thames and Hudson.

Herren, M. (ed.) (1988) *The Sacred Nectar of the Greeks: The Study of Greek in the West in the Early Middle Ages*. London: University of London Press.

Kauffmann, C. M. (1975) *Romanesque Manuscripts, 1066–1190*. London: Harvey Miller.

Kelly, S. (1990) "Anglo-Saxon Lay Society and the Written Word." In R. McKitterick (ed.), *The Uses of Literacy in Early Medieval Europe*, pp. 36–62. Cambridge: Cambridge University Press.

Kessler, H. (1977) *The Illustrated Bibles from Tours*. Princeton: Princeton University Press.

Kiernan, K. S. (1996) *Beowulf and the Beowulf Manuscript*. Ann Arbor: University of Michigan Press.

Lapidge, M. (2006) *The Anglo-Saxon Library*. Oxford: Oxford University Press.

Lowden, J. (1997) *Early Christian and Byzantine Art*. London: Phaidon.

McKitterick, R. (1989) *The Carolingians and the Written Word*. Cambridge: Cambridge University Press.

— (1990) *The Uses of Literacy in Early Medieval Europe*. Cambridge: Cambridge University Press.

— (ed.) (1994) *Carolingian Culture: Emulation and Innovation*. Cambridge: Cambridge University Press.

Mayr-Harting, H. (1991) *Ottonian Book Illumination: An Historical Study*, 2 vols. London: Harvey Miller.

Muir, B. J. (ed.) (2004) *A Digital Facsimile of Oxford Bodleian Library MS Janius II* (CD-ROM). Oxford: Bodleian Library.

Mütherich, F. and Gaehde, J. (1976) *Carolingian Painting*. London: Chatto and Windus.

Needham, P. (1979) *Twelve Centuries of Bookbinding, 400–1600*. New York: Pierpont Morgan Library.

Nersessian, V. (2001) *Treasures from the Ark: 1700 Years of Armenian Christian Art*. London: British Library.

Noel, W. G. (1996) *The Harley Psalter*. Cambridge: Cambridge University Press.

Nordenfalk, C. (1988) *Early Medieval Book Illumination*. New York: Rizzoli.

Parkes, M. B. (1992) *Pause and Effect: An Introduction to the History of Punctuation in the West*. Aldershot: Ashgate.

Safran, L. (ed.) (1998) *Heaven on Earth: Art and the Church in Byzantium*. University Park: Pennsylvania State University Press.

Temple, E. (1976) *Anglo-Saxon Manuscripts, 900–1066*. London: Harvey Miller.

Turner, D. H., Backhouse, J. M., and Webster, L. (eds.) (1984) *The Golden Age of Anglo-Saxon Art, 966–1066*. London: British Museum.

van der Horst, K., Noel, W. G., and Wüstefeld, W. C. M. (eds.) (1996) *The Utrecht Psalter in Medieval Art*. 't Goy-Houten: HES & De Graaf.

van Regemorter, B. (1992) *Binding Structures in the Middle Ages*, trans. J. Greenfield. London: Maggs.

Walker, R. (1998) *Views of Transition: Liturgy and Illumination in Medieval Spain*. London: British Library.

Webber, T. (1992) *Scribes and Scholars at Salisbury Cathedral c.1075–c.1125*. Oxford: Clarendon Press.

— and Smith, C. Delano (2006) *The Cambridge History of Libraries in England*, vol. 1. Cambridge: Cambridge University Press.

Webster, L. and Backhouse, J. M. (ed.) (1991) *The Making of England: Anglo-Saxon Art and Culture AD 600–900*. London: British Museum.

— and Brown, M. P. (ed.) (1997) *The Transformation of the Roman World AD 400–900*. London: British Museum.

Weitzmann, K. (1977) *Late Antique and Early Christian Book Illumination*. London: Chatto and Windus.

Wright, D. H. (1993) *The Vatican Virgil*. Berkeley: University of California Press.

14

Parchment and Paper: Manuscript Culture 1100–1500

M. T. Clanchy

Manuscript culture persisted in its essentials across the whole medieval millennium from 500 to 1500: the use of parchment, the privileging of the clergy, the use of the Latin language and of Latin alphabetical script (even for writing vernacular languages), the practice of illumination, the form of the codex itself – all these features persisted, though in varied forms. The period after 1100 witnessed thinner parchment (together with the increasing use of paper), new orders of clergy, the Twelfth-century Renaissance in scholasticism and then Humanist Latin, Gothic and cursive scripts, illuminated books for lay people, and even some challenges to the codex form itself from the use of rolls: one thirteenth-century manuscript of the English lawbook *Glanvill* is in the form of a roll more than eight feet long.

The most obvious difference from the preceding period is that many more writings survive from the years after 1100 and there is no doubt that more writing was being done, both for purposes of secular government and commerce and for religious reasons. By 1200, most scribes were professionals instead of being monks. But the clerical orders reinforced their ideological control over literacy through the new institution of the university, instead of the monastery, and through the Dominican and Franciscan Friars who took the lead from monks in the thirteenth century. Their Bibles and other devotional texts, equipped with finding aids like numbered chapters and indexes, and their summaries of doctrine (notably the *Summa theologiae* of Thomas Aquinas) ensured that Christian teaching in Latin remained at the heart of literacy and book production. The first books to be produced by Gutenberg's printing press in the 1450s were the Latin Bible and the Psalter (book of Psalms) complete with all their Latin abbreviations.

Beginning in the twelfth and thirteenth centuries, increasing numbers of lay people, particularly among the aristocracy, became owners of books and patrons of writers. Most significantly, women, or more accurately "ladies" in social terms, came to possess personal prayer-books in the form of Books of Hours, which imitated the liturgical books used by the clergy. These books had the potential to familiarize their owners with reading and to enable them to educate their children in the elements of literacy.

Women patrons were also responsible in part for the development of books in vernacular languages, notably French and German, in the twelfth century. By the fourteenth century, the volume of writing in vernaculars was beginning to rival the Latin learning of the clergy. The growing number of literates and the increasing volume and variety of book production by 1400 motivated inventors to experiment with ways of reproducing texts through printing. The essential point is, however, that a vigorous book-using culture was the precursor to the invention of printing rather than its consequence. The Middle Ages had invented the book in its latinate Western form and created its readership, clerical and lay, and male and female. By 1300, "everyone knew someone who could read" (Orme 2001: 240) and there were books in every church and every village.

In 1492 Johannes Trithemius, the abbot of Sponheim, published his polemic *In Praise of Scribes* in reaction to the success of the printing press, which was then some forty years old. "How long will printing something on paper last?," he demanded. "At the most a paper book could last for two hundred years," was his answer (Clanchy 1983: 10). The abbot contrasted the apparent superficiality of the paper printed book with the permanence of "writing on parchment which can last for a thousand years." Parchment, in its choicest form as calfskin (vellum), had indeed been the ideal material for making the greatest illuminated manuscripts over the centuries. Notable examples in the period 1100–1500 are the giant Bible of San Vito in Pisa in the twelfth century, the Moralized Bibles of St. Louis in the thirteenth, the Luttrell Psalter in the fourteenth, and the dozen or so luxurious Books of Hours made for John, duke of Berry (at the time of his death in 1416 he had three hundred illuminated manuscripts in his library).

Scribes and their Status

As a monk, the abbot of Sponheim could look back over a millennium to the writing of the Benedictine Rule, with its provisions for "divine reading" (*lectio divina*) which had linked monks so closely with books and book production. The greatest Benedictine abbot of the twelfth century, Peter the Venerable, abbot of Cluny, had likened the act of writing to work in the fields: "The pages are ploughed by the divine letters and the seed of God's word is planted in the parchment, which ripens into crops of completed books" (Clanchy 1983: 10). The word which Peter used for "completed" here is *perfectus*: the monastic scribe produced "perfect books." In Peter's metaphor of plowing, the scribe is understood to incise the words of Scripture into the parchment with the point of his quill pen, whereas the abbot of Sponheim criticizes printing as an essentially superficial process which stamps text onto perishable paper.

In reality, however, most scribes never had been monks sowing the seed of God's word, but scriveners and clerks doing paid work. "I neither meddle with plow nor harrow," Thomas Hoccleve declared. He insisted that scribal work was not some sort of game; it was arduous labor, as "we stoop and stare upon the sheep's skin" (Hoccleve

1981: 35). A good depiction of a scribe stooping over his work occurs in one of the Moralized Bibles made for St. Louis (Alexander 1992: 56). Working in the king's Chancery in the 1400s, Hoccleve wrote on parchment, whereas paper was making inroads into the book trade by 1400. In England, the Red Book of King's Lynn (a legal register) and the court book of Lyme Regis are exceptional in using paper before 1310; both are ports where paper could be obtained. Of the eighty-three manuscripts of Chaucer's *Canterbury Tales*, all written in the fifteenth century, 61 percent are on parchment, 34 percent are on paper, and 5 percent are mixed. In the long term, paper became much cheaper than parchment, but this was not the case until the industry had developed.

By elaborating the sacred page of Scripture, monks had sanctified writers as much as books. This ideal is exemplified in the twelfth century in the thinking of Peter the Venerable and the full-page portrait of Eadwine in the Canterbury Psalter. He is praised as *princeps scriptorum*, "the prince of writers" (or scribes) (Gibson 1992: 180). In the twelfth century there were likewise distinguished nun scribes. Guda who "wrote and painted this book" has her portrait, presumably a self-portrait though much smaller than Eadwine's, in a collection of Latin homilies (Alexander 1992: 20). An anonymous *scriptrix* (a female scribe) is known from St. Mary's Abbey in Winchester in the twelfth century. Nuns as makers of books are best documented in the twelfth century in Bavaria: at Wessobrunn, the recluse Diemut was specially commemorated as the maker "with her own hands" of the abbey's library (Beach 2004: 32); more than a dozen of her books still exist. A copy of Isidore (a work of secular learning) from Munsterbilsen in Westphalia declares: "these are the names of those who have written this book"; eight names of nuns follow (Robinson 1997: 88). The German tradition of nuns as writers continues. A liturgical book made for the convent of Rulle in Westphalia is inscribed in Latin: "The venerable and devout virgin Gisela de Kerzenbroeck wrote, illuminated, notated, paginated and decorated with golden letters and beautiful images this excellent book in her own memory in the year of the Lord 1300" (Oliver 1996: 109). This seems admirably specific, but it has been questioned whether Gisela did do all this, as the book contains a variety of scripts and artwork.

The use of Latin as the standard language of literacy was another element in the unbroken continuity of medieval manuscript culture that linked the ancient world with the present. Latin continued to be taught, as it had always been taught, through the Augustan classical authors, especially Cicero, Virgil, and Ovid, and Latin school texts are among the commonest books to survive from the Middle Ages. Some of the most original Latin prose and verse was composed in the Twelfth-century Renaissance, in the letters of Bernard of Clairvaux for example and the anthology of poems and music in the *Carmina Burana* codex. From the fourteenth century, in Florence in particular, schoolboys' books have survived. "This book is finished, now let's break the master's bones! This book is Galeazzo's, a good boy. I have written this in 1335" (Gehl 1993: 48). This is part of the colophon of an anthology of Latin verses copied out by Galeazzo. The process of copying meant boys compiled their own textbooks, while committing the texts to memory and perfecting their handwriting. (This sort of formal education in Latin was only for boys and not girls.) At the same time, Latin proved the perfect tool for the scholastic philosophers and lawyers. An important element in writing Latin, which, though developed earlier, had generally been firmly established by 1100 and was passed on to the vernacular languages, was the practice of separating the words by consistently sized spaces. This enabled the reader to scan the text silently instead of identifying each word by pronouncing it out loud.

Just when this medieval Latin seemed to be getting set in its ways, Petrarch and the Italian Humanists reinvigorated classical Latin and literally gave it a new look. A letter from Coluccio Salutati, chancellor of Florence from 1375 to 1406, or Poggio Bracciolini actually looked different, as the Humanists created a new script and new punctuation in the Italic letter forms which are standard today on computer screens and in printed books. Petrarch in 1373 had criticized the division of labor for producing books in the commercial workshops, the greatest of which were in Paris. "There are those who prepare the parchment," he described, "others who write the books, others again who correct them, others who illustrate them, and finally still others who bind them and decorate the outside surfaces" (Petrucci 1995: 193). He wanted Humanist scholars to restore the integrity of books, though not by reviving monastic illuminated manuscripts. Instead, scholars who had made themselves into exquisite scribes and designers, like Poggio Bracciolini, copied the books of the classical authors themselves (particularly Cicero in Poggio's case). Poggio's pages have a few colored initials but no other ornament. Their beauty depends on the whiteness of the parchment, the spacing of the lines and words, and the elegant simplicity of the roman capitals and lower-case script. The Humanists caused books in black-letter Gothic script ("bookhand" as it is often called) to look old-fashioned and barbarically obscure; Germany proved most resistant to the new style. With their ideal of a Renaissance reinvigorating the roots of classical culture, the Humanists were the most successful propagandists there have ever been in the book business.

Books in Vernacular Languages

Furthest in distance and in spirit from the Latin manuscripts of the Italian Humanists are the Icelandic books in Old Norse, which survive in relatively large numbers from the fourteenth and fifteenth centuries. The Icelanders, like all Scandinavians, had a dual literacy in runes and alphabetical script. Because they had two forms of vernacular writing and a relatively egalitarian society in which clerics had little power, non-Latin literacy was probably more widespread here than anywhere in Europe, with the possible exception of the great Italian cities like Milan, Florence, and Siena. The book that survives most frequently is the *Jónsbók* law code. Deluxe manuscripts of this, with miniatures in tones of red and green and lines of black script consistently ruled, are not unlike German or English vernacular manuscripts. Texts of Iceland's great medieval literature of the sagas are less common; some of these books are very plain in appearance, like the Codex Regius of the Poetic Edda dating from the late thirteenth century.

Undecorated manuscripts intended for reading aloud are a common feature of early vernacular literature.

In defending writing in the vernacular in the 1300s, Dante had argued that anything could be as well expressed in Italian as in Latin; the sun was setting on Latin's long day, now that the future of literature lay with the vernaculars. In the breadth of vision and diction of the *Divina commedia* he demonstrated what Italian could achieve. A generation later Boccaccio showed in the *Decameron* that the vernacular could be as effective for storytelling as for poetry. The writing of Italian had come late among the latinate languages; Spanish and French in various forms had begun developing literatures two centuries earlier. The most notable of these twelfth-century writings are the poems of the first troubadours (beginning with William IX, duke of Aquitaine), the Poem of the Cid, the Song of Roland, and the romances of Chrétien de Troyes. Like Dante, Chrétien had explicitly challenged the supremacy of Latin. No one now says anything much about the Greeks and Romans, he claimed in the 1170s, "there is no more word of them; their glowing embers are extinguished" (Clanchy 1993: 205).

Vernacular authors secured the fame of their books not primarily through arguments with Latinists but by the quality of their work. Often the earliest surviving manuscripts are modest in appearance, as has already been seen with Iceland's books. The earliest manuscript of the Song of Roland, probably dating from before 1150, is a small book written on unbleached parchment without decoration and with inconsistent spacing and ruling. It has been compared with the books used by students in the schools and nascent universities (it may have been written in Oxford). A writer in the French vernacular before 1150 was doing something novel and it would be appropriate if he emanated from a university environment (this is the time when universities first develop at Paris, Oxford, and Bologna). The somewhat amateur appearance of the Oxford manuscript may be a consequence of the writer doing something unfamiliar.

Dante had argued that vernacular literature must be illustrious and courtly if it were to measure up to Latin. This was achieved by making superb illuminated manuscripts of the French romances in the thirteenth century, especially the stories of the Holy Grail, and of the writings of Dante and Boccaccio in the fourteenth. These books contain numerous and detailed illustrations of the narrative so that the lay aristocrat, whether male or female, who owned the book, could study them during the reading or recap on the story afterwards. Dante's *Inferno* proved popular with illustrators because of the details of the punishments. The most magnificent patron and creator of vernacular writing was Alfonso X of Castile (1252–84). The principal manuscript (now in the Escorial in Madrid) of his *Cantigas* (songs) in praise of the Virgin Mary contains more than 1,250 miniatures arranged six to a page with explanatory captions. These are paintings of exceptional quality unified on the page by a strong decorative design. In their narrative clarity and coherence, they turn the genre of the illuminated manuscript into something like a technicolor film. Alfonso was also responsible for producing the multivolume lawbook, the *Libro de las leyes*, and an anthology of chronicles in Castilian comprising a history of Spain.

Dante had likewise argued that the vernacular must be "cardinal" and "curial": that is, it must be consistent enough in its spelling and syntax to be fit for legal purposes.

In Spain and France by 1250 the vernacular was fast supplanting Latin as the language of legal documents and hence of treatises on law, like Philippe de Beaumanoir's *Coutumes de Beauvaisis* (completed in 1283) which became a model for other books of customary law in France. Written law in the vernacular encouraged the growth of a non-clerical legal profession. The *Sachsenspiegel* (dating from the 1220s) by Eike von Repgow had a comparable wide success, where it was adapted and translated into Swabian and other variations of German. It was a systemization of Saxon law that was made user-friendly by being illustrated as well as being in the vernacular. For example, a widow could see depicted alongside the text on the page what she was entitled to on the death of her husband: her marriage chest, books, sheep and poultry, shears, cloth, bed and bed linen, and so on. This contrasts with the English lawbook put together by the judge Henry de Bracton at much the same time. It is a scholastic *summa* written in Latin and addressed to his fellow judges rather than the general public. Legal texts begin to be written in French (instead of Latin) in England in the 1250s, but English was not used for legal purposes until the fifteenth century or later.

As a consequence of the Norman Conquest, writing in English was not made illustrious and courtly (in Dante's terms) until Chaucer achieved this at the end of the fourteenth century. The Ellesmere manuscript of the *Canterbury Tales* celebrates this, as does John Shirley's copy (dating from 1400) of *Troilus and Criseyde*. This shows Chaucer or a narrator reading to an aristocratic audience, in which ladies are prominent, in a fairytale landscape of rocks, golden sky, trees, and a castle. The Chaucerian narrator stands in a red and gold pulpit; there is not a cleric in sight. At much the same time, the poet Thomas Hoccleve had Chaucer depicted in his manuscript in a very high-quality portrait. Deluxe editions and portraits were intended to make the new vernacular authors the equals of the Greeks and Romans.

The most impressive series of portraits of medieval vernacular authors are those in the Codex Manesse in Heidelberg. This magnificent book was started by Rüdiger Manesse of Zürich around 1300. It includes 137 authors and over five thousand poems and songs. The greatest names in German medieval literature are there: Wolfram von Eschenbach, Gottfried von Strasburg, Walter von der Vogelweide. Many of the authors are depicted as knights with their personal heraldic shields and crested helmets. The pioneer of the new German, Hartmann van Aue, rides out with his shield, banner, and surcoat displaying white eagle heads on a dark blue ground. The writers of chivalric romances and love songs are thus depicted as if they were actors in their own stories. The idea of celebrating German writers as chivalric heroes may have had particular appeal in Zürich because the city stands at the intersection of the German-speaking world with its French and Italian competitors. The Codex Manesse demonstrated the richness of German culture.

Books of Theology and Law

The continuing dominance of the illuminated manuscript carried with it the success of the codex format as the principal matrix in which texts were made and circulated. Its pre-eminence is displayed at Chartres Cathedral in the sculpture of Christ at the south door (this figure, now known as Christ the Teacher, dates from the 1200s). He holds a large book whose ornamented leather binding is visible. The bindings of medieval books have mostly been destroyed. A notable survival of a plain binding is that of the de Brailes Book of Hours now in the British Library (Donovan 1991: 31). Around the Scriptures, theologians and law professors built up a body of new learning which took the form of commentaries and collections of citations. In manuscript culture, these texts had a tendency to expand and to spread out over the page in the form of glosses, as readers and commentators added more material in the margins and between the lines.

The basic treatise on canon law, the *Decretum*, created by the Bolognese master Gratian around 1140, is the best example of this. His original book was a concise analysis of the sources or "canons" of ecclesiastical law. It found such favor with readers, however, that within twenty years many more sources were added and the papacy gave it official authority. Around 1210, Johannes Teutonicus added a massive paragraph-by-paragraph commentary, which became known as the Ordinary Gloss. This was supplemented in its turn, along with additional volumes of papal rulings (the Decretals) in 1235. The result was a multivolume text in which Gratian's original work was overlaid by a patchwork of glosses so bewildering that law students required years of study to understand them. The number of texts that a canon lawyer needed to know in 1300 had increased by perhaps as much as an hundredfold compared with 1100. As no individual could know so much, lawyers had to specialize and rely on formal qualifications to impress their clients. The legal profession and professional books grew together out of the multiplication of texts.

Much the same is true of theological books. Before 1100, there was already a massive corpus of material to read, as there were the writings of the Church Fathers as well as the Scriptures themselves. The works of St. Augustine stood in pride of place and his books remain the most frequently copied of the Church Fathers throughout the Middle Ages. When Peter Abelard came as a student to Paris in 1100, his masters, William of Champeaux and Anselm of Laon, were famed for their lectures on logic and divinity which students flocked to hear from all over western Europe. These masters do not seem to have written treatises of their own, as they depended on attracting students to their schools through their oral lectures. However, summarized statements (called "sentences") of these masters circulated among students. Around 1120, an anthology was made of these entitled *Liber pancrisis* (meaning the "all-gold book"). This contained "sentences" of the Church Fathers matched by those of the "modern masters," by which was meant William of Champeaux, Anselm of Laon, and the canon lawyer Ivo of Chartres. Once "modern masters" were given prestige equal to that of the Church Fathers, the way was open for the proliferation of texts, and university stationers began to provide for this by supplying copies of lectures piece by piece. New expositions of theology therefore established themselves, of which the most successful were Peter Lombard's *Books of Sentences* dating from the 1150s.

Abelard in the 1120s had commented in *Sic et non* (Yes and No) on the overwhelming mass of words that students had to cope with; a century later, this had increased enormously. By the fifteenth century, Peter Lombard's *Sentences* was symbolically depicted as topping a high tower of knowledge, with the ancient Greeks and Romans (Aristotle and Cicero) below him, and grammar (or beginner's Latin) at the foundation of everything. Abelard had called his own doctrinal treatise *Theologia* (Theology), the first use of this Greek term as a book title. (In manuscript culture not all books were given titles. Abelard gave provocative titles to his books in order to emphasize the importance of his work.) He was twice condemned as a heretic and his books were ordered by the pope to be burned wherever they might be found. However, at least one cardinal in Rome held on to his copies of Abelard and some of his works continued to be copied into the thirteenth century and beyond. Banning books seems to have been no easier to enforce in manuscript culture than in print culture, though the public burning of heretical books was quite common. The books of Wyclif and Huss have likewise survived despite being condemned. Even the preachers' pocket-books of the Cathar and Waldensian heretics have survived. A group of very small Waldensian books, translating the Scriptures into Occitan, exist from around 1500. Possibly heretics' books were made very small in order to conceal them.

In the course of the thirteenth century, theology and the interpretation of Scripture came to be dominated by the Dominican Friars. They were the "hounds of the Lord" (*Domini canes*) who led the papal Inquisition against heretics and aimed to control the written word. Friars differed from monks, as they worked in smaller units which were more centralized and more focused on mission. They needed numerous books, primarily for purposes of consultation and reference rather than for liturgical use. They disseminated the single-volume copies of the Bible that were being produced in Paris. By using very fine parchment and miniature script, the scribal workshops of thirteenth-century Paris produced texts the size of pocket-books. These Bibles usually have colored initials, in blue and red for example, but they are not lavishly illuminated manuscripts. The Friars introduced alphabetical indexing, which in its turn demanded consistent numbering of the books and chapters of the Bible. By 1239, the Dominicans in Paris had an alphabetical concordance of the Bible. By 1300, the Franciscan Friars in England were making a union catalogue of books in more than 180 ecclesiastical libraries. They gained access to the most exclusive and ancient cathedral and monastic libraries, such as Canterbury and St. Albans, and treated the books they found in them as so many units of information. In the Rule of St. Benedict, a monk had been allocated a single book to mull over for a whole year, now the Friars were demanding immediate information from many books so that they could go out and preach.

Round the Chapter House of the Dominicans at Treviso (north of Venice) there are imaginary portraits of the leading men of the order, all of whom are shown reading or writing. It is as if the Chapter House is a gigantic scriptorium with the Dominican scholars laboring at their books in the gallery. This painting was done in 1352 by Tomaso of Modena. To make the portraits look realistic, he recorded a wide range of readers' and writers' actions, even though each scholar sits at an identical desk with a bookshelf above it. Tomaso's pictures emphasize that the Friars were capable of writing their own books like professional scribes. Thomas Aquinas (who was a Dominican) was exceptional in having a secretary with him day and night. According to his hagiography, while he was having dinner with St. Louis, king of France, he suddenly called on Brother Reginald to get up and write at his dictation another paragraph of the *Summa theologiae*. Among the Dominicans portrayed at Treviso is Hugh of St. Cher (d. 1263), who had taught theology in Paris like Aquinas. Hugh is shown wearing reading spectacles. These would have been familiar to Tomaso the painter, as they were a north Italian invention probably of the late thirteenth century, but they would not have been used a century earlier when Hugh of St. Cher was teaching in Paris. By the fifteenth century, reading spectacles were quite common. *The Book of Margery Kempe* describes in 1436 how the priest, who was writing for her, tried a pair of spectacles which made his eyesight worse. As Margery lived at the port of King's Lynn, these spectacles had probably been imported from Germany.

Making Personal Books

In manuscript culture, individuals might make books of their own, either by writing them themselves or employing scribes. Even when a person knew how to write, it might be difficult to get hold of parchment, pen, and ink. (In the case of Margery Kempe, however, she had considerable difficulties finding anyone capable or willing to write down her spiritual experiences.) The sketchbook of the artist Villard de Honnecourt dating from 1200 serves as a how-to-do manual as well as a personal record. It has explanations (in French) for sixty-six pages of drawings which serve as models: they show, for example, how to depict a lion from the front, or design the apse of a church, or make a crane or a siege catapult. Likewise from the thirteenth century is Richard Hotot's estate book, which was probably intended as a how-to-do book for his heirs. He was a middling Northamptonshire landowner who practiced law in London, and compiled a list of his tenants. What is unusual about his book is that he used his own system of signs to make a series of footnotes on the pages.

The chronicle of Matthew Paris, written between 1235 and 1258, can likewise be understood as a personal book, as he did his own drawings as well as writing and emending the text himself. Like the Codex Manesse, he used heraldry as an integral part of his design. When a great man died, Matthew showed his coat of arms reversed in the margin; if he died shamefully, the shield is shown shattered. From fourteenth-century Florence come the earliest "secret books" (*libri segreti*) of Italian merchants in which the owner notes details of his family, his business partners, his finances, and occasionally his hopes and fears, as if writing gives a secure point of reference for the future. In London between 1360 and 1375 James le Palmer compiled his own alphabetical encyclopedia, with illuminated initials of novel design, entitled *Omne bonum* (Everything Good). The strangest books are those of Opicinus de Canistris, who found favor with Pope John XXII in the 1320s. He identified the geography of Europe with his own body: rheumatic aches signified the strife of Germany and France; Britain represented the pain of purgatory. Opicinus' books, with their maps and diagrams, are like a parody of a scholastic treatise, although they were meant in all seriousness.

Interacting with books was theoretically the monopoly of the clergy because they alone were officially literate. Their privileges were as great in the period after 1100 as they had been before, and they were reinforced by the energy of the Friars. Nevertheless, after 1100 they no longer had as exclusive a control over books as they had formerly claimed. In any century there had always been some literate lay men and women among the aristocracy, but from the twelfth century this became more general. After 1100, social class is of more significance in literacy than whether a person is technically clerical or lay. Lords and ladies had books in their homes. Guy de Beauchamp, earl of Warwick, possessed at least forty books in 1306, including the Bible, saints' lives, romances and histories, a book of physic and another of surgery, a child's reading primer, and an encyclopedia. Most of these books were in French, the language of the English aristocracy until the fifteenth century.

Among writers of French, an extraordinary phenomenon is Christine de Pisan (c.1364–c.1430), who composed, wrote, and published her own books by winning the support of the French royal family, including the millionaire bibliophile, John, duke of Berry. Much of her work was written in praise of women; her last publication was a poem defending Joan of Arc. Christine may have been taught to write like a professional scribe by her father, who was an official in the royal chancery. She was an adroit self-publicist, who had herself depicted writing at her desk and presenting her book to the queen in the intimacy of her bed chamber. As Christine succeeded as a writer – in every sense of that word – why could not other lay women of her class do likewise? Making books was a business well suited to medieval ladies, as it could be done in the home in the comfortable living-room in which traditional skills like embroidery were done. In addition to German nuns, a few female lay scribes and illuminators are known who assisted their husbands. Christine is unique in the scale of her ambitions – she intended her books to circulate throughout the world – and in the superb quality of the manuscripts she produced. Making books was no longer the province of monks and friars in their harsh cells, but of ladies like Christine in their luxurious houses.

Learning to Read

The reading primer listed among the Beauchamp books is significant. Chaucer in the Prioress's Tale describes a boy aged seven sitting in school at his primer, learning his little book. This is the first recorded use of the word "primer" in English. One such "little book" from around Chaucer's time is now in the Plimpton collection at Columbia University. Its eight folios form an unbound booklet measuring 12 cm by 8 cm. Like all primers, it begins with the alphabet – because that was the first thing to learn – and there then follow the three basic texts of late medieval Christianity: the Our Father, the Hail Mary, and the Creed. These prayers are all in English. The remaining pages list other sections of the catechism to learn by heart: the seven deadly sins, the cardinal virtues, and so on. The assumption of the primer is that the principal purpose in learning to read is to learn to pray and to make a confession of faith correctly.

The primer must once have been the commonest of all manuscript books, though now it is among the rarest. Usually the only ones that have been preserved are expensively illuminated collector's pieces, like the primer of the Emperor Maximilian (b. 1459) and that of Princess Claude of France (b. 1499). Claude's primer shows her learning to read through the intercession of St. Anne. According to the popular cult which started in the late thirteenth century, St. Anne taught her daughter, the Virgin Mary, to read. In wall paintings, stained glass, sculpture, and book miniatures, particularly in England, St. Anne is depicted instructing the Virgin as a girl from a Book of Hours. Similarly, the Virgin in her turn is shown instructing the child Jesus from her prayer-book. This is why the primer is called "Jesus's book" (*Liber Jesus*), for example in the primer of Massimiliano Sforza in 1493.

Beginning in the fourteenth century, the Virgin Mary at the moment of the Annunciation is almost invariably shown kneeling in an oratory with a Book of Hours open on her lectern. In her prayerful reading, she becomes a model for the person using the Book of Hours in which she is depicted. In one fifteenth-century image of the Annunciation the lady owner of the book is interposed between the Angel Gabriel and the Virgin, as if the angel were introducing her to the Virgin. Some artists depict additional books in Mary's oratory among commonplace household objects. In Carlo Crivelli's Annunciation (painted in 1486) in the National Gallery in London, four books sit casually on a shelf: one supports a candlestick, two are under a decanter next to some crockery, and another leans alongside it.

Before 1100, book production had been primarily ecclesiastical and monastic. By 1400, it was mainly commercial, whether it was aimed at the schools and the professions (including the clergy) or at wealthy lay people in town and country. Illuminated manuscripts continued to be produced but their patrons now were kings, dukes, and knights. "Sir Geoffrey Luttrell had me made," the Luttrell Psalter declares (Camille 1998: 49). By 1400, lay women were perhaps as likely as lay men to be the owners of books, particularly Books of Hours and vernacular literature. The clergy had made illuminated books so covetable that lay people wanted them too. This is a sufficient explanation for the luxury book market. Among ordinary books, the simplest – and probably the most common – was the reading primer. In the centuries between 1100 and 1500 books of many sorts, religious and secular, made their way from churches to palaces, town houses, and manor houses, where they were domesticated – as it were – by the lady of the house. In bed chambers and private oratories, books had begun to furnish a room a century or more before the invention of printing.

Did the existence of more books mean that more people were literate? Unfortunately, there is no statistical information that allows generalizations to be made in terms of numerical proportions or percentages, either for rates of literacy among the medieval population or for annual book production. (In ecclesiastical documents individuals are occasionally described as *literatus*, but this concerns their competence in Latin rather than their literacy in a modern sense.) Rough estimates can be made, however, of the number of books and documents that still exist; these suggest that the materials for literacy increased century by century between 1100 and 1500. Even so, this increase may indicate only that more has been preserved from later centuries – especially from the fifteenth century – than from earlier times. This demonstrates an increase in libraries and archives, rather than in literacy and book production. Nevertheless, the growth of books in vernacular languages and of prayer-books for lay household use, like the Luttrell Psalter, suggest that domestic and familial literacy was indeed increasing among the well-to-do. Could Sir Geoffrey Luttrell and his family read his Psalter, which is all in Latin? Are the magnificent pictures in this and other illuminated manuscripts so prominent and elaborate because the owners of these books made more sense of them than of the text?

Describing the prayer-book of Lady Margaret Beaufort (the great benefactor of Cambridge University who died in 1487), Bishop John Fisher praised her for having "a little perceiving" of the Latin text: by using the rubrics and headings (Fisher explained) she could find her place for the service of the day without assistance (Clanchy 2004: 109–10). It was a commonplace of medieval schoolroom practice that *legere* (meaning "reading" in the sense of pronouncing the text correctly) preceded *intellegere* (meaning "understanding" the text through grammar and vocabulary). Children might learn "reading" at home from their parents using a primer, but they could only achieve "understanding" in a grammar school – and these schools were restricted to boys. Because women got no schooling in grammar (which meant Latin), they missed out on learning to write as well, since writing was taught by copying out the alphabet and Latin vocabulary. Even though signatures (instead of seals) were increasingly being required from women as well as men to authenticate legal documents, the numbers of women who could write in 1500 may have been as low as 1 percent of the population.

Inability to write contrasts with the large numbers who might have been able to read, at least in the restricted medieval sense of *legere*. Derek Brewer estimates that in England "probably more than half the population could read, though not necessarily also write, by 1500" (quoted in Clanchy 1993: 13). This estimate depends on the number who might have been instructed – in the home rather than at school – in the basics of the reading primer. Certainly by 1500, and probably as early as 1200, writing had become familiar to the whole medieval population: as noted above, "everyone knew someone who could read" (Orme 2001: 240). Book-learning had been integrated into the life of the male clerical elite of monks and priests by the beginning of our period in 1100. The achievement of the years 1100 to 1500 was to extend book-learning from monasteries and churches into the domestic sphere of the family. The reading primer, which reinforced the link between religion and learning as strongly as the clergy did, had the potential to make everyone a literate and a book-owner. Shortly after 1500, booksellers' catalogues were selling primers, described as "abc"s, for a penny each. These were printed booklets, but their form was the same as it had been for centuries.

References and Further Reading

Alexander, J. G. (1992) *Medieval Illuminators and their Methods of Work.* New Haven: Yale University Press.

Beach, A. I. (2004) *Women as Scribes: Book Production and Monastic Reform in Twelfth-century Bavaria.* Cambridge: Cambridge University Press.

Binski, P. and Panayotova, S. (eds.) (2005) *The Cambridge Illuminations: Ten Centuries of Book Production in the Medieval West.* Turnhout: Brepols.

Camille, M. (1998) *Mirror in Parchment: The Luttrell Psalter and the Making of Medieval England.* London: Reaktion.

Carruthers, M. (1990) *The Book of Memory.* Cambridge: Cambridge University Press.

Clanchy, M. T. (1983) "Looking Back from the Invention of Printing." In D. P. Resnick (ed.), *Literacy in Historical Perspective*, pp. 7–22. Washington: Library of Congress.

— (1993) *From Memory to Written Record: England 1066–1307*, 2nd edn. Oxford: Blackwell.

— (2004) "Images of Ladies with Prayer-books: What Do They Signify?" In R. N. Swanson (ed.), *The Church and the Book*, pp. 106–22. Woodbridge: Boydell.

Coates, A. (1999) *English Medieval Books: The Reading Abbey Collections from Foundation to Dispersal.* Oxford: Oxford University Press.

Crick, J. and Walsham, A. (eds.) (2003) *The Uses of Script and Print, 1300–1700.* Cambridge: Cambridge University Press.

Derolez, A. (2003) *The Palaeography of Gothic Manuscript Books.* Cambridge: Cambridge University Press.

Donovan, C. (1991) *The de Brailes Hours: Shaping the Book of Hours in Thirteenth-century Oxford.* London: British Library.

Gehl, P. F. (1993) *A Moral Art: Grammar, Society and Culture in Trecento Florence.* Ithaca: Cornell University Press.

Gibson, M., with Heslop, T. A. and Pfaff, R. W. (1992) *The Eadwine Psalter.* Philadelphia: Pennsylvania State University Press.

Griffiths, J. and Pearsall, D. (eds.) (1989) *Book Production and Publishing in Britain, 1375–1475.* Cambridge: Cambridge University Press.

de Hamel, C. (1994) *A History of Illuminated Manuscripts*, 2nd edn. London: Phaidon.

— (2001) *The Book: A History of the Bible.* London: Phaidon.

Harthan, J. (1977) *Books of Hours and their Owners.* London: Thames and Hudson.

Hoccleve, T. (1981) *Selections from Hoccleve*, ed. M. C. Seymour. Oxford: Oxford University Press.

Kelly, S. and Thompson, J. J. (eds.) (2005) *Imagining the Book* [in the Middle Ages]. Turnhout: Brepols.

Kristjánsson, J. (1993) *Icelandic Manuscripts*, trans. J. Cosser. Reykjavik: Icelandic Literary Society.

Lewis, S. (1987) *The Art of Matthew Paris in the Chronica Majora.* Berkeley: University of California Press.

Oliver, J. (1996) "Worship of the Word." In L. Smith and J. H. M. Taylor (eds.), *Women and the Book: Assessing the Visual Evidence*, pp. 106–22. London: British Library.

Orme, N. (2001) *Medieval Children.* New Haven: Yale University Press.

Petrucci, A. (1995) *Writers and Readers in Medieval Italy*, trans. C. M. Radding. New Haven: Yale University Press.

Robinson, P. R. (1997) "A Twelfth-century *Scriptrix* from Nunnaminster." In P. R. Robinson and R. Zim (eds.), *The Making of Books: Medieval Manuscripts, their Scribes and Readers; Essays Presented to M. B. Parkes*, pp. 73–93. Aldershot: Ashgate.

Rouse, M. A. and Rouse, R. H. (1991) *Authentic Witnesses: Approaches to Medieval Texts and Manuscripts.* Notre Dame: Notre Dame University Press.

Shailor, B. A. (1988) *The Medieval Book.* Toronto: University of Toronto Press.

Smith, Lesley J. (2003) *Masters of the Sacred Page.* Notre Dame: Notre Dame University Press.

15

The Gutenberg Revolutions

Lotte Hellinga

The invention of printing with movable type, which took place in Mainz in the middle of the fifteenth century, is one of the few instances where we can pinpoint a dramatic acceleration in the slow evolutionary process of the history of script. The introduction of the new technique is often regarded as a revolution in the dissemination of knowledge and in communication, but it was by no means a revolution in the sense of a movement intended to overthrow the old order. By the middle of the fifteenth century, readership and ownership of books by men and women were no longer a privilege of the very few (see chapter 14). Book ownership had sufficiently grown to foster a departure from long-established scribal methods of book production and welcome a new technique that allowed books to be manufactured at a rate that caused amazement and delight. "All that has been written to me about that marvelous man seen at Frankfurt is true," wrote Cardinal Juan de Carvajal early in 1455 in a letter to the future pope Pius II, after he had seen sheets of the by then almost completed Latin Bible, which apparently had been put on display by the inventor and printer, Johann Gutenberg, at a political summit meeting of diplomats and prelates held at Frankfurt. The letter, although short, is revealing; it expresses admiration for the clarity of the graphic forms ("your grace would be able to read it without your spectacles"), it gives an estimate of the number of copies printed (between 158 and 180), and reports that they are difficult to obtain for demand is high: buyers were lining up even before the work was finished (Davies 1996). Finally, the circumstances under which the cardinal had seen sheets of the book allow us to guess that Gutenberg was well aware that active marketing strategies were required in order to get a return on his very large investment, perhaps even to raise cash in order to finish the work and repay his loans.

The novelty of print was celebrated in many colophons of early books, in convoluted Latin verse with difficult to interpret circumscriptions of the technique, but also famously by Caxton in plain English: "this said book . . . is not wreton with penne and ynke as other bokes ben to thende that every man may have them attones" (in the first book he printed, the *Recuyell of the Histories of Troy*, 1473). When the novelty had worn off, but not the appreciation of what the invention meant for Western civilization, centenaries were celebrated at various dates, according to the convenience and beliefs of the organizers. The most recent was in the year 2000.

Without a rising demand for texts produced in highly legible, well-manageable codex form, Johann Gutenberg might not have persisted in developing his ingenious invention, or promising trials might have met with indifference. From what we learn about Gutenberg's biography from legal documents, the long process of experiment and development had indeed been turbulent, beset with financial problems, political uncertainty and violence, and conflict between individuals (Bechtel 1992; Davies 1996; Kapr 1996). The modern era of mechanical book production was heralded by notions of the need for venture capital and of property rights to an invention.

The Technique: (1) Manufacturing Movable Type

Gutenberg's invention took full advantage of the degree of abstraction in representing language forms that was offered by the alphabet and by the Western forms of script that were current in the fifteenth century. From sparse relics of Gutenberg's early experiments, and from his great Latin Bible itself, it is possible to detect that the development of the technique took place in phases, and recent research based on modern imaging technology even suggests that Gutenberg's technique was indeed a precursor to the definitive process (Agüera y Arcas 2003). We may now surmise that the method of manufacture of type with steel punches and matrices, which became the standard for more than four centuries of typography, was introduced a few years later by Nicolas Jenson, who from early days on was praised as a co-inventor. Jenson's contribution was apparently based on the early part of his career at the Mint in Paris, where striking medals with elaborate lettering would have given him specialized expertise. Jenson became one of the most influential type-designers of all ages – as well as an excellent printer – when he worked in the 1470s in Venice, but this may have been preceded by an interlude in Mainz, where he probably made a type, first used in 1459, which, unlike Gutenberg's types, was able to withstand many years of intensive use (Hellinga 2003).

In spite of the existence of archival documents and a very considerable amount of printing surviving from the earliest decades, much of the detail and circumstances of the invention remains open to interpretation, and even has a long tradition of acrimonious dispute. We can, however, be confident about the technique once it had become stable. For each character, a punch was cut in steel, the hardest available metal. The steel punch was used to stamp the character in a copper matrix of fixed dimensions. The matrix was carefully adjusted to fit exactly into a mold, a hinged form which, when closed, was filled with hot, liquid metal with a low melting point, an alloy of lead, tin, and traces of other metals (commonly antimony). The mold would determine exactly the dimensions of the resulting character: of its surface at the top with the character-image (or body, in typographical terms) and its height to paper (Gaskell 1972: 11–39).

The number of characters to be cast would vary; most languages need, for example, many "e"s and "n"s, but very few "z"s. Cast characters were kept in type-cases, the capitals in the "upper case," the minuscules in the "lower case," and each character had a separate box in the case (Gaskell 1972: 35–7). With a complete fount, that is a set of cast characters, uniform in size but representing every element of the alphabet and in the quantities required for each letter, compositors could build up tightly fitting, solid pages of text. These were combined into forms from which the sheets of paper, subsequently to be folded, were printed. After the necessary number of copies had been printed on the press – on paper or, less frequently, on vellum – the pages of type could be taken off, washed, and disassembled. The individual characters would then be distributed over the type-cases, to be used again.

For printing in Latin, "international" styles were soon established, first a rotunda style developed in Venice, which became familiar to the whole world of learning, and later roman types, based on humanist script, which were pioneered by Nicolas Jenson. For liturgy, a "Gothic" fractura style remained appropriate, which had also been the style chosen by Gutenberg for his Latin Bible. In vernacular printing the style of types echoed the styles of script that had become associated with vernacular texts in manuscript, and varied between languages: the *schwabacher* from South Germany for German, the *bastarda* for French, the script of the Brethren of the Common Life in the Low Countries. English printing was influenced by several of these models, while printers attempted to "anglicize" them by introducing some traditionally English forms (BMC xi: 335–45).

The Technique: (2) The Printing Press

The printing press itself was subject to development. At first, it was a fairly simple adaptation of the press that had been known since antiquity for producing wine and oil. In this contraption, a flat platen was built under which a device could be pushed that held a sheet of paper. The platen would then be driven down by a screw powered by a lever. This press was capable of printing one folio leaf (on half of a sheet of paper or vellum) corresponding to the size of the platen. In the early 1470s, an improvement was introduced (probably first in Rome), a movable carriage which enabled the printer to place a whole sheet on the press and print it in two pulls with two successive moves of the carriage. This new procedure spread from Italy to other countries, and by the middle of the 1480s it had become generally available. This improvement, which speeded up the process of printing, had a profound effect on the production of texts (Hellinga 1997; illustrations of presses with moving carriages in Gaskell 1972: 119–23).

To understand this, we have to take a closer look at the printing process. Printed books were produced as codices, the form in which already for over a millennium established texts had been transmitted. To make a codex, sheets of paper or vellum are folded together to form quires, which are sewn together to form volumes, which can then be protected by a binding of various degrees of solidity. The production of codices, whether manuscript or printed, requires advance planning of their structure, which means that this form of reproduction is suitable only for texts with a predetermined beginning and end. For books printed in the hand-press period, the "format" of the book was determined by the number of times the full sheet was folded, while its dimensions would be determined by the size of the full sheet. The larger the number of pages that must be combined within the sheet to produce a small book, the more intricate the pattern of combination of pages (Gaskell 1972: 88–105). The practice of writing on full sheets before folding them was known to some scribes of manuscript codices, but with the introduction of the printing press, the sheet had to be the standard unit of production. Pages, once set in type, had therefore to be combined in a chase as forms corresponding to the size of the platen – a process known as "imposition." Initially, the typeset form would have the size of a half-sheet, later of a full sheet.

Since printers normally worked with a fairly limited supply of type, they needed to set pages in the combination required to complete the printing of a sheet, which (except for middle sheets in the quire) would not be in the order in which the text was to be read. A forecast of the contents of each page was therefore made on the manuscript used by the printer (usually by a line-count), a process which is called "casting off." The division of text in this way rapidly became an established routine. Compositors were adept at making the text they were setting fit the thus allotted space, by using variations in spelling, abbreviation, and contraction, or even by introducing variations in the text. There is evidence of the practice of casting off from the early 1470s (and it may have been practiced before) but it is much more difficult to provide a date for its discontinuation. It may well have varied between printing houses, and their investment in type. We can be certain that, for example, in England by the end of the seventeenth century the practice had become unknown (Hellinga 1999: 82), whereas it had been used for the printing of Shakespeare's First Folio in 1623, at a time when it was probably the normal procedure in all but the largest printing houses. It is important to realize that, until the discontinuation of the practice, texts were split up into building blocks to be assembled during production. Books were perceived by their makers as structures in which intellectual content had no more than a secondary part.

The main invention, the principle of composing pages of movable type, had been quickly accomplished to an astonishing degree of perfection. Nevertheless, further development was possible. Within a short time, pages in metal type were combined with woodcut illustrations, later to be followed by metal engravings. Hebrew and Greek, with their vowel points and accents, and music posed problems of vertical as well as horizontal composition which were solved only gradually: Hebrew in the early 1480s, Greek by the Venetian typographers of the 1490s. The first composition of mathematical figures in metal in the first edition of Euclid's *Elementa*, published in 1482 in Venice by the highly inventive printer Erhard Ratdolt, was exuberantly celebrated by him in a preface, which he even printed in gold in several copies.

Early in the sixteenth century a reaction against the growing uniformity in the appearance of printed books, especially books in Latin, can be observed. Printed books had penetrated new markets. It had become much more common for individuals to own books, and, paradoxically, printed books had become impersonal objects. At this time we find exceptional manuscripts of great splendor, works of art such as could never be produced mechanically. As part of the same reaction against uniformity, type-founders began to design typographical styles that were also works of art in their own right, commissioned for a particular person or to be used for a particular purpose. In the balance between the very general, so easily accepted by the eye that it becomes "invisible," and the very particular, the typeface that deliberately intrudes into the awareness of the reader, is comprised the whole long history of typography.

The Printing House

Compared with manuscript production, even within a scriptorial organization, the preparation, investment, organization, and technical skills required to produce books in print were very much greater. Even a modest early printing house employed a variety of personnel: compositors, press-crews, one or more correctors, an overseer or master printer. Type design, punch-cutting, and type-founding were specialized skills of the very few and would only exceptionally be found in a printing house such as, for example, Aldus Manutius in Venice. In every printing house, space was required for presses, for the storage of paper and perhaps vellum, and for the finished product. Above all, every printer had to foster trade connections to ensure that books were dispatched and sold in time to yield sufficient return on investment for the business to continue.

The relatively large investment in paper, equipment, and the complicated proce-dures encouraged careful control over texts before they were committed to print and during production. Printing houses initiated procedures for editing, text preparation, and proofreading right from the beginning of printing, checked the sequencing and imposition of pages (which were particularly vulnerable to error), and sometimes con-tracted learned or specialist correctors to oversee the accuracy of texts according to the standards of their time. The quality of the publications and the ensuing fame of a printing house stand in direct relation to the level of care in such procedures. Some printing houses which specialized in learned texts, for example Aldus Manutius in Venice and Johann Froben in Basel, employed famous scholars. Erasmus, who worked with these two printers, is the leading example, but there were many other correctors whose names we do not know: ecclesiastics ensured the accuracy of liturgical printing and of biblical and patristic texts. In a different area that required strict accuracy, lawyers of the Inns of Court in London are known to have corrected texts for the spe-cialist printer of this material, Richard Pynson (Baker 1999: 430). Other, less ambi-tious printers did not employ scholarly correctors at all. Conversely, authors, who generally had no control once their work was in the hands of printers, with or without their foreknowledge, complained bitterly about printing-house negligence and igno-rance. When early in the sixteenth century legal protection began to appear in the form of "privileges" issued by a local authority, it was the printer who was protected against competitors reprinting the text within a stated period of time, not the author (Armstrong 1990: 1–13).

In the early years, when Latin was the principal language in which books were printed (overall estimated at more than 70 percent of books printed before 1501), there was an almost constant migration of printers: the great centers of printing in Italy became home to printers from the Rhine area, from Paris, and from the Low Countries, before Italians became established in the industry. Printers who had learned the art and the business in Venice, Padua, and Rome, or in Cologne, returned to their native towns in the Low Countries, or went to Paris and London as founders of a trade that was to flourish in these more westerly centers of commerce. Among the eight early printers in England known as individuals, only William Caxton was born an Englishman, and his first steps in the publishing business were taken in Cologne and Bruges. The consequence of this mobility is that initially there was much uniformity in printing-house practice, but in the course of the sixteenth century the uniform character of the printing trade changed. Several influences brought this about. National identities became stronger, and printing in the vernacular increased; during the Reformation and the political turmoil of the sixteenth century, the printing press became more subject to controls and censorship imposed by authorities, as the power of the press in opposing authority by spreading heresy and dissidence was recognized. In many places the trade itself became organized in self-regulating companies or guilds, excluding outsiders.

As a result of this progressive separation, printing-house practices began to diverge between countries, but the basic technical equipment remained stable until the end of the "hand-press period" early in the nineteenth century. There were a few minor modifications to the press, and the last years of the sixteenth century saw the introduction of a rolling press for the printing of copper engravings. The history of type design is one of steady evolution, but type-founding remained the same as invented in the fifteenth century until the wide-scale application of stereotyping, first used in Bible printing in Holland in the late seventeenth century, but not fully developed until the nineteenth. Not long after that period rapid developments in printing technology wrought a definitive change in book production, which could from then on be carried out on an industrial scale.

The Spread of Printing after the Invention

The geographical spread of printing in the fifteenth century can be mapped with fair accuracy (Nieto 2003). In the two decades after its invention, printing spread in many directions over Europe and with gathering speed, emanating from Mainz (1455) and Strasbourg (1465): in the Rhine valley to Cologne (1465) and Basel (by 1468) and many smaller places in between, in the other German lands to Bamberg (not after 1461), Augsburg (1468), Nuremberg (1469), and northwards to Lübeck (1475) and Rostock (1476), in Italy to Subiaco (1465), Rome (c.1467), Venice (1469), Naples (c.1470), Milan (c.1470), Florence (1471), Bologna (1471), and Padua (1471), to Paris (1470) and Lyon

(1473), to Segovia (c.1472) and Barcelona (c.1473), and to cities in the Netherlands (1473, but probably already in the 1460s), and in Eastern Europe to Cracow (c.1473), Pilsen (1476), and Budapest (1473). England, where Caxton began printing in 1476, was rather late to be engulfed by this tide, but printing arrived there before it reached the Scandinavian countries in 1482 (in Odense). The rapid branching out of the technique, mainly between 1465 and 1475, was followed by further ramifications to very many small towns, some enterprising monasteries, and to universities, wherever there was demand for printed material. However, maps of the spread of printing reveal a reverse movement of concentration by the 1490s. In many small towns and other centers printing turned out to be of an incidental nature and was discontinued once an immediate need was fulfilled.

Through recording the surviving editions of texts, whether large or small, all printed before 1501, in a bibliographical database, we now have solid grounds for estimating that there are between 27,000 and 28,000 separate editions of that period still extant, although even with automated records it is difficult to provide a figure for the total surviving copies of these books. (The estimate is based on the short-title catalogue of incunabula, ISTC, recorded on the database held at the British Library, now an almost comprehensive record of surviving editions.) It is more difficult to estimate how many editions are lost, since rates of survival vary enormously according to the nature of the text and the book: a small schoolbook, for example, once it had served its purpose, had much less chance of surviving the centuries than a substantial, dignified edition of the Bible. Print-runs would also vary according to the expected demand, and much remains unknown, but there is just enough documentation to know that in the earliest years an edition size of 275–300 copies was not uncommon, while in the 1490s a print-run of 600 copies may have been considered normal. Extant contracts and accounts show that an exceptionally ambitious enterprise, Hartmann Schedel's *Liber chronicarum* printed in 1493 in Nuremberg by Anton Koberger, had a print-run of about 1,400 copies of its Latin version, but that the German version had a print-run of half that size.

Printing-house equipment, type metal and printing types, paper and parchment, could be transported down rivers, over mountains, and across seas, but printed books required a much more complex distribution system. This is the main reason why printing became concentrated in the most important centers on the trade routes that had traditionally linked the European countries. Commercial centers were also the places where one might find financial backing for the manufacture of a product that usually took a long time to sell and produce a return on investment. Thus, in the 1480s and 1490s, Venice took the lead in both book production and the book trade over all other cities, providing scholars and professionals across Europe with Latin works of the highest academic standard. Venice had quickly overtaken the early printers in Rome, which was never an international trade center, but Florence and Milan flourished at the expense of the many small towns in Italy where presses operated at one time or other. Similarly, north of the Alps, there were great concentrations of book production in Strasbourg, Nuremberg, Basel, and Cologne, in Paris, later followed by Lyon, and in Antwerp. Leipzig as a gateway to Eastern Europe became one of the most important centers of the book trade. Book production in Spain did not entirely conform to this pattern and remained relatively isolated. After absorbing early on a number of printers of German and Polish origin who seem to have worked mainly with materials from Italy, the Spanish presses came to provide for the requirements of the Iberian peninsula, in Latin, Hebrew, and the vernacular languages.

The British Isles constitute a case apart, for here, with London as a major center of trade, importation of Latin books from the continent dominated the book market. Printers in England hardly competed with the "Latin trade" as the flow of importation is known, and they were often importers themselves (Christianson 1999; Ford 1999; Needham 1999; Roberts 2002). A record of owners of printed books in the British Isles until the middle of the sixteenth century, combined with the places where the books they owned were printed, demonstrates that most books in Latin were imported from the great continental centers: above all from Venice and Paris, but also from Lyon, Cologne, Basel, and in smaller quantities from other centers of printing (Ford 1999: 189). Recent research into the book production that did take place in England before 1501 complements this finding: 63 percent of the surviving production of English printers are in English, and only 28 percent are in Latin, much of these consisting of works, liturgical and other, conforming to the use of the diocese of Salisbury. The remaining 9 percent are works in law-French, the language of texts of the common law of England (BMC xi: 43–7). Many of the English texts can be rated as a publishing success, not only because they were reprinted, but also because records of ownership show that they soon began to reach a new lay readership, especially among male readers and owners, while the tradition continued of book ownership among high-born and religious women, which had begun early in the fifteenth century with manuscripts (see chapter 14; BMC xi: 61–70.)

Fifteenth-century Books

With the steady geographical spread of printing from the early 1460s, application to a variety of uses grew at equal pace. The late fifteenth century was more an age of invention than of great literary creation. The earliest printers concentrated on the age-old cornerstones of Western civilization, most of them published in huge volumes: Latin Bibles, patristic texts, moral theology, civil and canon law, and liturgical works were soon followed by the authors of classical antiquity and by the great medical works of Arabic origin. Such lists and such large books characterize the production of Gutenberg's successors in Mainz, Johann Fust and Peter Schoeffer, and the early printers in Strasbourg, Rome, Venice, and Padua, and were followed by many later in the century.

Others deliberately took a different course. In Cologne, one of the first cities where early printers settled, a multitude of small quarto editions were printed from 1465 onward, many of them texts that were linked to the traditional curriculum of the university, prepared for publication by teachers (Corsten 1987). The first press in Paris, situated from 1470 at the Sorbonne, was even more closely associated with the university by the active participation as editors and authors of two prominent professors, Guillaume Fichet and Jean Heynlin. In contrast to the Cologne printers, they undertook the publication of new works in a spirit of renewal of teaching methods. They also used their books as instruments for intricate diplomacy, inserting in numerous copies of their printed works individual dedications to the pope, princes of the Church, and worldly rulers (Veyrin-Forrer 1987). The first press in Oxford (run by someone only identified as "the printer of Rufinus") was a modest enterprise and produced only three small books mainly for local use, but presented in a modern, humanist style (BMC xi: 13, 15). Later in the century, the newly established university in Leipzig followed the model of printing small quartos required for the curriculum of many of the universities in Eastern Europe. In the sixteenth century, the small, often short-lived university presses reflected a penchant for renewal and the originality of individual professors (Goldschmidt 1955). As witnesses for the interaction of authors and printers, their work is of great value. In quantitative terms, however, they represent only a small proportion of book production in Latin in the early years of printing.

Among the earliest printed books are traditional texts for the elementary teaching of Latin, almost all surviving only as fragments, which makes it impossible to arrive at a reasonable estimate of the total once produced. Modernizing textbooks and reading texts, written by schoolmasters and humanist scholars, began to appear in print in the 1480s. Apart from liturgical works, often commissioned on ecclesiastical authority, a large proportion of books in Latin were destined for the priesthood, which remained a stable client base for printers. Works for clerical use, such as Duranti's *Rationale divinorum officiorum* (ISTC records 45 editions), the much smaller *Manipulus curatorum* by Guido de Rochen (117 editions), and the *Stella clericorum* (at least 60 editions) were all frequently reprinted. Books of Hours and Psalters for the private devotion of lay people were printed many times, and were for printers a secure source of income but, as with the elementary schoolbooks, we know that much of this material is lost, and it is difficult to arrive at sensible estimates of how much was once printed.

Books for practical instruction were also published in Latin. The often-reprinted *Regimen sanitatis*, or more specifically the *Regimen contra pestilentiam*, is an example that shows that such popular texts could still be disseminated in the language of learning. A significant part of publishing in Latin consisted of historical works, some by contemporary authors. One of them was Werner Rolewinck whose *Fasciculus temporum* went from 1474 through many editions and translations, and was a strong influence on vernacular historical works, including William Caxton's version of the *Chronicles of England* and his edition of John Trevisa's translation of Higden's *Polychronicon* to which he added an extension (BMC xi: 127–30). Pseudo-historical works, such as versions of the history of Troy, could be equally successful. In 1493, a major enterprise in historiography was the publication of the *Nuremberg Chronicle*, a world history compiled by the learned Dr. Hartmann Schedel with the support of other scholars in Nuremberg, and spectacularly illustrated by a team headed by Michael Wohlgemut and Wilhelm Pleydenwurff in which the young Albrecht Dürer played a modest part. A German version was prepared in parallel and issued later in the same year (Reske 2000). Most historical works were frequently reprinted and they survive in many more copies than any other category of early printed book, clear indications that their publication was successful and that they came to be regarded as works of lasting value.

Practical and historical works in Latin appear therefore to have reached lay readers as well as scholars and ecclesiastics, but they were also published in most vernacular languages of the geographical area in which presses operated. The proportion of book production in the vernacular shows enormous variation in distinct language areas. What they have in common is that most printing in the vernacular consisted of devotional texts for a lay readership. Hagiography, sermons, and texts providing moral guidance were widely distributed, went through translations, and obviously fulfilled the need of a rapidly growing market, especially in countries north of the Alps. Few literary works by contemporary authors in vernacular languages were published in the period, even fewer with enduring fame. Sebastian Brant in German and François Villon in French stand out as exceptions. Instead, printers turned to the canon of medieval vernacular literature and improved access to texts that had already been transmitted in manuscript: Dante, Boccaccio in translation, Wolfgang von Eschenbach and, on a somewhat lower level but in much greater quantity, the many romances of medieval literature, as well as Aesop in various medieval translations. The fragmentary survival of popular texts, later known as chapbooks, suggests that by the 1490s they were already known as a cheap source of entertainment.

Printing in English is distinct from the general pattern. Taken together, the three main printers of the period 1476–1500 (William Caxton, Wynkyn de Worde, and Richard Pynson) published much more in English than in other languages, and their English books were unambiguously destined for a lay readership. William Caxton created this market. He combined editions of the English literary canon (Chaucer, Lydgate, Gower) with the publication of a large number of translations from French, most of them by himself. Uniquely, he added prologues and epilogues to these texts, explaining to readers his choices. His oeuvre in prose also includes his substantial extensions of existing chronicles which he brought up to date to recent times. Caxton's fame as England's first printer obscures the fact that he is one of the few contemporary authors to appear in print in a vernacular language, and who addressed his readers directly, in a voice that is still capable of speaking to us.

Initially, Caxton's preference was for literary and historical works, but with the translation of the *Golden Legend*, a massive collection of saints' lives probably published early in 1484, he began to concentrate on devotional texts. After his death in 1492, his immediate successor, Wynkyn de Worde, continued to concentrate on devotional works, while Richard Pynson's reprints from Caxton included *The Canterbury Tales*. A few years later, the roles reversed, and de Worde reprinted some of Caxton's literary publications, including *The Canterbury Tales*, but his approach was more critical than Pynson's had been, and he initiated rigorous revisions (BMC xi: 49–50).

De Worde's revision of *The Canterbury Tales*, based on the comparison of several manuscript sources (BMC xi: 214–16; Tokunaga 2006), is a good example of a remarkable phenomenon that began to develop as an effect of the much-expanded availability of textual sources, which is in direct contradiction to what must have appeared initially to be the major advantage of the multiplication of texts in print. A printed version might indeed be accepted as a standard and be copied in subsequent editions without being subjected to further critical assessment. However, multiplying a text in many copies might initiate a critical process. It frequently happened that on publication in print a text was compared with other sources and improved in later editions, sometimes on the grounds of greater completeness, but also by the introduction of variant readings, by conjecture, through collation with manuscripts, or in due course with other printed editions with versions from independent sources. The process can be observed from the very first years of printing, and can be demonstrated particularly well in the successive editions of *The Canterbury Tales*. It accelerated to become in the sixteenth century the basis for the critical assessment of the complete European literary heritage from classical times onward. Its immediate impact on religion and society was never felt more dramatically than in the sixteenth century, but in essence the process continues to the present day.

The Trade in Printed Books

The production of printed books soon created problems of marketing. As we have seen, a manuscript text, once set in type and printed, would spawn hundreds of copies. Along with the printing press, the already existing book trade had to be reinvented. The first printers in Rome, the partnership of Conrad Sweynheym and Arnold Pannartz, were shocked to discover that between 1467 and 1472 they had produced a warehouse full of printed books (they counted over 12,000 volumes) that they found hard to sell. They printed an appeal for help addressed to the pope, possibly also serving as an advertisement for their wares (BMC iv: 15). Selling books, printers discovered, takes as much ingenuity as printing them.

Only gradually, through owner's inscriptions, and the study of decoration and bindings, are we beginning to grasp the complexity of the early book trade. The illumination of copies of Gutenberg's great Latin Bible shows that within a short time it was decorated by artists in cities as far apart as Mainz, Leipzig, Vienna, Lübeck, Bruges, and London (König 1991). The major printers shared risks with distant colleagues, and operated in an international world through wholesale arrangements, resulting in the distribution of books over a wide area. Commonly, books eventually reached stationers in sheets ("in albis"), and could be decorated and bound according to customers' wishes. But through an entrepôt system (for example in Mainz and Louvain) an agent might receive copies of books in sheets, to have them decorated and bound before they were sold on to markets to which he had access.

In England, London's St. Paul's Churchyard was a center for the retail trade from early in the fifteenth century on, as was Cat Street in Oxford, but Caxton's shop in Westminster was new, conveniently situated near the royal court and parliament (BMC xi: 8–9). Less documented is the role of fairs in England, although some ownership inscriptions mention Stourbridge, but no inscription is known to record the fact that a book was bought from a peddler, although this must have happened quite often.

REFERENCES AND FURTHER READING

Agüera y Arcas, B. (2003) "Temporary Matrices and Elemental Punches in Gutenberg's DK Type." In K. Jensen (ed.), *Incunabula and their Readers*, pp. 1–12. London: British Library.

Armstrong, E. (1990) *Before Copyright: The French Book-privilege System 1498–1526*. Cambridge: Cambridge University Press.

Baker, J. H. (1999) "The Books of the Common Law." In L. Hellinga and J. B. Trapp (eds.), *The Cambridge History of the Book in Britain*, vol. III: *1400–1557*, pp. 411–32. Cambridge: Cambridge University Press.

Barnard, J. and McKenzie, D. F., with Bell, M. (eds.) (2002) *The Cambridge History of the Book in Britain*, vol. IV: *1557–1695*. Cambridge: Cambridge University Press.

Bechtel, G. (1992) *Gutenberg et l'invention de l'imprimerie*. Paris: Fayard.

BMC (1908–2007) *Catalogue of Books Printed in the XVth Century Now in the British Museum/British Library*, vols. i–ix: London: British Museum; vols. x, xii: London: British Library; vols. xi, xiii: 't Goy-Houten: HES & De Graaf.

Christianson, C. Paul (1999) "The Rise of the London Book-trade." In L. Hellinga and J. B. Trapp (eds.), *The Cambridge History of the Book in Britain*, vol. III: *1400–1557*, pp. 128–47. Cambridge: Cambridge University Press.

Corsten, S. (1987) "Universities and Early Printing." In L. Hellinga and J. Goldfinch (eds.), *Bibliography and the Study of 15th-century Civilisation*, pp. 83–123. London: British Library.

Davies, M. (1996) *The Gutenberg Bible*. London: British Library.

Ford, Margaret L. (1999) "Importation of Printed Books into England and Scotland" and "Private Ownership of Printed Books." In L. Hellinga and J. B. Trapp (eds.), *The Cambridge History of the Book in Britain*, vol. III: *1400–1557*, pp. 179–204 and 205–28. Cambridge: Cambridge University Press.

Gaskell, P. (1972) *A New Introduction to Bibliography*. Oxford: Clarendon Press.

Goldschmidt, E. P. (1955) *The First Cambridge Press in its European Setting*. Cambridge: Cambridge University Press.

Hellinga, L. (1997) "Press and Text in the First Decades of Printing." In *Libri, Tipografi, Biblioteche*, pp. 1–23. Istituto di Biblioteconomia e Paleografia, Università degli Studi, Parma. Florence: Leo S. Olschki.

— (1999) "Printing." In L. Hellinga and J. B. Trapp (eds.), *The Cambridge History of the Book in Britain*, vol. III: *1400–1557*, pp. 65–108. Cambridge: Cambridge University Press.

— (2003) "Nicolas Jenson et les débuts de l'imprimerie à Mayence." *Revue française d'histoire du livre*, 118–21: 25–53.

— and Trapp, J. B. (eds.) (1999) *The Cambridge History of the Book in Britain*, vol. III: *1400–1557*. Cambridge: Cambridge University Press.

Kapr, A. (1996) *Johann Gutenberg: The Man and his Invention*, trans. D. Martin. Aldershot: Scolar.

König, E. (1991) "New Perspectives on the History of Mainz Printing." In S. L. Hindman (ed.), *Printing the Written Word: The Social History of Books circa 1450–1520*, pp. 143–73. Ithaca: Cornell University Press.

Needham, P. (1999) "The Customs Rolls as Documents for the Printed-book Trade in England." In L. Hellinga and J. B. Trapp (eds.), *The Cambridge History of the Book in Britain*, vol. III: *1400–1557*, pp. 148–63. Cambridge: Cambridge University Press.

Nieto, P. (2003) "Géographie des impressions euro-péennes du XVe siècle." *Revue française d'histoire du livre*, 118–21: 125–73.

Reske, C. (2000) *The Production of Schedel's Nuremberg Chronicle*. Wiesbaden: Harrassowitz.

Roberts, Julian (2002) "The Latin Trade." In J. Barnard and D. F. McKenzie, with M. Bell (eds.) (2002) *The Cambridge History of the Book in Britain*, vol. IV: *1557–1695*, pp. 141–73. Cambridge: Cambridge University Press.

Tokunaga, S. (2006) "The Textual Transmission of *The Canterbury Tales*: The Case of Wynkyn de Worde." Unpublished PhD thesis, Keio University, Tokyo.

Veyrin-Forrer, J. (1987) "Aux origines de l'imprimerie française: l'atelier de la Sorbonne et ses mécènes (1470–1473)." In *La lettre et le texte*, pp. 161–87. Paris: L'École Normale Supérieure de Jeunes Filles.

16

The Book Trade Comes of Age: The Sixteenth Century

David J. Shaw

Incunables and Post-incunables: Continuity and Innovation

Although it has been traditional among book-collectors and printing historians to distinguish the fifteenth century with its own label of "incunable" (and to call the years 1501–40 the "post-incunable" period), the defining date of December 31, 1500 has no real importance in terms of the technologies used nor in the appearance of the books produced. However, there is no doubt that the typical book of 1530 looked significantly more modern than the typical book of 1490. The changes were, however, gradual and regional and, even by 1600, the books produced in most countries in Europe retained a recognizable national appearance in typography or in the layout of text as well as in the styles of bindings found on individual copies.

The Italian book had a stylistic reputation among purchasers, collectors, and book-trade personnel which encouraged the spread of a more "modern" appearance: increasing use of roman (and italic) type, instead of Gothic; greater use of white space and geometrical patterns in page layout (centered text, triangular and other shapes); and illustrations in a more "classical" style, with a clean black-on-white-ground appearance.

Although the invention of printing is commonly thought of as a "revolution," it is clear that the change was in the volume of material available for purchase, not in the nature of the texts offered. Italian printers in the 1470s over-supplied the market with new Humanist books and quickly reverted to supplying traditional texts, especially for the professional university-educated market: law, theology, medicine, as well as more basic school and college texts. Rabelais was still complaining in the 1530s of the durability of the old medieval educational texts: "Don Philippe des Marays, Viceroy of Papeligosse . . . answered that it was better for the boy to learn nothing than to study such books under such masters. For their learning was mere stupidity, and their wisdom like an empty glove; it bastardised good and noble minds and corrupted the flower of youth" (Rabelais 1955: 71).

Older texts gained a wider currency thanks to printing (Goldschmidt 1943). Study of the great scholars of the Middle Ages, theologians and lawyers in particular, was greatly facilitated by the availability of printed texts of their works and of commentaries on them. Typically produced in very large folio volumes, this aspect of the industry must have been as welcome to the printers as it was to students who had access to easily consultable copies of basic texts, either in their own possession or in the growing libraries of the universities and religious houses of Europe.

Parish clergy and ordinary lay people were also catered for by the growth of printing. In these cases, the texts tended to be smaller and cheaper. Works by (or attributed to) famous names such as St. Bonaventura or anonymous texts such as the *Dialogus linguae et ventris* (Dialogue of the Tongue and the Stomach) received an extra burst of life into the mid-sixteenth century. One of the staples of religious printing in many centers was the production of Books of Hours for lay people to use in their devotions. Each diocese had its own variety until the Council of Trent (1545–63) attempted to impose a standard set of liturgical texts such as the Tridentine Missal (1570), an attempt that was not entirely successful. Printers in Paris, for example, were producing several dozen editions a year of Books of Hours with woodcut illustrations in the 1520s, as well as other liturgical texts for churches and religious houses, such as breviaries and missals. Several centers specialized in the production of Bibles.

Vernacular literature also received a new lease of life through the printing press. The Arthurian legends, which had been immensely popular in the twelfth and thirteenth centuries, were modernized by translation into modern prose versions. These romances of chivalry were often very large books, designed at first for wealthy nobles or middle-class purchasers, but there were also "pot-boiler" versions of medieval tales which were produced in editions of eight or twelve leaves for a more popular market by specialist firms such as the Trepperel and Lotrian families in Paris. In the mid-century, a new vogue for this sort of literature arose with the creation of a range of new works such as the *Orlando furioso* and *Amadis de Gaule*, which unhinged poor Don Quixote.

Paradoxically, the avant-garde cultural craze of sixteenth-century Europe was the revival or "renaissance" of the literature of ancient Greece and, especially, ancient Rome. Colleges and "grammar" schools set up to educate boys for the professions and the universities saw their syllabuses captured by "Humanists" who taught the ancient languages and their culture. The publishing industry benefited immensely, first of all in Italy where the movement began, and then across the whole of Europe. New grammar books and other teaching aids were needed and suitable editions of the basic texts were produced in ever-increasing quantities. Popular Latin school authors, such as the poets Virgil, Terence, and Ovid or the prose writers Cicero and Caesar, made the fortunes of printers like Sebastian Gryphius in Lyon or the Wechel family in Paris and then in Frankfurt later in the century. Scholars such as Desiderius Erasmus (1466–1536) or William Lily (c.1466–1522) wrote grammar books, readers, and reference works. Erasmus's *Adagia* was a collection of classical proverbs each accompanied by an explanatory essay; his *Colloquia* provided specimen dialogues to help pupils learn to speak a good classical Latin. These and similar texts were printed in countless editions across Europe through the century and beyond, with print-runs as high as a thousand copies even at the start of the century.

The emphasis of this "Humanist" education was philological: a strong bias toward the study of the languages and literatures of the classical world. A related category of texts (one in which Erasmus also specialized) was the revival of the study of the early Church Fathers, especially those of the Greek Church, and also the study of the original languages of the Bible: Hebrew and Greek. These topics were looked on with suspicion at first by the ecclesiastical authorities, but gradually became part of the mainstream of intellectual activity in the Catholic as well as the Protestant traditions. Again, the publishers sought to meet a need with the provision of newly researched editions of the relevant texts, not always a profitable venture, as these were typically very large folio texts with extensive commentaries. Print-runs for these more learned works would inevitably be smaller.

So far as we know, the technology of printing was essentially unchanged from that of the incunable period but its practitioners were tending to specialize more: punch-cutting and type-founding in particular, and also bookbinding in the larger centers; papermaking and distribution had always tended to be in the hands of separate trades-men. The physical appearance of texts on the page did undergo changes which gradually gave the printed book a more modern and less medieval appearance. One of the main developments was the emergence of the title page, partly for practical reasons to protect the opening page of the text from wear and tear, partly for advertising reasons: the title of the book and the name and location of its producer could be displayed prominently on this otherwise blank first page (Smith 2000). Another development of the modern page layout was the introduction of page numbers, which did not really become common until the early sixteenth century. This went hand in hand with the develop-ment of indexes in scholarly works: without a page number, an index reference or a list of errata is very difficult to use.

One consequence of the ever-increasing growth of the consumer market for printed materials was pressure for a reduction in prices. The costs of producing an edition of a printed book depend on three factors: fixed overheads (accommodation, investment in equipment), the cost of labor, and the cost of paper. Of these, the greatest area of flexibil-ity was in reducing the page size and type size of the book so that the same amount of text could be fitted onto fewer sheets of paper. This had the effect of making the large formats (folio and quarto) less popular and the small formats (octavo and smaller) much more common. The producers of classical texts, for example, turned away from large format books with text accompanied by multiple commentaries to small-format editions with either plain text or texts with simple marginal notes intended for the wider school and college markets. In 1565, the Antwerp printer Christophe Plantin produced 1,250 copies of the satires of Juvenal and Persius in octavo format (8°) which needed ten sheets; the following year he produced 1,600 copies in the smaller "sixteen-mo" format (16°) occupying six sheets; twenty years later, his Leiden office issued an even smaller 24° edition which took up only two and a half sheets.

Illustrations were found in the earliest days of printing. The sixteenth century saw the development of woodcut and copper-engraved illustrations in a wide range of books, scientific, religious, and popular. There was also a spread in popularity of the use of sets of ornamental initials to decorate the starts of chapters, woodcut at first and later produced in type metal. These were accompanied by other ornamental elements: head-bands and tail pieces and the development of fleurons, small squares of type with a pattern which could be assembled to make decorative title-page borders and similar ornamental features.

Scholar Printers

During the course of the sixteenth century, hundreds of printers exercised their trade in towns and cities across Europe, their names largely unknown except to specialists in historical bibliography. In fact, the printers increasingly declined in importance in the book trade compared with the bookseller–publishers. In London, for example, it was the booksellers who became dominant in the Stationers' Company. Some printers, however, achieved a celebrity in their day which they have never lost, partly because of their technical and commercial abilities but also because of their own scholarly attainments or those of the circle of collaborators they attracted. Some created family dynasties, such as Manuzio, Estienne, and Plantin.

Aldo Manuzio (in Latin, Aldus Manutius, c.1449–1515) was already known in the 1490s as an innovator in the design of his Roman and Greek types and the quality of scholarship in his editions of classical texts. In the sixteenth century, he launched a series of small-format editions of classical texts printed in the very first italic type, designed by Francesco Griffo. These innovations in format and type were quickly copied and became fashionable throughout Europe. The celebrated French book-collector Jean Grolier (1479–1565) owned several copies of many of Aldus's pocket classics, often with elaborate ornamental bindings.

Aldus's trend-setting work extended beyond the vogue for classical texts. He also produced similar editions of Italian literary texts which had themselves achieved classical status by this time: an edition of Petrarch's *Canzoniere* (love sonnets) had been prepared for publication in 1501 by Pietro Bembo (1470–1547), humanist scholar and later a cardinal, who went on to produce an edition of Dante's *Divina commedia* in 1502. Aldus's business was carried on after his death by his father-in-law Andrea Torresano (1451–1529) and his sons and eventually by Aldus's own son, Paolo Manuzio (1512–74), and a grandson, also called Aldus Manutius (1547–97).

Five generations of the Estienne family were engaged in printing and bookselling in Paris and Geneva in the sixteenth and seventeenth centuries. Counting alliances by marriage, at least thirteen members of the family were engaged in the book trade, many of them using the emblem of the olive tree as their device. The founder, Henri Estienne (known as "Stephanus" in Latin), worked in Paris from 1502 until his death in 1520, producing scholarly editions of classical and philosophical texts for the university market, edited by the leading intellectuals of the day, especially Jacques Lefèvre d'Etaples. His son Robert (1503–59) was more famous still, as a scholar, dictionary-maker, and editor of classical texts, as well as a printer. His interests in the texts of the

Hebrew and Greek Bible led him into disfavor with the Catholic religious authorities in Paris. In 1551, he transferred to Calvinist Geneva to be able to carry on this work. Several other members of the family were also important scholars and authors as well as printers or publishers, including Robert's son, Henri Estienne the younger (1531–98), who took over the running of the Geneva office where he published his monumental Greek dictionary, the *Thesaurus Graecae linguae* (1572).

Although Christophe Plantin (1520?–89) was French, it was in Antwerp that he established what was to become one of the largest printing shops of the whole of six-teenth-century Europe, employing 150 men and sixteen presses at the height of his career. No scholar himself, he was nevertheless the friend and business partner of many of the greatest names of the second half of the century, classicists such as Justus Lipsius, artists (his grandson commissioned family portraits from Rubens), churchmen like Benito Arias Montano, and statesmen including King Philip II of Spain. The printing house which he established "at the sign of the golden compasses" and which he left to his son-in-law and business partner Jan Moerentorf (Moretus) still stands today in the Friday-Market in Antwerp. It passed through generations of the Moretus family until it was bequeathed to the city of Antwerp as a museum of printing in 1876. Plantin was a highly successful international businessman with offices or agents in all the major European capitals. His enthusiasm for typography has left a double legacy in the quality of the volumes that he produced and in the scope and importance of the historical col-lections of typographical materials preserved in the Plantin–Moretus Museum.

Many other successful dynasties of printers or publishers could be cited from this period but the emphasis on famous names whose works are sought after by book-col-lectors to this day distorts the true picture of the growth of the book trade in the six-teenth century. The expansion in the demand for printed books was met, not by the output of the presses of these famous names, but by a much greater army of invisible artisans: small firms, with their journeymen and apprentices, helped by family members, turning out the less well-produced, less well-considered mass of printed material that survives from the period.

Religion

Religion was an inescapable feature of daily life in early-modern Europe, and the new publishing industry inevitably derived considerable profit from supplying its varied needs. At first, this meant exclusively the needs of the Catholic Church: specialist texts for theologians and canon lawyers, practical manuals for parish clergy for preaching sermons or hearing confessions, service books for monasteries, cathedrals, and parish churches, Books of Hours for lay devotions, and reading matter in the vernacular lan-guages too, not to mention Latin Bibles. In the 1520s, for example, Latin Bibles were published in Antwerp, Basel, Cologne, Lyon, Nuremberg, Paris, and Strasburg. The advent of the Reformation in its various European manifestations inevitably altered the pattern of religious published materials and enormously increased its volume.

It is much disputed whether the Reformation could have happened without the power of the printing press to distribute its message. Its development would certainly have been different. Martin Luther (1483?–1546) initiated the German Reformation with his protest against the sale of indulgences (at Wittenberg, 1517). The controversies which followed were characterized by floods of pamphlets from all sides of the dispute, many written by Luther himself (two dozen in 1520 alone). In France in the 1520s, the group known as the *évangéliques*, influenced partly by Luther and partly by the work of Erasmus, had their own publishing program, supported by elements at court with intermittent periods of repression, such as the ineffective decree by King François I to ban printing in his kingdom (January 1535) following a spate of anti-sacramentarian pamphlets (the *affaire des placards*). The decree had no noticeable effect on the volume of printed materials recorded for that year.

One of the reformers' goals was to give a better scholarly understanding of the texts of the Bible through study of their Hebrew and Greek originals and to provide direct access to the Bible for the laity. Erasmus's edition of the Greek New Testament first appeared in 1519; his Latin paraphrases of the Greek New Testament (1517 and later) were frequently reprinted. Luther's translation of the Bible into German (New Testament 1522, complete Bible 1534) was the first of a series of new vernacular translations: Dutch (1526), French (1530), Italian (1530), English (1535), Spanish (New Testament 1543), Polish (1561), all opposed officially by the Catholic Church.

If Luther's Reformation was essentially German-speaking, the other main Protestant group, led by Jean Calvin (1509–64), was French-speaking, though based in Geneva, just outside the territory of the French crown and therefore beyond the reach of French ecclesiastical authority. The first edition of Calvin's *Institution of the Christian Religion* was printed in Latin in Basel in 1536, with a dedication to the king of France. By the time of Calvin's death, there had been ten editions of the work in Latin, seventeen in French, as well as editions in English, Italian, and Dutch. Calvin's Geneva was a publishing phenomenon: from being an unimportant printing town in the 1530s, it became the center of a propaganda industry by the 1550s. Robert Estienne transferred his business there from Paris in 1551, as had Josse Badius's son Conrad in 1549. Another important printer established in Geneva was Jean Crespin (c.1520–72), who printed much material for the Calvinist Church as well as educational and classical texts. His great personal contribution to the Calvinist Reformation was his *Book of Martyrs*, which graphically documented their sufferings at the hands of the Catholic authorities. First published in 1554, it was constantly revised and augmented and went through fifteen editions in twenty years. The presence of English Protestant exiles in Geneva during the reign of Queen Mary led Crespin to a collaboration with John Foxe (1517–87), whose own *Book of Martyrs* (1563), frequently reprinted, played a similar role in the documentation of the English Reformation and was regularly found among the books in English churches. Another important Calvinist bestseller was the metrical psalms composed by the French royal poet Clément Marot (1496–1544) and often published with copies of the French Calvinist Bible. The English equivalent was the metrical Psalter of Sternhold and Hopkins, first published in 1549 and remaining in use until the nineteenth century.

The Council of Trent (1545–63) was originally intended to address some of the abuses which the Lutherans had protested about, but soon embarked on a wholesale restatement of Catholic doctrine and liturgy to mark out the ground against the reformers. The three sets of sessions of the Council generated a whole literature of position statements, distributed all over Europe. The new liturgies required the abandonment of old service books and the printing of large quantities of new missals, breviaries, Books of Hours, and so on. Some printers exploited these opportunities very successfully. Christophe Plantin who, in spite of his own apparently unorthodox religious beliefs, held privileges from the Spanish crown for the production of the new liturgies in Spanish territories, including the Low Countries and the New World, was less successful, as his royal Spanish patron was not a good payer of bills.

Another aspect of the Counter-Reformation that had an impact on the market for books was the founding of new religious orders, especially ones with an educational mission. The Jesuit order established colleges all over Europe which attracted the sons of the nobility and gentry. Their educational reforms created an opportunity for whole series of new textbooks and further stimulated the demand for editions of the classical authors who provided the staple reading of the Jesuit schools.

A further characteristic of religious practice at the time was the attempt to control what could be safely read by the populace and to suppress what could not. In the Catholic world, the major development here was the creation of a series of Indexes of Prohibited Books (*Index librorum prohibitorum*), the printing of which provided further useful employment for printers. Books surviving from libraries of the period often show the marks of censorship as college or monastic authorities tried to expurgate texts which were otherwise thought to be worth studying.

The religious turmoil of the second half of the century stimulated a flood of printed propaganda. The French Wars of Religion (1562–98) generated an immense volume of pamphlets from all sides as the focus of the conflict shifted between Catholic and Protestant, crown and aristocracy, Spain and France. In England, Calvinist literature was smuggled in from Geneva or the Low Countries in Mary's reign; in Elizabeth's, heterodox works had to be imported or produced clandestinely by the Protestant Marprelate press (1588–9) or the Catholic English secret presses (1587 onward).

England's own Reformation also had a role for printed books. Henry VIII and Bishop John Fisher published anti-Lutheran tracts in the early 1520s, but by the mid-1530s the beginnings of the English Reformation saw the publication of English-language versions of tracts by German reformers. The history of the English Bible and the English prayer-book is well known, but the statistics of publication are worth stressing: the *Short-title Catalogue of Books Printed in England, Scotland and Ireland (1475–1640)* lists twelve editions of the Book of Common Prayer printed in 1549, the first year of publication; fifty years later, four or five editions a year were still being produced. The continuous availability of the Bible in English is similarly impressive: there were seven editions of the Great Bible in 1539 and 1540; in the 1590s, there were twenty-two editions of the Geneva Bible and two of the Bishops' Bible. The existence of the Church of England as an English-language state church ensured a continuous demand for Bibles, prayer-books, and expository materials, including controversial works published abroad by its Puritan and Catholic opponents.

The book trade also attempted to meet the needs of other religious communities beyond the main areas of Catholic, Lutheran, and Calvinist Europe. In particular, the liturgical needs of the Orthodox Churches, both Greek and Russian, started to appear in print, necessitating the preparation of special Greek and Cyrillic founts. For a long time, Venice remained the center for the printing of Orthodox liturgical books, mainly in Greek but also in Slavonic. The first Cyrillic liturgical text was a Book of Hours, printed in Moscow in 1565, the second dated book produced in Russia, the first being an edition of *The Acts of the Apostles* printed in 1564. Jewish religious texts in Hebrew were also produced, especially in Italy and in Eastern Europe.

Regulation

Although the civil and ecclesiastical authorities felt the need to keep an eye on the activities of printers, booksellers, and even purchasers of books, members of the book trade often looked to the same authorities for support and protection in their activities. In Paris, members of the book trade fell under the general jurisdiction of the university, which appointed twenty-four *libraires jurés* (sworn booksellers) as their intermediaries in administering oversight of the trade. In addition to the status that this gave, the *libraires jurés* had exemptions from taxes as members of the university. Authors and producers in France enjoyed protection for their wares through *privilèges* issued by the state authorities: a new work could be protected from reprinting by the award of a privilege for a limited number of years. The award was made by a court: the royal court, or, in Paris, the Parlement or the Prévôt, or one of the provincial *parlements*. Infringement of the privilege could be pursued through the courts, but the privileges sometimes stated the maximum price which could be charged for the book. Privileges were first issued by the Senate in Venice and were also found elsewhere in Italy and in Germany; they represented a step in the development of the concept of copyright.

In England the system was somewhat different. The Stationers' Company under its royal charter of 1557 was empowered to regulate the book trade (essentially in London) on behalf of its members and of the civil authorities. The Company kept a register in which its members could pay to have their new publications recorded. This gave them protection against reprinting, with the Company as the body that was empowered to enforce seizures and fines for infringements.

State and religious authorities in a number of countries had a system whereby new books had to be "licensed" before publication to ensure their religious conformity. The role of the *Index* in Catholic countries has already been mentioned. The other authority that came to concern itself with book censorship was the Inquisition, especially in Spanish territories.

Geography: The Continued Spread of Printing Centers

By the beginning of the sixteenth century, printers had established themselves in all the major cities of Europe, with Paris, Venice, and Lyon as the three main publishing centers. Paris was a university and administrative centre; Venice was the hub of an extensive trading empire; and Lyon had one of the most important European trade fairs, held four times a year, where merchants could arrange deals and settle accounts. By the end of the century, Venice had declined; the Lyon fairs had become less important; Antwerp had become more significant as a trading center; and the German fairs at Frankfurt and at Leipzig achieved a predominant role in the European book-supply system.

In all the major towns of Europe which had a university or college or a significant legal or administrative center, the printing industry had probably already been active since the fifteenth century. Cities such as Strasburg or Basel continued to have a significant presence in the book trade well into the sixteenth century. In the smaller centers, a printer may have done little book printing but would have had work producing material for local needs: pamphlets, administrative documents, and so on, and would also have functioned as a bookseller, a bookbinder, and often as a more general merchant. As the century progressed, this pattern of diversification into smaller urban centers continued, stimulated by young men looking for new opportunities to establish themselves in the trade and civic pride on the part of municipalities eager to support a modernizing initiative. In France, Toulouse continued to have a significant publishing industry throughout the century, supported by a university and the regional *parlement*. Bordeaux likewise had a succession of booksellers who occasionally published titles themselves, even if only edicts of the *parlement* or books for the local college; later in the century, Simon de Millanges established a successful printing business (1572–1623) which served the needs of the Collège de Guyenne and the new Jesuit college. On the other hand, only a handful of imprints are recorded for a small town like Saumur, and most of these are Wars of Religion pamphlets from around 1590. In Italy and Germany, the existence of many smaller, independent cities and principalities led to a good spread of regional printing and publishing businesses. The index to the British Library's *Short-title Catalogue of Books Printed in Germany up to 1600* shows 150 German and Austrian towns with printing or publishing activities. For Italy, the figure is 130 towns.

The situation in England was slightly different. Although spasmodic attempts to establish presses are recorded for provincial towns (York, 1506–19; Canterbury, 1533–56; Ipswich, 1548; Worcester, 1549–53), printing was essentially concentrated in the capital, with some other activity in the two university cities of Oxford and Cambridge. This situation was formalized with the establishment of the Stationers' Company when printing and publishing essentially became a monopoly of the Company and its members.

Many towns which did not yet have a printer would nevertheless have a bookshop, especially if there was a college or other local market to be supplied. Although literacy in the early-modern period was predominantly an urban phenomenon, chapmen carried small texts into the country districts, and even shepherds are recorded as making determined efforts to learn to read, particularly if they had religious interests.

The Book Trades

The book trade had a multiplicity of specializations. If the pressmen and compositors are the most obvious, behind them we find punch-cutters and type-founders, ink-makers and papermakers, all developing into quite distinct crafts by the mid-century. Sale of the output of the presses required the services of bookbinders and of booksellers, and more often than not a distribution network, especially for scholarly works in Latin, which required an international market to recover their costs. In the first half of the century, Parisian printers produced books for distribution in many provincial towns (especially Lyon and Rouen) as well as abroad (for example, London and Louvain). Already by the early years of the century, the dominant figure in the book trade was the *marchant libraire* or merchant bookseller, what we would call today a publisher and wholesaler. Even a major figure such as Aldus Manutius needed backers who provided financial support for his operations. Some of these financiers operated on a European scale, such as Anton Koberger in Nuremberg or the Giunti family in Venice or Jean Petit in Paris. As has already been mentioned, the major fairs provided the opportunity for publishers and booksellers to meet, place orders, and settle accounts.

The importation of books was usually subjected to control by the state authorities to guard against the introduction of religious or politically seditious works. The inevitable consequence was that such texts would be smuggled: there were cases of smuggling Lutheran writings into East Anglia in the 1520s and 1530s; printers in Geneva set up extensive networks for getting Calvinist works to their markets in the Protestant communities in France; at the end of the century, Catholic texts were produced by presses in Douai and Rouen for distribution to recusant communities both in England and on the continent. In Spain, it is generally believed that excessive censorship caused stagnation in the book trade by the mid-century.

Customers

Authors in sixteenth-century Europe had few rights. They owned their copyright so long as they held the only copy of their work. To get a new work printed, they had to persuade a bookseller or a printer to invest capital, labor, and materials in its production. This would frequently involve paying some or all of the costs in return for a share in the copies printed. Increasing numbers of contracts of this sort have been formed from this period, typically specifying payment for the cost of paper (Richardson 1999: 58–69).

Purchasers of books dealt with a retail bookseller, as today, either in person or by correspondence. The title page of a book would typically state the address of its publisher, and customers no doubt knew who specialized in what. In Paris in the first half of the century, scholarly texts might be bought from Henri Estienne at the Sign of St. John the Baptist opposite the Law Schools or from Gilles de Gourmont at the Sign of the Three Crowns on the rue Saint Jacques. Simon Vostre specialized in Books of Hours at the Sign of St. John the Evangelist on the rue Neufve Nostre Dame. In London and in Paris, the booksellers and printers tended to congregate in one area, the university quarter in Paris, and St. Paul's Churchyard in London. In the provinces, a customer would get a local bookseller to order from a supplier in the capital or might get a relative there to buy for him.

Who bought books? A lot can be deduced from the range of titles produced. Three-quarters of the books published in the fifteenth century were in Latin; by the end of the sixteenth century, over half were in the vernacular languages (Hirsch 1967: 132). This indicates that a large proportion of book buyers still belonged to the educated and professional classes who had learned Latin at school and university: doctors, lawyers, clerics, teachers, as well as those from well-to-do families who had received a similar education. Nevertheless, the growing proportion of books in the vernacular languages shows the growth of literacy in the general population, especially in urban areas in Protestant countries which put a high value on the ability to read the Bible.

How much did a customer have to pay for a printed book? In mid-sixteenth-century England, the popular pamphlet-sized *A lytell geste of Robin Hood* cost two (old) pence, whereas Chaucer's *Works* cost five shillings bound or three shillings unbound (Bennett 1950: 176–7). Inflation was, of course, a constant factor at this time and it is difficult to relate prices to wages. Clearly, books did sell and in considerable quantities. For the first time, a living author could become aware that he had access to a far wider public than his immediate circle of patrons. Clément Marot, *valet de chambre* and royal poet to King François I, was also a bestseller: his *Adolescence Clementine* went through about forty editions between its first appearance in 1532 and 1538 when he published his collected poems, which had gone through a further twenty editions by the time of his death in 1544.

Look to the Future

Just as the book trade in 1501 was not radically different from that in 1499, so the advent of the seventeenth century would not bring an immediate change in trends. The academic world still needed a good range of classical and religious texts; religious controversies continued to flourish; literacy continued to spread and the proportion of Latin books continued to decline. The economics of the printing trade favored the rise of consortia of booksellers such as the Compagnie de la Grand' Navire in Paris (1585–1641), forming what we would consider to be a publishing company specializing in the financing of editions of the Church Fathers. Scientific and reference publishing was not unknown in the sixteenth century (Nicolaus Copernicus's *De revolutionibus* was first published in 1543) but was to see a great increase in the next century as the scientific revolution progressed. Similarly, the demand for news books would develop strongly but was not unknown during the upheavals of the Wars of Religion. Newspaper publication, however, was still for the future.

REFERENCES AND FURTHER READING

Armstrong, E. (1986) *Robert Estienne, Royal Printer: An Historical Study of the Elder Stephanus*, rev. edn. Abingdon, Berkshire: Sutton Courtenay Press.

Barnard, J., McKenzie, D. F., and Bell, M. (eds.) (2002) *The Cambridge History of the Book in Britain*, vol. IV: *1557–1695*. Cambridge: Cambridge University Press.

Bennett, H. S. (1950) "Notes on English Retail Book-prices, 1480–1560." *The Library*, 5th ser., 5: 172–8.

Clair, C. (1960) *Christopher Plantin*. London: Cassell (reprinted London: Plantin, 1987).

— (1976) *A History of European Printing*. London: Academic.

Febvre, L. and Martin, H-J. (1976) *The Coming of the Book*, trans. D. Gerard. London: Verso (reprinted 1997; originally published 1958).

Gilmont, J-F. (ed.) (1998) *The Reformation and the Book*, trans. K. Maag. Aldershot: Ashgate (originally published 1990).

Goldschmidt, E. P. (1943) *Medieval Texts and their First Appearance in Print*. London: Bibliographical Society.

Hellinga, L. and Trapp, J. B. (eds.) (1999) *The Cambridge History of the Book in Britain*, vol. III: *1400–1557*. Cambridge: Cambridge University Press.

Hirsch, R. (1967) *Printing, Selling and Reading, 1450–1550*. Wiesbaden: Harrassowitz.

McKitterick, D. (2003) *Print, Manuscript and the Search for Order, 1450–1830*. Cambridge: Cambridge University Press.

Rabelais, F. (1955) *Gargantua and Pantagruel*, trans. J. M. Cohen. Harmondsworth: Penguin.

Richardson, B. (1999) *Printing, Writers and Readers in Renaissance Italy*. Cambridge: Cambridge University Press.

Smith, M. M. (2000) *The Title-page: Its Early Development 1460–1510*. London: British Library.

Steinberg, S. H. (1996) *Five Hundred Years of Printing*, rev. John Trevitt. London: British Library.

17

The British Book Market 1600–1800

John Feather

The World of the Book

In 1600, Elizabeth I sat on the throne of England, as she had done for more than forty years. During her reign, the kingdom had faced many great challenges, not least of which was that from a foreign power – Spain – which had tried and failed to invade and conquer. The queen's armies were still fighting in Ireland to try to bring that rebellious kingdom more fully under her control. In Scotland, James VI reigned over – and sometimes ruled – a kingdom that was less stable than its southern neighbor. He looked forward to the day (which was to come in 1603) when he would inherit the English crown to add to his own.

In 1800, George III was monarch of a United Kingdom of Great Britain and Ireland; in Ireland there were simmerings of revolt, but Scotland had been pacified after the failure of the rebellion of 1745. His people had won an empire in North America and India, lost part of it in 1776, and were beginning to build yet more colonies in the remote southern oceans. The great challenge was again from abroad, but this time from France which, under Napoleon, controlled virtually the whole of continental Europe and was actively planning an invasion of Britain. During the two hundred years between the reigns of Elizabeth I and George III, the political, social, intellectual, and cultural life of the British underwent great change. In 1800, even greater changes were becoming apparent; in the England of George III, new industries and new skills were remaking social and economic relationships and were causing the development of a different kind of society. It is against this background of profound and continuing change that we have to see the little world of the book.

At the turn of the seventeenth century that world was paradoxically both narrow and wide. It was narrow in the sense that the production of books in England was, for all practical purposes, confined to a small and closely knit group of booksellers and printers in London. It was wide in the sense that the London book trade (and the handful of printers in Scotland), although it produced books almost entirely in English,

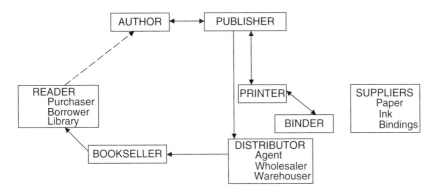

Figure 17.1   The circuit of the book.

also dealt with books in Latin – still the principal written language of the learned elite – that were imported from elsewhere in Europe. The "Latin trade," as contemporaries called it, is always part of the context of the early-modern book trade in Britain; its existence explains why scholarly publishing developed only slowly in the British Isles, even in the universities, and why the native trade was inward-looking both linguistically and geographically (Roberts 2002). The positive consequence was that the London book trade had a near-monopoly of the trade throughout England; there was slightly greater diversity in Scotland, but in a much smaller market. In 1600, the Irish trade was negligible, as was the Welsh trade.

The "book trade," however, is not a simple entity; it is a complex concatenation of trades and activities involving many players. The American historian Robert Darnton has developed the concept of the "circuit" of the book as a means of modeling these relationships (Darnton 1982, 1990). His approach has the merit of showing the connections between author and reader of which the book trade is merely the facilitator. A version of this circuit, using twenty-first century terminology, is given in figure 17.1. The principles embodied in the concept of the circuit have remained essentially unchanged since the sixteenth century; the players, however, have been through major transformations. In figure 17.2 the circuit concept is adapted to represent the English book trade in 1600.

The most important difference between the contemporary and early-modern models lies in the division of roles and skills between the various players involved in the trade. Nevertheless, it remains the case that at the heart of the printed book trade there is a person or firm which turns the author's work into a form in which it can be distributed and sold. Since the early nineteenth century, this functionary has been called the publisher, but long before the word was used in this sense the functions which it describes were central to the trade. In the early seventeenth century, the term used was "bookseller" or sometimes (but perhaps already rather old-fashioned) "stationer." We should confuse none of these terms with their modern equivalents. The seventeenth-century bookseller (the word which will be used here) did indeed sell books to the general

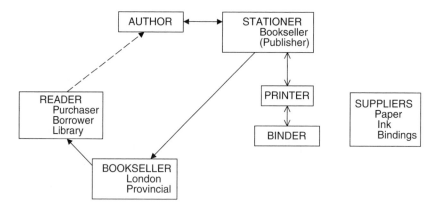

Figure 17.2   The book trade in the early seventeenth century.

public but he (rarely she, although there was an increasing number of women in the trade) might also be a publisher, a wholesaler, and a distributor. Sometimes – but less commonly after about 1600 – all of this was combined with printing and perhaps bookbinding. During the early seventeenth century, however, the separation of printing from the other functions was largely completed, at least in London. In Ireland and Scotland it remained common throughout the seventeenth century for a single business to combine all the functions of the trade, and when printing was allowed to develop in English provincial towns from the mid-1690s onward, it continued to be the normal practice for printers to sell and bind books, and occasionally even to publish them, as well as being printers and (in the modern sense) stationers. The final separation between booksellers and publishers (again using both words in the modern sense on this occasion) did not begin to happen until the last quarter of the eighteenth century, and only then do we find a handful of pioneers coming into the trade specifically to publish books.

Authors: The Primary Producers of the Book Trade

Everything that is printed and published has been written by someone. His or her identity may be concealed, disguised, or forgotten, but there is a human intelligence behind every word that has ever been put into print. The idea of the author as creative genius is a comparatively modern concept, a product of late eighteenth- and early nineteenth-century Romanticism. At the beginning of the seventeenth century, no such romantic notions prevailed. Authors wrote, as they always have, from a variety of motives: to persuade, to advance their careers, to say something they thought was worth saying, to give pleasure to themselves and perhaps to others, to make money. By 1600, the idea of writing for reputation and perhaps for money was no longer as unusual as it had been even within living memory. It was the development of the trade in printed books that had made this possible. For as long as books were written by hand, comparatively few copies could be put into circulation, and there was little chance of recouping significant sums of money from their sale. Authors "published" their work by allowing a scribe to copy it, and perhaps received a one-off payment from a patron for their trouble (Woudhuysen 1996). The development of a trade in printed books at the end of the fifteenth century increased the demand for new books as well as for printed versions of older ones. To meet this demand, authors were employed by printers to create books by editing existing texts or by composition. As the dominant role in the London book trade passed from printers to booksellers in the second half of the sixteenth century, so too did the initiative for developing new books and dealing with authors.

By the last quarter of the seventeenth century, writing for money – what came to be called "writing for the booksellers" – was an established, although far from respectable, occupation. A handful of such writers from every generation are remembered, usually because they were distinguished in other fields, or because they were writers of exceptional skill or interest. The financial rewards were comparatively small. The bookseller bought the book from the author, and the author's financial interest in it came to an end at that moment. The word which contemporaries used for what was bought was "copy," derived from the use of the word by printers to mean the manuscript followed by the compositor in setting the type. Even before 1600, there was an assumption in the book trade, reinforced by custom and in due course by law, that when a bookseller bought a copy, he or she had the unique right to print it or cause it to be printed. One consequence of this assumption was the evolution of the law of copyright (see chapter 38); another was the recognition of the author's role as the initiator of a chain of commercial transactions. By 1700, it was recognized in practice that when the bookseller bought a copy, the author was selling a product that he or she had created, and that the "rights" therefore originated with the author.

This was recognized in the first British Copyright Act (1710). Very soon, a few authors were exploiting the Act for their own benefit, manipulating the sale of their rights to give themselves some measure of control over the finished product. Alexander Pope was particularly adept at this. From about 1720 until the end of his life (he died in 1744), he exploited the book trade much more than it exploited him. In a reversal of traditional roles, he was the financial supporter – the patron – of a printer and a bookseller, and gave significant help to others in the trade. In return, he made demands on them about the physical appearance of his works, and insisted on payments that related to the number of copies sold and the number and form of reprints rather than simply accepting a single payment for the outright sale of his rights. No other eighteenth-century English authors (and few since) were able to exercise such control over the publication of their works. Pope's unique achievement was, however, of wider importance: he established that the author was a partner in the process of book production, and that the new law of copyright could be used to help authors as well as booksellers (Feather 1994).

During Pope's lifetime there were other developments which put authors in a more favorable position. The most important of these was the rapid development of newspapers and magazines. News books had existed before 1640, and proliferated during the Civil War (1642–9), but from 1650 until the Restoration (1660) they were tightly controlled, and effectively published by government. Under the 1662 Printing Act, pre-publication censorship of all printed matter, and the restriction of printing to London and (in a very limited way) Oxford, Cambridge, and York, meant that the newspaper press was again carefully controlled. Indeed, for some time after 1665 the only legal newspaper was the official *London Gazette*. During the 1670s, however, new titles did begin to appear, and from the mid-1690s onward they proliferated. The first London daily, *The Daily Courant*, began publication in 1702; the first provincial newspaper, the weekly *Norwich Post*, began publication in 1701. During the reign of Queen Anne (1702–14), party political strife was rampant; newspapers appeared on every side, sometimes subsidized by political leaders, including those in government. The first great English journalist, Daniel Defoe (1660–1731), learned his trade as a writer during this time, while also working as a government agent and spy. He was later to put his skills to other uses in *Robinson Crusoe* (1719) and *Moll Flanders* (1722).

Defoe was not the only writer to emerge form the journalistic maelstrom of early eighteenth-century politics. Joseph Addison (1672–1719) and Richard Steele (1672–1729), both active politicians, worked together on a journal which they founded, and whose name still survives: *The Spectator*. Each of the more than five hundred issues published in 1711 and 1712 consisted of a single extended essay on some social or political theme. *The Spectator* was a commercial success from the start, and it became a classic. In book form, the essays were reprinted in scores of editions throughout the eighteenth century and later, while Addison and Steele both continued to have parallel literary and political careers. The essay periodical itself became a well-established format for eighteenth-century magazines. Among those who benefited was Samuel Johnson (1709–84) whose *Rambler* (1750–2) and *Idler* (1758–60) imitated both the format and the commercial and literary success of *The Spectator*. Unlike Addison and Steele, however, Johnson was entirely dependent on his pen for his living for much of his life. His essay periodicals were written for the booksellers and were a straightforward commercial transaction. It was a measure of how far authors had come in less than fifty years.

The essay was not the only form of periodical. Indeed, the dominant form was quite different: the general interest magazine. Again, these have a seventeenth-century origin, but the most important was *The Gentleman's Magazine* which began in 1731, and survived in various forms into the twentieth century. The originator, editor, and publisher was Edward Cave, a former Post Office official with some knowledge but no experience of the book trade, who saw a niche in the market for a monthly publication which would carry a digest of the month's news (including fictionalized versions of parliamentary debates which it was illegal to report verbatim), lists and summaries of new books, and some general interest articles. It was aimed at a middle-class audience, and to some extent at a provincial one. It was a huge success. For writers it was a boon. It was an invaluable source of both income and training. Johnson was a parliamentary reporter for Cave, as well as epitomizing books and contributing many general articles. So too was Oliver Goldsmith (1728–74) who, like Johnson, used his work for Cave as a source of income while he established himself as a literary author. Many followed in their footsteps. And many followed in Cave's. General interest magazines were one of the characteristic products of the eighteenth-century English book trade.

Growing the Market

Authorship became an economically viable activity during the eighteenth century because the market for books, newspapers, and magazines grew substantially. There were many factors in this change. First, there was a growth in population. From the 1740s onward, the birth rate throughout the British Isles steadily increased, and outpaced the death rate. Secondly, this increasing number of people became wealthier; real incomes grew at all levels of society, although the greatest growth was among those who were already rich. Together, these two trends created a potentially larger market for printed matter, for it was precisely among the comparatively wealthy and the comparatively leisured that the book trade had traditionally found its customers.

But there were other factors at work. While illiteracy was still common, its incidence was decreasing. Although the growth of literacy was comparatively slow in rural areas, and women still lagged behind men for a variety of social and economic reasons, in the towns it was not uncommon for even working men to be able to read, and among the middle class literacy was all but universal. Philanthropic and religious schools provided some sort of access to education even for the very poorest. By the end of the eighteenth century, illiteracy was, for the first time in British history, a positive disadvantage both socially and economically. Ireland and the remoter parts of Wales and Scotland were less literate than England, but even in those places there was progress. Again, this created new and larger markets for the book trade. It also began to create a different kind of market. The traditional products of the London book trade were designed for its traditional markets. But at least some of the new readers wanted something different.

First, there was a growing demand for provision for children. Although this was certainly linked to changing perceptions of the nature of childhood itself, it was also a commercial venture. John Newbery (1713–67) was the first bookseller to make children's books a substantial part of his publishing business; he was to have (and still has) many successors. Some of these books also appealed to less well-educated adult readers, or to those whose hold on literacy was tenuous. An important manifestation of this part of the book market was the chapbook, a simple eight- or twelve-page booklet, usually with a crude woodcut illustration on the front cover, which retold some familiar story such as Robin Hood, or contained a highly abbreviated and simplified version of a more modern fiction such as that of Robinson Crusoe. Chapbooks and children's books were both responses to the development of new markets for the book trade.

Secondly, the new market wanted books that were cheap. There were several ways to achieve this by changing the physical manifestation of the text. The most obvious was to use smaller type and cheaper paper to produce books that could be sold profitably at a lower price. After 1774, when the House of Lords determined that the 1710 Copyright Act meant that all books went into public domain after twenty-eight years, there were hundreds of popular books which anyone could reprint in any format they chose. The cheap reprint was to be one of the mainstays of nineteenth-century publishing; its twenty-first century form is the paperback. Its origin, however, is in the late eighteenth century when it catered to the rapidly growing demand for cheap books. Books could also be made cheaper by spreading the cost of buying them. This was achieved by serial publication. Although this is probably most familiar in its nineteenth-century revival as the serialized novel, so beloved by Dickens, Thackeray, and others (and by their readers and publishers), it too is of eighteenth-century origin. There are some examples from the late seventeenth century, but it was from the 1740s to the 1760s that serial publication ("part books" in contemporary trade parlance) had its first heyday. In the eighteenth century, although some serial fiction was published, most part books were actually non-fiction, including some very serious works such as biblical commentaries, historical and topographical works, and biographies. Some were older works, but many were original publications. These new physical forms of printed matter, together with the newspapers and magazines, had a wider appeal primarily because they were cheaper, and to some extent because their contents were not designed for a cultural elite but for the contemporary equivalent of a mass market.

The market was not confined to London. Books were available for sale in the major English provincial towns before the invention of printing, but the development of an organized and reasonably efficient provincial trade is another phenomenon of the eighteenth century. This development was intimately linked with the growth of provincial newspapers. In its turn, this was facilitated by the lapse of the Printing Act in 1694–5 which, among its many unintended effects, legalized printing throughout England and Wales. In practice, change was slow, but by 1720 there were printers in some major towns and cities (such as Norwich and Bristol), in some regional centers (Northampton, Exeter), and in a handful of places which through historical and geographical accident were on major trading routes (such as St. Ives in Cambridgeshire on the Great North Road). An important part of these small but growing businesses was the production of a weekly newspaper, which typically had news taken from week-old London papers but advertisements from its own circulation area. These areas were huge, sometimes covering several counties, although circulation was small in numerical terms. The pioneering provincial printers were also typically booksellers. Because they had arrangements for the sale of their newspapers through agents in neighboring towns, they could also build a system for the distribution of books. A pattern developed. London remained the center of publishing activities in the book trade, but the London booksellers advertised their new titles in the London and provincial press and the provincial newspaper printers would take orders for those titles, transmit them to London, act as intermediaries for payment, and undertake to deliver books to customers. This delivery was through the agents who also sold their newspapers. In this way, networks of book distribution developed throughout most of England in the first half of the eighteenth century, together with shops in most towns which, if not actually bookshops, at least sold books (Feather 1985).

Through these networks, the London booksellers were able to reach the potentially large provincial markets. This opened up even quite remote parts of the country to metropolitan cultural and political influence. While the upper classes continued to make their annual pilgrimages to the county town, and perhaps also to London and (later in the century) to a fashionable watering place or spa such as Bath or Brighton, the middle classes who did not have these annual migratory patterns could also get access to books. At the same time, improvements in postal services, largely as a result of the work of Ralph Allen (1693–1764), who was postmaster in Bath but also had a contract to manage a large part of the national postal service, made direct delivery of London newspapers, magazines, and part books to provincial customers both physically possible and reasonably economic. Indeed, Cave (drawing on his background in the Post Office) always emphasized the importance of the provincial market, and the part books were probably specifically designed for it in many cases.

The market for books in Britain was therefore increasing in every dimension during the eighteenth century. There were more people; they were richer; many of them had more leisure time; more of them could read; there were more bookshops; there were better communications; and there were, partly as a consequence, more books and other printed matter than ever before. It was in Georgian England, not in its Tudor precursor, that the transition to a print-dependent society was completed. Even in Scotland, Wales, and Ireland there is evidence of the same phenomenon, albeit on a smaller scale. The predominance of small, scattered, and poor rural populations over large parts of all three countries militated against the development of the essentially urban culture of the book. Despite this, we find the trade expanding geographically and commercially.

The Distribution of Books: The Circuit Completed

Between the producers of books – authors, publishers, printers – and the consumers – the readers – there is a chain of supply that has become longer and more complicated as the trade has evolved. Centralized production and wide distribution are features of many specialized crafts and industries. But in early-modern England it was a pattern that was comparatively unusual. Some raw materials were nationally distributed from the only points of production: coal from the north-east and rock salt from Cheshire are two obvious examples. But most products were consumed within a short distance of where they were produced. London's food supplies were perhaps the great exception to this, but even in and around London there was both agrarian and pastoral farming which supplied the capital's ever-growing appetite. Some luxury goods were imported, and distributed from the ports: spices from Asia symbolize this trade at the beginning of our period, but by the end these commodities included sugar (from the Caribbean through Liverpool and Bristol), and tea from India (largely through London). Many of these luxury imports were subject to customs and excise duties, so that centralized distribution systems were essential to the legal conduct of trade.

Books, newspapers, and magazines fell somewhere between all of these categories. London was the only significant center of book production in England throughout the seventeenth and eighteenth centuries. It was also the center of the intellectual and literary culture which produced and consumed books. As a production center, it was largely unchallenged. The production of books in Scotland was on a very small scale; the Scottish booksellers did not seriously compete in England until the second quarter of the eighteenth century, and only then (as we shall see) in rather special circumstances. The same was true of Ireland, where the scale was even smaller, although by the middle of the eighteenth century the Dublin booksellers had developed a flourishing trade in the export of books to the British colonies in North America. Wales was yet further behind. Printing in both Welsh and English was a late and slow development. The Welsh book trade was almost entirely devoted to the distribution of books printed in England until the nineteenth century. In England itself, the production of books outside London was limited by law until 1694 and by economic reality after that time. Oxford and Cambridge had both had university presses since the sixteenth century, but despite occasional flurries of activity (notably in the second half of the seventeenth century in both places), they were of little commercial significance. Book production in other provincial towns developed only slowly after 1694, and even by the end of the eighteenth century, serious provincial publishing was very limited in scope and typically confined to books of regional or local interest. This was less true of Scotland and to some extent of Ireland. Some of the most influential British books of the eighteenth century were written by Scots living in Scotland, and were published there. They included many of the works of the philosopher David Hume (1711–76) and the economist Adam Smith (1723–90).

The London booksellers' control of the English – and to some extent British – book trade was maintained by the use of legal, economic, and cultural instruments, but all of these would have failed if they had not been able to meet the growing demand for books outside London. The final – and in some ways most important – link in the chain that competed the circuit of the book was the distribution system which brought together producer and customer, and hence author and reader.

The legal framework changed between 1600 and 1800 but, by a combination of accident and design, its consequences remained remarkably similar. At the beginning of the seventeenth century, the London book trade was carefully controlled. Crown officers and senior churchmen were directly involved in the control of content; even though censorship was fairly light-handed for most of the time, it was real and could occasionally be very heavy indeed. Part of the system of control was to restrict the right to print to a limited number (usually about twenty) of members of the Stationers' Company, the trade guild to which all members of the London book trade had to belong. Even during the upheavals of the middle decades of the seventeenth century, this tightly controlled system survived largely intact. It was re-enforced in the 1662 Printing Act, and effectively survived until that legislation finally lapsed in 1694–5. By that time, the London oligopoly of English book production was firmly entrenched, economically and technically as well as legally. Before the end of the seventeenth century, groups of booksellers were working together both in publishing and in distributing books. These groups, known as "congers," were a conscious attempt (largely successful) to protect existing oligopolies and to make it difficult for new entrants to the trade to set up in competition with existing business. The prospect of unfettered competition, remote as it might be, was very unattractive to the leading members of the London trade in the 1690s. When they realized (after about a decade) that the old legislation was never going to be revived, they changed their tack, petitioned for copyright legislation, and were successful in 1710. The 1710 Copyright Act was essentially a booksellers' law. It had the effect – unintended by parliament but certainly the objective of the booksellers – of further embedding the dominance of the London oligopoly.

The London booksellers were always capable of acting together when their oligopoly was threatened. They did so several times during the eighteenth century. They took action against Scottish printers and booksellers who illegally reprinted London books and sold them in the north of England and the Midlands. They tried – with rather less success because they were on less certain legal ground – to do the same against the Irish booksellers. They worked together for new legislation – to limit the import of English-language books, for example – and supported each other in what was sometimes long, complex, and expensive litigation in the courts of both England and Scotland. The mutual dependence of the London booksellers was perhaps best exemplified in the operation of the so-called "share-book" system. Rights in copies were regularly bought and sold at closed auctions which could be attended only by certain members of the trade. There was an understanding that rights bought at such sales (known as "trade sales") would only be sold through the same channel; hence the rights remained within the inner circles of the trade, although occasional newcomers were admitted, thus increasing the pool of capital among the participants. From the early decades of the eighteenth century onward, it became increasingly common for copy-owners to sell shares (from as much as a half, to as little as one sixty-fourth) in a copy, thus creating complex jointly owned copyrights. These are reflected in the long imprints to be found in many London books of the period. The consequence of the share-book system was that all those who participated in it had an interest in defending it, and in defending the interpretation of the 1710 Act which guaranteed the value of their investments.

There was greater competition in the trade, but it was between the London booksellers themselves, rather than between them and others. It was only in the last quarter of the century that the London booksellers' attempt to protect their traditional stranglehold on the trade began to fail. They lost a critical case in the House of Lords in 1774 which effectively opened the way to unlimited reprinting and sale of books whose copyright was in public domain. Booksellers in the north and the Midlands – the areas of greatest economic growth in these early decades of industrialization – could legally obtain books from Scottish and Irish suppliers if these were cheaper than their London rivals. Law and economics interacted, and did so in the environment of rapidly developing industrial capitalism.

The protection of the law, however, would have had little point if the London booksellers had not been able to operate efficiently at a national level. The economic mechanisms for the maintenance of London's domination of the trade revolved around the distribution system. We know little of this in the early seventeenth century. The upper and middle classes bought their books in London, or from London booksellers directly or through their agents. There were bookshops in the major provincial towns, and books were sold at markets and fairs. The chapmen and peddlers who took goods into the most remote parts of the country also included a few books among their other wares. It was the development of the networks of agents built up by the provincial newspaper producers that transformed the distribution system of the English book trade. By the middle of the century, most towns of any size had a printer and a weekly newspaper. Circulating areas actually contracted geographically, but print-runs and sales, and hence the networks of local agents, increased significantly. Where detailed investigation has been possible, as in Wiltshire and the surrounding areas of south-west England, it is clear that these networks were a critical channel for book distribution (Ferdinand 1997). Books were advertised in the newspapers and could be ordered through their agents. They transmitted the orders to the London booksellers, either directly or through the newspaper proprietor. Thus the provincial newspaper proprietors became the linchpins of a national book-distribution system. They had the contacts in the London trade (for stocking their own shops, as well as for supplies of essential items, such as paper and ink), they had relatively easy access to transportation (since they were typically based in major towns), and – critically – they had lines of credit with the London book trade and had developed means of payment which could overcome or circumvent the obstacles presented by a still primitive system of banking and credit transfer.

The consequence of these developments was that by the second half of the eighteenth century it was possible, without too much difficulty, to obtain a copy of almost any book anywhere in England, and in much of the rest of the British Isles. To facilitate this activity, the London trade also began to develop a supporting infrastructure. Various attempts had been made to produce regular lists of newly published books dating back to the Term Catalogues first published in 1668. The lists published in *The Gentleman's Magazine* were perhaps the first that were both authoritative and widely available. Before the end of the century, there were various attempts to produce a regular listing of new titles for the benefit of the trade rather than the public. A *Complete Catalogue of Modern Books*, first published in 1773, marks the beginning of a more or less continuous series. By the end of the eighteenth century, it was not difficult for a provincial bookseller or reader to keep up with what was being published. Moreover, these various lists also indicated to the provincial booksellers how each title could be obtained. Specialist book wholesaling is a phenomenon of the last quarter of the eighteenth century; until that time, the bookseller was typically his own distributor, although there is evidence that consortia of booksellers worked together to make the system more effective. In 1785, there appeared the first of many directories intended to help both

London and provincial booksellers to identify each other and to know how to communicate. This guide, *The London and Country Printers, Booksellers and Stationers Vade Mecum* by John Pendred, was as important for the Londoners, who could identify their primary provincial customers, as it was for the provincials, who could find out how to contact (and pay) the Londoners (Pollard 1955).

All the evidence taken cumulatively suggests that an effective system for book distribution was operational by about 1750 (Pollard 1978). Of course, it was far from perfect. The physical transport of books was problematic; they had (and have) a comparatively unfavorable ratio of weight to value, so that any form of transport for which the charges are based on the former, will disadvantage books. Books seem to have cost more in the provinces than in London as a result. However, the transport infrastructure was changing for the better. Indeed, it could hardly move in any other direction. The main roads were improved and maintained properly in the eighteenth century for the first time since the Romans left in 410. Before the end of the seventeenth century, the rivers were being partly canalized to make them more suitable for transport; artificial waterways began to be dug from the 1760s onward. Although the real revolution came in the nineteenth century with the building of the railways, by 1800 inland transport in Britain was easier than it had ever been, and provision was far more widespread. On the major roads there were regular coach services, carriers with carts and wagons, and – most important of all – state-controlled postal services which were both a cause and a consequence of the improvement of the roads. The book trade was a beneficiary of all of these developments; it was, in terms of the economy in general, a minor player, but for the trade itself the improvements in transport were another mechanism for securing the effectiveness of the distribution system.

The cultural dimension of the London oligopoly is less tangible but no less important. London was the center of English – and increasingly of British – literary life in the seventeenth and eighteenth centuries. Indeed, the book trade had its place in asserting and ensuring that dominance. The decline of royal and aristocratic patronage effectively left the book trade as the paymasters of the authors. In turn, the trade had to satisfy the wishes of its customers. Because the trade was in London, authors also had to be in London, or to go there to make their names and their fortunes. The mid-eighteenth-century writer Henry Fielding (1707–54) illustrated the process perfectly in one of his novels: the story of *Joseph Andrews* (1742) turns on one of the characters – Parson Adams, a country clergyman – going to London to try to find a bookseller to publish his (almost certainly unsaleable) book. Printed culture was very largely a metropolitan culture, underpinned by the legal and economic power of the London book trade. It was not until the industrial towns of the north and the Midlands began to develop their own distinctive cultural lives in the nineteenth century – including powerful and influential newspapers quite unlike the anodyne imitations of the London press which typified the eighteenth century – that this was to change. Even then, the London book trade was so well entrenched that it was to remain at the heart of British publishing for another two centuries. At the beginning of the twenty-first century, its position is still substantially intact.

Buyers and Readers: The End and the Beginning

The book trade was sustained by demand. Demand came from readers. Without readers there can be no book trade. The pattern which evolved in Britain in the seventeenth and eighteenth centuries, however, and which remains essentially intact even now, was that the producers – the booksellers (in the eighteenth-century sense) – dealt with intermediaries who were part of the same trade rather than with the general public. For much of the seventeenth and eighteenth centuries, these intermediaries were retail booksellers. In London, where it had been customary for booksellers to be retailers as well as publishers, specialization in retailing developed during the century. This development was as much social as it was economic. By the end of the century, the fashionable areas of London were no longer in the City where the trade was traditionally based, but to the west and the north, in rapidly developing Piccadilly, St. James's, and Islington. The retailers moved with their market, and developed their own distinctive branch of the trade. A simultaneous development, largely aimed at the opposite end of the socio-economic scale, was of selling books at low prices in great quantities, and the evolution of the practice of remaindering. The pioneer was James Lackington (1746–1815) whose Temple of the Muses was probably the largest bookshop in the world at the end of the eighteenth century. The link between public and publisher was finally broken. In the provinces it had never existed. Provincial books buyers bought through their local bookseller; the larger shops in the larger towns had a stock of books – typically an eclectic mixture of new and secondhand, dominated by Bibles, prayer-books, and school books – but could also order books for their customers. The would-be reader in Cumberland or Cornwall could read a review or epitome in *The Gentleman's Magazine* and then order the book through the same chain of supply that had brought the magazine in first place.

The price of books was always, of course, an issue for readers. Lackington's success demonstrated that by the end of the eighteenth century there was a market for cheap books. Retail book prices were remarkably stable from the late seventeenth century until the 1780s. Large books (folios and quartos to use contemporary trade terminology) were about 10s or a little more, octavos (perhaps the most typical format in the mid-eighteenth century) about 5s, and the smallest books even less. The smallest pamphlets sold for 6d, as did some tracts and chapbooks. Prices rose fairly steeply toward the end of the period (Altick 1957: 51). A three-volume novel typically sold at about 9s in the 1790s, but this had gone up to about 12s within a decade (St. Clair 2004: 203). This reflected broader trends in prices of goods and commodities in the period (Mitchell 1988: 719–20). Prices, however, need to be set in the context of wages and the cost of living. The latter was stable for much of the eighteenth century; indexing 1700 at 100, the cost of living fell slightly, reaching a low point of 81 in 1732, but after the middle of the century there was a steady increase to 109 in 1762, 130 in 1771, 140 in 1792, and 153 in 1796. In this context, the prices of books roughly reflect the general economic trends of the period, although in real terms they were probably marginally cheaper by the end of the century than they had been at the beginning, and there were far more cheap editions, partly as a consequence of the greater competition introduced into the trade from the mid-1770s onward.

But could people afford to buy books, however cheap they were? Even at the end of the eighteenth century, a female domestic servant could be earning as little as £4 a year, although her accommodation, food, and clothing were typically provided (Berg 2004: 377–8). A laborer (male) earned an average of £19 in 1710 and £25 in 1797. Among the most likely customers for books, a schoolteacher earned an average of £16 in 1710, and £43 in 1797. Both clerks and skilled men in the printing trade itself were better paid than this (£44 and £43 respectively in 1710; £135 and £66 in 1797). A clergyman's average income was £100 in 1710 and £238 in 1797, although these averages (and no doubt others) conceal very large variations between individuals (Mitchell 1988: 153).

Buying books, however, was not the only way to obtain them. In 1661, the London bookseller Francis Kirkman opened the capital's first circulating library, in which customers could borrow books for a limited period of time for a fee. A small circulating library became a profitable sideline for many booksellers throughout the country during the eighteenth century. For some, it was far more than that. In London, in the major provincial cities, and in the pleasure resorts, the circulating library brought the book trade into the developing leisure industry. Especially in the resort towns, the temporary residents needed amusements when not taking the waters or going to the assembly rooms or paying and returning "calls." The literature of the time – Sheridan's plays, Austen's novels – perfectly captures the life and the place of the circulating library in it. By the 1780s, circulating libraries had become an important part of the book-trade economy. The publishers of novels (and by this time we can use the word "publisher" in the modern sense) were particular beneficiaries. The Noble brothers in the 1780s, William Lane in the 1790s, and some others even less well remembered, built successful businesses on commissioning and publishing scores of novels designed specifically for sale to the libraries. Lane's Minerva Press, for example, specialized in Gothic fiction for the library market. These were never intended as literary masterworks; they were unashamed leisure reading, and had themes which are still familiar in that market: romance, horror, glamorized history, and the like.

By 1800, Britain had a print-dependent economy and culture, an increasingly literate and rapidly growing population, and an efficient book trade in which specialization in the various activities that constitute the trade was creating new businesses and laying the foundations for success and prosperity. The market and the means of reaching it developed in parallel, each feeding off the other. New genres and formats were developed to meet market demand. New methods of trading were devised. New distribution systems evolved. In the England of Elizabeth, books were still a luxury; in George III's United Kingdom, they had become a part of the fabric of life.

REFERENCES AND FURTHER READING

Altick, R. D. (1957) *The English Common Reader: A Short History of the Mass Reading Public 1800–1900.* Chicago: Chicago University Press.

Berg, M. (2004) "Consumption in Eighteenth- and Early Nineteenth-century Britain." In R. Floud and P. Johnson (eds.), *The Cambridge Economic History of Modern Britain*, vol. I: *Industrialisation 1700–1860.* Cambridge: Cambridge University Press.

Cranfield, G. A. (1962) The *Development of the Provincial Newspaper 1700–1760.* Oxford: Oxford University Press.

Darnton, R. (1982) "What is the History of Books?" *Daedalus*, 111: 107–35.

— (1990) *The Kiss of Lamourette: Reflections in Cultural History.* London: Faber and Faber.

Feather, J. (1985) *The Provincial Book Trade in Eighteenth-century England.* Cambridge: Cambridge University Press.

— (1994) *Publishing, Piracy and Politics: An Historical Study of Copyright in Britain.* London: Mansell.

— (2006) *A History of British Publishing*, rev. edn. London: Routledge.

Ferdinand, C. Y. (1997) *Benjamin Collins and the Provincial Newspaper Trade in the Eighteenth Century.* Oxford: Clarendon Press.

Johns, A. (1998) *The Nature of the Book: Print and Knowledge in the Making.* Chicago: University of Chicago Press.

Mitchell, B. R. (1988) *British Historical Statistics.* Cambridge: Cambridge University Press.

Pollard, G. (1955) *The Earliest Directory of the Book Trade.* London: Bibliographical Society.

— (1978) "The English Market for Printed Books." *Publishing History*, 4: 7–48.

Roberts, J. (2002) "The Latin Trade." In J. Barnard and D. F. McKenzie, with M. Bell (eds.), *The Cambridge History of the Book in Britain*, vol. IV: *1557–1695*, pp. 141–73. Cambridge: Cambridge University Press.

St. Clair, W. (2004) *The Reading Nation in the Romantic Period.* Cambridge: Cambridge University Press.

Woudhuysen, H. R. (1996) *Sir Philip Sidney and the Circulation of Manuscripts 1558–1640.* Oxford: Clarendon Press.

18

Print and Public in Europe
1600–1800

Rietje van Vliet

Imagine a man who must manage the daily business of three bookshops [in Berlin, Stettin, and Danzig] with all of the accompanying annoyances and worries, who is forced to spend eight weeks visiting two Leipzig fairs and occasionally the Danzig fair as well, who writes and signs some 400 letters a year concerning the [learned journal] Deutsche Bibliothek, not counting other correspondence, [and] who is not safe from interruption at any hour of the day, because anyone may enter a public shop.

These weary words were written by Friedrich Nicolai, one of the greatest publisher–booksellers of eighteenth-century Germany (Selwyn 2000: 99). His shop could be found in the center of Berlin, and was recognizable by the bust of Homer above the doorway. That in itself was an indication that business was blossoming; for most booksellers had to make do with striking lettering on the façade, or a shop sign. Title pages of recently published books, in addition to prospectuses, pamphlets, broadsheets, subscription lists, and other eye-catchers hung on the doorposts, the window frames, and on the wooden notice boards on the front of the bookshop – an effective way of advertising that had existed before the invention of the printing press. Inside, the bookcases reached to the ceiling. Most of the bookshelves contained stacks of paper, the unbound books. In the seventeenth century, these were in folio or quarto format; in the eighteenth century, chiefly octavos or small handy-sized duodecimos. Often there was room in the shop itself for folding and binding the quires. Only a limited number of books were already fitted with a parchment or leather binding. Not only books were sold: office supplies, lottery tickets, and even drugs were available over the counter. Outside, servants were busy unloading the sturdily packaged, waterproof barrels and crates full of printed sheets, quires that had been ordered by colleagues at home and abroad (Lehmstedt 1999).

The appearance of the bookshop and the activity surrounding it changed little in the seventeenth and eighteenth centuries. Illustrations, regardless of where and when they were made, show little variation. But the growth in this sector of industry itself showed huge differences. In terms of speed, the book trade in Europe developed unequally. Important factors were the extent of urbanization, the Church's influence, and the sovereign's ambitions. Venice, which until 1700 was responsible for a quarter of the total production in Italy – for the most part consisting of religious and school books destined for the Iberian peninsula – was now faced with formidable competition from Rome, with its large community of scholars (Santoro 2003: 115–24). The book trade in rural Czechia (Bohemia and Moravia) and Slovakia, which as parts of the Habsburg empire were subject to Austria's severe censorship legislation and language politics, scarcely got off the ground (Šiměck 2002: 29, 87). In the Southern Netherlands (Belgium), where in the sixteenth century Antwerp booksellers such as Plantin belonged to Europe's best, the book trade did not amount to much in the centuries thereafter. The dependence upon Spain and later upon Austria hampered further development. In Austria itself, the book trade only really blossomed under enlightened monarchs such as Maria Theresa and Joseph II (Bachleitner et al. 2000).

In seventeenth-century Spain the *Imprenta real* in Madrid was the most active publisher. Cities like Barcelona and Valencia also functioned as centers of the book trade. The monarchs of the Bourbon dynasty, who had been on the Spanish throne since 1700, were favorably disposed toward the arts and sciences and, therefore, toward the book trade. However, protectionist measures, in combination with the ever-watchful eye of the Catholic censors, prevented a lively trade with the rest of Europe (Fouché et al. 2005: 111–13). Finally, in Moscovia, only *the Moskovskii pechatnyi dvor* was allowed to print books throughout the seventeenth century. It was controlled by the Russian Orthodox Church. After 1721, when Peter the Great had himself declared emperor of Russia, the center of the book trade moved to St. Petersburg, where the Imprimerie de l'Academie des Sciences' *Knižnaja palata* obtained a monopoly position in the distribution of enlightened ideas. Catherine the Great also allowed private individuals to enter into the publishing trade, but when the French Revolution broke out, she decided at once to close Novikov's printing office, which had been responsible for one-third of Russian book production (Barenbaum 1991: 41–57). The largest players in international book trade were the Dutch Republic and, in the second half of the eighteenth century, France and the German states.

International Book Trade

During the seventeenth century, the international book trade was dominated by the Netherlands, and this did not change until the middle of the eighteenth century. Two events contributed to the Dutch booksellers' success. First, Antwerp fell into Spanish hands at the height of the Dutch Revolt in 1585. This gave Amsterdam the opportunity to assume an economically leading position as the center of international trade. Amongst the Protestant refugees who moved from Antwerp to the north were many printers and publisher–booksellers. For example, the famous Dutch publishing family Elzevier, which was responsible for approximately 16,000 editions between 1580 and 1712, came from the Southern Netherlands (Dongelmans et al. 2000). The Republic's political structure, its enormous economic growth, excellent commercial relations, comparatively broad religious tolerance, and the presence of trade and investment capital gave the Dutch book trade the opportunity to develop into the *"magasin de l'univers."* Finally, the persecution of the Jews in Spain and Portugal, which resulted in an exodus of well-to-do Sephardic Jews to Amsterdam, had a similar impact on the Hebrew book trade. To the farthest corners of Eastern Europe, this market was dominated by Jewish Amsterdam booksellers (Berkvens-Stevelinck et al. 1992).

The Revocation of the Edict of Nantes in 1685, resulting in a large influx of refugees, also added to the flourishing Dutch book trade and gave an additional boost to its quality. Many Huguenots brought little else with them other than their considerable intellectual abilities. A number of them established themselves as booksellers and created a ferment in international trade, in part thanks to the complex international network of scholars and fellow-booksellers of Huguenot descent. Of these, the most important were the brothers Huguetan and Henry Desbordes of Amsterdam, Abraham Acher of Rotterdam, Jean Neaulme of The Hague, and Elie Luzac of Leiden.

In the middle of the eighteenth century, however, the Republic's dominant position as a producer of books came to an end. In 1750, Malesherbes became director of Louis XV's office of pre-publication book censorship. He was to be a great defender of the economic interests of the French publishing industry, and opposed the rival censorship prerogative claims of France's parliaments and episcopacy. As a result, the French book trade was able to develop, and the Dutch had to contend with competition from the south. This also applied to the large book-trade firms just outside the borders of France, such as the Société Typographique de Neuchâtel in Switzerland and the Bassompierre Company in the Principality of Liège.

A second factor that brought the supremacy of the Dutch book trade to an end was strong economic growth in the German states. These had finally recovered from the consequences of the Thirty Years' War (1618–48). It was not until 1765 that book production returned to the level it had been in 1620 (Blanning 2002: 142). For all those years, Dutch booksellers had been active and had opened branch offices in German cities. For example, Amsterdam citizens Arkstee and Merkus owned one of the largest bookshops in Leipzig; Janssonius van Waesberge had a branch in Danzig, Neaulme in Berlin, and Luzac in Göttingen (van Vliet 2005: 189–90). The quality of their printing was better, the Dutch paper was superior, and their trade network was much more closely knit than that of their German counterparts.

Under the influence of Frederick the Great, king in Prussia from 1740, Berlin grew to become the center of the scholarly world. The presence of many internationally famous scholars, among whom were many Huguenots, ensured a thriving book trade there. The international book fairs, traditionally the logistic junctions of the printed word, also strengthened the German book trade. Initially, the center was in Frankfurt, where in 1650 twice as many books were sold than in Leipzig. However, the strict censorship legislation in this Catholic trade center on the Main, a tributary of the Rhine, prevented a free trade in enlightened ideas. By 1700, the situation had completely reversed and Leipzig had taken over Frankfurt's role as the city for international book fairs. The enlightened climate in the Protestant electorate of Saxony, to which Leipzig belonged, gave writers and booksellers far more opportunities. Frankfurt's last book fair catalogue appeared in 1750 with only seventy-two titles, whereas the annual production in the German states at that time already amounted to 1,350 titles (Steinberg 1996: 131–2). After that, the number of titles offered by national and international booksellers via the Leipzig book fair catalogues grew explosively. In 1755, there were just 1,231 titles; in 1775; there were 2,025 titles; and by 1795 the number had risen to 3,368 titles. But by then, Leipzig's importance as Europe's intellectual center was already on the wane. Due to the rise of commission selling, in which publishers sent retailers requested and unrequested books on commission, and due to the distribution of books via main correspondents, it was no longer necessary for a bookseller to do his purchasing twice a year at the *Buchmesse*. In 1784, the last Dutchman with his own book stand was spotted at the book fair (van Vliet 2005: 190–7).

Although at the beginning of the eighteenth century the first German quality printers had already begun to resist the presence of the Dutch in their home market, it was thanks to the Leipzig bookseller Philip Erasmus Reich, in particular, that the booksellers from Germany's many principalities collectively took action to recapture their position from the Dutch. He obtained support from, amongst others, Georg Conrad Walther of Dresden who maintained close relations with many French philosophers, and from the Breitkopf Company in Leipzig which, in the second half of the eighteenth century, would develop into one of the most famous music printing firms in Europe.

There was also a push factor that made the Dutch publisher–printers give up their dominant position in the international book trade. It was a step in a development that led to further specialization in the book business. As long as the custom of exchange trade existed and payments were made in printed sheets of the same value, booksellers were generally both printers and publishers. In the international book trade, particularly, exchange remained common for a long time. It is evident, however, that by the middle of the seventeenth century, most of the publisher–booksellers generally contracted their printing out to specialized printers. Only 13.7 percent of all books published in Berlin between the years 1751 and 1825 were manufactured by publisher–booksellers in their own printing shops (Selwyn 2000: 103). After the 1750s, further specialization took place: buying on an annual account made the combination of publishing and distribution less necessary. The new means of distribution, after all, offered discounts of up to 30 percent. It became attractive to focus on wholesale and retail trade and leave the production of books to countries with low salaries and cheap paper and ink (Selwyn 2000: 113–15; van Delft and de Wolf 2003).

The Expansion of the Public Sphere

One of the most conceptual studies of culture in the eighteenth century is Jürgen Habermas's *The Structural Transformation of the Public Sphere* (first published in 1962; first English edition 1989). He defined the public sphere as the medium by means of which private persons can debate in public. In doing so, they make use of a rich array of cultural media: reading societies, literary societies, learned societies, libraries, theaters, museums, coffee houses, salons, and so on. Free debate could occur orally, of course, but also in books, newspapers, and other periodicals. The production of these printed forms increased spectacularly throughout Europe in order to satisfy the emancipating citizen's ever-increasing hunger for reading. In the years 1701–10, sixty-four new periodicals appeared in the German states alone; from 1741 to 1750, there were 260 new titles in that area; from 1781 to 1790 no less than 1,225 new periodicals were added. In total, between 1700 and 1790, German readers saw the appearance of 3,494 new periodicals (Blanning 2002: 5–14, 159).

To a large degree, the expansion of the public sphere was caused by rapidly increasing levels of literacy. These varied from country to country and were often related to the area's level of urbanization. At the same time, there were significant differences in literacy between men and women, and between countries, depending on whether these were Catholic or Protestant. Percentages are difficult to establish with accuracy because research is mainly based upon available signatures or crosses on official acts. Moreover, this information reveals little about the reading abilities of those concerned.

In 1680, 29 percent of the French male population could read and write. A hundred years later, in 1780, this percentage was 47 percent. For women, the percentage rose from 14 to 27 percent. By contrast, in Paris in 1789, 90 percent of men were able to put their signature to a will with 80 percent of women being able to do so. In Amsterdam in 1730, 76 percent of men and 51 percent of women signed their marriage certificate; in 1780, the percentages were 85 percent and 64 percent, respectively (Houston 1988: 130–54; Blanning 2002: 111–18). Estimates indicate that in the middle of the eighteenth century only 10 percent of the adult population of German-speaking Central Europe could read and write. In 1770 this had gone up to 15 percent and in 1800 to 25 percent. In countries like Poland and Russia where levels of urbanization were low, illiteracy was high (Schenda 1977: 441–5).

For the German sociologist Rolf Engelsing, the growth in the number of readers, combined with an enormous increase and diversification in the number of titles, was reason enough to speak of a reading revolution. In the German states, this took place in the second half of the eighteenth century. The use of Latin, the language of scholars, diminished in favor of the vernacular. New genres appeared on the market, such as periodicals, novels, and more general works. Moreover, booksellers founded commercial circulating libraries enabling them to provide less wealthy customers with books; reading societies appeared which likewise reached new reading groups. The reading public began reading in a different way: from endlessly and intensively re-reading and memorizing a limited group of predominantly devotional writings to extensively reading a larger, more varied, and newer set of texts (Engelsing 1974). This reading revolution must have occurred in the rest of Europe too, although opinions differ as to how and when it occurred (van Delft and de Wolf 2003).

To discover what was read in the seventeenth and eighteenth centuries, it is important to distinguish between scholars and the bourgeois middle classes. An international scholarly community existed in Europe from the age of Erasmus and before. The significance of this Republic of Letters really manifested itself in the seventeenth century. The mechanization of the world picture, combined with new empirical and Cartesian research methods, led to an explosive growth of scholarly publications. The language of these cosmopolitan scholars was initially Latin and later French. From the last decades of the seventeenth century, their exchange of ideas took place in learned journals.

The oldest learned journal in Europe is the *Journal des savants* (1665) edited by Denis de Sallo. Following its example, Italy started the *Giornale de' letterati* (1668); Leipzig got its *Acta eruditorum* (1682). Every self-respecting university founded an academy of sciences that was to guarantee free scholarly activity. Research results were invariably recorded in learned journals. Thus, *Commentarii academiae scientiarum imperialis Petropolitanae* (1726) appeared under the auspices of the Russian Academy of Sciences in St. Petersburg, and almost directly after its foundation, the University of Göttingen started its *Göttingische Zeitungen von Gelehrte Sachen* (1739).

Most learned journals, however, were started on the initiative of a scholar or a bookseller. It was in the bookseller's interest to publish such journals which could act as a form of showcase to display their wares to potential customers. The learned journals had a freer format than institutional journals, although they were comparable as regards content due to the noticeable presence of the many book reviews. In the Netherlands, the French scholar Pierre Bayle, settled in Rotterdam because of the intellectual climate, started his famous *Nouvelles de la république des lettres* (1684). Afterwards, a great many learned journals, or "bibliothèques" as they were often called, were to follow.

Of course, not only scholars read journals. The average citizen read his newspaper, and informed as well as entertained himself by means of periodicals. The *Gazette de France* (1631), the *Leipziger Zeitung* (1660), the *Oprechte Haerlemse courant* (1662), and the *Gaceta de Madrid* (1697) are amongst the earliest newspapers. As early as the seventeenth century, the first satirical magazines appeared in which authors criticized the events of their time in scarcely veiled ways. By contrast, 'Spectators', which started to appear from the early eighteenth century, had a more didactic–moralistic character. These very popular essay magazines were named after the renowned British *Spectator* of Addison and Steele. In Italy, the famous *Il caffè* (1764–66) appeared, not coincidentally named after the coffee house. This periodical is generally considered to be the precursor of the modern cultural and philosophical magazines in Italy (Santoro 2003: 112–13).

Women and children were identified as new reading groups, evidenced by the introduction of children's and women's magazines. Thus, publications such as the *Magasin des enfants* (1756) and the *Magasin des jeunes dames* (1772), educational literature written by Marie le Prince de Beaumont, were snapped up greedily throughout Europe. By the end of the eighteenth century, every European country was familiar with a wide range of periodicals in the fields of literature, fashion, music, theater, and the fine arts. The originally broadly oriented learned journals changed into special interest magazines concerned with, for example, psychology, educational theory, technology, or physics.

From the seventeenth century onward, the European citizen also read novels. In France, in particular, the novel developed early, with highlights such as *Cassandre* (1642) by La Calprenède and *Le Roman comique* (1651) by Paul Scarron. Annually, on average, twelve novel... ...on found their way to foreign countries in translation. In th... ...vould reach full maturity. On the cultural fringe, pornographi... ...ks were written. Both *La puttana errante* (c.1650), attributed t... ...*cole des filles* (1655) obtained international fame. These texts... ...f a series of highly sought-after, albeit forbidden books. Nev... ...devotional literature always remained popular throughout Europe. Publishers were always interested in such lucrative religious publishing projects. Marc-Michel Rey of Amsterdam, known for his daring editions of Jean-Jacques Rousseau and other anti-religious writings, made no bones about publishing hymn books. Besides this, in politically turbulent times, people read leaflets and pamphlets of which, at the time of the French Revolution alone, close to ten thousand titles were published (Darnton and Roche 1989: 165).

For the reader at the end of the seventeenth century there was so much knowledge available that books were needed in which that knowledge was systematically organized. The *Grand dictionnaire historique* (1674) by the French scholar Louis Moréri was the first encyclopedic reference work, followed shortly afterwards by the *Dictionnaire historique et critique* (1697) by Pierre Bayle. The demand for works like this was such that publication of encyclopedias in the vernacular was also profitable, such as the unfinished *Biblioteca universale sacro-profana* (1701) by the Venetian Vincenzo Coronelli and the *Grosse vollständige Universallexikon aller Wissenschaften und Künste* (1732), popular in the German states, by the Leipzig publisher–bookseller Johann Heinrich Zedler. The book of books, however, was the 38-volume *Encyclopédie* (1751) in folio format by Diderot and d'Alembert. This monument of Enlightenment publishing was the product of the efforts of 135 "encyclopedists," amongst whom were Voltaire, d'Holbach, and Rousseau, who used their entries to argue for economic, political, and religious reform.

Although the anti-clerical and atheistic passages led to severe penalties and stiff fines, the *Encyclopédie* became one of the bestselling reference works of the century. On the 25,000 copies printed, the publisher–booksellers made a fortune. The competition was ferocious, especially when Fortuné-Barthélemy de Félice in Switzerland started his 58-volume *Encyclopédie d'Yverdon*. Here, too, a choice selection of leading international authors collaborated. Anticipating the wishes of the reader, the publisher chose the handier quarto format. The more compact composition of the entries and the more moderate theological opinions also ensured an unprecedented number of sales in northern Europe (Darnton 1979).

The Emancipation of Writers

By early in the seventeenth century, writers had begun to resist the power of the publishers. Increasingly, they wished to be paid for the products of their pens. Traditionally, they received remuneration by dedicating their texts to a prince who, flattered by the great honor lavished on him in the panegyric, would reward the author financially as a patron. Publishers, too, made use of this kind of funding. Yet most of the writers got little or nothing for their work. At best, they received a number of "author's copies."

The publisher received the full right to exploit the ideas of the writer. In France, this right was coupled to a strict system of privileges; in the Dutch Republic, publishers were free to apply for a printing privilege. With such a patent they had, for a given period and within the territorial boundaries, the exclusive right to do what they saw fit with the copy. For the rest, the work was a free commodity. Therefore, a fierce struggle arose between internationally operating publisher–booksellers in which they competed with each other with many illegal editions of books (*contrefaçons*). Because they could also apply for a privilege for these piracies, in the Electorate of Saxony, for example, they could prevent the original edition from being sold at the *Leipziger Buchmesse*. Piracy functioned here, as in other countries, as a corrective principle in the market against monopolies, inadequate distribution, and high prices.

Initially, the Dutch publishers in particular were guilty of aggressive piratical practices. In the second half of the eighteenth century, Lyon, Rouen, Avignon, Trévoux, Geneva, and Neuchâtel, too, were places infamous for pirate printing (Fouché et al. 2002). In the Principality of Liège, Bassompierre went to work so shamelessly that in 1772 he put a publication of the works of Montesquieu on the market with not only his own printer's device but also the complete impressum of its original London publisher, Nourse. In Vienna in 1775, Maria Theresa forbade booksellers to jeopardize the domestic book trade, arts and sciences by their publications, but in doing so she gave the court printer, Thomas von Trattner, permission to reprint illegally everything in the large Habsburg empire he deemed worthwhile – and that was a great deal. It made him the greatest pirate-printer in Europe.

Such practices contributed to the self-assurance of a growing legion of writers who had to live off their writing. For a long time, their reputation demanded that they kept pretending to perform their intellectual labor solely as a pastime, in addition to their proper jobs as clergymen, scholars, doctors, and so on. But, around the turn of the century, an increasing number of writers started to demand appropriate payment. They negotiated hard with their publisher about their honorarium. In 1748, Samuel Formey, a Huguenot refugee and scholar living in Berlin, who maintained contacts with innumerable booksellers, was given the following choice by the Dutch publisher Elie Luzac for his work as editor in chief of the *Bibliothèque impartiale*: seven guilders per sheet and twenty complimentary copies, or eight guilders per sheet. The publisher thought this was a generous offer because, according to him, most writers usually got paid five guilders per quire (van Vliet 2005: 107). Diderot had a less flattering impression of Dutch publishers. In his *Voyage en Hollande* (1773), he complained: "Publishers in Holland print everything that is offered to them, but they never pay."

The gap between author and publisher became wider than ever. For this reason, writers decided to take publication of their work into their own hands. The seventeenth-century orientalist Thomas Erpenius started his own printing business because he did not trust the stingy publishers who had their books printed as cheaply as possible. Early in the eighteenth century, the Dutch hack Jacob Campo Weyerman published many of his texts at his own expense, assured in advance of good sales. Other writers combined forces and founded collective publishing companies. The German scholar Leibniz, for example, resisted the publisher–booksellers who, according to him, were vultures. In 1715/16, plans were made for a *Societas subscriptoria inter eruditos* where scholars could subscribe to quality books for little money. This plan, however, was never put into practice. Later in the eighteenth century, scholars succeeded in starting their own book-store–publishing business (Steiner 1998: 334). The emancipation of writers had reached a point at which they could begin to exploit their reputations in a modern way.

This development was accompanied by an increasing awareness that, initially at least, the author not the publisher owned the text. In 1643, the French playwright Pierre Corneille was one of the first authors who fought for his rights. Nevertheless, in France, it would take until the end of the eighteenth century before there was any question of copyright. Still in 1763, in his *Lettre sur le commerce de la librairie*, Diderot observed that, although censorship was strictly regulated, there was not a single law protecting the intellectual property of the writer. It was not until 1791 and 1793 that the *Déclarations des droits du génie* were adopted. This is almost a century after the Copyright Act of 1710 had in England designated writers as the rightful proprietors of their printed texts. In Norway and Denmark (1741) and Spain (1762), too, there was already some form of copyright. In the Netherlands this was not settled until the annexation by France (1812). In the German states, the *Allgemeine Landrecht für die Preussische Staaten* (1794) marked an important turning point in the history of copyright.

Constraints on Books

Everywhere in Europe the freedom of the press was curtailed by censorship, but the severity varied. The Dutch Republic was most tolerant, although even here freedom of the press definitely had its limits. Everyone was expected to endorse public Church doctrine, to refrain from undermining the business of the state, and to promote good morals. Otherwise, books were confiscated, sometimes burned, and both the author and publisher–printer were fined. They could also be imprisoned or exiled. It was a repressive form of censorship after the fact, resulting in measures prohibiting the distribution, possession, and reading of the book in question (van Delft and de Wolf 2003).

But censorship legislation in the Netherlands was less severe than, for example, in France where between the years 1659 and 1789 a total of 942 people connected to the book trade landed up in the Bastille. The royal censors had to approve each and every manuscript before the printer could begin his task. Before 1700, this was a maximum of four hundred manuscripts per year; around 1750, it was some five hundred manuscripts; and by 1780 it had exceeded a thousand. The percentage of rejected manuscripts varied, despite self-censorship, from 10 to 30 percent. This system of prior restraint included general privileges that gave a publisher the monopoly on a book for a specific period of time, and tacit permissions (*permissions tacites*) for books that could not be suppressed but could also not be approved (Chartier and Martin 1990: 88–94, 99–109).

Comparable censorship was generally practiced in countries with an absolute monarchy, especially in those where the Catholic Church had great censorship powers through the Inquisition; for instance, in Italy and Spain. The *Index* would not begin to lose its power until the nineteenth century.

The French physician La Mettrie discovered to his grief just how far the power of orthodoxy reached. He had fled France in 1747 because of his writings about the materiality of the soul. This idea directly opposed Church doctrine about the dualism of body and soul. In the Netherlands, his writings were not welcome either. That very year, his *l'Homme machine* was published anonymously by the young bookseller Elie Luzac. Luzac, however, had ostentatiously placed his publisher's name on the title page. The Church and, in its wake, the secular government immediately took action against him. The entire print-run was confiscated and a large fine was imposed upon him. This did not appear to upset him much. He assisted La Mettrie in getting out of the country while his presses printed the subversive work anew. Because the book was forbidden far beyond the borders of Holland, it was in great demand. Luzac made a substantial profit on it (van Vliet 2005: 68–73).

But that was not the only reason he took the risk of printing *l'Homme machine*. Luzac was convinced that truth could only be discovered in debate, and that potentially incorrect ideas could only be refuted through argument and not through censorship. He recorded these opinions in his *Essai sur la liberté de produire ses sentimens* (1749). The debate about the freedom of the press was pursued internationally but did not, just yet, lead to the abolition of censorship. Sweden was the first country to make this move, in 1767, although the possibility of censoring works that were Spinozistic or atheistic was maintained. Denmark followed suit in 1770, and here no restrictions to the legislation were added (Laursen and van der Zande 2003).

In the seventeenth and eighteenth centuries, many works were published with false imprints. Sometimes this was done to give the customer the impression that he or she was dealing with a domestic publication, whereas the edition originated, for example, from Amsterdam. Usually these books concerned dangerous ideas. According to their title pages, many controversial works were published in London which had no censorship legislation and thus de facto freedom of the press from 1695 onward. The Amsterdam bookseller Marc-Michel Rey published many works by Baron D'Holbach, controversial because of their materialism, with an imprint mentioning only London. Other fictitious imprints contained the names of virtual publishers, such as Pierre Marteau of Cologne who, if we rely on his name, must have worked for 340 years. In 1670, Spinoza's *Tractatus theologico-politicus* appeared in Amsterdam, published by the non-existent Hamburg printer "Henricus Kunraht." A fictitious imprint which stands out immediately is, for example, "Alethobathopseudopolis, chez Bold Truth, rue du Mock," belonging to the *Traité des dissensions entre nobles et le peuple* (1733) by Jonathan Swift.

In France in the eighteenth century, separate catalogues dedicated to these forbidden bestsellers circulated. The way in which they were transported, too, required a certain level of resourcefulness to prevent them from being confiscated. Guillaume Bergeret, from Bordeaux, ordered eleven hard-core "philosophical" titles from the Société

Typographique de Neuchâtel. "Please marry all the books with the others," he wrote, indicating his wish for the supplier to mix those sheets with obscene texts with others whose content was not dangerous (Darnton 1996: 17). The clandestine activities were more complex than this relatively simple hide-and-seek game by publisher–booksellers. The literary underground could be accessed by a European network of smuggling routes. Dutch publishers of forbidden books for the French market made use of the overseas trade routes via Rouen, or sent their contraband over the French borders through Maastricht, Liège, and Bouillon. The Société Typographique de Neuchâtel hired smugglers, or insurers (*assureurs*), to transport the crates of illegal books to the Swiss–French border. They insured the publisher a safe passage. The carriers did the actual work and carried these heavy packs across winding mountain paths to a secret address, just over the border (Darnton 1996: 17–21).

As early as the second half of the seventeenth century, the first signs of the expansion of the public sphere can be seen. This was accompanied by an explosive increase in books, newspapers, periodicals, pamphlets, and other printed matter. The Enlightenment ideal – the propagation of knowledge and civilization – was an especially motivating force in this development. But the speed with which the book trade expanded in seventeenth- and eighteenth-century Europe was highly influenced by the political situation in individual countries. By the end of the eighteenth century, specialization, rationalization, and innovation in the book trade had been put into motion nearly everywhere. The political unrest just before the end of the century, culminating in the French Revolution, temporarily set back this development, but also ushered in a century of huge print-related technical innovation, of modern ways of distribution, and of the commercially oriented book trade.

REFERENCES AND FURTHER READING

Bachleitner, N., Eybl, F. M., and Fischer, E. (2000) *Geschichte des Buchhandels in Östenreich*. Wiesbaden: Harrassowitz.

Barbier, F., Juratic, S., and Varry, D. (eds.) (1996) *L'Europe et le livre: réseaux et pratiques du négoce de librairie XVIe–XIXe siècles*. Paris: Klincksiek.

Barenbaum, I. E. (1991) *Geschichte des Buchhandels in Russland und der Sowjetunion*. Wiesbaden: Harrassowitz.

Berkvens-Srevelinck, C., Bots, H., Hoftijzer, P. G., et al. (eds.) (1992) *Le magasin de l'univers: The Dutch Republic as the Centre of the European Book Trade*. Leiden: Brill.

Blanning, T. C. W. (2002) *The Culture of Power and the Power of Culture: Old Regime Europe 1660–1789*. Oxford: Oxford University Press.

Burke, P. (2000) *A Social History of Knowledge: From Gutenberg to Diderot*. Cambridge: Polity.

Chartier, R., and Martin, H-J. (eds.) (1989) *Histoire de l'édition française*, vol. I: *Le livre conquérant. Du Moyen Age au milieu du XVIIe siècle*, 2nd edn. Paris: Fayard/Promodis.

— and — (eds.) (1990) *Histoire de l'édition française*, vol. II: *Le livre triomphant 1660–1830*, 2nd edn. Paris: Fayard/Promodis.

Darnton, R. (1979) *The Business of Enlightenment: A Publishing History of the Encyclopédie 1775–1800*. Cambridge, MA: Belknap Press.

— (1982) *The Literary Underground of the Old Regime*. Cambridge, MA: Harvard University Press.

— (1996) *The Forbidden Best-sellers of Prerevolutionary France*. London: Fontana.

— and Roche, D. (eds.) (1989) *Revolution in Print: The Press in France 1775–1800*. Berkeley: University of California Press.

van Delft, M., and de Wolf, C. (eds.) (2003) *Bibliopolis: History of the Printed Book in the Netherlands*. Zwolle: Waanders.

Dongelmans, B. P. M., Hoftijzer, P. G., and Lankhorst, O. S. (2000) *Boekverkopers van Europa; Het 17de-eeuwse Nederlandse uitgevershuis Elzevier*. Zutphen: Walburg Pers.

Engelsing, R. (1974) *Der Bürger als Leser: Lesergeschichte in Deutschland 1500–1800*. Stuttgart: Metzler.

Fouché, P., Péchoin, D., and Marshall, A. (eds.) (2002–5) *Dictionnaire encyclopédique du livre*, 2 vols. Paris: Electre, Éditions du Cercle de la Librairie (vol. 3 forthcoming).

Habermas, J. (1989) *The Structural Transformation of the Public Sphere: An Inquiry into a Category of Bourgeois Society*. Cambridge, MA: MIT Press (originally published in 1962).

Houston, R. A. (1988) *Literacy in Early Modern Europe: Culture and Education 1500–1800*. London: Longman.

Laursen, J. C., and van der Zande, J. (eds.) (2003) *Early French and German Defenses of Freedom of the Press*. Leiden: Brill.

Lehmstedt, M. (1999) " 'Le rendezvous de tous les gens de lettres et de tous les nouvellistes': Gestalt und Funktion des Buchladens im Zeitalter der deutschen Aufklärung." *Leipziger Jahrbuch zur Buchgeschichte*, 9: 11–75.

Santoro, M. (2003) *Geschichte des Buchhandels in Italien*. Wiesbaden: Harrassowitz.

Schenda, R. (1977) *Volk ohne Buch: Studien zur Sozialgeschichte der populären Lesestoffe 1770–1910*, 2nd edn. Munich: Deutscher Taschenbuch Verlag.

Selwyn, P. E. (2000) *Everyday Life in the German Book Trade: Friedrich Nicolai as Bookseller and Publisher in the Age of Enlightenment 1750–1810*. Pennsylvania: Pennsylvania State University Press.

Šiměck, Z. (2002) *Geschichte des Buchhandels in Tschechien und in der Slowakei*. Wiesbaden: Harrassowitz.

Steinberg, S. H. (1996) *Five Hundred Years of Printing*, 2nd edn., revised by J. Trevitt. London: British Library.

Steiner, H. (1998) *Das Autorenhonorar: seine Entwicklungsgeschichte vom 17. bis 19. Jahrhundert*. Wiesbaden: Harrassowitz.

van Vliet, R. (2005) *Elie Luzac (1721–1796): Boekverkoper van de Verlichting*. Nijmegen: Vantilt (translation forthcoming: Leiden: Brill, 2008).

Wittmann, R. (1991) *Geschichte des deutschen Buchhandels: Ein Überblick*. Munich: Beck.

19

North America and Transatlantic Book Culture to 1800

Russell L. Martin III

The book history of early America begins almost with the history of the printed book itself. Like the other cultural developments that followed in the wake of Gutenberg's invention of printing with movable type – the humanistic learning of the Renaissance and Enlightenment, the religious controversy of the Protestant Reformation, and the ideological shifts leading to political revolutions in America and France – the discovery of what was for Europeans a "new world" was very much articulated, mediated, and promoted by the printed word. Starting with the publication in Barcelona of Christopher Columbus's "Letter" of 1493, *Epistola Christofori Colom*, news of his voyage and discoveries spread rapidly through print. Eleven other editions in Latin and Italian appeared within a year, published in Rome, Paris, Antwerp, Basel, and Florence. When Columbus wrote of the "islands of the Indies," he set off not only geographical, cultural, political, and social change but a publishing phenomenon as well.

Indeed, without the printing press, one doubts whether the European encounter with America could have proceeded at the same pace or at the same level of general interest. Norsemen may have voyaged to America around the year 1000, but the outlines of those discoveries were not made available in print until much later, the Greenland Saga appearing in 1688 and the Vinland Saga in 1705. The explorers and colonists who followed Columbus (within a decade of his first voyage, at least eighty transatlantic crossings are documented) ultimately defined European notions of the New World, in large part because they were able to use the printing press to announce their discoveries to a wide audience.

This chapter focuses on (1) the European publication and reception of accounts of the New World; (2) the development of the art of printing in the Americas, touching especially upon the role of printing in the American Revolution; (3) the distribution of books both within the colonies and through transatlantic networks of trade, including the role of libraries as centers of print culture; and (4) popular works reprinted in early America. For our purposes, "early America" means primarily British North America and what became the United States: that is, writings in English (printed on both sides of the Atlantic) documenting the Anglo-American experience down to about 1800. But that Anglo-American book culture needs to be placed in a larger European context as well, for book history in early America was an international and polyglot phenomenon. All of the European powers with colonial ambitions in the Americas – Spain, Portugal, France, the Netherlands, and England – contributed to a vast literature. Other languages, including those of Native Americans, added to the mix as well.

The multiple editions of the Columbus letter are typical of the reception accorded to numerous other early works documenting the European encounter with the New World. An English landmark in the literature of discovery and exploration was Richard Hakluyt's *Principall Navigations, Voiages and Discoveries of the English Nation* (London, 1589). The first two parts of Hakluyt's text deal with British adventurers in Asia, Africa, the Middle East, the Mediterranean, and Europe. The third part is devoted to America and provides detailed (and in some cases the first) accounts of voyages in search of a Northwest Passage; settlements in the Carolinas, in Virginia, and at Roanoke; exploits in Caribbean waters; and the narratives of Cabot, Hawkins, Gilbert, Frobisher, Drake, Lane, and Hariot. The Drake narrative gives a complete account of the circumnavigation of 1577–80, including his exploration of the California coast. Critics have long accorded Hakluyt's text a place as an epic of the modern English nation, but from the point of view of book history it has a different function: as an anthology that served as a model for later travel narratives. When John Smith came to write his accounts of Virginia and New England, he did so in the tradition of Hakluyt.

Setting the pattern for natural history was Jose de Acosta (1540–1600) and his *Historia natural y moral de las Indias*, first published in Seville in 1590. An encyclopedic treatise, based on first-hand observation in the New World and familiarity with ancient science and the teachings of the Church, Acosta's work was reprinted in more than twenty Spanish editions from 1590 to 1792 and translated into Italian (1596), German (1598), French (1598), and English (1604). Acosta was especially interested in the pre-Columbian civilizations of the Aztecs and Incas, whose religions, customs, and governments he compared.

Thomas Gage, an English Dominican cleric, began in 1625 his travels as a stowaway, smuggled in a biscuit barrel aboard a ship bound for the Philippines, in violation of the Spanish royal decree excluding foreigners from Spain's new territories. Gage spent most of the next twelve years in Mexico, Guatemala, Nicaragua, and Panama, living among the Indians and occasionally serving as parish priest or professor of philosophy. Upon his return to England, he converted to the Church of England and published *The English American, His Travail by Sea and Land; or, A New Survey of the West Indies* (London, 1648), which caused an immediate sensation for its revelations of the wealth and defenselessness of the Spanish American colonies. It remained in print for almost a century, in more than twenty editions, being translated into French, German, and Dutch. After its long run through the publishing centers of Europe, its last publication came about in colonial America, where James Parker reprinted an abridged version in Woodbridge, New Jersey in 1758 as *The Traveller*. Parker's plan was to publish the entire account as well in monthly installments in the *New American Magazine*, but the journal folded before the serialization could be completed.

The sheer staying power of a work such as Antonio de Solis's (1610–86), *Historia de la conquista de Mexico* is instructive. First published in Spanish in Madrid in 1684, it appeared in more than eighty editions through 1800 and was translated into French, Italian, German, Danish, and English. An English translator of 1724 noted that the popularity of Solis offered "conclusive testimony to the charm exercised over the reading public by a thoroughly unreliable work, through the elegance and purity of its literary style." Reading more like a novel than a work of history, Solis's grand narrative did more to preserve the heroic view of Cortes and the conquest in the popular mind than any other source.

Although almost unknown today, William Robertson's *History of America* was among the most popular works of its time. A Scots clergyman and author, Robertson had already established his reputation with his *History of Scotland*. From its first publication in 1777, *History of America* went through more than thirty editions before 1800 and remained a steady seller through the early decades of the nineteenth century. The American Revolution may have contributed to its immediate appeal, but Robertson won readers with his meticulous scholarship and lucid prose.

The popularity enjoyed by Jonathan Carver's *Travels through the Interior Parts of North America* (London, 1778), one of the earliest books on the Middle West, is unrivalled in the literature of early Native American travel. Thirty-two separate editions of the work are recorded. It was a major stimulus to Alexander Mackenzie and Lewis and Clark. After the Seven Years' War, in which he served in five campaigns against the French, Carver set out from Boston in 1766 to explore the territory beyond the Mississippi and to find a northwest land passage between the Atlantic and Pacific oceans. The work contains one of the earliest descriptions of what is now known as Minnesota and Wisconsin. Carver made important contributions to the mapping of the region and the knowledge of its natural history. Indian life and customs are described with great detail, particularly their methods of war.

The basic tool for the study of the New World's impact on the old in print is John Alden and Dennis C. Landis, *European Americana: A Chronological Guide to Works Printed in Europe Relating to the Americas, 1493–1776* (1980–). Continuing the tradition begun by Joseph Sabin's *Bibliotheca Americana* (begun in 1868, completed in 1936, and also still worth consulting), *European Americana* is the most comprehensive bibliographical guide to the entire printed record of the earliest period, with more than 30,000 entries, arranged chronologically. A more restrictive lens is provided by R. C. Simmons, *British Imprints Relating to North America, 1621–1760: An Annotated Checklist* (1996), which lists British reprintings of American works, often brought about by a combination of American hunger for publicity and legitimacy with British curiosity about the colonial scene. Simmons provides entries for 3,212 publications dealing with some aspect of North America through 1760. By comparison, there are 9,085 North American imprints through the same period. The universe of (predominantly) English-language Americana thus extends to 12,297 imprints through 1760, with British imprints accounting for roughly one-quarter of that total. The earlier the date, the higher the ratio. For example, there are 1,170 British imprints in Simmons through 1700; the North American Imprints Program (NAIP) database yields 992 imprints for the same period. (Sponsored by the American Antiquarian Society, NAIP is an ongoing effort to create bibliographical records in machine-readable form for all surviving American imprints, from 1640 onward, with the goal of eventually reaching the year 1876.)

The individual authors most frequently represented in Simmons's list include John Cotton (39 entries), George Whitefield (38), George Keith (27), Cotton Mather (25), Thomas Hooker (25), Increase Mather (23), and Thomas Bray (19). All of these are familiar names to students of colonial America; less familiar, perhaps, is the transatlantic pattern of their publications. Only seven works authored solely by John Cotton were printed in America, and only one of Thomas Hooker's – all posthumously, according to NAIP. (That is not surprising given the fact that Cotton died in 1652 and Hooker in 1647, not long after the first printing press was set up in Cambridge.) George Whitefield, on the other hand, had more works printed in America before 1760 (90 imprints) than in Britain. George Keith's numbers (30 American imprints) were about the same on either side of the ocean. Cotton Mather and Increase Mather were, of course, fixtures of the Boston press; 414 of Cotton's works and 132 of Increase's were printed in America before 1760. Only two works by Thomas Bray (well known for his support of colonial library societies) were printed in America.

These bare figures suggest that comparative studies can add to our knowledge by analyzing exactly which titles by which authors were printed in Britain and America, where, when, and by whom. For example, the Virginia Presbyterian minister Samuel Davies has fourteen entries in Simmons and only nine in NAIP, with little duplication. What were the conditions which led to some of his works being printed in Britain and others in America? To understand Davies better, to re-read him, we need to consider his writings in a transatlantic context. For many colonials, London publication offered legitimacy and a much wider audience. The classic example is Benjamin Franklin's London edition of his *Experiments and Observations on Electricity, made at Philadelphia in America* (1769). But, as we shall see, by the end of the eighteenth century American printers were also actively reprinting British authors.

Printing came to the New World in 1539, when Juan Cromberger sent a press and a printer, Juan Pablos, to Mexico City. Exactly a century later, Stephen Daye became the first printer of English-speaking North America. He established his press at Cambridge, Massachusetts late in 1638 or early in 1639 and printed the famed Bay Psalm Book there in 1640. This is the first substantial book and the earliest extant example of printing from what is now the United States. The Cambridge press continued under Daye's son Matthew until his death in 1649, after which it was managed by Samuel Green.

The next press to be established was at Jamestown, Virginia, by the printer William Nuthead. The Nuthead press was quickly suppressed by the colonial government, however, and nothing of its output has survived. After leaving Jamestown, Nuthead established another press at St. Mary's City, Maryland, sometime before August 31, 1685. It was carried on until Nuthead's widow removed it to Annapolis around 1695, yet nothing more than a broadside and a few forms survive. Thomas Reading established a second press at Annapolis in 1700. William Bradford brought printing to Pennsylvania in 1685, when he established a press at Philadelphia. He also established the first press in New York in 1693. Thus, by the end of the seventeenth century, there were permanent presses in Cambridge, Boston, New York, and Philadelphia. Their productions were modest, mainly government printing, forms, and sermons.

Thomas Short was the first printer in Connecticut, arriving in New London in 1709 to do the official printing of the colony. It is unclear when printing first came to New Jersey. William Bradford issued a book of laws, *Anno Regni Georgii Regis*, with the imprint Perth Amboy 1723, though some scholars doubt whether he would have moved his press from New York simply to issue this book. The first permanent printer in New Jersey was James Parker, who established his press at Woodbridge in 1757. James Franklin, after running afoul of the authorities in Boston for publishing the *New England Courant*, settled in Newport in 1727, bringing his press and establishing a tradition of lively journalism and literature in Rhode Island. Printing returned to Virginia in 1730 with the arrival of William Parks. In 1731, a monetary incentive offered by the South Carolina government attracted three competing printers to Charleston: George Webb, Eleazer Phillips, and Thomas Whitmarsh. All three soon died or left, though Louis Timothy, a protégé and business associate of Benjamin Franklin, took over the Whitmarsh press. James Davis, trained by William Parks in Williamsburg, became the first printer in North Carolina in 1749, when he settled in New Bern and began to print the journal of the House of Burgesses. Punished by the Massachusetts Assembly for supposedly printing an objectionable pamphlet in 1754, Daniel Fowle consequently moved to Portsmouth, New Hampshire and started the colony's first press in 1756. Delaware's first printer was also a Franklin apprentice: James Adams served more than seven years with Franklin and Hall in Philadelphia before he established his press in Wilmington in 1761. Finally, James Johnston, newly arrived from England, set up the first press in Savannah, Georgia in 1762: he printed the colony's statutes and began the *Georgia Gazette* in 1763.

With this chronology in mind, it is useful to think of the pre-1801 period of American printing in three distinct phases: the beginnings to about 1740, 1740 to 1776, and 1776 to 1800. By 1740, the printing trade was firmly established, and, as James N. Green has argued, there was by this time a good deal of competition (see Hall and Amory 2000). There were fifteen printing shops operating in nine towns, with five in Boston, two each in New York and Philadelphia, and single shops in Charleston, Williamsburg, Annapolis, Germantown, New London, and Newport. The number of newspapers had tripled to twelve, with fiercely competitive markets in Boston, New York, and Philadelphia. Newspapers provided printers with a new source of income that freed them from the economic control of colonial governments and provided a forum for opinions that the authorities found increasingly difficult to hold in check. By 1740, the five printers in Boston were each issuing their own newspapers. More than any other factor, the rise of newspapers changed the nature of printing in the British colonies.

At the same time, the rate of printing of books and pamphlets accelerated rapidly. The output of the presses became more and more varied as a wider market developed for materials beyond subsidized governmental publications, broadsides, sermons, and theological works. Consider the case of the Bible and its marketability. While Psalters, New Testaments, and other selections from the Bible were printed with some frequency in early America, the Bible itself was rarely attempted. It was far too complex and expensive for the average printing shop. In any case, only the universities of Oxford and Cambridge and the king's printer enjoyed the privilege of publishing the Authorized Version. As a result, Bibles were a staple of the import trade. The first Bible printed in the New World was the Eliot Indian Bible (1663), a monumental effort typographically and linguistically. The first American Bible printed in a European language was in German in 1743. The first English Bible was printed by Robert Aitken in Philadelphia in 1782, more as an exercise in patriotism than as a bookselling venture: it included a resolution of Congress "recommend[ing] this edition of the Bible to the inhabitants of the United States . . ." This Bible was, in fact, a subscription book, and not a very successful one. But in a few more years Bible printing would become a sound business venture. More than thirty American editions of the English Bible appeared between 1788 and 1800, led by the efforts of Isaiah Thomas in Worcester.

One of the first publications to issue from the press in English North America was *An Almanack for New England* for 1639, printed by Stephen Daye in Cambridge (no copy has survived). In a preindustrial, predominantly rural country, the almanac was a necessity, used by individuals from all walks of life, a household fixture that was often kept hanging on a string from the fireplace mantle. Many almanacs were also used as diaries, George Washington being perhaps the most famous almanac diarist. In addition to monthly calendars and tables of astronomical events, almanacs included advice for farmers, medical and domestic receipts, and miscellaneous literary fare. In all its diversity, the almanac had one great theme: time itself. As Nathaniel Ames expressed it in his almanac for 1744:

> This little book serves well to help you date
> And settle many petty worldly Things,
> Think on the Day writ in the Book of Fate,
> Which your own final dissolution brings.

Unlike their English counterparts, which often emphasized astrology and necromancy, the earliest almanacs in America stressed practical instruction and improvement, a reflection first of Puritan influence (seventeenth-century Harvard students, most of them destined for the ministry, were some of the earliest compilers of almanacs) and later of the more enlightened intellectual climate of the eighteenth century. Even so, most almanacs featured the "man of signs" or "the Anatomy," a crude woodcut of a human figure, with corresponding links to the signs of the zodiac governing various parts of the body. While the compilers were always quick to say that they themselves were not practitioners of astrology, they included "the Anatomy" to appeal to "common" readers.

As printing spread in the colonies, almanacs followed as a matter of course. William Bradford published the first almanacs in Pennsylvania (Philadelphia, 1686) and New

York (1694), Timothy Green the first Connecticut almanac (New London, 1709). In Newport, James Franklin, elder brother of Benjamin, assumed the pseudonym "Poor Robin" and printed the *Rhode-Island Almanack* for 1728. In Maryland, John Warner produced *An Almanack for 1729*, and *The South-Carolina Almanack* was advertised for sale in Charleston in 1733. In Williamsburg, Theophilus Grew's *Almanack for 1735* was advertised by the printer William Parks, who had moved to the Virginia capital from Annapolis. New Hampshire's first was *An Astronomical Diary* for 1757, printed in Portsmouth by Daniel Fowle. *Poor Roger 1760: The American Country Almanac* was printed in Woodbridge, New Jersey by James Parker, *The Wilmington Almanack* for 1762 was printed in Delaware by Thomas Adams, and *The Georgia and South-Carolina Almanack* for 1764 was printed in Savannah by James Johnston. Not until after the War of Independence were almanacs printed in North Carolina (New Bern, for 1784), Vermont (Bennington, 1784), and Maine (Portland, 1786).

The most famous compiler of almanacs in the eighteenth century was, of course, Benjamin Franklin. Assuming the mantle of Richard Saunders, Franklin issued his first *Poor Richard* in Philadelphia in 1733, and remained personally involved in the series until 1758. "I endeavored to make it both entertaining and useful," he wrote in his *Autobiography*, "and it accordingly came to be in such demand, that I reap'd considerable profit from it, vending annually near ten thousand." Records indicate that *Poor Richard* was distributed not only in Philadelphia but throughout the colonies. The reasons for its success are not hard to find. Franklin had a knack for coining or adapting a proverbial phrase ("Men & melons are hard to know," "Hunger never saw bad bread," "Early to bed, early to rise, makes a man healthy, wealthy and wise") but so did many other compilers of almanacs. Franklin's genius was revealed in the personal essays that accompanied each edition. Through his prefaces, Franklin created a fictional character who assumed a life of his own – Poor Richard's wife Bridget even contributed an essay one year. Engaging, witty, and lively, Franklin's almanacs still make for entertaining reading.

Readers had certain expectations for their almanacs, and unnecessary innovation was not welcomed. As a rule, almanacs came with an explanation of the calendar, a list of eclipses for the year, the names and characters of planets, signs of the zodiac, and "the Anatomy." They included such practical things as interest tables, courts and court days, lists of government officials, population tables, postal rates, bank officers, exchange rates, and time and place of religious meetings. For studying the development of local economies on the frontier, almanacs are useful sources. They are also anthologies of popular literature: epigrams, ballads, songs, satires, elegies, odes, epistles, essays, jokes, legends, proverbs, and anecdotes.

Almanacs were used effectively as propaganda in the American Revolution, supporting the patriots' cause through verse, essays, and graphic illustrations. Before and during the War of Independence, the American press produced hundreds of polemical pamphlets, posted thousands of broadsides, and filled their newspapers with essays, letters, extracts of speeches, satirical and patriotic poetry, as well as official proclamations. In the year of the Stamp Act, John Adams noted in his diary: "Innumerable have been the Monuments of Wit, Humour, Sense, Learning, Spirit, Patriotism, and Heroism, erected in the several Colonies and Provinces, in the Course of the Year. Our Presses have groaned, our Pulpits have thundered, our Legislatures have resolved, our Towns have voted . . ." (December 18, 1765). Compared to the more modest output of the preceding years, the publications of 1765 (354 surviving imprints) must have seemed "innumerable" to Adams or any other observer. The number of American imprints would continue to rise, peaking in the eventful years of 1774 (819 surviving), 1775 (997), and 1776 (741), falling off during the rest of the war, and rising again once peace was established in 1783. By 1790, American printers were producing more than a thousand titles, and by 1800, more than two thousand.

Writing to Thomas Jefferson in 1815, Adams looked back at the transforming events he had witnessed and shaped, concluding:

> The Revolution was in the minds of the people, and this was effected, from 1760 to 1775, in the course of fifteen years before a drop of blood was shed at Lexington. The records of thirteen legislatures, the pamphlets, newspapers in all the colonies, ought to be consulted during that period to ascertain the steps by which the public opinion was enlightened and informed concerning the authority of Parliament over the colonies.

Following Adams's suggestion, consider "the steps," the distribution, of the Declaration of Independence. On July 8, 1776, four days after it was adopted by the Continental Congress, the self-evident truths of this document were proclaimed to an assembled crowd in Philadelphia. In New York on July 8, the Declaration was read to George Washington's troops. However dramatic and forceful these oral presentations might have been, most Americans learned of the political separation from Great Britain through printed sources. The Declaration was printed in at least seventeen American editions in 1776 and 1777, while also being reprinted in virtually all the newspapers. The first printing in Massachusetts, for example, was in the July 17 edition of the *Massachusetts Spy*, a patriot newspaper published by Isaiah Thomas in Worcester.

Of course, the Declaration of Independence did not appear in a vacuum. When readers opened the *South Carolina & Georgia Almanack* for 1777, they found a text of the Declaration along with more mundane information that helped them order their daily lives. Those almanac readers had grown accustomed to political as well as practical advice over the years. William Pitt's "Speech for the Removal of the Stamp Act" was printed in the *South Carolina & Georgia Almanack* for 1767. "A Question of Taxation without Representation by a Gentleman of South Carolina" appeared in the almanac for 1771, and was followed in 1775 by the essay "Liberty the Birthright of Man." The Declaration of Independence, then, was part of an ongoing print debate in all the colonies.

Print performed several key functions in transforming subjects of the British crown into independent citizens of the United States. First, there was a new emphasis on the diffusion of learning. "Without Knowledge among the People," wrote Isaac Collins in his prospectus for the *New-Jersey Gazette* in 1783, "Liberty and publick Happiness cannot exist long in any Country; and this necessary Knowledge cannot be obtained in any other way than by a general Circulation of publick Papers." This point was made more emphatically a few years later by John Fenno in the first issue of the *Gazette of the United States* (New York, April 15, 1789): "The great and momentous subject of Education is hourly appreciating in its importance: That part of the NEW CONSTITUTION, which opens the door to every man of rank, possessing VIRTUE and ABILITIES, to the highest honours in the great American Republick, has expanded the views of every American." Of course, it had long been a commonplace in Anglo-American culture that newspapers in particular (and books in general) were meant to be both "useful and entertaining." But the American Revolution had changed many of the social ground rules. The idea of equality – opening the door to "every man of rank, possessing virtue and abilities" – gave education a new significance in the United States, unlike "any other country upon the face of the earth." Fenno went on to say, "The MIDDLING and LOWER CLASS of CITIZENS will therefore find their account in becoming subscribers for this Gazette, should it pay a particular regard to this great subject." In other words, by paying for a paper devoted to education, subscribers were in effect paying themselves ("their account"). Their money would not be wasted, especially if they could rise "to the highest honours" by reading their newspapers.

Secondly, there was a new emphasis on political liberty. Isaac Collins concluded his prospectus of 1783 with the injunction: "But if to save a few Pence, or a little Time in reading publick Papers, we should neglect them, Ignorance may gradually overspread this new enlightened land, and Tyranny advance as Knowledge decays, until Darkness and Slavery wrap this glorious Land in all the Horrors of despotick Sway." For most African Americans, slavery was not a rhetorical flourish but a reality. As one reads the revolutionary newspapers and their constant appeals to liberty (of persons and the press), one is struck by the numerous times that slavery is mentioned in the same breath, not to mention the numerous advertisements for runaway slaves. Yet the language of the press is often biblical in phrasing and image. As Sam Adams wrote in the *Boston Gazette*: "*Your* Press has spoken to us the words of truth: It has pointed to this people their dangers and their remedy: It has set before them Liberty and Slavery; and with the most perswasive and pungent language, conjur'd them, in the name of GOD, and the King, and for the sake of all posterity, to chuse Liberty and refuse Chains . . ." Noticeable here is the quasi-divine power of the press: it speaks "the words of truth," it conjures. In "The Art of Printing, a Poem" one finds the same attribution of supernatural power to the press: "Hail mystick art! which men like angels taught, / To speak to eyes, and paint unbody'd thought!" (*The Lancaster Almanack*, 1775).

Still, despite the limits and contradictions of the press during the Revolution (the treatment of James Rivington and other loyalist printers is a conspicuous illustration of how unwilling Americans often were to extend the freedom of the press to unpopular causes), a consensus did emerge that the free exercise of printing would invariably promote the public good. The question of human rights may have led to odd juxtapositions on the page, but it also led to Benjamin Rush's *An Address to the Inhabitants of the British Settlements in America, Upon Slave-Keeping* (1773) and other early abolitionist literature. The printed word gave women a broader audience as well and helped to focus attention on their altered roles in the newly established republican order. As expressed in *The Sentiments of an American Woman* (Philadelphia, 1788), women too were "Born for liberty, disdaining to bear the irons of a tyrannic government." And as John Mycall of Newburyport, Massachusetts, put it in his prospectus for *The Temple* in 1782: "The interests of Liberty are inseparable from those of learning and of virtue." This is one of the enduring legacies of the Revolution. While *The Temple* itself may have failed as a weekly newspaper – and while the Revolution may not always have lived up to its ideals – the "simple facts, plain arguments, and common sense" of Thomas Paine's galvanizing revolutionary pamphlet, reprinted in twenty-seven editions in 1776, took on a life of their own.

In 1771, Benjamin Franklin observed that subscription libraries "have improved the general Conversation of Americans, made the common Tradesmen and Farmers as intelligent as most Gentlemen from other Countries, and perhaps have contributed in some Degree to the Stand so generally made throughout the Colonies in Defence of their Priviledges." Franklin would know. With the support of his Junto, a group of young tradesmen interested in self-improvement, Franklin was instrumental in founding in 1731 the Library Company of Philadelphia (an institution still very much with us and in the vanguard of book history research).

Although more than one hundred book catalogues of various kinds (college, subscription, rental, private, booksellers') were published in America before 1801, relatively few of them have been given the scrutiny they deserve. (For a comprehensive listing, see R. B. Winans, *A Descriptive Checklist of Book Catalogues Separately Printed in America, 1693–1800* [1981].) Yet library catalogues can help us situate authors, titles, and ideas in the broader world of colonial and revolutionary America.

Sir Isaac Newton's presence in the Harvard College Library (founded 1638) is instructive. In the 1723 catalogue he was represented by only one work, his *Opticks* (London, 1704). In the supplementary list of 1735, Newton's *Chronology* (London, 1728) and his *Observations on Daniel and the Apocalypse* (London, 1733) were included. The 1773 catalogue included a multivolume set of his *Works*, in Latin and English, of unspecified date. Between 1773 and 1790, however, Newton reached his zenith, as measured by his presence in the library, which by the later date held his *Chronology of Ancient Kingdoms Amended* in both the London and Dublin editions of 1728; the *Arithmetica universalis*, second edition (London, 1722) and its English translation (London, 1748); the seventh edition of *Tables for Leases* (London, 1758); *Optics* (London, 1704, 1719, and 1721); *Lectiones opticae* (London, 1729); *Philosephiae naturalis principia mathematica* (London, 1726 and 1729; Geneva, 1729); *De mundi systemate* (London, 1731); *Opuscula* (Lausanne and Geneva, 1744); *Observations on the Prophecies of Daniel and John* (London, 1733 and 1754); and *Two letters to M. LeClerc* (London, 1754).

What are we to make of this? Were Americans, at the far end of the Atlantic world, simply slow to catch the latest waves in science? Not necessarily. We know from John Adams's diary and from Professor John Winthrop's lecture notes that Newtonian science was taught at Harvard while Adams was an undergraduate in the 1750s. The Harvard book collection, then, is not a completely trustworthy measure of Newton's influence in early America. When we also take into account the disastrous fire of 1764, which almost completely destroyed the Harvard collection, it becomes apparent that the space given to Isaac Newton in the catalogue of 1790 is less an indication of a new-found interest in Newtonian science and more a measure of the college's attempt to re-establish an important figure in the curriculum. But in other areas the catalogue does offer us a window on the pressing questions of the day. This is perhaps most evident in the numerous political tracts in the 1790 catalogue: almost one hundred titles under the heading "America."

Unlike imprint catalogues, such as the English Short Title Catalogue or NAIP, library catalogues are not limited by geography or nationality and thus provide a different lens on the past – a broader, richer contextual view. Cotton Mather (for example) looms inordinately large in the annals of American imprints and, even after the fire of 1764, he looms large in the Harvard catalogue of 1790 as well. But among the theological tracts listed therein, one finds Mather in the company of a wide assortment of bishops, dissenters, and even freethinkers (more than twenty-five works by Joseph Priestley). This bibliographical variety is evident not just in the theological works but in every topic covered by the Harvard collections, which broadly represent the interests of learned culture.

However, for popular genres (almanacs, school books, novels, Psalters) one must look elsewhere. From 1640 to 1800, the most frequently reprinted American work, based on surviving records in NAIP, was the *New England Primer*, with 154 records (62 editions appeared in the last decade of the eighteenth century). Noah Webster's *Grammatical Institute* comes next, with 101 editions recorded from 1783 to 1800. In third place is another pedagogical mainstay, Thomas Dilworth's *New Guide to the English Tongue* (68 editions between 1747 and 1800). The United States Constitution is next with 66 imprints between 1787 and 1800, followed by the Brady-Tate version of the Psalms, with 64 editions between 1713 and 1800. In fact, if all biblical texts (Psalters, Testaments, complete Bibles, adaptations, and abridgements, in German as well as in English) are considered as an aggregate, there are 407 American imprints in this category, from the Bay Psalm Book of 1640 to the Authorized Version of the Bible printed by Isaiah Thomas in Worcester in 1800. The NAIP database suggests that early Americans had one overriding concern: how does one get through this world? The answer is found in their surviving books, pamphlets, and broadsides, which cluster under three main headings: religion, the affairs of daily life, and politics.

In addition to the inspired oracles of God, Americans read Isaac Watts's *Divine Songs* (reprinted 58 times between 1730 and 1800) and his *Hymns and Spiritual Songs* (45 editions between 1742 and 1800), the Westminster Assembly's *Shorter Catechism* (40 editions between 1682 and 1800), Martin Luther's *Kleine Katechismus* (37 editions from 1744 to 1800), and the *Heidelberger Katechismus* (30 editions from 1712 to 1800, not counting its frequent appearance as part of the Psalter). Robert Russel's *Seven Sermons* was reprinted 29 times between 1701 and 1800 and *The History of the Holy Jesus*, a juvenile work by "A Lover of Their Precious Souls," also survives in 29 editions, the earliest from 1746. More than forty other religious titles were reprinted from five to twenty times.

Textbooks, professional manuals, guides for hearth and home, personal narratives, and a few works of imaginative literature were frequently reprinted. In addition to the *New England Primer*, Webster's *Grammatical Institute*, and Dilworth's *A New Guide to the English Tongue*, one should also mention Ezekiel Cheever's *A Short Introduction to the Latin Tongue* (printed first in 1709 and reprinted in every decade until 1785), *The Youth's Instructor in the English Tongue* (11 editions), Daniel Fenning's *Universal Spelling Book* (10 editions), Thomas Dilworth's *The Schoolmaster's Assistant* (24 editions), and William Perry's *The Only Sure Guide to the English Tongue* (17 editions). Benjamin Franklin's *Way to Wealth*, published 16 times between 1758 and 1800, encouraged the Protestant ethic to flourish in the counting house as well as the meeting house. For earning a living, Thomas Goodman's *Experienced Secretary* was a durable guide (12 editions between 1703 and 1730), along with George Fisher's *The American Instructor* (7 editions between 1748 and 1787) and Daniel Fenning's *Ready Reckoner* (16 editions from 1774 to 1800). While printers were busy issuing the laws of colonies and states, lawyers and justices frequently relied on such works as the *Conductor Generalis*, printed in 11 editions from 1711 to 1800. William Buchan's *Domestic Medicine* survives in 29 American editions from 1772 to 1800, along with William Cadogan's *A Dissertation on the Gout* (7 editions from 1771 to 1785). In sickness and health, many Americans pondered John Johnson's *The Advantages and Disadvantages of a Married Life* (15 editions from 1757 to 1800) and William Secker's *A Wedding Ring, Fit for the Finger* (6 editions from 1690 to 1773), which offered "directions to those men that want wives, how to choose them; and to those women that have husbands, how to use them."

Personal experiences, such as Mary Rowlandson's famous captivity narrative, *The Sovereignty and Goodness of God* (16 editions from 1682 to 1800), Eleazar Wheelock's *Plain and Faithful Narrative* (8 editions, 1763 to 1775), and John Williams's *The Redeemed Captive, Returning to Zion* (10 editions, 1707 to 1800) apparently always found an audience. Visionary and remarkable occurrences were retailed: *A Wonderful Dream* (16 editions, 1753 to 1800), *A Wonderful Discovery of a Hermit* (10 editions, 1786 to 1800), *The French Convert* (22 editions, 1725 to 1800), and *A Dialogue between Death and a Lady* (7 editions, 1732 to 1800).

After the United States Constitution and Thomas Paine's *Common Sense*, the most popular political work was *The Manual Exercise* of Great Britain, reprinted 22 times between 1757 and 1780 and undoubtedly put to good use by combatants on both sides of the war. (The vigorous pamphlet literature of the Revolution is well surveyed by Bernard Bailyn [1967] and T. R. Adams [1980].) Not only was the reprinting of political pamphlets in such numbers a new phenomenon, but the pace and geographic spread of their publication were unprecedented as well. Twenty-seven editions of *Common Sense* were printed up and down the sea coast, all with the space of a year, 1776. Jonathan Shipley's *A Speech Intended to Have Been Spoken on the Bill for Altering the Charter of the Colony of Massachusetts Bay* appeared in twelve editions in 1774, in Boston, Philadelphia, Lancaster, New York, Hartford, Salem (Massachusetts), Newport, and Williamsburg.

Perhaps it was no accident that the American popularity of Daniel Defoe's *Robinson Crusoe* (as measured by reprinting and abridgements) reached its peak after the Revolution. Although one American edition appeared in 1757 and another in 1774, thirteen more *Crusoes* were printed from 1784 to 1790, with an additional 29 editions forthcoming in the last decade of the eighteenth century. *Robinson Crusoe* is the American book *par excellence.* After all, it is the story of a man who disobeys his English father, builds an empire in the New World, reads his Bible daily, and converts and conquers "savages." In short, the novel distilled the religious, practical, and political lessons that had long figured among the staple products of the early American press.

REFERENCES AND FURTHER READING

Adams, Thomas (1980) *The American Controversy: A Bibliographical Study of the British Pamphlets about the American Disputes, 1764–1783.* Providence: Brown University.

Alden, John and Landis, Dennis C. (1980–) *European Americana: A Chronological Guide to Works Printed in Europe Relating to the Americas, 1493–1776.* New York: Readex.

Amory, Hugh (2005) *Bibliography and the Book Trades: Studies in the Print Culture of Early New England*, ed. David D. Hall. Philadelphia: University of Pennsylvania Press.

Bailyn, Bernard (1967) *The Ideological Origins of the American Revolution.* Cambridge, MA: Harvard University Press.

Barber, Giles (1976) "Books from the Old World and for the New: The British International Trade in Books in the Eighteenth Century." *Studies on Voltaire and the Eighteenth Century*, 151: 185–224.

Bond, W. H. and Amory, Hugh (eds.) (1996) *The Printed Catalogues of the Harvard College Library 1723–1790.* Boston: Colonial Society of Massachusetts.

Brigham, Clarence (1947) *History and Bibliography of American Newspapers*, 2 vols. Worcester: American Antiquarian Society.

— (1958) *Bibliography of American Editions of Robinson Crusoe to 1830.* Worcester: American Antiquarian Society.

Clement, Richard W. (1996) *The Book in America, with Images from the Library of Congress.* Golden: Fulcrum.

Davis, Richard Beale (1978) *Intellectual Life in the Colonial South, 1585–1763.* Knoxville: University of Tennessee Press.

Evans, Charles (1903–55) *American Bibliography*, 13 vols. Chicago: Charles Evans. Completed by Clifford K. Shipton through 1800; with *Index* (vol. 14), 1959 and *Supplement* (1970) by Roger P. Bristol.

Fiering, Norman (1976) "The Transatlantic Republic of Letters: A Note on the Circulation of Learned Periodicals." *William and Mary Quarterly*, 3rd ser., 33: 642–60.

Green, James N. (1995) *At the Instance of Benjamin Franklin: A Brief History of the Library Company of Philadelphia.* Philadelphia: Library Company of Philadelphia.

Hall, David D. and Amory, Hugh (eds.) (2000) *The Colonial Book in the Atlantic World.* Cambridge: Cambridge University Press.

Hayes, Kevin J. (1996) *A Colonial Woman's Bookshelf.* Knoxville: University of Tennessee Press.

— (1997) *The Library of William Byrd of Westover.* Madison: Madison House.

Honour, Hugh (1975) *The New Golden Land: European Images of America from the Discoveries to the Present Time.* New York: Pantheon.

Joyce, William L., Hall, David D., Brown, Richard D., and Hench, John B. (eds.) (1983) *Printing and Society in Early America.* Worcester: American Antiquarian Society.

Remer, Rosalind (1996) *Printers and Men of Capital: Philadelphia Book Publishers in the New Republic.* Philadelphia: University of Pennsylvania Press.

Sabin, Joseph (1868–1936) *Bibliotheca Americana: A Dictionary of Books Relating to America, from its Discovery to the Present Time.* Continued by Wilberforce Eames and completed by R. W. G. Vail. New York: Bibliographical Society of America.

Simmons, R. C. (1996) *British Imprints Relating to North America 1621–1760: An Annotated Checklist.* London: British Library.

Stowell, Marion Barber (1977) *Early American Almanacs: The Colonial Weekday Bible.* New York: Burt Franklin.

Tanselle, G. Thomas (1971) *A Guide to the Study of United States Imprints.* Cambridge, MA: Harvard University Press.

Thomas, Isaiah (1970) *A History of Printing in America*, ed. Marcus McCorison. New York: Weathervane.

Winans, Robert B. (1981) *A Descriptive Checklist of Book Catalogues Separately Printed in America, 1693–1800.* Worcester: American Antiquarian Society.

Wroth, L. C. (1938) *The Colonial Printer.* Portland, ME: Southworth-Anthoensen.

20

The Industrialization of the Book
1800–1970

Rob Banham

At the end of the eighteenth century the making of books was still very much a craft. Papermaking, punch-cutting, type-casting, composition, inking, and binding were all done by hand, and printing was still a process using a wooden hand press – little had changed since the end of the fifteenth century. In contrast, the period 1800–1970 was one of continuing innovation which saw the introduction of many new technologies, only the most significant of which are covered here. By the end of the nineteenth century, the process of printing books with metal type was almost entirely mechanized and, by 1970, letterpress technology was on the way out, having been superseded by phototypesetting and offset lithography. The printing, publishing, and selling of books increasingly became separate activities: by 1970, it was extremely unusual for books to be printed and published by the same company.

Many of the technological advances in printing and its allied trades during the nineteenth century were driven by the requirements of newspaper and periodical printers who needed to meet an ever-increasing demand for their products. *The Times* newspaper, in particular, was at the forefront of many new developments. There were also social changes that led to a greater demand for printed matter, all of which were inextricably linked to one another: increasing literacy rates; better education; the huge increase in the size and number of manufacturing and retail businesses; and improvements in communication, particularly through the introduction of the railway network and the penny post.

Papermaking

The mechanization of the papermaking process was crucial to the industrialization of the book: without a papermaking industry capable of supplying large quantities of paper, increases in printing output would simply not have been possible. The breakthrough was made by Nicholas-Louis Robert, who worked in the paper mill of Didot

Saint Leger in Essonnes. After several experiments in the 1790s, Robert was awarded a patent for his papermaking machine in 1799. Didot felt that there were better prospects for developing the machine in England and, with this in mind, his brother-in-law, John Gamble, was sent to London. Gamble was introduced to the Fourdriniers, who were involved in the stationery and papermaking trades. They agreed to finance the project and an English patent was granted in 1801. Several improved versions of Robert's original machine were made by the engineer Bryan Donkin. By 1807, Fourdrinier papermaking machines had become commercially viable and were able to produce more paper in a day than a single vat for hand production could make in a week. Improvements continued to be made, most notably the addition of steam-heated drying cylinders. By the 1830s, machine-made paper was commonly used in all kinds of printing, including the production of books. The printer George Clowes is recorded in 1837 as declaring that "The Fourdrinier machine had been very beneficial to the printing trade, materially reducing the price of paper and enabling them to produce books at a much cheaper price" (Clapperton 1967: 292).

By 1850, production of paper in the UK had risen from around 2.5 lb per capita in 1800 to about 8 lb (Hills 1988) and the papermaking industry was struggling to meet the demand due to a shortage of rags, the main raw material of traditional Western paper. This led to a search for other materials from which paper could be made. In 1854, *The Times* offered a reward of £1,000 for the invention or discovery of a cheap substitute for cotton and linen rags. In the UK, the answer to this problem was to use esparto grass, which was imported from southern Spain and North Africa. During the two world wars supply lines were cut and so straw was used for papermaking instead. Numerous experiments were made in the eighteenth and nineteenth centuries which attempted to make use of wood pulp in papermaking, some mechanical, some chemical, and some a combination of the two. By the end of the nineteenth century, a significant amount of paper was being made from wood pulp. In the twentieth century, this became the primary source of material for papermaking and the amount of paper produced increased enormously – the amount of wood pulp imported into the UK increased from 79,000 tonnes in 1887 to 2,738,000 tonnes by 1970 (Hills 1988). Paper made from esparto grass and wood pulp is not as strong as rag paper, but these substitute materials allowed virtually unlimited production of low-cost paper which greatly reduced the unit cost of books and other printed items.

New Presses

The first significant improvement on the wooden hand press was the introduction of a new iron press, invented by Earl Stanhope in around 1800. Several other iron presses followed the Stanhope, of which the Columbian and Albion were by far the most successful. The Albion (figure 20.1), patented in 1820, was the English answer to the Columbian, which had been brought to England from America by its inventor George Clymer in 1817. The iron press had several distinct advantages over the wooden press.

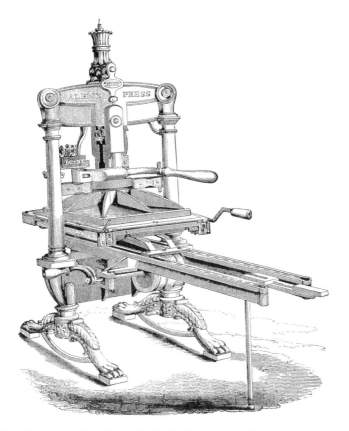

Figure 20.1 The Albion press. From J. and R. M. Wood, *Specimens of Polytype Ornaments*, c.1855 (St. Bride negative 513).

It required less physical effort to use but delivered much greater pressure, more evenly, with a much larger platen. The increased platen size meant that large forms could be printed in one pull, whereas the wooden press had required two. The new iron hand press soon became popular with book printers, but in reality the superior power made little difference to them. The iron press was faster but not significantly so and, while the extra power would have made printing easier, it had a much greater impact on jobbing printers as it allowed them to print posters with large, heavy display type.

However, the added power of the iron press did mean that it was better suited to printing wood-engraved illustrations. Early illustrated books employed woodcut illustrations, which had the advantage that they were cut in relief so that the blocks could be printed together with the metal type. Woodcut images were rather crude, although in the hands of a great artist, such as Albrecht Dürer, a much more sophisticated effect could be achieved. Later, copperplate images, which provided a much greater level of detail, were preferred to woodcuts. This was a much slower and more expensive process – the copper plates had to be printed separately from the type on an intaglio press. A happy medium was found in the late eighteenth century when Thomas Bewick improved and popularized the technique of wood-engraving. Wood-engravings were produced by working on the end grain of a piece of hard wood, such as box, with tools similar to those used by copper engravers. This meant that much finer lines could be cut than could be done with woodcuts where a knife was used to cut into the side of a plank of wood. Wood-engraving was still not as fine as copperplate but, as a relief process, it could be printed together with the type and quickly became a popular means of illustrating books, newspapers, and magazines.

Wood-engraving remained very much a craft and the only way of increasing the speed of production was by having illustrations engraved piecemeal. Large illustrations had to be made up from a number of small blocks bolted together because trees that provided suitable wood for engraving did not usually grow large enough to provide woodblocks much bigger than 120 × 170 mm (5 × 7 inches). Each of the component blocks could be engraved by a different worker to speed up production. However, technology was developed which allowed duplicates of blocks to be produced by stereotyping or electrotyping (see below) so that multiple copies could be printed at the same time, on different presses or by different printers.

The first mechanized printing presses followed hot on the heels of the iron hand press. Friedrich Koenig, a German engineer living in the UK, began experimenting with steam-driven presses soon after the Stanhope press had been introduced. Initially, he attempted to apply steam power to the platen press but he soon switched to modifying the cylinder press used by copperplate printers which provided a simpler and more efficient means of applying pressure to the form (figure 20.2). Soon machines built by Koenig were installed at *The Times*, which triumphantly announced the first issue to be printed on a steam-powered press on November 29, 1814.

Koenig's machines printed 1,100 sheets an hour compared with around 300 sheets an hour on an iron hand press, but they cost £900, almost ten times as much as the Stanhope, and it appears that this was prohibitive for most book printers. By the 1830s, some large book-printing firms were running steam presses. However, for most book printers, smaller, hand-powered cylinder presses remained the norm until the middle of the nineteenth century at which point they began to move over to steam presses that were specifically developed for book printing (such as the Wharfedale).

A series of improvements to Koenig's press were made by Edward Cowper and Augustus Applegath, who were employed by *The Times* after Koenig returned to Germany. Although presses had been mechanized, the paper was still fed into the machines by hand in the form of single sheets (these were easier to tax and stamp than rolls of paper). In response, Applegath built a new press with four feeding stations that printed four sheets during one movement of the form and produced over 4,000 sheets an hour.

Newspapers and periodicals continued to drive the development of printing machines. Output was increased when Applegath constructed a vertical rotary press in 1848 which marked the first move away from a flat bed of type and significantly increased the speed of production. This was further improved in 1858 with the introduction of horizontal

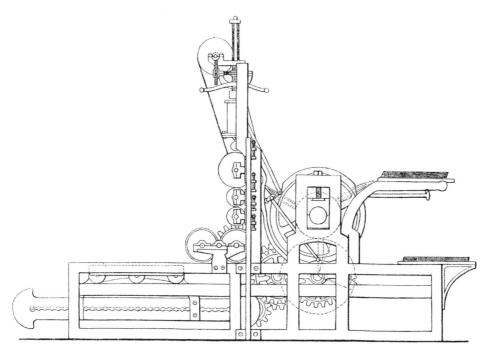

Figure 20.2   Koenig printing machine of 1811. From T. Goebel, *Frederick Koenig und die Erfindung der Schnellepresse*, 1906 (St. Bride negative 182).

rotary presses imported from America. These huge machines, produced by R. Hoe & Co., had up to ten feeding stations and were capable of up to 20,000 impressions an hour (figure 20.3). Applegath's rotary press still used flat forms of type – his "cylinder" was in fact a polygon with flat sides that carried columns of type – and early Hoe machines employed a special means of securing ordinary printer's type to the cylinder.

However, soon after *The Times* introduced the Hoe machine, successful trials were undertaken to print from curved stereotype plates (see below) and by 1870 new machines had been installed that took advantage of this technology. During the 1860s, the problem of having to feed paper in by hand was finally solved by the abolition of paper duty in 1861 and by the introduction of web-fed machines that could print on both sides of a continuous reel of paper. By the end of the century, folding and cutting mechanisms had been added to machines that could produce 24,000 copies of a complete newspaper in an hour. Throughout this period of relentless advances in newspaper printing, the book trade continued to limp along behind (figure 20.4). Most book printers used presses derived from Koenig's designs but, toward the end of the nineteenth century, some paperbacks were being printed on either sheet- or web-fed rotary presses. Little changed in the twentieth century except that presses were driven by electricity rather than steam, and on sheet-fed presses vacuum suction was introduced to feed the sheets in automatically.

Figure 20.3   Hoe's eight-cylinder printing machine. From *Typographic Messenger*, September 1866 (St. Bride negative 313).

Figure 20.4   Hoe's bed-and-platen book-printing machine. From *Typographic Messenger*, July 1867 (St. Bride negative 442).

Stereotyping and Electrotyping

Stereotyping is the method of creating a cast-metal printing plate using a mold taken from a form of type (or from a woodblock illustration). There are a number of reasons why it might have been desirable for book printers to use stereotyping, all of which have to do with saving time, money, or both. A printer who used stereotyping would not need to replace his type as often because it would not suffer as much wear and tear. It also meant that printers did not need to stock so much type, thus cutting down on what was otherwise an expensive investment.

The main advantage of stereotyping was the ability to reprint something at a later date without having to pay composition costs a second time. Paper was an expensive commodity and therefore not many printers (or publishers) could afford to print more copies of something than it was estimated that they could initially sell. Unfortunately, this meant that they might miss out on sales if they happened to underestimate the number of copies required. If there were sufficient demand for more copies of a particular title, the printer would have to undertake another print run. This required starting the job again from scratch and incurring for a second time all the costs that this entailed. This problem could be solved by leaving all the forms for a particular title standing. However, most printers would not have had large enough stocks of type to set a whole book and at any rate this was only practical for books that were in more or less constant demand. Stereotyping meant that reprints could be produced without expending further time and money to compose the pages afresh and without having to leave the type standing.

Stereotyping using casts made in sand or plaster had been in use since the 1700s, and the technique of "dabbing" to make stereotype copies of woodcuts and wood-engravings had probably been around for even longer (Mosley 1993). However, a reliable means of stereotyping forms of type was not in place until a method of casting plates from plaster of Paris molds was patented in 1784 by Alexander Tilloch, editor of *Philosophical Magazine* and part-proprietor of *The Star*, and printer Andrew Foulis. Their invention did not really take off until Earl Stanhope approached them in 1800 wanting to develop and use their process. In 1803, a printer named Wilson, under the patronage of Stanhope, set up as a stereotype printer. Both Cambridge University Press and Oxford University Press soon had agreements with Wilson for the printing of Bibles, Testaments, and prayer-books.

Casting stereos using plaster of Paris was expensive and time-consuming. It required specially cast type and took around two hours to make a single plate, not including the time it took to bake the mold. The protracted nature of the process was exacerbated by the fact that each mold could only be used to make one plate because it was always destroyed during casting.

Around 1828–9 the papier mâché method of casting stereotype plates was rediscovered (having previously been used as early as the seventeenth century) by Claude Genoux in France. This superseded Stanhope's method and continued to be used, more or less unchanged, until the use of metal type for commercial printing came to an end. Genoux's process replaced plaster of Paris with papier mâché or "flong." The wet flong was laid on top of the form and beaten with a stiff brush to force it into the gaps. It was then removed and dried, ready to be used for casting plates. A special "drying and casting press" was used to dry the mold, initially while it was still pressed against the form. The same piece of equipment was used to cast the plates: the press was moved from a horizontal to a vertical position, which allowed the air to escape when metal was poured in. The flong, or wet-mat, process was much faster than the Stanhope process and did not require special type. Most importantly, the flong molds were not destroyed in casting, meaning that they could be used repeatedly and also that they could be stored for possible future use without having to undertake the actual casting of plates, thus saving time, money, and storage space. The molds could also be packaged and transported safely so that they could be made in one place and the plates cast and printed elsewhere. The flong molds were soft and pliable and so could be curved into a hemispherical shape and then used to cast curved plates for use with rotary presses.

The spread of stereotyping early in the nineteenth century generated an explosion in the number of "stock blocks" that were available from type-foundries; some companies traded in nothing but stereotype blocks. This meant that printers now had access to cheap images to enliven their printed pages, a system similar to the picture libraries of today.

From the late 1830s, electrotyping was also used for plate-making, especially for the duplication of wood-engraved blocks. A mold was made using wax or plastic and a thin layer of metal was deposited on the mold using electrolysis. The resulting "shell" was an exact copy of the original, faithfully reproducing even the finest lines. This had to be strengthened, by backing with a lead alloy, and then mounted onto a block of wood before it could be used for printing.

Bookbinding

In 1800, books were still bound by hand, usually after being sold to the bookseller or private individual as flat sheets or in paper-covered boards which were not intended to be durable. By the end of the century, all the various aspects of bookbinding had been mechanized and most books were sold ready bound. The first machine to enter the bookbinding trade was the rolling press which was used to flatten the folded sheets before binding:

> a process that had hitherto been performed by a workman hammering the sheets with a fourteen-pound beating hammer – a monotonous job concerning which Arnett gave this warning: "When employed at the beating stone the workman should keep his legs together to avoid hernia, to which he is much exposed if, with the intention of being more at ease, he contracts the habit of placing them apart." (Darley 1959: 29–30)

By 1830, the rolling press was in use at most binderies, but the folding of printed sheets and binding of books continued to be done by hand well into the nineteenth century. As in other areas, it was the newspaper trade that led the way: the first folding machines were in use by the 1850s, attached to cylinder presses for folding newspapers as they were printed. By the end of the century, machines to fold sheets for binding into books were in use, and paper-cutting, gathering, stitching, stapling, and gluing were all automated. Mechanical means of attaching the covers and stamping the lettering on them had also been devised. In large binderies, all these machines were connected by a system of belts and pulleys to one or two steam engines that provided the power.

One of the most important developments was not a new machine but a new material. In 1820, Charles Pickering published the first of his "Diamond Classics" series (set in 4½ point "diamond" type) which were bound in cloth. In 1830, Pickering applied lettering to the spine of his cloth bindings using the new arming press – an iron printing press adapted for this purpose. The covers had to go into the arming press flat and this meant that they had to be made separately, so the lettering could be stamped on, before being glued to the book.

> Shortly after this, it was discovered that even sewing could be dispensed with. The sections of a book were guillotined down the back, so that the book, instead of being, say, ten sections of thirty-two pages, became three hundred and twenty loose sheets of paper. By using a special kind of adhesive called caoutchouc, or gutta-percha, these pages could be made to adhere to the case quite satisfactorily. (McLean 1972: 6–7)

For reasons of economy, most books conformed to one of a number of standard sizes that related to the size of the paper that they were printed on. After the adoption of DIN (Deutsche Industrie Norm) paper sizes, books began to be printed in A4 and A5 formats, particularly after these sizes became common due to the spread of the photocopier after World War II.

Hot Metal

Preparing pages of metal type for printing was a time-consuming and expensive process, but it was not until the end of the nineteenth century that punch-cutting, type-casting, and composition were all automated, and all three continued to be done by hand well into the twentieth century. The first breakthrough came with the introduction of type-casting machines: David Bruce's pivotal caster, invented in the US in 1838 and introduced to the UK in the middle of the nineteenth century, was capable of casting 6,000 pieces of type in an hour – around twelve times as many as a hand caster. Later machines improved output further, casting over 50,000 pieces of type an hour.

The slowest part of the process of manufacturing type by hand was punch-cutting – cutting a single punch and making a matrix from it could take a day or more. Punch-cutting was finally mechanized in 1885 with the invention of Linn Boyd Benton's punch-cutting pantograph. This worked in a similar way to the pantograph for cutting wood type, but instead of making wood letters it made metal punches. The starting-point is a large drawing around 25 cm (10 inches) high. In cutting punches by hand, the only function of drawings is to provide a visual reference for the punch-cutter. In mechanized punch-cutting, drawings were an integral part of the system – for the first time in the history of type production the designing and making became separate parts

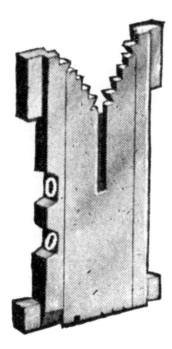

Figure 20.5   A double-letter Linotype matrix. From W. Atkins (ed.), *The Art and Practice of Printing*, 1932.

of the process. The drawing was used to make a pattern, usually in metal, which the pantograph machine could trace around to produce punches in whatever size was required.

A number of abortive attempts were made to mechanize the composition of type during the nineteenth century, which failed due to a combination of poor engineering and opposition from compositors. The answer was found at the end of the nineteenth century in the shape of machines which both cast and composed type. The first was the line-casting system introduced by Ottmar Mergenthaler in 1885 and developed subsequently by the Mergenthaler Linotype Company. The Linotype machine was first used by *The New York Tribune* newspaper. The machine carried a magazine of matrices similar to those used for hand-casting which were released by pressing keys on a keyboard to fall into a line. The operator then cast the whole line as a solid slug, a "line o' type," which gave the machine its name (figures 20.5 and 20.6).

At the same time as Mergenthaler was developing his Linotype system, Tolbert Lanston was working on a rival machine called the Monotype which cast and composed individual pieces of type. Lanston's machine had two parts, a keyboard and a caster. In the Monotype system, text was composed at a keyboard that punched character codes into a paper ribbon. The Monotype caster had all the matrices for a single typeface in a matrix case. The matrix case moved under instruction from the codes on the paper

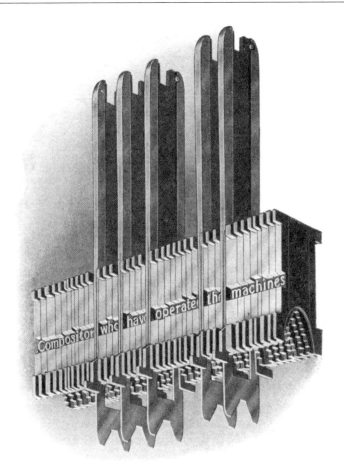

Figure 20.6 A line of single-letter Linotype matrices and spacebands, ready for casting a line of type. From L. A. Legros and J. C. Grant, *Typographical Printing-surfaces*, 1916.

ribbon. Each character code in the paper ribbon produced at the keyboard was made up of two holes. At the caster, these controlled a pair of pins in the mechanism that positioned the matrix case over the mold. One pin selected a column of matrices in the case; the other a single matrix within the column. Because it cast and composed individual pieces of type, corrections could easily be made to typesetting done on a Monotype machine (figure 20.7).

In the first half of the twentieth century, both Linotype and Monotype introduced many of their own typefaces which, now in digital form, remain the staples of book design today. The majority of these typefaces were historical revivals based on typefaces used by great printers of the past, such as Manutius, Plantin, Baskerville, and Bodoni. They also produced some entirely new types, the best known being Monotype's Gill Sans and Times New Roman.

Figure 20.7   A Monotype matrix case. Department of Typography and Graphic Communication, University of Reading.

Lithography

Arguably one of the most important developments in the industrialization of the book was the invention of lithography by Alois Senefelder in Munich in 1798. Lithography was the first entirely new method of printing to have been invented for hundreds of years. The key to the process is the basic principle that grease and water do not mix. If marks are made on a flat, porous stone surface with a waxy crayon or other greasy substance it will stick to the stone and be partially absorbed. The whole surface can then be moistened and the water is attracted to the stone but repelled by the grease. If the stone is then inked up with greasy printing ink, the ink will adhere to the greasy marks but be repelled by the water. The ink can then be transferred to a sheet of paper through the application of pressure. Unlike relief printing where the printing surface is raised, or intaglio where the ink is contained in incised grooves in a metal plate, in lithography the printing surface is flat.

Soon after its invention, lithography was being used to print books, mostly very small in both extent and print-run, but for the most part it was used for jobbing work and the reproduction of works of art and had very little impact on the book trade. In many ways, letterpress printing was extremely restrictive: the nature of type made of small, rectangular blocks of metal imposed limits on what could easily be printed. Lithography, on the other hand, allowed a great deal of freedom: any mark that could be made on the stone could be printed and so it had a great advantage over letterpress when it came to printing tables, diagrams, music, equations, maps, and the like. It was also capable of reproducing handwriting and so enabled the printing of non-Latin languages without the need to invest in expensive typefaces that would rarely be used. However, lithography was much slower than letterpress, and while powered machines were developed for letterpress printing early in the nineteenth century, lithographic printing relied on the hand press until after 1850. This meant that lithography was only used for printing short runs of books in circumstances in which the most could be made of its flexibility.

In the second half of the nineteenth century, powered machines with automatic inking and damping mechanisms were introduced, but further development was hindered by the fact that the rotary principle could not be applied to lithographic stones. The answer was the development of offset printing and the introduction of metal plates to replace the lithographic stones. In offset printing, the ink is transferred from the lithographic stone or plate to an intermediate rubber cylinder and then on to the paper. In the first quarter of the twentieth century, both sheet- and web-fed rotary presses for offset lithographic printing were in use. However, the vast majority of books (and newspapers) continued to be printed by letterpress. In part this was due to the fact that lithography was thought to be inferior to letterpress in terms of clarity of impression and density of ink. Because lithography deposited less ink, the printed result often had a rather "flat" look compared with letterpress, where the ink was caused to spread by the enormous pressure of the press. The use of water in the process tended to grey the ink and cause a certain amount of paper distortion, with resultant problems in register. Lithography was also hindered by the fact that text had to be composed in metal first.

> The original method was to set type by hand, proof it on special transfer paper, and then transfer the image to stone; later, type was set on a composing machine, proofed, and then photographed down onto a plate. But in both methods there was an initial stage when the text could just as well have been printed in an edition by letterpress. (Twyman 1970a: 29)

Letterpress printing finally began to be superseded by lithography in the 1960s when the advent of phototypesetting meant that text could be composed without using metal type (see below).

Although most books were originally printed by letterpress in the first half of the twentieth century, some were then reproduced using offset lithography – often when US and UK publishers collaborated on a title. The normal procedure was to have the book printed and typeset in one country, then to send the other publisher printed sheets or a finished copy that could be photographed for printing by offset lithography. This would save around 50 percent of the cost of typesetting and was also a very quick way of working.

Color

After some experiments in the incunable period, it became unusual to find color in books because it was difficult to justify the added expense. After 1800, color printing became more widespread, mainly driven by the demands of the advertising industry, but there was also an increase in the use of color in books. Text printed in color was generally limited to the occasional two-color title page, although there were exceptions, such as the version of the New Testament produced by De la Rue and Giles Balne in 1829 which was printed throughout in gold on special porcelain-coated paper. Illustrations printed in color were much more common, although the vast majority were still in black only. The best-known developments in this area are probably those of Savage, Baxter, and Knight, in the first half of the nineteenth century, although they were by no means the first to experiment with printing images in color.

William Savage's book, *Practical Hints on Decorative Printing*, was published in two parts in 1818 and 1823. Savage used oil-less inks to print a series of wood-engraved blocks, each in a different color, to build up a full-color image.

> The book is a virtuoso performance. One of the plates, "Ode to Mercy", was printed from as many as twenty-nine different wood-blocks and is a masterpiece of technical skill if not in conception. Savage's major contribution was to refine and extend the technique used by John Baptist Jackson in the eighteenth century by introducing rich colours and a great many more workings. (Twyman 1970a: 38)

Baxter's method was similar to that used by Savage, using a series of woodblocks to print different colors in order to produce the effect of full color. Unlike Savage, Baxter used oil-based inks and an intaglio key plate for the black working, which was usually a complete picture in its own right.

Charles Knight's career began at around the same time as that of Baxter. In 1832, he founded the *Penny Magazine* and this was followed by numerous books, often issued in parts, and all of these early works were illustrated with woodcuts. In 1838, Knight patented a method of color printing which he termed "illuminated printing." Like Baxter, Knight used oil-based inks, although his process differed in that he printed the colors first, from metal plates, with the black added last from a woodblock. The key to his idea was to apply four colors to a single sheet during the course of a single pass through the press. The sheet of paper remained stationary in the press until all the colors had been applied. This was achieved by fitting the press with a revolving frame in the place of the usual platen. Each color was printed on top of the preceding one whilst the ink was still wet, meaning that further colors could be created by mixing the inks together. In the field of lithographic printing, Godefroy Engelmann in the 1830s pioneered a similar method, called chromolithography, of building up color images using different stones to print different colors. Chromolithographed illustrations were used in books, sometimes with spectacular results, as in Owen Jones's masterpiece, *The Grammar of Ornament* (1856). All of these methods required the separation of the original into its constituent colored plates by eye, each plate then being engraved by hand. Later this was done using photography (see below).

Photography

The first role of photography in books was simply as tipped-in illustrations, one of the best-known early examples being the four-volume *Reports by the Juries* of the Great

Exhibition in 1851, which contained 155 pasted-down photographs. From around 1860 photographic images were transferred onto wood blocks by sensitizing the surface of the block before being engraved by hand as before.

By the 1870s it was possible to use photography to reproduce line drawings or other images with no tonal values. The original was photographed and the negative exposed onto a metal plate coated with a light-sensitive emulsion that hardened where it was exposed to light.

> Development removes the unexposed emulsion and leaves the drawing represented by lines of hardened emulsion on the surface of the bare metal. The plate is now treated to convert the emulsion into an acid resist, and it is then ready for etching. Etching with acid eats away the surface of the metal wherever it is unprotected, leaving the resist protected lines standing in relief. (Jennett 1967: 130)

However, paintings and photographs that had shades of grey could not be reproduced this way with black ink and white paper. The answer came in the shape of the halftone screen. "This was a device used to break down the tonal image of a photograph into a series of small dots. The size of the dots depended on the amount of light passing through a mesh of lines engraved on glass and on the coarseness of the mesh itself" (Twyman 1970a: 31). The negative was exposed onto the plate through this mesh of tiny holes (the "screen") resulting in a "halftone" block broken up into raised dots of greater or smaller size in correlation to the light and dark areas of the photograph. The same principle is still used to reproduce images today. When printed, and viewed at reading distance, the dots appear to reproduce the tonal values of the original photograph. In crude halftone screens, with larger dots, the dot pattern can sometimes be seen with the naked eye, but usually the dots are so small that they can only be seen with a magnifying glass.

The same method was later applied to reproducing color photographs using three or four colors to give the effect of full color. The original is photographed through a red, a green, and a blue filter. The halftone plates made from these photographs are called color separations and are printed in cyan, magenta, and yellow respectively (in four-color printing black is added). The resulting printed image is actually composed of different-sized dots in these three colors, but the human eye is fooled into seeing a complete range of colors.

Halftones printed better on coated or "art" papers, which were not suitable for printing text by letterpress, and so most books featuring halftone reproductions had them printed on different paper from the text paper to form a discrete section of the book, usually at the back or in the center. As the quality of reproduction improved, more "integrated" books were produced where the text and halftones were placed together on the pages.

Metal plates for lithographic or offset lithographic printing could also be made photographically. A metal sheet coated with a light-sensitive substance that would also attract greasy printing ink was exposed to light through a negative film. The coating hardened in the parts hit by the light and the rest remained soft. The soft parts were washed out, leaving the metal plate bare in these areas. Finally, a water-receptive substance was applied which adhered only to the bare metal, leaving only the area to be printed receptive to ink.

In the early 1960s, a new technology, called photosetting or filmsetting, began to become a significant force. This was a means of setting type using photography, based on a very simple principle: by shining light through a photographic negative of a character, an image of that character could be made on photosensitive material. The character images were negatives carried on a matrix – transparent images on a black background. As with hot metal machines, there was a selection mechanism that responded to input from a keyboard, choosing and positioning the correct characters. However, instead of positioning the character over a jet of molten metal, it was positioned over a high-intensity light source and then exposed onto a photosensitive film or plate. Most phototypesetting systems also had a screen where the typesetter could see the text they had entered, allowing them to edit and correct it.

There were many different phototypesetting machines, some simple, some complex. In some, the different components were separate, others were combined into a single master unit. Typefaces for phototypesetting systems came in a variety of forms (discs, disc segments, film strips, and grids), which were not interchangeable between different systems. In some systems, the fount matrix remained stationary while the light source moved; in others, the matrix spun or rotated, while the light source remained stationary.

Phototypesetting allowed much greater freedom than metal type. Metal type was limited to a small number of different sizes and the space between the characters could be increased by set amounts but not decreased. With phototypesetting, characters of any size could be produced and the spacing between them altered as required. As with most new printing technology, there was initially some resistance to phototypesetting, but it was ideally suited to offset lithographic printing and together these two technologies offered a serious alternative to hot metal and letterpress printing. During the 1970s, phototypesetting became the predominant method of setting type.

The Mass-market Paperback

Paperback books were introduced to the market in the 1870s and books with few pages, such as chapbooks, had long been "self-covered" (the jacket or wrapper printed on the same paper as the text pages). However, it was not until the twentieth century, and the founding of Penguin Books in 1935, that the mass-market paperback really took off. The company was founded by Allen Lane with the aim of making good-quality writing cheaply available. The first Penguins cost just 6d, which was the price of a packet of ten cigarettes. They were modeled on the English-language reprints published by Albatross in countries outside the British empire and the US. They shared the same format and the Albatross books also had an easily recognizable bird logo and color coding for different genres. Penguins were a great success, selling over three million books by the end of 1936. Production of the mass-market paperback relied on long print-runs and low production costs in order to remain cost effective: Penguin titles had to sell over 17,000 copies before becoming profitable. This meant that Penguin print-runs were large enough to take advantage of the technology available to newspapers. The huge numbers of books printed by Penguin meant that many different printers were used and this often led to inconsistencies across the different series or even within different copies of a single title. It became increasingly necessary for the publisher to provide detailed specifications for the compositor and printer, a new stage in the production of books that was fulfilled by the typographic designer. The design of Penguin books was revolutionized by the typographer Jan Tschichold who joined the company in 1947. Tschichold revamped the whole of Penguin's output, making subtle improvements to the design of some series and completely redesigning others. Arguably his most important contribution, however, was to re-educate printers about standards and consistency in typesetting. He produced a four-page leaflet of precise instructions on typographic style called the *Penguin Composition Rules* which became an industry standard.

The Shape of Things to Come

By 1970, the entire process of making books was automated. Most books were printed on machine-made paper, from type produced by a Monotype caster, and the sheets folded and bound by machine. No doubt printers from the days before the industrial revolution would have been stunned by the sheer volume of books that twentieth-century technology could produce, not to mention the fact that some books featured full-color photographic reproductions. Nevertheless, it was still based on the method of letterpress printing used by Gutenberg over five hundred years earlier, although this technology was on the decline. Phototypesetting and offset lithography were about to take over as the standard means of printing books; soon, and for the first time, letterpress would not be the dominant technology in printing. However, the reign of phototypesetting was to be short-lived: by 1970, the first steps had already been taken toward a new world of desktop publishing and digital printing.

References and Further Reading

Baines, P. and Haslam, A. (2002) *Type and Typography*. London: Laurence King.

Burch, R. M. (1981) *Colour Printing and Colour Printers*. London: Garland.

Clapperton, R. H. (1967) *The Papermaking Machine: its Invention, Evolution and Development*. Oxford: Pergamon.

Darley, L. (1959) *Bookbinding Then and Now: A Survey of the First Hundred and Seventy-eight Years of James Burn & Company*. London: Faber and Faber.

Gaskill, P. (1972) *A New Introduction to Bibliography*. Oxford: Oxford University Press.

Hills, R. L. (1988) *Papermaking in Britain 1488–1988*. London: Athlone.

Huss, R. E. (1973) *The Development of Printers' Mechanical Typesetting Methods 1822–1925*. Charlottesville: University Press of Virginia.

Ivins, W. (1953) *Prints and Visual Communication*. Cambridge, MA: Harvard University Press.

Jennett, S. (1967) *The Making of Books*. London: Faber and Faber.

Kubler, G. A. (1941) *A New History of Stereotyping*. New York: J. J. Little and Ives.

Lee, M. (1965) *Bookmaking: The Illustrated Guide to Design and Production*. New York: R. R. Bowker.

Legros, L. A. and Grant, J. C. (1916) *Typographical Printing-surfaces: The Technology and Mechanism of their Production*. London: Longmans, Green, and Co.

Lewis, J. (1970) *Anatomy of Printing: The Influence of Art and History on its Design*. London: Faber and Faber.

McLean, R. (1972) *Victorian Book Design and Colour Printing*. London: Faber and Faber.

Moran, J. (1973) *Printing Presses: History and Development from the Fifteenth Century to Modern Times*. London: Faber and Faber.

Mosley, J. (1993) Introduction to *Ornamented Types: Twenty-three Alphabets from the Foundry of Louis John Pouchée*. London: I. M. Imprimit.

Southall, R. (2005) *Printer's Type in the Twentieth Century: Manufacturing and Design Methods*. London: British Library.

Southward, J. (1887) *Practical Printing: A Handbook of the Art of Typography*. London: J. M. Powell and Son.

Strauss, V. (1967) *The Printing Industry: An Introduction to its Many Branches, Processes and Products*. Washington: Printing Industries of America.

Tomlinson, C. (ed.) (1854) *Cyclopedia of Useful Arts*. London: George Virture.

Twyman, M. (1970a) *Printing 1770–1970*. London: Eyre and Spottiswode.

— (1970b) *Lithography 1800–1850: The Techniques of Drawing on Stone in England and France and their Application in Works of Topography*. London: Oxford University Press.

— (1990) *Early Lithographed Books: A Study of the Design and Production of Improper Books in the Age of the Hand Press*. London: Farand Press and Private Libraries Association.

Unwin, S. (1946) *The Truth about Publishing*. London: George Allen and Unwin.

Whetton, H. (ed.) (1948) *Practical Printing and Binding*. London: Odhams.

Wilson, F. (1886) *Stereotyping and Electrotyping*. London: Wyman and Sons.

21

From Few and Expensive to Many and Cheap: The British Book Market 1800–1890

Simon Eliot

The 1800s and 1890s

Imagine yourself as an enthusiastic reader of novels in 1800 wanting to buy the latest fashionable novel. What would it look like, and how much would it cost you? Early nineteenth-century novels were often published in two, three, or more volumes; commonly in duodecimo size – smaller than most modern octavo novels. The type would usually be large with generous spacing between the lines and wide margins (this was a way of bulking out a novel to fill three volumes). Because there was no such thing as standard publisher's binding until the 1830s, most novels would have been issued in temporary bindings of grey cardboard – with a printed paper label on the spine – on the assumption that those who bought them would wish to bind them in their own library style.

Each volume would be priced between 5s and 6s, so a three-volume (or "three-decker" as it became known) novel would cost a buyer between 15s and 18s. As this was at a time when a skilled builder would be earning a weekly average of 21s, a printer 27s, and a teacher about 17s (Mitchell 1988: 153), the buying of a new novel for most of the population was an unaffordable luxury.

By 1821, Constable, the publisher of Sir Walter Scott, had traded on his popularity by bumping up the price of each volume to 10s 6d, thus pricing a three-decker novel at 31s 6d: more than the average weekly wage for most of the nineteenth century. If you could not afford a first edition, you might have to wait a long time for something cheaper. Jane Austen's novels, published in multivolumes between 1811 and 1817, only emerged in cheaper editions published by Richard Bentley in his "Standard Authors" series in 1833.

A novel-buyer in the last decade of the nineteenth century had more choice. After 1894, the three-decker first edition of the novel disappeared and was replaced by a single volume selling at 6s. This volume would be in standard publisher's cloth, possibly with a colored designed stamped on it. A few months later, a second edition at around 2s 6d would appear, and within a couple of years, it might be available as a paperback at 6d. With an increase in real incomes between the 1860s and the 1890s, 6d was a price that most readers could afford.

The novel is but one example of the transformation in form, price, and readership that all sorts of printed text underwent during the period covered by this chapter. Take newspapers as another example. In 1803, *The Times* had a circulation of fewer than 2,000 and cost a reader 6d an issue: a few pages in length, composed entirely of letterpress, with no illustrations, and with its front page devoted exclusively to advertisements. In contrast, by the later 1880s, W. T. Stead's evening *Pall Mall Gazette* was splashing news across its front page with banner headlines and cartoons – and all for 1d. In 1896, Lord Northcliffe launched *The Daily Mail* at a halfpenny for eight sheets, and sold 397,215 copies on its first day. By World War I, it was the first newspaper in the UK to sell over 1 million copies a day.

A final example comes from what one might call "the ownership of printed images." Around 1800, unless you were comfortably off, it was unlikely that you would own many, or any, pictures with which to decorate your walls. Picture-producing technology was slow, difficult, and therefore expensive. Magazines and newspapers did not include illustrations. If you were an artisan or a clerk, or anyone earning less than they did, you might have access to a few crude, small, monochromatic woodcuts – and that would be all. By the 1890s, there was a plethora of systems for producing and reproducing cheap images, including wood-engraving, lithography, and halftones from photographs. Wood-engraving had its greatest impact in the middle of the period and made possible periodicals that to a significant extent were carried by their illustrations, such as *Punch* (1841) and the *Illustrated London News* (1842).

By the 1890s, readers had access to a range of high-quality, large-scale images, some in color and many derived from cheap sources, such as magazines, newspapers, and advertisements. Your walls, if you chose, could be plastered with printed images. But it was not just interior walls. The explosion of printed ephemera (all those items printed for an occasion and then thrown away: advertising posters, tickets, invitations, visiting cards, labels, forms, handbills, programs, and so on) meant that by the end of the period the average person would be swimming in a sea of print: with inadequate or nonexistent planning laws, virtually every vertical surface would be plastered with printed sheets and the streets would be littered with ephemera.

Communications and Literacy

One feature of the broader industrial revolution that was to have an immense impact on textual culture was the development of the railway system in Britain. Within a generation (roughly 1830–60) the country acquired a fast, all-weather goods and people transport system that could carry bulky materials (such as printing machines, paper, or type) easily and cheaply to virtually any town in the country. It ensured that newspapers and magazines were transported in a matter of hours (rather than days or weeks by horse-drawn vehicle or by sea) to almost any part of mainland UK. Train travel was much smoother and better lit than coach travel, and this created a new environment in which reading and writing could be done comfortably – and not just on long journeys. Once the main routes were established, intermediate stations became available which made it possible for the middle class to move out of the densely popu-lated cities and commute to work. Commuters needed newspapers and magazines that could be read in the space of their daily return journeys. For longer trips, the "railway novel" or "yellowback" was marketed: selling at 2s or less with a racy illustration on a (usually) yellow background, it was the airport lounge novel of its day. To cater to this new demand, railway bookstalls were established, many originally by individual entre-preneurs, though by the mid-century most of these were being run by W. H. Smith in England (who did not move into high street shops until the 1900s), John Menzies in Scotland, and Easons in Ireland (Wilson 1985).

Another influential change was the growth in literacy through the period. Roughly speaking, in 1800 in England and Wales (literacy rates in Scotland were a few percent higher in most decades) about 60 percent of males and 45 percent of females could read. By 1841, this had risen to 67 percent and 51 percent respectively; by 1871, 81 percent and 73 percent; and by 1891, 94 percent and 93 percent. These rates were not uniform either geographically or socially so these averages hide differences. For instance, by 1800 it was safe to assume the almost everyone in the middle classes and above could read; and literacy levels were always higher in urban areas than rural ones. Nevertheless, such overall increases were impressive, particularly when one couples them to a rising popu-lation: in 1801, the population of England, Scotland, and Wales was just over 10 million; in 1851, over 20 million; and by 1891 over 33 million (Mitchell 1988: 11–12).

Then, as now, reading skill varied and thus it is important not to underestimate the importance of oral culture, in particular listening to books and newspapers being read aloud. Even those near the bottom of society and themselves not literate might be related to, or might know, someone who was literate and who might provide access to the printed word by reading to them (Vincent 1989).

Literary Property and its Consequences

There were a number of additional copyright acts during our period, the most of impor-tant of which was in 1842 which extended copyright to 42 years or seven years after the author's death, whichever was the longer. Additionally, it re-enforced the law on the legal deposit of any new printed work at the British Museum Library. At first this was not vigorously enforced, but in the mid-1850s the Principal Librarian of the Library, Antonio Panizzi, began to threaten publishers with legal sanctions – and the books flowed in. Since that time the legal deposit collection of the Library has been a much better and more accurate, if not comprehensive, record of British publishing.

Copyright legislation had other consequences. In creating defensible literary rights, it gave authors the potential to make serious money out of their writing. Driven by hope, the volume of manuscripts submitted to publishers increased enormously, one of the factors that encouraged many to introduce a filter system in the form of the publisher's reader. Readers such as Geraldine Jewsbury for Bentley and John Morley for Macmillan had a significant impact on their employer's list and thus helped to define the publishing house.

In practice, most published writings did not sell well enough to make much, if any, money. In any case, many authors still sold their copyrights outright to a publisher so that, even if the book were a success, they had no further pecuniary interest in it. Until the late nineteenth century when the royalty system was introduced from the USA, most writers who did not sell outright had some sort of "half-profits" arrangement in which profits – if the publisher declared any – were split 50 : 50. Despite this, a small number of writers made substantial sums, and a significant minority made a living. This led to various attempts to "professionalize" authorship, the most successful of which saw the creation of the Society of Authors (SoA) in 1884. Partly in response, the Associated Booksellers of Great Britain and Ireland was founded in 1895, and the Publishers' Association in 1896.

The fact that by the end of the period literary property could be chopped up into a multitude of subsidiary rights that could be sold off separately (UK book rights, European, translation rights, serial rights, secondary serial rights, and so on) encouraged the emergence of the literary agent who, usually for a 10 percent fee, would undertake to represent the author in all these negotiations. Sir Walter Besant, prime mover of the SoA, was also one of the first novelists to use a professional literary agent: A. P. Watt from 1882.

Patterns of Production

The number of copies of stamped newspapers rose from 16 million in 1801 to over 78 million by 1849; the number of book titles published in the decade went up from roughly 14,550 in the 1800s to around 60,812 in the 1890s (Eliot 1994: 117, 147). Book titles do not represent numbers of copies, and many of these titles would be produced in print-runs of no more than 500–1,000. However, a popular novel in 1800 might have a combined print-run in its early years of up to 12,000. By the 1890s, a similarly popular novel might see 100,000 copies and more produced in its first five years in different editions.

Between 1800 and 1830, the annual pattern of production was a traditional one: there was a substantial bulge of new titles in spring; production dipped during the summer months and rose slightly in autumn. By the 1840s, this had changed: the spring season was still visible but now a new season emerged that ran from October to December: Christmas. This Christmas season got progressively larger as the century progressed. The emergence of Christmas as a major commercial festival is confirmed by the circulation of the first modern Christmas card (by Henry Cole in 1843) and the series of Christmas books, starting with *A Christmas Carol* (1843), produced by that most commercially responsive of great authors, Dickens. By late in the century, cards and postcards were a significant feature of our printed culture: in 1850, more than 500,000 Valentines were sent; and at Christmas 1877, 4.5 million cards went through the post (Vincent 1989). In the early decades, the majority of titles listed in the trade journals were at high (above 10s) or at medium price (between 3s 6d and 10s); by the 1890s, more than two-thirds of titles listed were priced at under 3s 6d.

One factor that affected the price of texts in the earlier part of the century was the series of taxes and duties applied to paper, newspapers, advertisements, and so on – the so-called "taxes on knowledge." These were at their height between 1800 and the 1830s at a time when the need to control and limit information (particularly to the lower classes) seemed most pressing in the shadow of the French Revolution. In the early 1800s, the tax on newspapers was 4d per copy; in 1836, this was reduced to 1d and was finally abolished in 1855. Paper duty was finally repealed in 1861.

Cheap Books and Part-works

One form of printing that carried on through most of our period did not need cheapening because it was already at rock-bottom prices. These were traditional cheap publications designed for the literate or semi-literate poor. The chapbooks (so called because they were sold in markets – "chepe" is the Old English for market – not bookshops) had been around since the seventeenth century but came into their own in the eighteenth century. They were small, paperbound pamphlets, usually 6 × 4 inches (15 × 10 cm), and with about 24 pages containing retellings of traditional and fairy stories, such as Robin Hood, Guy of Warwick, or the Seven Champions of Christendom. These usually sold for a 1d, as did an early nineteenth-century innovation in popular literature: the broadside ballad. This consisted of a long sheet of paper printed on one side and containing a sensational story, a description of an execution, or a song, or both illustrated by crude and frequently reused woodcuts – a real multi-media experience. Broadside ballads tended to favor stories of violent murders and executions, the most popular titles selling 1–2 million copies over a number of years and produced by such publishers as John Pitts and James Catnach (Neuburg 1977: 138–40).

Flowing into this flood of popular print was another tributary that shared some features with the broadside: it was a mishmash of memoirs, portraits, and accounts of boxing matches called *Boxiana*, which began publication in cheap parts in 1818 and lasted until 1824. This was written by Pierce Egan who can claim to have popularized part-publication twenty years before Dickens. *Boxiana* was nonfiction, but Egan's next and most successful venture, *Life in London*, issued in monthly parts 1820–1 was fiction enlivened by illustration. At 1s a part, these were too expensive for a working-class audience, but Egan's works were soon reprinted or condensed in much cheaper forms by Catnach and others.

Another source of cheap and plentiful text that had been available from the beginning of our period was the printed play: a small, commonly board-covered book priced
at 6d and containing a recent or current play performed on the London stage and elsewhere. There were many series of these produced by such publishers as John Duncombe,
John Cumberland, and T. Dolby. One suspects that many of these texts, often with
short lines and clear indication of who is speaking at any given time, might well have
been easier to read for those whose grip on literacy was still quite loose. That having
been said, one should not underestimate the instinct for domestic performance (just
think of the number of plays performed in the Austen or Dickens households) – and
not just for drama: "Duncombe's Acting Editions" frequently carried on their back
pages advertisements for "Music for the Million" – that is, scores selling for 3d each.

Most literary fashions gradually percolate down the social strata, but the illustrated
monthly part reversed the trend and what was a down-market form was, from the late
1830s, taken over by Dickens and his publishers – most notably Chapman and Hall
and Bradbury and Evans – who, almost single-handedly, made it a respectable mode of
publication: eighteen monthly parts at 1s a part with a final double number at 2s. Each
issue was surrounded by pages of advertisements, the sale of space for which boosted
the income from each part. The level of Dickens's success can be measured by the fact
that a number of his novels were almost immediately dramatized for the London stage
(sometimes even before they had completed serialization) (Patten 1978: 90–1) and that
various manufactures "merchandised" his characters: "Pickwick" cigars and figurines
were but two examples.

Where Dickens led other distinguished authors (such as Thackeray, George Eliot,
and Trollope), and many less distinguished, followed. Working-class fiction began to
imitate the inimitable, and many novels were produced in 1d weekly parts that ran for
as long as readers were prepared to buy them. G. W. M. Reynolds's *The Mysteries of the
Court of London* published by George Vickers, for instance, ran from 1849 to 1856 and
contained, it has been estimated, no fewer than 4.5 million words (James 1974: 47,
109). Reynolds was a journalist and publisher as well as a novelist, and produced such
popular papers as *Reynolds's Miscellany*, a detail which again illustrates the close connection between fiction and periodical publication.

John Dicks became G. W. M. Reynolds's managing clerk and printer and publisher
of the *Miscellany* in 1847. Dicks had a long and remarkable career in cheap publishing,
which included publishing *Dicks' Penny Standard Plays* weekly from the 1860s and twice
weekly from 1882. He moved into the canon by producing *Dicks' Shakspere's Works* at
the rate of two plays for a 1d; he then produced a complete works for 2s, which was
followed in due course by a 1s edition; together, these two editions sold over 750,000
copies. In the late 1860s, *Dicks' English Novels* appeared, each a complete novel in paperback selling at 6d, and this more than sixty-five years before Penguin Books. Dicks
did not neglect periodical publication: *Reynolds's Miscellany* was combined with Dicks's
own *Bow Bells* in 1869. Niche markets we also catered for: *Builder's World* was launched
in 1876 and the *Boy's Herald* in 1877 (Dicks 2004).

With the death of Dickens in 1870, monthly part-fiction began to die, but the need to keep novels cheap led to a growing tendency to serialize within the pages of middle-class magazines and newspapers: commonly before a novel was published as an expensive three-decker it would be serialized in a monthly magazine over a year. This pattern was another that had been rehearsed in the down-market publications of the 1840s when 1d weeklies, such as *The Sunday Times* (although the title suggested a newspaper), devoted almost all of its pages to three or four serialized novels illustrated by wood-engravings.

As we have seen with *Boxiana*, part-publication was not exclusively for fiction. All forms of lengthy text could be chopped up and re-marketed as parts building to a greater whole. In the early nineteenth century, Thomas Kelly sold, among many other things, a history of the French Revolution, a life of Christ, and a history of England all in parts, or "numbers," as they were frequently called; he also published a Bible in no fewer than 173 parts (Altick 1957: 264–5). Between 1833 and 1844, Charles Knight, publisher to the Society for the Diffusion of Useful Knowledge, produced a *Penny Cyclopaedia* in weekly 1d parts, finally amounting to twenty-seven volumes.

Part-publication was not restricted to cheap works. In the 1820s, the firm of A. J. Valpy of Took's Court, Chancery Lane, later absorbed into Longmans, undertook the republication of the "Delphin" edition of Greek and Roman classics. These were issued in monthly paperback parts of 627 pages (exactly forty-two printed sheets) at the price of 21s per part; it was assumed that owners would collect them and bind them up into complete volumes at a later date. So confident was Valpy of this that monthly parts might end in mid-sentence only to be completed in the following part. The whole enterprise was planned for ten years and 120 parts. Despite its length, high price, and unwieldy publication process, Valpy attracted over 900 subscribers to his edition which would cost each at least 120 guineas.

Lending and Selling

Another means of cheapening access to texts was to loan rather than sell them. In the early nineteenth century, newspapers such as *The Times* could be hired out for an hour or so for a penny: W. H. Smith began as a "newswalk" in the late eighteenth century, one of whose functions was to hire out periodicals (Wilson 1985). This was made possible by the rag-based paper – which was much tougher than modern newsprint – on which periodicals were printed. However, economically, the lending of books was the more important, and in this trade the circulating libraries were predominant. Circulating libraries emerged as a significant force in the eighteenth century, but it was the inflated book prices of the early nineteenth century, in particular the three-decker novel, that made them essential to many middle-class readers. These libraries charged an annual fee – usually 2–4 guineas – for the right to borrow one volume at a time. Higher subscriptions allowed more volumes to be borrowed. It was in 1842 that the largest and most successful circulating library, Mudie's, was founded. Mudie's scale and efficient organization (he even used standard, lead-lined boxes – a sort of containerization – to distribute books abroad) allowed him to charge the low annual fee of one guinea and yet distribute books throughout Britain and its empire (Griest 1970). Others followed suit: W. H. Smith in the 1860s, the Boots Booklovers Library from 1898, and The Times Book Club from 1905.

Although the Public Libraries Act (13 and 14 Vict. C.65) was passed in 1850, the rate at which these free institutions were established was very low until the 1880s. Even then, many of the libraries on offer were daunting places where you could not browse the shelves but had to use a printed catalogue to order what you wanted from a librarian behind a counter (Kelly 1977).

By the 1880s, many of the circulating libraries were facing a problem: they were no longer being given long enough to circulate three-decker editions before the publisher produced much cheaper second editions (often at 3s 6d or less). The only way circulating libraries could counter this was to sell these no-longer-circulating titles off at a substantial discount. The great libraries would sell job lots to smaller or more local circulating libraries and they, after circulating them for a time, would sell them on to even cheaper or smaller libraries until they were sold off to individuals or ended up on the open-air book barrows in such places as Farringdon Road in London.

As recorded by the trade journals, many new booksellers moved from selling new to selling second-hand books because the investment was much less and titles stocked had already been market-tested. The sellers of new books faced many problems, including the fact that, from the 1850s to the 1890s, and in accordance with the free-trade principles of the time, there was no form of retail price maintenance which meant that cash buyers would expect up to a 25 percent discount (Barnes 1964). "Underselling," as discounting was called, meant that booksellers' profits were squeezed. However, in 1891, under the guidance of the publisher Frederick Macmillan, the net book system (which protected a standard price below which a book would not be discounted) was established, this becoming the Net Book Agreement by 1901 which survived intact until the 1990s.

Things were made more difficult by the fact that those of the middle class who did not buy for ready money might expect a long line of credit, perhaps up to six months or more. Many booksellers failed because of cash-flow problems. Even those who survived rarely did so on books alone. Specialist bookshops were rare, and most would sell more profitable and fast-moving lines, such as newspapers, stationery, fancy goods, and patent medicines (one of the reasons why so many cheaper books contain advertisements for medical goods).

One thing that did help support bookshops of all sorts was the efficient system of wholesaling that evolved during the period. W. H. Smiths certainly performed the role, but the outstanding service was that offered by Simpkin, Marshall which, apart from being considerable publishers in their own right, and agents for small publishers in the provinces, also offered a centralized book-supply system that flourished until the firm was bombed-out in late December 1940.

Although commonly associated with three-decker novels, Mudie's catalogues – which by the 1880s were over a thousand pages long and issued annually – actually listed many more two- and one-volume novels. However, eclipsing all novels put together was the nonfiction stock. We should never forget that, even at its height, Victorian fiction accounted for only about a third of the titles listed in the book-trade journals, such as *Publishers' Circular* (a thin paper edition of which was "printed for the Colonies and Abroad") and *The Bookseller*. Overwhelmingly, the titles produced during our period were devoted to nonfiction, although it has to be said that few would be characterized by the long print-runs that would mark out a bestselling work of fiction.

Poetry, too, featured more strongly in Mudie's catalogues than one might have expected. Sir Walter Scott and then Byron sold spectacularly well in the first three decades of the nineteenth century. In the 1850s, Tennyson came to the fore and, as the Romantic poets came out of copyright in the mid-Victorian period, Wordsworth and others were extensively reprinted – few Romantic poets other than Byron sold well during the Romantic period (St. Clair 2004). As there was no copyright arrangement with the US until 1891, American poets such as Longfellow could be reprinted cheaply, and as early as 1862 his works had been issued by at least fifteen publishers. Overall, however, the popularity and profitability of poetry declined through the period and by the end many publishers were expecting poets to help subsidize their own publication. The areas in which poetry continued to flourish in the late nineteenth century were in cheap classic reprint series (sometimes associated with the promotion of the canon as in "Lubbock's Hundred Best Books" series) – and as school textbooks (Eliot 2006).

Other Bestsellers

Until the second half of the nineteenth century, religion was the predominant subject of published books: this was a substantial category that ranged from Bibles, New Testaments, Psalms, and Common Prayer-books to collections of sermons and Sunday school literature for children. The mass production of sacred texts was not a wholly commercial venture: many charitable organizations, such as the Religious Tract Society and the British and Foreign Bible Society, would subsidize the production and distribution of these texts, though rarely would they be distributed for free (on the Samuel Smiles principle that nothing that was given free would be properly valued). Printers and publishers with traditional Bible-printing privileges (such as Oxford University Press, Cambridge University Press, and the King's or Queen's printer) made substantial profits on this trade, at least until the later nineteenth century when the growing secularization of British society gradually reduced demand. In the short period 1848–50, for instance, OUP, CUP, and the Queen's printer in England and Scotland produced 4,634,274 Bibles and New Testaments between them (Eliot 1994).

Religious texts were commonly used to teach children to read (hardly surprising as many of the literate from the lower classes had been taught in Sunday schools). As the century progressed, and as the opportunities for schooling were extended socially and geographically, sometimes through charitable efforts but more frequently, in the later nineteenth century, by legislation (for example, Forster's Education Act of 1870), so the demand for textbooks of all sorts expanded. Public and grammar schools had for centuries generated a demand for Latin and, to a lesser extent, Greek teaching texts, but the new syllabuses required a wider range of subjects, including mathematics, history, and English. Textbooks that were widely adopted could generate substantial profits for publishers, particularly as they could be sold steadily to generations of pupils. Commonly, publishers would pay writers a flat fee for producing textbooks and, later, hire them or others to revise the text. Stereoplated or electrotyped, these textbooks had a longevity unmatched by most other books apart from the Bible and Shakespeare. Macmillan, a major textbook producer founded in Cambridge in 1843, sometimes kept the same titles in print for 40–60 years (Eliot 2002: 24–5). Suitably adapted, such textbooks could be exported to the empire, and that created yet another lucrative market which was exploited by Macmillan, Longman OUP, CUP, Bell, Murray, Cassell, Chambers, Edward Arnold, Sampson Low and Blackwood, among others. This textbook market was reinforced and steered by systems that had at their heart the creation and secure printing of examination papers and the syllabuses that drove them. Great university presses, such as OUP and CUP, carried the status of their institutions and marketed their prestige along with their textbooks.

Additionally, there was a growing market catering to the characteristically Victorian drive for self-improvement. "How-to" books flourished from Mrs. Beeton's *Household Management* (published in parts 1859–61 by her husband, who had made a considerable profit reprinting Mrs. Stowe's *Uncle Tom's Cabin*), through books of etiquette to conjuring tricks, public speaking, and the right way to play games (such as Longman's "Badminton" series from 1885). In the mid-nineteenth century, this craving for guidance was also satisfied by periodical publication whether it was the back-page correspondence columns of 1d weeklies, such as the *Family Herald* (from 1842) or the *London Journal* (from 1845), or later by weeklies devoted almost exclusively to the genre, such as *Answers to Correspondents* (published by Harmsworth from 1888).

The market for children's books was also a highly dynamic one. This market shaded into religious publishing, textbooks, and school prize books at one end, but acquired an almost wholly independent nature at the other. As the century progressed, there were more and more works of fiction written specifically for children. As the illustration revolution increased in speed, the opportunities to produce richly illustrated books were not missed: by the 1890s, annuals and comic books were being produced in huge quantities, particularly for the Christmas season.

Less seasonal but equally dynamic was the substantial increase in the publication of information. Not merely encyclopedias of all sorts, but parliamentary reports and papers, exhibition catalogues (most notably the illustrated catalogue of the Great Exhibition of 1851 printed by Clowes), and railway timetables. The demand for guide books increased hugely. An early provider was Murray with their "Handbook" series which started in 1836 with Holland. The development of lithography made it much easier and cheaper to print maps and music, so the rapid expansion in production of Ordinance

Survey maps, school atlases, and sheet music (for choral societies and home entertainment) was to be expected. By the end of our period, two huge publishing projects were underway: *The Dictionary of National Biography*, initiated by the publisher George Smith in 1882 and only later taken over by OUP (in 1917), and *The Oxford English Dictionary*, which was itself issued in parts (called "fascicles") between 1884 and 1928. Slightly less grand but equally typical of this information revolution were such publications as *Bradshaw's Railway Companion* (from 1839/40), *Who's Who* (from 1849), *Wisden Cricketers' Almanack* (from 1864), and the multitude of street and trade directories which helped contemporaries navigate the growing towns and cities of the period.

The World We Have Lost

The cost of print in the early nineteenth century forced even middle-class families into strategies that now seem quite odd. If you could not own but only borrow a novel or a book of poetry then one way of retaining the text was to copy parts of it out into a commonplace book. These were frequently shown to friends, and texts were swapped between them (and sometimes parodied). Later, as print of all sorts became cheaper, commonplace books gave way to albums and later to autograph books. All these are examples of the very important production of the stationery trade which included diaries, blank forms, and all the material required by commerce, such as letter and ledger books, in an age that saw the typewriter, carbon copy, and filing cabinet only introduced at its end.

Both private and commercial reading and writing were constrained by the nature of available light at a time when the window tax applied (only abolished in 1851) and artificial light was mostly in the form of tallow candles that required attention every few minutes, or expensive oil lamps. By the mid-nineteenth century, gas lighting had improved things markedly for the middle classes, but it was only with the introduction of electric lighting at the end of our period that modern conditions of domestic lighting prevailed.

Much of the material that the average nineteenth-century reader read can now only be found in specialist collections or has been lost altogether. Most losses are accidental but we should not forget that certain types of text, such as pornography, were actively suppressed. Some early Victorians commented on the wide availability of pornography. This was available at all prices from the expensive with scholarly pretensions down to the collections of obscene songs selling for a few pence. John Camden Hotten, a versatile and adventurous general publisher of the 1860s, had a particular line in flagellation literature, though he also seems to have supplied pictures – using the new technologies including photography. Most of Hotten's pornography was privately printed in small runs (often no more than 300 copies) and sold expensively to interested parties (Eliot 2000). Henry Vizetelly, with probably more principled motives than Hotten, made the mistake of publishing Zola's naturalistic novels unexpurgated, in translation and at a low price between 1884 and 1888. To the guardians of morality, a low price meant availability to women, children, and the lower orders, all of whom were much more corruptible than middle-class men. Vizetelly was prosecuted twice in 1888–9, on the second occasion being sent to prison for three months, an experience that broke him (Landon 2003).

By the 1890s, books were rather a small part, economically speaking, of the publishing and printing industry. In 1907, books (including blank books) accounted for only 17.1 percent of total value. The two most important sectors were jobbing printing (41.7 percent) and periodical publishing (28.2 percent; Eliot 1994: 105). In that sense, 1800–90 was a dress rehearsal for the twentieth century.

REFERENCES AND FURTHER READING

Altick, Richard D. (1957) *The English Common Reader.* Chicago: University of Chicago Press.

Barnes, James J. (1964) *Free Trade in Books.* Oxford: Clarendon Press.

Cross, Nigel (1985) *The Common Writer.* Cambridge: Cambridge University Press.

Dicks, Guy (2004) *The John Dicks Press.* New York: Guy Dicks.

Dooley, Allan C. (1992) *Author and Printer in Victorian England.* Charlottesville: University Press of Virginia.

Eliot, Simon (1994) *Some Patterns and Trends in British Publishing 1800–1919.* London: Bibliographical Society.

— (2000) "'Hotten, Rotten, Forgotten'?: An Apologia for a General Publisher." *Book History,* 3: 61–93.

— (2002) "'To You in your Vast Business': Some Features of the Quantitative History of Macmillan." In Elizabeth James (ed.), *Macmillan: A Publishing Tradition,* pp. 11–51. London: Macmillan.

— (2006) "What Price Poetry? Selling Wordsworth, Tennyson and Longfellow in Nineteenth- and Early Twentieth-century Britain." *Publications of the Bibliographical Society of America,* 100 (3).

Feather, John (1994) *Publishing, Piracy and Politics.* London: Mansell.

Griest, Guinevere L. (1970) *Mudie's Circulating Library and the Victorian Novel.* Bloomington: Indiana University Press.

Hepburn, James (1968) *The Author's Empty Purse.* London: Oxford University Press.

James, Louis (1974) *Fiction for the Working Man.* Harmondsworth: Penguin.

Kelly, Thomas (1977) *History of Public Libraries in Great Britain 1845–1975.* London: Library Association.

Landon, Richard (2003) "A Man under Fire: Henry Vizetelly and the Question of Obscenity in Victorian England." In *Vizetelly & Compan(ies),* pp. 107–22. Toronto: Thomas Fisher Rare Book Library.

Mitchell, B. R. (1988) *British Historical Statistics.* Cambridge: Cambridge University Press.

Neuburg, Victor E. (1977) *Popular Literature: A History and Guide.* Harmondsworth: Penguin.

Patten, Robert L. (1978) *Charles Dickens and his Publishers.* Oxford: Oxford University Press.

Rose, Jonathan (2001) *The Intellectual Life of the British Working Classes.* New Haven: Yale University Press.

St. Clair, William (2004) *The Reading Nation in the Romantic Period.* Cambridge: Cambridge University Press.

Sutcliffe, Peter (1978) *The Oxford University Press: An Informal History.* Oxford: Clarendon Press.

Sutherland, J. A. (1976) *Victorian Novelists and Publishers.* London: Athlone.

Vincent, David (1989) *Literacy and Popular Culture: England 1750–1914.* Cambridge: Cambridge University Press.

Wilson, Charles (1985) *First with the News: The History of W. H. Smith 1792–1972.* London: Jonathan Cape.

22

A Continent of Texts: Europe 1800–1890

Jean-Yves Mollier and Marie-Françoise Cachin

If one compares the production of books in Europe at the end of the twentieth century with that of a hundred years earlier, one gets the erroneous impression that things began to accelerate after 1918. If we look the other way around, and compare the 1850s–1890s with the 1750s–1790s, the difference is obvious. The explosion of book production and of all kinds of print production actually took place in the nineteenth century, and more precisely after 1850, after what has long been called the "industrial revolution." It did not occur in all the countries of continental Europe at the same time or at the same speed, and to understand each country's specific rhythm, it is necessary to take into account the growth of literacy. Thus, northern and western Europe stand in contrast to the eastern and southern parts of the continent where illiteracy was still high until the beginning of the twentieth century. Yet popular literature had penetrated deeply even in the countries around the Mediterranean – Spain, Portugal, Italy, and Greece – before 1900. Poland, Romania, and even Russia also experienced some of the effects of that enormous transformation taking place all over the continent.

At that time, people were aware of a rapid change in their habits or, to put it another way, of witnessing a kind of "cultural revolution," a silent but violent one, in all that concerned the written word (Mollier 1993). As early as 1740–60, at a time when Richardson's *Pamela*, Goethe's *Werther*, or Rousseau's *La Nouvelle Héloïse* had brought torrents of tears to readers' eyes, strong criticism had been leveled in Germany at *die Lesewut*, the reading craze that seemed to have taken hold of part of the population (Wittmann 1997). Robert Darnton, commenting upon the extraordinary success of Jean-Jacques Rousseau's novel, the greatest bestseller of the ancien régime, finds it impossible to overestimate the violence of this passion for reading (Darnton 1985: 134). In countries dominated by the Roman Catholic Church, as well as in those in which Protestantism ruled, reading was considered something that distracted Christians from their duties. Yet an important change had occurred during the period variously known as the *Lumières*, *Aufklärung*, Enlightenment, or *Illuminismo*: alongside the philosophical movement, a pre-Romantic literary current seems to have encouraged people to buy or borrow books and to rid themselves of all kinds of censorship that might have inhibited the spread of new ideas.

Less than a century later, around 1830, the French writer Charles Nodier worried about the development of book publishing and estimated that the books produced in France in a year could encircle the world. In 1839, Augustin Sainte-Beuve, one of the most highly esteemed critics of his time, stigmatized the birth of "industrial literature" (Sainte-Beuve 1839). With the appearance of serialized novels, writing had acquired a new nature and literature a new function. Published in periodicals and magazines before being gathered into volumes, fiction, it was said, penetrated all areas of life, from the cottage to the castle kitchen. As early as 1848 in London, thanks to W. H. Smith, and 1853 in Paris, thanks to Louis Hachette, railway stations would overflow with new books, a flood that nothing could stop. France would endeavor to contain it with the "Riancey amendment" (a form of tax on fiction) voted in July 1850, and Austria, some Italian states, and Portugal would reinforce censorship.

All this was to no avail, and books, like newspapers and print in general, increased inexorably. In addition to traditional Bibles, school textbooks were published, as well as innumerable series of practical books and adventure stories, soon followed by the portable dictionaries and encyclopedias of the 1860s–1870s. Soaked through in printing ink, smothered under tons of paper, the men and women of the times reveled in the works of Charles Dickens, Honoré de Balzac, Alexandre Dumas, Anthony Trollope, Eugène Sue, and Harriet Beecher Stowe, to mention only a few of the novelists whose audience was worldwide – one sign among many of the early advent of mass culture in some of these countries before 1900 (Mollier 2004).

A Second Revolution of the Book?

Some specialists have proposed a division of the time separating us from Gutenberg into three distinct periods. After the printing of the 42-line Bible in Mainz in the 1450s, and the preservation for nearly four centuries of the old regime of typography that this created, the use of a steam-powered press to print *The Times* in 1814 could be considered as the beginning of a "second revolution" in the modes of producing books. The third phase would start at the end of the twentieth century with the advent of electronic texts whose ultimate effects no one today can predict (Mercier 2002).

Besides the fact that this division into three periods appears too linear and does not take into account the various economic crises (in 1826, 1831, 1835, 1848 for Britain and France), the phrase *L'Apparition du livre* (The Coming of the Book), used by Lucien Febvre and Henri-Jean Martin (1958) to indicate the change introduced by Gutenberg, is problematic. As has been shown in earlier chapters of this volume, the book in its most characteristic material aspects – the codex – was conceived in the Western world between the end of the first century AD and the fifth. Therefore, one cannot use the word *"apparition"* for the book *stricto sensu* as regards the fifteenth century. The phrase "printing revolution" used by Elizabeth L. Eisenstein in her book *The Printing Revolution in Early Modern Europe* (Eisenstein 1979, 1983) has also been strongly questioned in recent years (Chartier 1995).

This division also does not take into account the typographical art of China, Korea, and Japan, which developed long before that of Europe, and consequently one should rather speak of three "revolutions of reading" or of "modes of reading" to indicate the three media represented by the *volumen* (roll), the *codex*, and the screen, which, however, leaves out the use of bone, ivory, stone, and clay in high antiquity.

Even if we cannot agree on the terminology, the expression "second revolution of the book" can be accepted as makeshift, enabling us to throw light on the unique nature of the nineteenth century. Coming together with the rapid development of schooling, urbanization, industrialization, and a revolution in the means of communication, the spread of the book took place amidst considerable changes in a number of countries. London, the world capital of print at the end of the eighteenth century, was the center of continuous exchanges with its empire after 1840. Leipzig and Frankfurt yielded ground to London, but Germany – the cradle of the printed book – could still boast a remarkable number of publishing cities, among which were Stuttgart, Munich, and Berlin. In traditionally centralized France, Paris was to take advantage of the weakness of the provinces and concentrate within its walls most of the publishing business after 1830.

Austria-Hungary, Belgium, and Switzerland, all with an early high level of literacy, Italy and (to a lesser degree) Spain and Portugal, all reveal similar phenomena. Printing presses developed, followed by their mechanization and industrialization with the introduction of rotary presses around 1865, and of Linotype and Monotype systems from the 1890s. By that date, large printing companies, such as Thomas Nelson's in Edinburgh, Paul Dupont's in Paris, or the Brockhaus family's in Leipzig, employed at least one thousand workers. Printers and specialists in mechanical binding – Mame in Tours, Nelson in Scotland, or Reclam in Leipzig – were industrial manufacturers similar in status to the captains of the textile and steel industries. In fact, the firm of Reclam was the first fully to rationalize the various production processes and resort to a division of labor, the Taylorization of tasks, and economy of scale by making up standardized metal dispensers for books sold at a very low price – 20 pfennigs – installed in railway stations, hospitals, spas, or on transatlantic liners in 1912 (Barbier 1995: 97). With a thousand such dispensers in use in 1914, distributing one million and a half volumes per year, Germany proved its capacity for coping with the "craze for reading" characteristic of readers of Goethe's works and spreading it to all those who earlier could not have shared in it because they lacked either education or access to printed materials.

As firms manufacturing paper, ink, glue, thread, or books grew larger, so too did the number of points of sale increase throughout the century. Not only were there bookshops in every European city of any importance, but also another network appeared: the railway station bookstalls, based on the model started by W. H. Smith in London in 1848 (Wilson 1985). Partly replacing peddlers, this network was itself in competition with the opening of book departments in the department stores of most big cities from the 1860s onward. Before the end of the century, Europeans could buy their favorite authors through the three networks that today remain the main means of distribution: department stores, railway station bookstalls, and local bookshops. Distribution of successful writers' novels through the mail and by train was quite different in kind and size from the transmission of small volumes of poetry or plays in the sixteenth and seventeenth centuries. In this respect, the expression "second revolution of the book (or the press)" for the period after 1840–5 is quite appropriate.

Other quantitative criteria can be used to prove this point. Let us begin with those so-called "backward" countries, such as Spain and Italy. In the former, about 500 titles were published every year in the 1870s, but the *Bibliografia española* was recording 1,000 titles ten years later and 2,000 in 1905. At the same time, newspaper titles increased from 521 in 1868 to 2,000 in 1913. In Italy, the number of titles rose from 2,000 in 1820 to 8,000 in 1890. In Paris, the increase was even more spectacular: the *Bibliographie de la France* recorded about 6,300 titles in 1840, over 10,000 in 1855, 20,000 in 1880, 28,000 in 1900, and 32,000 in 1913 (Botrel 1988: 229; Botrel et al. 2003). There was the same progression in Germany with 6,200 titles in 1840, 10,000 in 1870, 20,000 in 1894, and over 35,000 in 1913. If in Britain taxes on newspapers inhibited the progress of the press before 1836 and even until 1855, after that date circulation soared for Sunday papers, such as *Lloyd's Penny Sunday Times*, and daily papers, such as *The Daily News* (Lee 1976). In Britain, the existence for several decades of prestigious publishing houses, such as Longman, Murray, Routledge, and Macmillan, testified to the healthy condition of the trade.

During the period, publishers became progressively more prepared to offer large amounts of money to writers whose works brought a high return of equity to those publishing houses that had invested in the means of reaching the mass reading public. With the arrival of what can be called "publishing capitalism" (Mollier 1988), in Britain as well as in France and Germany, publishers looked for male or female writers capable of reaching the largest possible number of readers: in Britain, Dickens, Trollope, Wilkie Collins, and Mary Elizabeth Braddon; and in Paris, Dumas père, Eugène Sue, Balzac, Paul Féval, Ponson du Terrail, and, later, Zola.

Industrial Literature

In a satirical novel serialized in Paris in 1845, Louis Reybaud's *Cesar Falempin* published by Michel Levy frères, one of the characters, the manufacturer Granpré, is described as the inventor of the "first steam serial." In his factory, an army of ghostwriters each work on a particular part of a given chapter or on a precise task. "Each deals with what he knows best, explains the orchestra director and, as Adam Smith says, the serial reaches its highest level of development." It was quite easy to recognize the most prolific European writer of the time in this caricature, the one who, in the very same year, had been the target of a pamphlet entitled *Fabrique de romans: Maison Alexandre Dumas et Cie* (Manufacture of Novels: Alexandre Dumas & Co.). Six years after the publication of Sainte-Beuve's article aimed at Honoré de Balzac, Dumas, and all those who had agreed to give their literary works for serialization in the press, a recurring debate denounced the transformation of literature and its accelerating degradation. Considering that the nature of writing changed when the novelist was no longer trying to write a masterpiece in the silence of his study or to give birth painfully to a world he had been carrying within him for a long time, critics reproached genuine men of letters – Balzac, Dumas, and Sue were undoubtedly such men – with transforming themselves into vulgar serial writers paid per line and trying to get the maximum profit from the increasing number of periodicals that were publishing fiction. A similar phenomenon also took place in England. Shortly afterwards, following the *roman à quatre sous* published in sixteen-page issues, France would imitate Britain by inventing the *journaux-romans*, that is, periodicals specializing in mass-market literature.

In London, the novelist Wilkie Collins forged a highly significant phrase to describe the anonymous reader of this kind of prose: "the future of English fiction may rest with this Unknown Public, which is now waiting to be taught the difference between a good book and a bad" (Lyons 2003: 379). He had in mind the three million readers of cheap illustrated weeklies recruited from among the lower classes of society. In that context, the creation of public libraries in 1850 was partly meant to moralize the reading material of the masses, an obsession then pervading all European countries, whether Catholic or Protestant. In Paris, as we have observed, a conservative member of parliament had a bill voted in 1850 to impose a tax on novels, which aimed to discourage the craze for penny novels spreading like an epidemic throughout the country, but which did not succeed in preventing the increase of serial fiction writers. When the first popular penny paper, *Le Petit Journal*, was launched in 1863, Millaud, its owner, called on the novelist Ponson du Terrail, the father of the *Rocambole* series, in order to ensure the success of the enterprise. By asking another serial fiction writer, Timothée Trimm – alias Léo Lespès – to edit the paper, he demonstrated how extraordinarily easy it was for fiction to penetrate the press so that it was difficult to know where the frontier between fact and fiction stood. As *le fait divers* (news in brief) began to change the paper's content profoundly, media culture was born and imposed its law on all those who lived by it (Thérenty and Vailant 2003).

The last third of the nineteenth century moved further in that direction by inventing the literary series. Book series started in Europe at the very end of the eighteenth century, but before 1800 they existed only in limited numbers. It is only after that date, and particularly in fiction, that they began to multiply, and so much so that in 1837 one of the characters in Balzac's *Illusions perdues* explains to the young writer Lucien de Rubempré that he must himself become a "series" if he wants a fiction publisher to become interested in his works. By having the same characters appearing repeatedly in several of his works, Balzac himself experimented with this technique. The name of one of the best-known French publishers, Gervais Charpentier, is associated with this revolution through the launching of a series bearing his own name, the "Bibliothèque Charpentier," in 1838 (Olivero 1995). In England, in 1849, George Routledge launched the first "Railway Library" on the model of Simms and McIntyre's "Parlour Library" (Altick 1957), soon to be imitated by Bentley and many other publishers. In Germany, Philip Reclam's "Universal Biblothek," launched in 1867 at a very low price, had 3,470 titles by 1896 and, in France, Louis Hachette's "Bibliothèque des chemins de fer" or Michel Lévy's one-franc series followed the same path. By offering readers and hurried travelers books that were easy to read, publishers expected to see their print-runs multiply and further to stimulate the demand for reading material which by then existed in all developed societies.

In the 1870s and 1880s, this process was extended by the creation of other kinds of serialized literature, such as sentimental fiction for women and detective fiction for men. With the popular press choosing crime for its front page, just as, in the same period, the crimes committed by Pranzini then Soleillant inflamed the French reading public, one witnesses the appearance of characters such as Sherlock Holmes or Arsène Lupin, Chéri-Bibi or Fantômas. Nick Carter's adventures, created in the United States and rapidly exported to Europe, together with Western fiction and its youthful hero Buffalo Bill, met with enormous success at the end of the century. Similar to the American dime novels, one could find one-shilling books in England, the *romans à quatre sous* in France, one-lira books in Italy, and books at 10 or 20 pfennigs in Germany, which means that the stream of high circulation, popular fiction was spreading throughout Europe. In France, such an evolution was even more striking when in 1904–5 the publisher Arthème Fayard launched two series, one at 0.95 francs, the other at 0.65 francs, starting with print-runs of 50,000–100,000 copies. Such high figures anticipated the 1935–40 paperback revolution, even though the content of Arthème Fayard's "Livre Populaire" was closer to twentieth-century north-American pulp fiction. The *littérature de gare*, as it is contemptuously called in France, or *trivialliteratur* in Germany, could boast thousands of readers, even though in England, for example, its expansion was limited by Victorian morality whose forcefulness can be seen in the trials of Henry Vizetelly, Zola's publisher, and in the imprisonment of Oscar Wilde.

Guidebooks, Practical Books, and Mass-market Dictionaries

Originally, guidebooks interested only pilgrims traveling to the Holy Land or, a thousand years later, young English aristocrats going on the Grand Tour. At the end of the eighteenth century, the first genuine guidebooks for the city of Rome appeared, followed by books about the Alps, Switzerland, spas, or cities like Paris, London, Vienna, and Hamburg. A study of the publication of guidebooks in France from the Middle Ages to the twentieth century has shown that the phenomenon actually started between 1800 and 1830 since as many guidebooks were published during these three decades as between 1600 and 1799. However, the publication of these kinds of work then rapidly increased. Whereas 114 titles were registered between 1800 and 1830, 160 titles were published between 1837 and 1852, and 348 between 1853 and 1870, with 50 titles in 1851, the year of the Great Exhibition in London (Chabaud et al. 2000: 573–6).

Following the success of the Galignani Brothers and of Samuel Leigh, the modern concept of "handbooks for travelers" was to be associated in England with the name of a family of publishers, the Murrays (Monaghan 1998). In Germany, Karl Baedeker is as famous in that field as Giuseppe and Petro Vallardi or Ferdinand Artaria in Italy. In France, the same type of work was popularized by Adolphe Joanne. With the railways, universal exhibitions, tourism, seaside resorts, and soon ski resorts, guidebooks experienced their first golden age between 1851 and 1900. In most European countries, thousands of similar volumes were published. Often marketed on railway station bookstalls, but also in the more traditional bookshop or department store, they show the emergence of leisure and of tourism long before it became widespread following the extension of paid holidays to the majority of workers.

After John Murray launched the first series of twenty-six red hardback guidebooks for travelers in 1836 (these covered almost all of the European continent and, later, the countries around the Mediterranean, and then India, Japan, and New Zealand), the phenomenon became worldwide (Guilcher 2000: 81–93). Murray was immediately imitated by George Bradshaw, Francis Coglan, and then by the German publisher Karl Baedeker, his great rival, who would deprive him of a large part of the British market after 1870; Murray did not understand the audacity of the latter, who, by offering his guidebooks in three languages, German, English, and French, soon became the model. In France, Louis Hachette managed to adapt by taking over the guidebook publisher Louis Maison's backlist and entrusting Adolphe Joanne with the task of making attractive books whose blue covers became known throughout the century before the appearance of Michelin's green guidebooks after 1900. If, to those famous forerunners, one adds Thomas Cook's "Tourist's Handbook" series, amounting to twenty-five titles published from 1874 onward, Longman's, Macmillan's, Stanford's, and Baddeley's "Thorough Guide" series in Britain, Treves guidebooks in Italy, Griben and Meyer for Germany, and Conty and Garnier for France, one gets an idea of the international expansion of guidebooks and of the market that such books catered for up to the beginning of World War I. Though, in general, print-runs never exceeded 5,000 copies, the multiplication of titles and of editions is evidence of a large market in these traveling companions.

At the same time, another market, that of practical books, started. In France, the fashion began with a new kind of manual: *Bon Jardinier, Bonne Cuisinière,* or *Parfait Secrétaire.* It was not such an original idea as conduct books and letter-writing manuals had existed long before the nineteenth century. However, here again, the phenomenon was so vast that it is vain to compare it with the situation of previous centuries. Extending the range of his products to all possible subjects that could be popularized, the French publisher Roret was in the forefront of this market; the introduction of electricity around 1880 allowed him to launch a still wider range of do-it-yourself volumes, as they are called today. Just as lively in Britain and Germany, the publication of practical books all over the continent benefited from the appearance of a market for foreign-language teaching books. Methods of learning French or English were quickly offered by the Galignani Brothers, followed by Ollendorff's method of learning German.

Connected to the publication of books for schools and universities, this market rapidly attracted the great publishing houses in Britain and on the continent, such as Macmillan, Nelson, Hachette, Garnier, Larousse, Brockhaus, and Mayer. In fact, these powerful publishers, selling millions of copies of printed books after 1870, benefited from the mass extension of literacy and schooling in many European countries by increasing the list of their publications thanks to the reputation of their names, which were often used almost as common names. When one says "I bought a Larousse or a Baedeker," one forgets that, behind these trade names, there exist real men and women, often the founders of immense publishing empires.

The development of dictionaries and encyclopedias is one of the most obvious characteristics of societies in which a mass market appears quite early. Pierre Larousse, who edited the *Grand dictionnaire universel du XIXe siècle*, defined his century as that of dictionaries without risk of being contradicted by his contemporaries. A very old genre, but transformed into an object of real worship after 1850, the dictionary attracted German publishers first. Friedrich Brockhaus, whose *Konversationslexicon* met with immense success during that period and was imitated all over the continent, is the most famous name in the field. Besides him, one must mention another German, Meyer, whose large dictionaries, illustrated first with engravings, and later with photographs, became known all around the world. In France, Pierre Larousse's name has remained associated with the very concept of dictionaries. In Britain as in Italy, in Spain as in most other countries, the dictionary craze was boundless. The launching in 1905 of Claude Augé's *Petit Larousse illustré*, with a print-run of 300,000 copies, marks the beginning of the mass-market circulation of this kind of work. In the 1860s–1870s, the possibility of obtaining credit to buy books had allowed the less wealthy middle and lower middle classes to purchase those huge 6–15-volume encyclopedias. But after 1900, smaller or even pocket format dictionaries were printed and sold to a widening circle of readers.

A flood of religious books flowed over Europe after 1800. An instrument to spread the gospel to native populations before becoming the privileged tool of foreign missions, the Bible had also been used in Britain to counteract the influence of the French Revolution and of Thomas Paine's book, *The Rights of Man* (1791). Millions of copies of the publications of the Religious Tract Society, the British and Foreign Bible Society, and the London Missionary Society were printed, and similar organizations in Geneva or in other countries reached almost the same figures. The Roman Catholic Church preferred alternative genres, such as the lives of saints or "good" novels, but religious books were not neglected, particularly after the adoption of the Roman liturgy everywhere in France, which made the fortune of the publisher Mame in Tours who was given the responsibility of producing the new unified prayer-book. During the whole period, religious books and textbooks, dictionaries and practical books, guidebooks and treatises of popular medicine, all books destined for a mass readership, competed with the most widely circulated novels, a fact that should not be forgotten when one examines the deluge of books that rained down on the whole of Europe in the nineteenth century.

The Internationalization of the Novel

It was during the period 1800–90, the time of Chateaubriand and Zola, that the novel captured the whole world, as has already been shown. We return to the novel, in the conclusion of this chapter, in order to underline its transmedia character: that is, its capacity to pass from one mode of production to another and to migrate throughout the world. Harriet Beecher Stowe's *Uncle Tom's Cabin* is a very good case in point. In the first stage of the book's career, between 1852 and 1879, over 1,500,000 copies were sold in the original language, and eight different translations into French and many other translations into German, Italian, Spanish, Portuguese, Russian, Danish, Finnish, and other languages (Winship 1999; Parfait 2000) were also published. But probably even more important was the serial publication of the novel in daily papers and weekly or monthly periodicals, whether national, regional, or local, in the United States and in Europe. Moreover, what is now called merchandizing was on the same scale. This tragic story was adapted for the theater, and later on made into a film. Popular songs praising Uncle Tom's courage were written, and his face was reproduced on glasses, plates, shawls, shirts, and all kinds of objects. This proved the novel's ability to move from one medium to another and from one country to another throughout the world.

Another similar example is that of Alexandre Dumas's *Comte de Monte Cristo* (1844–5). In the 1860s, cigar manufacturers in Cuba paid one of their workers to read the successful serialized novels of the time to his fellow-workers. The cigar-makers' craze for the character of the Count of Monte Cristo was such that they decided to give their hero's name to one of their best products, the famous "Monte Cristo" cigar. Here again one can witness the plasticity of the novel which can be read silently and individually, or aloud to a large audience, or performed by a temporary actor, or transformed into an item of public consumption. In the nineteenth century, besides Harriet Beecher Stowe's and Alexandre Dumas's novels, Eugène Sue's *Les Mystères de Paris*, Victor Hugo's *Les Misérables*, Zola's *Germinal*, as well as Charles Dickens's *Pickwick Papers* and Robert Louis Stevenson's *Treasure Island* and *Dr. Jekyll and Mr. Hyde* went around the world. The authors of these books impressed their contemporaries' imaginations by representing unforgettable characters, and consequently erasing or keeping in the background the memory of most other books. In that respect, there is no possible comparison between a popular scientific work and one of Sherlock Holmes's investigations, or between a textbook and the exciting adventures of the hero of *Treasure Island*. Even if these different kinds of books have contributed to the making of the modern reader's identity, novels have remained the most potent in that reader's memory.

There is no denying that poetry and drama were still read at school. The lasting fame of Byron or Lamartine, Goethe, Keats, Heine, or Hugo could not be understood if they had not been published in textbooks at the end of the nineteenth century, and neither perhaps would the fervor for Shakespeare, Schiller, Hugo, Ibsen, or other playwrights have survived without the work done in the various kinds of schools which, over the whole continent, contributed to the creation of the pantheon of literature about whose heroes everyone was expected to know.

Many writers became celebrities: besides the best-known writers already quoted, one should mention the Russian novelist Turgenev and the Scottish writer Walter Scott (who inspired Balzac and was probably one of the most translated novelists at the beginning of the century), Goethe, Manzoni, Stendhal, Flaubert, George Sand, Dostoevsky, Tolstoy, Jules Verne, Lewis Carroll, Andersen, Mark Twain, Collodi, Eça de Queiros, Perez Galdos, Clarin, D'Annunzio, Hamsun, Thomas Hardy, Wilde, Zola, and Svevo. However, this incomplete and partial picture of the celebrities of the time largely conceals reality since apart from Scott and Dumas, Perez Galdos, Clarin, and Jules Verne, popular literature is missing. Yet a marked phenomenon of the time is the emergence of national novelists who, in a certain way, illustrate the capacity of the countries importing fiction to give birth to gifted male and female writers. Spain is probably the best example, for after naturalizing French novelists under the names of "Pablo Féval" or "Alejandro Dumas," the country enthusiastically welcomed Benito Perez Galdos's prose whose mission was to raise Spain's reputation and to make it known in all Latin America (Botrel 1993). In Italy, the popular novelist Carolina Invernizio's works fascinated Antonio Gramsci so much that he called her "a rabbit-like breeder of fictional worlds" when he mentioned her 123 novels published during her lifetime by Adriano Salani, one of the most expert professionals in mass-market literature and in the promotion of the large circulation press (Solari 1992).

Even Brazil fervently welcomed Eugène Sue's, Paul Féval's, and Alexandre Dumas's serials and, at the end of the nineteenth century, all of Alexandre Dumas's works whose influence on the young Jorge Amado is well known. In Mexico, the craze for historical novels after 1850 was the direct consequence of the translations of Scott and Dumas, even if plots generally took place in the New World. The backgrounds of Ignacio Manuel Altamirano's and Rafael Delgado's fiction owe a lot to the French realistic novel, notably to Balzac, who also inspired the Argentine novelist Lucio Vicente Lopez's *Le Grand Village*. On the other hand, Julien Martel's novel *La Bourse* was strongly influenced by Zola's *L'Argent*. Thus, the internationalization of the novel developed in almost all continents (though at a varying pace), and its success was due to the fact that this specific literary genre can be defined as "a general cognitive matrix" (Saint-Jacques 2001: 446), almost universal but not quite so, whose cross-media qualities allowed it to fill up the space of newspapers, periodicals, reviews, and books almost endlessly between 1800 and 1914. Largely represented at the first conference on literary and artistic property that took place in Paris in 1878, novelists were to encourage the development of the Berne Convention in respect of international copyrights in 1886, followed at the turn of the century by the birth of institutions like the Pen Club and the Nobel Prize for Literature, as well as by the creation of the Goncourt and Pulitzer prizes. Showing solidarity to one another in spite of their competition in the race for celebrity, they were the first to benefit from the universal reform of education. If today, the German Karl May's novels, inspired by the Far West, or Carolina Invernizio's, Perez Galdos's, Paul Féval's and others' are hardly read, one should not forget that these novelists reflected the craze for reading that developed throughout the world in the nineteenth century, spreading to all classes of society and transforming the most popular novelists of that period into some of the first celebrities.

REFERENCES AND FURTHER READING

Altick, Richard (1957) *The English Common Reader: A Social History of the Mass Reading Public, 1800–1900*. Chicago: University Chicago Press.

Barbier, Frédéric (1995) *L'Empire du livre*. Paris: Cerf.

Botrel, Jean-François (1988) *La diffusion du livre en Espagne 1868–1914*. Madrid: Casa de Velasquez.

— (1993) *Libros, penser y lectura en la Espana del siglo XIX*. Madrid: Fundacion German Sanchez Ruiperez.

—, Infantes, Victor, and Lopez, Francois (eds.) (2003) *Historia de la edicion y de la lectura en Espana, 1472–1914*. Madrid: Fundacion German Sanchez Ruiperez.

Cachin, Marie-Françoise (2002) "Rapports de lecture et autres archives de l'éditeur Macmillan." *Cahiers Charles V*, 32: 39–62.

Chabaud, Gilles, Cohen, Evelyne, Coquery, Natacha, et al. (eds.) (2000) *Les Guides imprimés du XVIe au XXe siècle: villes, paysages, voyages*. Paris: Belin.

Chartier, Roger (1995) *Forms and Meanings: Texts, Performances, and Audiences from Codex to Computer*. Philadelphia: University of Philadelphia Press.

Darnton, Robert (1985) "Rousseau und seine Leser." *Zeitschrift für Litteraturwissenschaft und Linguistik*, 57–8: 134.

Eisenstein, Elisabeth L. (1979) *The Printing Press as an Agent of Change: Communication and Cultural Transformations in Early Modern Europe*. Cambridge: Cambridge University Press.

— (1983) *The Printing Revolution in Early Modern Europe*. Cambridge: Cambridge University Press. (A condensed version of *The Printing Press as an Agent of Change*.)

Febvre, Lucien and Martin, Henri-Jean (1958) *L'Apparition du livre*. Paris: Albin Michel.

Guilcher, Goulven (2000) "Naissance et développement du guide de voyage imprimé: du guide unique à la série, une stratégie de conquête des lecteurs." In Gilles Chabaud, et al. (eds.), *Les Guides imprimés du XVIe au XXe siècle: villes, paysages, voyages*, pp. 81–93. Paris: Belin.

Lee, Alan J. (1976) *The Origin of the Popular Press in England, 1855–1914*. London: Croom Helm.

Lyons, Martyn (2003) "Le XIXe siècle et la naissance d'un nouveau public." In Yves Noël Lelouvier and Gilles Quinsat (eds.), *Le Monde des littératures*. Paris: Encyclopaedia Universalis.

Mercier, Alain (2002) *Les trois révolutions du livre*. Paris: Imprimerie nationale.

Mollier, Jean-Yves (1988) *L'Argent et les lettres: histoire du capitalisme d'édition, 1880–1920*. Paris: Fayard.

— (1993) "Le Manuel scolaire et la bibliothèque du people." *Romantisme*, 80: 79–95.

— (2004) "La naissance de la culture de masse en France et dans le monde." In Greg Burgess (ed.), *Revolution, Nation and Memory: Papers from the George Rudé Seminar in French History*, pp. 138–63. Hobart: University of Tasmania.

Monaghan, Charles (1998) *The Murrays of Murray Hill*. New York: Urban History Press.

Olivero, Isabelle (1995) *L'Invention de la collection*. Paris: IMEC Editions.

Parfait, Claire (2000) *Les Editions américaines d'Uncle Tom's Cabin, de Harriet Beecher Stowe, de 1852 à 1999*. Paris: University Paris 7.

Sainte-Beuve, Augustin (1839) "De la littérature industrielle." *Revue des Deux-mondes*, 17.

Saint-Jacques, Denis (2001) "Le roman au-delà du livre et de la nation." In Jacques Michon and Jean-Yves Mollier (eds.), *Les Mutations du livre et de l'édition dans le monde du XVIIIe siècle à l'an 2000*, pp. 442–7. Quebec: Les Presses de l'Université Laval.

Solari, Gabriela (1992) "La littérature à un sou, à deux sous, à trois sous: permanences et transformations de l'impression populaire en Italie à la fin du XIXe siècle." In Dominique Julia (ed.), *Annuaire du département d'histoire et civilization*, pp. 59–88. Florence: Institut Universitaire Européen.

Thérenty, Marie-Eve and Vaillant, Alain (2003) *1836: L'An I de l'ère médiatique*. Paris: Nouveau Monde Edition.

Wilson, Charles (1985) *First with the News: The History of W. H. Smith, 1792–1972*. London: Jonathan Cape.

Winship, Michael (1999) "The Greatest Book of its Kind: A Publishing History of *Uncle Tom's Cabin*." *Proceedings of the American Antiquarian Society*, 109: 318–24.

Wittmann, Reinhardt (1997) "Une révolution de la lecture à la fin du XVIIIe siècle." In Guglielmo Cavallo and Roger Chartier (eds.), *Histoire de la lecture dans le monde occidental*, pp. 331–64. Paris: Seuil.

23

Building a National Literature: The United States 1800–1890

Robert A. Gross

There was no American literature in the nineteenth century. So said a chorus of British and European critics of the new nation. "Literature the Americans have none – no native literature . . . It is all imported," the Rev. Sydney Smith pronounced in the *Edinburgh Review*. In 1820, Smith famously insulted American pride: "In the four quarters of the globe, who reads an American book?" Two decades later, Alexis de Tocqueville was obliged to agree. During his 1830s' tour of the United States, the liberal aristocrat found much to admire about "democracy in America" but not its literary productions: "The inhabitants of the United States have . . . at present, properly speaking, no literature." What did exist was best hidden from foreign guests. "If the American nation be judged of by its literature," the English traveler Harriet Martineau concluded in 1837, "it may be pronounced to have no mind at all." That verdict persisted, even as the United States was rising to world power. In 1888, the English critic Matthew Arnold echoed Sydney Smith. For all their industrial success and national wealth, Americans were lacking in civilization: "In literature they have as yet produced little that is important."

Many Americans unhappily agreed. With high hopes for the Revolution, aspiring poets had anticipated a "rising glory" of the arts in a free republic. That expansive vision soon faded. Far from heeding Noah Webster's dictum that "America must be as independent in *literature* as she is in politics," most writers in the early republic took their cues from the former mother country. America remained a cultural colony of the Old World well into the nineteenth century. In 1837, Ralph Waldo Emerson summoned the "American Scholar" to answer "the postponed expectation of the world." "We have listened too long to the courtly muses of Europe." This call for literary independence was but one in a litany of complaints about native mediocrity heard throughout the century. American literature was deemed inferior either because it failed to realize European models or because it tried too hard to imitate them.

Perhaps the critics were looking in the wrong place. In the eighteenth century, literature carried a distinctive meaning it no longer bears today. Samuel Johnson defined it in 1756 as "learning," the acquisition of which required education in the Greek and Roman classics. Learned men (and a few women) were the citizens of the republic of letters, communicating freely across national borders to advance the "improvement" and enlightenment of mankind. Every branch of knowledge invited their interest, from "natural philosophy" (the progenitor of modern "science") to history and politics to languages, rhetoric, and *belles lettres* (encompassing essays, drama, poetry, and fiction). When Noah Webster embarked on the linguistic inquiries that culminated in his monumental *American Dictionary of the English Language* (1828), he appealed to "the Friends of Literature in the United States" for financial aid. "Similar undertakings in Great Britain have been supported by contributions," he explained. Would not "the lovers of learning" in America do the same "to enlarge the sphere of knowledge"? Apparently not: Webster was in constant need of funds to carry on his scholarly project, an experience shared by other literary men in his day and confirming the view that in the absence of aristocratic patrons and well-endowed institutions, the Muses could not thrive in the infant republic. In fact, Americans did establish diverse associations and launch numerous journals to promote the progress of knowledge. Still, their reputation was fixed, in Emerson's words, as "a people too busy" with business ever "to give to letters" more than token regard.

If "letters" did have a future in the new nation, that lay in the wider field opened up over the nineteenth century, when "literature" ended its narrow alliance with elite learning and admitted into its ranks the entire body of writing produced in a time or place. In the age of Enlightenment, men of letters competed to contribute to the world's stock of knowledge. The agenda shifted with the currents of nationalism and democracy. Now every Western nation claimed a distinctive character, given form in original works of literature and art from the common life of its people. By this standard, Emerson would identify the "English traits" of "strong common sense" and "mental materialism" as characteristic of the nation that produced Chaucer and Shakespeare, Macaulay and Dickens, while seeking the essence of American experience in the popular realm of "the familiar" and "the low." This quest for national distinctiveness has shaped literary history ever since. Until recently, critics have told the story of American literature as the long struggle to find an original, authentic voice for the unprecedented realities of experience in the New World. Such a narrative is suggested by the very title of this chapter, "Building a National Literature." But book history alters the angle of vision. It goes beyond the particular agendas that writers and historians attribute to books and comprehends the wide array of interests and participants, the diversity of institutions, and the host of cultural practices that were bound up in the world of print Americans made, through their domestic engagements and their international entanglements, over the nineteenth century. By these means and media, writers and readers carried on the conversations among themselves and with the wider world that can appropriately be called "American literature."

The United States embarked on independence with a print culture that was at once local and cosmopolitan but hardly national. America's arrival on the world stage was heralded in print, with the Declaration of Independence circulating in thirty newspapers and fourteen broadsides before it was even signed. The republic was dependent on its constituent parts, the very news of its existence spread by a decentralized network of printers among a loosely connected people. The success of the new nation required better communications, and so the federal government that came into being with the Constitution in 1789 set about promoting a greater sense of nationality. Newspapers were central to that goal. "Whatever facilitates a general intercourse of sentiments," James Madison wrote in 1791, "as good roads, domestic commerce, a free press, and particularly *a circulation of newspapers through the entire body of the people* . . . is equivalent to a contraction of territorial limits, and is favorable to liberty."

Under the fostering arm of government, the press enjoyed special privileges accorded to no other genre of print. The Post Office Act of 1792 allowed newspapers to circulate through the mail at cheap rates, subsidized by high charges on personal letters; books were banned from the mailbags. Editors could also exchange issues at no cost, and they were free to reprint whatever they pleased. Government put few obstacles in their way. Liberty of the press was guaranteed by state and federal constitutions, and following the storm over the 1798 Sedition Act, official efforts to regulate newspapers faded. In contrast to Britain and France, the new republic eschewed the state powers customarily employed to police opinion. In the Old World, heavy taxes on newspapers restricted their circulation to an economic elite; in the United States, news was potentially accessible to all. Subscriptions, to be sure, were costly – as much as ten dollars a year for a daily, five for a weekly, the bill payable in advance – but copies were readily available in coffee-houses and taverns, where it was common to see men sociably gathered, as the poet Philip Freneau noticed, "to spit, smoke segars, drink apple whiskey, and *read the news.*" Politicians encouraged the habit by providing a variety of subsidies – printing contracts, official advertising, and patronage jobs – to ensure the well-being of the press. Thanks to all these measures, newspapers took on the character of public utilities, and reading them became a conscientious act of citizenship. As early as 1800, the *Portfolio* dubbed Americans "a nation of newspaper readers."

Serving both public purpose and private interest, newspapers proliferated at a dizzying pace up and down the coast and deep into the Western frontier, faster even than the burgeoning population of the new nation. Some 200 papers circulated in 1800; a quarter-century later, that figure had grown four-fold to 861, then swelled to 1,400 by 1840. Everywhere, except the rural South, where printers were seldom seen, the press played an integral part in the conduct of business and politics. Like their eighteenth-century predecessors, urban dailies supplied valuable commercial "intelligence" about prices and markets far and near. They rightly called themselves "advertisers"; commonly, half or more of these four-page sheets were given over to paid notices of goods and services for sale.

The political columns of the press were no less devoted to salesmanship. At the dawn of the republic, editors vowed to be "open to all parties but influenced by none," as the *Freeman's Journal* of Philadelphia declared in its masthead, while the ambitious entrepreneur John Fenno hastened from Boston to New York with the dream of founding a "gazette of the United States" as official organ of the national establishment. But hardly had the new government gone into operation than it split into competing factions, centered around Alexander Hamilton and Thomas Jefferson, that developed after 1800 into full-fledged partisan bodies contending for power in Washington and the states. Each party cultivated its own network of newspapers to carry on the contest in print; from editorial offices functioning as party headquarters flowed the official messages calculated to rally the faithful and win over the undecided. In election seasons, urban advertisers and country gazettes made politics their main business, selling candidates and platforms like any other product. Up to 1820, newspapers preferred to cloak their partisanship in seemingly impartial language stressing the common good; in succeeding decades, they took up the cudgels and waged the fight for Democrats and Whigs, Anti-Masons, Know-Nothings, and Republicans without inhibition. Editors, more often politicians than printers, denounced their rivals as scurrilous skunks, dirty dishcloths, and "lickspittle tools" and brawled with them in the streets. Epithets and opinions were the stuff of the party press in campaign mode.

Where was the *news* in these papers? It consisted chiefly of official documents – the annual message of the president, laws enacted by state legislatures, proceedings of political conventions, trial records – along with extracts from the foreign press, prices current, and accounts of ships arriving and departing. From the 1820s on, editors competed fiercely to be the first to put such items into print, employing schooners, pony expresses, even carrier pigeons to win the race. But independent reporting was lacking. Journalists did show initiative by attending sessions of Congress and taking stenographic notes on the debates. Unfortunately for contemporaries and historians interested in what exactly was said, such transcripts were not what the public read. Politicians were accorded the right to review the notes and "improve" them before speeches went into print – a practice known as "speaking to Buncombe" whereby the people's representatives said one thing to their colleagues and another to their constituents. If national "news" was bowdlerized in the press, events close to home could go missing entirely, partly because everyone already knew them, but even more because such matters were beside the point. Scattered across an extensive republic, local newspapers served to connect readers to wider worlds beyond the community. They constituted a national bulletin board, posting stories from all over the land. Noah Webster, an erstwhile editor himself, was quick to discern the significance of this process. Newspapers, he observed in the very first issue of his *American Minerva* in December 1793, were "common instruments of social intercourse, by which the citizens of this vast Republic constantly discourse and debate with each other."

The boundaries of American journalism expanded dramatically with the birth of the penny press. In September 1833, a new era of mass communications dawned with the inauguration of Benjamin Day's *New York Sun*. This brash upstart adapted recent innovations in the London press to American circumstances and challenged the business model for an urban newspaper. It was soon followed by a host of imitators in New York and beyond, most notably, James Gordon Bennett's *New York Herald* (1835) and Horace Greeley's *New York Tribune* (1841). Unlike the high-priced "mercantile advertisers" aimed at New York's political and business elite, the penny papers catered to the broad middle and working classes of the surging city. The papers were tiny: at $8\frac{1}{2}$ by 11 inches, the *Sun* easily folded into a man's pocket, whereas its established rivals, three times that size, were "blanket sheets." They were cheap, a penny an issue (soon raised to two cents) and available in single copies hawked by newsboys on the streets. They were independent in politics and populist in style. And they promised to print "ALL THE NEWS OF THE DAY." This was an entirely new formula for commercial publishing. With its handy format, low price, and appealing contents, the penny press gathered up readers en masse and sold them to advertisers for huge profits. The *Herald*'s daily circulation climbed to 60,000 by the eve of the Civil War, an achievement made possible by the introduction of steam-powered printing presses and machine-made paper. Popular journalism was at once a cause and consequence of the industrial revolution.

In the hands of Bennett, a Scottish immigrant who had labored long and futilely in the party press, the modern tabloid emerged in its quintessential form, capturing all the "human interest" of the day: crime, violence, sex, high society, sports (boxing matches, horse races, yachting regattas), Wall Street, show business, and celebrities. But the *Herald* did not ignore politics, which Bennett pursued as aggressively as he sniffed out scandal. Seizing on the invention of the telegraph, *Herald* correspondents broke the news of American victories in the Mexican war and the discovery of gold in California; the provisions of the Treaty of Guadalupe Hidalgo surfaced in the paper the same day as the US Senate received the confidential document from President Polk. (Furious at the leak, senators ordered the arrest of the *Herald* reporter and demanded to know his source – to no effect; after a month, the defiant newsman was released.) The scoops and sensations brought to public view in the popular press constituted a distinctive contribution to American literature. In the pages of the penny papers unfolded the daily life of a great metropolis with "a variety, a piquancy, a brilliancy, an originality," according to Bennett, "that will entirely outstrip the worn out races of Europe, who have been degenerating for the last twenty generations." Capturing the excitement, novelty, and dangers of an ever-changing city, these heralds and tribunes of the people reflected urban society to itself.

The popular appetite for news was insatiable. In 1869, the British journalist Edward Dicey characterized the American as "a newspaper-reading animal." A periodical existed for virtually every breed of *genus Americanus*. Where the party and penny press targeted readers in particular cities and towns, other enterprises identified groups with specialized interests and fashioned them into regional and national audiences. Vocational publications abounded, with farmers getting the most attention and advice. No self-respecting denomination of Christians was without its house organ. Temperance advocates drank from the *Fountain* and enlisted in the *Cold Water Army*; health reformers looked to the *Sanitarium*; abolitionists championed the cause of the slave in the *Emancipator* and the *Liberator*. Starting with *Freedom's Journal* in 1827, African Americans fought not only for their own liberty but for the *Rights of All* (as the paper was renamed). The Cherokee Nation advertised its progress in civilization in the bilingual *Cherokee Phoenix*, and although that effort failed to stop forcible removal from Georgia, the paper, true to its original name, was reborn in Oklahoma as the *Cherokee Advocate*. There were "amulets," "garlands," "mirrors," and "toilets" for ladies (and an *Agitator* for women's rights); "assistants" and "companions" for mothers; "friends" for orphans and youth. Alas, "sporting papers" like the *Flash* and the *Whip*, modeled on English originals, led young men astray with titillating tales of vice in the nation's cities and detailed guides on where to find it.

Those preferring the safer precincts of fiction could turn to the "story papers" that flourished in the mid-1840s, when canny businessmen took advantage of a loophole in the postal laws and began churning out cheap editions of foreign novels in newspaper format. In the spirit of James Gordon Bennett, the editors of *Brother Jonathan* and *New World* in New York and *Universal Yankee Nation* in Boston (which claimed to be "the largest paper in all creation") won the hearts of "the Reading Million" and threatened the interests of established publishers by snapping up the latest works of Charles Dickens, Edward Bulwer-Lytton, and other popular writers as soon as they arrived on the transatlantic steamers and getting them into print well before they appeared as books. "We are friends of the people," boasted the *New World*, "and our motto is 'The greatest good to the greatest number.'" Though that practice was soon halted, newspapers never stopped running fiction. Harriet Beecher Stowe's *Uncle Tom's Cabin* first created a sensation in the anti-slavery weekly *National Era*, where it was serialized in forty installments in 1851. *Frank Leslie's Illustrated Magazine*, launched by an English engraver-turned-publisher in New York, played a prominent part in popularizing such novelists as Wilkie Collins in the Civil War decades and after, while literary syndicates marketed works by the leading American and British writers to newspapers all over the country during the last two decades of the century. Thanks to the post office, the railroad, and the telegraph, the newspaper could chart diverse paths – local, regional, national, or perhaps all at the same time – in the building of a literary marketplace.

In histories of American literature, book publishing usually holds pride of place and with good reason. Books carried a cultural prestige lacking in periodicals. Whether bound in leather or cloth, they were made to last, embodying "timeless" knowledge across the generations; newspapers, by contrast, were typically as short-lived as the information they contained. Ephemera comprised the bulk of items issued by colonial printers: almanacs, broadsides, newspapers, pamphlets in political and religious debates, primers, and spellers. For their books, Americans went to London, Edinburgh, and Dublin in a habit that survived the Revolution. It was simply cheaper to import the latest literature from Britain than to patronize the native press, and it signified a cosmopolitan desire to participate in the international republic of letters. For that situation to change, entrepreneurs would have to find new ways of conducting the book business, and consumers would have to alter their literary tastes.

In the early 1790s, the printer Mathew Carey, a radical Irish nationalist who had fled prosecution for sedition by the English authorities and set up shop in Philadelphia with an endorsement from Benjamin Franklin, devised an ingenious route into publishing. With the backing of well-heeled merchants, he ordered thousands of pounds worth of books from several leading British booksellers, stocked a store on Market Street, and turned the inventory to immediate profit. Carey's ambitions went beyond the import trade. Instead of paying his suppliers, he pocketed the money and invested it in two risky ventures, expensive reprints of William Guthrie's *New System of Geography* (1786) and Oliver Goldsmith's *An History of the Earth and Animated Nature* (1774), which had gone through multiple editions in London and Dublin. Carey aimed to cover his costs by signing up advance subscribers, some 1,200 in all, for Guthrie's two volumes, which were adapted for American readers by the Philadelphia astronomer David Rittenhouse and Massachusetts geographer Jedidiah Morse. So ambitious was this design that Carey was obliged to give up printing altogether and concentrate on marketing his wares – no easy task, as it turned out, since the ready audience for the project in the Middle States and New England was quickly tapped out and the newspaper advertisements Carey placed brought in few others. Facing an imminent crisis of debt, Carey seized on the expedient of hiring a footloose Anglican parson named Mason Locke Weems to peddle his books wherever they could be sold. A born salesman, Weems traveled throughout the Chesapeake, winning over the gentry with visions of "Worlds upon Worlds" about "to burst upon their senses" from the pages of Guthrie. The sales pitch did more than rescue Carey from financial ruin. It pointed up the opportunities and the obstacles in publishing books for a people dispersed across the countryside of an extensive republic. In the bid to bring books to readers, rather than wait for them to come into his store, Carey learned a crucial lesson: picking titles was only part of a publisher's task; marketing and selling them demanded equal attention.

Carey's example was repeated by other printers-turned-publishers in the 1790s, not all of whom obtained working capital by expropriating British creditors. The patriot printer Isaiah Thomas of Worcester, Massachusetts, launched his publishing career with a line of "toy" books for children, reprinted from London originals, and with substantial quarto and folio editions of the Bible. However they entered the business, these entrepreneurs built American publishing on the recycling of British and European books. This specialty was made profitable by the Copyright Act of 1790, which, in keeping with the Constitution's mandate to "promote the Progress of Science and useful Arts," granted authors "the exclusive right to their Writings" for a limited term of fourteen years (renewable, in the author's lifetime, for another fourteen) – a provision modeled on English precedent (the 1710 Statute of Anne, the first copyright law in the world). There was a catch: only American citizens (and resident aliens) need apply. Foreigners could claim neither protection against nor payment for unauthorized reprints of their works by the likes of Carey and Thomas. In effect, the vast body of British and European literature constituted a public domain free for the taking. Like squatters on the frontier, booksellers seized the opportunity; from the 1790s on, the bestselling books in London were being reprinted in the United States within one or two years.

The loose copyright laws fostered a "culture of reprinting" that made the American reading public the largest and most up-to-date in the Western world. In Britain, where the "intellectual property regime" tightened sharply in the early nineteenth century, publishers exploited their legal monopoly over current titles and kept book prices high and edition sizes low. As a result, the great works of the Romantic age, especially the poetry and novels of Walter Scott, gained a wider audience across the Atlantic than in their native land. With no legal obligations to foreign authors, American booksellers saved on royalties, and they cut costs further by altering texts at will. In the course of reprinting, "three-decker" English novels shrank to two volumes (and often two-in-one), shorn of unnecessary verbiage. One Boston publisher had no apologies for condensing Scott's Waverley novels: "there is a great deal of rubbish – such as the long introductions &c." Every branch of knowledge, from theology to biography to natural history, suffered such cavalier treatment. In 1820, 70 percent of the titles issued in the United States were pirated from overseas; three decades later, following a great expansion of original American publishing, that figure remained a substantial 43 percent. Even with all those reprints in circulation, Americans had not lost their taste for imports. Serious learning still carried an Old World lineage. Well into the nineteenth century, book collectors, colleges, and library societies provided a sturdy market for British books, which such businessmen as George Palmer Putnam serviced by setting up quarters in London as agent for customers back home. In similar fashion, prosperous Americans were accustomed to celebrate Christmas by presenting loved ones with fancy gift books from England. Far from retreating before American books, the import trade boomed, growing nearly tenfold over the middle decades of the century.

British models shaped virtually every aspect of American publishing during its formative decades. Technology came from abroad, as did the craftsmen trained to use it. What books and periodicals Americans did not import or reprint they imitated and made their own. Many genres – the evangelical magazine, the gift book, the picturesque "tour," the illustrated weekly, even the Valentine writer – originated in the Old World, then spread to the New, where they won large followings. In one crucial respect the fledgling book trade departed from the norm. Unlike the highly concentrated business of London and Paris, publishing developed as an infant industry in diverse cities and towns, from Boston to Charleston on the coast and west to Pittsburgh and Cincinnati. Decentralization was due both to the transportation barriers obstructing a national market and to the economic opportunities afforded by the copyright laws. Anybody could enter the field, issue a new title, or reprint an existing one by a foreign writer, so long as he had the capital to hire printer and binder and the willingness to assume the financial risk. But how to get books to potential readers beyond a locality? Publishers combined forces to enlarge the geographical scope of bookselling, while regulating regional and national competition. In emulation of an English practice known as "courtesy of trade," they devised a rule for reprinting: whoever first issued a foreign text was its rightful owner, notwithstanding the absence of copyright. Under this compact, a single reprint of an English work could circulate throughout the nation, free from competing editions. Booksellers, like newspaper editors, would exchange publications with one another, thereby increasing and diversifying their stock. Or they might join together in co-publishing ventures and divide up the territory for sales. Other methods of dissemination were to purvey books on commission, supply them at standard discounts, establish branch stores, and send traveling salesmen into the countryside. These cooperative arrangements rested upon a shared sense of identity and common interests. Splitting off, like Carey, from printers and devoting themselves to publishing and selling books, the leading figures in the book trade cultivated a collective image as urban gentlemen, promoting the economy and culture of the republic. In reality, they were following in the well-marked trail of English stationers, collaborating to uphold prices, curb competition, and limit risks.

The pace of change was actually set outside the established book trade. From the 1820s to the 1850s, the leading agents of the "benevolent empire" – the American Bible Society, the American Tract Society, and the American Sunday School Union – produced and distributed millions of pious pamphlets and books. Intent on propagating the word and winning converts for Christ, these religious publishers employed stereotype plates and steam-powered presses well in advance of their commercial counterparts. But delivering the divine message to needy souls proved a more difficult challenge. The benevolent societies relied on a network of local auxiliaries to finance and distribute their publications, and therein lay the problem. Rich, respectable communities, abounding in professed Christians, were quick to answer the call, while hardscrabble frontier settlements went unserved. The prevailing localism of American life circumscribed the reach of philanthropy. To overcome those limits, the national agencies enlisted an evangelical army of divinity students and ministers willing to work for minimal pay and deployed them to the dark corners of the land. Their mission was to be traveling salesmen for the Lord, going from door to door handing out Bibles and tracts to starving souls at whatever price, if any, they could afford. Employing these colporteurs brought additional complications: they had to be recruited, trained, supervised, paid, and held to account. By the 1850s, the benevolent societies were operating as modern corporate bureaucracies, their central headquarters overseeing a chain of regional offices that directly employed scores of agents in the field. Ironically, they did so in order to combat the immoral influence of the literary marketplace, which supplied people with what they wanted in this life, not what they needed for eternal salvation. Reversing that equation, the tract and Bible societies reinforced older habits of reading. Inside the peddlers' packs were the steady sellers of seventeenth- and eighteenth-century divinity – Baxter's *Call*, Alleine's *Alarm*, Flavel's *Touchstone* – along with newer evangelical titles like *The Dairyman's Daughter*, nearly all the products of English pens. In urgent matters of the spirit, numerous Christians still found inspiration in the mother country.

The transformation of commercial publishing developed in tandem with the broader economy. From the 1820s to the Panic of 1837, the United States experienced a long wave of sustained growth, bringing unprecedented prosperity to a burgeoning middle class and swelling demand for consumer goods, including books. The changes stirred the book trade, whose ranks were still small and scattered in various cities, chiefly Boston, New York, and Philadelphia, but with outposts along the trade routes to the West. Just as newspapers raced for the latest news from Europe, so booksellers hastened to reprint the most popular works in London. Driving this enterprise was the craze for the historical romances of Walter Scott, which gave a new respectability to reading fiction. No longer could publishers afford to wait and see if a title sold well enough in England to merit reprinting. With speed of the essence, booksellers paid to obtain advance sheets from London – a compensation of sorts to the publishers and writers being pirated. The "author of Waverley" and his imitators appeared in print as soon as they arrived in harbor. Courtesy of trade dissolved. Publishers invaded each other's territory with rival editions of the same work, only to find themselves ultimately out-flanked by the story papers, which nearly ruined the trade. There was no alternative but to satisfy the demand. The key to success lay in publishing new books. Mathew Carey, who had built his firm on the solid foundation of reprints and the Bible (which he kept in standing type and reissued as warranted), could not fathom why his son and successor was expanding the list of publications so rapidly. "There is nothing on earth worse than an old stock of books," the son patiently explained. "Five-sixths of the whole sales are of books manufactured within the year." Even that was not enough to beat the competition. Carey & Lea battled for dominance with the Harper Brothers for a decade; ultimately, the Harpers won. In a striking pattern of concentration, Manhattan emerged as the publishing capital of the nation, followed by Philadelphia, Boston, and Cincinnati.

The new business model reorganized publishing along modern lines. With flexibility and speed crucial to success in the competitive marketplace, the leading firms embraced technological innovation. Stereotyping, which preserved cast type on metal plates, allowed for printing on demand; firms could now reproduce works in smaller or larger lots, in response to changing needs. Papermaking machines and steam presses lowered costs, expanded output, and accelerated production. Even the centuries-old art of binding was mechanized. Taken together, these inventions transformed the appearance of books. Attractively packaged in cloth covers, illustrated with engravings, and neatly printed in large editions, each year's titles from companies like Boston's Ticknor & Fields, the industry leader in design, arrived, for the first time in book history, as uniform com-modities on the market. It thus became easy to assign them fixed prices. Distribution was regularized in turn. Older cooperative arrangements gave way to an impersonal division of labor, as most publishers ceased to be old-style "booksellers." Their special-ized business was to organize the process of publication, bringing works into print at their own expense and risk and then selling them wholesale to jobbers and retailers nationwide. Thanks to the railroad, which extended steadily in the Northeast from the 1830s on and completed its transcontinental journey in 1869, a national book-trade system gradually emerged. From grand offices in Manhattan and other publishing centers issued an ever-expanding volume of books – some 1,350 in the year before the Civil War – to be disseminated across the country by wholesale jobbers, traveling sales-men, and retail shops. The independent bookstore was the hub of the system. In every major city and town, shopping for books became a convenient, everyday experience.

Sarah Payson Willis Parton was a prominent beneficiary of these changes. Better known by her pen name Fanny Fern, Parton achieved celebrity and riches as a newspaper columnist and novelist after years of struggling as a single mother to support herself and three young children. Born in 1811, she came of age with the press, witnessing in her own family the changing practice of journalism and the opening of new opportuni-ties for commercial writing. Her grandfather had edited a patriot newspaper in Boston during the Revolutionary War; her father had enlisted in the fight against federalism as editor of the *Eastern Argus* in Portland, Maine, before giving up politics for religion and starting one of America's earliest religious newspapers, the *Boston Recorder*; her older brother, Nathaniel P. Willis, fashioned a literary career as an urbane poet and genteel magazine editor. Yet, when financial disaster struck, the young mother, first widowed, then divorced, was cast on her own resources, with no help from her literary kin. To make ends meet, she tried teaching and sewing, then picked up the pen, submitting articles in the early 1850s to several Boston family magazines (the *Mother's Assistant*, the *True Flag*, and the *Olive Branch*). For the sake of propriety, as well as to conceal her identity from inquisitive relatives, she adopted the pseudonym Fanny Fern. But her ambition burned bright, and it was rewarded by a shrewd publisher who collected her periodical pieces and issued them as a book with the title *Fern Leaves from Fanny's Portfolio*. The volume was an instant success, selling 70,000 copies within a year. With a satirical wit that gave bite to sentimental prose, Fanny Fern won a huge following for her forthright pieces portraying the sufferings of poor children on New York's streets and the burdens of women in a patriarchal world. As a literary professional, she reveled in her large sales and loyal fans. Her novel *Ruth Hall* (1854), a *roman-à-clef* about a brave woman writer trying desperately to feed her children, culminates in a remarkable financial reward: 100 shares of stock in a local bank, worth $100 each. For pouring "her own heart's history" onto the pages of a book, the author has unknowingly earned a fortune of $10,000 – roughly what Parton herself had by then garnered in royalties from her books. That was far more than Parton's grandfather and father had ever gained from political and religious newspapers.

The astonishing career of Fanny Fern is tribute to the forces behind the expansion of the literary marketplace by the mid-nineteenth century: the rise of national periodicals; the huge popularity of novels; the profitability of writing as a vocation, especially for women; the appeal of celebrities in popular culture; and the collaboration of author and publisher in creating and disseminating American literature. As much as anyone writing in her time, Sarah Parton demonstrated just how valuable intellectual property could be. Her financial coup was the product of the smart bargain she had made in selling the copyright to her works in exchange for a share of the revenues their publication brought in – a royalty agreement that remains standard practice today. Right from the start of the 1790 Copyright Act, Noah Webster had seen its economic uses, as had such female writers as the historian Hannah Adams and the feminist Judith Sargent Murray. So, too, had booksellers like Henry C. Carey, who was quick to buy the copyrights and finance the publications of James Fenimore Cooper and Catherine Maria Sedgwick in the 1820s and 1830s – investments that only gained in value after Congress extended the copyright term in 1831 to twenty-eight years (with a possible renewal for another fourteen). The complaints of literary nationalists notwithstanding, copyright facilitated the making of American literary careers. Both native and foreign works could come from the same presses.

It was not Fanny Fern, rooted in journalism and popular culture, whom the builders of American literature had in mind during the late nineteenth century when they established a canon of the nation's major writers, but rather a coterie of New England males: Ralph Waldo Emerson, Nathaniel Hawthorne, Oliver Wendell Holmes, Henry Wadsworth Longfellow, and a few lesser poets. The elite roster owed its existence to Boston publisher James T. Fields, who had the inspiration to market these authors, all issued by his company and its successors, as a rare breed of artists creating superior works of the imagination that truly deserved recognition as "literature." Set apart from ordinary books by their elegant format and gathered into standard editions and distinguished series, such masterpieces claimed the status of American "classics" on a par with England's best. "It is literature . . . that holds in precipitation the genius of the country," decreed Houghton Mifflin editor Horace Scudder, "and the higher the form of literature, the more consummate the expression of that spirit . . ." This canonizing frame of mind, with its sacral view of art and its ranking of writers in a finely graded hierarchy, was well suited to the mood of the publishing establishment in the Gilded Age. The heirs and successors to the leading family firms – Appleton, Harper's, Putnam, Scribner's – liked to downplay the commercial aspects of their trade. Publishing for them was not so much a business as a profession with a high cultural mission. Happily, philanthropy coincided with self-interest. Through national magazines (*Atlantic, Harper's, Scribner's, Century*), major publishing houses served the cause of literature, while promoting their authors and advertising themselves.

It would be a mistake to idealize the publishing world of the late nineteenth century. Like any entrenched interest, industry insiders treated newcomers as interlopers. In the 1870s and 1880s, another wave of cheap fiction rose, with the appearance of George Munro's Seaside Library and similar series. Consisting of foreign novels reprinted in magazine format, these books in disguise, like the earlier story papers, took advantage of postal regulations and circulated as second-class mail. Mainstream firms denounced this violation of courtesy, which Munro scorned as " 'a right of possession' based primarily on the principle, or lack of principle, of *first grab.*" Only with US ratification of international copyright in 1891 were the reprinters driven out of business. Even so, the establishment continued to face stiff competition from subscription publishers, who did a handsome business selling Mark Twain, Ulysses S. Grant, and other popular writers by advance order to the vast countryside. Despite their huge sales, such volumes, sneered spokesmen for the regular trade, were "absolutely worthless," with a "gaudy" appearance belied by shoddy construction – "gorgeous binding, usually in very bad taste, thick but cheap paper, outrageously poor wood-cuts, the largest type with the thickest leads." Only the ignorant, seduced by silver-tongued salesmen, would accept such "humbug." Clinging to a conservative vision of publishing as an elevated, gentlemanly affair, the leading firms stood apart from the expanding mass market cultivated by the purveyors of cheap books and the entrepreneurs of popular journalism.

Elite and mass media together strengthened national perspectives in American life at the expense of the local and the cosmopolitan. The process of change made for a more uniform, standardized print culture. It eroded the position of country editors as mediators between small towns and the wider world. It turned once-proud printers with dreams of owning their own presses into a permanent industrial working class. It converted the civic organs of the early republic into sales bureaus for consumer culture. And it gave vast license to the newspaper barons – Joseph Pulitzer, William Randolph Hearst – who built on the legacy of James Gordon Bennett and fashioned the "yellow journalism" of the 1880s and 1890s. But national institutions of print also spread literary culture at home and abroad, winning grudging respect for American writers even in London, where Fanny Fern was pirated not long after her US debut. Ultimately, the advance of the publishing media enabled Americans to see themselves and the larger world through native eyes. In that rise to literary independence, we can also discern an ebbing of the cosmopolitanism that once was central to American print culture. In a globalized world, where old habits of cultural nationalism clash with the urgent need for international understanding, the making of American literature was not an unmixed blessing.

REFERENCES AND FURTHER READING

Amory, Hugh and Hall, David D. (2000) *A History of the Book in America*, vol. I: *The Colonial Book in the Atlantic World*. Cambridge: Cambridge University Press.

Baldasty, Gerald J. (1992) *The Commercialization of News in the Nineteenth Century*. Madison: University of Wisconsin Press.

Barnhurst, Kevin G. and Nerone, John (2001) *The Form of News: A History*. New York: Guilford.

Brodhead, Richard H. (1986) *The School of Hawthorne*. New York: Oxford University Press.

Brown, Candy Gunther (2004) *The Word in the World: Evangelical Writing, Publishing, and Reading in America, 1789–1880*. Chapel Hill: University of North Carolina Press.

Casper, Scott, Chaison, Joanne D., and Groves, Jeffrey D. (eds.) (2002) *Perspectives on American Book History: Artifacts and Commentary*. Amherst: University of Massachusetts Press.

—, Groves, Jeffrey D., Nissenbaum, Stephen W., et al. (forthcoming 2007) *A History of the Book in America*, vol. III: *The Industrial Book, 1840–1880*. Chapel Hill: University of North Carolina Press.

Crouthamel, James L. (1989) *Bennett's New York Herald and the Rise of the Popular Press*. Syracuse: Syracuse University Press.

Ellis, Joseph J. (1979) *After the Revolution: Profiles of Early American Culture*. New York: W. W. Norton.

Greenspan, Ezra (2000) *George Palmer Putnam: Representative American Publisher*. University Park: Penn State University Press.

Gross, Robert A. and Kelley, Mary (forthcoming 2008) *A History of the Book in America*, vol. II: *An Extensive Republic: Books, Culture, and Society in the New Nation, 1790–1840*. Chapel Hill: University of North Carolina Press.

Henkin, David M. (1998) *City Reading: Written Words and Public Spaces in Antebellum New York*. New York: Columbia University Press.

Horowitz, Helen Lefkowitz (2002) "Another 'American Cruikshank' Found: John H. Manning and the New Sporting Weeklies." *Proceedings of the American Antiquarian Society*, 112: 93–126.

Johanningsmeier, Charles A. (1997) *Fiction and the American Literary Marketplace: The Role of Newspaper Syndicates in America, 1860–1900*. New York: Cambridge University Press.

John, Richard R. (1995) *Spreading the News: The American Postal System from Franklin to Morse*. Cambridge, MA: Harvard University Press.

Kaser, David (1957) *Messrs. Carey & Lea of Philadelphia: A Study in the History of the Booktrade*. Philadelphia: University of Pennsylvania Press.

Kelley, Mary (1985) *Private Woman, Public Stage; Literary Domesticity in Nineteenth Century America*. New York: Oxford University Press.

Leonard, Thomas C. (1986) *Power of the Press: The Birth of American Political Reporting*. New York: Oxford University Press.

— (1995) *News for All: America's Coming-of-age with the Press*. New York: Oxford University Press.

McGill, Meredith L. (2003) *American Literature and the Culture of Reprinting 1834–1853*. Philadelphia: University of Pennsylvania Press.

Mott, Frank Luther (1962) *American Journalism: A History, 1690–1960*, 3rd edn. New York: Macmillan.

Nord, David Paul (2001) *Communities of Journalism: A History of American Newspapers and their Readers*. Urbana: University of Illinois Press.

— (2004) *Faith in Fiction: Religious Publishing and the Birth of Mass Media in America*. New York: Oxford University Press.

Pasley, Jeffrey L. (2001) *"The Tyranny of Printers": Newspaper Politics in the Early American Republic*. Charlottesville: University Press of Virginia.

Raven, James (2002) *London Booksellers and American Customers: Transatlantic Literary Community and the Charleston Library Society, 1748–1811*. Columbia: University of South Carolina Press.

Schudson, Michael (1978) *Discovering the News: A Social History of American Newspapers*. New York: Basic.

Sheehan, Donald (1952) *This Was Publishing: A Chronicle of the Book Trade in the Gilded Age*. Bloomington: Indiana University Press.

Starr, Paul (2004) *The Creation of the Media: Political Origins of Modern Communications*. New York: Basic.

Stewart, Donald Henderson (1969) *The Opposition Press of the Federalist Period*. Albany: State University of New York Press.

Tebbel, John (1972–81) *A History of Book Publishing in the United States*, 4 vols. New York: R. R. Bowker.

Tucher, Andie (1994) *Froth and Scum: Truth, Beauty, Goodness, and the Ax Murder in America's First Mass Medium*. Chapel Hill: University of North Carolina Press.

Warner, Michael (1990) *Letters of the Republic: Publication and the Public Sphere in Eighteenth-century America*. Cambridge, MA: Harvard University Press.

Winship, Michael (1995) *American Literary Publishing in the Mid-nineteenth Century: The Business of Ticknor and Fields*. Cambridge: Cambridge University Press.

Zboray, Ronald J. (1993) *A Fictive People: Antebellum Economic Development and the American Reading Public*. New York: Oxford University Press.

— and Zboray, Mary Saracino (2005) *Literary Dollars and Social Sense: A People's History of the Mass Market Book*. New York: Routledge.

24

The Globalization of the Book
1800–1970

David Finkelstein

Until the early nineteenth century, the production of books in Western Europe could be explained fairly simply in business terms. Early printers combined the roles of printer, publisher, and bookseller in one. They commissioned and bought rights to works, then produced and attempted to make a profit from the results. As trade increased to include international links, these roles began to be separated: by the late eighteenth century, many Western European cities had traders specializing specifically in publishing, subcontracting to printers, illustrators, and other related production specialists to complete material work on books and other printed texts, and subsequently selling the finished products to established, specialist book retailers.

The industrial revolution in nineteenth-century Britain allowed it to become a world leader in book production and dissemination. It used increased advances in technology to produce books more cheaply and transport them faster and further than its competitors. Britain's empire also proved an ideal space for the development of a transnational, globalized book market. Books and texts were an important aspect of British intellectual domination of its English-speaking colonies, but it was never a one-sided activity. Technological innovation, working practices, and textual material circulated round: initially exported, absorbed, and adapted, it was then returned to be inserted and utilized in British settings to improve the book-trade system.

The results were emulated by other nations from the 1840s onward. As part of this evolution, by the turn of the twentieth century, international copyright treaties had been agreed and trade organizations had been founded to regulate, manage, and standardize world trade, further supporting the transnational circulation of texts. After World War II, international book publishing began a process of shifting from self-contained, nationally based organizations into large, transnational, corporate organizations. Multinational media mergers, begun in the 1960s, would reshape the economics of book publishing, accelerating a process begun earlier in the century of viewing books as one of many content sources within a larger mass-media communication industry.

Copyright and Technological Innovation

The rise of a reading public in Britain in the late eighteenth century (with interests in and ability to pay for printed works) created changes in the economic fortunes of authors and book traders, generating an audience from whom they could earn money if successful in capturing its imagination. Crucially, it would be the development of copyright as a legal concept that would lead to an international economic revolution, a result of eighteenth-century legal battles in Britain between English and Scottish factions.

Interpretations of who owned the results of an author's efforts would be clarified in 1774 following a landmark legal case in London between a Scottish and an English bookseller. The case was argued with the legal help of James Boswell, the literary recorder of Samuel Johnson's life. *Donaldson* v. *Becket* established the legal precedents and concepts of individual copyright ownership that would shape all following international interpretations of copyright. The judgment confirmed that no individual printer or publisher could claim perpetual copyright over intellectual property generated by authors, and confirmed earlier statutes that had granted sole reproduction rights to entrepreneurs who had purchased these rights for 14, then 28 years. France followed in 1778 with its own legal interpretation of copyright protection (rights that were subsequently strengthened in 1793 with further statutes). Austria followed in 1832, as did Germany in 1835. Over the next sixty years, other nations slowly adopted similar copyright laws (with increasing lengths of time assigned for copyright protection: 50, then 75 years from initial publication), but international copyright regulation was only to be achieved after much struggle with the ratification of the Berne Convention in 1887.

Changes in legal rights happened in tandem with major technological and market change. Book production was transformed by scientific and industrial innovations (see chapter 20). Steam-driven trains and boats speeded up delivery of books and print across national and international borders. Telegraph cables, based on technological breakthroughs in Britain and the US in the 1830s and 1840s, were laid across national, transatlantic, and international borders. The first underwater telegraph cable linking Britain and continental Europe was laid in 1850 and joined London to Paris; the first successful transatlantic telegraph cable between Europe and North America was laid in 1858, running between Ireland and Newfoundland. These developments, along with the establishment of dependable postal services, enabled quick and efficient circulation of information between authors, editors, publishers, and their readers.

This industrialization of printing and publishing systems was part of a larger industrialization of business across Western Europe. Mechanization enlarged market potential, shifting power in the book trade at the same time. As Robert Escarpit notes, "Faced with a developing market, printing and bookselling underwent a major change, as nascent capitalist industry took charge of the book. The publisher appeared as the responsible entrepreneur relegating the printer and bookseller to a minor role. As a side effect, the literary profession began to organize . . ." (1966: 22–3).

Among the first book-trade economies to change, partly in response to the techno-logical advances made during the industrial revolution of the late eighteenth and early nineteenth centuries, was that of Britain. After 1780, we see a shift from small, indi-vidualized firms to large, multi-focused, family-led, corporate entities. Major publishing houses emerged which acted both as general and specialist list publishers. Family firms such as Blackwood & Sons, John Murray, Chambers, Smith, Elder & Co., Macmillan, and others, founded in the late eighteenth and early nineteenth centuries, would become pre-eminent in their field by the 1860s, dominating trade in Britain and profiting from exports to anglophone colonies worldwide. Some had printing operations attached to their editorial and production offices, but on the whole firms moving to consolidate reputations as "publishers" shifted the bulk of their printing onto the shoulders of spe-cialist printing firms, who took advantage of new technologies to produce orders for several publishers simultaneously and at speed. By the late nineteenth century, the economic structure of the book market in Britain (and in turn Western Europe) would be firmly established, and firms that profited from its stability would dominate both local and overseas colonial markets.

Global Book-trade Expansion

Such success encouraged the free flow of books beyond national borders. Britain and its empire, it can be argued, was the first transnational, globalized economy to emerge as a beneficiary of the advances supported by industrialization (a point discussed further below). With Britain leading from the 1830s onward, its economic initiatives and success would be replicated across the Atlantic and in other European states, and the printing trade would be completely transformed over the second half of the nineteenth century. By 1848, Germany, the US, the Nordic countries, and elsewhere had modern-ized and adapted technology within their own book trades. In tandem with such changes there was a growth in an increasingly active bourgeois and reading public keen to consume the products of the printing press. Important European and US firms rising to prominence during this period include Hachette in France, Samuel Fischer and Bernhard Tauchnitz in Germany, George Putnam, Houghton Mifflin, and Harpers & Co. in the US, Gyldendals in Denmark, and Norstedts and Albert Bonnier in Sweden (Chartier 1981; Gedin 1982: 34–9; Hall 1996: 44).

Individual nation-states harnessed the British experience to their own ends. In the US, while printing had formed an important part of the eighteenth-century colonial experience, the "golden age" of US publishing and printing activity took place after 1830 with the advent of new technology which increased capacity and communication and allowed firms, such as Harpers in New York, or Carey, Lea in Philadelphia, to become nationally and internationally known (Hall 1996: 44). Their ability to dominate local markets was also due to their size and production rates: typically, American edi-tions were three or four times larger than British print-runs (which averaged about 750–1,000 copies per impression), and prices a third or a quarter less. Inexpensive printings were partially enabled by widespread unauthorized printing, a particular concern of British sources from whom such material was "borrowed." The problem of "piracy," as it was viewed by British publishers affected by these actions, and US protectionist regulations against non-US manufactured material (justified by the industry as necessary for protecting national printing industry interests), would prove endemic through to the 1890s, when the US reluctantly adopted some measure of international copyright legislation under the Chace Act.

In France, change dated from the July Revolution of 1830, when state censorship was relaxed and liberal trade laws were instituted, and 1833 when general education became compulsory, thus encouraging an increase in the number of literate readers. The emergence of a mass press, catering to an increasingly literate urban French readership, dates to the appearance in 1836 of Emile de Girardin's commercial daily *La Presse* and its rival *Le Siècle*. Within a year, general daily newspaper sales across Paris had risen from 70,000 to 235,000 copies a day; by 1870, sales had reached one million; by 1880, they had topped two million (Escarpit 1966: 28; de la Motte and Przyblyski 1999: 2). Textual innovations included featuring serialized novels (the *roman feuilleton*), a method copied from British publishing practice. Among now canonical authors of nineteenth-century French literature initially published in this way were Balzac, Dumas, Emile Zola, and Flaubert.

Nineteenth-century French distribution sources also drew inspiration from British models – in the first instance, from the circulating library system begun by C. E. Mudie in London in 1842 (and which for over fifty years monopolized and dictated the terms by which Victorian fiction in particular was produced and distributed), and also from the newspaper and railway bookstall network developed by W. H. Smith. Guinevere Griest comments on Smith's start: "In the early part of the nineteenth century Smith's had been the leading newspaper agent of Britain, a position which was not relinquished when the firm started to expand with the railway bookstall business in 1848" (Griest 1970: 31). By 1862, Smith's had obtained a monopoly on bookstall operations in almost all of the English railways (another retail competitor, John Menzies, would dominate the Scottish market), a position it would continue to occupy through to the late twentieth century. It would also venture into the publishing market, issuing in conjunction with Chapman and Hall from 1854 onward inexpensive, two-shilling paperback reprints of popular novels for sale specifically at railway stations (they were termed "yellowbacks" on account of the yellow tint of the paper covers).

French operators would imitate such innovations in distribution. The French publisher Louis Hachette, who had begun operations in Paris in 1826, had by the 1860s, through astute engagement with the French government as a major supplier of school textbooks, turned his firm into France's largest publishing house. On his death in 1864, the firm employed 165 people and generated a gross annual turnover of one million francs. Visiting Britain in 1851, Hachette observed W. H. Smith's railway bookstall successes. When he returned home he successfully lobbied for rights to establish similar bookstalls at French railway stations. As the railway network expanded (growing 600 percent between 1850 and 1870), so too did Hachette's railway bookshop empire, extending to several thousand stalls and shops across the nation.

Hachette also copied Smith's reprint series with his own "Railway Library" editions in the 1850s: he issued 107 titles in the first year of production, and another sixty in the second. Five hundred titles were published during the life of the series. Successful titles included works by Dickens, who accounted for twenty-eight volumes (of which *David Copperfield* was the most popular, selling 100,000 copies, and *Oliver Twist* a close second with sales of 83,000), Thackeray, George Sand, Victor Hugo, and the Comtesse de Ségure's *Malheurs de Sophie*, which throughout the 1860s sold a steady 40,000 copies a year, eventually totaling 1.7 million sales (Gedin 1982: 39–40). Hachette would grow from strength to strength over the coming decades, opening outlets and selling in overseas book markets, such as Algeria and Turkey. On the eve of World War I, its annual turnover would exceed sixty million francs. After the war, however, Hachette ceased functioning as a family-owned firm, and throughout the twentieth century it would undergo a series of restructuring moves that led to its reformulation as an international, multimedia conglomerate empire, covering a wide area of entertainment work.

Nineteenth-century publishing successes such as these were matched by the publishing opportunities available amongst a cornucopia of published mass-media sources that included daily, weekly, monthly, and quarterly journals. The rise in the number of journals seeking contributions enabled many authors to earn a living from writing. Literary property proved an increasingly valuable commodity, particularly as individuals gained stronger legal rights in their texts through crucial national and international rulings and trade agreements hammered out over the course of the nineteenth century. Publishers realized that leisure reading material could boost sales of journals and newspapers, as well as serve as useful advertising for their firm's brand of fiction and nonfiction. The use of serialized material from the 1840s onward became ubiquitous in literary periodicals and newspapers, and a market developed through to the 1880s and beyond whereby texts (either pirated or legally purchased) would be serialized and circulated internationally: "stories from New York, fashion from France, information from Australia filled the democratic pages of the mid nineteenth-century miscellany" (Johnson-Woods 2000: 355).

International trade organizations and agreements were created to standardize and manage world trade in both general and book-specific areas. It is not coincidental that, as Eva Hemmungs Wirtén points out, "the first major international public unions, the International Telegraph Union (1865), soon followed by the Universal Postal Union (1874), are concerned with the intensification in international communication" (Wirtén, 2004: 31). These were followed by, among others, the organization and standardization of time through the creation of the International Date Line (Greenwich Meridian Time) in 1884; the setting up of the International Bureau of Weights and Measures in 1875; the founding of the International Labour Office in 1901; and the development of the Universal Radiotelegraph Union in 1906. The reasons underpinning the founding of these organizations and unions in the early stages of each emerging technology "was not the creation of a single authority to manage world affairs," but rather "the establishment of regulatory regimes for, in principle, the predictable and orderly conduct of pressing transnational processes" (Held et al. 1999: 43).

Exporting the Industrialized Book-trade Model

European print communication practices as remodeled in the wake of nineteenth-century technological innovations were successfully exported to other countries, drawing on European investment, technology, and skilled labor. Printing networks and activities would flourish or falter as determined by the specific needs of, and levels of support provided by, the ruling powers. In the case of the British, the setting up of print shops in their overseas possessions and colonies was initially part of missionary settlements and/or the official administration's communication system. These would be followed by the export of skilled personnel, equipment, and working practices, enabling a local print culture economy to develop, though generally still dependent on the mother country for many of its needs (including the lucrative educational market, dominated by Scottish and English firms such as Thomas Nelson & Sons, Oliver & Boyd, Macmillan, Longman, and Oxford University Press).

New Zealand's print heritage, for example, begins with the tradition of the missionary book, produced in the indigenous language of the area – in this case between 1815 and 1845 as part of missionary efforts at printing religious material in indigenous languages to be read by those they tried to convert. A second strand, English-language printing, developed in New Zealand from 1840 with the publication of a newspaper, *The New Zealand Gazette and Britannia Spectator.* Newspapers would become the primary expression of printing activity in New Zealand's colonial development. As J. E. Traue notes, the growth was rapid: there would be "28 newspapers founded between 1840 and 1848 for a European population of 59,000; 181 newspapers founded between 1860 and 1879; 150 founded between 1880 and 1889" (Traue 1997: 109).

The establishment of print culture traditions in New Zealand, and their initial expression through the production of newspapers, is one mirrored in other colonial territories such as the West Indies, Hawaii, Tahiti, Indonesia, Kenya, and India (Anderson 1983; Cave 1986; Bayly 1996; Finkelstein and Peers 2000; Chakava 2001; Traue 2001). India, for example, witnessed the development of its print communication networks from the mid-1700s onward. While the technology and culture of mass media was at least initially largely borrowed from Europe, its audience was much more fragmented by language, region, and race. Interestingly enough, the British were among the last of the European powers active in India to introduce the printing press into their enclaves. It was not until 1761 that the British in India acquired a press, and even then it was a press that had been taken from the French. Its role was primarily the production of official documents and texts. Printing for popular consumption came much more slowly. The first newspaper in Calcutta was published in 1780, followed by one in Madras in

1785 and Bombay in 1789. By the mid-nineteenth century, newspapers and magazines were common elements in Anglo-Indian life. As one commentator noted in 1851, "The newspaper is as necessary an adjunct to the breakfast table in Calcutta as it is in London" (Hobbes 1851: 362).

Australia witnessed a similar trajectory of printing development. Throughout the nineteenth century there was little domestic book publishing undertaken in Australia; indigenous print production developed after the Gold Rush of the 1850s, and focused on the newspaper and magazine market, along with the undertaking of general trade work. Australian wholesale book distributors, such as George Robertson of Melbourne, circulated mainly British and North American produced titles, albeit with a focus on material of likely colonial interest. Australian writers found outlets for their work through two routes. The first consisted of publication or serialization in diverse local and regional newspapers and literary journals, of which there were many, often short-lived, examples. The second was seeking publication (or, in the case of initial Australian serialization, re-publication) with British publishers, particularly after the successful launch in the 1880s of rival inexpensive paper and cloth bound "colonial series" by Bentley, Sampson and Low, Macmillan, and others. The result was a flowing back to Britain of "raw" material, in this case literary work, which was then recycled in British colonial arenas through being published and sold in the Canadian, Australasian, and Indian markets.

In the last quarter of the nineteenth century, Australian booksellers began to venture into publishing, often through co-publication ventures with British publishers. From the 1890s through to the 1960s, however, the Australian book market would be dominated to an exclusionary extent by British publishers, particularly after the adoption of the Australian Copyright Act of 1912, which "ensured that overseas publishers could dictate the terms of trade and oblige retailers to obtain their supplies from prescribed sources, thus fixing prices and maintaining them at a higher level . . ." (Kirsop 2001: 326). As late as 1961, 40 percent of British books were exported, of which 25 percent were destined for Australia alone (Johanson 2000: 254–82).

Printing and book culture developed at a different pace and much earlier in Canada, but was equally slow in moving beyond "job printing" (handbills, stationery, account books, and so on) and journalistic work to indigenous literary and prose production. As one survey suggests:

> Publishing in Canada began with handwritten manuscripts, circulated privately. This gave way to the newspaper and general publishing output of printing presses using hand-set type, and thence to new technologies as they became available. Distribution of books, in the earliest years, was often by private importation or by purchase from the local printing office, before the population was great enough to support separate bookstores and distribution agents. (MacDonald 2001: 92)

The development of printing followed progressive settlement across Canadian provinces: the printing press arrived first in Halifax in 1751, then Quebec in 1764, Niagara in

1793, and Toronto in 1798. Work undertaken in this early period was usually jobbing printing; other main areas of production included state and religious material as well as newspaper publication. Until the late nineteenth century, the economy of print production and distribution in Canada was a combination of pragmatic, individualistic, and regionalized activity, with individuals functioning along older models combining printing, publishing, and distribution roles. As one commentator notes, "It was not until consolidation began with the arrival of large non-Canadian firms at the beginning of the twentieth century that this changed" (MacDonald 2001: 93).

Literary Agents

This range of national examples demonstrates the extent to which print production and book publishing often evolved along similar lines when successfully exported from Western Europe. At the same time, such print production and communication systems also proved part of a "distinctive, determinate set of interlocking, often contradicting practices" (Feltes 1993: 17). The increasing value ascribed to literary property, for example, created a role for new intermediaries such as literary agents to manage such commodities. Literary agenting would be one of the many innovations that characterized the twentieth-century book market. Agents' expertise in negotiating intellectual property rights in a variety of areas beyond conventional book rights (such as the emerging mass-media areas of film, radio, and, from mid-century onward, television) shifted power to determine literary "value" from publisher to author. Their skill lay in recognizing and perfecting the mediating role of the agent as arbiter and evaluator of literary property, or, more precisely, as one commentator noted, in "participating in, and in fact becoming the source of, the valuation of copyright" (Gillies 1993: 22). Early agents such as A. P. Watt, who began his career in the later 1870s, James Brand Pinker, who began his agency in January 1896, and the formidably successful transatlantic American agent Curtis Brown, who began working in London in 1899, refined and expanded negotiations of material reproduction rights to cover a bewildering range of new outlets extending beyond standard print media boundaries. By 1925, for example, there were common cases of agents negotiating over twenty-six different rights to a book, including rights to playing card and cigarette packet pictures (Joseph 1925: 92–3).

As publishing grew more international in scope, particularly following the creation in the late twentieth century of multinational media conglomerates, the role of the literary agent evolved in scale and importance; agents became the main, initial "filter" of textual material presented for trade publication, replacing the publisher and publisher's reader as the initial arbiter of literary value. The agent became a major mediator in print culture, as well as a significant presence in other media, negotiating contracts and the valuation of individual talent in sports, film, television, radio, and other entertainment arenas. The expansion signaled the continuing enfolding of print culture activity within other communication networks.

Globalization and the Twentieth Century

Such changes in nineteenth-century legal statutes, technology, business practices, and social formations created circumstances by which printed texts, manufactured more quickly and at increasingly cheaper cost, could be sold to more people, generating larger profits for publishers, and allowing individual authors to claim more profits from work produced. Much remained static during the first half of the twentieth-century, though the introduction in Britain of inexpensive Penguin paperback books by Allen Lane in 1935 was a significant moment in international book production. Penguin Books built on past experiments in paperback production, but the combination of visually distinctive covers, unconventional sales outlets, and profitable, original titles in paper rather than cloth covers demonstrated that there was an international mass market eager to purchase cheap paperback versions of popular texts. Lane followed this with the launch of the Pelican label in 1937, designed to market nonfiction titles (McCleery 2002). Other publishers moved to exploit the opportunities of the paperback: in the US, for example, Robert de Graaf founded Pocket Books in 1939, marketing populist titles with gaudy covers to reach wide audiences across the United States; in Britain, Pan Books was started in 1944, while Panther was created around the same time by two ex-servicemen interested in tapping into the market opportunities represented by armed forces personnel. All signaled a shift of focus to mass-market production.

These developments, along with further activities during the second half of the twentieth century, marked a steady move in book publishing to a position strongly dependent on mass-market strategies. As Richard Ohmann comments, "Publishing was the last culture industry to attain modernity. Not until after World War II did it become part of the large corporate sector, and adopt the practices of the publicity and marketing characteristic of monopoly capital" (Ohmann 1998: 22). To increase economies of scale, there was a tendency from the 1960s onward to join publishing houses together through mergers to form large, often transnational conglomerates. The general traits and practices of family-run and focused publishing houses began to be replaced by international corporate and economic business structures. It became part of a move by some to join together different "media platforms" for maximum efficiency and profitability (thus bringing books, newspapers, television, film, and music industries together under one roof).

One of the first corporate moments signaling this shift was the leading US firm Random House's move to public ownership in 1959, its acquisition of the publishers Alfred Knopf in 1960 and Pantheon Books in 1961, then sale to the media giant RCA (Radio Corporation of America) in 1966. Other mergers and acquisitions occurred during the same period: the illustrious Scottish firm Thomas Nelson & Sons, founded in 1798 and for long a pre-eminent source of religious, educational, and such affordable pocketbook series as the famous "Nelson Sevenpenny Classics" (which offered cloth-binding reprints of well-known works at this low price), was taken over by the Anglo-Canadian media corporation Thomson in 1962, then systematically dismantled and amalgamated with other media acquisitions. The photocopying pioneer Xerox moved into the educational and ancillary print and information market through purchasing and merging University Microfilms, Inc. in 1962, American Education Publications in 1964, and R. R. Bowker Co. in 1967. On the European continent in 1965 the eminent German publisher S. Fischer (founded as a family firm in 1887) was sold to Holtzbrinck, a large financial firm that included Germany's largest book club in their holdings. The US educational giant Houghton Mifflin became a public stock company in 1967. In 1968 the long-established British family firm of Longman was bought out and amalgamated with the multinational conglomerate Pearson. Longman Pearson in turn took over Penguin in 1970. Such takeovers matched the general trend in national and international publishing sectors; the annual merger rates in US publishing, for example, grew similarly quickly throughout the 1960s, peaking in 1968 at 47 and declining only slightly to 44 in 1969 (Coser et al. 1985: 25–6).

A noticeable trend in the latter part of the twentieth-century global book economy was its phenomenal expansion. It has been estimated that in 1850 annual world book title production totaled 50,000; in 1952, it had risen to 250,000 titles; by 1963, it equaled 400,000; in 1970, 521,000 (Escarpit 1966: 57–8; Milner 1996: 70; Zaid 2004: 21). Four language groups (English, French, German, and Spanish) dominated, accounting together for between 34 and 36 percent of these titles (Escarpit 1966: 61–2). As the dominance of multinational organizations in the book market increased, there was also a shift in who dominated international book markets, particularly in the anglophone world. Whereas in the nineteenth century, Britain led the way in terms of creating, defining, and exporting book-trade initiatives, in the mid-twentieth century, with the loss of its colonies as captive markets and the takeover and merger of many of its family-based firms, there was a noticeable shift toward the US and European rivals as significant players in the world market.

Three other important developments also took place in the global book market between 1800 and 1970, as Andrew Milner points out. First, there was a move away from fiction to nonfiction titles, or what Robert Escarpit has called "functional books," particularly textbooks, providing "powerful testament to the commercial significance of the captive market delivered to the book trade by the systems of higher and secondary education" (Milner 1996: 70) Secondly, there was an expansion of "non-bookshop" distribution networks: mass-market distribution of book titles through non-traditional retail outlets (such as newsagents, supermarkets, department stores, and book clubs). A survey in the US in 1969, for example, found that "four general books out of five bought by or for individual American adults came to them from book-club or mass-market channels" (quoted in Milner 1996: 70). The phenomenon was replicated in other countries with developed book-distribution structures. Finally, the rise of the paperback as a significant vehicle for mass-market distribution of books in inexpensive formats enabled texts to reach far wider audiences worldwide than ever before. Whether that reach was enough to maintain the position of books as important communication tools in the increasingly globalized world media and information economy of the last quarter of the twentieth century is the subject of other chapters in this book.

References and Further Reading

Anderson, Benedict (1983) *Imagined Communities.* London: Verso.

Bayly, C. A. (1996) *Empire and Information: Intelligence Gathering and Social Communication in India 1780–1870.* Cambridge: Cambridge University Press.

Briggs, Asa and Burke, Peter (2002) *A Social History of the Media, from Gutenberg to the Internet.* London: Polity.

Cave, Roderick (1986) *Printing and the Book Trade in the West Indies.* London: Pindar.

Chakava, Henry (2001) "The Origins and Development of Publishing Systems in English-speaking Africa: In Search of an Independent Model." In Jacques Michon and Jean-Yves Mollier (eds.), *Les Mutations du livre et de l'édition dans le monde du XVIIIe siècle à l'an 2000,* pp. 339–49. L'Harmattan: Les Presses de L'Université Laval.

Chartier, Roger (1981) "L'ancien regime typographique: reflexions sur quelques travaux recents." *Annales ES,* 36: 191–209.

Coser, L. A., Kadushkin, C., and Powell, W. W. (1985) *Books: The Culture and Commerce of Publishing.* Chicago: University of Chicago Press.

Duguid, Paul (1996) "Material Matters: The Past and Futurology of the Book." In Geoffrey Nunberg (ed.), *The Future of the Book,* pp. 63–101. Berkeley: University of California Press.

Eggert, Paul (2003) "Robbery under Arms: The Colonial Market, Imperial Publishers, and the Demise of the Three-Decker Novel." *Book History,* 6: 127–47.

Escarpit, Robert (1966) *The Book Revolution.* London: George G. Harrap.

Feltes, N. N. (1986) *Modes of Production of Victorian Novels.* Chicago: University of Chicago Press.

— (1993) *Literary Capital and the Late Victorian Novel.* Madison: University of Wisconsin Press.

Finkelstein, David and McCleery, Alistair (2005) *An Introduction to Book History.* London: Routledge.

— and Peers, Douglas Mark (2000) " 'A Great System of Circulation': Introducing India into the Nineteenth-century Media." In David Finkelstein and Mark Douglas Peers (eds.), *Negotiating India in the Nineteenth-century Media,* pp. 1–23. Basingstoke: Macmillan.

Gedin, Per (1982) *Literature in the Marketplace,* trans. G. Bisset. London: Faber and Faber.

Giddens, Anthony (1990) *The Consequences of Modernity.* Stanford: Stanford University Press.

Gillies, Mary Ann (1993) "A. P. Watt, Literary Agent." *Publishing Research Quarterly,* 9 (spring): 20–34.

Greco, Albert (1995) "Mergers and Acquisitions in the US Book Industry, 1960–1989." In Philip G. Altbach and Edith S. Hoshino (eds.), *International Book Publishing: An Encyclopedia,* pp. 229–42. New York: Garland.

Griest, Guinevere (1970) *Mudie's Circulating Library and the Victorian Novel.* Bloomington: Indiana University Press.

Hall, David D. (1996) *Cultures of Print: Essays in the History of the Book.* Amherst: University of Massachusetts Press.

Held, David, McGrew, Anthony, Goldblatt, David, and Perraton, Jonathan (1999) *Global Transformations: Politics, Economics and Culture.* London: Polity.

Hobbes, Robert George (1851) "Calcutta." *Bentley's Miscellany,* 30: 361–8.

Johanson, Graeme (2000) *Colonial Editions in Australia, 1842–1972.* Wellington, NZ: Elibank.

Johnson-Woods, Toni (2000) "The Virtual Reading Communities of the *London Journal,* the *New York Ledger* and the *Australian Journal.*" In Laurel Brake, B. Bell, and D. Finkelstein (eds.), *Nineteenth-century Media and the Construction of Identities,* pp. 350–62. Basingstoke: Palgrave.

Joseph, Michael (1925) *The Commercial Side of Literature.* London: Hutchinson.

Kirsop, Wallace (2001) "From Colonialism to the Multinationals: The Fragile Growth of Australian Publishing and its Contribution to the Global Anglophone Reading Community." In Jacques Michon and Jean-Yves Mollier (eds.), *Les Mutations du livre et de l'édition dans le monde du XVIIIe siècle à l'an 2000,* pp. 324–9. L'Harmattan: Les Presses de L'Université Laval.

McCleery, Alistair (2002) "The Return of the Individual to Book History: The Case of Allen Lane." *Book History,* 5: 85–114.

MacDonald, Mary Lu (2001) "The Modification of European Models: English Canada before

1890." In Jacques Michon and Jean-Yves Mollier (eds.), *Les Mutations du livre et de l'édition dans le monde du XVIIIe siècle à l'an 2000*, pp. 84–93. L'Harmattan: Les Presses de L'Université Laval.

Michon, Jacques and Mollier, Jean-Yves (eds.) (2001) *Les Mutations du livre et de l'édition dans le monde du XVIIIe siècle à l'an 2000*. L'Harmattan: Les Presses de L'Université Laval.

Milner, Andrew (1996) *Literature, Culture and Society*. London: UCL Press.

de la Motte, Dean and Przyblyski, Jeannene M. (eds.) (1999) *Making the News: Modernity and the Mass Press in Nineteenth-century France*. Amherst: University of Massachusetts Press.

Ohmann, R. (1998) *Selling Culture: Magazines, Markets, and Class at the Turn of the Century*. London: Verso.

Schiffrin, André (2001) *The Business of Books: How the International Conglomerates Took Over Publishing and Changed the Way We Read*. London: Verso.

Secord, James A. (2000) *Victorian Sensation: The Extraordinary Publication, Reception, and Secret Authorship of Vestiges of the Natural History of Creation*. Chicago: University of Chicago Press.

Traue, J. E. (1997) "But why Mulgan, Marris and Schroder?: The Mutation of the Local Newspaper in New Zealand's Colonial Print Culture." *Bibliographical Society of Australia and New Zealand Bulletin*, 21 (2): 107–15.

— (2001) "The Two Histories of the Book in New Zealand." *Bibliographical Society of Australia and New Zealand Bulletin*, 25 (1): 8–16.

Williams, Raymond (1966) *Culture and Society 1780–1950*. London: Pelican.

Wirtén, Eva Hemmungs (1998) *Global Infatuation: Explorations in Transnational Publishing and Texts*. Uppsala: University of Uppsala Literature Department.

— (2003) *No Trespassing: Authorship, Intellectual Property Rights, and the Boundaries of Globalisation*. Toronto: University of Toronto Press.

Zaid, Gabriel (2004) *So Many Books*. London: Sort of Books.

25

Modernity and Print I: Britain 1890–1970

Jonathan Rose

Around 1890, the British book trade became modern, in several important senses of the term. First, it organized to protect its interests. The Society of Authors had been launched by Walter Besant in 1884, followed by the Associated Booksellers of Great Britain and Ireland in 1895 and the Publishers' Association in 1896. On January 1, 1900, these three organizations brought into force the Net Book Agreement, under which publishers could force booksellers to sell their books at a fixed price. This prevented the kind of ruinous discounting which, by the 1880s, was bankrupting booksellers and squeezing all but the best selling books out of the marketplace.

The main objective of the Society of Authors was to secure international copyright protection, which soon became a fixture of the modern literary world. The Berne Convention was ratified in 1887, and the Chace Act of 1891 brought the United States into the global system of literary property. Macmillan and Oxford University Press took advantage of the newly protected American market in 1896, when they both set up subsidiary companies in New York.

Meanwhile, the balance of literary trade was shifting. Through much of the nineteenth century, the American book trade had been "postcolonial": dependent on cheap British imports and British literary models. Consequently, it did not serve American interests to respect international copyright. But, by 1891, the United States was finally becoming a major literary power: the Chace Act was ratified largely because Mark Twain and Bret Harte were now valuable export industries that were worth protecting. As the twentieth century progressed, American authors increasingly penetrated the British market, while it became less easy to market British authors to Americans. Between the world wars, Winston Churchill's books did not sell well in the United States, though they were published by the distinguished house of Scribner. In contrast, *Inside Europe* (1936), by American journalist John Gunther, sold more than 100,000 copies in the UK in less than two years: it alerted the British public to the Nazi menace at a time when their own media treated Hitler with complacency, if not sympathy. The obscenely violent *No Orchids for Miss Blandish* (1939) sold half a million copies, making it the most popular novel in wartime Britain, where many readers assumed that the author (James Hadley Chase) was American. In fact, he was the son of an English army officer, but Chase knew what British readers wanted: he learned the conventions of hard-boiled American crime fiction from James M. Cain, and (with the help of an American slang dictionary) he banged out *No Orchids* over six weekends.

By 1890, most publishing firms were no longer one-man enterprises. They had become modern corporate business organizations, where publishers delegated responsibilities to specialized employees or departments dealing with editorial matters, marketing, or publicity. Screening of manuscripts was commonly devolved to professional readers, which had probably existed in some form since the 1830s. Edward Garnett was the most brilliant publisher's reader of his day: he worked at various times for T. Fisher Unwin, Gerald Duckworth, and Jonathan Cape, nurturing the talents of Joseph Conrad and D. H. Lawrence. Frank Swinnerton lifted Chatto and Windus out of a literary slump, securing Aldous Huxley, *The Great Gatsby*, and Constance Garnett's translations of Chekhov (though he would have nothing to do with Ezra Pound and William Carlos Williams).

The literary agent was a more recent invention. The first, A. P. Watt, began work around 1875, followed by J. B. Pinker (1896) and Curtis Brown (1899). Initially, publishers denounced them as parasites and useless middlemen, and a few of them were frauds: Arthur Addison Bright cheated J. M. Barrie out of £16,000 before killing himself in 1906. But the agent clearly provided a necessary service in a modern and increasingly complex literary marketplace. As the number of publishers increased, each one developing a specialized list, the literary agent knew how to match the right author with the right firm, maximizing earnings for both. When a publisher purchased the copyright to a book, an agent could help sell the serial, overseas, translation, dramatic, film, and broadcast rights to other outlets. The agent also served useful editorial functions, helping authors to refine manuscripts and tailor them to specific markets and reading publics. Inevitably, agents began to specialize, with Watt retaining mainstream authors such as Rudyard Kipling, H. Rider Haggard, Lewis Carroll, and Arthur Conan Doyle. More experimental writers (Conrad, Lawrence, H. G. Wells, James Joyce, Henry James) were cultivated by Pinker, who had to work harder to sell them to editors and often advanced them money while they were still struggling to find an audience. By 1939, there were fifty-six UK literary agencies, rising to seventy-eight by 1974.

Dickens, George Eliot, and Anthony Trollope were probably the last novelists who addressed the entire English reading public, which, by 1890, was fragmenting into several different publics reading different kinds of books. Accordingly, publishers began to develop focused lists. Ward Lock specialized in light bestsellers by H. Rider Haggard, E. Phillips Oppenheim, and Edgar Wallace. Routledge and Kegan Paul developed a strong philosophy list, edited first by C. K. Ogden and later by A. J. Ayer. Swan Sonnenschein concentrated on sociology and socialism, including the first English translation of *Das Kapital* (1886). George Allen and Unwin also published leftist intellectuals (J. A. Hobson, Bertrand Russell, Harold Laski, Gandhi), as did Secker and Warburg (George Orwell) and Victor Gollancz, though Gollancz also had a strong stable of detective writers (Dorothy L. Sayers). B. T. Batsford specialized in architecture for both professional and general readers: the term "Batsford book" immediately called to mind their distinctively designed volumes on country life. Basil Blackwell focused on poetry, classic reprints, textbooks, and (later) science and medicine. Burns and Oates published for Roman Catholics, A. R. Mowbray for Anglo-Catholics. Frederick Warne produced children's books written by Beatrix Potter and illustrated by Kate Greenaway, Walter Crane, and Randolph Caldecott. Mills and Boon began as a general publisher in 1908, but when the Great Depression created a demand for escapist romance, the company concentrated on that subgenre. And when Stanley Paul found that it could not compete with larger literary houses, it turned to its forte, sports and hobbies.

A small circle of publishers was responsible for all the great works of Victorian fiction, but around 1890 several new and innovative firms opened for business. William Heinemann scored a stunning success with his very first book, Hall Caine's *The Bondsman* (1890), with sales of 450,000. His subsequent publication of Caine's *The Manxman* (1894) in a one-volume, six-shilling format helped render the Victorian three-decker novel obsolete. His firm would publish Henrik Ibsen, Henry James, H. G. Wells, John Masefield, D. H. Lawrence, George Moore, Robert Louis Stevenson, Israel Zangwill, W. E. Henley's magazine the *New Review*, and John Galsworthy's *Forsyte Saga*. As an editor for Methuen (founded 1889), W. E. Henley recruited Kipling, Wells, Henry James, and W. B. Yeats. The firm also published T. S. Eliot, Edgar Rice Burroughs, the complete works of Oscar Wilde, and Albert Einstein's *Relativity*. Edward Arnold (founded 1890) had E. M. Forster and Leonard Woolf; Archibald Constable (also 1890) had George Meredith and George Bernard Shaw. After Oscar Wilde was imprisoned in 1895, Leonard Smithers published the avant-garde literature that other firms were afraid to touch, including Aubrey Beardsley, Arthur Symons, and Wilde's own *Ballad of Reading Gaol* (1898). Grant Richards (founded 1897) produced typographically innovative editions of Shaw's plays, as well as Samuel Butler, Baron Corvo, Ronald Firbank, Osbert and Sacheverell Sitwell, A. E. Housman's *A Shropshire Lad*, and James Joyce's *Dubliners*. Gerald Duckworth (1898) published Lawrence, Virginia Woolf (his half-sister), the early works of Evelyn Waugh, and the plays of John Galsworthy (though he refused *The Man of Property*).

These new publishers were all exploiting a growing niche market for modernist literature. Until fairly recently, critics took the modernists at their own valuation: as pure artists who utterly rejected commercialism. But once book historians like James G. Nelson (1989), Peter McDonald (1997), Joyce Piell Wexler (1997), and Lawrence Rainey (1998) began looking at publishers' ledgers and literary agents' correspondence, it became apparent that modernist authors and publishers were in fact shrewd profit-maximizing entrepreneurs. The Bodley Head, founded in 1889 by Charles Elkin Mathews and John Lane, was the fount of the poetry revival of the 1890s, publishing Richard Le Gallienne, John Davidson, Oscar Wilde, and the *Yellow Book*. Mathews and Lane worked out an ingenious formula for making poetry pay: they bought at bargain prices leftovers of fine paper, on which they printed a few verses, using large type, generous leading, and enormous margins, and they left the pages "uncut." The visual effect was wonderfully artistic. Their advertisements emphasized the small print-runs (often no more than 500), which persuaded customers that they were acquiring something like a private press book. Only a philistine would have pointed out that they were getting very little poetry for the money, or that the royalties paid were minimal. As Margaret Stetz recognized, "John Lane devised the first modern sales campaign in publishing: the first to focus not on individual authors or titles, but on an entire line of new and unfamiliar merchandise; the first to create and to sell an image of the publishing firm itself" (Stetz 1991: 75). It also sold its customers an alluring self-image: anyone who bought a Bodley Head book was clearly a person of taste and discernment. Leonard Woolf likewise claimed that the Hogarth Press published books that commercial publishers would not touch, but he was a good businessman, and the press eventually generated a steady profit from the novels of Virginia Woolf and translations of Sigmund Freud. Joyce and Lawrence resorted to publishing limited editions of *Ulysses* (1922) and *Lady Chatterley's Lover* (1928) with private presses in France, a lucrative strategy for "marketing modernism," although (argues Joyce Wexler 1997) it limited their readership and deprived them of the editorial discipline they would have found in the mainstream literary marketplace.

That said, highbrow critics were not entirely wrong to perceive a disturbing trend toward lower-middlebrow literature. According to the *Bookseller*, before 1914 a publisher could print 1,000 copies of a novel, sell half of them, and still break even; but after the war, one had to sell as many as 2,000 to make a profit, thanks to sharply increased production costs. To hold down those expenses, the typical length limit for novels was reduced from 200,000 to 130,000 words. These economic forces discouraged experimentalism and well-developed narratives in favor of quick and easy formula fiction.

The modernists also had good reason to protest that they were victims of puritanism. The Obscene Publications Act became law in 1857, and in 1889 Henry Vizetelly was jailed for publishing Zola, though he claimed that the translations cleaned up the most offensive passages. Grant Richards published *Dubliners* (1914) only after he prevailed upon Joyce to remove some risqué language. When D. H. Lawrence's *The Rainbow* (1915) was suppressed, Methuen did not attempt to defend it. In 1928, Jonathan Cape fought the ban on Radclyffe Hall's *The Well of Loneliness*, but his barrister bungled the defense, falsely claiming that the novel did not portray lesbianism, and the case was lost.

In 1953, Secker and Warburg secured an acquittal for Stanley Kauffmann's *The Philanderer*, on the grounds that a book must be assessed as a whole and not condemned merely for a few obscene passages. That decision led to a more liberal Obscene Publications Act in 1959, which exempted books with real literary value. Allen Lane tested the new law by publishing an unexpurgated *Lady Chatterley's Lover* as a Penguin paperback. This was a serious gamble: it seems to be a universal law of censorship that the likelihood of suppression varies inversely with the price of the book. As chairman of the Bodley Head, Lane had slipped James Joyce's *Ulysses* past the Home Office by publishing first an expensive limited edition (1936) and later a cheaper trade edition (1937). But the authorities chose to prosecute the Penguin *Lady Chatterley*, priced at only 3s 6d, a point hammered home by the prosecuting attorney. "Is it a book you would even wish your wife or your servants to read?" he asked, evidently unaware that three of the jurors were women (who quite possibly enjoyed reading it). Penguin spent £12,777 on the trial and stockpiled 200,000 copies, but their victory made it a worthwhile investment. In just six weeks, two million copies of the paperback were sold, generating a profit of £62,000. Its success allowed the company to go public in April 1961: the shares (popularly known as "Chatterleys") sold spectacularly (McCleery 2002: 169–78). *Lady Chatterley* was not the last literary work to be prosecuted for obscenity: Calder and Boyars had to defend Hubert Selby, Jr.'s *Last Exit to Brooklyn* in 1966 and ultimately won on appeal.

The era of modern literature was also the heyday of cheap uniform reprints. These series had proliferated ever since *Donaldson* v. *Becket* (1774) established that copyrighted works eventually entered the public domain. But after 1890, near-universal literacy, rising working-class and lower middle-class incomes, cheap mass-market publishing, and an ethic of "self-improvement" made it possible to sell inexpensive classics on an unprecedented scale. W. T. Stead began his Penny Poets series in May 1895; by October 1897, he had sixty volumes and well over five million copies in print. J. M. Dent's "Everyman's Library" was inaugurated in 1906 with a plan to publish one thousand volumes of the best works of world literature, though that goal would only be reached fifty years later. It offered all the predictable standbys, but it was not so narrow as some critics of the "traditional canon" have charged: American, Russian, and female authors were well represented, and some effort was made to include modern and Asian literature. By 1975, more than 60 million Everyman volumes had been sold worldwide, an invaluable resource for students and autodidacts.

A more modern method of selling still cheaper and more popular reprints was pioneered by Allen Lane's Penguin Books. Lane certainly did not invent the paperback: in the nineteenth century, American dime novels, the Tauchnitz series of Germany, and most books published in France had paper covers. Penguins were very similar in format to (and undoubtedly inspired by) Albatross Books, a paperback series that had been published out of Germany for the British tourist market since 1932. Like Tauchnitz and Albatross, Lane purchased paperback reprint rights from various publishers and authors, the first British publisher to do so. But his real innovation lay in his marketing strategy: very low price (sixpence), very high volume (initial print-runs of at least 20,000, with a break-even point at 17,500), and sales though unconventional outlets (Woolworth's). Penguins were perhaps the first truly classless books in Britain: affordable for everyone, yet packaged in an attractively democratic format that would appeal to all readers, however genteel. And Lane chose authors who combined literary talent with popular appeal: the first batch of Penguins in 1935 included Mary Webb, Dorothy L. Sayers, Compton Mackenzie, and Ernest Hemingway's *A Farewell to Arms*. Penguin Classics began in 1945 with a prose translation of *The Odyssey*, which sold more than a million copies in fifteen years. Soon Penguins had serious competitors. Pan Books was launched in 1944; by 1965, it was selling 21 million copies, of which James Bond was responsible for 6 million. In 1969, Penguin was still the market leader, selling 27 million paperbacks, but it had to share the field with Fontana (13 million), Corgi (13 million), and Panther (9 million); the last had been launched by two RAF veterans with no publishing experience.

Modern mass-market publishing inevitably produced a nostalgic reaction: the private press movement. When William Morris founded the Kelmscott Press in 1891, he radically rethought the art of printing, which he mastered from scratch at a fairly advanced age. Based on a careful study of incunabula, he designed type founts and watermarks, secured supplies of fine papers, and even insisted on ink made from traditional ingredients. His typography involved eliminating white space through narrow leading and tight word spacing; integrating and balancing text, ornaments, and illustrations; and designing facing pages as a visual whole. Many of the fifty-three titles produced by his hand presses were works of medieval literature, some of them originally printed by William Caxton. As a socialist influenced by Marx, Morris was convinced that the alienation of labor could be ended only by reviving handcraft methods of production. He paid his workers reasonably well and gave them considerable autonomy. However, Morris was still in charge of the press, and he was not completely averse to using modern print technology, such as electrotypes. And, of course, like all the best private printers, he produced expensive works for affluent collectors.

In 1898, C. R. Ashbee bought William Morris's two Albion presses and carried on the Kelmscott tradition with his own Essex House Press. T. J. Cobden-Sanderson set up a bindery to serve the Kelmscott Press, and when it closed, he established his own Doves Press. Its most famous book, the Doves Bible (1903–5), employed strikingly clean and simple typography that contrasted sharply with Kelmscott ornateness. C. H. St. John Hornby's Ashendene Press printed an edition of Dante (1906–9), which has been compared to the Kelmscott Chaucer. James Guthrie bought one of Kelmscott presses for his own Pear Tree Press, but went much farther than Morris in abolishing the division of labor: for the most part, he edited, hand printed, and marketed his own books. As managed by Elizabeth Yeats and her brother, William Butler Yeats, the Dun Emer Press (later renamed the Cuala Press) combined an Arts and Crafts movement sensibility with Irish cultural nationalism and feminism (the production workers were women). The Gregynog Press (founded 1927) emphasized Welsh culture and exceptionally fine bindings. And the gorgeous colors of French Impressionism were introduced into English typography by the Eragny Press, begun in 1894 by the husband-and-wife team of Lucien and Esther Pissarro.

Book artistry was not necessarily incompatible with mass marketing. J. M. Dent had been a master bookbinder, and his early "Everyman's Library" volumes were designed in a William Morris style by Reginald Knowles, with hand-lettered titles and floral ornaments stamped on the spine in gold. St. John Hornby not only created the Ashendene Press, he was also a partner of W. H. Smith, which would retain Eric Gill to design a distinctive Trajan type for their shop fronts, hire Douglas Cockerell to run a quality bindery, and acquire Bernard Newdigate's Arden Press. The latter published a number of finely printed guides on bookshop management, emphasizing the importance of attractive interiors and window dressing. Smith's appreciated the importance of aesthetics in modern bookselling: the cluttered seediness of their nineteenth-century railway bookstalls gave way to a more tasteful, clean décor that appealed to twentieth-century consumers.

One distinctively modern method of book marketing bypassed bookshops altogether. In 1905, the Times Book Club had been established as a circulation-boosting device: subscribers to the newspaper were entitled to borrow books from the club or purchase them at a large discount. The first true UK book club was the Book Society, founded in 1929. Unlike its American predecessors, the Book of the Month Club and the Literary Guild, the Book Society did not print books itself: it purchased them in bulk from publishers and retailed them at the net price to its members. Victor Gollancz's Left Book Club (founded 1936) published original books with distinctive orange covers and had 50,000 members by 1939. His club was not (strictly speaking) Communist, but before 1940 it rarely strayed far from the party line. Its most famous book, George Orwell's *The Road to Wigan Pier*, aroused some indignation with its criticisms of the Soviet Union: Gollancz only published it after adding an apologetic preface. The Readers' Union (founded 1937) took the step of offering reprinted books at steeply discounted prices. Not until 1968 did the Publishers' Association and the Booksellers' Association agree to allow book clubs to publish books for their members simultaneously with trade editions available in bookstores. Book clubs proliferated in the 1960s, many of them under the umbrella of W. H. Smith. But since most readers had access to good bookshops, clubs never accounted for more than 5 percent of book sales in this period, far less than in the United States.

Of course, book readers were not necessarily book buyers. A 1940 survey found that while 55 percent of working-class adults read books, only 24 percent bought books, and just 16 percent patronized public libraries. In this social stratum, books were still often borrowed from workmates, inherited from grandparents, won as school prizes, or scavenged from rubbish bins. Many families acquired the complete works of Shakespeare or Dickens by clipping promotional coupons from cigarette packets and newspapers. For middle-class patrons in search of light mysteries and romances, W. H. Smith and Boots offered circulating libraries. Boots Booklovers Library flourished from 1898 to 1966. During World War II, the company had a million subscribers and purchased 1.25 million volumes a year, which made it a force to be reckoned with in the publishing world.

The Public Libraries Act of 1850 permitted (but did not require) localities to levy property taxes to support libraries. At first, only a few were created, and they were often intimidating places, where readers had to ask librarians to fetch books from closed stacks. Only after 1890 was there a characteristically modern effort to make libraries user-friendly. In 1894, Clerkenwell inaugurated the first lending library with open stacks, though most libraries did not adopt that practice until after World War I. Open access did not dramatically increase book thefts, as pessimists had predicted, but it could result in overcrowding, as new patrons flocked to the shelves. Around the turn of the century, Croydon public library pioneered innovative outreach activities, including public lectures, a magazine for readers, exhibits of technical books, a lending library of photographs, an index to periodical literature, topical reading lists, and a public information service. After 1920, the word "information" became more and more common in library literature, emphasizing the provision of the kind of data necessary to a modern industrial economy. In the 1920s, library vans were introduced in rural areas, where a great effort was made to set up village branch libraries. The first urban bookmobile, or "bibliobus," was inaugurated in Manchester in 1931.

All these efforts contributed to a striking increase in library coverage and usage. In 1884–5, just 23 percent of the British population were served by public libraries, rising to 60 percent by 1913–14 (though only 46 percent in Wales) and nearly universal service by 1934–5. In 1875–7, libraries annually issued only 0.92 books per head of population in the areas they served, increasing to 1.33 issues in 1913–14, 3.69 issues in 1934–5, and 11.67 issues in 1971–2.

Public libraries were a countercyclical business: usage surged in economic slumps and declined again when prosperity returned. In the 1920s and 1930s, workers "on the dole" spent much of their time in the stacks, where they could easily get through three or four books a week. Cheap crime thrillers, romances, and westerns could be had at two-penny circulating libraries, which proliferated in the slums: in York in 1938, they loaned out half as many volumes as the public libraries. Although many librarians feared that the picture palaces were distracting the masses from true literature, a movie version of a classic could send readers scrambling to borrow the book, as was the case with *Romeo and Juliet* (1937) and *Pride and Prejudice* (1940).

A 1962–3 survey of London found that, while professionals, executives, and managers made up 17 percent of the national population, they accounted for 45.8 percent of library members. Manual or lower clerical workers, 58 percent of the total population, were just 33.1 percent of library members. This represented a dramatic shift from the Victorian period: in 1876, Leeds reported that 81 percent of its lending library patrons were working class.

Because public libraries were slow to penetrate the coal valleys of South Wales, colliers set up their own libraries, more than a hundred by 1934. They were supported by deductions from their wages and (after 1920) by taxes on coal production. The average collection was about 3,000 volumes, though the impressive Tredegar Workmen's Institute circulated as many as 100,000 annually, and at one point devoted £60 of its £300 acquisitions budget to philosophy. Mainly these libraries loaned out thrillers, romances, westerns, and other popular fiction, but there was also demand for English classics and (in a few leftist coal towns) Marxist literature. Cooperative societies also sponsored workers' libraries: the Royal Arsenal branch at Woolwich had a collection of 10,000 volumes in the 1930s. Nearly all of these independent proletarian libraries were defunct by 1970, victims of universal public-library service and the decline of a working-class tradition of intellectual self-improvement.

That tradition was still very much alive in the first half of the twentieth century. After the first large bloc of Labour Party MPs was elected in 1906, the *Review of Reviews* asked them which books and authors had shaped their worldviews: John Ruskin was named most often, followed by Charles Dickens, the Bible, Thomas Carlyle, Henry George, Walter Scott, John Stuart Mill, and William Shakespeare (very few mentioned

Karl Marx). A 1940 study found that in working-class secondary schools, where education ended at the age of 14, students averaged six to seven books a month outside
required school reading. Impressively, 62 percent of boys and 84 percent of girls read
poetry outside school: they were partial to Kipling, Longfellow, Masefield, Blake,
Tennyson, and Wordsworth. Fervent literary discussions could take place in mineshafts,
as one Nottinghamshire collier recalled: "Tha wants ter read Shelley's stuff. That's
poetry!" (quoted in Rose 2001: 242). But employers did not always approve of well-read
workers. Housemaid Margaret Powell was fond of Dickens, Conrad, and Proust, so she
asked the lady of the house:

> if I could borrow a book from her library to read, and I can now see the surprised look
> on her face. She said, "Yes, of course, certainly you can, Margaret," adding "but I didn't
> know you could read." They knew that you breathed and you slept and you worked, but
> they didn't know that you *read*. Such a thing was beyond comprehension. They thought
> that in your spare time you sat and gazed into space, or looked at *Peg's Paper* or the
> *Crimson Circle*. You could almost see them reporting you to their friends. "Margaret's a
> good cook, but unfortunately she reads. Books, you know." (quoted in Rose 2001: 25)

Granted, Margaret was hardly a typical case. Which books, then, were average
British readers buying and reading? Those are two different questions, and the answers
depend on the methodologies used by historians. Collating eighty-three public library
catalogues published between 1883 and 1912, Simon Eliot (1992) concluded that the
most heavily stocked novelists were Mary Elizabeth Braddon, Walter Scott, Mrs. Henry
Wood, and Charles Dickens, followed by Margaret Oliphant, E. Bulwer Lytton, Char-
lotte Yonge, and R. M. Ballantyne. Note the prominence of female authors. Troy Bassett
and Christina Walter (2001) used booksellers' reports published in *The Bookman*, a literary monthly, to reconstruct bestseller lists for 1891–1906, and arrived at different
results. Their top ten authors (in descending order) were S. R. Crockett, Marie Corelli,
Rudyard Kipling, Ian Maclaren, Stanley Weyman, Robert Louis Stevenson, Arthur
Conan Doyle, Elizabeth Thorneycroft Fowler, J. M. Barrie, and Mrs. Humphry Ward.
Note the insularity: the most popular writers were all British. The bestselling foreign
author was Emile Zola, in fourteenth place, in spite (or perhaps because) of efforts to
censor his work. Far lower on the list were Mark Twain and Leo Tolstoy. Eighty years
after his death, Walter Scott was still in fifteenth place. Nonfiction bestsellers predict-
ably included war and imperial memoirs, as well as a guide to bodybuilding by Eugene
Sandow, but also some remarkably serious philosophy and religion, such as A. J.
Balfour's *The Foundations of Belief* and Bishop Charles Gore's *Lux Mundi*.

Measured by documented sales, the most popular novelists of the early twentieth
century included the romance writers Marie Corelli (who averaged 100,000 books annually) and Ethel M. Dell (whose formulas would be explicitly copied by Barbara Cart-
land). Hall Caine's 1901 *The Eternal City* sold more than a million, and Charles Garvice
enjoyed better than 7 million total sales between 1899 and 1920, while Nat Gould
hammered out several popular racing novels each year. Mrs. Henry Wood's 1861

tearjerker *East Lynne* had nearly a million copies in print by World War I, most of them sold after 1889. Florence Barclay's 1909 romance *The Rosary* surpassed the one-million mark, and Elinor Glyn's notoriously sexy *Three Weeks* (1907) topped two million. These authors made "bestseller" a dirty word among more serious writers like H. G. Wells, though his *The Outline of History* would be one of the most widely read nonfiction books of the 1920s. A. J. Cronin's *The Citadel* (1937), which sold more than 40,000 copies in nine days, proved that a novelist could address a serious social issue (in this case, national health-care policy) and still break sales records.

All the same, a 1947 survey of Middlesex libraries found that the most popular authors were still fairly lightweight: Hugh Walpole, Warwick Deeping, Jeffrey Farnol, P. G. Wodehouse, A. E. W. Mason, and John Buchan. Only one-eighth of the fiction loaned represented "acknowledged classics and modern novelists who are appreciated in particular for the power and style of their writing" (Kelly 1977: 382). The intellectual difficulty of modernist literature initially limited its appeal, though it would eventually find a mass audience: E. M. Forster's *Howards End* (1910) sold not quite 10,000 copies in its first three years, but a quarter of a million as a Penguin paperback (1942).

As George Orwell noted in his essay "Boys' Weeklies," school stories were a strikingly popular subgenre of children's literature. By 1940, school stories accounted for one of every eight books read by boys in working-class secondary schools, and one in four among the girls. These yarns efficiently and thoroughly indoctrinated their readers in public-school values, as hatter Frederick Willis cheerfully recalled:

> We learnt that boys of the higher class boarding schools were courageous, honourable, and chivalrous, and steeped in the traditions of the school and loyalty to the country. We tried to mould our lives according to this formula. Needless to say, we fell very short of this desirable end, and I attributed our failure to the fact that we were only board school boys and could never hope to emulate those of finer clay. Nevertheless, the constant effort did us a lot of good. We thought British people were the salt of the earth . . . The object of our education was to train us to become honest, God-fearing, useful workmen, and I have no complaints against this very sensible arrangement. (quoted in Rose 2001: 323)

Literary criticism was dominated by the mainstream *Times Literary Supplement* (founded 1902), which peaked at 49,000 circulation in 1950. Highbrow reviews appealed to much smaller "minority" audiences: the leftist *Calendar of Modern Letters* started with 7,000 subscribers and dropped to 1,000; T. S. Eliot's *Criterion* had only 800; *Scrutiny* never more than 1,500. The brilliant, irascible, dogmatic F. R. Leavis used *Scrutiny* as a personal platform to denounce middlebrow writers and champion the very few authors he thought worth reading. Leavis himself wrote 15 percent of the articles in the journal: most of the rest were produced by his acolytes, including his wife, Queenie. She sneered at *John o' London's Weekly* (published 1919–54), a literary review aimed at the not-very-educated classes, but it attained a circulation of 100,000 in the 1930s.

The stress of World War II actually increased demand for books, out of a need for distraction, for understanding the world situation, or for something to do during long blackouts. In Halifax, public library loans jumped from 716,000 in 1938 to just over a million in 1945. A librarian reported that in Coventry, devastated by the Luftwaffe, "the distribution of reading matter to the people has become almost as necessary as the distribution of food," and bombed-out areas were served by bookmobiles (quoted in McAleer 1992: 51). In February 1940, 62 percent of adults were reading a book, falling to 51 percent in 1941 and 45 percent in 1946–7. And in 1944, Dickens, Hardy, and Jane Austen were the second, third, and fourth most frequently borrowed novelists at the Bristol public libraries. In the face of rising demand "You just sold out," one publisher remembered. "You didn't have to do anything in fact – people *begged* you for them, the suppliers, the booksellers, the wholesalers" (quoted in McAleer 1992: 52).

Yet the war also constricted the supply of books. Paper was rationed, beginning in March 1940, when publishers were allowed only 60 percent of what they had used in 1938–9. The proportion fell to 37.5 percent by January 1, 1942, when the Book Production War Economy Agreement took effect. This scheme mandated smaller type, less white space, and inferior paper and bindings. It resulted in some remarkably ugly books, but it conserved raw materials. Publication of new titles declined to roughly half prewar levels, and the production of reprints fell even more precipitously. German bombers damaged about fifty libraries and destroyed some 750,000 volumes, nearly a third of them in the British Museum. On December 29–30, 1940, a raid gutted Paternoster Row, the center of the book trade: 5 million volumes were lost in the warehouse of wholesaler Simpkin Marshall. Overall, about twenty firms were devastated in the Blitz, including Eyre and Spottiswoode, George Allen and Unwin, Ward Lock, Hodder and Stoughton, Methuen, George G. Harrap, Hutchinson, Michael Joseph, Nelson and Sons, Gerald Duckworth, and even Hurst and Blackett, the UK publisher of *Mein Kampf* (surely an historic low point in author–publisher relations). The resulting loss of company records has seriously handicapped book historians, though the Luftwaffe was not solely to blame for that: some archives were patriotically sacrificed to waste-paper drives.

After World War II, the world of British publishing expanded (rising from 320 firms in 1939 to 572 in 1950) and became distinctly less insular. While studying at the University of Zurich, John Calder read European books and noted that many of them were not available in English. His firm, founded in 1949, published Eugène Ionesco, Fernando Arrabal, Alain Robbe-Grillet, Nathalie Sarraute, and Marguerite Duras, as well as Samuel Beckett and Henry Miller. John Lehmann's imprint, in the span of its brief existence (1946–52), published Tennessee Williams, Saul Bellow, Gore Vidal, Paul Bowles, Theodore Roethke, Nikos Kazantzakis, Jean-Paul Sartre, and André Malraux. In addition to Henry Miller, Anaïs Nin, Jean Cocteau, Octavio Paz, and Yukio Mishima, Peter Owen had the foresight to publish Hermann Hesse, in time for the *Siddhartha* craze of the 1960s. Jonathan Cape took the lead in introducing British readers to Latin American authors, including Gabriel García Márquez, Pablo Neruda, Octavio Paz, Isabel Allende, Jorge Luis Borges, Mario Vargas Llosa, and Carlos Fuentes. This globalizing trend was due in part to the entry of some enterprising central European émigrés into the clubby circles of UK publishing, among them George Weidenfeld (Weidenfeld and Nicolson), Paul Hamlyn (Octopus Books), Walter Neurath (who made Thames and Hudson a major art publisher), and André Deutsch. Deutsch's list included Norman Mailer, Mordecai Richler, Philip Roth, John Updike, Jack Kerouac, Andrei Sakharov, John Kenneth Galbraith, Simone de Beauvoir, and V. S. Naipaul.

The British book industry was still able to generate some staggering pop-culture successes. By 1964, there were more than 40 million copies of Ian Fleming's James Bond thrillers in print, accounting for almost all of Jonathan Cape's profit margin. Overall, by 1970, 23,500 titles were published, more than twice the figure for 1950.

Modern British publishers owed much of their prosperity to imperial and other overseas markets. Macmillan had launched its successful "Colonial Library" in 1886. The following year, Thomas Nelson and Sons issued a Nyanja-language reader for what is now Malawi, and went on to develop a lucrative imperial trade in textbooks, with branch offices in Canada, Australia, Nigeria, South Africa, and Kenya. By the mid-1950s, Penguin was selling 10 million books a year, just over half of them overseas. In 1969, UK book sales totaled 77 million copies valued at £145.7 million, of which 47 percent were exported. Under the British Commonwealth Market Agreement, UK publishers agreed to retain Commonwealth rights to books whenever they sold US rights to American publishers, and to acquire Commonwealth rights whenever they bought UK rights to American books. That meant that Australasian readers sometimes had to pay more for British books than they might have had to pay for American editions. The agreement was terminated in 1976, having run foul of US antitrust laws.

Thus, by 1970, British publishing was a mature, modern industry. Along with rock music, books were one of Britain's few flourishing exports. Old established firms and upstart houses were prospering, exploiting large markets for both light and serious literature. Public libraries were ubiquitous and well funded, and moral censorship was no longer a problem for serious literature. In contrast, after 1970, independent publishers would be swallowed up by conglomerates, book exports would be reduced by the growth of indigenous publishing in the former colonies, public library funding would be constricted, and Salman Rushdie's *The Satanic Verses* (1988) would incite a censorship threat more dangerous than anything Joyce and Lawrence had faced. But that would be in another era.

References and Further Reading

Alloway, Ross (2003) "Selling the Great Tradition: Resistance and Conformity in the Publishing Practices of F. R. Leavis." *Book History*, 6: 227–50.

Bassett, Troy J. and Walter, Christina M. (2001) "Booksellers and Bestsellers: British Book Sales as Documented by *The Bookman*, 1891–1906." *Book History*, 4: 205–36.

Black, Alistair (1996) *A New History of the English Public Library: Social and Intellectual Contexts, 1850–1914*. London: Leicester University Press.

— (2000) *The Public Library in Britain 1914–2000*. London: British Library.

De Bellaigue, Eric (2004) *British Book Publishing as a Business since the 1960s*. London: British Library.

Eliot, Simon (1992) *A Measure of Popularity: Public Library Holdings of Twenty-four Popular Authors 1883–1912*. Oxford: History of the Book on Demand Series.

Feather, John (1991) *A History of British Publishing*. London: Routledge.

Gillies, Mary Ann (1993) "A. P. Watt, Literary Agent." *Publishing Research Quarterly*, 9 (1): 20–33.

Kelly, Thomas (1977) *A History of Public Libraries in Great Britain 1845–1975*, 2nd edn. London: Library Association.

McAleer, Joseph (1992) *Popular Reading and Publishing in Britain 1914–1950*. Oxford: Clarendon Press.

McCleery, Alistair (2002) "The Return of the Publisher to Book History: The Case of Allen Lane." *Book History*, 5: 161–85.

McDonald, Peter D. (1997) *British Literary Culture and Publishing Practice 1880–1914*. Cambridge: Cambridge University Press.

Mumby, Frank Arthur and Norrie, Ian (1975) *Publishing and Bookselling*, 5th edn. London: Jonathan Cape.

Nelson, James G. (1989) *Elkin Mathews: Publishers to Yeats, Joyce, Pound*. Madison: University of Wisconsin Press.

Rainey, Lawrence (1998) *Institutions of Modernism: Literary Elites and Public Culture*. New Haven: Yale University Press.

Rose, Jonathan (2001) *The Intellectual Life of the British Working Classes*. New Haven: Yale University Press.

— and Anderson, Patricia (eds.) (1991) *British Literary Publishing Houses, 1820–1965*, 2 vols. Detroit: Gale Research.

Stetz, Margaret Diane (1991) "Sex, Lies, and Printed Cloth: Bookselling at the Bodley Head in the Eighteen-nineties." *Victorian Studies*, 35: 71–86.

Wexler, Joyce Piell (1997) *Who Paid for Modernism? Art, Money, and the Fiction of Conrad, Joyce, and Lawrence*. Fayetteville: University of Arkansas Press.

Wilson, Charles (1986) *First with the News: The History of W. H. Smith 1792–1972*. Garden City: Doubleday.

26

Modernity and Print II: Europe 1890–1970

Adriaan van der Weel

At the start of the twentieth century, Europe, along with the rest of the Western world, was gripped by a veritable reading frenzy. Agriculture as a way of life for the majority was coming to an end, and urbanization spread, favoring literacy. Photographs, especially of cityscapes, reveal how much lettering confronted people in their daily life. In all capital cities, countless kiosks sold a choice of newspapers, national and international, that would never again be rivaled. In Paris, in 1910, with a population of around 2.5 million, 5 million papers were printed every day. In 1900, *Le Petit Parisien* alone printed 1.5 million copies daily; it was to go on to become the bestselling international daily in the years leading up to World War I (Martin et al. 1986). People were reading on a scale never seen before, and newspapers and illustrated magazines were the first of the twentieth-century mass media. But books were becoming cheaper too, and available more widely and more readily than ever before.

The scale on which print was now spreading brought about tremendous changes in the production, distribution, and consumption of books everywhere. Just as the age of the mass-consumer society at large was dawning, so was the age of the cheap book series and the mass paperback. The individual ownership of books (as against, for example, borrowing from libraries, commercial or otherwise) grew alongside that of other consumer goods. Buying books was made easy by the large numbers of cheap, paper-covered series that appeared on the market. Many of these had started, in the nineteenth-century vein of improvement of the lower orders, as classics series. Some contained only national, others international literature. Still in existence today in Germany, for example, is Reclam's "Universal-Bibliothek" (1867–), which published German as well as other classics. There were series aimed at a wide variety of readerships and uses, such as the Dutch series "Voor den Coupé" ("For the Railway Compartment," 1893–1918) for railway travel, or the Swedish "Verdandis småskrifter" ("Brochures of the Verdandi Student Union"), small books of popular science for self-improvement published by the Bonnier publishing company from 1887 to the early 1920s. Cheap reprint series had usually been limited to books that the publisher already owned, or which were out of copyright, such as the series "Le Livre populaire" started by Arthème Fayard in 1904. Published at 65 centimes, these were well within popular reach. But now some series even began to offer current writing. In the Netherlands, where foreign rights were not protected, reprint series could also include the latest foreign (especially English, American, or German) books, either in translation or in the original language.

In a way, little of this was new. It simply continued the reading revolution of the nineteenth century, fueled on the demand side by rising literacy, increasing leisure time, and population growth, and, on the supply side, by cheaper and faster print production. But the dedicated reprint series that started to appear in the first few decades of the twentieth century, buying titles from other publishers, did represent a more market-oriented approach: for example, "Th. Knaur, Romane der Welt," a series edited by Thomas Mann. What was most striking was the sheer scale on which print was now spreading, and especially percolating down into the lower reaches of society. The age of print as a mass medium ushered in the age of the masses.

Among the types of publication designed to reach these new readers all over Europe were endless series of cheap "penny dreadfuls" (*Groschenhefte, romans à quatre sous*), covering a wide range of genres, but especially serving poorer and less-educated readers, and children's books and magazines. For example, aimed particularly at children – the readers of the future – was the French adventure series *Journal des voyages et des aventures de terre et de mer* (1877–1929). To supply the insatiable demand for the most popular genres, publishers in many countries, but especially those with a smaller home market, looked abroad. Translations, involving various degrees of adaptation – names, local color – were common. And so this French series found itself published in Italy as *Giornale illustrato dei viaggi e delle avventure di terra e di mare* (1878–1931). Similarly, the "Biblioteca dei miei ragazzi" was modeled on and largely translated from the "Bibliothèque de Suzette," a series started in 1919 by the publishers of the very successful children's weekly, *La Semaine de Suzette* (1905).

In such children's series, suitable texts by any author about any subject could be published (often written to order), but some of the most popular series were entirely devoted to one hero. One of the best-known examples was the Nick Carter series (New York, Street & Smith, 1886), stories about a master detective which were syndicated in most European countries by the firm of A. Eichler, and inspired many local imitations. Along with thrillers and westerns (such as the equally popular Buffalo Bill series), detective and crime novels are a typical example of the many new popular entertainment genres that made their appearance toward the end of the nineteenth century. The huge popularity of Sherlock Holmes (based on the model of Émile Gaboriau's *l'Affaire Lerouge* of 1863), together with that of the penny-dreadful form, created the mold for much European detective fiction. Well-known examples were the French anti-hero Fantômas (sometimes dubbed the "Lord of Terror") and Arsène Lupin (the "Gentleman Cambrioleur" or Gentleman Burglar) series. Arsène Lupin became no less famous than Nick Carter, and was translated into almost all European languages, as was the Lord Lister series (1908). Originally written by Kurt Matull in German and published throughout Europe by Eichler, after the tremendous success of the first 110 issues it was continued locally in many languages. The last issue in Dutch by Leo Felix Hageman (no. 3687) did not appear till 1967.

Detective novel series also appeared in regular book form. In the Netherlands, a series of *Amerikaansche detective-romans* in translation flourished from 1899 to 1905. Georges Simenon, a Belgian writer living in Paris, had already produced more than two hundred books of cheap fiction under several pseudonyms when, in 1931, he started writing the Maigret novels that were to make him famous. They were published by Fayard, with a photographic cover. English and American detective novels continued to set the tone, and "l'Empreinte" ("The Fingerprint," 1932) was a well-known French detective series publishing most of the famous anglophone detective writers. In 1933, the weekly series "Détective" was the first to sport a photographic cover in color.

Cartoons were preceded, around the turn of the century, by the illustrated *historiette*: drawings with running text beneath. In France, the famous example was *La Famille Fenouillard*. The influence of American popular culture was strong in the case of cartoons, too, with such publications as *Buster Brown* (1902–26) and *Felix the Cat* (1931). By the 1920s, the use of speech balloons was common. The publication of the weekly *Journal de Mickey* (Mickey Mouse, from October 21, 1934) paved the way for further Americanization of the illustrated press in France. But European cartoonists were quick to pick up the craft. Among the famous European cartoon heroes was Belgian Hergé's Tintin (1929) published by Casterman.

Distribution of such cheap reading matter was chiefly through kiosks and tobacco shops. In the late 1920s in the Netherlands, a sensational novel in a cheap series could be bought for between 17.5 and 45 cents, or an issue of Nick Carter for 15 cents (compare a carpenter's weekly wage of about 16 guilders). By 1935, two-thirds of all books were published at less than 2 guilders. But despite the cheapness of these mass-produced publications, not everyone could, or wanted to, actually buy them. Commercial lending libraries remained significant at least until World War II. In Germany, they had been the most important channel for entertainment fiction from the late Enlightenment period until the Third Reich. In the late 1920s, partly as a result of the economic crisis, the lending libraries experienced a lift in their fortunes in Germany. In 1932, there were still some 18,000 such libraries.

It has been estimated that in Germany some 60 million *Groschenhefte* were published in the period 1933–9 (Wittmann 1991). With the extreme popularity of these cheap, weekly series, translated and adapted throughout Europe in the first few decades of the twentieth century, the internationalization of the entertainment industry began. It was the American flavor even of the German imitations of the heroes and their adventures that caused them to be blacklisted in Germany in 1940. In the genre of pulp fiction, Anglo-Saxon authors like Zane Grey and Edgar Wallace vied with Hedwig Courths-Mahler for popularity. Accordingly, in this period we witness a change from a predominantly national trade in books to one that was once again becoming international. But this time the traffic did not so much convey science, or the European classics, but a torrent of popular culture translated out of and into various continental languages. It was from this time that the fairly heavy admixture of Anglo-American ideas and forms began to promote a certain homogenization of European culture.

Mass culture rose on a tide that would not retreat. Even though many regarded reading and the knowledge it brought as a civilizing force, for others the wider spread of literacy was not a cause for rejoicing. The former reading elite, in particular, regarded the ubiquitous consumption of books and newspapers with disapproval. Apart from begrudging the masses a share in a reading culture that had previously been reserved for them, many people feared the new underbelly of literature with its mass-culture characteristics. Literary authors especially had grown increasingly self-conscious as artists. Many felt that they should not have to bow to the vulgar tastes of the plebs. The gap between the popular taste and those who catered to it and that of the cultural elites – who despised the masses and their tastes, and favored the expressions of a higher art – was widening. As a consequence of the growing dichotomy between artistic success and success in the marketplace, the book market was increasingly felt to be divided between high culture and popular consumption.

Amid the commodification of the work of the mind that could be observed taking place everywhere shortly after the turn of the century, the *Kulturverleger* made his appearance. The *Kulturverleger* zealously embraced his cultural mission, served as a partner to his authors, and was interested in making public a particular type of literature. In Germany, Stefan George and his circle (not just of authors, but also of artists, illustrators, publishers, printers, and binders) could be said to epitomize this phenomenon. Samuel Fischer was a patron of modernity, publishing foreign naturalists and expressionists like Ibsen and Zola, and German authors like Thomas Mann, Hermann Hesse, and Arthur Schnitzler. Kurt Wolff was the publisher of Franz Kafka, and a host of other expressionist authors. A similar role was played by Querido in the Netherlands, and Gallimard (founded in 1911 to publish Les Éditions de *La Nouvelle revue française*) in France, with writers such as Proust, Gide, Saint-Exupéry, Valéry, and Larbaud. In 1933, Gallimard bought the famous Éditions de la Pléiade, founded by Jacques Schiffrin.

These *Kulturverleger* were also the main publishers who stimulated the *Buchkunstbewegung*, advocating new attention to typography and book design. The *fin de siècle* had created a distinctive typography of letter forms to look at rather than texts to read. The reverse tendency – emphasis on the purity of geometric form – could be observed in De Stijl, Bauhaus, and Nieuwe Zakelijkheid. Insel Verlag, for example, harmoniously integrated the aesthetics of book production with an impressive literary program, publishing Hofmannsthal, Rilke, and Borchardt. The aim of the *Kulturverleger* was not necessarily to publish for an elite; most were eager to spread serious fiction to a wider readership by publishing it also in carefully crafted but cheap reprint series. They thus did much to present the well-designed (*schönes*) book to a wider audience. This relationship between the author-as-artist and the publisher-as-civilizing-force served to emphasize the symbolic role of books. Distinguishing the discriminating owner from those who merely read for entertainment, many of these books were not necessarily bought to be read.

One of the attractions of the book series was the guidance this form of publication offered to the less-experienced book buyer. Membership of a book club offered a similar appeal, in addition to the lower price. But initially the club aspect, which gave its members a sense of belonging to a circle of like-minded readers, also played a role. When book clubs first made their appearance, in the Weimar Republic after World War I, it was their ideological nature that characterized them. Originally books were published by the club for the exclusive benefit of its members, with the obligation to buy all titles offered by the club. This model represented the ideal from a production point of view. Minimizing the risk of both overproduction and underproduction, it allowed for the lowest price for the consumer. In the course of time, many other business models have been tried. Books might be bought from publishers, or clubs might enter into co-publication arrangements. The model that became the standard in the 1970s was that of licensing existing book titles from other publishers. This had the advantage to members of providing a much wider choice of titles. Members agreed to purchase a minimum number of books annually (usually one per quarter), with the club offering a "club selection" for anyone who had not made a personal selection by a certain date.

In France, the first book club began operations in 1924; in the Netherlands, in 1937; in Italy, the Club degli editori was not founded till 1960. In Norway, the publication, both before and after World War II, of subscription series shared many characteristics with book clubs, but the first actual book club only appeared in 1961. The importance of book clubs in Europe, especially in the 1950s and 1960s, can hardly be overestimated. In 1960, the fifteen German book clubs had 5 million members between them, accounting for 20 percent of total book sales by value. In the 1990s, the number of members had risen to 6.5 million, or a member in one in four households (Wittmann 1991). Perhaps because the book-club phenomenon began in Germany, the German media conglomerate Bertelsmann continues its hold on the market in Europe, as it does elsewhere in the world. In the Netherlands, it started the Europaclub (later ECI) in 1965; in France, the joint venture France Loisirs with Presses de la Cité in 1970. These Bertelsmann-owned clubs are by far the largest in their respective countries.

The fact that books became cheaper, and that competition in price was obviously effective and becoming more prevalent, posed a problem to the book trade. The "fixed book price" presented itself as one solution. In the Netherlands, prices had to all intents and purposes been fixed since the foundation of the Dutch *Vereeniging ter Bevordering van de Belangen des Boekhandels* in 1815 (the oldest of the modern book-trade associations) with the express purpose of preventing any form of piracy or undercutting of prices. Sweden's book prices were similarly effectively fixed from the foundation of the Swedish Publishers' Association in 1843. In Germany, the *Buchhandlerische Verkehrsordnung* of the *Börsenverein* (the German book-trade organization) took effect in 1888, limiting the discount that booksellers could give on books. The Swiss and Austrian book-trade regulations were adjusted to the German rules. In an attempt to defend themselves against competition by kiosks, the booksellers' syndicate in France, in cooperation with the publishers' syndicate, set a maximum discount too. In 1943, this turned into a real fixed book price. In spite of this book price cartel, in the period 1890–1938 book prices in France went up by a factor of four only, compared with a factor of nine for retail prices in general (Martin et al. 1986).

The fixed book price could not disguise the fact that publishers, authors, and the new book-buying public began to enter into more direct commercial relationships. The potential for authors to earn real money with their writing, for example, caused authors to organize themselves, with a special focus on their economic interests. The ratification of the Berne Convention in 1887 was in some ways a direct consequence of this pressure. The Deutsche Schriftstellerverband in 1877 united two existing rival organizations. In 1909, the Schutzverband deutscher Schriftsteller (SDS) was founded, becoming an important force during the book crisis in the second half of the 1920s when writers (especially "serious" ones) were in a very weak position. Membership rose from 1,400 in 1920 to 2,404 in 1932 (Wittmann 1991). In Italy, the Authors' Society was founded in 1882; it later became the Società italiana degli autori ed editori (SIAE). In smaller countries, where due to the smaller market authors had less to gain, such organizations generally occurred later. In the Netherlands, the Vereeniging van Nederlandsche letterkundigen was founded in 1905; in Flanders, the Vereeniging van Vlaamsche letterkundigen in 1907.

At the same time, this more commercial footing and publishers' more finely tuned commercial antennae did not stop more ideologically informed publishing ventures from being successful. Especially in Germany, the ideals of worker emancipation and socialism informed many initiatives for the publication and distribution of books, such as J. H. W. Dietz (1881), Buchhandlung Vorwärts (1894–1924), who published, for example, the *Berliner Arbeiterbibliothek* and an edition of the *Communist Manifesto*, Malik-Verlag (1916–38), with the satirical artist George Grosz as its most prominent employee, and book clubs such as Der Bücherkreis and Büchergilde Gutenberg (both founded in 1924). In France, the Librairie du Travail (1918–37), and in the Netherlands Arbeiderspers (the continuation of Ontwikkeling, 1916–), did much to spread the ideology of socialism.

Religious publishing slowly declined, but remained an ideological force in the twentieth century. In Catholic Belgium, Brepols (1796), publisher of playing cards and liturgical books in thirty languages, became "Éditeur Pontificale" in 1905. In the Netherlands, the Roman Catholic part of the population was served by its own Catholic publishers. Their close links to the hierarchy safeguarded Catholic readers from the dangers of moral corruption and Protestant influences. But it was in Protestant countries, where religious publishing had always been more substantial, that the decline was particularly noticeable. From accounting for about one-fifth of titles in the middle of the nineteenth century, by 1920 the publication of religious books had already more than halved in Germany and the Netherlands. It was to dwindle to below 5 percent by the middle of the twentieth century.

The shift with the most wide-ranging consequences in the period we are concerned with is that from a demand-led book economy to a supply-led one. This was the result of many factors. We have already encountered some of the nineteenth-century technological changes in print production. The invention of the rotary press particularly affected print production by favoring larger print-runs. But the combination of increased title production, on the one hand, and increased book consumption, on the other, made for a much more diffuse market.

The increases in production (starting in most European countries at various stages in the nineteenth century) eventually gave rise to a perceived problem of overproduction. This widely heard complaint may have had some basis in fact (during World War II it was possible for publishers to keep active despite paper shortages by divesting themselves of accumulated overstock). Mostly, however, it was less a matter of overall quantity than of a growing challenge to match supply and demand. In a market in which the number of both book titles and readers was expanding, it was simply increasingly difficult to locate potential readers for a particular title in the sea of potential book buyers.

Another factor was that of competition to the print media, not only from other media, but also from other forms of entertainment. If the nineteenth century had been the "Age of the Book," the book's position was certainly challenged in the twentieth. In absolute terms, the book market kept growing steadily, in title production as well as total volume, and leisure time was expanding too. But a spate of new media was beginning to compete with print for news, information, and entertainment. First there was the cinema (initially silent; from the end of the 1920s, talking), then radio, and, finally, television. In addition, there was the popularity of music, both live and recorded, and of going out to the movies and dance halls. Yet the book profited from these other media, too: through serialization of fiction, radio plays, and readings. Often films stimulated public awareness of a book, and could make the difference between commercial success and failure. Many authors – such as Thomas Mann – took a great interest in the filming of their books.

Last but not least, there was the more general economic crisis of the 1920s, fueled by postwar inflation, which eventually led to the Great Depression. This severely cut the purchasing power of the middle class. All these factors contributed to the "book crisis" of the late 1920s and 1930s. It hit the Netherlands and Germany in the 1920s; Italy in the 1930s.

One of the most notable effects of these various factors on the book industry was the growing need for a greater emphasis on marketing. This could be seen in the attention lavished on covers (for example, the use of photographs and color), and the rise of advertising. But it also led to book-promotion activities on a national scale. In Germany, National Book Day (March 22, the day of Goethe's death) was instituted in 1929 by the Börsenverein. From 1934, this was replaced by the annual National Socialist book week to promote the German book. In the Netherlands, CPNB (Collective Propaganda for the Dutch Book) was founded in 1930, organizing its first "book week" in 1932. When the Associazione Editoriale Libraria Italiana (AELI, founded in 1922) handed over its responsibilities to the fascist regime, the fascists took the promotion of the Italian book firmly in hand. Book promotion was part of a wider program of state control, which included standardizing state school books and making sure that they carried a recognizable fascist tone. But the fascists also proposed to institute formal rules for economic competition. It was hoped that centralized control would solve other aspects of the book crisis: the sense of overproduction and that pre-unification heritage, the chaotic nature of the book market. Thus these measures could actually count on wide support even if censorship and enforced conformity to fascism were not objectives shared by everyone (Santoro 2003).

In the face of increasing pressure from other media, and competing leisure-time activities, booksellers, too, realized the need for a more active approach to the potential buying public. No longer could they afford to sit waiting passively in their shops; they needed to reach out through such sales and marketing techniques as prospectuses, advertising, attractive window displays, and greater attention to interior decoration. Overall, this development is epitomized by the move in the 1920s and 1930s from the closed bookshop where buyers were served by an expert bookseller to open-shelf shops where the customers could browse and handle the books. A more outward-looking attitude on the part of regular booksellers was also stimulated by the competition from other sales outlets, such as railway station kiosks, department stores selling books, book clubs, and the flourishing practice of colportage. Kiosks, tobacconists, and similar points of sale were also used for the distribution of cheap series of entertainment fiction published by newspapers and high-circulation illustrated periodicals. It was easy for them to market such "exclusive readers' offers" to their readers, and production was cheap on newsprint using the rotary presses they already owned.

The increased media use in general (radio and film besides newspapers and illustrated weeklies) caused a greater awareness of the world outside the traditional community, whether local or regional or even on the scale of the nation-state that had for so long provided the natural range for so much European publishing. The importation of elements of mass culture from the US and, to a somewhat lesser degree, from Britain that we have observed must be seen in this context. After World War II, it would contribute to the rise of English as a *lingua franca*.

While we can recognize this pattern of media use in many Western countries, in the Soviet Republic – and later in all of its Eastern European vassal states – the situation was very different. Since state propaganda was regarded as an effective means of eradicating bourgeois thought and establishing a socialist ideology, the entire chain of print production (paper production, typesetting, printing, binding) and distribution were brought under state control. Printing had come to Russia late, and it was only late in the nineteenth century that a serious commercial publishing industry had come into being. In the brief window before the October Revolution of 1917, Russian publishing showed itself to be very cosmopolitan, publishing more or less everything that was appearing elsewhere in Europe. The industry's domination after the Revolution by the huge state conglomerate of Gosizdat (1919) smoothed the way for the even tighter state and party control of the Stalinist era. It is a measure of the success of this control that in Russia during the Cold War, which lasted from 1945 to 1990, 80 percent of all publications were issued by the state. Official censorship, carried out by the censorship agency Glavlit (1922), was ultimately in the hands of the Central Committee's

Propaganda Department. Through the effective mechanism of granting the right to publish only to approved institutions, conformity to party ideology could be ensured. In addition to official censorship, Russian libraries also exercised self-censorship – a practice prevalent in Nazi Germany too – which was sometimes even more rigorous (Remnek 1991; Line 2003).

The relaxation of censorship and control after Stalin's death in 1953 was only very gradual. But all sorts of materials unacceptable to the regime did eventually begin to circulate in the clandestine *samizdat* or self-publishing circuit. During the Cold War period, books that had been smuggled out of the Eastern bloc were regularly published in the West. An example of such propagandist publishing was the first printing of *Dr. Zhivago* in the Netherlands at the request of the CIA.

The same complete, centralized, state control was imposed in one after another of the Eastern European states as they fell under the communist sphere of influence. Finland, too, came briefly (1944–6) under a "Soviet Controlling Commission," which used methods of censorship similar to those in the USSR. This censorship involved removing politically incorrect (anti-Soviet and Nazi) books and other materials to the *spetskhran* – the closed collection housing books that were forbidden but nonetheless catalogued and stored (Ekholm 2001).

The situation in Germany too was, of course, decidedly atypical. Apart from the widespread effects of the economic depression (which actually hit the book trade less badly than it did other sectors of the economy), the 1930s saw the first effects of the Nazi regime in Germany. Within four months of the National Socialists taking power in 1933, the first book burnings took place. The exile of German writers and publishers for political reasons started long before persecution for race became instituted in 1938. In all, some 1,800 writers and journalists are known to have fled the country. German book publishers settled in many countries, not necessarily German-speaking, attempting to supply banned books from exile. With the new German departments they created in the period immediately after 1933, Dutch publishers Querido and Allert de Lange published some 200 titles by over one hundred authors between them. The Swiss publisher Oprecht published 145 titles by 115 exiled authors; Malik in Prague 40 titles by 22 authors. After brief stays in Austria, Italy, and Switzerland, Bermann Fischer settled in Stockholm, where he made use of offset lithography for reprints for the Scandinavian market of Werfel, Schnitzler, and the Mann brothers. Despite the fact that so many authors and publishers emigrated to the US, the only successful publisher was Friedrich Ungar (from Phaidon, Vienna), who published about one-third of the roughly 350 exile publications that appeared in the US in the period 1933–55 (Wittmann 1991).

Earlier, France had similarly been home to a large number of exiles, though of another kind. Each for their own reasons, a host of writers, especially from an Anglo-Saxon background, found Paris a congenial place to work and be published. Apart from James Joyce (*Ulysses,* published by Sylvia Beach's Shakespeare & Co in 1922), famous authors who availed themselves of the greater freedom to publish in France included Henry Miller (*Tropic of Cancer,* published by Jack Kahane's Obelisk Press, 1934), Samuel Beckett (*Watt,* 1953), Vladimir Nabokov (*Lolita,* 1955), and J. P. Donleavy (*The Ginger*

Man, 1958). The last three were published by the Olympia Press, founded by Kahane's son Maurice Girodias, who published numerous other expatriate authors.

In spite of all the attempts to enforce the political conformity of publishers, authors, and booksellers, the role of the book as an instrument of propaganda in the Third Reich was actually much less important than it was in communist Russia. It was also much less important than film, radio, illustrated periodicals, and newspapers, for the methods of totalitarian regimes of controlling their citizens also move with the times. The notable exception, of course, was Hitler's blockbuster *Mein Kampf* (1925). By April 1933, sales stood at 340,000; by April 1940, after the book had been decreed the compulsory official gift for all German newlyweds, the total number of copies in print had reached 6 million (Wittmann 1991).

As had been the case in World War I, the conditions of World War II disrupted the book trade in many ways. The international trade was an obvious victim: in particular, the regular import of English-language books to the continent, as well as the continental publication of English books, came to a virtual standstill (though both revived with unprecedented vigor after the war was over). In Germany, Jewish, French, and English books, as well as light reading with an Anglo-American character (such as Wild West and detective novels), were banned. Paper shortages as well as widespread and often far-reaching censorship led to a shortage of any but the safest titles everywhere. There was no room for any sort of speculation, and new titles were rare. For publishers, an unlooked-for benefit was the opportunity to sell off unsold stocks, sometimes decades old. To alert entrepreneurs, opportunities offered themselves occasionally. In 1943, the appearance on the French market, starved of Anglo-American comics, of *Le Téméraire: journal pour la jeunesse* met with huge popular acclaim, moving from 100,000 to 150,000 copies within a year (Martin et al. 1986).

While the production of printed matter for National Socialist propaganda purposes used many resources, a small but vigorous clandestine press did manage in most German-occupied territories to put out news sheets as well as books. De Bezige Bij in Amsterdam and Les Éditions du minuit in Paris were examples of publishers that grew out of illegal activities to turn into leading literary publishers in their countries. With the onset of the Allied campaign in continental Europe, service editions began to find their way into civilian hands. These were soon joined by a wide range of publications specifically designed for European distribution by the British and American propaganda offices. After the war had ended, many British publishers were quick to seize the opportunities engendered by the wartime scarcity of non-propagandist reading matter and an interest in the Anglo-Saxon culture of the liberators.

As soon as paper supplies began to revert to normal after the war, the book industry took off. From the mid-1950s, but especially during the 1960s and 1970s, it began to experience a boom. In the 1920s and 1930s, experiments in pocket-sized, mass-produced books had occurred in various countries, but the concept of the mass paperback, as we know it today, did not take off on the continent till after World War II. Belgium (Bibliothèque Marabout, 1949) and Germany (Rowohlt's Rotations-Romane, RoRoRo, 1950) were the first to adopt this new form on a large scale. Rowohlt had been one of the first publishers to gain licenses for all sectors of occupied Germany. The paperbacks, which had initially appeared in newspaper format, were printed in massive print-runs (of 55,000 and up) on two sides simultaneously, used the innovative "perfect binding" technique invented by Lumbeck, and carried advertising in the middle of the text (Wittmann 1991). The Netherlands soon followed with Prisma pockets (1951); France with Livre de poche (1953). In Italy, the mass paperback did not really take off till the 1960s (Oscar Mondadori, 1965). In conjunction with the postwar economic boom, new series were started everywhere. Especially popular were current *belles lettres* (both in the national language and in translation), detectives, and other similar entertainments.

Apart from the more predictable economic causes of the postwar publishing boom, the effect of the Cold War is worthy of note. This was both a direct influence, resulting from all sorts of propaganda activities, and a much more diffuse one. Among the more diffuse effects of the Cold War was the tendency to redefine national culture. This resulted in many new publications, but also notably in new editions and revisions. The rewriting of history books, both general and textbooks, is an obvious example.

Textbooks were always in need of minor revisions to reflect new knowledge, changing geopolitical circumstances, spelling, and so on. Mostly, these were of a kind that could easily be made in new printings as the market absorbed them. From time to time more major revisions were required. Italy and Germany show peaks in textbook production in the 1930s, as a result of the ideological changes instigated by the National Socialist and fascist regimes. In France, the first major impetus for the school-book industry after the various nineteenth-century national education acts came from the confluence of a number of changes after World War II. These included new notions about the nature of childhood and the role of education, the professionalization and concentration of school-book publishing, as well as updates of the books' factual and ideological content. With 750 new titles, textbook production in France in 1950 returned to levels seen last in the 1880s (compared with an average of 300 in 1930–40; the average between 1880 and 1890 was 750; Martin et al. 1986). In the Netherlands, textbooks had grown to become the largest category by volume in the period after the introduction of compulsory primary education in 1900.

Especially notable among postwar developments was the surge in interest in English and American culture, and the rise of English as a *lingua franca* in Europe. The general book-buying public displayed an apparently insatiable demand for English-language books. Berhard Tauchnitz, who had started publishing his "Collection of British and American Authors" in 1837, had already proved that a sizable market existed for them in continental Europe. Even before World War II, publishers John Holroyd-Reece (Britain) and Kurt Enoch (Germany) had founded the "Albatross Modern Continental Library" (1931) in the same fashion – going on to buy Tauchnitz in 1934. It was the successful Albatross series that provided Allen Lane with a great deal of inspiration for his famous Penguins. He took not only the idea of the bird name, along with a stylized black-and-white picture of it, but also the color coding of the covers. The very first Albatross – in yellow, indicating "psychological novels, essays, etc." – was James Joyce's *Dubliners*; other early authors included Aldous Huxley, Sinclair Lewis, and Virginia

Woolf. During the war, the Continental Book Company of Stockholm and London joined the market with their "Zephyr Books: A Library of British and American Authors."

However, it was after World War II that books in English began their triumphal march in earnest. Old stalwarts Tauchnitz and Albatross continued to be available, but a host of new competitors made an appearance. Star Editions, "To be sold on the Continent of Europe only," were produced in England. In 1946, the Swiss company of Scherz & Hallwag started publishing their "Scherz Phoenix Books" in Berne and Paris, with A. J. Cronin's *The Keys of the Kingdom*. Soon, however, in recognition of the European hunger for books in English, many British publishers began to organize their own networks of European representatives. In 1953, William Heinemann, for example, set up a subsidiary company in The Hague. This took care of warehousing but when, following the general postwar paper shortage, supplies of paper became available, it also published and printed a number of Heinemann titles. In fact, the Netherlands went on to become the biggest non-English-speaking per capita consumers of books in English.

Translations were another form in which Anglo-American culture spread on the continent. The French "Série Noire" (Gallimard, 1945–) was a series of hard-boiled crime novels, mainly of American origin. During the Cold War period, the French Communist party resisted the perceived intellectual and moral damage this and other series represented. It was also committed to combating the adverse effects on children of American cartoons by offering non-capitalist French parallels. Illustrated weeklies for children were very big business. In France just after World War II, there were some thirty titles, at around 3 million copies per week, not counting the fortnightlies or the issues of complete stories, which brought the total up to 22 million per month (Martin et al. 1986; Fourché 1998).

At the end of the nineteenth century, the German book had been a global commodity, with almost 500 shops selling exclusively or preponderantly German books in America alone, and 245 foreign members of the German Book Trade Association scattered across the globe. Before World War II, a great deal of international scientific publishing had taken place in German, as well as in various national languages. After the war, when Germany had lost so many of its scientists, the epicenter of scholarly publishing was clearly shifting. European scholarly publishing became increasingly international, and increasingly looked to English as its main vehicle. There were many exceptions to this general trend, such as the use of Russian in Eastern-bloc countries after 1948. Also, in science, the tendency was more pronounced than in other disciplines (notably the humanities). What aided the trend, and helped the growth of scholarly publishing at large, was the postwar growth of the academic population, and of its international mobility. The resulting competition placed greater pressure on scholars to publish outside of dissertations (Altbach and Hoshino 1995).

However unhappy editors of national scientific journals were with this development, internationalization, especially in scholarly publishing, was unstoppable in the postwar period. With their roots in the nineteenth century, the big European multinationals in publishing, Hachette (1826), Bertelsmann (1835), Wolters Kluwer (Wolters, 1836; Kluwer, 1889), Springer (1842), and Reed Elsevier (Elsevier, 1880; Reed, 1894) had all gone through a period of sustained growth before World War II. It was the science publishers that were the first to publish multinationally. Elsevier, one of the first publishers in Europe to be founded as a limited liability company, entered into a joint venture in New York in 1937 for the publication in English of German scientific works. In 1939, Elsevier opened an office in the UK. Springer, too, first looked to the US, setting up an international venture in New York in 1965. The international expansion of Kluwer, especially in the field of law, began in the late 1960s, with the acquisition of a number of smaller Dutch scholarly publishers with an international portfolio: Martinus Nijhoff, Junk and Stenfert Kroese, and later through the acquisition of German law publishers and a joint venture with British Harrap. For Hachette and Bertelsmann, general publishers with a sizable home market, international expansion came later. With its emphasis on solid religious publishing and its old-fashioned taste in children's literature, Bertelsmann had only just managed to survive the German book crisis of the second half of the 1920s. Not long after the end of the war, Bertelsmann began its media diversification, starting with music in the 1950s, and moving into film in the 1960s. Bertelsmann became a limited liability company in 1971, but is still not publicly traded. While Bertelsmann's international expansion started in the 1970s, that of Hachette began even later, although it had begun to experiment with co-publications in Germany and England before World War II.

While scholarly publishing at large, and scientific, technical, and medical publishing in particular, were undergoing a process of concentration and internationalization, the democratization of print production offered new opportunities for more marginal publishing ventures. From the end of the 1960s, political, "countercultural," and feminist publications were availing themselves of the opportunities of offset printing, photocopying, and mimeographing. While offering exciting opportunities for new entrants to the field of print production, the photocopying machine was perceived as a serious threat to profitability, especially of scholarly publishing. But, once again, the book managed to weather these technological challenges.

References and Further Reading

Altbach, Philip G. and Hoshino, Edith S. (eds.) (1995) *International Book Publishing: An Encyclopedia*. New York: Garland.

Bachleitner, Norbert, Eybl, Franz M., and Fischer, Ernst (2000) *Geschichte des Buchhandels in Österreich* [History of the Book Trade in Austria]. Wiesbaden: Harrassowitz.

Biblioteca dei miei ragazzi (www.bibliotecadeimieiragazzi.it).

Bibliothèque de Suzette (www.bibliothequedesuzette.com).

Börsenblatt für den deutschen Buchhandel [Newspaper for the German Book Trade].

Datenbank Schrift und Bild 1900–1960 [Database Text and Image 1900–1960] (www.polunbi.de).

Le droit d'auteur [The Author's Right]: *revue du* [Newsletter of the] *Bureau de l'Union Internationale pour la Protection des Oeuvres Littéraires et Artistiques*.

Ekholm, Kai (2001) "Political Censorship in Finnish Libraries from 1944 to 1946." *Libraries and Culture*, 36 (1): 51–7.

Fourché, Pascal (ed.) (1998) *l'Édition française depuis 1945* [French Publishing since 1945]. Paris: Éditions du Cercle de la Librairie.

Glas, Frank de (1989) *Nieuwe lezers voor het goede boek: De Wereldbibliotheek en Ontwikkeling/De Arbeiderspers vóór 1940.* Amsterdam: Wereldbibliotheek.

Hall, Murray G. (1985) *Österreichische Verlagsgeschichte 1918–1938* [Austrian Publishing History 1918–1938], vol. 1: *Geschichte des österreichischen Verlagswesens* [History of the Austrian Publishing World]. Vienna: Böhlau.

Kuitert, Lisa (1993) *Het ene boek in vele delen: De uitgave van literaire series in Nederland 1850–1900* [One Book in Many Parts: The Publication of Literary Series in the Netherlands 1850–1900]. Amsterdam: De Buitenkant.

Lehmstedt, Mark (ed.) (2000) *Geschichte des deutschen Buchwesens* [History of the German Book Trade]. Berlin: Digitale Bibliothek.

— and Herzog, Andreas (eds.) (1999) *Das bewegte Buch: Buchwesen und soziale, nationale und kulturelle Bewegungen um 1900* [The Eventful Book: The Book Trade and Social, National and Cultural Movements around 1900]. Wiesbaden: Harrassowitz.

Line, Maurice B. (2003) "Libraries, Reading and Publishing in the Cold War." *Journal of Documentation*, 59 (1): 105–8.

Martin, Henri-Jean, Chartier, Roger, and Vivet, Jean-Pierre (1986) *Histoire de l'édition française* [History of French Publishing], vol. 4: *Le livre concurrencé 1900–1950* [The Book in Competition 1900–1950]. Paris: Fayard/Cercle de la Librairie.

Nieuwsblad voor den boekhandel [Newspaper for the Book Trade].

Remnek, Miranda Beaven (1991) *Books in Russia and the Soviet Union: Past and Present.* Wiesbaden: Harrassowitz.

Santoro, Marco (2003) *Geschichte des Buchhandels in Italien* [History of the Book Trade in Italy]. Wiesbaden: Harrassowitz.

Simons, Ludo (1984–7) *Geschiedenis van de uitgeverij in Vlaanderen* [History of Publishing in Flanders], 2 vols. Tielt: Lannoo.

Tveterås, Harald L. (1992) *Geschichte des Buchhandels in Norwegen* [History of the Book Trade in Norway]. Wiesbaden: Harrassowitz.

Weel, Adriaan van der, Coppens, Chris, Dongelmans, Berry, et al. (eds.) (2003) *Jaarboek voor Nederlandse boekgeschiedenis* [Yearbook for Dutch Book History], vol. 10. Leiden: Nederlandse Boekhistorische Vereniging.

Widmann, Hans (1975) *Geschichte des Buchhandels vom Altertum bis zur Gegenwart* [History of the Book Trade from Antiquity till the Present], vol. 1. Wiesbaden: Harrassowitz.

Wittmann, Reinhard (1991) *Geschichte des deutschen Buchhandels: Ein Überblick* [History of the German Book Trade: A Survey]. Munich: Beck.

See also publishers' corporate websites.

27

Modernity and Print III:
The United States 1890–1970

Beth Luey

The history of the book in the United States from 1890 to 1970 can be summed up in two words: *new* and *more*. More publishing houses, organized in new ways, and owned by more people from new social groups, published more books in new genres and formats, by an expanded group of authors, to be sold in new ways to more readers. In less than a century, American publishing ceased to be regional and became national and international. Small family firms became large corporations. Trade houses were joined by flourishing scholarly publishers and by textbook houses whose size and profits outpaced the rest of the industry. I will tell most of this story from the point of view of publishers and authors, but I will begin with a banker, for in this period the always uneasy balance between culture and commerce in the world of books shifted visibly toward commerce.

The Business of Publishing

In the 1890s, J. Pierpont Morgan made two major investments in books. In 1896, he acquired his first Gutenberg Bible at a cost of $13,500, launching his extensive bibliophilic activities. Morgan began by raiding the treasures of Europe, but over time he invested in American manuscripts as well, adding Twain to Milton. Other wealthy men acquired valuable books and manuscripts throughout the first two decades of the twentieth century, and these form many of the collections of today's research libraries, including the Huntington Library in California, the Folger Shakespeare Library in Washington, and the Ransom Library at the University of Texas, as well as the Morgan Library in New York. Beginning in the 1890s, another wealthy man, Andrew Carnegie, donated more than $41 million to build 1,679 free public libraries in 1,412 municipalities in the United States alone. (Another 828 Carnegie libraries were constructed in other Anglophone countries.)

Although Gutenberg Bibles were beyond the reach of all but the wealthiest, books attracted middle-class collectors in the early decades of the twentieth century. As printing became more of an industry than a craft, the United States developed a parallel tradition of fine presses whose products were sought as works of art and as investments. Megan Benton describes "a 'craze' for finely made, physically distinctive books in the fifteen or so years that followed the First World War, an era in which buyers demonstrated a frenetic 'willingness to absorb limited editions in limitless numbers'" (2000: 3). The Great Crash of 1929 ended this craze, but manuscripts and first editions – limited or not – again became collectible in the 1940s and remain the subject of a lively trade.

Throughout the 1890s, J. P. Morgan had made another sort of investment in books: as a banker, he loaned money to the publishing house of the Harper Brothers. Most nineteenth-century publishing companies were owned by families or by partners. Morgan's involvement in the Harper firm started the shift in ownership from families, first to private investors, and then to the public corporations that began to dominate the industry in the 1960s. When Harper's had first issued stock in 1896, the Harper family bought most of it, and Morgan allowed the Harpers to direct the firm. Three years later, however, bankruptcy again loomed. Morgan demanded that the firm reorganize and took an active role in its restructuring and recovery. The directors, with Morgan's approval, installed new management from outside the family. Morgan loaned Harper's nearly $2.5 million over the years because, in his words, "the downfall of the House of Harper would be a national calamity" (Strouse 1999: 366). He never recovered his investment, nor did he press Harper's for repayment. In the decades that followed, many publishing houses incorporated and sold stock, but few found investors as tolerant as Morgan.

Traditional publishing historians (as well as older publishers) once described the period from 1890 to 1910 as the time when publishing ceased to be an occupation for gentlemen and became a purely commercial venture. Modern publishing historians argue that publishing was always a business and that, even in its twenty-first-century conglomerate incarnation, it retains a claim to cultural status. The Harpers, Putnams, Appletons, and Scribners were all in the business to make money. As long as they controlled family firms and maintained close personal ties to authors, the profit motive was overshadowed by the cultural value of their wares. As the firms grew and issued stock, it became more difficult to ignore the fact that they were businesses.

Gentlemanly, high-culture values were also hard to affix to the fastest-growing sector of the industry: textbooks. As public education expanded, school books became big business. In 1890, a textbook trust called the American Book Company was capitalized at $5 million. Many of the companies that published textbooks did nothing else, including names still familiar: Ginn, Heath, and Scott, Foresman. Meanwhile, trade houses like Harper and Houghton Mifflin expanded their textbook divisions.

There were other indications that the book industry was growing more businesslike. The turn of the century saw the formation of both the American Booksellers Association and the American Publishing Association, organizations designed to promote the sometimes conflicting interests of these two groups. Authors, too, began to organize, though their efforts were largely ineffective: the Society of Authors was formed in 1884, and the Authors' Syndicate in 1889. More important was the rise of the literary agent, who represented authors in their dealings with publishers. Literary agencies had operated since the middle of the nineteenth century, but in the 1890s agents like Paul Revere Reynolds and Flora May Holly became influential enough to raise the hackles of traditional publishers. Henry Holt described the literary agent as "a very serious detriment to literature and a leech on the author, sucking blood out of proportion to his later services" (Bonn 1994: 55). American authors, however, felt differently, and their agents helped them profit from their work.

The Rise of the American Author

By the middle of the nineteenth century, the United States could claim a literary canon, but few American authors could support themselves by writing. British writers dominated the market. An 1893 survey of libraries found the most popular authors to be Sir Walter Scott, Charles Dickens, William Makepeace Thackeray, Henry Bulwer-Lytton, and George Eliot; the lone Americans were Nathaniel Hawthorne and James Fenimore Cooper. In contemporary literature, though, Americans were doing better. The most popular recent books were *Ramona* by Helen Hunt Jackson, *Little Lord Fauntleroy* by Frances H. Burnett, and *Ben Hur* by Lew Wallace. British novelists remained popular in the first decades of the twentieth century, but Americans gained ground. Historical novels set in Europe were joined by romances set in the United States, especially in the South and West. American authors conquered the market with rural novels like *Mrs. Wiggs of the Cabbage Patch* and *Rebecca of Sunnybrook Farm* – all as Pollyannish as *Pollyanna,* which was published in 1913. Western novels by Jack London, Zane Grey, and others sold well in the United States and were translated into many European languages. These books were not, by some standards, serious literature, but their success indicates that the number of readers and book buyers in the United States had expanded beyond an urban elite. American authors could now claim more than a canon: they had an audience. The term *bestseller* was coined in 1895, and a number of lists were established during that decade, suggesting that books were at last becoming a mass medium.

American authors were helped by copyright legislation. Until 1891, the works of British authors enjoyed no copyright protection in the United States. Naturally, American publishers preferred publishing already popular English writers, without paying them, to publishing less well-known American authors who expected royalties. Charles Dickens and Anthony Trollope lobbied passionately for an international copyright agreement, but American publishers remained obdurate. In 1891, a compromise was reached that protected both British authors and American publishers: under the Chace Act, foreign works could be granted American copyrights, but only if the books were manufactured in the United States. British publishers could not simply export books across the Atlantic and thus could not compete directly with American houses, and British and American authors found themselves on a more equal footing.

After World War I, American literary authorship entered a golden age. F. Scott Fitzgerald, Sinclair Lewis, Ernest Hemingway, Thomas Wolfe, and Theodore Dreiser were all writing in the 1920s. They earned more for their writing than would have been possible twenty years earlier, though not always from their book royalties. Having profited from advances in printing technology, the inexpensive periodical rates of the 1879 Postal Act, and growing advertising revenues, national magazines could now pay authors handsomely for short stories. "Between 1919 and 1936, F. Scott Fitzgerald earned some $225,784 for his magazine fiction as opposed to only $66,588 for his novels. Theodore Dreiser, in the early 1920s, was still relying heavily on fees for magazine work to meet his day-to-day expenses" (West 1988: 107). A story's appearance in a mass-market magazine not only paid well, it also promoted the author's name and books. In fact, some of these magazines – for example, *Harper's*, *Collier's*, and *Scribner's* – were owned by book publishers who used them to attract and spotlight authors.

By some accounts, the interwar period was also a golden age of editing. Fitzgerald, Hemingway, Wolfe, Marjorie Kinnan Rawlings, and many others benefited from the editorial attention of Maxwell Perkins at Scribner's. Along with his contemporaries, such as Hiram Haydn at Crown and Saxe Commins at Random House, Perkins is credited with nurturing authors, befriending them, and guiding their careers. Activist editing was a fairly recent phenomenon: until the late nineteenth century, editors generally decided whether a manuscript was publishable but did not work with authors to develop their writing. The first well-known exception was Ripley Hitchcock, at Harper's from 1890 to 1918, who directed Edward Noyes Westcott's revision of what would become the bestselling novel *David Harum.* Hitchcock reorganized the manuscript, deleted subplots and characters, and altered the style. By the 1920s, such work had become common, though it was performed with different degrees of skill and tact. As the role of literary agents expanded and publishing became less personal, the editor's role as friend, confidant, and mentor diminished, but thoughtful editing did not end with World War II. Editors such as Jason Epstein, Roger Straus, Robert Gottlieb, and Michael Korda continued the tradition well into the 1960s.

A national market for books required an efficient distribution system. The railroads helped, but few Americans outside big cities could easily buy books: as late as 1931, the nation had fewer than eight hundred bookstores. The Book of the Month Club (BOMC), established in 1926, made up for this dearth by allowing people anywhere in the country to order books by mail. The club did not merely distribute books but publicized and promoted them. By 1929, the BOMC had more than a hundred thousand members. Rather than competing with booksellers, as retailers feared, the book clubs increased sales for everyone.

Publishers took advantage of that expanded market by reissuing classics, modern classics, and near-classics. Many firms offered elegantly bound sets of their most successful authors' earlier works, while Grosset and Dunlap promoted inexpensive reprints. The Modern Library had been established in 1917; purchased in 1925 by Donald

Klopfer and Bennett Cerf, it became the foundation of Random House. In its new incarnation, the Modern Library merged cultural status, fine design, and low prices in a highly profitable and critically acclaimed series. Of course, publishing in this decade was not all high culture: Simon & Schuster began in 1924 by producing crossword puzzle books.

A New Generation of Publishers

The established publishers of the 1920s came from the white Anglo-Saxon Protestant establishment, and they rarely welcomed ideas or employees with other ethnic origins. Fortunately, a number of ambitious young men – mostly Jewish – managed to raise the capital to start their own houses. Their ventures opened opportunities to new talent and ideas, and by the 1920s and 1930s they were offering the older houses real competition. Benjamin Huebsch founded his own company in 1905, publishing Maxim Gorky, James Joyce, and D. H. Lawrence. Alfred and Blanche Knopf launched their firm in 1915, the first American publishers to promote Russian literature. Boni and Liveright went into business two years later. These houses brought Americans the works of Nikolai Gogol, Ivan Turgenev, Emile Zola, Anatole France, Friedrich Nietzsche, Arthur Schopenhauer, and Sigmund Freud. They also promoted modernist and controversial American authors, including Eugene O'Neill, Ezra Pound, John Reed, and Upton Sinclair. Random House, founded in the 1920s, sought a larger audience but was noticeably more adventurous than the established firms.

These houses promoted new business methods as well as new authors. Their advertisements were less staid and more effective, and some of the publishers became near-celebrities. "Knopf's egotism became part of the firm's promotion. When announcing several minor volumes in 1919, he told booksellers that he would like them to have 'the same confidence in my *Publishers' Weekly* advertisements that I flatter myself you have in what I tell you when I meet you face to face" (Madison 1966: 324). Horace Liveright invested in Broadway plays and became well known in theater circles, while Bennett Cerf eventually became a television quiz-show personality.

Some of the new generation were also more willing to challenge the nation's censorship laws. The newer houses were the most frequent targets of censors, and when in 1923 the Clean Books League sponsored legislation in New York, Horace Liveright led the opposition. It was at the legislative session considering this bill that New York state senator Jimmy Walker uttered his famous pronouncement: "No woman was ever ruined by a book." The bill was defeated. The American Civil Liberties Union, founded in the 1920s, formed its National Committee on Freedom from Censorship in 1932 and became an effective advocate for the right to read. In 1933, *Ulysses* was found not obscene in a trial that Random House precipitated by importing a copy in a way guaranteed to be detected by the Customs Service. In 1946, the courts gave *Esquire* the right to use the mails, and the postmaster general's powers to censor were limited. The two 1957 cases that continue to govern the federal courts' decisions on obscenity – *Butler* v.

Michigan and *Roth* v. *US* – established the idea that community standards must be applied to decide what is obscene. Since then, few attempts have been made to limit what adults may read; instead, censorship efforts have focused on children's reading. Censorship cases relating to national security surface from time to time, and although no single doctrine has emerged, it is clear that the courts are reluctant to restrict publishers in any medium from disclosing matters of public interest.

The Impact of War

World War II disrupted American publishing. Paper was rationed, printing plates were melted down, and many publishing employees enlisted in the war effort. But the end of the war marked the beginning of a period of tremendous expansion in reading and publishing, and of the dominance of American books in the world market.

The longer people stay in school, the more likely they are to read. In the 1940s and 1950s, the federal government began funding education and research, encouraging more Americans to attend high school and college. The GI Bill, passed at the end of the war, accelerated the growth of higher education by providing financial aid to veterans. Between 1940 and 1950, college enrollment in the United States increased by 78 percent. Cold War competition – especially after the launch of Sputnik in 1957 – generated increased funds for school libraries, innovation in science and mathematics education, financial aid to students, and large research grants to universities.

The impact of enrollment growth on publishing was immediate: college students need books. John Wiley, a publishing house that specialized in college and graduate-level textbooks, grew from 99 employees in mid-1945 to 229 in 1948. W. W. Norton expanded its college division, and other houses quickly moved into the business.

But veterans did not devote themselves entirely to school. They also started the families they had postponed for military service. Consequently, publishers expanded or launched children's divisions. Theodore Geisel, better known as Dr. Seuss, began writing for children before the war, but sales of his work made a quantum leap in 1954 when he began the "Beginner Book" series, designed to help baby-boomers learn to read by providing entertainment in a structured, limited vocabulary. (The idea was Bennett Cerf's.) *The Cat in the Hat* launched the series, which remains enormously popular. "Golden Books," a series of inexpensive children's volumes sold in many non-bookstore outlets, began with twelve titles in 1942 and was selling a hundred million books annually by 1957. Throughout the 1960s, children's book sales exceeded adult trade book sales.

When baby-boomers started school in the early 1950s, they needed textbooks. Companies that had never published school texts entered the market; those already active expanded their lists. When the boomers graduated from high school, more and more of them attended college. Educational aspirations expanded to those whose parents had attended college under the GI Bill and, especially in the 1960s, to women and members of minority groups. Between 1960 and 1980, direct federal student aid increased from

$300 million to $10 billion, and college enrollment went from 3.7 million to 12 million. Even in the baby bust of the 1970s, enrollment increased.

As universities grew, they founded new university presses and expanded existing ones. The oldest American university press in continuous operation, that of Johns Hopkins, published its first book in 1887. The University of Chicago followed suit in 1891. By 1929, there were twenty presses, and by 1949, forty-four. In the 1950s, ten new presses were founded. These presses provided a noncommercial outlet for the growing number of specialized scholarly books produced by the expanding – and increasingly research-oriented – professoriate.

Worldwide demand for American books also grew. Before the war, American book exports were negligible – only 5 percent of total sales. During the war, Australia, New Zealand, and Latin American countries were unable to get the British and German textbooks they had relied on. The US State Department and the Office of War Information organized publishers' visits to these countries. Publishers opened international sales departments and hired international representatives, beginning in 1946. After the war ended, sales of US publications abroad soared. Some publishers' export sales increased by as much as 20 percent a year in the 1950s and 1960s, and annual growth rates of more than 10 percent were common until at least 1980. The initial export expansion was mostly in textbooks and scientific materials, as English replaced German as the international language of science. Interest in American popular culture allowed trade houses to participate in the export business, mostly by selling foreign and translation rights rather than through direct export of books. Literary fiction, serious nonfiction, genre fiction, cookbooks, inspirational titles, and self-help books all made their way abroad.

The Paperback

Some book historians attribute the postwar success of paperback books to another World War II phenomenon. During the conflict, publishers worked with the armed forces to distribute free paperbound books to US troops: the Armed Services Editions. They bore little resemblance to paperback books: they had no real covers and were produced in a horizontal format. Few of them survive because (like cheap, popular literature of other eras) they were read to death. Whether these paperbound books made readers more receptive to paperback books is an open question, but something certainly did.

Paperbound books had existed since before the Civil War. Dime novels, inexpensive reprints, and "cheap libraries" provided small volumes for a nickel or a dime throughout the nineteenth century. What differentiates the "paperback revolution" beginning in the 1930s is not the paperback format or the low prices of the books. Indeed, the lurid covers of early paperbacks recalled the reputation of their predecessors. The important differences are the quality – or perhaps the respectability – of the titles, the strong ties of the new houses to mainstream publishing, and the broad distribution the new paperbacks achieved.

Robert de Graff founded Pocket Books in 1939, with nearly half the funding provided by the owners of Simon & Schuster. The new company thus acquired instant respectability and access to a large hardcover list that could be mined for reprints. Penguin Books, founded in England in 1935, opened a New York office in 1939 as well. Avon was founded in 1941; its financing came from the American News Company, a magazine distributor. Popular Library and Dell were launched in 1943, Bantam in 1945, and New American Library (NAL) in 1948.

Paperback houses published both original titles and reprints. Genre fiction reminiscent of dime novels and pulp fiction appeared on some of the original lists, but most of the books were reprints of classic and current fiction and nonfiction. Paperback publishers bought rights from hardcover houses rather than from authors, usually for five years. The limited term may have become customary because trade houses were initially leery of paperback publication. They feared that paperback sales would reduce their revenues, and they shared authors' fears of cheapened reputations. Those fears diminished as the paperback houses issued more quality reprints. New American Library, through its Signet and Mentor imprints, counted William Shakespeare, William Faulkner, and Edith Wharton among its authors, lending new respectability to paperbacks. Soon they were publishing Truman Capote and J. D. Salinger along with Mickey Spillane. Large advances and royalty payments also helped to win over authors and publishers. Early advances ranged from $500 to $2,000, but NAL paid a $35,000 advance for Norman Mailer's *The Naked and the Dead* in 1951 and more than $100,000 for James Jones's *From Here to Eternity* in 1953. Mario Puzo's advance for *The Godfather* in 1968 was $410,000.

Booksellers had little interest in handling books that sold for only a quarter and that featured scantily clad heroines or leering racial stereotypes on their covers. In any case, there were not enough American bookstores at that time to sell the numbers of books needed for the paperback houses to turn a profit. Instead, paperback publishers used the magazine distribution system, selling through drugstores, five-and-dimes, tobacco shops, railroad stations, and other outlets frequented by people who had never entered a bookstore. By 1942, Pocket Books could be found in more than a thousand outlets nationwide; after the war, more than a hundred thousand outlets sold them.

This distribution system was extremely effective, but it left paperbacks open to a new source of censorship. When news distributors objected to a book because of its depictions of race or sexuality or because of its political views, paperback houses had to reconsider publication. In some cases, they simply did not issue the titles. At other times, they deleted offensive words or passages (sometimes without the author's knowledge). Faulkner, Mailer, John Steinbeck, and James Baldwin were among the authors whose works raised distributors' hackles.

With their low prices, paperback books had to sell in huge numbers to be profitable. The smallest initial print-runs were typically 150,000 at a time when only the bestselling hardcover books sold 100,000 copies. Some books had first printings of half a million copies, and Erle Stanley Gardner's mysteries began life in printings of a million. The prices rose gradually, to 35 cents in the mid-1950s and to a dollar by the early

1960s, but the increases did not deter purchasers. In 1947, 95 million paperback books were sold for $14 million. Five years later, 270 million copies were sold for $40 million, and in 1959 nearly 286 million copies sold for $67 million. By 1960, Americans were spending more on paperbacks than on hardcover trade books, even though paperbacks cost roughly one-fifth of what hardcover books cost.

As early as the 1940s, paperback houses began issuing larger-format, more durable, and more expensive trade paperbacks along with their inexpensive mass-market paperback books. Penguin had its Pelican series, which became NAL's Mentor Books, and in 1953 Doubleday started its Anchor series. The Vintage, Everyman, Touchstone, Galaxy, and Compass imprints soon joined them. These books were priced at 75 cents to a dollar, with print-runs of around 20,000. The books were aimed at the college market, and they changed curricula. College literature classes now replaced or supplemented anthologies with paperback editions of novels (a trend that gradually made its way into high schools); history classes could add paperback document collections and classic monographs. Trade paperbacks also opened the doors of bookstores: by 1960, 85 percent of booksellers sold paperbacks.

By the mid-1970s, paperbacks were fully integrated into the universe of authors, publishers, booksellers, and readers. Although a few houses published only hardcover or only paperback books, most published both. The paperback format was not limited to trade books but had spread to university presses and textbook houses. Paperbacks were sold in nearly every bookstore. Paperbacks were the Model T of publishing – though they came in more colors than black. They made book ownership possible for Americans who did not live near bookstores or did not feel comfortable walking into their often stuffy atmosphere, and for those who could not afford to buy hardback books. Like the expansion of higher education, they democratized learning and book ownership.

Engulf & Devour

In his 1976 film *Silent Movie,* Mel Brooks created Engulf & Devour, a fictional conglomerate that was trying to buy all the Hollywood studios. Beginning in the 1960s, many publishers feared that the same sort of takeover mania was at work in the book business. Engulf & Devour was probably a takeoff on Gulf & Western, which was busy acquiring media properties and was itself eventually acquired by Viacom, which now owns both Paramount Pictures and the Simon & Schuster companies. The book industry experienced a great deal of consolidation beginning in the 1960s, but not because of a megalomaniac plot. The methods of consolidation and the reasons behind it were complex.

The mergers became possible because publishers that had been privately owned, or whose stock was closely held, went public to raise capital. The first of these was Random House, which sold 30 percent of its stock to the public in 1959. John Wiley (which remains independent) made its first public stock offering in 1962, while Houghton,

Mifflin and Putnam's did so in 1967. These and other public offerings created a great deal of interest among magazine and newspaper publishers, which saw book publishers as having related interests; among movie studios, which viewed books as material for their films; and among foreign publishers, who wanted an efficient way to enter the US market.

Much of the consolidation took the form of mergers between publishing houses. Mergers made possible diversification into new areas. For example, several trade houses bought or merged with paperback houses rather than start their own divisions: Random House bought Ballantine; Holt, Rinehart & Winston bought Bantam and Popular Library; and Doubleday bought Dell. Harper's merged with Row, Peterson in 1967 to re-enter the textbook market. Mergers also allowed companies to raise capital for growth, which was the motivation for the sale of E. P. Dutton to Elsevier and of the later merger of Scribner's and Atheneum.

Many of the sales took place, not because of the urge of big fish to eat little ones, but because of the desire of the little fish to retire to a nice, quiet pond. The entrepreneurs of the 1920s and 1930s wanted to reduce their activity or retire altogether, and in many cases their children had no desire to take over the business. In 1960, Alfred and Blanche Knopf, approaching retirement, sold their company to Random House. Their son Pat had left the Knopf firm in 1959 to help found Atheneum. The following year, Kurt and Helen Wolff, also nearing retirement, sold Pantheon to Random House. Both Knopf and Pantheon remained independent subsidiaries for some years. The founders of New American Library sold out to Times Mirror in 1963, as did Harry Abrams in 1966.

In some cases, companies far removed from the industry bought publishing houses for the wrong reasons. In the 1960s, when schools and textbook publishing were expanding, some technology companies believed that schools would rely increasingly on technology for teaching and that textbook companies would provide the content that they needed to add to their hardware. Xerox bought two publishing houses in the 1960s, and by 1974 was the nation's second-largest school textbook publisher. RCA, Bell & Howell, CBS, ITT, Litton Industries, and a joint venture between General Electric and Time also went on buying sprees. Most of these alliances vanished during the 1980s, when it became clear that the anticipated synergy was not going to materialize and that the profit margin in book publishing was not adequate to satisfy the shareholders of technology companies.

Despite the mergers of the 1960s, independent publishing survived. Wiley and McGraw-Hill are family-controlled, and W. W. Norton is employee-owned. New presses started, and some of them succeeded, becoming medium-sized or even large publishing houses. Workman Publishing, founded in 1968, has a list focused on cooking, cats, and calendars, but with the acquisition of Algonquin in 1989, it added literary fiction and nonfiction to its list. Its bestselling book, *What to Expect When You're Expecting,* was published in 1984 and has ten million copies in print. Ten Speed Press, which began in 1970 as the publisher of cycling books, created a long-term bestseller with *What Color is your Parachute?,* and now, with three additional imprints, issues about 150 titles each year. Many of these serve niche markets – regional audiences, minority groups, and religious groups. The largest group of independent publishers is formed by the nonprofit houses, which grew in number and expanded their publishing programs between World War II and 1970. These include university presses, museums, historical societies, academic societies, and research institutes. Their output is small compared to that of the commercial houses, but their cultural influence is disproportionate to their size.

Concerns about consolidation extended well beyond the publishing houses. Authors and their agents worried that they would face reduced choices and lose negotiating power. Social commentators worried that the quality of American books would plummet, that innovation would be stifled, and that unpopular political views would find no outlet. These fears were understandable, but they were not realized.

Although conglomerates were theoretically in a position to reduce authors' incomes from subsidiary rights, they were never able to do so. Before companies producing a variety of media merged, authors generally transferred their copyrights to a hardback publisher, who then sold – to the highest bidders – paperback, translation, film, television, and other rights, sharing the revenues with authors as specified in their contracts. Authors feared that, after mergers, their rights would be "sold" internally and that the prices would be artificially held down. This did not happen, because the hardback divisions had to meet *their* revenue expectations, so they continued to sell to the highest bidders, whether within the conglomerate or outside. In some cases, one division of a conglomerate ended up bidding against another.

It did become more difficult for authors to find publishers for first novels and for what publishers call "mid-list" books – those expected to sell fewer than ten thousand copies. In most cases, smaller houses and some nonprofits picked up the slack. Moreover, publishers are notoriously poor at predicting sales. Alfred Knopf once told a visitor that, among the dozen manuscripts on his desk, one was a bestseller. When the visitor asked which it was, Knopf replied that if he knew that he would not have to publish all twelve. Where one editor sees a mid-list book, another may see a bestseller.

The impact of consolidation on readers was mitigated by the fact that, even after being swallowed up by conglomerates, book publishing remained essentially a cottage industry. Large corporations could reduce costs by combining business functions, but they were generally unable to combine editorial offices. For the most part, imprints within publishing houses retained their own editorial staffs, their own standards, and their own identities even when they had to meet new revenue expectations.

The impact was also mitigated by the fact that publishing thrives on controversy. When one house turns down a book because it offends the political or moral sensibilities of its corporate owner, the story promptly shows up on the front pages of a newspaper (often one owned by a competing conglomerate), and within days the book has been sold to another house that is less easily offended (or is offended by other views) and is eager to cash in on the notoriety. In 1990, staff members at Simon & Schuster protested the imminent publication of Brett Easton Ellis's *American Psycho* because of its vivid depiction of violence against women. Richard Snyder, president of the firm, canceled publication of the book, already in page proof. The book was immediately picked up by the Vintage imprint of Random House and published three months later.

Nevertheless, the shift from private to public ownership was significant. A publicly held company is far different from an entrepreneurial house. Editors might still choose titles that reflected their own literary values, but their decisions then went before committees with more stringent views on profitability. Personal relationships between authors and editors became business relationships between agents and contract departments. When publishing houses were integrated into conglomerates (or larger publishing houses), their position became tenuous: a shift in corporate emphasis, or poor financial performance, might lead to the sale of a publishing division or the replacement of editorial directors. Management responsible to Wall Street could not be as generous or civic-minded as J. P. Morgan. The acquisitions of the 1960s led in some cases to the resale of all or part of a publishing house, to resignations or the firing of editors, and to increased emphasis on the bottom line.

Whether the dominance of commerce mattered to books and their readers is an open question. Innovative authors continued to break new ground, while established authors reliably turned out the same kinds of books that had won them an audience in earlier years. Readers continued to have a broad choice of literary novels, serious nonfiction, political diatribes, poetry, self-help books, religious and spiritual inspiration, health advice, romance novels, science fiction, mysteries, humor, and even crossword puzzles. Books may have become commercial commodities, but they remained objects of desire, inspiration, and imagination.

References and Further Reading

Benjamin, Curtis G. (1984) *US Books Abroad: Neglected Ambassadors.* Washington: Library of Congress.

Benton, Megan L. (2000) *Beauty and the Book: Fine Editions and Cultural Distinction in America.* New Haven: Yale University Press.

Berg, A. Scott (1978) *Max Perkins: Editor of Genius.* New York: E. P. Dutton.

Bonn, Thomas L. (1989) *Heavy Traffic and High Culture: New American Library as Literary Gatekeeper in the Paperback Revolution.* Carbondale: Southern Illinois University Press.

— (1994) "Henry Holt A-spinning in his Grave: Literary Agenting Today and Yesterday." *Publishing Research Quarterly,* 10 (1): 55–65.

Cerf, Bennett (1977) *At Random: The Reminiscences of Bennett Cerf.* New York: Random House.

Cole, John Y. (ed.) (1984) *Books in Action: The Armed Services Editions.* Washington: Library of Congress.

Dardis, Tom (1995) *Firebrand: The Life of Horace Liveright, the Man who Changed American Publishing.* New York: Random House.

Davis, Kenneth C. (1984) *Two-bit Culture: The Paperbacking of America.* Boston: Houghton Mifflin.

Hart, James D. (1950) *The Popular Book: A History of America's Literary Taste.* New York: Oxford University Press.

Hawes, Gene R. (1967) *To Advance Knowledge: A Handbook on American University Press Publishing.* New York: Association of American University Presses.

Korda, Michael (1999) *Another Life: A Memoir of Other People.* New York: Random House.

Madison, Charles A. (1966) *Book Publishing in America.* New York: McGraw-Hill.

Miller, Laura J. (2000) "The Best-seller List as Marketing Tool and Historical Fiction." *Book History,* 3: 286–304.

Portrait of a Publisher, 1915–1965 [Alfred Knopf] (1965) New York: Typophiles.

Rubin, Joan Shelley (1992) *The Making of Middlebrow Culture.* Chapel Hill: University of North Carolina Press.

Samuels, Edward (2002) *The Illustrated Story of Copyright.* New York: St. Martin's.

Satterfield, Jay (2002) *"The World's Best Books": Taste, Culture, and the Modern Library.* Amherst: University of Massachusetts Press.

Schwed, Peter (1984) *Turning the Pages: An Insider's Story of Simon & Schuster, 1924–1984.* New York: Macmillan.

Strouse, Jean (1999) *Morgan: American Financier.* New York: Random House.

Van Slyck, Abigail (1995) *Free to All: Carnegie Libraries and American Culture, 1890–1920.* Chicago: University of Chicago Press.

West, James L. W., III (1988) *American Authors and the Literary Marketplace since 1900.* Philadelphia: University of Pennsylvania Press.

Wright, Louis B. (1976) *Of Books and Men.* Columbia: University of South Carolina Press.

28

Books and Bits: Texts and Technology 1970–2000

Paul Luna

Looking back on book production in the period 1970–2000, it is clear that changes in text composition were driven by economic imperatives, first to reduce the cost of turning an author's text into publishable data, and subsequently to extract maximum value from that data. The gradual standardization of computer systems prompted the convergence of the typesetting and printing industries, previously with separate and highly specific technologies, with the larger, business-driven world of document creation, transmission, and retrieval. While more lay people than ever before have access to the tools and terminology that were previously the preserve of typesetters and printers, those industries are no longer the sole determinants of the development of the technologies they use. The boundaries between the tools that printers use to typeset and make books, and the tools that authors use to write, and publishers use to edit, have dissolved. This convergence means that typesetting in particular has been dethroned, or democratized. Authors, copy-editors, and designers have become implementers of editorial and typesetting decisions when previously they had specified their requirements to typesetters (Hendel 1998: 105–25; Morgan 2003; Mitchell and Wightman 2005: xi). This chapter will consider individual books produced in this period as a way of reflecting on aspects of these changes.

At the start of our period, the hot-metal letterpress tradition was still alive, and used alongside the photo-composition methods and lithographic printing that would supersede it. The roles of copy-editor, designer, compositor, and proofreader were still distinct and separate. For the Oxford and Cambridge university presses, the production and publication of the various editions of the complete New English Bible (NEB) in 1970 were major events. (The New Testament had been published separately in 1961.) These were businesses with investment and expertise in traditional composition and printing methods, but their close ties to the Monotype Corporation gave them access to its latest equipment, and they acted as test sites for each new generation of typesetting device. Cambridge produced the three-volume library edition of the NEB; it was set with hot metal in Monotype Ehrhardt, and printed letterpress, continuing the design that had been established for the New Testament. Oxford produced the one-volume standard edition and an illustrated schools edition (1972). The standard edition was set in Mono-photo Plantin, while the illustrated edition was set in Monophoto Times Semibold; both were printed lithographically. For these volumes, with expectations of long print-runs and a continuing reprint life, photo-composition and lithographic printing was the forward-looking choice. However, the popular paperback of the NEB (Penguin 1974) was printed by rotary letterpress, using relief plates made from the Oxford setting. Rotary letterpress was still the norm for mass-market paperback imprints.

For books to be printed letterpress, composition by Monotype (and occasionally Linotype, never a large player in the British book-composition field) was still practical. Firms had invested over many years in equipment and typefaces in a stable technological environment, meaning that, for academic work in particular, resources existed for spe-cialist language, mathematical, and technical setting that would have needed much investment to replicate for photo-composition. By 1970, photo-composition was cost-effective for straightforward composition, such as magazine text, or for high-volume, repetitive work, such as telephone directories, and would gradually become practical for all book work.

Photo-mechanical composition systems had started as attempts to replace the hot-metal casting mechanism with a photographic exposure mechanism, but retaining most of the rest of the machinery. The Monophoto Filmsetter introduced in 1952 used a keyboard almost identical to its hot-metal equivalent. The Mark 4 Filmsetter (1967) used for the NEB was driven by a 31-channel tape, and was configured in much the same way as a composition caster. Instead of brass matrices held in a grid, which was positioned over the casting mechanism on instruction from the punched-paper tape, the Filmsetter had a grid of glass negatives, positioned over a light source and shutter. Film or paper output replaced metal type (Wallis 1997).

The adaptation of well-tested mechanical principles provided some continuity in engineering and maintenance, but film or paper output was initially difficult to correct. The individual types cast by the Monotype could be corrected easily by hand, letter by letter, from the case; a single-line slug of Linotype setting could also be replaced, with rather more labor, by having it recomposed and cast. Correction to film was more troublesome. The tape produced by the keyboard was effectively uncorrectable, so the Monophoto Filmsetter lost the advantage of single-type correction that its predecessor had over the Linotype. The line containing the error had to be re-keyed, re-exposed, and the resultant piece of film or paper carefully stripped into the original. Metal type is inherently self-squaring and self-aligning. Aligning pieces of film requires a light-box, a grid, and a careful eye to ensure alignment. Moreover, if the chemicals used to develop the material, or the strength of the light source, varied from the original setting, then it would result in text of a different density (Heath and Faux 1978).

The first-generation photo-composition machines were slow. For higher-volume work, second-generation machines, such as Higonnet and Moyroud's Lumitype (1949, also known as the Photon), had photo-matrices as glass discs or strips, and instead of using a stationery light source, had a timer and flash to freeze the image of each letter while the disc was still spinning (Southall 2005: 79ff). By the end of the 1960s, these machines could be driven by keyboards producing correctable punched-paper tape, allowing complete jobs to be re-run with corrections. At the lower end of the market, Compugraphic were able to produce much more affordable photo-composition machines from 1968. While the NEB had been set on film, with a resulting high-definition image, low-cost composition was based on bromide-paper output. This rapidly advanced the use of photo-composition in jobbing typesetting – it was easy to combine page elements using paper output, which could be pasted up and re-photographed. An even cheaper alternative to the Compugraphic was the IBM Selectric Composer (1961). The IBM can be considered as the earliest word-processing machine, a term coined for it by its manufacturers in 1974, when it was combined with a magnetic tape drive to store keystrokes as they were typed. Information could now be stored, retyped automatically from the stored information, corrected, reprinted as many times as needed, and then erased. However, storage capacity on the reusable tapes, and from 1969 on magnetic cards, was very limited (Seybold 1977: 317). In composition terms, the IBM was an electric typewriter with interchangeable golf-ball heads containing variable-width characters in designs based (with considerable loss of subtlety) on leading hot-metal typefaces (Steinberg 1996: 221–2). Display type could be provided by Letraset dry-transfer lettering or hand-set photo-lettering.

Composition by hot metal, early photo-composition systems, and typewriter shared one feature: all text had to be specifically keyboarded for composition, and those key-strokes were useless for any further work; they were effectively lost. The reusability of keystrokes, the manipulation rather than sequential recording of data, and high speeds of final output were the main goals of developers. *The Random House Dictionary of the English Language: The Unabridged Edition* illustrates early approaches to computer-assisted composition. Conceived in 1959, it was the first dictionary prepared this way. Text was data-captured and tagged to represent both kind of content and appearance. Laurence Urdang, its inspirer and editor, wrote:

> The coding of different levels of information – main, entry word, pronunciation, definition(s), variant(s), etymology, run-in entry, illustration – and more than 150 fields to which definitions were assigned – botany, chemistry, computer science, etc. – made it possible to prepare information for each level and in each field independently, thus ensur-ing better uniformity of treatment and far greater consistency among related pieces of information than had been achieved on other dictionaries. With all the data appropriately coded, programs enabled the computer to sort all of the bits and pieces into dictionary order. Once that had been accomplished, it remained only to read through the entire dictionary to make certain of the continuity and integrity of the text. (Urdang 1984: 155–6)

The intention was to keyboard the text only once. Entering dictionary text into the computer was a problem because the number of characters and character variations available was limited. The punched-paper tape used was based on US newspaper tele-typesetting conventions, which envisaged a 90-character repertoire, similar to the limitations of a manual typewriter. To represent the wider range of typographic possibilities (italic, bold, superiors, accents, Greek, and so on), the keyboarded text had to contain codes to indicate these different alphabets whenever a change from one to another was required. The typewritten proofs produced by the tape-perforating keyboard repeated these codes. The huge newspaper market for straightforward English-language typesetting in the US tended to make it easy for manufacturers to ignore complex composition requirements.

The actual typesetting of the dictionary shows the limitations of the composition equipment at the time (1965). The two possible contenders (both ruled out by the publishers) were the RCA VideoComp and Photon, the first machines to accept magnetic-tape input. While the sheer bulk of the dictionary might have seemed like ideal fodder for these machines, the heavy typographic coding of the text (averaging two-and-a-half style changes in every line) meant that the VideoComp, which had little memory to store variant founts, could not be made to work at peak efficiency. The text was eventually conventionally set by hot metal on the Monotype. To produce copy for the keyboarders, the finally edited text was output to a Datatronix, a CRT (cathode ray tube) screen linked to a microfilm camera, each screen-full of text being photographed to microfilm, which was then printed out on a high-speed Xerox. As in the first proofs, this printout was coded rather than being rendered in true typographic founts.

The convolutions of the *Random House Dictionary*'s production method point out the problems before a relatively uniform set of text-processing methods was developed. The missing component in the 1970s and early 1980s was any kind of common platform or device independence. This lack was not new. While a hand-compositor could combine the types of any foundry in his stick as long as they had a common height-to-paper, all mechanized composition systems were proprietary: Monotype hot-metal matrices could not be used on Linotype machines; Monophoto film matrices could not be used on Compugraphic machines. Device independence became important when data exchange began to be considered, and when the globalization of print production meant that data-capture, text-processing, and final output might happen on different continents.

Following Random House's lead, early computer-assisted composition focused on books with a large data-manipulation requirement: dictionaries, catalogues, directories, and encyclopedias, all text-heavy and with relatively straightforward, static columnar layouts. Oxford University Press, like its rival Collins, experimented with computer-assisted composition in the 1970s. Spare capacity on mainframe computers was used for text-processing: Collins used British Leyland's IBM mainframe in Cowley to run pagination programs on edited dictionary text (Luna 2000); Oxford used the ICL mainframe at its London warehouse in Neasden to process text for the *African Encyclopaedia*, *Crockford's Clerical Directory*, and the *Advanced Learner's Dictionary*. These projects involved new relationships within the publishing firm between publisher and computer suppliers (Urdang relates how in 1959 IBM salesmen were baffled by the idea of handling the text of a book on a computer); new roles for computer personnel within firms; and new frustrations for production people, used to placing work with printers with clear expectations of deadlines and costs, who gradually realized that new programs took time to develop, test, and de-bug, even if the actual processing they did took only hours to run.

Editors had to learn a whole new way of approaching proofs. Line-printer proofs provided either only the crudest typographic variation, or were simply print-outs of the text as it had been keyed, complete with codes, without any typographic formatting. Proofreaders had to decipher codes, and line-ends and dubious hyphenation decisions had to be reviewed separately, before expensive film or bromide was run through the typesetter. Proofing, which had always integrated a read for textual accuracy with an assessment of visual accuracy, disintegrated into a series of separate checks. Designers were often on the periphery of early computerized typesetting – with so much coding, keying, and processing to worry about, intrusions from someone who might want to change the way things looked were not always welcome. Oxford tried hard to make its computer-set catalogues and directories look as similar to their hot-metal predecessors as possible, but physical separation (some forty miles away at Neasden in OUP's case) from the traditional locations of composing room and layout studio helped reinforce the differences of the process.

By now, typesetting devices could break single-column text into pages and add headlines and folios; or could set a multi-column page by reversing at the end of each column and then setting the subsequent column beside it. If illustrations were involved, page make-up (the combination of different elements that make a page) remained a manual operation. True interactivity in page make-up had to await the development of page description languages in the 1980s. Before then, computerized composition moved from the "heroic" age of ad hoc programming and machine-specific configurations to the more systematic phase of front-end systems (Seybold 1984: 170). These multi-user systems supported the third generation of fast photo-composition machines based on imaging type on a CRT screen, which was transferred to film or paper by an optical system (Seybold 1984: 112). These included the Linotron 505 (1968), and various Autologic APS machines. These latter stored founts digitally, rather than as photo-graphic masters (Southall 2005: 143–7).

Front-end systems had their origins in the need to automate newspaper composition, especially in the United States, where there was a large domestic market relatively unfettered by union restrictive practices. The first such system was installed by Xylogics at the Daytona Beach *News-Journal* in 1971. (In the UK, restrictive practices prevented the introduction of such systems in newspapers until Eddie Shah's *Today* in 1986.) Copy could be entered by journalists, and routed to sub-editors and page-layout operators, thereby achieving the goal of single-keystroking. From 1970, keyboards were combined with visual display units (VDUs) to provide feedback to the keyboarder (Seybold 1977: 281). On multi-terminal systems, these entry terminals only had sufficient memory to store the text being worked on at the time: data was held and processed centrally. Front-end systems such as the Miles 33 400 system and the Ferranti CS7 were used in the composition of the *Oxford Shakespeare* and the second edition of the *Oxford English Dictionary* (1989). These systems were not used in the same way as for newspaper production, to capture new keystrokes: in the case of the *OED*, all text editing was done on specially designed editing software, and then transferred to the CS7 on magnetic tape; there was editorial keyboarding by *Oxford Shakespeare* staff, but it was essentially to amend and add formatting codes to existing texts prepared by Trevor Howard-Hill for the Shakespeare concordance project. Essentially, both systems were used for formatting rather for text entry and editing (Luna 1990; Ragg and Luna 2003).

The second edition of the *OED*, like the *Random House Dictionary*, was conceived as a database that would hold the components of the dictionary. Urdang's compartmentalization of data into fields had been overtaken by the more sophisticated approach of describing a document's structure. This was called "standard generalized mark-up language" (SGML) and was developed by Charles Goldfarb and others for IBM in the 1960s. SGML described the underlying structure of a document rather than its visual attributes; it delineated the structural elements, and also described the hierarchical relationships between them (Alschuler 1995). For example, the elements of a dictionary entry might be divided into a headword group, a definition group, and an etymology group; each tagged group would then have its component elements tagged: within the headword group would be the headword, variant spelling, and pronunciation. A document type definition (DTD), separate from the specific data, and usable for as many documents as necessary, describes these elements and relationships. While it seeks to separate structure and content from visual implementation, usefully from the typesetting point of view it allows the definition of entity references, codes which represent any character, such as an accented one, not accessible from a normal keyboard, or a combination of characters, such as a fraction. This was an important step in overcoming the mismatch between the limited capabilities of the typewriter-derived computer keyboard with a hundred or so keys, and the relatively wide character sets of traditional systems such as the Monotype.

The composition of the *OED* confirmed the globalization of text composition and book production in this period: data-capture took place in the US, much of the software was written in Canada, system management and text-processing were done in Oxford, typesetting in the north of England, and printing and binding in the US. In comparison with the production of the first edition, as John Trevitt has written, "what was a connected sequence of interdependent activities carried out under one roof has become a set of discrete functions each of which may be performed anywhere in the world" (Steinberg 1996: 239). Data-capture was done manually, optical character recognition still, as in the 1960s, regarded as having an unacceptably high error rate. SGML tagging was added at the keyboarding stage, based on the logical typographic coding of the original edition's typography.

For supply to the typesetter, both the *OED* and the *Oxford Shakespeare* text were tagged with proprietary codes describing typographic attributes and also more sophisticated text-processing routines, such as conditional text, line numbering, cues for indexing, and extracting headlines. These systems used were efficient at performing multi-column pagination, implementing complex rules about how columns and pages should be broken, and how footnotes and sidenotes could be inserted. The Miles 33 system, for example, was designed to handle the complex typography of parliamentary papers produced by the Stationery Office. But such systems did not support SGML, and all SGML tags in incoming data had to be converted to typographic tags in a "tags-to-typography" specification. Nor was it possible to interact with the system. Tags were added to text, manually or by search-and-replace routines, and then galley files were sent for batch processing into pages. In the case of a long file, or one with many conditional or variable commands, this processing could run overnight. Errors in tagging were only revealed if the resulting page files were incorrect, or if they failed to emerge. At this stage, there was no "what you see is what you get" (WYSIWYG) functionality, and screens represented all text, of whatever style, in generic founts with visible codes, while proofing prior to output on a high-resolution typesetter was carried out using low-resolution printers with generic founts rather than true type designs.

This process was suited to the text-heavy, multi-column, multivolume *OED*, or the two-column, line-numbered *Oxford Shakespeare*. Editorial work concentrated on the construction and correction of the text; design concentrated on describing rules for the combination of repetitive elements and for page make-up. Automatic line-end word division (which in the *OED* was not used to assist justification) could be handled by the front-end, using either algorithms or an exception dictionary; it could also, in some cases, be handled by logic in the final typesetting device. Fourth-generation phototypesetting devices were capable of imaging a whole page at a time using proprietary page description languages (Seybold 1984: 386–91). A scanning (rasterizing) laser built up a whole-page image in horizontal scan lines at a resolution of at least 1,000 lines to the inch. The page could contain type, line artwork, and halftone images. Monotype's Lasercomp (1976), used for the *OED* and *Oxford Shakespeare*, was the first such machine: it set a broadsheet newspaper page in less than a minute. The more modest Linotron 202 or Compugraphic 8400, using the previous-generation CRT technology, were more likely to be used for straightforward book composition.

The proprietary nature of the software controlling different machines caused problems in the control that designers and production staff could exercise over their suppliers. Computerized phototypesetting systems worked to many different sets of standards: increments could be points, half-points, decipoints, or eighths of a point. Changing output resolution could change point size. Italic could be created by slanting roman type. It was difficult to keep up with the differences in capability between Compugraphic, Linotron, and Monophoto machines. Partly because versions of the typeface were available on all systems, Times New Roman started its second lease of life: originally a superior newspaper typeface, it became the default for computerized composition, a role it holds to this day.

These production changes did not directly affect the author–publisher relationship (unless the complaints about the quality of computerized word division count). That came when the author's text, keyed on a word-processor, became a direct source of copy. The 39th edition of *Hart's Rules* (1983) makes no concession to computerized typesetting: the only hint is a mention of the "96-unit system" used on the Lasercomp that had replaced the Monotype hot-metal 18-unit system. The same year saw the first issue of the *Chicago Guide to Preparing Electronic Manuscripts*, followed in 1984 by *Oxford Rules for the Preparation of Text on Microcomputers*. Both described sets of generic codes that authors were asked to use rather than the (then) variety of word-processor commands for bold, italic, and levels of heading.

The *Chicago Guide* also demonstrates how the use of authors' keystrokes changed the role of the copy-editor, who now had to check on the author's presentation of the text, as well as prepare it for the typesetter. When all text had to be re-keyed, the imposition of house style imposed relatively little extra cost. Author-supplied text would now have to be put into house style by the author under instruction from a copy-editor, or else by the typesetter, which would reduce the savings promised. The *Guide* suggested that, "because an electronic version of the manuscript already exists, the printout should be marked more as if it were a proof than original manuscript." It went on to comment that it might not be appropriate to insist on "certain mechanical or arbitrary things that a copyeditor does to conform to house style – things that, if done in some other consistent reasonable way, should not detract from the quality of the writing." A list of issues such as the use of serial commas and the use of en-rules rather than hyphens in figure extents, as well as grammatical points, followed. The *Guide* continued: "We try to eliminate as candidates for electronic publishing those manuscripts that are likely to cause eventual problems if they are handled electronically: manuscripts whose authors may balk at being asked to enter changes to their prose."

While the large publishing, front-end driving, high-speed typesetters were indispensable for projects such as the *OED* and the *Oxford Shakespeare*, the need to reduce the cost of composition meant that relatively few formerly integrated typesetting and printing houses survived by adopting this technology. Economic pressures were forcing a division of labor on the industry. In the early 1970s, the IBM Selectric Composer offered a low-cost alternative to the phototypesetter. It could produce camera-ready copy at low cost, and, most importantly, it could be operated by a typist rather than a trained compositor (Steinberg 1996: 221–2). Printers such as OUP experimented with IBM composition in-house; then, against a background of trade union difficulties, encouraged the start-up of small, independent typesetting bureaus, often run by ex-compositors. The development of small, independent typesetters was important because it allowed specialization. The replacement of large hot-metal composing rooms with skills across a wide variety of kinds of book composition (mathematical, scientific, dictionary, foreign-language) was partly achieved through the fragmentation of these individual skills into a range of small suppliers. These suppliers typically started with IBM composition, moved on to direct-entry photo-composition systems, such as the Linotype CRTronic (1979), and finally to desktop publishing. Academically prestigious but economically problematic publications, such as *The New Testament in Greek: The Gospel According to St. Luke* (Clarendon Press, 1984), showed how complex setting that would previously have been handled on the Monotype could be set on the IBM with efficiency, if with considerable reduction in the aesthetics of the typesetting.

The IBM's range of typefaces and point sizes was severely limited, and any display type had to be set separately. It is interesting to note that the non-Greek text of *St.*

Luke was set in IBM's version of Times New Roman, hardly ever used in OUP's hot-metal composing rooms, while display type is phototypeset in a version of Baskerville. IBM composition cut the cost of one-off composition but, as we have seen, did not allow for the manipulation or reuse of data. For this, a new generation of desktop machines would have to be developed.

Another niche market was mathematical composition. Hot-metal composition of mathematics was highly expensive because of the handwork required to convert the elements of equations, which could be keyboarded, into displayed equations. Monotype developed its four-line composition system, first for hot metal (1956), then for photo-composition, and similar capabilities were developed for the Linotron 505, but a radically different approach was taken by Donald Knuth, who between 1977 and 1989 developed his own mathematical typesetting system, TeX. TeX allowed mathematicians to do their own typesetting by using a mark-up system that was conceptually half-way between procedural (system- or machine-specific) and structural (e.g. SGML) mark-up. Aimed at scientists who had access to mainframe computers, it achieved device independence partly through the use of a linked fount description system, MetaFont, and its own Computer Modern Roman founts, which were essentially copies of Monotype's hot-metal mathematical fount designs. The sophistication of the composition features that Knuth included in TeX, such as its ability to optimize justification and page-breaks across a whole document, did not prevent it from being seen as only a solution for niche scientific typesetting, where it has maintained a following. Knuth's own *Digital Typography* (1999) displayed its strengths, and an unusual example of TeX being used for non-mathematical setting can be seen in John Sutherland's *Who Betrays Elizabeth Bennet?* (1999), which used PostScript founts rather than Computer Modern Roman. LaTeX, a development of TeX, was easier to use, and found a niche amongst academic authors from the humanities as well as the sciences.

By 1985, many pieces of the puzzle were in place. Phototypesetters such as the Lasercomp could output any combination of type and graphics over a whole newspaper-size page on film or bromide, using their own proprietary raster image processor (RIP). Personal computers with word-processing applications allowed authors to key and save text to floppy disks that could be transferred from one device to another (Steinberg 1996: 228).

The key development that changed all kinds of text composition was the device-independent page-description language. Adobe's PostScript language (1984) rapidly became dominant. It interpreted the layout of text and images that could now be created, using Adobe's PageMaker software on an Apple Macintosh desktop computer (1984), so that it could be printed out on a PostScript-enabled Apple desktop LaserWriter (1985). Promoted as "desktop publishing," this powerful model of device-independent standards and WYSIWYG software, which enabled complex graphic material to be created interactively, became the new norm for all publishing and typesetting activities. The economies of scale of the personal computer market made it inevitable that desktop composition systems would be far cheaper than dedicated typesetting front-ends; the few that survived reconfigured themselves around now-standard desktop components.

The description of PageMaker as a page-layout application indicates its significance: the composition process changed from one that was concerned with the creation of individual columns of type, which were combined with images in a separate operation, into one that was concerned with the dynamic creation of whole pages. This change of function meant that typographic output devices previously known as phototypesetters became image-setters: no longer did type have a means of output all to itself. Monotype and Linotype allowed their image-setters to be driven by the device-independent Adobe PostScript RIPs as well as their proprietary ones, beginning the convergence of the "high-end" of professional typesetting with the "low-resolution" end of desktop publishing.

This convergence was seen immediately in the availability of common typefaces for desktop use and for professional publishing applications. No longer were typefaces proprietary to composition systems: any PostScript (or later TrueType) fount would work on any PostScript device. Office documents changed from mono-spaced typewriter styles that had been used even on electric typewriters, to "professional" proportional designs. Linotype and Monotype rapidly digitized large parts of their type libraries, originally created as part of the marketing of their composition equipment, but now viewed as separate assets. However, the real innovations came from the much smaller digital foundries that immediately developed – and from Adobe itself. In particular, the concentration of type design in Britain, Germany, and the United States was challenged by type designers redressing the imbalance between Latin and non-Latin types, helped by the establishment of Unicode, a standardized approach to defining character positions within founts (Hudson 2002). By the end of the period, the names Linotype and Monotype were associated only with the marketing of digital type, not with typesetting equipment.

The combination of the introduction of the Apple Macintosh and the IBM PC as standard hardware, and of Adobe's PostScript page-description language, had changed the paradigm for composition. From a PostScript file created in Adobe's PageMaker software, the Apple LaserWriter could print a page at good-enough resolution for a desktop; the Linotronic 300 could output the same page, with the same Adobe founts, at professional print quality. As well as integration, the Mac and PC offered ease of use. The front ends that were so competent at handling text composition lacked the interactivity that was necessary for highly illustrated books. Previously, the composition of pages for illustrated books could be handled in one of two ways. Designers could prepare layouts for a typesetter to implement by piecing together film of text and images, or themselves prepare artwork boards by pasting up text elements and indicating positions for illustrations (which had to be separately inserted at the final film stage). An example of this is the *Reader's Digest Repair Manual* (1972). Both approaches required the initial setting of all text type and headlines as galleys, which would be divided into the necessary chunks to fit the page layout: in this respect photo-composition differed little from metal composition. Now that images could be scanned and digitized, PageMaker took the artwork board as a metaphor and allowed designers to cut, paste, and arrange text and images electronically – with every element visible on screen exactly as it would print.

The transfer of author-keyed text to the typesetting process was simplified. Files from word-processing applications could now be imported into page-layout applications by designers or typesetters. The need for authors to add generic codes to identify text elements disappeared – PageMaker could understand Word's internal codes for italic, bold, and so on. The *Oxford Children's Encyclopedia* (1991) and the *Oxford Illustrated Encyclopedia* (1993) demonstrate the adoption of desktop techniques into professional book production. The *OCE* was produced by importing Word files into PageMaker. Writing to fit a layout was a major beneficiary of this change. Whereas copy-fitting had previously required either meticulous cast-off or a willingness to re-set type at galley stage to suit a page layout, the interactivity of desktop publishing allowed editors and designers to work collaboratively to resolve questions of copy-fitting and make-up. While most of the *OCE*'s illustrations were conventionally drawn and scanned, the *OIE* rapidly moved to preparing all its artwork on a Macintosh, using PostScript drawing applications such as Freehand. Drawings produced using PostScript, like PostScript founts, could be sized independently of output resolution. This allowed easy integration with pages constructed in Quark XPress, the desktop composition software introduced in 1987 that became more widely used than PageMaker. It was also possible to systematize keyboarding of copy in the word-processing application, by using either Quark XPress's proprietary tags or matching style-sheet definitions, thus automating the formatting of text as it was imported into the page-make-up application.

Although Quark XPress came to dominate small-scale typesetting, developments of front-end systems maintained a role for more complex titles. Interset's Quoin (1990) and Advent's 3B2 (which included a TeX module for mathematical composition) provided publishing-system functionality on desktop hardware; they were particularly good at setting dictionaries and reference works, where publishers required that the data they had supplied be returned in SGML or extensible mark-up language (XML) format. (XML offered more flexibility in reflecting document structure than SGML, and could be used to generate Internet pages as well as printed pages.) Adobe's Framemaker text-processing application (from 1986), which could accept SGML (and later XML) files as input, also retained a niche in the market, but generally for technical documentation rather than one-off book typesetting, where XPress, though less capable of automation, was more flexible. XPress, and its Adobe rival InDesign (1999), also allowed designers directly to create templates and styles for typesetters to use, while Quoin and other front ends still required a specification that was implemented by the typesetter.

The production of *Common Worship: Services and Prayers for the Church of England* (2000) allows us to consider some broader aspects of publishing policy, as well as the methods of composition used (Morgan 2003). The design process followed the desktop publishing model. The Church of England (who acted as their own publishers) commissioned a design company (rather than a typesetting or publishing house) to design and typeset the book. The simultaneous print and electronic publication shows that, even for such a formal text, the typeset, printed, bound version no longer has automatic primacy. *Common Worship* provided an authorized alternative to the 1662 *Book of Common*

Prayer and a replacement for the 1980 *Alternative Service Book*. The *Book of Common Prayer* had been reprinted in the period, but from existing metal settings. The *Alternative Service Book* was "conventionally" typeset on a Linotron 202 in Palatino, very much a typeface of this period, and a departure from the workaday typefaces previously used for the majority of prayer books. It was the last service book to be published for the Church of England by the Oxford and Cambridge university presses and the Queen's Printer.

Common Worship was a response to its publisher's requirement that it should be designed for use, and that consideration should be given to users with visual impairment or lack of manual dexterity. It was decided that page breaks should fall so that no prayers were broken across pages: the longest single prayer was identified, and decisions on type size and page size based on that. Like its previous publishers, the Church of England developed a detailed liturgical house style guide, transferring responsibility for detailed textual consistency to the designers of the book. This hands-on approach, using Quark XPress, ensured the necessary control over the page make-up, and also allowed design refinements to be introduced during the production of the book as different sections were proofed (the whole production being to a tight schedule). A disadvantage of a desktop system that focused mainly on page layout was the lack of any structural tagging of the text, which had implications for its continuing life as an electronic document.

Common Worship was also made available for download from the Church of England's website in Adobe's portable document format (PDF) and in Microsoft Word-compatible rich-text format (RTF). The PDF preserves exactly the typographic formatting and page layout of the printed edition. It can be printed out, but it cannot easily be manipulated, for example to create a service sheet with a particular combination of liturgical options. To do this, the RTF is required, as selected text can be copied from it and pasted into another document. The RTF preserves the text, but does not use style sheets to control the typographic styling of particular elements; paragraphs carry typographic formatting but are not identified structurally, so the formatting can easily be lost or become inconsistent. Moreover, the typographic styling of the RTF is only an approximation of that used in the printed text: the typeface Arial, a default on all computers, is used instead of the less widely available Gill Sans used in the printed book; subtle differences of type weight and spacing are lost, as is the identification of congregational responses by the speech-prefix "All." It is an irony that, given the great care with which editors and designers considered the fall of text on the printed page, such user-focused considerations are lost when the text is used to produce a derivative document. A solution for documents of this kind is the use of XML tagging, which allows reference to external schema (similar to the document type definition required by SGML) which can allow output formats to be designed for different production circumstances. At the time of writing, this functionality does not exist within Microsoft Word.

This period saw typesetting change from systems that capture data for a specific typographic output system to part of an integrated chain of document production, which may have printed output as only one of its aims. Authors and copy-editors began to work interactively with their texts. Designers, using page-layout applications, took a hands-on role in composition (Hendel 1998: 189–90). Typesetting moved to a generally more stable technological environment after 1985, after a period of competing and incompatible photo-composition and typewriter-based systems. Standardization on PostScript as a page-description language enabled a rebirth of creative type design. This addressed issues of optical scaling and correct weighting for output systems – essentially making type look right at any size rather than using uncorrected linear scaling – that had been integral to metal type production, but which were usually inadequately implemented in phototypesetting (Tracy 1986: 54). Large character sets were made practical by the increase in computer storage capacity and the development of the Unicode standard. Although workflows became more integrated, word-processing, design and layout, automated composition, and web distribution were still handled through separate applications. While the aim of the designer and typesetter was still to give each text an ideal typographic form, it was now understood that the dominant requirement for any text processing was the need for flexible reuse and universal distribution: any print publication should be considered as just one instance of that text, and not necessarily the form that would be most widely available.

REFERENCES AND FURTHER READING

Alschuler, Liora (1995) *ABCD . . . SGML: A User's Guide to Structured Information.* London: International Thomson Computer.

Bringhurst, Robert (1992) *The Elements of Typographic Style.* Vancouver: Hartley & Marks.

Chicago Guide to Preparing Electronic Manuscripts. Chicago: University of Chicago Press, 1983.

Hart's Rules for Compositors and Readers at the University Press Oxford, 39th edn. Oxford: Oxford University Press, 1983.

Heath, L. G. and Faux, Ian (1978) *A Manual of Phototypesetting.* Manchester: Lithographic Training Services.

Hendel, Richard (1998) *On Book Design.* New Haven: Yale University Press.

Hudson, John (2002) "Unicode: From Text to Type." In John D. Berry (ed.), *Language, Culture, Type,* pp. 24–44. New York: Association Typographique International.

Knuth, Donald E. (1999) *Digital Typography.* Stanford: CSLI.

Luna, Paul (1990) "The Oxford English Dictionary." *Baseline,* 13: 34–7.

— (2000) "Clearly Defined: Continuity and Innovation in the Typography of English Dictionaries." *Typography Papers,* 4: 5–56.

Mitchell, Michael and Wightman, Susan (2005) *Book Typography: A Designer's Manual.* Marlborough: Libanus.

Morgan, John (2003) "An Account of the Making of *Common Worship*." *Typography Papers,* 3: 33–64.

Oxford Rules for the Preparation of Text on Microcomputers. Oxford: Oxford University Press, 1984.

Ragg, Edward and Luna, Paul (2003) "Designing the Oxford Shakespeare." *Typography Papers,* 5: 5–22.

Seybold, John W. (1977) *Fundamentals of Modern Composition.* Media, PA: Seybold.

— (1984) *The World of Digital Typesetting.* Media, PA: Seybold.

Southall, Richard (2005) *Printing Type in the Twentieth Century: Manufacturing and Design Methods.* London: British Library.

Steinberg, S. H. (1996) *Five Hundred Years of Printing,* ed. and rev. John Trevitt. London: British Library.

Sutherland, John (1999) *Who Betrays Elizabeth Bennet?* Oxford: Oxford University Press.

Tracy, Walter (1986) *Letters of Credit.* London: Gordon Fraser.

Urdang, Laurence (1984) "A Lexicographer's Adventures in Computing." *Dictionaries: Journal of the Dictionary Society of North America*, 6: 150–65.

Wallis, Lawrence W. (1997) "Monotype Time Check." *Monotype Recorder*, n.s. 10: 46–55.

29

The Global Market
1970–2000: Producers

Eva Hemmungs Wirtén

Despite the fact that books had already proved themselves to be a highly adaptable commodity that prospered in the booming market conditions of mass production as early as the time of Charles Dickens and Victor Hugo, "one might almost as convincingly hold that book publishing was the last culture industry to attain modernity. Not until after World War II did it become part of the large corporate sector, and adopt the practices of publicity and marketing characteristic of monopoly capital" (Ohmann 1996: 22). Today, the book is fully integrated into our information age with its global media market. The last three decades of the twentieth century undoubtedly witnessed a radical transformation of a trade that had always seen itself as slightly apart and different from others. As trades go, publishing is a highly contextual business which operates under various different conditions, and thus looks very different in different parts of the world. Substantial local and regional variations in cultural identity, political and legal frameworks, language, economic structure, and social demographics, obviously influence the way in which books are produced. The diversity that results from such complexity cannot be fully accounted for here. Instead, the following chapter takes a different approach and suggests that the story of producers can be told by describing three interrelated themes that suggest a *structural* and far-reaching reorganization of contemporary publishing, the consequences of which reverberate both locally and globally. These themes are: conglomeratization, content, and convergence.

Conglomeratization

Perhaps the most obvious change in the business of publishing during this period is the way in which it moved from being mainly a privately and independently run and owned, small-scale endeavor to being part of larger, increasingly transnational, media conglomerates, so-called TMCs. This is a term used to describe the apparently haphazard amalgamation of disparate corporate entities sheltered by one huge corporation

which buys everything in its way. Gulf and Western is an early example of such conglomeratization, at one time owning land in the Dominican Republic, insurance companies, racehorses, sports teams, and lingerie manufacturers, as well as the publisher
Simon & Schuster and Paramount Pictures (Bagdikian 2000: 28–9).

The integration of publishing into these larger conglomerates began in the 1960s
and can be described as a three-stage process. Though close scrutiny will prove that we
are not witnessing a perfectly chronological sequence, but rather seeing a fluid process
in which some of these broader tendencies overlap in time, we can still summarize it
as: (1) beginning with the buying of textbook publishers by companies which had little
or no previous experience of publishing; (2) continuing with the buying of trade publishers by larger media corporations; (3) the vertical and horizontal consolidation of the
contemporary transnational media corporation including its holdings in print.

The acquisition of textbook publishers by corporations like IBM, ITT, Westinghouse,
and Xerox was initially prompted by an anticipation that buying software or "content"
would – in combination with the hardware already at the disposal of these companies
– serve as the ideal strategy at a time when teaching and education were perceived as
one of the largest potential markets. Together with trade and professional books, education is one of the three major segments of the publishing industry. While much of this
discussion centers on trade publishing – mostly for its cultural rather than financial
significance – professional and educational publishing can hardly be discounted in a
society that increasingly pivots around the acquisition of information and knowledge.
Consequently, textbook publishers are major businesses in their own right displaying
similar characteristics of concentration and consolidation as trade publishing. Evidence
of this strategic role is the fact that the period's largest acquisition in printing and
publishing history was the sale by Viacom of Simon & Schuster's textbook unit to
Pearson PLC in 1998 (*Mergerstat® Review* 2000: 288).

The second wave of corporate invasions of publishing occurred when corporations
such as RCA, CBS, and Gulf and Western began to purchase trade publishing houses.
The story of Random House is a good example of the buying and selling pattern typical
of this consolidation. Bought by RCA for $40 million in 1966, Random House had
already purchased Knopf in 1960 and Pantheon in 1961. Sold to the Newhouse group
(Advance Publications) in 1980, they then in turn traded Random House to the German
company Bertelsmann for $1.4 billion in 1998. Currently, Random House acts as the
corporate umbrella for over a hundred publishing houses in thirteen countries, owning
imprints such as the previously mentioned Knopf, but also Ballantine Books and
Bantam Dell in the US, Plaza & Janés in Spain, Goldmann in Germany, as well as
several venerable British publishing houses such as Jonathan Cape, Chatto and Windus,
and the Bodley Head.

The third stage – which is the most interesting for us – can perhaps be best described
as a further consolidation of stage two, in that we now see these developments operating
in a distinctly transnational media market. Publishing has by now left behind its tradition of being a set of family-run businesses and become integrated into transnational
media conglomerates, conglomerates that look very much like a Russian *Babushka* doll,

where the largest doll holds a smaller one, which in turn holds a still smaller one, until the most minuscule is reached. Translated into publishing, this means that if Jonathan Cape is now an imprint within Random House, Random House is only one of many companies owned by Bertelsmann. Within these larger media conglomerates, book publishing rarely constitutes more than a small part. In 2000, Time Warner Trade Publishing's contribution to Time Warner's total revenues stood at a mere 1 percent. HarperCollins provided 7 percent of its parent company News Corporation's total sales, and Simon & Schuster's contribution to the Viacom total revenue was expected to decline, as a result of the purchase of CBS in 2000, from 5 percent to 3 percent. In 2000, Random House had sales of $2 billion, representing approximately 12 percent of its parent company's total revenues (Milliot 2001: 62–3). The emergence and consolidation of the media conglomerates must also be seen against a much larger backdrop of general transnationalization and globalization where the growth of transnational corporations in all types of businesses has been most dramatic in the developed countries.

On the one hand, this period appears to be one in which the market for books expands and becomes truly global; on the other hand, this development is matched by another, in which the control and ownership of publishing through the media conglomerates becomes ever more concentrated. Names and owners come and go, since the *modus operandi* of the conglomerate process is a continuous state of mergers and acquisitions, alliances and licensing deals that, during the 1990s, resulted in a "tiered global media market" (Herman and McChesney 1997: 52), where a handful of companies represented the most important and powerful. Although several of these were American, most notably Time Warner, Disney, and Viacom, the increasing transnational nature of the media market also meant that many companies rising to global prominence at this time were located outside the United States, but with substantial investments in American publishing, leading to a growing recognition that the United States was by no means immune to what some referred to as a possible "takeover" by European interests (Barnet and Cavanagh 1994: 105). Major players based outside the United States at the beginning of the twenty-first century were Rupert Murdoch's News Corporation, the German firm Bertelsmann, the Dutch–British Reed Elsevier, the Dutch Wolters Kluwer, the Canadian Thompson, the British Pearson PLC, and the two French giants Lagardère and Vivendi Universal. It is interesting to note that all of the above non-US corporations have a history in print culture, several of them starting out as publishing houses, whereas firms such as Time Warner, Disney, and Viacom have stronger ties to movies, music, and television.

Undeniably, conglomeratization meant a structural transformation in the way in which publishing as a business was conducted. What emerged was a new economy and with it came new players onto the field, not necessarily because they desired to work with books, but rather because they were equipped with the know-how demanded by a new type of market. For instance, the literary agent knew how to negotiate and promote the deals that some authors now expected: in particular, the subsidiary-rights race that began in the wake of a truly successful book with paperback publishing, but would then branch out into major licensing deals for everything from movies to duvet covers. Other developments that had a considerable impact on the industry were the technological breakthroughs in inventory control, in particular the arrival of computerized systems that would indicate how well a book was selling. This was the corporate technologizing of books: the idea that everything could be tracked, understood, and made profitable by the new gadgets of surveillance. Add to this that the product itself – the text – faced massive challenges in the shape of things to come – e-books, hypertext, and more – and it all added up to a reconfiguration of a business that had existed without fundamental changes since the emergence of the mass market for such writers as Dickens and Hugo.

Of course, it was only to be expected that such profound restructuring would have a less tangible, but every bit as revolutionary, impact on those who worked in publishing: it caused an identity crisis that took many by surprise. Thomas Guinzburg, who sold Viking to Penguin in 1975, expressed a sense of lost innocence when reflecting on the deal, which looked ideal on paper, but quickly turned sour in real life. Penguin did not understand, Guinzburg said, after being ousted from the company, that "our *instinct* for books was always central" (quoted in Whiteside 1980: 145).

Despite statements to this effect, the business of publishing was never at any time or place a homogeneous and harmonious field – quite the opposite, in fact – and yet it is generally assumed as a truth of sorts that it used to be a calling where profit margins were low but steady and thus offered you a line of business you rarely entered for profit but because you had some sort of relationship with books and reading. In other words, publishing was "run by its editors rather than its accountants" (Schiffrin 2000: 81). The rewards you could hope to reap in such a system were intangible, coming to you in the shape of cultural and social capital rather than in dollars or pounds. Building a reputable stable of writers was a long-term rather than a short-term commitment, where investments were made in authors based on what they might achieve in the future and dividends put on hold until they eventually – many years in the future perhaps – provided a return on that initial investment. One of the basic premises that made such reasoning possible was that publishing operated on a principle of swings and roundabouts. If the publishing house was fortunate enough to secure a bestseller, then the substantial revenues that could be expected from that book would subsidize the losses incurred by less-successful and perhaps occasionally controversial books, books that nonetheless were judged important as part of the overall publishing program. Although having the occasional bestseller was important, it was the offerings of the house in its entirety, as well as a well-managed backlist, that finally justified the work of a publisher.

In his memoir *The Business of Books* (2000), André Schiffrin described a meeting in January 1990 with Albert Vitale, the man brought in to lead Random House when Newhouse purchased the publisher. The topic for their discussion was the spring 1990 list, one that the editors were particularly pleased with, partly because it included books about that highly popular cartoon family, *The Simpsons*:

> Vitale looked through the books that we were to publish . . . "Who is this Claude Simon?" he asked disdainfully, having clearly never heard of the Nobel Prize-winning

novelist, "and this Carlo Ginzburg?" probably Italy's best-known historian. I then noticed that he would begin reading on the right side of the page, where the print runs were listed, and only then moved to the puzzling titles. For him, it was as if we were a shoe manufacturer, making sizes too small to fit most customers. "What is the sense of publishing books with such small printings?" he shouted. Were we not ashamed of ourselves? How could I face myself in the mirror each morning knowing that I wanted to publish such hopelessly unprofitable titles? The list included Groening's books, which, according to our reckoning, would more than amply pay for the losses that might be incurred by the more difficult books. But Vitale's new policy was that each book should make money on its own and that one title should no longer be allowed to subsidize another. (Schiffrin 2000: 91)

Schiffrin's account expresses in a nutshell the clash between the old ("swings and round-abouts") and the new ("bean-counting") approach to publishing. The relentless search for bestsellers and the demand that each title carry its own weight – both ideas seen as the result of conglomeratization – placed the two men in opposite corners: one following in the tradition of those who know how to "read" and the other belonging to those who know how to "count" (Bourdieu 1999: 16).

Even if we are compelled to accept this description of a widening split in attitude toward publishing, it is one in dire need of additional clarification. Publishing has always been two things at once: a commercial activity as well as a cultural one. The scales might have tipped in favor of the former during this period, and being subjected to the whims of the market no doubt provided an unwelcome wake-up call to the realities of corporate life. As it developed during this period, the identity crisis of the business can be related to this built-in dichotomy in which publishing – and trade publishing in particular – is seen as an entity that needs to make a profit, on the one hand, and, on the other, clings to a die-hard self-image as a unique undertaking operating according to its own economic laws.

The importance of publishing in monetary terms borders on the insignificant, yet the symbolic capital at stake was and is substantial. The impact of this trade reaches therefore far beyond what its relatively modest contribution to the media conglomerates and other transnational corporations suggests, and we must rather search for the reason behind the continued importance of print properties elsewhere. Albert Greco's point that "the U.S. book industry was the prestigious keystone of the entire mass communications industry, primarily for the 'content' it generated" is therefore an interesting one to consider (Greco 1997: 45).

Content

A privileged word in the language of the media conglomerates is *content*. Content ownership was a major incentive behind the conglomeratization and concentration in media and publishing. But few things are as prone to politics as statistics. While some say that the title output has never been so impressive, growing by 256 percent in the United

States between 1960 and 1989 (Greco 1997: 54), others disagree and point out that since a handful of companies now controls the market, this is only a smoke-screen argument, since it hides the fact that true publishing clout of the kind only available to the media conglomerates is necessary in order to sell and display a publisher's books in chain bookstores that "are now able to demand almost whatever terms they wish from the major publishers, who are pressed to pay large amounts of co-op advertising money if they want their books to be placed prominently in the stores" (Schiffrin 2000: 124). Be that as it may, a common observation is that the market tended to become increasingly polarized. It was also characterized by the emergence of the "brand" authors at the beginning of the 1970s, many of whom were women – Judith Krantz, Jackie Collins, and Shirley Conran come to mind. These authors not only tapped into a new market but could also command advances and advertising budgets that marked a new era in publishing.

In his survey of the symbolic boundaries marked out in French and American publishing, Daniel Weber noted that French publishers were more prone to "justify a desire to launch a bestseller as a means of subsidizing a more difficult or experimental work" than their American counterparts (Weber 2000: 128). In general, the American publishers Weber interviewed were largely utilitarian in their approach to literature, relying on the market to determine what constituted a good book. The French interviewees, on the other hand, were more sensitive to the possible effects of recent publishing trends, such as conglomeratization, and expressed concern for the possible fate of French literature and language in the wake of importation and translations (Weber 2000: 141). The concern of the French editors can, of course, be attributed to many things, among them the desire to appear to be an alternative to mass-market mainstream publishing and to the specter of "Americanization."

While it is practically impossible to capture the range of content made available by book publishing, one can at least observe that is it mostly written and published in English. According to UNESCO (2004), almost 50 percent of all translations are made from English into various languages, but only 6 per cent of all translations are into English. Merely 2.96 percent of the books published in the US in 1990 were translations; in Britain, the number was 2.4 percent for the same year (Venuti 1995: 12). In 1994, 1,418 of the 51,863 books published in the US, or 2.74 percent, were translations (Venuti 1998: 160). Between 1968 and 1992, only 2 percent of the books on *Publisher's Weekly* annual list of bestsellers came from non-English language authors (Lemieux and Saint-Jacques 1996: 285). A comparison of book translations in the so-called SIACS (States in Advanced Capitalist Societies) – France, Germany, Japan, the Netherlands, Spain, Sweden, UK, and the United States – between 1983 and 1985, substantiate these findings. English is the language from which most translations occur. This tendency to dominate is corroborated by the reciprocally minimal ratio of translations going the other way (Held et al. 1999: 346). This subject is further discussed by Claire Squires in chapter 30 of this volume.

According to one of the very few sources we have on the global production of books, *The UNESCO Statistical Yearbook 1999*, most countries have a negative trade balance when it comes to the import/export of print culture and, if we accept these numbers at their face value, then we can conclude that – with a few notable exceptions – the entire world engages in the importation of textual material that the UK and the US exports. However, we need to interpret these statistics with some care. We can almost certainly discern tendencies of exclusion, whereby entire continents such as Africa display negative trade balances over time, whereas the US and the UK consistently display positive trade balances (UNESCO 1999: iv. 134–50). However, most accounts of the advantages and disadvantages of being an "importer" as opposed to being an "exporter" are far too sweeping in their generalizations. For instance, cultural movements of this sort are not simple, and their benefits and drawbacks can rarely be found only on one side.

While the global economy thrives on increasingly complex flows which no longer can be explained by a straightforward connection between language and nation-state – and several of the most powerful transnational media corporations today are non-US based and non-US owned – most TMCs are still building their empires on the English language: in research, in entertainment, in literature. In order to reach a global audience for an author writing in a "minor" language, translation first into English is absolutely necessary. If all we needed in order to prove linguistic power were numbers, then Chinese would appear to do well. As it is, English remains the vernacular of the world.

Convergence

If one of the major motives behind conglomeratization was the accumulation and control of that valuable asset "content," then it was a consolidation in two dimensions: vertical – the mergers and acquisitions of publishing houses according to the principles discussed previously – but also, and perhaps even more importantly, horizontal, ensuring the same kind of control over all possible distribution channels used in order to distribute the content in question. And this is the point at which the third element enters the picture – the component of *convergence* – the possibility of drawing on a number of new technologies in order to exploit their potential to the fullest: on telecommunications, cable, and the Internet. By the end of this period, convergence suggested not only that the traditional functions of telephones, television sets, and personal computers were about to merge, but also that this represented the erasure of traditional boundaries between media forms, and the commingling of diverse platforms in media, telecommunications, and software. This was a development that promised to bring together the compounded assets achieved by years of consolidation in a hitherto unprecedented manner.

The year 2000, a significant year in terms of mergers, saw two major, well-publicized deals with a clear impact on the global media market: the acquisition of Time Warner by America Online, and the arrival of Vivendi Universal. On December 8, 2000, Vivendi (the result of the 1998 merger between Compagnie Generale des Eaux and Havas, one of the largest publishing groups in France) announced its merger with

Seagram (owner of, among other things, the Universal Music Group and Universal Studios and ranked twenty-third among the world's one hundred largest transnational corporations in the *World Investment Report 2000*) and Canal+ (one of Europe's largest pay television providers) to produce Vivendi Universal.

As with media, telecommunications were also becoming global, through alliances and cross-national mergers, partnerships and acquisitions. Even more than in the former area, deregulation was central to the expansion of telecommunications. Increased global cultural flows, digitization, the importance of information, and, above all, the critical breakthrough of the Internet into millions of homes, created market euphoria within the media conglomerates. Even publishers' backlists, once guarded as valuable property but rather ignored in the pursuit of the next bestseller, now seemed to offer an opportunity for revival. In his book *The Agent: Personalities, Politics, and Publishing* (2001), Arthur Klebanoff, one of the founders of the electronic press Rosetta Books, tells of his experience of trying to secure electronic rights to books by Kurt Vonnegut, something that caused the original publisher, Random House, to take Rosetta Books to court, arguing that these rights were included in the original contracts, an argument the court rejected. The material and immaterial repercussions of e-books, a new kind of "book" that few publishers knew what to make of, were very real in Klebanoff's world:

> Delivery to the consumer by almost instantaneous download; a reading experience limited only by the pace of new technology, with the appliances and software packages which make it work; easily adjusted fount size for those who prefer larger type; search engines that find words in context, anywhere throughout a book, instantly; dictionaries that define and even pronounce a highlighted word; on-screen note taking and highlighting, used to collect and summarize information for writing papers; and a storage capability equal to forty books in a single handheld device, with compression technologies coming to market which will multiply that amount by ten. (Klebanoff 2001: 7–8)

The promise of a golden technological future may have triggered the AOL–Time Warner and Vivendi mergers, but both conglomerates fell on hard times in 2002. The combination of a brutal stock-market backlash and the September 11 terrorist attacks on New York and Washington in 2001 swiftly turned a technological dream into a nightmare. Shares plummeted and heads began to roll. Throughout the summer of 2002, it became clear that the grand edifice that the media moguls had built was nothing more than a house of cards. Bigger had not meant better, and very little, if anything, of the hopes of synergy and convergence had been realized in an economy that showed no signs of recovery. The days of the media-shopping spree were over, at least for the time being. As 2002 drew to a close, nobody was heard promoting convergence, the Internet hype was long gone, and more conservative executives stepped in to replace those that had been associated with the dot.com era, and selling instead of buying became a favored corporate activity.

Conclusion

The story of publishing during the three final decades of the twentieth-century is easily read as a tragedy that, in a way, has altered (for the worse) the business of books. However, an alternative view could claim that publishing before conglomeratization was a backward, inefficient, and even at times an unprofessional business (Whiteside 1980: 13–14), which was in dire need of modernization.

It was a trade not only marked by bursts of eccentricity, but also by a distinct gender bias and equally apparent class distinctions that operated to increase rather than reduce the differences between highbrow and lowbrow. But perhaps more than anything, the story of how publishing became part of the media conglomerates is a *male* story. Perpetuating a nostalgic longing for a mythical time when publishing was a profession for gentlemen is a stratagem that increases in strength as the market pressures from consolidation and concentration transform the global media landscape.

During this period, women became part of publishing and the book business to an unprecedented degree, and they made their mark as publishers, editors, writers, and readers, perhaps most visibly within the mass-market domain of paperbacks and best-sellers. The history of their impact on the events I have described still remains to be written. "All publishing was run by many badly-paid women and a few much better paid men: an imbalance that women were, of course, aware of, but which they seemed to take for granted", writes Diana Athill, long-time editor (and partner) at André Deutsch in her book *Stet: A Memoir* (2000). An exception to the lack of documentation on the role of women in publishing, Athill's fifty-year career as editor represents a first-hand experience of how publishing once was allowed to operate according to charmingly idiosyncratic rules but then became just one cog in the media machine that in the end is just there to enhance the total value of the parent conglomerate. Today, books are by and large expected to meet much higher profit margins. Since it is equally desirable that they perform well individually rather that in the context of a complete publishing program, internal subsidization and long-term investments are no longer considered part of a viable publishing strategy.

Where once there was a publishing house relentlessly searching for quality or a bookshop with an owner passionate to promote a good read, now stretches the desert-like corporate spaces of major multinational media conglomerates whose understanding and appreciation of books and reading is close to nil. In fact, this is no doubt an over-simplified account of the current state of affairs, if for no other reason than that it assumes too much, both of the present *and* of the past.

In trying to summarize these developments, one finds, perhaps inevitably, both pros and cons. Despite the fact that they made independent booksellers go out of business, the arrival of the multi-stores Barnes & Noble, Borders, and Waterstones have helped to create a new form of public space. The technological advances of print-on-demand and e-books might solve permanently the problem of keeping seldom-asked-for titles available. However, looked at from another perspective, this technological wonderland can be counterproductive, hindering public accessibility to a wide range of literature by celebrating a market dedicated to a mass audience. However, the mushrooming of transnational media conglomerates have not been an obstacle to the simultaneous growth of small and specialized publishers which can be both successful and quality-conscious, and the Internet holds the potential for fostering new, niche presses. The mergers and acquisitions will no doubt continue, just as assuredly as the players and corporations involved will have different names.

Perhaps the most accurate account of what has taken place in this highly volatile business is to suggest that it illustrates an inherent polarization: between centralization and decentralization, between consolidation and diversification, between expansion and contraction, between art and business. Whatever else can be said, the growth of an increasingly transnational and global media market, conglomeratization, content, and convergence proved a combination that dramatically, and permanently, changed the face of publishing between 1970 and 2000.

REFERENCES AND FURTHER READING

Altbach, Philip G. and Hoshino, Edith S. (1997) *International Book Publishing: An Encyclopedia.* London: Fitzroy Dearborn.

Athill, Diana (2000) *Stet: A Memoir.* London: Granta.

Bagdikian, Ben H. (2000) *The Media Monopoly,* 6th edn. Boston: Beacon.

Barnet, Richard J. and Cavanagh, John (1994) *Global Dreams: Imperial Corporations and the New World Order.* New York: Simon & Schuster.

de Bellaigue, Eric (2004) *British Book Publishing as a Business since the 1960s.* London: British Library.

Bourdieu, Pierre (1999) "Une révolution conservatrice dans l'édition." *Actes de la Recherche en Sciences Sociales,* 126–7: 3–28.

Epstein, Jason (2001) *Book Business: Publishing, Past, Present, and Future.* New York: Norton.

Feather, John (1991) *A History of British Publishing.* London: Routledge.

Fouché, Pascal (ed.) (1998) *L'Édition Française depuis 1945.* Paris: Cercle de la Librairie.

Greco, Albert (1997) *The Book Publishing Industry.* Boston: Allyn and Bacon.

Gründ, Alain (2000) "Opening Remarks." Given at the 26th Congress of the International Publisher's Association, Buenos Aires, May 1–4, 2000 (available at www.ipa-uie.org).

Held, David, McGrew, Anthony, Goldblatt, David, and Perraton, Jonathan (1999) *Global Transformations: Politics, Economics and Culture.* London: Polity.

Hemmungs Wirtén, Eva (1998) *Global Infatuation: Explorations in Transnational Publishing and Texts.* Uppsala: Uppsala University.

— (2004) *No Trespassing: Authorship, Intellectual Property Rights, and the Boundaries of Globalization.* Toronto: University of Toronto Press.

Herman, Edward S. and McChesney, Robert W. (1997) *The Global Media: The New Missionaries of Corporate Capitalism.* London: Cassell.

Klebanoff, Arthur (2001) *The Agent: Personalities, Politics, and Publishing.* New York: Texere.

Korda, Michael (1999) *Another Life: A Memoir of Other People.* New York: Random House.

Lemieux, Jacques and Saint-Jacques, Denis (1996) "US Best-sellers in French Quebec and English Canada." In Emile G. Mcanahy and Kenton T. Wilkinson (eds.), *Mass Media and Free Trade: NAFTA and the Cultural Industries,* pp. 279–305. Austin: University of Texas Press.

Mergerstat® Review 2000. Los Angeles: Mergerstat.

Michon, Jacques and Mollier, Jean-Yves (2001) *Les Mutations du livre et de l'édition dans le monde du XVIIIe siècle à l'an 2000.* Quebec: Les Presses de l'Université Laval.

Milliot, Jim (2001) "The Land of the Giants." *Publisher's Weekly*, January 1: 61–3.

Murray, Simone (2004) *Mixed Media: Feminist Presses and Publishing Politics*. London: Pluto.

Nunberg, Geoffrey (ed.) (1996) *The Future of the Book*. Berkeley: University of California Press.

Ohmann, Richard (1996) *Selling Culture: Magazines, Markets, and Class at the Turn of the Century*. London: Verso.

Radway, Janice (1984) *Reading the Romance: Women, Patriarchy, and Popular Literature*. Chapel Hill: University of North Carolina Press.

— (1997) *A Feeling for Books: The Book-of-the-Month Club, Literary Taste, and Middle-class Desire*. Chapel Hill: University of North Carolina Press.

Schiffrin, André (2000) *The Business of Books: How International Conglomerates Took Over Publishing and Changed the Way We Read*. London: Verso.

Thal Larsen, Peter (2001) "The Year the Giants Chose to Merge." *Financial Times*, May 9 (available at http://specials.ft.com/ft500/may2001/FT319FOVHMC.html; accessed December 28, 2004).

UNESCO (1999) *Statistical Yearbook 1999*. Paris: UNESCO.

— (2004) www.unesco.org/culture/xtrans/html_eng/index6.shtml (accessed December 28, 2004).

Venuti, Lawrence (1995) *The Translator's Invisibility: A History of Translation*. London: Routledge.

— (1998) *The Scandals of Translation: Towards an Ethics of Difference*. London: Routledge.

Weber, Daniel (2000) "Culture or Commerce? Symbolic Boundaries in French and American Book Publishing." In Michèle Lamont and Laurent Thévenot (eds.), *Rethinking Comparative Cultural Sociology: Repertoires of Evaluation in France and the United States*, pp. 127–47. Cambridge: Cambridge University Press.

Whiteside, Thomas (1980) *The Blockbuster Complex: Conglomerates, Show Business, and Book Publishing*. Middletown: Wesleyan University Press.

30

The Global Market
1970–2000: Consumers

Claire Squires

The chronological period covered by this chapter is one that saw "the most substantial change in the structure of general trade publishing and bookselling since publishing and bookselling first began to differentiate themselves from each other [during the eighteenth century]" (Willison 2001: 574). This change is documented in the companion chapter to this one (chapter 29), in which Eva Hemmungs Wirtén discusses the conglomeratization and globalization of the worldwide publishing industry since 1970. In the realm of production, publishing saw an enormous upheaval, transforming the industries – or at least those of Western Europe and North America – from small and middle-sized, independently run businesses to global, multimedia conglomerates. But what impact has this had on consumers of books?

Reading, as Robert Darnton famously writes in "What is the History of Books?," "remains the most difficult stage to study in the circuit that books follow" (Darnton 1990b: 122), and the attempt to trace a very recent history of readers in the global market can present as many problems as that of more distant periods. There is, first, the question of the correspondence between the terms "reader" and "consumer." If a reader can read without having bought (by borrowing or stealing), and a consumer can buy without reading (buying on behalf of others or leaving the purchase languishing on a pile of unread books), how can patterns of consumption and reading be understood and meaningfully analyzed? Secondly, there is the issue of the extent to which the realms of both readership and consumption can actually be charted. What information is available to researchers studying the near-contemporary? What mix of quantitative and qualitative data is available, and how does this influence prevalent analyses of the global market?

These broader theoretical and methodological questions of how we can know about patterns of consumption are addressed toward the end of the chapter. There are severe limitations on the extent of current knowledge about very recent consumer activity, and these are forceful reminders of Darnton's dictum. As recently as 2005, the UK trade journal *The Bookseller* remarked in an editorial that "Publishers are stuck in the

Stone Ages when it comes to customer data: beyond vague ideas that reading increases with age, class and education, they have little or no idea who their customers are, where they live, or what their tastes may be" (*The Bookseller* 2005: 32). However, this chapter also sets out to explore, as best it can, and in the short space available to it, some prevailing themes and trends in the very recent history of global book consumption.

The Global Market

From 1970 onward, then, via mergers and acquisitions, the ownership of publishing companies became increasingly globalized. Alongside this development, there was a considerable display of cultural anxiety from commentators on the publishing industry, who feared that conglomeratization and globalization would cause (indeed, had already caused) a homogenization of content and with it the hegemony of the English language, market censorship, and restrictions in access to the market masquerading as free trade (see, for example, Bagdikian 1983; Schiffrin 2000). Such critiques did not bode well for the consumer, and echoed Steven Connor's argument that the greatest challenge to publishers in this period, from the perspective of a postmodernist cultural politics, was the "preservation of diversity" (Connor 1996: 23).

Are these negative analyses of the global publishing market justified? Elsewhere, I have argued the need for a greater degree of both quantitative data and interpretive analysis in order to assess this question, and the end of this chapter returns to methodological issues with regard to recent publishing history (Squires 2004). Nonetheless, this chapter now addresses evidence for the plurality (or otherwise) of output in a globalized marketplace, and the impact of this for the consumer.

The licensing of foreign and translation rights in overseas markets is one indicator of the worldwide nature of publishing output. Bestsellers, such as J. K. Rowling's series of *Harry Potter* books, Umberto Eco's literary-philosophical novels, John Grisham's courtroom thrillers, and Stephen King's gothic horrors, to name but a few global publishing phenomena in this period, are translated and published throughout the world, sold in multiple territories and consumed by an international readership. Although, on the one hand, this might seem to promote a positive internationalism, on the other, this scenario is a potentially troubling one, and a result of the conglomeratization and globalization of recent publishing history. As Miha Kovač comments, this can potentially lead to the "'standardiz[ation]' of world book production" via a control over the market operated by major companies, "thereby opening the gates to 'McDonaldization' of the world book business" (Kovač 2002: 44). The thrust of this argument is a standard anti-globalization one, applied specifically to publishing and its output.

Kovač questions the opening assumption of his own article, however, via an analysis of recent changes in two small Central European publishing cultures, those of Slovenia and Hungary. This analysis is based on a comparison of the proportion of translations within total book output in different European countries, a proportion which demonstrates "significant differences" from country to country (2002: 49). However:

there is a striking similarity in the nature of these translations: the majority of them are English. In countries such as Germany, for example, around 15 percent of total book output is translations. In France, translations represent around 10 percent of the total book output. In Italy, similar to Hungary or Slovenia, translations represent between one-third and one-quarter of the total book output. In all these countries, those originally in English represent between 60–80 percent of the translations. On the other hand, in 1990, only 2.4 percent of the total British output of books was translations; in the United States it amounted to 2.96 percent. (Kovač 2002: 51)

Despite regional variations within Europe, Kovač concludes that in the 1990s, "the flow of translations from the United Kingdom and United States to European countries was between five and fifteen times greater than the flow of translations from European countries to the UK and USA," meaning that "almost 50 percent of all translations in the world are made from English into various languages, but only six percent of all translations are made into English" (Kovač 2002: 49–50). This is the situation that led the book-translation researcher Lawrence Venuti to criticize the Anglo-Saxon book business as "imperialistic abroad and xenophobic at home" (Venuti 1995: 17; cited in Kovač 2002: 50).

Such quantitative analysis would seem to suggest the global hegemony of Anglo-Saxon culture and its conduit, the English language. However, the impact on both production and consumption, Kovač claims, is more ambiguous (2002: 50). For Anglo-Saxon producers – the writers and their literary agents, and the primary US or UK publisher (even if owned by a non-US or UK conglomerate) – this is good economic news. The evidence suggests that their products are both successfully reaching global markets and competing extremely effectively in home markets. For consumers, however, the picture is arguably reversed. Typically, UK and US audiences, unless they read in foreign languages and make the effort to acquire foreign-language editions, have a very limited access to texts created beyond their own cultures. The book consumers of European nations outside the UK have access to a much wider range of cultural reference, even if a majority of the work translated into their own languages is derived from original English-language publications. If the top figure of 80 percent of the translations from English is assumed, this still leaves, based on Kovač's figures, 2 percent of total book output into French, 3 percent into German, and between 5 and 6 percent into Italian, Hungarian, and Slovene, translated from languages other than English. In other words, European nations typically have access to a large number of books translated from English, but also a percentage from other languages that is at least equivalent to, and often more than, that to which British and American readers typically have access.

In this analysis, it is the British and American readers who are culturally impover-ished, while their publishing industries derive financial benefit from foreign and transla-tion rights. There is here a marked distinction between the impact of globalization on producers and consumers. The impact of globalization on consumers in non-English-speaking markets is, however, arguably not attractive either. US- and UK-originated texts can and do exert pressure in national marketplaces, bringing them into competition with locally produced materials. What is the impact for consumers, then, of a preponderance of English-language originated texts in a local market? Is the only interpretation of the global publishing market one of "McDonaldization?"

Globalized Content and the Consumer

In her work on Harlequin Enterprises, Eva Hemmungs Wirtén explores this question from the perspective of the alteration of texts through translation, a process she terms "transediting" (Wirtén 1998, 2001). Although Harlequin's headquarters is actually in Canada (rather than the US or UK), its publication program, which reaches six continents and operates in twenty-four languages, could well be considered as "a prime example of 'Americanization' " or globalization determined by "bad mass culture" (2001: 569). While noting that cultural production is dominated by writers from anglophone countries, but that cultural reception extends to nations from which writers are not derived (for example, Sweden, Russia, Italy, or China), Wirtén goes on to describe the process of "transediting," which places a different perspective on patterns of global production (2001: 569). The process is one whereby translators and editors effectively rewrite texts via "internalized values" which are expressed in the course of "transediting" for different local markets (2001: 571). This process is "a systematic adaptation that sometimes result[s] in the construction of a totally new text"; "transediting" is therefore "a mode of rewriting, creating something new, or [even] blatant interfering and tampering with the text" (2001: 570). Harlequin texts are therefore both globalized and localized: a practical example of *"glocalization."* To a greater or a lesser degree, this process always takes place when translated texts are produced, in terms of their selection, translation, and editing.

But what is the impact on consumers of globalized and/or glocalized production? For a children's book critic such as Jack Zipes, the global publishing success constituted by the millions of consumers of the *Harry Potter* series, to take a prime example, is troubling. Zipes attacks *Harry Potter* on several fronts, but his most swingeing criticism is reserved for the way in which the books have been turned into global commodities that privilege a particular worldview. Zipes sees the series as intrinsically bound up in global capitalism, writing that: "Phenomena such as the Harry Potter books are driven by commodity consumption that at the same time sets the parameters of reading and aesthetic taste" (Zipes 2002: 172). The complaint he makes is that this taste is a homogenizing one, which makes Harry – who is male, white, middle class, and English-speaking – a universal hero. *Harry Potter* and similar global commodities are, to Zipes, examples of cultural imperialism.

Are all global products – and the consumption of them – to be condemned? An anti-globalization stance such as this might well miss the finer nuances of actual reading practices. Discussing television – another cultural medium in which anxieties about the impact of globalization are rife – John Tomlinson comments that critics readily condemn the global distribution of US television soap operas, such as *Dallas*, with "scant regard to the way in which the audience may read the text" (Tomlinson 2000: 307). He argues instead for an assessment of empirical studies of people watching and interpreting tele-visual texts within different cultural contexts, which pays attention to the "negotiations" audiences make with the text (Tomlinson 2000: 310). Several claims could be made for the "negotiations" made with the *Harry Potter* texts by different groups around the world, if such attention is applied to global publishing phenomena.

An initial reinterpretation of *Harry Potter* is made by publishers for their own markets through their choice of cover designs, each of which subtly or blatantly reinterpret the series. Even within national markets such reinterpretations are made: Bloomsbury, the UK publisher of *Harry Potter*, famously publishes children's and adults' editions of the books with the same text but different cover designs. Further negotia-tions also occur even before books reach consumers. Each foreign-language edition is, necessarily, translated, and hence is open to the vagaries of the translation process. This is a process whose analysis, as Wirtén states, is only open to scholars with both a high degree of linguistic ability and access to archival materials in the form of translation and editorial drafts, which understandably – if regrettably – limits study and dissemi-nation in this area (Wirtén 2001: 573). This also, it could be argued, maintains a hegemonic concentration on Anglo-Saxon versions, with scholarship following the cul-turally imperialistic lines of English-language publication. Studies of the translations of *Harry Potter* do nevertheless already exist, with published scholarly articles on the transition of the text from UK to US English (Nel 2002), and into French, German, and Spanish (Jentsch 2002). The linguistic competence required to construct the latter study, however, confirms Wirtén's point.

In some geographical sectors, book piracy is rife, and so publishers illegally present alternative editions to consumers. In China, for example, in the hiatus between the publication of the fourth and fifth books in the *Harry Potter* series, a completely fake "fifth" book appeared, with a title roughly translated as *Harry Potter and Leopard Walk up to Dragon*. The book claimed to have been written by Rowling and to have been translated by the translators of the official books (BBC News 2002). Indeed, a radical interpretation of copyright and the control it exerts over textual production would say that it is a form of market censorship, with piracy representing a "true" free market unshackled by legislative restrictions (Jansen 2001).

But what of the negotiations made by consumers, rather than those presented to them by intermediary producers (be they local publishers or pirates)? How do consum-ers make their purchasing decisions, and how do readers read? What appropriations are made by readers? The link between book history and reader-response theory has been well established, notably by Darnton himself in "First Steps Towards a History of Reading," which calls for "a history as well as a theory of reader response" (1990a: 157), and by Guglielmo Cavallo and Roger Chartier in the introduction to their *History of Reading in the West* (1999).

A more recent exploration of the link was made by Christine Pawley in her article "Seeking 'Significance': Actual Readers, Specific Reading Communities" (2002). Pawley uses Benedict Anderson's concept of the "imagined community" in order to foreground empirical study and "real" readers (Anderson 1983; Pawley 2002: 145). Tracing the evidence of actual US reading communities in the form of library records from 1890s' Iowa and 1950s' Wisconsin, Pawley builds up quantitative data in order to analyze patterns of readership and develop theories about the social interactions that were indicated by them. Pawley goes on to discuss other researchers' investigations into more recent reading communities, and the more ethnographic methods that contemporaneous study allows but is lost to the longer-term historical researcher. She refers to Janice A. Radway's (1984) observational work on women's readings of romance fiction and Elizabeth Long's (2003) study of reading groups and book clubs, to which should also be added the surveys of Jenny Hartley (2001, 2002) and DeNel Rehberg Sedo (2002). (Leah Price's 2004 article, "Reading: The State of the Discipline," gives a more thorough overview of studies in readership.)

It is worth noting that much of this recently undertaken ethnographic investigation into reading habits and practices specifically addresses issues of gendered or ethnic reading communities. These studies therefore have a strongly focused ideological under-pinning. They also have a clearly empirical basis, using techniques of both quantitative and qualitative social science research. Hartley's book, for example, is reliant on a large sample response to a questionnaire survey, observation, and focus-group-style discussion (Hartley 2002). Through this combination of quantitative and qualitative methods, Hartley addresses such issues as the composition and purpose of reading groups, their strategies for choosing and discussing texts, prevailing trends in the choice of texts, as well as touching on the historical background to book and reading societies and group-ings and their specific contexts. With regard to the composition of reading groups, for example, Hartley's survey unsurprisingly demonstrated their domination by women, with 69 percent of the groups being all female. Women in reading groups commented on the lack of men in their group, giving a range of remarks from "Can't find any men who read" to "All female – we want to keep it like that" to "We enjoy being independent from men with meaningful, intelligent conversations." However, some of the longest-established reading groups responding to her survey were all male, with histo-ries and sometimes formalized codes of behavior stretching back into the eighteenth century (Hartley 2002: 27–8). These issues are sociological, historical, economic, and literary in nature, and their interdisciplinary fusion clearly accords with that of book history in general.

Another recent example of research focused on reader activity and response is that of Paul C. Gutjahr (2002). Taking as a broader historical context the attitudes of American Christians toward the novel, Gutjahr examines the emergence of one particu-lar series of Christian novels (the "Left Behind" books) and reader responses to them via the customer reviews section of the Internet bookseller Amazon.com. By coding the content of the customer reviews, and thus quantifying responses to the series, and then by a follow-up questionnaire sent to reviewers (at the time of research Amazon.com included the e-mail contact details of reviewers), Gutjahr was able to establish demo-graphic information (including reviewers' denominations and perception of their faith), the attitudes of readers toward the series, and their use of it for devotional, evangelical, and exegetical purposes. Gutjahr's findings allow him to make a broader argument about the relationship of American Christian readers to the novel, claiming that the gap between Bible reading and novel reading has narrowed, and "a clear and influential connection exists between the reading of sacred and nonsacred works. Such a connection forces one to reconsider how best to redefine the term *sacred text*" (Gutjahr 2002: 227). Once more, empirical research into reader response allows an understanding of book consumption, set within an historical and ideological framework.

And yet it is this sort of study, which allows researchers to analyze the negotiations readers make with texts, textual producers, and critical authority figures, that is largely missing from the evidence-base of recent book history. In order to investigate the consumption patterns of a global commodity such as *Harry Potter*, substantial surveys of reader-response data would have to be devised, applied, and analyzed. Information sources, such as customer reviews on Amazon.com and its various international partners, could certainly be addressed, while being aware of the limitations of a sample derived from Amazon, as Gutjahr discusses:

> First, Amazon.com appeals to a specific, computer-literate, credit-able clientele. It is impossible to say just how accurate a representation this clientele is of the nation's reading public as a whole, as it is also impossible to say how representative these readers are of those who read [a given] series.
>
> Second, it is impossible to tell much about the readers themselves. Aside from offering the content of their reviews and an occasional note on geographical location, the reviewers remain largely anonymous. There is no way to confirm either the content or the identity of those who write these reviews.
>
> Finally, those who write the reviews tend to have strong opinions about the book upon which they are commenting. They need to be motivated to get back online to key in their thoughts . . . (Gutjahr 2002: 219)

Despite these reservations, however, the Internet and the way in which it has allowed readers to express their responses to texts in a public forum, provides a rich research tool for scholars, and a potential testing-ground for various theories of the popularity (or otherwise) of books and the uses to which they are put. Gutjahr explicitly set out to discover via his Amazon analysis and subsequent survey the ways in which readers use the "Left Behind" series to affirm and develop their Christian perspectives. In my own construction of a case study of Helen Fielding's bestselling novel *Bridget Jones's Diary* (1995), reviewers' comments on Amazon.co.uk (the British version of the Internet bookseller) were similarly revealing (Squires 2007). Among many others, these two views of the novel and its eponymous protagonist had been posted:

[1]   This is about as funny as being stuck in a police cell. Bridget Jones should be shot, and Helen Fielding let off with a caution. This is unrealistic, unfunny, uninteresting, unoriginal pap. The editor should also be shot for allowing this weak, angsty, old hat creation to grace our bookshops. What a relief that Bridget Jones is too sad to find a partner and we're spared any genetic reproduction on that front. I wonder,

is Ms Fielding aware that a movement known as feminism occurred this century. Please, no more of this rubbish.

[2]   Yes, yes, yes. I am quite aware that this is not the most liberated of portrayals of the inner workings of a woman's mind. No doubt strident feminists are at this very minute burning the book and it's [sic] author in effigy. But come on girls, which one of us can honestly say you haven't thought along the same lines as Bridget at least once? I would not consider myself a slave to my need for emotional fulfilment, or see it as tied to my finding a bloke but I can see where Bridget is coming from. None of us wants to end up dead, half-eaten by an Alsatian. This is a tender, funny and inspiring book. It certainly made me laugh. (Amazon 1999)

These two responses to the novel use the same frame of reference to opposing effect. In terms of the readers' respective attitudes to the novel's perceived humor and relation to reality, the first finds it "unrealistic, unfunny, uninteresting," while the second appeals to fellow female browsers to admit that none "can honestly say you haven't thought along the same lines as Bridget at least once," and freely admits that it "made me laugh." Both refer to Bridget Jones's situation as a single girl to indicate either a personal affinity or anger about the portrayal of a perceived social type. Both also mention feminism as a key reference point to express their reactions. Within these two reader responses, then, are the suggestions of a debate that call upon questions not only of literary value but also of literary fashion and form, empathy and audience appeal. If analyzed, reader responses such as these two can begin to suggest why some books take a hold in the consumer consciousness. Indeed, when combined with textual study, an exploration of publishers' and book retailers' marketing activities, and media reception, such analysis can begin to hint at why some books become bestsellers rather than others.

Similar studies could certainly be constructed with regard to other global book phenomena. As well as reader surveys and ethnographic methods, advancing technology in the period 1970–2000, most particularly during the past decade, have allowed other avenues of research into consumer activity. Global commodities such as *Harry Potter*, J. R. R. Tolkein's *The Lord of the Rings* trilogy, and Terry Pratchett's *Discworld* series spawn a growing number of fan websites, chatrooms, and online fan fiction. The latter trend, in particular, is symptomatic of the ways in which, as both Tomlinson and Wirtén discuss, consumers negotiate, appropriate, rewrite, create anew, interfere and tamper with the text. Moreover, as Rebecca Sutherland Borah (2002) investigates in her ethnographic observations of online *Harry Potter* fan communities, such a study can document the very real resistance of readers around the world to attempts by global, multimedia conglomerates (in this case Warner Brothers) to control intellectual property, merchandising, and appropriations by readers in the form, for example, of fan fiction and websites.

A group of schoolboy fans of *Harry Potter* in the Czech Republic, like the opportunistic pirate in China, also tired of waiting for the fifth book to appear and, with the English-language edition readily available to them, began to translate and post on the Internet a Czech-language version well in advance of the appearance of the official version. This violation of copyright law prompted comments from the Czech publisher, who adopted the tone of a stern Hogwarts teacher: "We have contacted our lawyer and we are speaking with the Czech police," he said. "We know their [the boys'] names and addresses . . . They are fans of Harry Potter. They just don't know how complicated and dangerous this is. [The boys] . . . think it's funny. But it's not funny for us or Ms Rowling . . ." He also criticized their translating work, and said: "There are a lot of mistakes" (News24.com 2003).

This is a striking example of readers who, by becoming "authors" of a translated text, place themselves in strict contravention of intellectual property law, the means by which global commodities are defined, controlled, and exploited. The global might of Rowling and her associated business partners can undoubtedly quash such malefactors through the courts, but global and highly visible commodities such as *Harry Potter* inevitably attract appropriation: this is simultaneously a sign of their success and a challenge to the owners of the intellectual property. As Borah mentions, appropriations by younger readers of the series include readerly acts as inoffensive and innocent-seeming as drawing pictures or making costumes and wands. She describes how corporations attempt to control their properties and thereby inhibit imaginative appropriations:

> younger fans are discouraged from creating their own texts and making their own objects in favor of buying "genuine" goods and joining "official" fan clubs. Rather than being encouraged to connect with other readers/viewers and to participate in shared communal activities (which don't directly benefit a company), youngsters are often treated as passive consumers, ready to accept whatever is hailed as the newest fad to be viewed and collected. Generally, as young audiences age, many fans lose interest in their initial pursuits, due in part to being over-targeted with mass-produced consumables that quickly become obsolete memorabilia. As they move into adolescence, these fans often shift their attention to different pastimes such as sports, video games, or social activities, which may lead them into other types of fan communities. (Borah 2002: 349–50)

More specifically, she discusses the extreme merchandising of *Harry Potter*, and the heavy-handed legal efforts made by Warner Brothers to close down unofficial *Harry Potter* websites (including legitimate, non-profit sites which did not contravene copyright law). Some of these attempts amounted, in Borah's words, to "harassment" (2002: 355). The resilience of some of these sites, and of reader activity generally, however, makes clear that consumers can become pitted against producers, and is a fascinating example of how text is used, owned, and appropriated by a variety of frequently conflicting stakeholder groups. The consumer here is clearly not just a passive recipient of the production and marketing strategies of global, multimedia conglomerates.

Market Research

These few examples show a variety of ways in which research into reader activity can be used to understand more about trends in recent global consumption, and to suggest lines along which further research can be conducted. And yet they cannot do much more than hint at global patterns, and they do not provide a complete overview of the global market from the perspective of consumers. To do this would require a comprehensive and consistent set of both quantitative and qualitative data, the likes of which – even in this age of information – does not exist.

Consumption has become much easier to quantify in the post-1970 period in some countries with the introduction of EPOS (electronic point of sale) systems, which record sales as they occur through the shop till, thus generating instant and accurate sales data. These data can then be profitably used by retailers and publishers to inform their reordering, reprinting, and commissioning decisions, though an argument remains about how this market knowledge is used, and whether it leads to creative or copycat publishing (see Rickett 2000; Hutton 2002). However, this system currently operates in only a handful of countries and, despite its sophisticated delivery of sales information, it does not delve further into the psychology of book consumption. It is fair to say that publishers, particularly in the general trade market, really know very little about what motivates their consumers. Market research is only infrequently conducted on anything other than an anecdotal basis. The fanfare that greets the occasional forays into consumer research indicates this. One recent example is the several pages (including the front cover) taken out by Random House UK in *The Bookseller* to advertise the consumer research it had commissioned into "The Power of John Grisham." The opening text of the advert reads:

> The Power of John Grisham
> All readers love the escapism of reading him
> Women are hooked by the moral dilemmas
> Men are fascinated by the issues
> Everyone enjoys the pace
> Everyone thinks he's a star
> How do we know?
> Easy, we asked them . . . (Random House 2004)

Such self-congratulatory copy would suggest not just the power of John Grisham, but also the infrequency with which such consumer research is carried out, and hence the paucity of knowledge that even a multimedia conglomerate such as Random House has about its consumers and the reasons for their purchasing decisions.

General book consumer surveys exist in various publishing markets, but their coverage is patchy, and they often use non-comparable statistical bases. The variable levels of data provided via the International Publishers' Association website (www.ipa-uie.org) clearly demonstrate this knowledge gap, and confirms Darnton's statement about the difficulties inherent in the study of reading. Moreover, given the variable ways in which readers acquire books, patterns of consumption do not strictly mirror patterns of reading. Kovač notes how, despite a lack of exact figures, "a trend is apparent which disconnects high publishing revenue performance with a high number of per capita library loans" (2004: 31). He concludes that:

a bigger demand for books in a given society could be met through channels other than book sales. Even more, the case might be that a greater demand for books does not bring much financial benefit to the book publishing industry at all, as the link between the growth of library networks and the performance of the book publishing industry seems to be contradictory in that a too successful library network might mean less financial success for the publishing industry. (2004: 32)

In order to analyze patterns of global book readership, then, there is more to study than trends in consumption. Library borrowing is one important additional area of study, but there is also the aspect of actual book use: are bought books read, and in what ways? These are questions that have bedeviled historians of reading of all periods, but are also pertinent to an age in which it might be assumed that we know more about patterns of consumption, and can find out more – through ethnographic and observational research – about reader activity.

And yet, although it is arguably too early to establish patterns and trends in this near-contemporary period, it is a perfect moment at which to discuss the methods for collecting and analyzing data, and for beginning to carry out this research activity. Moreover, there is an urgent political impetus which extends beyond market information and the scholarly desire for knowledge. The recent fiftieth anniversary of the charity Book Aid International, an organization established with the specific aim of encouraging Westerners to assist developing countries by the donation of books, demonstrates all too clearly how book consumption is very unevenly spread across the globe, principally due to economic factors (Graham 2004). In the West, book production and consumption increased – in some cases remarkably – during the period 1970–2000. Yet in some other countries, book consumption and basic literacy is a privilege rather than a right, with the products of the publishing industry inaccessible to many citizens. Researching global patterns of book consumption, and their regional variations, should render these discrepancies apparent, and can potentially, therefore, make the study of very recent publishing history a potent political tool.

REFERENCES AND FURTHER READING

Amazon (1999) www.amazon.co.uk/exec/obidos/tg/stores/detail/-/books/0330332767/customer-reviews/qid=1035649491/sr=1-4/ref=sr_1_3_4/ref=cm_cr_dp_2_1/026-5624646-4387602 (accessed March 5, 1999).

Anderson, Benedict (1983) *Imagined Communities: Reflections on the Origin and Spread of Nationalism.* London: Verso.

Bagdikian, Ben (1983) *The Media Monopoly.* Boston: Beacon.

BBC News (2002) "Fake Harry Potter Novel Hits China" (available at http://news.bbc.co.uk/1/hi/entertainment/arts/2092661.stm; accessed January 14, 2005; article first appeared July 4, 2002).

Bookseller (2005) "Rethink Publishing . . . and Expand the Market with Books People Want." *The Bookseller,* March 11: 32.

Borah, Rebecca Sutherland (2002) "Apprentice Wizards Welcome: Fan Communities and the

Culture of Harry Potter." In Lana A. Whited (ed.), *The Ivory Tower and Harry Potter: Perspectives on a Literary Phenomenon*, pp. 343–64. Columbia: University of Missouri Press.

Cavallo, Guglielmo and Chartier, Roger (eds.) (1999) *A History of Reading in the West*, trans. Lydia G. Cochrane. Cambridge: Polity (originally published 1995).

Connor, Steven (1996) *The English Novel in History 1950–1995*. London: Routledge.

Darnton, Robert (1990a) "First Steps towards a History of Reading." In *The Kiss of Lamourette: Reflections in Cultural History*, pp. 154–87. London: Faber & Faber.

— (1990b) "What is the History of Books?" In *The Kiss of Lamourette: Reflections in Cultural History*, pp. 107–35. London: Faber & Faber.

Graham, Gordon (2004) "The Editor's Place." *Logos*, 15 (3): 116–17.

Gutjahr, Paul C. (2002) "No Longer Left Behind: Amazon.com, Reader-response, and the Changing Fortunes of the Christian Novel in America." *Book History*, 5: 209–36.

Hartley, Jenny (2001) *Reading Groups*. Oxford: Oxford University Press.

— (2002) *The Reading Groups Book 2002–2003 Edition*. Oxford: Oxford University Press.

Hutton, Tatiana (2002) "Bookscan: A Marketing Tool or Literary Homogenizer?" *Publishing Research Quarterly*, 18 (1): 48–51.

Jansen, Sue Curry (2001) "Market Censorship." In Derek Jones (ed.), *Censorship: A World Encyclopedia*, pp. 1542–5. London: Fitzroy Dearborn.

Jentsch, Nancy K. (2002) "Harry Potter and the Tower of Babel." In Lana A. Whited (ed.), *The Ivory Tower and Harry Potter: Perspectives on a Literary Phenomenon*, pp. 285–301. Columbia: University of Missouri Press.

Kovač, Miha (2002) "The State of Affairs in Post-Communist Central and Eastern European Book Industries." *Publishing Research Quarterly*, 18 (3): 43–53.

— (2004) "Patterns and Trends in European Book Production and Consumption: Some Initial Observations." *Javnost/The Public*, 11 (4): 21–36.

Long, Elizabeth (2003) *Book Clubs: Women and the Uses of Reading in Everyday Life*. Chicago: University of Chicago Press.

Nel, Philip (2002) "You Say "Jelly," I Say "Jell-O"?: Harry Potter and the Transfiguration of Language." In Lana A. Whited (ed.), *The Ivory Tower and Harry Potter: Perspectives on a Literary Phenomenon*, pp. 261–84. Columbia: University of Missouri Press.

News24.com (2003) "Potter Fans Face Piracy Charges" (available at http://www.news24.com/News24/Entertainment/Abroad/0,,2-1225-1243_1382962,00.html; accessed January 14, 2005; article first appeared July 7, 2003).

Pawley, Christine (2002) "Seeking 'Significance': Actual Readers, Specific Reading Communities." *Book History*, 5: 143–60.

Price, Leah (2004) "Reading: The State of the Discipline." *Book History*, 7: 303–20.

Radway, Janice A. (1984) *The Romance Reader: Women, Patriarchy, and Popular Literature*. Chapel Hill: University of North Carolina Press.

Random House (2004) "The Power of John Grisham." *The Bookseller*, September 17.

Rickett, Joel (2000) "Publishing by Numbers?" *The Bookseller*, September 1: 20–2.

Schiffrin, André (2000) *The Business of Books: How International Conglomerates Took Over Publishing and Changed the Way We Read*. London: Verso.

Sedo, DeNel Rehberg (2002) "Predictions of Life after Oprah: A Glimpse at the Power of Book Club Readers." *Publishing Research Quarterly*, 18 (3): 11–22.

Squires, Claire (2004) "Novelistic Production and the Publishing Industry in Britain and Ireland." In Brian Shaffer (ed.), *A Companion to the British and Irish Novel, 1945–2000*, pp. 177–93. Oxford: Blackwell.

— (2007) *Marketing Literature: The Making of Contemporary Writing in Britain*. Basingstoke: Palgrave Macmillan.

Tomlinson, John (2000) "Cultural Imperialism." In Frank J. Lechner and John Boli (eds.), *The Globalization Reader*, pp. 307–15. Oxford: Blackwell.

Venuti, Lawrence (1995) *The Translator's Invisibility: A History of Translation*. London: Routledge.

Willison, Ian R. (2001) "Mass Mediatisation: Export of the American Model?" In Jacques Michon and Jean-Yves Mollier (eds.), *Les Mutations du livre et de l'édition dans le monde du XVIIIe siècle à l'an 2000*, pp. 574–82. Quebec: Les Presses de L'Université Laval.

Wirtén, Eva Hemmungs (1998) *Global Infatuation: Explorations in Transnational Publishing and Texts. The Case of Harlequin Enterprises and Sweden.* Uppsala: Department of Literature, Uppsala University.

— (2001) "Glocalities: Power and Agency Manifested in Contemporary Print Culture." In Jacques Michon and Jean-Yves Mollier (eds.), *Les Mutations du livre et de l'édition dans le monde du XVIIIe siècle à l'an 2000*, pp. 565–73. Quebec: Les Presses de L'Université Laval.

Zipes, Jack (2002) *Sticks and Stones: The Troublesome Success of Children's Literature from Slovenly Peter to Harry Potter.* London: Routledge.

PART III
Beyond the Book

31

Periodicals and Periodicity

James Wald

Accustomed to a diet of information in bite-sized morsels, readers increasingly lack the patience and even ability to digest serious books. The collective and ephemeral nature of the new media in turn encourages authors to dash off flimsy essays that would never stand scrutiny on their own. The result is a vicious circle. Although this lament could have been drawn from today's debates about the web, it comes from eighteenth-century German critiques of the periodical (Raabe 1974). It even entered the literary canon. The Theatre Manager in *Faust* worries how to please a jaded public:

> If one comes bored, exhausted quite,
> Another, satiate, leaves the banquet's tapers,
> And worst of all, full many a wight,
> Is fresh from reading of the daily papers.

Elsewhere, Goethe complained that ceaseless periodical reading fostered passivity, reducing culture to something "only supposed to distract" (Lowenthal 1961: 34, 21). The parallels command our attention. One ironic benefit of the digital revolution has been renewed interest in the history of "print culture," though often marred by a tendency to view the latter monolithically and focus comparisons narrowly on "technology." Many paradoxes are more easily resolved, and phenomena better understood, if we instead view them from the perspective of genre, with historically conditioned conventions of writing and reading.

The normative status of the codex, reflected in the name of our discipline and even the title of the present volume, leads many to view difference as hierarchy:

Book	*Periodical*
venerable	recent
complete	fragmentary, open-ended
univocal	polyvalent

individual	collective
individualistic: authorial	individualistic: subjective
authoritative	suspect, provisional
creative	derivative
permanent	ephemeral

The periodical was arguably the first original genre to arise following Gutenberg's invention. Like the latter, it was not *sui generis*. Rather, it combined and developed earlier practices, constituting something qualitatively new. The essence of the periodical is periodicity. The periodical is thus not a book *manqué*, but a nonlinear assemblage of parcels of text, the unity of which derives from a common program cumulatively implemented through repetition. Scorn is the price of success as well as novelty. Since the appearance of the first newspaper (1605) and journal (1665), roughly 1.5 million periodicals have conquered the globe: the vehicle of every major cultural and political movement, the preferred means of scientific communication, and the most popular reading matter.

The periodical was protean as well as prolific. It is relatively easy to see what links modern newspapers such as *Asahi Shimbun*, the *Guardian*, *Al Ahram*, and *El País* with one another and with the *Aviso Relation oder Zeitung* (1605), *Courante uyt Italien, Duytslandt &c* (1618), *Moniteur Universel* (1789), and *Shenbao* (1872), but what could possibly unite modern journals such as *African Zoology*, *Paris-Match*, *Cigar Aficionado*, *Hispanic Entrepreneur*, and *Fuck You: A Magazine of the Arts*? What can they, moreover, have in common with the *Rambler* (1750), *Revue des Deux Mondes* (1829), *Australian Gold Digger's Monthly Magazine and Colonial Family Visitor* (1852), or *Efemérides barometrico-medicas matritenses* (1743)? Much ink and effort have been wasted in the quest for a definition that can expand to cover all possible variations without succumbing to analytical entropy.

The German school of periodical research pioneered by Joachim Kirchner associates the newspaper with (1) public accessibility; (2) periodicity; (3) timeliness; (4) universality – ascribing to the journal only the former two qualities (Kirchner 1928; Dovifat 1962). Periodicity is a trait shared by the periodical proper (journal/magazine) and newspaper, which are our focus, with several variants of the codex, including annuals (almanacs, gift books, yearbooks), proceedings, monographic series, and part-publication, which began as a rationalization measure in the seventeenth century and became a literary vogue in the nineteenth. Allowing for the inevitable historical exceptions, we will therefore employ "periodical" in the British sense, equivalent to American "serial": "A publication in any medium in successive parts bearing numerical or chronological designations and intended to be continued indefinitely" (Woodward and Pilling 1993: 1).

Frédéric Barbier and Catherine Bertho Lavenir (2003) posit a tripartite history of media dominated, successively, by the principles of opinion, information, and communication:

(1) 1751 to 1870, the second revolution of the book: the democratic and industrial revolutions invest print with social and political significance.
(2) 1870 to 1950, the universalization of the media: heyday of the press, new media of picture and sound, in the mass age of national and global conflict.
(3) 1950 onward, the networked multimedia world: cultural and economic globalization.

The historian of the book, like the lawyer or evolutionary biologist, will look for the causal logic behind a phenomenon. Writing is some 6,000 years old, the codex over 2,000, and printing with movable type over 550, but the periodical only 400. Hunger for information may be "timeless," but its diffusion implies a social need; its mechanical reproduction, the existence of a market; and the rise of a new genre, a change in reading practices as well as cultural production.

Barbier and Bertho Lavenir begin with the phenomenon that so worried Goethe, the shift from "intensive" to "extensive" reading: from repeated and extended rumination over a few traditional texts, to quicker consumption of a wider range of changing titles. Although debate has focused on the extent of new popular literacy, extensive reading was already the *modus operandi* for intellectuals: at first a necessity for the few, and only later a choice for the many. The periodical proved ideally suited to both audiences, publicizing information formerly and sometimes jealously confined to the private communication networks of princes, merchants, or scholars.

Amidst a variety of overlapping rather than successive genres, we can discern the evolution from ad hoc, single-topic print publication (Germany 1480) to varied content and serial appearance: weekly newspapers (Strasbourg 1605) and dailies (Leipzig 1650, London 1702, Paris 1777). Three influential variants were the Dutch *coranto* (1618–50), a weekly or bi-weekly "running relation" of multiple stories under a changing title, in which form the first French and English "newsbooks" appeared (Amsterdam 1620); and Théophraste Renaudot's intelligencer and gazette (1633, 1631), official publications on commerce and foreign politics. Periodicity evolved in tandem with the rhythms and reach of the incipient postal services on which the inflow of information and distribution of publications depended. Early newspapers were international in content and orientation: local news required no new communication medium, and censors forbade coverage of internal affairs, along with other threats to state, religion, and morality.

Whereas the newspaper was a popular medium, the journal was an erudite one that displayed a dual tendency toward specialization and popularization as it evolved to address new topics and readership. Most learned journals contained diverse content but inclined toward what David Kronick (1976) calls the derivative (reviews, abstracts, excerpts) or the substantive, as exemplified by the first two titles (1665). Denis de Sallo's *Journal des Sçavans* offered a weekly overview of the "Republic of Letters" "because things age too much if one defers speaking of them for a period of a year or a month" (Martin 1984: 2.199). *The Philosophical Transactions* (later: *of the Royal Society*) emphasized experimental scientific research. The value of the new genre as a supplement and alternative to soaring book production (250,000 titles in the seventeenth century) and cumbersome epistolary exchanges is easily imagined: the largest German Baroque scholars' libraries numbered 20,000 volumes (typically 4,000–5,000). Leibniz, whose many periodical contributions included twenty-six on the calculus, had some 600 correspondents. The learned periodical henceforth became the principal forum of scholarly communication (1,858 scientific titles by 1790).

Its success inspired periodicals providing amusement or instruction for the growing non-academic market, although their precise genealogy and taxonomy are debated. The monthly *Mercure Galant* (1672, renamed *Mercure de France* in 1724) offered courtly news and culture for the social elite. Edward Cave's *Gentleman's Magazine* (1731) lent its name to a new type of periodical miscellany. The most original subgenre, however, was the essay journal represented by the *Tatler* (1709) and *Spectator* (1711) of Steele and Addison, which, as the latter put it, sought to bring philosophy out of the colleges and libraries to the coffee-houses and tea tables, so as to reach the "blanks of society," particularly the "female world" (Lowenthal 1961: 67–8). Both journals were extensively reprinted and imitated, above all in Germany, where, as Wolfgang Martens (1968) has shown, some 450 "moral weeklies" (1720–60) in effect created middle-class literary culture. Because the newspaper represented a more basic need, it seems everywhere to have preceded the journal: Italy 1631/1668, Sweden 1624/1732, Russia 1703/1755, American colonies 1690/1741, Australia 1803/1821. Until about 1725–30, a nation's first journal was likely to be a learned one; thereafter, general interest.

The periodical superseded the book as the dominant textual medium of intellectual exchange, social commentary, and entertainment in the age of Enlightenment and revolution, movements that emphasized popularization and debate. Continuing repression and stamp taxes notwithstanding, England between the Glorious and American revolutions established a "free" press based on metropolitan newspapers containing a mixture of political and business news, culture, and opinion, financed in part by advertising. In 1695, Kaspar von Stieler declared, "One reads newspapers not in order that one may become learned and skilled in judgment, but only in order to learn what is going on" (Kronick 1976: 17). Judgment was what journals promised: as Addison put it, not "what passes in Muscovy or Poland," but "knowledge of one's self" (Lowenthal 1961: 67). By combining the entertaining with the instructive, journals were to impart cohesion and aesthetic and moral skill to a growing reading public. Hence the importance of reviews: 433 contributors to Friedrich Nicolai's *Allgemeine Deutsche Bibliothek* covered 80,000 titles from 1765 to 1806. The shift from a rule-based to a taste-based, subjective aesthetic demanded that even expert judgment legitimize itself before the tribunal of opinion. Contemporaries spoke of the century of the journal and criticism, both of which increasingly extended to the social.

Politically and culturally fragmented Germany produced the richest periodical culture, a veritable supraregional communication network: between 1609 and 1700, 162 newspapers (200 concurrently by 1800), reaching all but the lowest social strata; 3,494 journals by 1790. Because authorship and reading were inseparably associated with journals, the resultant debate assumed paradigmatic significance. Against those who praised journals for "diffusing useful knowledge to all estates," critics (ironically, often writing in journals) charged careless authors and opportunistic "journal manufacturers" with feeding the new "plague" of "journal addiction," which joined the diagnosis of graphomania and reading frenzy as causes of cultural decline and (the intemperate soon added) the French Revolution (Raabe 1974: 122, 113, 112). Even defenders of journals worried that their proliferation was overwhelming readers, while dissipating the efforts of writers. Friedrich Schiller's *Horen* famously proposed, by bringing together the best authors and eschewing extreme erudition and populism alike, to eliminate competition and "reunite the politically divided world under the banner of truth and beauty" (Wald 1995: 118). It went from sensation in 1795 to silence in 1798, having failed to accommodate the demands of the genre and public taste. Like the web today, the periodical occupied a liminal realm between the elite and the popular, a site of continual contest between groups that valued reading for different reasons. As the first mass medium, the periodical summoned up deep anxieties arising from the breakdown of the putative unitary public and made visible a commodification of culture whose existence traditional interests preferred to ignore or deny.

In France, centralization and privilege relegated innovation to interstitial niches or sites beyond the legal and geographical boundaries of the kingdom. The 1789 Revolution liberated not just the nation, but the periodical, which in the form of the newspaper encompassed both information and criticism. The revolutionary press – 2,000 mostly short-lived newspapers and 12,000 pamphlets in the first decade – both covered and propelled events. Newspapers, in Jeremy Popkin's words, "served as the Revolution's real 'public space'" (1990: 180), the manifestation of the popular will and public opinion that legitimized the new regime and paradoxically demonstrated its actual disunity. As in the English Revolution before and others later, the initial flood of print dried up under revolutionary dictatorship and restoration. Napoleon permitted only thirteen newspapers under the Consulate and four under the Empire, and his vanquishers likewise sought to restore unity by compulsion.

The periodical was central to the democratic and national struggles that would dominate the next two centuries. For Jürgen Habermas (1991), in the absence of freedom, a critically reasoning, bourgeois, political public sphere emerged from the literary: above all, through journals, as both forums and subjects of discussion in homes and new sites of sociability. Benedict Anderson (1983) suggests that the simultaneous reading of newspapers, made possible by the combination of print capitalism and linguistic diversity, provided far-flung individuals with a concrete experience of belonging to the imagined community of the nation. Paul Starr, countering deterministic notions of technology or capitalism, has emphasized how "constitutive, political decisions" (2004: 3) regarding intellectual property, civil liberties, and systems of communication and transportation shaped the modern media and allowed the republican United States to become the precocious and continuing leader.

The century between Waterloo and Versailles commercialized, popularized, and professionalized the periodical. Publishers and governments, traditionally oriented toward elites, came to view popular reading – like nationalism and primary education – as a force more profitably harnessed than suppressed. With its unprecedented demand for volume and speed, the periodical rather than the book forced the innovation of production methods and trade practices. In 1814, König's steam-powered, flatbed-cylinder machine printed all 4,000 copies of *The Times* of London overnight. By 1896, a Hoe rotary press could print and fold 96,000 eight-page issues of Pulitzer's *New York World* (circulation nearly 1.5 million) in one hour, from stereotype plates, on rolls of pulp paper running at 32.5 miles per hour. The elimination of technological, juridical, and economic obstacles to the mass circulation of literary commodities rendered periodicals ubiquitous, increasingly cheap, and eventually colorful.

Already in 1826, Michael Faraday found the output of scientific periodical literature overwhelming. The signal development, however, was the rise of alternatives to elite newspapers and reviews, in two waves of popularization: the appearance of penny newspapers and weeklies around 1830, and the advent of the sensationalistic "new" or "American" journalism of Pulitzer and Hearst and their European imitators around 1880 (Harmsworth, Millaud). They coincided, respectively, with populist pressures and the introduction of mass schooling in the era of anti-revolutionary stabilization and national integration. The number of US journals rose from about 100 in 1825 to 3,300 by 1885, and newspapers from 200 in 1801 to 7,000 in 1880. In Britain, there were 267 newspapers in 1821 and 2,504 by 1914. Russian-language periodicals numbered 170 in 1860 and 606 in 1900. Inexpensive newspapers and monthly or weekly magazines provided multigenerational audiences with news, scandal, entertainment, practical information, fiction, and a dose of reformism, along with growing amounts of advertising and illustration. They were the textual equivalent of department stores: urban, democratic, commercial institutions that appealed to women, reshaped markets as well as consumption, and aroused similar anxieties.

Paradoxically, democratization reinforced hierarchy, establishing a periodical great chain of being descending from lofty quarterlies (*Edinburgh Review* 1802, *North American Review* 1815), via "high-quality" illustrateds (*Scribner's Magazine* 1887, *Strand* 1891), related family publications (*Harper's Weekly* 1857, *Gartenlaube* 1853), and cheap, mass-circulation magazines (*Munsey's* 1889, *Collier's* 1888) to fare for the newly or semi-literate (*Tit-Bits* 1881). Russians distinguished between monthly "thick journals" and illustrated weekly "thin magazines" – the appetite for which newspapers whetted rather than spoiled. Renewed debate on the periodical focused less on the quantity of reading matter than the quality of reading practices among a mass public figured as feminine and lower class.

All strata consumed serialized fiction, in part-publications inspired by the success of *The Pickwick Papers* (1836–7), in new family magazines, and (on the continent) in the *feuilleton* or non-political portion of the newspaper (one thinks of Verne, Thackeray, Dumas, Trollope, Conan Doyle). Some theories attempt to explain the appeal of serial literature by opposing "female" fiction to "male" nonfiction or positing complementary rhythms of textual pleasure (goal-oriented male installments within the periodicity of feminine delayed gratification). Certainly, the tangible benefits of the *ménage à trois* between author, publisher, and reader were clear. When Eugène Sue's *Juif Errant* ran in

169 *feuilletons* in the *Constitutionnel* (1844–5), it boosted sales from 5,944 to 24,771 and earned him 100,000 francs.

The key to cheap print was advertising income, which allowed publishers to sell below cost. The appearance and character of periodicals changed accordingly. Between 1908 and 1913, advertising space in the *Saturday Evening Post*, that juggernaut of bourgeois socialization, occupied 35–50 percent of a given issue, and advertising revenues grew by 600 percent, leading the Curtis Corporation to proclaim that its ostentatious new headquarters was "built on faith – faith in the power of advertising" (Cohn 1989: 64). Even as a feminist press emerged, mainstream publishers increasingly targeted women as consumers.

Commercialization fostered journalistic sensationalism and sobriety alike. Sensationalism (like bolder "American" design) compensated for the inherent redundancy of event-based content whose increasing blandness derived from shared wire services (Havas 1835, Wolff 1849, Reuters 1851) and pools (Associated Press 1848, United Press 1907), as well as the political reserve prompted by new ideals of journalistic "objectivity" and the triangulated cultivation of readers, stockholders, and advertisers. A profit-driven press emphasizing reporting replaced a crudely partisan one in the US in the 1830s, Britain by mid-century, and Japan in the 1880s. Critics pointed in vain to the spurious separation of editorial from commercial concerns.

Controversy assumed forms appropriate to the environment of public opinion ("jingoism," "muckraking"). Periodicals turned the Dreyfus case into "The Affair" that affirmed the power of the press and public intellectuals. One unintended consequence was the Tour de France (1903), a promotional device for a cycling magazine formed by arch-conservatives (including Michelin) who seceded from another over its Dreyfusard politics and advertising prices. Sales increased tenfold to over 250,000 by 1908. The simultaneous circulation of the bicycles, periodicals, and products they advertised epitomized the intimate and uneasy intermingling of the worlds of goods and ideas.

Consumerism, conflict, and consolidation in the era of the two world wars and the Cold War produced both the greatest efflorescence of, and threats to, periodical culture. On the one hand, periodicals embodied and celebrated the commercialization of leisure. Henry Luce's information and photojournalistic magazines (*Time* 1923, *Life* 1936) and their imitators satisfied the needs of a visually literate middlebrow public accustomed to a fast-paced life and desirous of being informed and modern but not overly intellectual or unconventional. On the other hand, periodicals continued to serve as artillery and fortresses (to use popular nineteenth-century metaphors) in political and cultural wars, as mass media met mass politics.

Both the Nazis and the Soviets sought to create new human types and societies and rejected a free, heterogeneous literary market, although with different rationales and consequences. Pursuing historical debates on overproduction to a draconian conclusion, the Nazis eliminated ideologically acceptable as well as subversive publications. What political "coordination" began, "total war" finished: by 1944, the number of journals had sunk from some 7,300 to 500, and the number of newspapers from 4,100 to 977. Enhanced diffusion of periodicals abroad was the goal of the equally draconian national switchover from "Gothic" to roman letters (1941), preposterously justified as another blow against malevolent Jewish influence. The Nazis sought to tame a nation of readers; the Bolsheviks, to create one. The latter viewed increasing literacy (21 percent in 1897) and publication, like industrial production, as measures of revolutionary success. Unable to allow either a traditional elite or a new but autonomous popular culture, they created the "Soviet reading 'myth'": a nation of voracious readers united through print by socialist values (Lovell 2000: 21). By the 1960s, the USSR produced some 6,800 periodicals in 60 languages with a circulation of 61 million, including 602 daily newspapers (c. 50 in 1913). This hothouse diversity was to be both the cause and proof of social cohesion, but neither long survived communism itself.

After 1945, the victorious Allies presided over an unprecedented rebuilding of the publishing landscape equivalent to the renewal of devastated cities: a simultaneous loss and opportunity. Although the toll of "totalitarian" dictatorship of right and left was obvious, capitalist democracy proved harsh in its own way. Concentration, which began in the late nineteenth century (Scripps, Hearst, Harmsworth), accelerated and spread. Competition declined. Both the cookie-cutter of communism and the gentle but relentless kneading of the capitalist invisible hand shaped what to many appeared as an increasingly homogeneous product. Put another way: *Der Spiegel* (1947) and *India Today* (1975) look like *Time* for the same reason that Frankfurt and Mumbai look like Chicago.

Precocious or analogous developments such as the Roman *acta diurna*, Chinese *ti pao*, or Mughal manuscript newsletters notwithstanding, the periodical was a modern European invention, a "civilian tool of Western empire-building" (Reed 2004: 10) that non-Westerners came to employ for their own ends. It shaped languages, created canons, and forged identities along a broad spectrum of responses: neither mere imitation nor negation of Western values, nationalism, or technology. Where cultural resistance to the letterpress book or commercialization was strong, periodicals sometimes eased the introduction of print culture. Middle Eastern modernizers such as Faris al-Shidyaq proselytized for the new technology as the means of overcoming backwardness while preserving and democratizing the scribal legacy. His *al-Jawa'ib*, the first non-governmental Arabic paper (Constantinople 1861) became a forum for nationalist cultural revival. In China, lithography, thanks to its low cost and closeness to traditional aesthetics, served as a "compromise technology" (Reed 2004: 89). Illustrated newspaper supplements and journals were the bridge between indigenous woodblock printing and the high-speed industrialized letterpress required for modern news periodicals that flourished after the Sino-Japanese war.

In the Western hemisphere, where the first news-sheet was published in Spanish in Mexico in 1541, local vernaculars never seriously challenged the dominance of colonial languages in print. India, by contrast, developed what Vinay Dharwadker calls "the first fully formed print culture to appear outside Europe and North America . . . distinguished by its size, productivity, and multilingual and multinational constitution, as well as . . . its inclusion of numerous non-Western investors and producers" (1997: 112). The rich print culture (including 14,000 nineteenth-century periodicals in forty languages) may even have forestalled the violence that accompanied other colonial struggles. The rise of nationalist movements was inextricably linked with periodicals: a fourfold increase in circulation of Bengali newspapers from 1883 to 1888, a quadrupling of Egyptian papers between 1892 and 1899 (and nearly thirty women's periodicals founded 1892–1920), and 474 Ottoman periodicals published in various languages following the Young Turk revolution in 1908.

The periodical flourished because it offered all the agents of the communications circuit distinct advantages: for publishers, financial calculability and a means of recruitment and publicity; for authors, regular income and exposure; for readers, affordable diversity of content. Periodicity allowed for continual intellectual or material response, whose virtual intimacy compensated for the anonymity of the market. Growing commercialization and scale of operations wrought changes in that relationship as well as the genre.

Johann Friedrich Cotta pioneered the integrated enterprise, offering high fees for contributions to an unparalleled complex of periodicals. His political and literary newspapers *Allgemeine Zeitung* (1798) and *Morgenblatt für gebildete Stände* (1807) relentlessly promoted his book catalogue, especially lucrative editions by luminaries such as Schiller and Goethe, won via journal contracts. Other publishers attached their names to flagship publications (*Blackwood's, Harper's, Scribner's, Westermann's*). Complexity and profitability grew hand-in-hand. By 1912, "A single edition of either the *Ladies' Home Journal* or the *Saturday Evening Post* consumed four square miles of paper and 60,000 pounds of ink and required sixty-five railway cars to distribute it" (Cohn 1989: 64). The British press barons used revenues from cheap magazines to subsidize still cheaper newspapers. The printer–publisher–retailer thus evolved into a "pure" publisher and sometimes manager of a multifaceted concern, which was to its forerunner as the railroad was to the textile mill: a network rather than single locus of activity, often requiring public ownership rather than family capital.

The understandable scholarly emphasis on books has distorted our view of authorship. Periodicals fostered the rise of professional writers, incidental writers, and professionals who wrote. A journal's title and the collective reputations of its established authors spread an umbrella of provisional credibility over its new writers. The birth of the periodical coincided with what Foucault (1984) controversially identifies as an epochal reversal in the author function, whereby scientific discourses came to be judged on their merits, and literary discourses required attribution to a named creator. Dieter Paul Baumert (1928) suggests a further differentiation of aesthetic and informational roles. He discerns a sort of bell curve of the authorial persona in journalism, as the dominant activity evolved from mere compilation in the pioneering phase, to individualized literary shaping of material in the Enlightenment and Romantic eras, and editorial selection and arrangement after 1848. As the profile of the average journalist receded, elite contributions (bylines, *feuilletons*) stood out all the more by comparison.

Even for prominent authors, the regularity of periodical work was sometimes both attraction and agony. Schiller, Hegel, Melville, and Robert Nicoll likened the routine of periodicity to the lot of the galley slave. Still, for writers willing to accept the constraints of serialization in mass-circulation magazines marketed as much to advertisers as readers, the rewards could be considerably more lucrative than book contracts: in F. Scott Fitzgerald's case, $225,784 versus $66,588 from 1919 to 1936.

The combination of consistent title and changing content in effect made periodicals objects of both intensive and extensive reading. The *Encyclopédie* expressed a classic ambivalence when it described journals as devised "for the comfort of those who are too busy or too lazy to read entire books . . . a means of satisfying their curiosity and of becoming wise at little expense" (Kronick 1976: 20). Even the latter advantage was only relative. Because print-runs of early journals were 500–1,000 copies and even newspapers rarely sold in tens of thousands prior to the advent of cheap print, a single copy may have been shared by ten or twenty persons, in homes, coffee-houses, clubs, or popular joint-subscription organizations (430 in the German territories between 1760 and 1800; 463 in Paris between 1815 and 1830). Ironically, when periodicals were scarce, the experience of reading them was often collective and oral, but became more individualized and silent after they became a mass medium, reflecting the shift from vehicle of public discussion to object of private consumption. Mass-circulation periodicals were immensely profitable and influential, but whether they succeeded in manipulating their readers is a question that only a history of audiences can confirm. British workers, Victorian ladies on both sides of the Atlantic, and Soviet "new women" all turned to periodicals for entertainment and self-improvement in ways as likely to resist as absorb indoctrination.

As the means of physical production and distribution of periodicals evolved, periodicity settled into normative rhythms: daily for newspapers, weekly or monthly for magazines, and quarterly for "weightier" titles. The periodical that most exuberantly flaunts its periodicity is *La Bougie du Sapeur* (*The Sapper's Candle*, 1980). Named after a cartoon character born on February 29, this humorous "daily" appears only every four years, now accompanied (only every 28 years, of course) by a Sunday supplement. The joke makes sense only in an age so saturated with periodicity that we no longer notice it unless jolted out of our routines. Periodicity of publication was part of the evolution from fluctuating feast-and-fast rhythms to a modern world of factory discipline and time zones (derived from the needs of railroads), in which both work and recreation proceed according to schedule. In *Adam Bede* (1859), George Eliot lamented the replacement of the old, slow leisure by the new, which she described as "eager" and marked by "that periodicity of sensations which we call post-time." In Arthur Schnitzler's stream-of-consciousness novella "Leutnant Gustl" (published in the Viennese daily, *Neue Freie Presse*, 1900), as the dishonored protagonist deliberates whether to kill himself at 7 a.m. local time or railroad time, his presumptive last act is to go to his café for coffee – and the morning paper.

Today, the periodical faces the challenges of rising costs, competition from other media, and changing habits of consumption. Television became the principal vehicle of both entertainment and news, depriving periodicals (especially magazines) of advertising as well as audience and, as a constant generator of narrative, even driving fiction from their pages. Major newspapers have compensated for the loss of immediacy through expanded analysis of the sort associated with the journal. The genre once reviled as a mendacious compilation of trivia now appears as the nostalgic voice of gravitas. Finally, the center of gravity of the newspaper is shifting. Between 1970 and 1997, the number of dailies, total circulation, and circulation per thousand inhabitants declined in the more developed countries but soared in the developing world (−25/+65, −13/+262, −23/+107 percent, respectively). In 2004, only thirty-five countries registered increases in newspaper circulation, notably China and India (35 and 23 percent). The decline of traditional mass-circulation magazines (particularly large-format illustrateds) has opened the market to larger numbers of consumer publications with lower circulations. Now, as earlier, quantity does not imply longevity. In the nineteenth century, US magazines typically lasted for two years. In 1989, only 20 percent survived more than four.

The challenge of the Internet soon eclipsed the "print versus video" debate. Web periodicals are still primarily pendants of paper versions, but increasingly online only (*Slate* dates from 1996). Their long-term economic and conceptual models remain unclear. One-fourth of adult Americans read news online daily, but the expectation of "free information" has militated against charging for "content." Most electronic periodicals are typical transitional products that recapitulate the aesthetics and functions of the previous technology, resulting only in enhanced diffusion of static texts (disparagingly known as "brochureware" or "long-distance photocopying").

A reconceptualization of both the periodical and its intellectual property regime is arising from the information explosion in the sciences (7,888 biomedical journals in 1959 versus 19,316 in 1977; 10,000 articles in *Physics Abstracts* in 1955 versus 146,500 in 1996). Soaring numbers and prices of scholarly periodicals issuing from monopolistic commercial presses devour library acquisition budgets at the expense of monograph purchases. The problem is compounded in developing countries, where the inability of scientists to keep up with current research prevents them from contributing to it. In 1991, the Third World accounted for only 1.5 percent of the journals and 5 percent of the papers in the Science Citation Index. Scholars and librarians associated with the "open-access" movement therefore urge a switch from paper to digital format and profit to reciprocity, on the principle that work produced without remuneration should be available online without restriction through peer-reviewed journals (over 2,000 so far) and repositories.

As David Kronick (1976), Joost Kircz (1998), and James O'Donnell (1998) have observed, the character of the learned journal as a means of disseminating, storing, and retrieving information highlights essential features of the periodical genre and the transformative possibilities of electronic publication, which expands the boundaries of the text and the reader's capacity for interaction with it. Decoupling the text from an inalterable physical incarnation renders diffusion in principle universal and instantaneous, and underscores the primary function of the publisher as middleman. A single article can share several journal titles, whose assignment as credentialing and locator mechanisms could follow "publication." The interactive capacity for continual updating allows the periodical to recapture the immediacy that it once ceded to audiovisual media, enabling users to respond to or even modify published texts, blurring the boundary between author and reader, and loosening the "fixity" that Elizabeth Eisenstein associated with print. Indeed, the new Anglo-American Cataloguing Rules replace "serial" and "monograph" with "continuing" and "finite" resources, both of them updatable.

Of course, ease of publication does not guarantee readership, not when "blogs" are being spawned at a rate of one per second. But research will become easier because we will search for information itself rather than the title of the journal or article that contains it. Pursuing this logic, some scientists envision a new form of scholarly communication in which "different types of information, at present intermingled in the linear article, can be separated and stored in well-defined, cognitive, textual modules" (Kircz 1998: 210), linked to one another both within and between publications. This possibility of boundless interconnection reminds us that, alongside the view of the periodical as inferior to the book existed others that claimed complementarity or even superiority. The early German Romantics, for example, developed a theory of the periodical as evolving encyclopedia or collectively authored book greater than the sum of its parts. By transcending the dilemma of selection versus expansiveness, the digital periodical may replace the book as the normative textual genre and become the portal through which we enter the coveted realm of the universal library. In the process, ironically, its hallmark – periodicity – may be radically transformed as we also enter a continually updatable hypertextual present.

REFERENCES AND FURTHER READING

Anderson, Benedict (1983) *Imagined Communities: Reflections on the Origin and Spread of Nationalism.* London: Verso.

Barbier, Frédéric and Bertho Lavenir, Catherine (2003) *Histoire des médias de Diderot à internet* [History of the Media from Diderot to the Internet], 3rd edn. Paris: Armand Colin.

Baron, Beth (1994) *The Women's Awakening in Egypt: Culture, Society, and the Press.* New Haven: Yale University Press.

Baumert, Dieter Paul (1928) *Die Entstehung des deutschen Journalismu: Eine sozialgeschichtliche Studie* [The Development of German Journalism: A Social-historical Study]. Munich and Leipzig: Duncker und Humblot.

Brooks, Jeffrey (1985) *When Russia Learned to Read: Literacy and Popular Literature, 1861–1917.* Princeton: Princeton University Press.

Cohn, Jan (1989) *Creating America: George Horace Lorimer and the Saturday Evening Post.* Pittsburgh: University of Pittsburgh Press.

Dharwadker, Vinay (1997) "Print Culture and Literary Markets in Colonial India." In Jeffrey Masten, Peter Stallybrass, and Nancy Vickers (eds.), *Language Machines: Technologies of Literary and Cultural Production*, pp. 108–33. London: Routledge.

Dovifat, Emil (1962) *Zeitungslehre* [Theory of the Newspaper], 4th edn., 2 vols. Berlin: de Gruyter.

Foucault, Michel (1984) "What is an Author?" In *The Foucault Reader*, ed. Paul Rabinow, pp. 101–20. New York: Pantheon.

Garvey, Ellen Gruber (1996) *The Adman in the Parlor: Magazines and the Gendering of Consumer Culture, 1880 to 1910s.* New York: Oxford University Press.

Habermas, Jürgen (1991) *The Structural Transformation of the Public Sphere: An Inquiry into a Category of Bourgeois Society*, trans. Thomas Burger. Cambridge, MA: MIT Press (originally published 1962).

Kirchner, Joachim (1928) *Die Grundlagen des deutschen Zeitschriftenwesens. Mit einer Gesamtbibliographie der deutschen Zeitschriften bis zum Jahre 1790* [Foundations of the German Periodical. With a Complete Bibliography of German Periodicals up to 1790]. Leipzig: Karl W. Hiersemann.

Kircz, Joost G. (1998) "Modularity: The Next Form of Scientific Information Presentation?" *Journal of Documentation*, 54 (2): 210–35 (available at www.science.uva.nl/projects/commphys/papers/jkmodul.htm; accessed August 12, 2004).

Kronick, David A. (1976) *A History of Scientific and Technical Periodicals: The Origins and Development of the Scientific and Technical Press 1665–1790*, 2nd edn. Metuchen, NJ: Scarecrow.

Lindemann, Margot and Koszyk, Kurt (1969–86) *Geschichte der deutschen Presse* [History of the German Press], 4 vols. Berlin: Colloquium.

Lovell, Stephen (2000) *The Russian Reading Revolution: Print Culture in the Soviet and Post-Soviet eras.* Houndsmills: Macmillan.

Lowenthal, Leo (1961) *Literature, Popular Culture, and Society.* Englewood Cliffs: Prentice-Hall.

Martens, Wolfgang (1968) *Die Botschaft der Tugend: Die Aufklärung im Spiegel der deutschen Moralischen Wochenschriften* [The Message of Virtue: The Enlightenment in the Mirror of the German Moral Weeklies]. Stuttgart: Metzler.

Martin, Henri-Jean, Chartier, Roger, and Vivet, Jean-Pierre (eds.) (1983–6) *Histoire de l'édition française* [History of French Publishing], 4 vols. Paris: Promodis.

O'Donnell, James J. (1998) *Avatars of the Word from Papyrus to Cyberspace.* Cambridge, MA: Harvard University Press.

Popkin, Jeremy (1990) *Revolutionary News: The Press in France, 1789–1799.* Durham: University of North Carolina Press.

Raabe, Paul (1974) "Die Zeitschrift als Medium der Aufklärung" [The Periodical as a Medium of the Enlightenment]. *Wolfenbüttler Studien zur Aufklärung*, 1: 99–136.

Reed, Christopher A. (2004) *Gutenberg in Shanghai: Chinese Print Capitalism, 1876–1937.* Vancouver: UBC Press.

Schröder, Thomas (1995) *Die ersten Zeitungen: Textgestaltung und Nachrichtenauswahl* [The First Newspapers: Text Formation and Selection of News]. Tübingen: Günter Narr.

Shattock, Joanne and Wolff, Michael (eds.) (1982) *The Victorian Periodical Press: Samplings and Soundings.* Leicester: University of Leicester Press.

Smith, Anthony (1979) *The Newspaper: An International History.* London: Thames and Hudson.

Starr, Paul (2004) *The Creation of the Media: Political Origins of Modern Communications.* New York: Basic.

Sullivan, Alvin (ed.) (1983–6) *British Literary Magazines*, 4 vols. Westport, CT: Greenwood.

Tebbel, John and Zuckerman, Mary Ellen (1991) *The Magazine in America 1741–1990.* New York: Oxford University Press.

Valdés, Mario J. and Kadir, Djelal (eds.) (2004) *Literary Cultures of Latin America: A Comparative History*, 3 vols. Oxford: Oxford University Press.

Wald, James J. (1995) "The 'Small Club of Connoisseurs' and the 'General Public': Schiller's *Horen* and Posselt's *Europäische Annalen.*" In Herbert Rowland and Karl J. Fink (eds.), *The Eighteenth-century Book Review*, pp. 113–35. Heidelberg: C. Winter.

Woodward, Hazel and Pilling, Stella (eds.) (1993) *The International Serials Industry.* Aldershot: Gower.

32

The Importance of Ephemera

Martin Andrews

By its very definition, book history concentrates on the contents and artifact of the book. But to explore and understand the subject in all its dimensions, we need to extend beyond the book itself to consider a breadth of contextual issues. In addition to literary content and organization, we need to study topics such as printing and production; readership and the act of reading itself; the buying, selling, and distribution of books; the availability of, and discussion about, books, libraries, and literary societies. Printed ephemera can contribute to all of these areas of research, providing a rich and important source of information.

What objects do we mean when we refer to ephemera? Even in the particular area of ephemera relating to the book, the range is enormous: prospectuses, catalogues, billheads and letterheads, bookmarks, posters announcing publications and literary events, handbills for circulating libraries, booksellers' labels, galley proofs, book tokens, dust jackets, advertisements − the list goes on. Individually, items of ephemera might seem trivial and peripheral, but cumulatively they can throw a very particular light on history, offering not only factual detail but also an atmospheric and evocative direct link with the past.

With the growth of literacy, communications, advertising, and marketing, there was a great proliferation of jobbing printing in the nineteenth century, but ephemera relating to the printing, publishing, and marketing of books have existed since the very beginning of printing with movable type. The first dated specimen of Western printing was not a book but a piece of ephemera: an indulgence probably printed by Johann Gutenberg or by his partners Fust and Schoeffer in 1454. Although rare, examples of ephemera from the earliest days of book printing have survived. Two copies of a short advertisement printed by William Caxton in about 1478 for his *Commemorations of Sarum Use* still exist (figure 32.1). The advertisement promises that the book is competitively priced ("good chepe").

Occasionally, items such as a prospectus or advertisement are bound into a book or more commonly found hidden away in the binding. The value of paper was such that

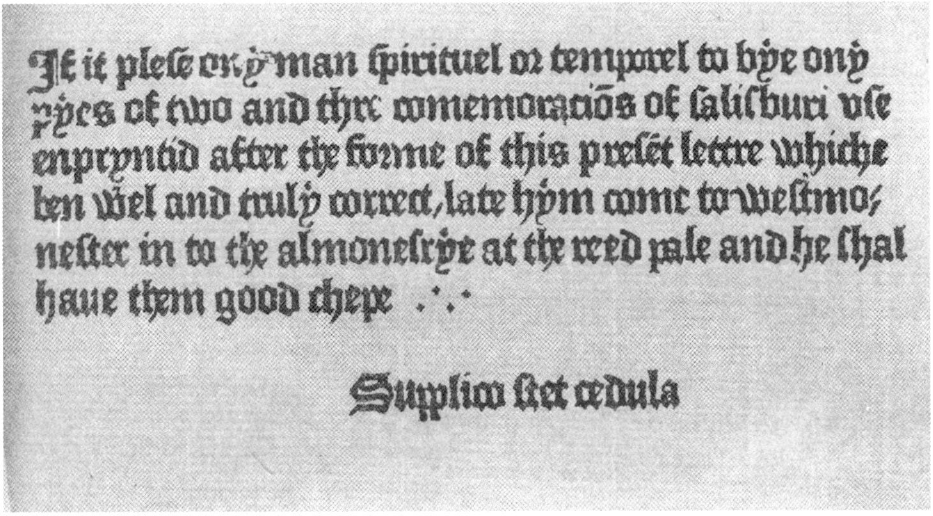
If it plese ony man spirituel or temporel to bye ony
pyes of two and thre comemoracios of salisburi vse
enpryntid after the forme of this preset lettre whiche
ben wel and truly correct, late hym come to westmo-
nester in to the almonesrye at the reed pale and he shal
haue them good chepe

Supplico stet cedula

Figure 32.1 William Caxton's advertisement for *Commemorations of Sarum Use*, c.1478. Reproduced from a photolithograph facsimile published in 1892. The original is in the Bodleian Library, Oxford.

redundant items were reused as one of the layers of pasteboard or pasted down to the wooden board. This was possibly the fate of a list of books for sale printed by Peter Schoeffer in 1470. The list was used by a traveling salesman who wrote his address at the bottom of the sheet. The final line of the list is picked out in a larger size of type as a specimen of the typeface used in the Psalter for sale. In 1498, Aldus Manutius circulated a list of books printed in Greek, classified by subject (grammar, poetics, logic, philosophy, sacred scriptures), and priced. In America, ephemeral items such as broadsides were the stock-in-trade of the first printers. The first book published in the English colonies was the Bay Psalm Book of 1640, printed by Stephen Daye. But he is also known to have printed a "Freeman's Oath" broadside and an almanac.

There have been many debates about a precise definition of printed ephemera, but there is much to be gained from a wide, embracing approach, accepting fuzzy edges. Broadly, the derivation of the word lies in the Greek *epi* (about or around) and *hemera* (a day). The word is also used as the specialist term for the freshwater insect, the mayfly (*Ephemera danica*), which, in its adult winged form, is commonly believed to live for only a day. For astronomers, astrologers, and navigators, the word *ephemeris* is used for a calendar or table of days. Even Dr. John Johnson, appointed printer to the University of Oxford in 1925 and founder of the extensive and celebrated collection of ephemera that is now housed in the Bodleian Library, found it difficult to be precise. He said his collection consisted of "common printed things . . . what is commonly thrown away – all the printed paraphernalia of our day-to-day lives, in size from the largest broadside to the humble calling card . . . from magnificent invitations to coronations of kings to the humblest of street literature sold for a penny or less." On another occasion, he defined it as "everything which would normally go into the wastepaper basket after use, every-thing printed which is not actually a book" (Rickards 1988: 14). But Johnson's defini-tions were not meant to be deprecating; on the contrary, he greatly valued ephemera as documentation of his world of printing and publishing: "I keep every trade card of every traveller who comes within the gates [at OUP], and treasure them in my archives. They are among the many gauges of our craft" (Johnson 1933: 46).

Today, there is wide recognition of ephemera as an important historical source. As Asa Briggs argues, "In the reconstruction of the past everything is grist to the historian's mill, and what was thrown away is at least as useful as what was deliberately preserved. As our sense of past times changes, we try to strip away the intervening layers and discover the immediate witnesses" (quoted in Rickards 1988: 9). Ephemera provide us with a very particular kind of evidence. They offer an opportunity for scholarly analysis as well as a more subjective quality, an almost emotional and tactile response to worn and fingered material, directly handled by the people whose concerns and activities we are trying to understand, material that, against the odds, has survived and come down to us, often in a fragile state. In an unpublished essay, "The Study of Ephemera, 1977", the ephemerist Maurice Rickards wrote:

> An implicit component of every item of ephemera is the reader over our shoulder – the eyes for which the item first appeared; the living glance that scanned the paper even as we ourselves now scan it . . . Not only can you "hear their voices", as Trevelyan put it, you can merge your glance with theirs . . . You become, as you read, an intimate part of the detail of their experience – not just overhearing them, but being momentarily *within* them . . . As we survey a battered public notice or a dog-eared printed paper, we are aware not only of the sum total of duration (implicit in its wear and tear), not only the buffetings and bruisings that its condition proclaims, but the countless scannings it has undergone – the multitude of readings and re-readings. It is, as you might say, "eye-worn" . . . (quoted in Rickards 1988: 16–17)

There are other areas of confusion and debate. One is the problem of distinguishing when a pamphlet, brochure, or other minor publication can be described as a book and therefore no longer ephemera. Librarians commonly define a book as being a bound work of thirty-two pages or more. Is a newspaper or magazine to be classed as ephem-era? Such publications are given bibliographical status and are kept in libraries and yet are also thrown away after use. This clearly is an issue when looking at essays, serialized novels, and short stories in journals and popular magazines. Furthermore, the artifactual description of "book" is given to a variety of documents: order book, stamp book, autograph book, ration book, and specimen or sample book. Another issue is how to categorize letters and manuscripts. Is the daybook of the publisher Longmans to be considered ephemera compared with a hand-scribbled note from the publisher to the printers? However, precise and rigid definitions are unhelpful. What is important is how this huge and diverse area of material can inform a study of the history of the book.

Figure 32.2 Receipt from Robert Allardice, bookseller and stationer, 1831. John Lewis Collection, Reading University Library.

Finding material is often a matter of chance, locating the odd relevant item in private collections of printed ephemera or among specialist traders or at regularly held ephemera fairs. But there are also major collections in libraries, museums, and company archives, such as the collection of typographer John Lewis at the University of Reading, organized with sections relating to bookselling, publishing, libraries, printing, and printers (figure 32.2). The seventeenth-century diarist Samuel Pepys had a particular passion for ballads, chapbooks, and other street literature, preserved in the Pepys Library at Magdalene College Cambridge. Amongst thousands of items that form "a throwaway conspectus of the life and times of a remarkable Londoner" (Rickards 1988: 39) are forty or so trade cards gathered from the businesses within walking distance of his home, including this card for a bookseller: "Roger Tucker. Bookseller at the Signe of the Golden Legg. At the corner of Salisbury Street in the Strand. Sells all sorts of Printed Books and all manner of Stationery Ware at reasonable Rates. Where allso one may have ready mony for all Sorts of books."

Another seventeenth-century collector of street ballads, John Bagford, was to become notorious as something of a vandal to those interested in books. Brought up as a

shoemaker in London with little formal education, Bagford nevertheless gained a reputation as a bibliophile. He was commissioned as an agent by many distinguished book
collectors and academics, including members of the Society of Antiquaries, to search
out specific and often rare volumes for their libraries. Ferreting around in attics, cellars,
street markets, and dusty bookshops in England and abroad gave him an opportunity
to research his own book, *Proposals for Printing an Historical Account of that Most Uni-
versally Celebrated, as well as Useful Art of Typography* (1707). Unfortunately, to inform
his study and provide illustrations, Bagford amassed a vast collection of title pages,
frontispieces, and illustrations, which some believe he wantonly cut out of precious
volumes – even destroying books for their bindings and endpapers. In *The Enemies of
Books* (1888), William Blades described Bagford as a "wicked old biblioclast" who "went
about the country from library to library tearing away title-pages . . ." (quoted in Rickards 1988: 44). Alongside his misdirected passion for books, Bagford was also fascinated
by social history and picked up and preserved a vast cross-section of printed oddments
of the time: tickets, bills, lottery puffs, price lists. Included in this mass of trivia was
material relating more closely to his interest in printing and publishing: galley sheets,
bookplates, specimens of paper and watermarks, and price lists. Bagford's collections
are now housed in the British Library.

From the very beginning of jobbing printing in America, certain collectors felt
compelled to preserve the ephemeral scraps that accompanied their everyday lives, recognizing their worth as, in Dale Roylance's words, a "persuasive graphic witness to their
times" (1992: 6). Perhaps the greatest of these early collectors was Isaiah Thomas
(1749–1831), founder of the American Antiquarian Society and a successful printer and
publisher. In his early career, Thomas produced radical newspapers (the most famous
being the *Massachusetts Spy*) and revolutionary patriotic rhetoric as a passionate supporter
of the cause of American independence. After the war, Thomas concentrated on his
business enterprises: settling in Worcester, Massachusetts, he eventually owned several
printing offices, bookstores, paper mills, and a bindery. As well as books, he published
newspapers, broadsheets, sheet music, periodicals, pamphlets, children's literature of all
kinds, and a yearly almanac. He retired at the age of 53 to dedicate himself to his
interest in documenting the history of the young nation, and in 1810 published his
book, *The History of Printing in America*. As the first librarian and president of the
American Antiquarian Society, Thomas amassed a vast collection of printed ephemera,
incorporating his own personal archives and also material he had purchased, such as a
large proportion of the Mather family collection. In his account of the society, published
in 1813, Thomas wrote: "We cannot obtain a knowledge of those who are to come after
us, nor are we certain what will be the events of future times; as it is in our power, so
it should be our duty, to bestow on posterity that which they cannot give to us, but
which they may enlarge and improve and transmit to those who shall succeed them"
(Thomas 1813: 4).

In the twentieth century, another collector, a contemporary and friend of John
Johnson, brought together a major collection of American and European printed ephemera spanning a period from 1856 to the 1970s. Bella Landauer began gathering material

in 1923 when she started collecting book plates. Her interests and obsessions quickly expanded to trade cards, advertising, and eventually all genres of material. Over 8,000 items were given to the New York Historical Society and now form the Bella Landauer Collection of Business and Advertising Ephemera. She also donated ephemera to many other national institutions.

Collections such as these provide serendipitous sources of information for the book historian. More comprehensive sources are publishers' archives: much can be gleaned from the ephemeral material they contain. The development of publishers can partly be traced through letterheads, detailing moves to new premises and the coming and going of partners and directors, quite apart from the contents of such letters and bills. Prospectuses and announcements are an obvious source of information about publications but can also give an overview of the philosophy and aspirations of a publishing enterprise – occasionally they become a manifesto. When Harold Midgley Taylor set up the Golden Cockerel Press in 1920, he outlined the aims and ideals of his literary and printing cooperative:

> Its members are their own craftsmen, and will produce their own books themselves in their own communal workshops . . . By their elimination of the middleman they are able to stake their work as printer-publishers on an artistic success in exactly the same way that an honest author stakes his. Wherever such an arrangement is possible, they are therefore willing, after the necessary outlay of paper and publicity has been paid off, to share the gross receipts with the author, without any separate payment for their work as printers. Except in the case of very large books and very short runs, the shares will be equal. This seems to be the only way in which the literary artist can get any adequate or fair remuneration for his work . . . As regards distribution, they base their method on Reputation rather than Publicity. They believe that a good piece of work has its natural public . . . They propose as a rule to dispense with travelers . . . They will use the word advertisement in its old sense of announcement and not eye-trap, announcing their publications regularly and adequately . . . (Golden Cockerel Press announcement 1920, John Johnson Collection, Bodleian Library, Oxford)

From such documents – and from publicity material, notices to travelers, catalogues, and the myriad of other trivial documents generated by a publisher – one can piece together the story of the firm and the stories of the books produced.

Ephemera can also provide first-hand evidence of the history of printing. Printers' advertisements and letterheads naturally boast of new processes and equipment: the adoption of lithography, photography, stereotyping, electrotyping, process engraving, Monotype, and Linotype can be dated by noting the appearance of such terms. Invoices, bills, and receipts can provide details of costings and profit margins (figure 32.3). The other trades and industries associated with book production, such as paper manufacturers and binders, also printed informative ephemera of a similar nature.

Many documents are generated during the production of a book: proofs, layouts, specifications, artwork, and design visuals. These documents are ephemeral as they only have value for a short time in production: once the book is published they become

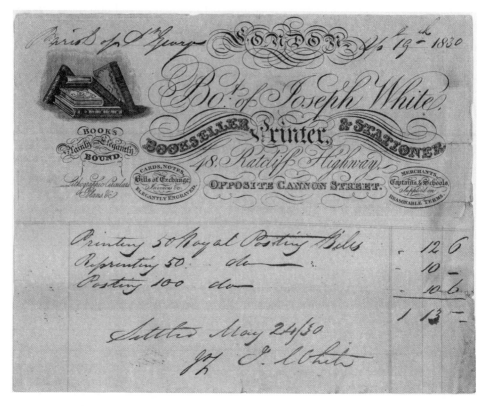

Figure 32.3   Bill from Joseph White, bookseller, printer, and stationer, 1830. Author's collection.

redundant and are often destroyed or stored in a cellar and forgotten. But they can tell us much about how a book was put together – about editing, style, intended audience, economic decisions, and the structure and presentation of the text. In the Plantin–Moretus Museum in Antwerp, the proofreading room of the *Officina Plantiniana* still survives intact: displayed there are examples of galley proofs dating from the seventeenth and eighteenth centuries, marked up with corrections and alterations. In the same building, the type foundry and composing rooms have type specimens on show. Framed in the early bookshop is an index of forbidden books printed by Christophe Plantin in 1569 by order of the Duke of Alba, and intended to be displayed in the bookshops of the Low Countries; it is the only surviving example of its kind.

In the twentieth century, with the emergence of the professional designer and camera-ready artwork, illustration and cover design became a crucial stage in the making of a book. Even for the work of well-known illustrators and artists, much of the ephemeral evidence has been neglected and lost. Design decisions, demonstrated through these artifacts, could have a major effect on the nature and success of a book.

Booksellers and libraries produced trade cards, posters, and book lists that help us understand the distribution, popularity, and availability of particular titles and authors.

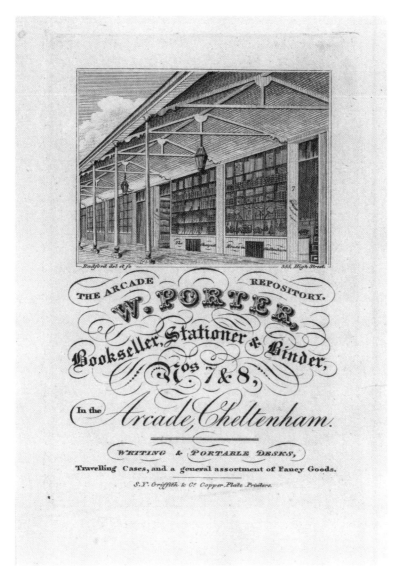

Figure 32.4　Trade card for W. Porter, bookseller, stationer, and binder, c.1830s. John Lewis Collection, Reading University Library.

Often such documents contain important details. A flyer for George Lovejoy's subscription library in Reading, England of 1860 proclaims: "G. L. would just observe, that by the New Postal Regulation books can now be sent to all parts of the kingdom at a cost of 6d, and thus the contents of his extensive Library may become accessible to Subscribers in any part of Her Majesty's dominions" (Local History Collection, Central Library, Reading, England). Illustrated advertising material sometimes depicts library façades and bookshop windows (figure 32.4) or detailed interiors (figure 32.5), giving

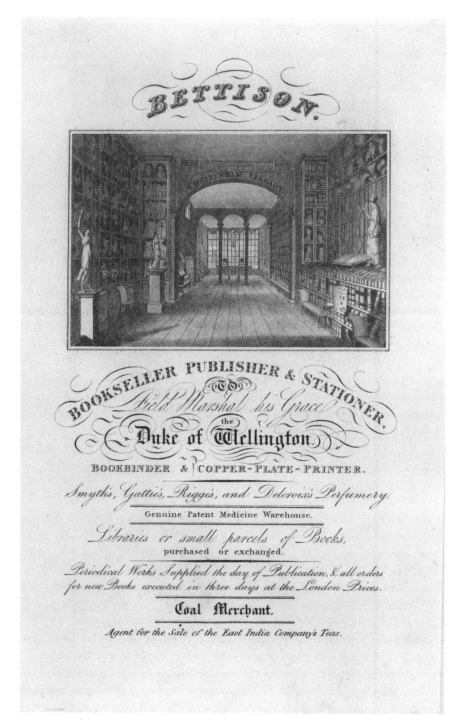

us a glimpse of their layout and atmosphere, and often showing the array of other goods that bookshops sold. Thus, we can understand the context within which the book purchaser or borrower browsed and read. For those in rural locations, away from bookshops, the book-hawker was an essential supplier, and much of the history of hawkers can be traced through their tracts, pamphlets, and circulars.

Private book owning and borrowing by individuals (figure 32.6) were not the only ways in which books were used and appreciated by the public. In Britain, the move toward self-education for the skilled members of the working class led to the proliferation of mechanics' institutes (from the 1820s) and literary societies. Public libraries were set up (figure 32.7) and lecture programs and public readings arranged. Posters and flyers that document their activities were circulated to promote these events. Penny Readings, aptly named, became a popular source of entertainment and education in town and country. Recitations and readings from the works of Shakespeare, Dickens, Scott, and other contemporary authors – serious, comic, sentimental, dramatic – were held in public halls for the modest admission of one penny. Such societies and public readings became a common feature of American life as well.

Another kind of ephemera that can throw light on the history of the book includes items found in or pasted in books themselves. Book plates are an obvious source of information about readership and ownership (figure 32.8). Booksellers' and bookbinders' labels, reflecting the period when gentlemen had their books hand-bound for their libraries, are often found pasted onto the inside of covers. They were miniature trade cards, often printed in black ink on thin tinted paper or in gold on a flat color. The donation of a book to a library is frequently acknowledged on a printed label, as in a volume in Aberdeen University Library: "The Gift of J. Bill (His Majesties Printer) to the New College of Aberdene. 1624." In the nineteenth century, magnificent, brightly colored, chromolithographed certificates adorned the inside pages of prize books, in recognition of high achievement and attendance at school.

The early Puritan colonists in America brought with them primers, horn books, and Bibles from the homeland. Setting up schools in the New World, they consulted manuals for schoolmasters, many of which gave good advice about the use of Rewards of Merit to promote morality and diligence amongst young pupils. Over the centuries, these precious decorative and colorful awards have been proudly carried home to parents by generations of schoolchildren (figure 32.9). The words and images used on Rewards of Merit are significant illustrations of the attitudes toward religion, education, achievement, and moral values that shaped American society.

Found in books but not usually attached to them is another item of ephemera – the bookmark. Known in the Middle Ages as a register, it began to be called a "marker" in the early nineteenth century. Variously made of strips of vellum, ribbon, paper, or cardboard, often decorated or embroidered by hand, the bookmarker of printed card became widespread from about the 1860s. As well as being useful for keeping one's place, they were often rich adornments that could reflect a certain cultural status. Markers illustrated with religious themes became popular, but by the end of the 1870s the printed bookmark had largely become a marketing tool for advertisers, given away

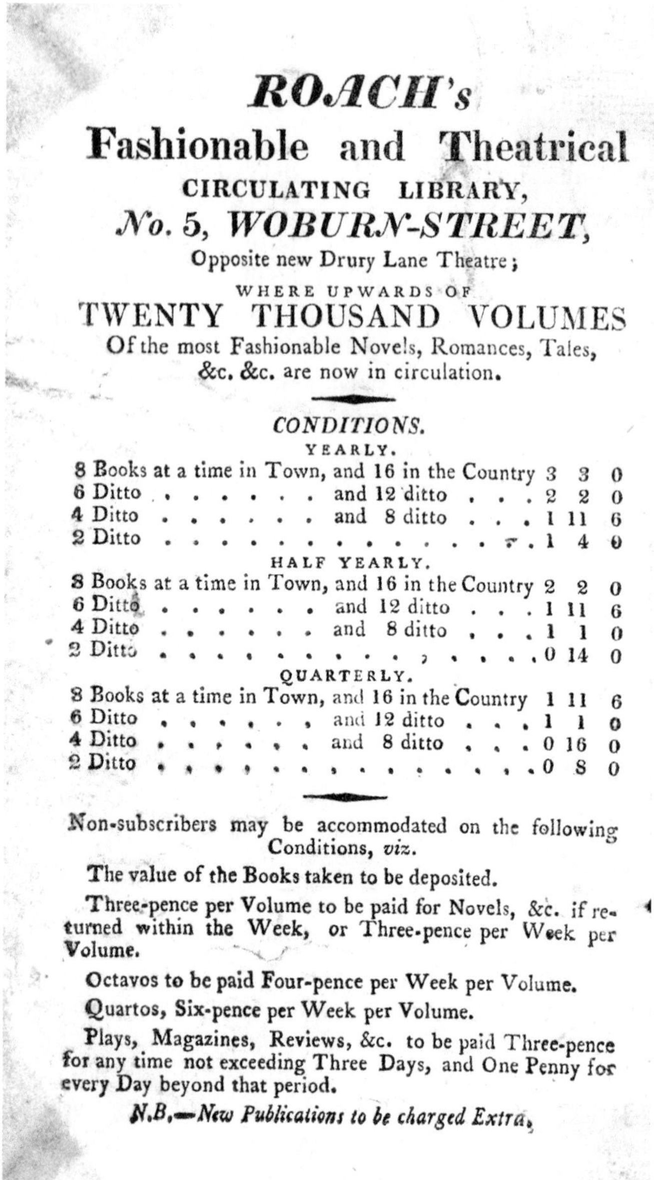

ROACH's
Fashionable and Theatrical
CIRCULATING LIBRARY,
No. 5, WOBURN-STREET,
Opposite new Drury Lane Theatre;

WHERE UPWARDS OF

TWENTY THOUSAND VOLUMES
Of the most Fashionable Novels, Romances, Tales,
&c. &c. are now in circulation.

CONDITIONS.
YEARLY.

8 Books at a time in Town, and 16 in the Country	3	3	0
6 Ditto . . . . and 12 ditto . . .	2	2	0
4 Ditto . . . . and 8 ditto . . .	1	11	6
2 Ditto	1	4	0

HALF YEARLY.

8 Books at a time in Town, and 16 in the Country	2	2	0
6 Ditto . . . . and 12 ditto . . .	1	11	6
4 Ditto . . . . and 8 ditto . . .	1	1	0
2 Ditto	0	14	0

QUARTERLY.

8 Books at a time in Town, and 16 in the Country	1	11	6
6 Ditto . . . . and 12 ditto . . .	1	1	0
4 Ditto . . . . and 8 ditto . . .	0	16	0
2 Ditto	0	8	0

Non-subscribers may be accommodated on the following
Conditions, *viz.*

The value of the Books taken to be deposited.

Three-pence per Volume to be paid for Novels, &c. if returned within the Week, or Three-pence per Week per
Volume.

Octavos to be paid Four-pence per Week per Volume.

Quartos, Six-pence per Week per Volume.

Plays, Magazines, Reviews, &c. to be paid Three-pence
for any time not exceeding Three Days, and One Penny for
every Day beyond that period.

N.B.—New Publications to be charged Extra.

Figure 32.6 Price list for Roach's Circulating Library, c.1830. Maurice Rickards Collection, Centre for Ephemera Studies, Reading University.

free. Sometimes a marker was made to have an additional use, such as a calendar, ruler, timetable, or puzzle.

A popular form of bookmark was made from silk ribbon, which was produced using the Jacquard weaving loom. The ribbons were elaborately woven by machine with

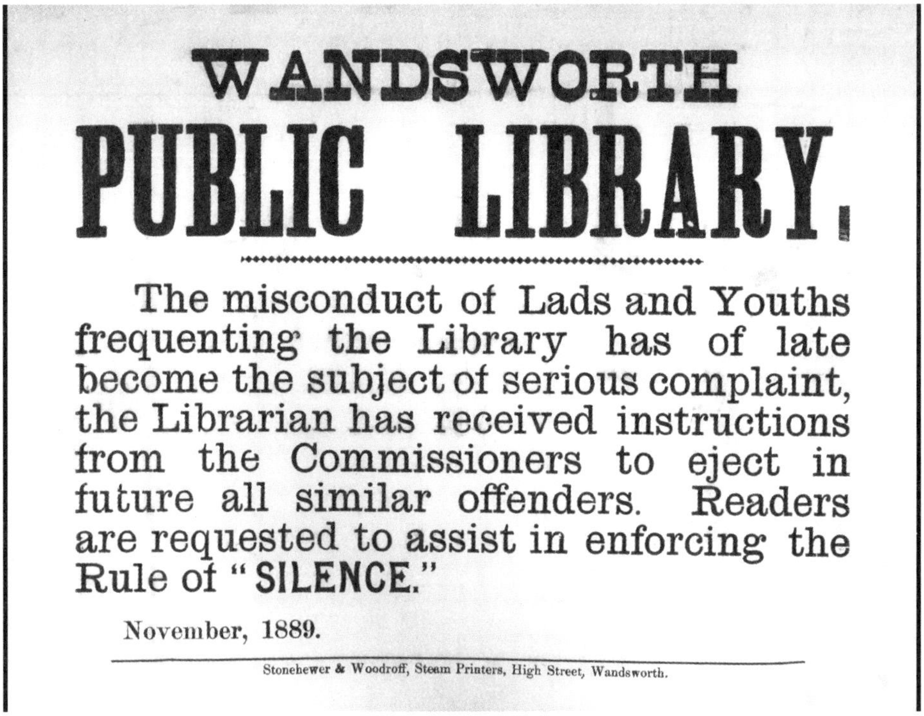

WANDSWORTH
PUBLIC LIBRARY.

The misconduct of Lads and Youths frequenting the Library has of late become the subject of serious complaint, the Librarian has received instructions from the Commissioners to eject in future all similar offenders. Readers are requested to assist in enforcing the Rule of "SILENCE."

November, 1889.

Stonehewer & Woodroff, Steam Printers, High Street, Wandsworth.

Figure 32.7 Notice from the Wandsworth Public Library, 1889. Maurice Rickards Collection, Centre for Ephemera Studies, Reading University.

intricate pictures, the loom being "programmed" to a preset pattern (anticipating certain elements of the computer). The best-known firm manufacturing these markers was Thomas Stevens of Coventry in England. They later became a speciality of the textile mills of Paterson, New Jersey, which was known as "Silk City, USA" in the 1880s.

Reference has already been made to the problems involved in a precise definition of a book. This leads to the consideration of a range of published materials that are book-like but, because of their short length and bindings, are categorized as booklets or leaflets. Chapbooks, playbooks, and short monographs fall into this category. The dissemination of texts through these cheaper forms of publication could introduce a new readership to particular authors and lead on to book reading. The chapbook takes its name from the itinerant "chapman" or street vendor who sold these cheap and crudely printed booklets of anecdotes, romantic tales, verses, riddles, and puzzles. Usually of a small size (about 145 × 90 mm, from four to twenty-four pages), they were frequently sold unstitched and untrimmed, the reader having to finish off the binding at home. For many readers, chapbooks had the advantage over the broadsheet in that they more closely resembled a proper book. They often relied on worn and battered old type and

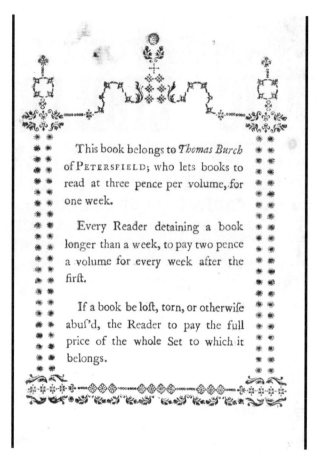

Figure 32.8   Bookplate, Thomas Burch of Petersfield, early nineteenth century. Maurice Rickards Collection, Centre for Ephemera Studies, Reading University.

woodcuts recycled from previous publications. The success of the chapbook led religious organizations to publish tracts and essays with a similar format but a higher moral tone. The texts of popular plays performed in nineteenth-century theaters were cheaply printed and sold as souvenirs. Single-section, stitched, paperbound textbooks of a more scholarly nature were also commonly available in the nineteenth century. Thomas Gray's *Elegy Written in a Country Churchyard* and James Shirley's *Death the Leveller* were published in Green's "Scholastic Series of Poetry." Extending to twelve pages and with extensive notes and biographical details, these little volumes sold for a penny.

Other ephemera can provide a context for the reading and handling of books: for example, the packaging of candles used for illumination (figure 32.10). Advertisements for chairs with bookrests and bedrests add to our general understanding of how books were used (figure 32.11). One of the most successful novelty biscuit tins produced by

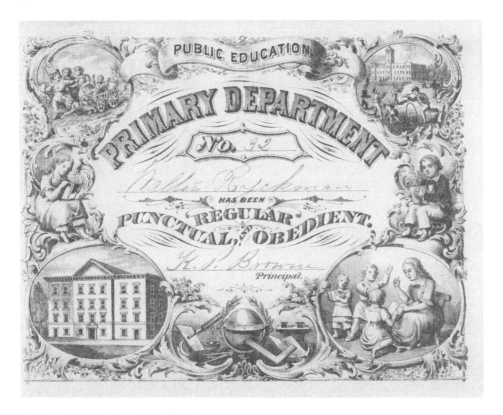

Figure 32.9   Reward of Merit, c.1870s, private collection.

Huntley and Palmers in the 1890s was in the shape of a set of books, complete with colored bindings and tooled titles – and the selection of titles says something about popular (or aspiring) tastes in literature.

In our own times, in ironic contrast to the promise of the "paperless society," our lives are littered with a seemingly ever-increasing amount of ephemeral paper documents that permeate every aspect of our daily existence. "Junk mail," mostly unwelcome and unsolicited, tempts us to acquire more credit or consume endless fast food. The vast amount of glossy, promotional material, the tedious, bureaucratic forms demanding our attention, the over-packaging of products, and streets strewn with drifts of litter are the bane of modern life. Yet, in their turn, these documents will reflect our age for the future. From the "transient minor documents of everyday life" (Rickards 1988: 7) we can have a direct contact with the past through artifacts that were once central to the functioning of society – the etiquette, protocol, private and business life of past centuries and societies around the world. Maurice Rickards has written that ephemera:

Figure 32.10   Packaging label for reading lamp candles, c.1890. Maurice Rickards Collection, Centre for Ephemera Studies, Reading University.

> has much more than passing validity. Above and beyond its immediate purpose, it expresses a fragment of social history, a reflection of the spirit of its time . . . which is not expected to survive, but which can prove to be very useful in research . . . Ephemera represents the other half of history: the half without guile. When people put up monuments, published official war histories they had a constant eye on their audience and their history would adjust to suit, whereas ephemera was never expected to survive . . . so it contains all sorts of human qualities which would otherwise be edited out. (Rickards 1977: 9)

Printed ephemera can document the world of trade and commerce, revealing the bureaucratic manipulation and control of society through rules, regulations, forms, records, certificates, and permissions. Ephemera can reflect the tastes and interests of a period: fashions, hobbies, entertainments, community and social events, sport, travel, art, and culture. The development of education and communication and the opening up of communities and social mobility can be traced through ephemera. After all, most events in life are themselves ephemeral. Often, the only record of great theatrical and dance performances, musical concerts, and art exhibitions are the programs, catalogues, posters, tickets, and flyers that have survived – particularly for experimental or fringe events.

However, for the librarian and archivist, ephemera can pose problems. This material does not lend itself to familiar conventions of classification, storage, and cataloguing. Alan Clinton has observed that:

> Traditionally librarians deal with books, museum curators with artefacts, and archivists with manuscripts. Yet at the edges of what was once regarded as the proper concern of each of these are large amounts of printed paper. These materials are often designated nowadays as "ephemera", and are generally distinguished by being difficult to arrange and to find. (Clinton 1981: 7)

A GREAT LUXURY TO ALL READERS.

AN ESPECIAL BOON TO INVALIDS AND PERSONS OF FEEBLE STRENGTH.

The fatigue of holding a book, and the inconvenience of stooping over the table when reading for any length of time, have frequently been experienced.

The Reading Easel has been contrived to obviate both of these disadvantages. It is easily applied to any bed, chair, or sofa, and is readily adjusted to the variations of sight, altitude of the head, and the most convenient attitudes of the body.

Any position in which a book may be required while being read, the Easel is capable of assuming; affording the reader a degree of ease and luxury unattainable when the hands are constantly occupied with holding the book, or the body incessantly stooping over a table.

The Easel may also be made use of as a stand for holding music, or as a light table for small articles, near a chair, or the bed side.

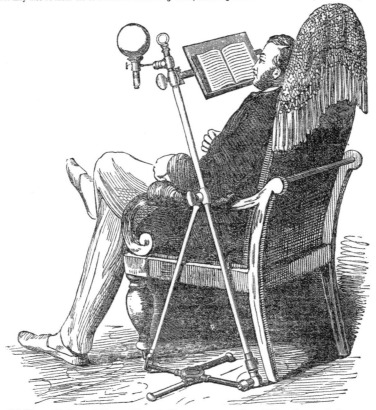

PRICE, with Brass Rods and Brass Thumb Pieces, 20s. each. Ditto, Bronzed Ornamental Stand and Telescope Rods, 45s. each. Lamps for Ditto, with Inkstand, 8s. and 16s. each.

TO BE HAD OF THE NEW LIBRARY COMPANY,

68, WELBECK STREET, CAVENDISH SQUARE, LONDON, W.

Or at the BRANCHES—64, KING WILLIAM STREET, E.C. (near the Statue) ; and 80, KING'S ROAD, BRIGHTON (near the Grand Hotel).

[W H. & L. Collingridge, City Press, London.

Figure 32.11 Advertisement for the "Reading Easel," c.1870s. Author's collection.

If the ephemera of the past are difficult to handle, then what of the future and the preservation of electronic documents and communications? Perhaps we will need a new definition of the word.

References and Further Reading

The two principal organizations devoted to the study of ephemera are the Ephemera Society of America, PO Box 95, Cazenovia, NY 13035-0095 (www.ephemerasociety.org); and the Ephemera Society, PO Box 112, Northwood, Middlesex HA6 2WT, United Kingdom (www.ephemera-society.org.uk).

Clinton, Alan (1981) *Printed Ephemera: Collection, Organisation and Access.* London: Clive Bingley.

Fenn, Patricia and Malpa, Alfred P. (1994) *Rewards of Merit: Tokens of a Child's Progress and a Teacher's Esteem as an Enduring Aspect of American Religious and Secular Education.* Cazenovia, NY: Ephemera Society of America.

James, Louis (1976) *Print and the People 1819–1951.* London: Allen Lane.

Johnson, John (1933) *The Printer, his Customers and his Men.* London: J. M. Dent.

Lambert, Julie Ann (2001) *A Nation of Shopkeepers: Trade Ephemera from 1654 to the 1860s in the John Johnson Collection.* Oxford: Oxford University Press.

Lewis, John (1962) *Printed Ephemera: The Changing Uses of Type and Letterforms in English and American Printing.* Ipswich: W. S. Cowell (paperback edn., London: Faber & Faber, 1969).

— (1976) *Collecting Printed Ephemera.* London: Studio Vista/Cassell and Collier Macmillan.

McCulloch, Lou W. (1980) *Paper Americana.* New York: A. S. Barnes.

Makepeace, Chris E. (1985) *Ephemera: A Book on its Collection, Conservation and Use.* Aldershot: Gower.

Rickards, Maurice (1977) *This is Ephemera.* Vermont: Stephen Greene.

— (1988) *Collecting Printed Ephemera.* Oxford: Phaidon/Christie's.

— (2000) *The Encyclopedia of Ephemera*, ed. Michael Twyman. London: British Library.

Roylance, Dale (1992) *Graphic Americana: The Art and Technique of Printed Ephemera.* Princeton: Princeton University Library.

Sullivan, Edmund B. (1980) *Collecting Political Americana.* New York: Crown.

Thomas, Isaiah, Sr. (1813) *Account of the American Antiquarian Society.* Boston: Isaiah Thomas.

Twyman, Michael (1970) *Printing 1770–1970: An Illustrated History of its Development and Uses in England.* London: Eyre & Spottiswood (repr. London: British Library, 1998).

33

The New Textual Technologies

Charles Chadwyck-Healey

In July 1945, *Atlantic Monthly* published an article entitled "As We May Think" by Dr. Vannevar Bush (1890–1974), Director of the Office of Scientific Research and Development. In overall charge of the Manhattan Project, Bush was one of the most powerful scientists in America at a time when a government at war was funding science on an unprecedented scale. In the article, he gives the earliest description of what is now called "hypertext" as he envisages the location of related information in large databases through a system of internal linkages. He also recognizes the need for new technologies to deal with the rapidly increasing output of scientific publishing, and writes: "Professionally our methods of transmitting and reviewing the results of research are generations old and by now are totally inadequate for their purpose." He goes on to describe a machine, the size of a desk, which he calls the Memex, in which users store information – many thousands of books, journals, and research notes – on microfilm, but regards the ability to locate information instantly as being as important as the storage of the information itself. This has been considered by many commentators to be the conceptual forerunner of the electronic database with hypertext links and searching by keyword. But the Memex is closer to an intermediate generation of machines that was developed in the 1970s in which data stored on microfilm was located through magnetic or optical blips on the edge of the film or between the frames, with motorized winders that took readers directly to the page that they had keyed in.

Bush influenced other computer scientists who became pioneers in their own right. His student, Claude Shannon (1916–2001) laid the foundations of modern information theory, described as one of the great intellectual achievements of the twentieth century,[1] and his paper of 1948, "A Mathematical Theory of Communication," has been called "the Magna Carta of the information age."[2] Shannon realized that by treating messages as strings of binary digits, it was possible to separate the message from the medium it traveled on. Out of this new thinking, data compression and error correction gave digital communications a speed and reliability that made computer networks and, ultimately, the Internet possible.

Douglas Englebart read "As We May Think" in the late 1940s and was a believer in Bush's machine. In the early 1960s, at the Stanford Research Institute, he and colleagues created "NLS" (oN-Line System) which was the first implementation of hypertext and also provided tools such as the computer "mouse," tele-conferencing, word processing, and e-mail, decades before they came into common use. The NLS team understood the need for a visual user interface at a time when most computer scientists had no direct contact with the computer; input was by punched cards and output was by paper tape.

Ted Holm Nelson was the first to use the term "hypertext" in the mid-1960s. In his second self-published book, *Literary Machines* (1981) he writes: "Individuals, unfortunately just don't get it. Most or 'all' of our reading and writing can or will, in this century, be at instant-access screens." He goes on: "I will deal simply with reading and writing from screens, and the universe that I think is out there to create – and then explore and live in. Vannevar Bush told us about it in 1945 . . . but the idea has been dropped by most people. Too blye-sky [sic]. Too *simple*, perhaps." Later he writes: "The Xanadu™ Hypertext System will be an unusual and probably unique repository in which all forms of material – text, pictures, musical notations, even photographs and recordings – may be digitally stored . . . and accessible from any port at any time' (Nelson 1981). Bob Bemer (1920–2004) was not connected with Bush, but from 1960 worked on a standard coding system for storing letters of the alphabet as binary digits. The resulting American Standard Code for Information Interchange (or ASCII) was finalized in 1963, remains in use today, and is fundamental to the creation and exchange of textual information.

While these pioneers were working on the building blocks of information technology, another technology, started before the war, was preparing the way for librarians and their clients to use information stored on media other than paper to be read using a machine. This medium was microfilm.[3] Microfilm publishing for libraries started in 1935 with an edition of *The New York Times* for 1914–18 by the Eastman Kodak Recordak Division. In 1937, Eugene Power (1905–93), the founder of University Microfilms, began selling a microfilm edition of English books published before 1640. In 1939, *The New York Times* became available on microfilm on subscription. From the late 1950s, microfilm publishing grew rapidly as libraries expanded as a result of the growth of higher-education funding. Librarians bought microfilm to save space and because it was inexpensive. It was an important bridge between print and the forthcoming electronic media but, unlike Bush's vision, was treated as a mass-storage medium and a means of obtaining research materials not available in other formats. It was not until the 1980s that publishers began to provide better access to the contents of large microfilm collections through cataloguing for each title and fuller indexes and bibliographies.

In contrast, the first digital texts were catalogues, bibliographies, and indexes – metadata, information about books, not the books themselves. In 1963, the Jones Report on the use of computers at the Library of Congress led to the birth of the MARC record (Machine Readable Cataloguing) that began to be used in the US in 1965.

Thomas J. Watson Jr. bet the future of IBM on the System/360 family of computers that was launched on April 7, 1964, and it was the introduction of third-generation computers with random access disks, CRT (cathode ray tube) terminals, and the ability to send information to other computers or "remote consoles" by phone line that enabled computers to be used for the dissemination of textual information.

At the New York World Fair in 1965 the American Library Association funded a computer-based project called Library/USA. Visitors could ask librarians questions on various subjects and the answers stored in a UNIVAC computer were printed out on a "high-speed" chain printer. While the computer answered questions, it was also used to store stolen car license plates. Operators in one of the New York tunnels would key in the license plates of cars as they passed and the computer would respond before the car reached the waiting police at the other end of the tunnel. In the same year, Ralph Parker (1909–1990), Director of Libraries at the University of Missouri, and Frederick G. Kilgour (1914–2006), then Associate Director of the Yale University Library, submitted a proposal of extraordinary vision for a computerized network of libraries in Ohio to provide a shared cataloguing program based on a central computer store. A book would only have to be catalogued once, and there would also be a union catalogue recording the location of books in libraries throughout the state.

Like Bush, Kilgour had an impressive war record as the highly respected Acting Chairman of the Interdepartmental Committee for the Acquisition of Foreign Publications. He took the Ohio College Library Center (OCLC) from a one-man operation in 1967 to a not-for-profit institution with assets of $13 million, serving more than 1,600 libraries ten years later. He retired in 1995. Today, OCLC is an international cataloguing behemoth accessed online by over 50,000 libraries with a catalogue that contains over 50 million items, still located in Dublin, Ohio.

Also in 1965, Dr. Roger Summit, employed by the Lockheed Missile and Space Company, started to work with NASA to provide better access to the NASA Scientific and Technical Aerospace Reports (STAR). As Bush had foreseen, such was the failure of existing information technologies to keep up with the outpouring of scientific research that there was a common view at Lockheed that it was usually easier, cheaper, and faster to redo scientific research than to determine whether it had already been done (Summit 2002). But in 1968, a year before America put men on the moon, Summit's team won a major contract from NASA to develop an online retrieval system called NASA/RECON (Remote Console Information Retrieval System), while Summit called the retrieval language itself "Dialog." Conceived by government-funded "big science," an important new information technology called "online" had been born. Of equal significance was the ARPANET contract led by the Advanced Research Projects Agency (ARPA) which, in 1969, connected four major university computers, one of which was Englebart's lab at Stanford. Larry Roberts, project director and "father of the ARPANET," wanted to link computers at ARPA-funded research institutions so that they could share computer resources. But ARPANET was also designed to provide a communications network that would function even if part of it were destroyed by nuclear attack, so that if a direct route was damaged, "routers" would find alternative routes. In the 1970s, the ARPANET became the Internet when a protocol called TCP/IP was developed by Bob Kahn and Vint Cerf to enable different computers using different software to communicate with each other.

In 1972, the Dialog Information Retrieval Service established by Lockheed began to offer other databases to subscribers with computer terminals and so became the first commercial online service. These included ERIC (Educational Resources Information Center) and NTIS (National Technical Information Service) and were used by a handful of customers. But through the 1970s many scientific and professional databases were added to the rapidly growing Dialog service, and in 1982 Dialog Information Services Inc. was spun out of Lockheed with Summit as President and CEO.

The online vision was compelling: scientists working at home with access through the terminal on their desks to a virtual library that contained a store of information greater than anything that might be found in a physical library. By the end of the 1970s, the still tiny online industry seemed to offer unlimited opportunities through the harnessing of computer technology to the access and distribution of information. Through the 1980s, Dialog did indeed grow at 20–30 percent per year and also had to compete with new competitors, including DataStar created by Radio Suisse, BRS, SDC-Orbit, and many smaller hosts or online providers.

The online industry had huge technical competence and Dialog was profitable from the outset, but the business model was flawed. This only became obvious after the introduction of a new medium, CD-ROM, in the mid 1980s. Dialog offered third-party databases because database publishers could not offer computer access to remote users themselves but, in doing so, Dialog separated the publishers from their end-users. This "separation" included taking a substantial part of the sales revenue – 60 percent was typical. Many publishers found that their online revenues were quite limited and, without being able to know who their users were, were not able to conduct effective sales and marketing themselves, yet suspected that their online host was not conducting effective marketing either.

Another weakness was the complexity of the search process. From the beginning, sophisticated search strategies such as the "logical sum" and the "logical product of logical sums" were possible but unlike the Boolean searching, "And" or "And Not," this sophistication required the user to be trained to carry out such searches or to use an intermediary, usually a librarian. It was a culture that revered the "priesthood of searchers" (Miller and Gratch 1989: 391) rather than making the user–machine interface easier to use. Online access was charged by the minute and a poorly planned search could be expensive for the library that hosted the service. Libraries either had the choice of charging their clients, which did not fit into the university library ethos, or have intermediaries manage access to the online terminals so that expenditure could be kept within budget, creating another potential barrier between the end-user and the information provider. An exception was LexisNexis, which was launched in 1973 as an online service for lawyers. This was a well-defined market which needed immediate access to legal texts, documents, and regulatory information, and LexisNexis soon became an essential resource in almost every law firm.

In 1988, Lockheed sold Dialog to Knight-Ridder, a US newspaper group, for $353 million. But, in comparison with the growth of CD-ROM publishing, in which Dialog and other online providers also became active, and the explosive growth of the Internet, the use of information delivered online was quite limited, even by scientists and engineers. At the time, the only way to disseminate information held in a computer was by phone line to terminals or "remote consoles." For publishers, the lack of a convenient, durable, portable vehicle that could be used as a publishing medium was a barrier to creating electronic publications. Electronic publishing would not take off until such a medium became available and the floppy disc was not that medium – it was too fragile, held too little information, and could too easily be tampered with.

One solution in use for the last twenty-five years of the twentieth century was the computer output microfiche (COM). This married two media, digital information and microfilm, and enabled computerized information to be distributed widely at low cost to be read on inexpensive microfiche readers. It was used widely for information that had to be frequently updated, such as library catalogues, parts catalogues, and internal business records, but never became popular as a general publishing medium because few people wanted to read continuous text on the screen of a microfiche reader. By the time "reader printers" that photocopied microfiche pages became sufficiently reliable for general use, the computer revolution was well underway. In the late 1970s, the 12-inch optical disc, also known as the video disc, seemed to have great potential for publishers, but by mid-1980 1.3 million videocassette recorders (VCRs) had already been sold in the US and the ability of the VCR to record programs made it more versatile than the video disc. Video discs failed as a consumer product but were used in training and education because they could display both still and moving images and be controlled or "programmed" by the new microcomputers.

At the beginning of the 1980s these new media both excited and confused book publishers who could see that computerized information could offer entirely new publishing opportunities but had difficulty in seeing how they could be realized. In 1981, the books of Dr. Spock had appeared on both video disc and video cassette, and in 1982 MCA released a video disc containing cooking lessons by Craig Claiborne and Pierre Franey. In May 1982, George Rosato, Vice President of Random House's schools division, speaking about educational software, stated: "One of the very early questions was, 'Is there business in this field?' Now it's 'How big is this business?'" Robert Dahlin, writing in the *Publishers Weekly Yearbook* (1983), looked back on 1982 and asked "Where is all this leading?" He went on: "The answer is not at all clear, but 1982 explorations underscored the fact that a book is a book and an electronic product is not a book." He then explained this Zen-like statement, but decades later book publishers are still trying to work out how to publish successfully both books and electronic publications.

One publisher that understood how to use the optical disc was Information Access Corporation (IAC), which published *InfoTrac,* an index of business, technical, and general interest magazines and newspapers for the student market in the US. By 1986, this index on optical disc was in use in three hundred academic and public libraries, and the full text of the articles was also available on companion sets of microfilm. Here was a combination of computerized indexing accessing text on microfilm that Bush would have recognized as a worthy rendering of the Memex concept. Libraries reported overwhelming user acceptance and waiting lines at workstations. It was far from the "priesthood of searchers," and some librarians were uncomfortable with the way that students abandoned print indexes and bibliographies and seemed to think that *InfoTrac* indexed everything, but librarians also saw that it brought users into the library who had never been there before (Tenopir 1986).

IAC was still using the optical disc in 1986, the year in which the CD-ROM (Compact Disc-Read Only Memory) became the exciting new publishing medium. Philips and Sony had announced the CD-ROM in 1984, and in 1985 Grolier brought out *Grolier's Electronic Encyclopaedia*, advertised as "The Knowledge Disk," on both video disc and on CD-ROM. Audio CDs were already established and the advantage of the CD-ROM over the optical disc was the large number of mastering and replicating factories that could manufacture CD-ROMs inexpensively. The attraction for publishers was that it was a robust, tamper-proof medium that stored thousands of pages on a single disc.

Apart from Grolier, the first publishers to use the CD-ROM medium were not the large book publishers but Microsoft, the software giant, and hardware manufacturers like Digital Equipment Corporation (DEC), online providers like Dialog and BRS, and new publishers like SilverPlatter Information Inc. Microsoft made an immediate impact on the consumer market with *Microsoft Bookshelf*, a collection of basic reference books, and *Encarta*, an encyclopedia on CD-ROM based on a print encyclopedia to which were added still images, video clips, and sound, creating something entirely new and immediately attractive to anyone who now had a CD-ROM reader connected to his or her PC.

Grolier had announced its "Knowledge Disk" with the promise "Gone are the hernia-inducing heavy volumes," and within a few years they were gone. Electronic media took over from print. *Encyclopedia Britannica* was sold and the new owners had to think how to position their electronic version. Yet this destruction of what had seemed an unassailable branch of consumer book publishing was not only due to the new technology but also to aggressive pricing and market domination by an international software giant that used its CD-ROM encyclopedia as a "loss leader" to sell something else.

By 1986, both DEC and SilverPlatter had signed up for publication on CD-ROM for the library market the same bibliographic databases that Dialog and others were already offering online. These included PsycLIT, ERIC, and PAIS. Since none of these were exclusive to one CD-ROM publisher, each publisher had to distinguish its own versions by the quality of its software, by price, and by service and availability. Silver-Platter soon established itself as the market leader with polished branding, good software, and a network of sales agents throughout the world that gave it a much greater international presence than most publishers of a comparable size.

For publishers like University Microfilms in the US (which changed its name to ProQuest in 2001) and Chadwyck-Healey in the UK, for whom microfilm was the principal publishing medium, CD-ROM was new and glamorous with an enthusiastic public acceptance that microfilm had never enjoyed. Unlike SilverPlatter, these publishers shied away from signing up non-exclusive databases and preferred to concentrate on CD-ROM publications that were exclusive to them or contained data that was owned or created by them. In 1986, University Microfilms was testing both optical discs and CD-ROMs, and one of its first products was its own database *Dissertations Abstracts*.

In 1989, Chadwyck-Healey with Her Majesty's Stationery Office published *UKOP*, the first complete catalogue of British government publications, issued bi-monthly on CD-ROM, and then with Saztec published a CD-ROM edition of the world's most famous library catalogue, *The British Library General Catalogue of Printed Books*. It cost £9,000, half the price of the last print edition, which had only been completed in 1987, and, unlike the latter, every element in the catalogue record could be searched. It was a spin-off from the costly conversion of the catalogue in its old guard-book format into a Public Access Online Catalogue (OPAC) which had become a requirement for all large libraries. In 1990, Chadwyck-Healey started to create its own databases by the manual keying of printed texts. By 1994, it had published all of English poetry from the Middle Ages to 1900 on five CD-ROMs sold to libraries for £25,000. To be able to search for any word or phrase in all of English poetry was revolutionary, but it also meant that a library would now have a more comprehensive collection of poetry than it could ever have in print; every title was already catalogued, and it took up no shelf space.

Large-scale electronic text-creation was only possible because of the existence of companies in India, Singapore, China, and the Philippines that carried out "data capture" by manually keying texts twice (for accuracy) at a very low cost. Of equal significance had been the development of Standard Generalized Mark Up Language (SGML), an encoding system that gave form and structure to ASCII files so that they appeared on the screen in a format similar to that of a printed page. SGML coding was software independent and was flexible: editors could draw up their own coding to suit each body of text, and this enabled Chadwyck-Healey to convert complex foreign-language texts, including the *Patrologia Latina*, a larger body of text than English Poetry, and the Weimar Edition of the works of Goethe in 143 volumes. Both were published in 1995.

Almost every major publisher started a multimedia department to publish CD-ROMs. The British publisher Dorling Kindersley (DK), already famous for its well-designed, fully illustrated, nonfiction books aimed at younger readers, was more successful than others. Microsoft bought a 25 percent stake in the company because it liked DK's clean graphical images which suited the limited resolution of the computer screens of the time. DK's first CD-ROM was on musical instruments with text, images, and sound. The DK CD-ROM list grew rapidly, fostered by the enthusiasm of its founder, Peter Kindersley. Microsoft's founder, Bill Gates, was also interested and personally reviewed CD-ROM publishing ideas. The bestselling title, *The Way Things Work*, sold 1.25 million copies, and at its peak in the mid-1990s CD-ROM publications had annual sales of £25 million. By the late 1990s, DK's CD-ROM sales began to decline. Difficulties of distribution and a downward pressure on prices were the main reasons.

The CD-ROM became a devalued consumer product as free CD-ROMs were increasingly used as promotional tools. The most enduring DK CD-ROM titles were those with the greatest practical use, the "Drilling Discs" – curriculum cramming and testing CD-ROMs.[4]

"The New Papyrus," as the CD-ROM has been called (Lambert and Ropiequet 1986), was the catalyst that enabled print publishers to become electronic publishers, but was then consumed in the process. In 1991, there were 1,200 CD-ROM titles worldwide. By 1993–4, there were 18,000 titles[5] and librarians began to tell publishers that they no longer wanted their databases on CD-ROMs; they wanted the publishers to maintain them and deliver them online. The CD-ROM had become an unmanageable medium in the larger library. There were too many different kinds of software, and a CD-ROM could not be widely networked because of limitations on the speed at which the laser beam head moved across the disc.

Online delivery required the publisher to invest in expensive proprietary client–server software, but there was now the Internet and a new universal "client" software (the software that sits on the customer's computer and enables it to access the publisher's database) called the "browser", and it was free. Tim Berners-Lee, a researcher at CERN, had had an inspired vision of the Internet as a network of distributed information. In 1990, he wrote the Hypertext Transfer Protocol (HTTP) that enabled hypertext documents to be sent over the Internet with addresses from which they originated, now known as "URLs." The pages of documents were formatted using his Hypertext Markup Language (HTML) and he also wrote a "browser", which he called the "World Wide Web" (W3), to retrieve and view hypertext documents. In 1993, Berners-Lee and Michael Dertouzos (1936–2001) founded the World Wide Web Consortium, which coordinates W3 development internationally.

The Internet was originally limited to research, education, and government. The culture of freedom from commercial pressures, a creators' and users' democracy, and a burning desire to keep the "net" out of the hands of publishers have resulted in most of the visible Internet being freely accessible. But library publishers were unconcerned about the anti-establishment culture of the "web" except when copyrights were infringed because their use of the Internet was as an online channel for delivering databases to their customers – who could only gain access to the database if they had paid an annual access fee, up front.

Journal articles, reference books, and bibliographic databases were the first to be delivered via the Internet. Publishers like SilverPlatter and its rival Ovid found that the functionality of their software, which had been their main selling point, could no longer be differentiated because of the limitations of the browser that was now common to all publishers. The lack of a physical delivery medium – a book, a roll of film, or a disc – made librarians even more price-aware. The mid-1990s was a challenging period of transition for library publishers for whom the CD-ROM had been so profitable.

But Internet delivery had enormous benefits in terms of access for users. University students and staff could connect to the Internet from their dormitories, offices, and even homes. Wherever they were, they could access databases subscribed to by their library which had become a buying agent for library users who no longer came to the library. The Internet also had advantages for publishers. Internet software was less expensive to develop than software for CD-ROMs, and there was greater protection against illegal copying because it was difficult to download a complete database from the Internet. Large databases previously published on multiple CD-ROMs were now quicker and easier to access. In 1998, Chadwyck-Healey launched a website called Literature Online (LION), with ten databases of English and American literature previously published as separate CD-ROMs. Biographies, criticism, and bibliographies were added, together with internal hypertext links as well as links to other websites that made the collection into one coherent, fully searchable database. Since its launch, LION has become one of the major teaching and research resources for English and American literature, which would not have happened if it had remained a collection of CD-ROM titles.

But the Internet was also disruptive. It changed the relationship between publishers and libraries. For centuries, libraries had owned outright the books and journals on their shelves. Now, publishers maintained their databases and sold "access" to libraries for a fee. Libraries did not necessarily accept the efficiency of this new paradigm. Each database could be regularly evaluated, dropped if no longer needed, and picked up again when required, in contrast to the library's capital-intensive practice of investing in books and journals, many of which quickly became redundant. But in 2004, in response to the librarians' traditional preference to buy outright, publishers introduced "Perpetual Access" to US libraries in which the libraries own the databases but must also pay the publisher a small annual online access fee.

The Internet changed the commercial relationship between libraries and library publishers in another way, a change that had started with CD-ROMs. US libraries formed buying groups or consortia, which would negotiate with a publisher for a supply of CD-ROMs or access to a database on behalf of the entire group for an all-in fee – a single deal could run to millions of dollars. The Joint Information Systems Committee (JISC) bought electronic publications on behalf of UK higher education. By 1999, countries like Denmark and Finland had national buying consortia embracing both public and academic libraries. In 2000, the government of Iceland bought access to LION for all of its 300,000 citizens. By this time, Chadwyck-Healey, the publisher of LION, had been bought by ProQuest.

CD-ROMs had been a rewarding medium for reference-book publishers. Almost every directory benefited from being able to be searched electronically. But much of the information in directories like *The Encyclopedia of Associations* was freely available on the web accessed by search engines. The web was no longer a neutral delivery channel, it was now a competitor. On the other hand, reference books like A. & C. Black's *Who's Who*, with proprietary biographical information which could not be found on the web, continued to sell well in print and on CD-ROM, but also generated royalty revenue as part of *KnowUK*, a website launched in 1999 containing core UK reference works. Book publishers like A. & C. Black used aggregators like Chadwyck-Healey, the publisher of *KnowUK*, to experiment with web publishing. Oxford University Press had its own multimedia department in the late 1980s, publishing a wide range of titles including CD-ROMs for children, but used an electronic journals aggregator, the HighWire Press at Stanford University Library, to create and host the online version of the *Oxford English Dictionary*. The organic nature of the web in which content can be changed or added at any time suits a big dictionary which is constantly being amended. OUP published a new edition of the *Dictionary of National Biography* in print and online in September 2004. The first online updates were added in January 2005. Already the online edition is more authoritative than the print edition and will continue to grow away from it. It seems unlikely that there will ever be another print edition.

Other publishers recognized the importance of the web by publishing books about it: Nicholas Negroponte's *Being Digital: The Road Map for Survival on the Information Superhighway* (1995) was typical of the genre. Sales of academic books continued to decline as libraries diverted more of their funds toward buying journals and other electronic resources. Some publishers hoped that electronic publishing would save the academic monograph but, unlike the journal which has been fully embraced in its electronic format, take-up of electronic editions of current books has not been sufficient to make the electronic book or "e-book" viable. But publishers used the new technology to extend the life of print editions by storing texts electronically and producing print copies on demand or in very small editions.

In the late 1990s, several new companies began to offer textbooks and academic books online. The investment made by them was huge in relation to the typical investment made by the established library publishers. NetLibrary and Questia Media Inc. each had funding of $100 million. Their plan was to convert books licensed from publishers into XML format and sell electronic access to these books to libraries. But restrictions on access designed to pacify nervous publishers, and a tendency for publishers to hold back their best titles, compromised the model, and in the case of NetLibrary the business failed. In late 2001, NetLibrary filed for bankruptcy under Chapter 11 and was bought by OCLC for $2 million. Questia still sells to libraries but has reduced the size of its operation.

Ebrary, founded in 2001 by Chris Warnock, the son of the founder of Adobe, and backed by several large publishers, offered electronic versions of books in PDF (Adobe's Portable Document Format). Ebrary was first aimed at individual users who would pay only for the pages they downloaded or printed, but it then offered libraries the entire collection of books on an annual subscription allowing simultaneous use by more than one reader, an important selling point for libraries. Safari Techbooks On-line, a partnership between O'Reilly & Associates, Pearson, and Books24x7, all based in Boston, have been more successful book aggregators by being more focused. Safari puts IT books online and enables them to be searched and downloaded by IT and programming professionals. Books24x7 offers electronic versions of business and technology books which can be searched and downloaded and which are aimed at business professionals.

While the new aggregators tried to break into the library field, librarians continued to buy electronic editions of old books from traditional library publishers like ProQuest and Thomson Gale, the very same books that they already had on microfilm, in reprint, and, in the largest libraries, in original editions. The 125,000 English books printed before 1700 that University Microfilms had begun to microfilm in 1937 were offered as *Early English Books On-line (EEBO)* by ProQuest. Thomson Gale published electronic editions of the majority of books printed in the eighteenth century.

Neither ProQuest nor Thomson Gale followed Chadwyck-Healey by offering SGML-coded, fully searchable, electronic editions produced by manual keying. This was considered to be too expensive for the academic library market. Their electronic editions are made by scanning microfilm, but early print cannot be satisfactorily searched by Optical Character Recognition (OCR) software so the main advantages over the microfilm edition are the convenience of having text delivered to computer screens. ProQuest, the University of Michigan, and Oxford University then set up the Text Creation Partnership in 1999 to address the limitations of only having scanned images. Now over 15,000 books have been converted directly from the scanned images into SGML-coded, fully searchable, electronic texts; the goal is a total of 25,000 texts to be made available to libraries who have already bought EEBO and who then make a substantial financial contribution to the partnership. This partnership model is proving to be popular with libraries and publishers. Oxford University and the University of Michigan have created a new partnership with Readex to convert 6,000 texts from the 40,000 texts in the Evans Early American Imprints collection, and in a separate partnership Thomson Gale is converting 10,000 texts from the 150,000 texts in the Eighteenth Century Collections Online.

But all these initiatives have been overshadowed by Google's announcement in December 2004 that, in partnership with some of the great research libraries (including Oxford, Harvard, and New York Public Library), it would underwrite the cost of scanning millions of books. Out-of-copyright books will be available in their entirety for free on the web through the Google site. Excerpts or "snippets" of in-copyright books are available to searchers in response to a search – only a few lines of text containing the searched-for term is displayed, even though the entire text has been scanned. It is this comprehensive copying of in-copyright books without permission that has incurred the wrath of publishers, who see it as a direct infringement of their rights, and in 2005 law suits were started against Google. Google has countered that it already scans the entire contents of websites in order to provide its much-admired search service and that the scanning of books to provide a comprehensive in-depth search capability is no different. The logic of Google's position seems unassailable. Specialized books sell in small numbers and sit on library shelves underused because the information in them is relatively inaccessible compared to what we are now used to on the web. An initiative on this scale to provide in-depth access to the world's books (albeit mainly in English) must be welcomed, but runs directly counter to the legal rights of authors and publishers which are carried over from another age.

In contrast to the nervous hostility of publishers, libraries have warmly welcomed Google's initiative because through it libraries achieve two longed-for goals. They become publishers at no cost and risk to themselves by carrying out both the selection of titles and the scanning, and the out-of-copyright scanned books are free to all. Previously, conversion into a new format put out-of-copyright books back into the ownership of the publisher/converter who could then charge what the market would bear. In the 1980s, libraries had tried to wrest the initiative from publishers by undertaking the microfilming of large numbers of older books for preservation purposes, funded by organizations such as the National Endowment for the Humanities and the Mellon Foundation. But, because there were usually only one or two copies of each microfilm, the millions of books that were filmed remained relatively inaccessible. Since the Google announcement, the rival search service Yahoo! has announced a book digitization project with partners such as the University of California, the Research Libraries Group (RLG), and the UK National Archives, together with commercial partners that include Adobe and Hewlett Packard. The Library of Congress has also announced plans to create a World Digital Library and has already received a donation of $3 million from Google. Other initiatives have been announced by Microsoft and AOL and, with a combined market capitalization of half a trillion dollars, the impact of these commercial companies on how we access and use textual information and images will be profound.

Libraries too have been changed. Visitors to the British Library look through monumental glass walls at the red and gold bindings of the King's Library unaware that this part of the library was originally designed to house the catalogue. The OPAC, first envisaged in the 1960s but only completed in the late 1980s, enabled the architect to think again and use the space to display the most magnificent of the library's founding collections.[6]

Bush's vision of organized and accessible scientific literature has already been achieved by the wide adoption of the electronic journal article accessed by electronic search tools. But the idea of the "e-book," a single book only published in electronic media, is misconceived because it regards the electronic version as only a replica of the printed book. Web 2.0, which is the new iteration of the web, envisages constantly developing services rather than individual products. Publications are not static but constantly evolve. Information not only flows from the publisher to the user but from user to user and from user to publisher. Wikipedia (www.wikipedia.org), the people's encyclopedia (created by web users with very little editorial intervention), now exceeds *Encyclopedia Britannica* in size, and publishers such as the Alexander Street Press are now creating Wiki-based services covering specialized subjects such as "Women and Social Movements" in which the content is under the control of academic editors. RSS feeds and push technologies, a part of Web 2.0, enable users to see when new items are posted or even to see when someone has linked to a site. Other sites like Flickr (www.flickr.com) hold millions of photographs provided by the public. The speed with which such huge databases can be searched and brought to the reader's screen is what sets apart electronic media. We quickly take for granted such speed and convenience and will always demand more. This demand drives the progress of electronic media, a progress that has already had a greater influence on the ways in which we access text and images than we have yet begun to realize.

NOTES

1   By Aaron D. Wyner (1939–97), the editor of Shannon's collected papers.

2   Quoted by John Naughton in *The Observer*, London, February 25, 2001.

3   "Microfilm" includes the other formats microcards and microfiche. The generic term is microform.

4   Interview with Alan Buckingham, Managing Director, Dorling Kindersley Multimedia/ Interactive Learning 1991–8, June 2004.

5   Commission of the European Communities DG XIII/E (1993) *New Opportunities for Publishers in the Information Services Market*, E5.

6   Address by Colin St. John Wilson, architect of the British Library, at the 23rd Congress of the Association Internationale de Bibliophilie, London, September 22, 2003.

REFERENCES AND FURTHER READING

Allison, Anne Marie and Allan, Ann (1979) *OCLC: A National Library Network*. Short Hills: Enslow.

Berners-Lee, Tim (1999) *Weaving the Web*. San Francisco: Harper Collins.

Ekman, Richard and Quandt, Richard E. (1999) *Technology and Scholarly Communication*. Berkeley: University of California Press.

Kenna, Stephanie and Ross, Seamus (1995) *Networking in the Humanities*. London: Bowker Saur.

King, G. W., Edmundson, Harold P., Flood, Merrill M., et al. (1963) *Automation and the Library of Congress*. Washington: Library of Congress.

Lambert, Steve and Ropiequet, Suzanne (1986) *CD-ROM: The New Papyrus*. Redmond: Microsoft.

Miller, W. and Gratch, B. (1989) "Making Connections: Computerized Reference Services and People." *Library Trends*, 37 (4): 387–401.

Negroponte, Nicholas (1995) *Being Digital*. New York: Knopf.

Nelson, Ted Holm (1981) *Literary Machines*. Swarthmore, PA: Ted Holm Nelson.

Power, Eugene B. with Anderson, Robert (1990) *Edition of One: The Autobiography of Eugene B. Power*. Ann Arbor: University Microfilms International.

Sigel, Efrem, Schubin, Mark, Merrill, Paul F., et al. (1980) *Video Discs: The Technology, the Applications, and the Future*. White Plains: Knowledge Industry.

Summit, Roger (2002) "Reflections on the Beginning of Dialog." *Chronolog Newsletter*, Thomson Dialog, June.

Tenopir, Carol (1986) "Infotrac: A Laser Disc System." *Library Journal*, September 1: 168–9.

Thompson, John B. (2005) *Books in the Digital Age: The Transformation of Academic and Higher Education Publishing in Britain and the United States*. Cambridge: Polity.

Veaner, Allen B. (1976) *Studies in Micropublishing 1853–1976: Documentary Sources*. Westport: Microform Review.

PART IV
Issues

34

New Histories of Literacy

Patricia Crain

The Trouble with "Literacy"

Everybody knows what literacy is. It is what digital media puts at risk and what "at-risk" students are not getting enough of. It is an object and a source of editorial polemic, political showboating, NGO imperatives, and bookish nostalgia. As a term of art, however, identifying an area of study, "literacy" possesses the vices of both its capacious abstraction and its apparent common-sense utility. Its bureaucratic aura aligns it with policy and the aggregate rather than with practice and the individual. No one says "I love my literacy," but lots of people love (or hate or are otherwise disaffected by or excluded from) reading and writing. And it is reading and writing that constitute literacy: the practices and processes, implications and consequences, origins and aims, poetics and politics, of reading and writing. Yet if reading and writing are its most obvious components, "literacy" and related terms nonetheless always stand for something beyond these practices. One might say, in fact, that "literacy" expresses everything that is left out when one speaks solely of reading and writing. If the excess that "literacy" captures might variously be identified as, among other things, ideology, culture, identity, power, pleasure, aspiration, and historical context, it is then small wonder that scholars struggle to define this thorny and unsatisfactory term.

Part of the problem is that "literacy" entered the English language precisely in order to augment mere reading and writing, to layer these practices with additional significance. (Other European languages, which registered a similar shift, tended to base their neologisms on the root "alphabet"; Baumann 1986: 17.) "Literacy" (from Latin *littera*, letter) comes into currency around 1883, according to the *Oxford English Dictionary* (*OED*), that monument to the Western ideal of literacy (whose first installment, not coincidentally, came out the following year). Here, "literacy" originates "as an antithesis to *illiteracy*," and signifies "[t]he quality or state of being literate; knowledge of letters; condition in respect to education, *esp.* ability to read and write." A noun of quality, state, or condition, "literacy" thus establishes the end to which the verbs "read" and "write" supply the means. In the transition to a substantive, what had been practices became hypostatized, and process gave way to product. Raymond Williams suggests that the word "was invented to express the *achievement* and *possession* of what were increasingly seen as general and necessary skills" (my emphasis; Williams 1985: 188). The literate had always represented a restricted class (of medieval European clergy or fifth-century BC Athenian gentry or seventeenth-century New Spanish *letrados*, for example), whose "possession" of literacy was assumed, if its "achievement" was the object of technical manuals and physical disciplines. A sense of distinction, of a distancing from vernacular spoken language as well as from everyday reading and writing, has always clung to "literate." The ancient *litteratus* often meant cultured, and the medieval *litteratus* usually meant educated in Latin. Dr. Johnson's *Dictionary* (1755) offers "literate" and "lettered" as synonyms meaning "educated to learning," while "illiterate" is "unlettered, untaught." Newly required by late nineteenth-century Americans and Western Europeans, literacy was ever more widely available and widely promoted. "Literacy" hints, if guardedly, at democratic access.

As Raymond Williams points out in *Keywords* (1985), language does not merely reflect "the processes of society and history." Rather, "important social and historical processes occur *within* language" and, furthermore, "[e]arlier and later senses coexist, or become actual alternatives in which problems of contemporary belief and affiliation are contested" (Williams 1985: 22). "Literacy" consolidates a range of reading and writing practices under one term, capturing in that gesture a moment in the history of Western and specifically US bureaucracy and educational theory. Jenny Cook-Gumperz nicely sums up the problem:

> the shift from the eighteenth century onwards has not been from total illiteracy to literacy, but from a hard-to-estimate multiplicity of literacies, a *pluralistic* idea about literacy as a composite of different skills related to reading and writing for many different purposes and sections of a society's population, to a twentieth-century notion of a single, standardised *schooled literacy.* (emphasis in original; Cook-Gumperz 1986: 22)

The *OED* cites as the first usage of "literacy" a squib from the 1883 *Journal of Education* (under its earlier name, the *New England Journal of Education*): "Massachusetts is the first state in the Union in literacy in its native population." The original passage goes on to say: "and the nineteenth only from its Irish and French-Canadian illiteracy" (Editorial 1883: 54). This brief editorial item blames a blow to Massachusetts's long and proudly held educational primacy on new immigrants. The prophetic ring of this first citing, prefiguring twentieth- and twenty-first-century anxieties over education and immigration, suggests that the mentalities and institutions which gave birth to "literacy" still, to a large extent, maintain.

In seeking a usable definition, scholars struggle with the inheritance of "literacy," not only as an elusive term but as one expressive of many of the factors that enabled the word to secure its status as a galvanizing cultural concept. These might include, among other things, nativism, sexism, competition among languages and dialects, challenges from other communications media, racial and class hierarchies, shifting locations of cultural production, and so on. Scholars, educators, and policy-makers have responded variously over the years to this intractable complexity. Some throw up their hands: as one scholar puts it, "the stunning fact is that we do not fully know what literacy is" (Szwed in Cushman et al. 2001: 423). Others have offered technical, local, or, in some other fashion, restricted definitions. The social historian Lawrence Stone, for example, in a foundational article (discussed further below), defines literacy as:

> the capacity to sign one's name, which for periods before the nineteenth century is nearly all we now know or indeed are ever likely to know in the future. We do not know now, and may never know, the precise relationship between the capacity to sign one's name – "alphabetism" might be a better word for it – and true literacy, that is the ability to use the written word as a means of communication. (Stone 1969: 98)

At the other end of the spectrum, the US government's National Center for Education Statistics defines literacy in broad, aspirational terms as "using printed and written information to function in society, to achieve one's goals, and to develop one's knowledge and potential." In a similar vein, and in an effort shared by most scholars to situate literacy in social networks, the historian of education Sylvia Harrop reads literacy as "an indicator not only of the educational and cultural interests, but also of the general well-being of a community" (Harrop 1983: 52). In what he characterizes as a "radical critique of the term literacy and its popular uses," Robert Pattison defines literacy as "foremost consciousness of the problems posed by language, and secondarily skill in the technologies, such as rhetoric and writing, by which this consciousness is expressed" (Pattison 1982: vii, vi). Most recently, David Vincent calls it "a tool for enabling individuals and social groups to extend their understanding of themselves and their world, and amongst the objects of comprehension is that of literacy itself" (Vincent 2000: 24).

Such definitions betray a self-conscious and self-reflexive strain, as if to say that literacy describes the mode of communication that broods about itself. Wary of these difficulties, the historian Harvey Graff, who has undertaken the most sustained and searching critique of traditional literacy scholarship, acknowledges that the "very notion of literacy is problematic" (Graff 1987: 373), and suggests that it

> represents a range of abilities or skills that may or may not lead to a distinctive personal, social-psychological condition or orientation. Its meaning is established only in precise historical contexts; it is not universally given or proscribed. It need not connote dimensions of the liberal, the polished, or the literary, and may not even contrast strongly with illiteracy. (Graff 1987: 374)

In a similar vein, the education historian E. Jennifer Monaghan writes that "something that schoolteachers have known all along has belatedly been recognized, that there is no strict demarcation between literacy and illiteracy" (Monaghan 2005: 3). Like Graff, Monaghan and other scholars seek to escape the binary opposition of the term's

origins. Others find literacy's monolithic and hegemonic qualities inescapable and identify them as essential to its meaning. The literary scholar John Guillory, for instance,
defines literacy "as *the systematic regulation of reading and writing*, a complex social phenomenon corresponding to the following set of questions: Who reads? What do they
read? How do they read? In what social and institutional circumstances? Who writes?
In what social and institutional contexts? For whom?" (emphasis in original; Guillory
1993: 18). Though some of its practitioners would quibble with Guillory's core definition, with its emphasis on discipline and social control, recent histories of literacy
address the questions he raises and other similar questions, drawing upon a broad and
varied archive. Before surveying some of these, it may be helpful briefly to sketch a
genealogy of the field.

A Short History of the History of Literacy

Theories of education and of reading and writing have an ancient provenance and might
be said to begin the history of literacy. Plato's *Phaedrus*, in which Socrates (whose own
opus was, of course, strictly oral) critiques writing as a threat to memory and as a weak
imitation of true knowledge, might be considered the *locus classicus* of the "consequences
of literacy" genre. Modern histories of education have often been, of necessity, interested
in literacy, from Werner Jaeger's monumental history of Greek education, *Paideia*
(1939–44) and the literary historian T. W. Baldwin's *William Shakspere's Small Latine
and Lesse Greeke* (1944) to Lawrence Cremin's three-volume history of American education (1970–88). Writing either before or against the grain of the mid-twentieth-century
New Critical concentration on the literary artifact, a number of literary scholars were
interested in historical and contemporary readers, and in the sociology of readership.
Working during the post-World War II expansion of British higher education, literary
and social historians of the left found common ground, often through their transformative work in adult education, especially in and around the Centre for Contemporary
Cultural Studies (CCCS) at the University of Birmingham (1964). The title, much of
the spirit, and some of the methods of *The Uses of Literacy* (1957) – a participant-observer
analysis of contemporary popular culture by CCCS founding director Richard Hoggart
– echoes through literacy studies decades later, while social historians trace their lineage
to E. P. Thompson's *The Making of the English Working Class* (1963).

   The history of literacy proper begins with two foundational articles. Social anthropologist Jack Goody and literary historian Ian Watt's "The Consequences of Literacy"
(1963) was published in an essay collection in 1968. The following year, social historian
Lawrence Stone's "Literacy and Education in England 1640–1900" appeared. Goody
and Watt posited (rather notoriously) what has become known as the "great divide"
theory of literacy and orality. Using fifth-century BC Athenian culture as their laboratory, they argued that the introduction of writing allowed a widely literate urban society
to create the conditions for key features of Western culture to emerge: among these
were a shift from a mythic to an historical sense of time, an awareness of a difference

between past and present, and a sense of the individual's alienation from tradition. Though they claimed to be rejecting a "dichotomy based upon the assumption of radical differences between the mental attributes of literate and non-literate peoples," they posited that "pre-literate" cultures were "homeostatic" and emphasized that "there may still exist general differences between literate and non-literate societies" (Goody and Watt 1968: 44). Despite their disclaimers, Goody and Watt attributed to literacy an array of social and cultural as well as cognitive and psychological phenomena. More recent research has called into question the extent of early Greek literacy (Harris 1989). Some scholars see Goody and Watt's determinism as part of a "literacy myth" (Ruth Finnegan in Keller-Cohen 1994; see also Graff 1987). Many now detect presentism, Western chauvinism, ethnocentrism, and "missionary" condescension in this work; Goody himself has substantially revised his own position over the years. Anthropologist Walter Mignolo has concluded that recent "ethnographic works done on the genres of speech in non-Western communities have shown that orality is an equivalent to, rather than an outdated precursor of, literacy" (Mignolo 1995: 213). Discredited in some quarters though it may be, the orality–literacy divide and its technological determinism remain influential, particularly through the works of classicist Walter Ong and media theorist Marshall McLuhan.

Lawrence Stone established some of the methodologies and asked some of the questions that have since characterized the field by categorizing levels and causes of literacy and offering demographic evidence of its spread between the English Civil War and 1900. Stone presented a largely, though not exclusively, statistical response in the first such regional analysis of literacy, concluding that "the conquest of illiteracy took place in three main stages, one fairly active and one very active phase being separated by over a century of relatively slow growth. The whole process took about four hundred years, starting at the top of the social pyramid and working downwards" (Stone 1969: 125). This "conquest" meant that in England about 40 percent of men were literate by 1675, a percentage that increased slowly until 1780 and rapidly thereafter, with two-thirds of the men and half of the women literate by 1840. After 1840, according to Stone, "the growth of elementary education in Victorian England was so rapid that it took only another fifty years virtually to wipe out illiteracy altogether, both for men and for women" (Stone 1969: 119).

Literacy has long been an object of quantitative speculation by those interested in the religious or political well-being of the state, from the Florentine Giovanni Villani's observation that there were "from eight to ten thousand boys and girls learning to read" in late 1330s' Florence to sixteenth-century assessments of the number of English readers by Thomas More and others (Ferguson 2003: 79, 76). The signature archive that Stone and others have mined relies on such documents as charters, oaths, marriage registers, and, by the nineteenth century in Europe and the United States, a variety of census and school records. In England, the Protestation Oath of Loyalty to Parliament implemented in 1642 was meant to be signed – or "marked" – by all English men; the 1754 Marriage Act required signatures on marriage registers; in France, from 1827, army recruits were asked about their education.

These dates, and a series of others (beginning, in England, from as early as the ninth century), which express the reach of church and government bureaucracies, loom large in the history of literacy research. Most historians surround with qualifications the figures drawn from these archives, and the numbers themselves get re-crunched and reinterpreted by succeeding scholarly generations. Signature evidence in particular arouses intense debate. By definition exclusive, it charts only men (in the case of most oaths) or only property owners (in the case of deeds and wills), threatening the historian with the familiar dilemma of reproducing the very conditions that restricted the archives in the first place. In literary historian Margaret Ferguson's assessment of signature data, "so long as literacy is bound up with questions of social status, people are going to misrepresent or 'produce' their kinds and degrees of this form of cultural capital" (Ferguson 2003: 79). Social historian David Vincent suggests that while signature evidence "offers no direct evidence of an ability to read, and the capacity to inscribe two words on just one occasion in an individual's life provides the slightest possible indication of command over the skills of writing," he is nonetheless swayed by the advantage of a "standardised body of evidence" that permits historical and regional comparison (Vincent 1989: 17). As a "measurable" trace of a literacy practice, signatures remain inescapable in many kinds of research, especially for the early modern period to the mid-nineteenth-century period of expansion.

While the evidence itself may have merit, it is often dearly paid for. The rhetoric of statistical certainty seems inevitably to bleed into the text that surrounds the charts and graphs. A triumphalist language of war, sport, and the hunt (on the one hand) or of pathology and disease (on the other) tends to infuse even the most careful of these works, as reading and writing are "conquered" or illiteracy is "wiped out" (as in the Lawrence Stone passage above), and as some group is always "catching up" and another is "gaining the upper hand" (these examples from Vincent 1989.)

The Ethics and Politics of Literacy History

Beyond the narrative of development that signature evidence tends to create, statistics generally tell a story of state interest in the reading and writing skills of citizens, and histories of literacy often begin by calling attention to the politics of literacy. "The history of literacy has aroused fierce passions in France," François Furet and Jacques Ozouf, historians affiliated with the Annales School, write at the beginning of their 1982 study of French literacy. "This is because it has been studied not for its own sake, but rather in order to furnish ammunition in the political debate over education which until recently constituted one of the major lines of cleavage between left and right" (Furet and Ozouf 1982: 1).

Unique, as all national cases are, the French case nonetheless mirrors other such histories. Linguistic, ethnic, and cultural hegemony and homogeneity have often been the implicit or explicit aim of literacy campaigns, whether subtly or aggressively prosecuted. In the United States, the history of literacy is interwoven with, and implicated in, the history of racial conflict, Indian "removal," and slavery. "Race in particular," Michael Warner writes,

> was made one of the social meanings of the difference between writing and speech by racial division in the reproduction of literacy, and by the consequent overlap between determinate features of the medium and traits of race. Black illiteracy was more than a negation of literacy for blacks; it was the condition of a positive character of written discourse for whites. (Warner 1990: 12)

Literacy testing has a long history in the United States as a device of racism and nativism, used to restrict voting in the post-Reconstruction South and (starting in 1917) to limit immigration nationwide.

Just as the Birmingham School was motivated in part by post-war British adult education, contemporary research often echoes scholars' engagement with institutions of literacy on their own campuses and in their own communities. Histories of literacy today, more than ever, cross disciplinary boundaries, influenced (for example) by work in composition and rhetoric, by "popular" or "informal" education movements in Africa and Latin America, and by the consciousness-raising, "problem-posing" pedagogy of the Brazilian theorist and activist Paulo Freire. Promoting an "ethnographic understanding," Brian Street (in Cushman et al. 2001: 433) has persuasively critiqued what he calls the "autonomous model" of literacy, which figures literacy as a neutral technology: "What is taken in the 'autonomous' model to be qualities inherent to literacy are in fact conventions of literate practice in particular societies" (Street 1984: 4). He poses instead an "ideological" model, viewing literacy as always embedded in, and expressive of, rather than somehow transcending, ideology. In tune with much recent theoretical work in the humanities and social sciences, Street urges a kind of defamiliarization: "Faith in the power and qualities of literacy is itself socially learnt and is not an adequate tool with which to embark on a description of its practices" (Street 1984: 1). In line with Street's critique, literacy as an aspect of "discipline" in Michel Foucault's terms, and as "symbolic capital" in Pierre Bourdieu's, has also influenced current thinking, while postcolonial approaches have contributed to understanding the hybrid nature of colonial and creole literacies.

Finding Literacy in All the Wrong Places

As some of their titles indicate ("consequences of," "development of"), earlier studies implied a theory of development, culminating in the current status and prestige of Western industrialized literacy. Recent histories attend instead to *mentalités* or the "mental world" of readers and writers, across a broad range of historical, social, and cultural situations. Marked by a heightened awareness of social power dynamics, by conversation across disciplines, and by a critique of modernity, these works attend less to demographics and more to individual readers and writers or groups of readers and writers. The archive has accordingly shifted to include such materials as library records, autobiographies, diaries, children's literature and literacy practices, scrapbooks, schoolbooks, visual representations of reading and writing, and histories of related media techniques and technologies. Recent histories tend to question prevailing "common-sense" assumptions about literacy: that literacy and economic progress automatically go hand in hand, that mass literacy depended on government support of schooling, that ordinary readers left no records and are therefore lost in the mists of history. As David Hall puts the current case, "To inquire into the uses of literacy is not to ask about the distribution of literacy as a skill, but to explore how reading [and, one might add, writing] functioned as a cultural style" (Hall 1996: 41).

New histories of literacy find reading and writing in unexpected places and tease out the historical significance of these newly discovered (or newly perceived) texts. In his study of the English peasant uprising of June 1381, Steven Justice uncovers the overlooked literacy of these revolutionaries and suggests that literate skills might have been "more widely diffused than we have thought." Countering long-held assumptions that the rebels' destruction of church and state documents expressed a kind of mute and abject (and "illiterate") rage against these symbols of power, Justice finds instead that the rioters destroyed only documents that bore on their demands, conveying thereby a "familiarity with and an investment in the documentary culture by which a realm was governed" (Justice 1994: 52). The rebels, then, were not longing for a return to orality and memory as depositories of institutional covenants: they aimed to "re-create, not destroy, documentary culture" through *"acts of assertive literacy"* (Justice 1994: 188, 24, emphasis in original). Justice speculates that the mysterious scraps of rebel writing embedded in contemporary chronicles may have circulated as manuscript broadsides. "[M]erely by existing, [the broadside] asserted . . . that those who read only English – or even could only have English read to them – had a stake in the intellectual and political life of church and realm" (Justice 1994: 30). Contemporary chroniclers, representing the authority that in the end crushed the insurgents, have been allowed to own the rebels' story; by examining the scant traces of rebel writing in the official story, Justice undermines the chroniclers' power using their own tools. The chroniclers so little expected the possibility of a peasant voice that they "did not efface those voices, because they could not understand them well enough to efface them" (Justice 1994: 261).

"[O]fficial culture," Justice concludes, "need not be read as it wishes" (Justice 1994: 261). This could be the motto of much recent work on contemporary and historical literacy. In the case of the fourteenth-century English peasants, literacy was used, as it so often has been, to demand economic and civil rights, but more than this, vernacular peasant literacy challenged the authority of French and Latin. Like the literacy of medieval peasants, the literacy of African-American slaves and Native Americans, with the exception of a few famous cases, has been until recently underrated and under-studied. Hilary Wyss counters "the assumption . . . that Native Americans were not literate before the end of the eighteenth century" (Wyss 2000: 3) by pointing to seventeenth-century wills, deeds, marginalia in Bibles, letters, conversion narratives, and the evidence of Indian literacy found within texts by whites. She draws out Indian "autoethnographies" (in Mary Louise Pratt's term) "in which colonized subjects undertake to represent themselves in ways that *engage with* the colonizer's own terms" (Pratt, quoted in Wyss 2000: 4).

While Native Americans were encouraged to become literate to "civilize" them and to incorporate them into English land-use conventions, African-American slaves were excluded (through social and often legal constraints) from access to literacy: "A form of capital themselves, slaves were strictly debarred . . . from acquiring any cultural or monetary capital of their own" (Nelson Salvino 1989: 147). And yet, Janet Cornelius estimates that against crushing odds as many as 10 percent of the antebellum United States' slave population became literate, sometimes taught by whites, sometimes, at the risk of amputation (a punishment so widespread that many thought it was legally mandated), teaching themselves or learning from other slaves. This hard-won literacy could have powerful real-life effects, including escape or manumission. But in the American South, as in most other historical and geographical sites, literacy alone, despite the blinding myth of its empowering force, often had very little social or economic payoff. "While blacks embraced and subverted the white ideology of literacy for the freedom it could provide from physical bondage," Dana Nelson writes, "their hard-earned literacy skills did not mean very much in terms of social and economic acceptance among whites" (Nelson Salvino 1989: 152). Studies of literacy among the enslaved also highlight what often gets effaced in discussions of literacy: the cultural and historical differences between the practices of and attitudes toward reading and writing. Reading traditionally came first in the curriculum, with writing, requiring more training to teach, reserved for more elite (and, until the mid-eighteenth century, usually male) students. For Native Americans, and to some extent for African Americans, reading pedagogy's gloss of Christian proselytizing made it culturally invasive; for the same reason, from the point of view of whites, teaching reading could seem benign. Writing, on the other hand, always seemed to represent the promise – or threat – of empowerment (Monaghan 2005).

While slaves risked gaining the literacy skills whose potential benefits, including escape or manumission, outweighed the potential dire punishments, northern, middle-class African-American men and women were establishing literary societies "as a means of self-defense and to fight for the right to enter the sphere of politics" (McHenry 2003: 57). At the same time, according to Thomas Augst, young, white, American men in the nineteenth century, attending lyceum lectures and confiding their aspirations to their diaries, "learned to pursue independence within a dense landscape of literacy" (Augst 2003: 2). For the young American man, writing

> in a blank book enables him to rectify past mistakes, to trust in God, to form the determination to "win" on which his success and freedom as a man depends. With his cursive "hand," an ambitious clerk invests his diary with moral utility, the power to shape the outcome of one's struggles in the protean world of market culture. Through such gestures, young men vested writing with magical, if not mythical, powers of freedom. (Augst 2003: 9)

Diaries offer to historians accounts of ordinary lives with the detail and intensity once reserved only for histories of elites. Letter writing, too, once a domain of privilege, became democratized in the eighteenth and nineteenth centuries. "The easy possibility of letter writing," wrote Franz Kafka, "must – seen merely theoretically – have brought into the world a terrible disintegration of souls. It is, in fact, an intercourse with ghosts, and not only with the ghost of the recipient but also with one's own ghost which develops between the lines of the letter one is writing" (quoted in Siegert 1999: 4). Along with silent reading and diary writing, letter writing evinces and creates a new relationship between self and others, and what seem to be distinctly modern reaches of both interiority and alienation. For David Vincent, "[l]iteracy in modern Europe came of age on 9 October 1874" with the Treaty of Berne, authorizing the Universal Postal Union, which would connect "[e]very inhabitant of every country" in Europe "in a common system of flat-rate postage" (Vincent 2000: 1). Valentine's Day emerges strikingly as an exemplary site of this transition: with the English penny post, something like 400,000 Valentines were mailed in 1841 and, in London alone, mail increased on February 14 by 1.5 million items in 1871 (Vincent 1989: 44). The cheap and speedy exchange of letters, postcards, and commercial holiday cards profoundly transformed everyday life, allowing affective bonds to withstand the increased mobility of modern life.

If "self-culture" and, somewhat later, "self-expression" became bywords of nineteenth- and twentieth-century literate culture, early schoolbooks – for example, trecento Florentine grammars (Gehl 1993), Renaissance handwriting manuals (Goldberg 1990), Anglo-American alphabet books (Crain 2000), and nineteenth-century rhetorics (Carr et al. 2005) – manifest a quite different ideology of literacy. Such texts reveal methods of training as well as a given culture's aspirations for reading and writing pedagogy. For Erasmus and other Renaissance pedagogues, the "human is made human through the letter" (Goldberg 1990: 175). The notion that alphabetic learning generally distinguishes the human extends through the Enlightenment, lending itself to colonial and imperial programs as well as to a still influential teleological model of literacy. Walter Mignolo's study of the "darker side of the Renaissance" finds in Spanish grammars a dual emphasis on "the unification of Castile and the expansion of the Spanish Empire": in Elio Antonio de Nebrija's important 1492 grammar "the letter was defined as the instrument to tame the voice," a theory with wide-ranging consequences for the methods of Spanish colonization (Mignolo 1995: 41, 43). Mignolo describes the resulting differences between Mexica (i.e., Aztec) and Spanish modes of communication in the sixteenth century, which

> had not only different material ways of encoding and transmitting knowledge but also . . . different concepts of the activities of reading and writing. Mexicas put the accent on the act of observing and telling out loud the stories of what they were looking at (movements of the sky or the black and the red ink). Spaniards stressed reading the word rather than reading the world, and made the letter the anchor of knowledge and understanding. Contemplating and recounting what was on the painting (*amoxtli*) were not

enough, from the point of view of the Spaniard's concept of reading, writing, and the book, to ensure correct and reliable knowledge. (Mignolo 1995: 105–6)

Over time, in common with many colonized groups, Amerindians adapted European writing systems and genres "in order to sustain their own cultural traditions" (Mignolo 1995: 204). Still, literacy is so often implicated as a set of disciplining and culturally destructive technologies, one might wonder why the subaltern ever submits to it except under duress. The Nigerian anthropologist John Ogbu suggests one answer: "If we don't know what you know, when we get up, our things will be gone" (quoted in Keller-Cohen 1994: 359).

The Poetics of Literacy

The French anthropologist and surrealist Michel Leiris described in his memoir his sensuous attachment to alphabetic letters: "If I think that when I say *alphabet* I am eating language, the illusion takes place by way of the book, this book whose materiality remains a ballast when I join together the primary elements of writing, which themselves lead me to the tongue, of which they are the algebraic summary or the broken reflection" (Leiris 1991: 32). The nostalgia-steeped, highly polished memories of a French intellectual; the diary of a working-class reader; a seventeenth-century Massachusett Indian's graffiti in the margins of his Bible – these are the kinds of sources that uncover the experience of and the significance of (for lack of a better word) literacy. These documents are far from transparent: scholars must appreciate that they are crafted not only by individuals but by generic conventions as well as by cultural, social, and historical contingencies. Even marginalia is a genre, with formal constraints.

Literacy has often been treated as a marker and a maker of cultural, social, and national histories; it has also been seen as part and parcel of modern constructions of personality, subjectivity, and interiority. As an object of study, then, literacy is a rich site for exploring the hinge between and the interpenetration of the public and the private, the social and the personal, the large and national or global, on the one hand, and the small and local, on the other. But the oppositions embedded in "literacy," rooted in its nineteenth-century origins – the ways in which it evokes the somewhat evacuated categories of "illiteracy" or "orality" – pose an ongoing challenge to the historian.

References and Further Reading

Altick, Richard (1998) *The English Common Reader: A Social History of the Mass Reading Public, 1800–1900*, 2nd edn. Columbus: Ohio State University Press (originally published 1957).

Augst, Thomas (2003) *The Clerk's Tale: Young Men and Moral Life in Nineteenth-century America.* Chicago: University of Chicago Press.

Baldwin, T. W. (1944) *William Shakspere's Small Latine and Lesse Greeke.* Urbana: University of Illinois Press.

Baumann, Gerd (ed.) (1986) *The Written Word: Literacy in Transition.* Oxford: Clarendon Press.

Boyarin, Jonathan (ed.) (1993) *The Ethnography of Reading.* Berkeley: University of California Press.

Carr, Jean Ferguson, Carr, Stephen L., and Schultz, Lucille M. (2005) *Archives of Instruction: Nineteenth-century Rhetorics, Readers, and Composition Books in the United States.* Carbondale: Southern Illinois University Press.

Cavallo, Guglielmo and Chartier, Roger (eds.) (1999) *A History of Reading in the West,* trans. Lydia Cochrane. Amherst: University of Massachusetts Press.

Cipolla, Carlo M. (1969) *Literacy and Development in the West.* Harmondsworth: Pelican.

Clanchy, M. T. (1993) *From Memory to Written Record: England 1066–1307.* Oxford: Blackwell.

Cook-Gumperz, Jenny (ed.) (1986) *The Social Construction of Literacy.* Cambridge: Cambridge University Press.

Cornelius, Janet Duitsman (1991) *"When I Can Read my Title Clear": Literacy, Slavery, and Religion in the Antebellum South.* Columbia: University of South Carolina Press.

Crain, Patricia (2000) *The Story of A: The Alphabetization of America from The New England Primer to The Scarlet Letter.* Stanford: Stanford University Press.

Cressy, David (1980) *Literacy and the Social Order: Reading and Writing in Tudor and Stuart England.* Cambridge: Cambridge University Press.

Cushman, Ellen, Kintgen, Eugene R., Kroll, Barry M., and Rose, Mike (eds.) (2001) *Literacy: A Critical Sourcebook.* New York: Bedford/St. Martin's.

Editorial (1883) "First Fruits of Butler's Inaugural." *Journal of Education,* 17 (4): 54.

Ferguson, Margaret W. (2003) *Dido's Daughters: Literacy, Gender and Empire in Early Modern England and France.* Chicago: University of Chicago Press.

Furet, François and Ozouf, Jacques (1982) *Reading and Writing: Literacy in France from Calvin to Jules Ferry.* Cambridge: Cambridge University Press.

Gehl, Paul (1993) *A Moral Art: Grammar, Society and Culture in Trecento Florence.* Ithaca: Cornell University Press.

Goldberg, Jonathan (1990) *Writing Matter: From the Hands of the English Renaissance.* Stanford: Stanford University Press.

Goody, Jack and Watt, Ian (1968) "The Consequences of Literacy." In Jack Goody (ed.), *Literacy in Traditional Societies,* pp. 27–68. Cambridge: Cambridge University Press.

Graff, Harvey (1987) *The Legacies of Literacy: Continuities and Contradictions in Western Culture and Society.* Bloomington: University of Indiana Press.

Guillory, John (1993) *Cultural Capital: The Problem of Literary Canon Formation.* Chicago: University of Chicago Press.

Hall, David D. (1996) "The Uses of Literacy in New England, 1600–1850." In *Cultures of Print: Essays in the History of the Book,* pp. 36–78. Amherst: University of Massachusetts Press.

Harris, William V. (1989) *Ancient Literacy.* Cambridge, MA: Harvard University Press.

Harrop, Sylvia (1983) "Literacy and Educational Attitudes as Factors in the Industrialization of North-East Cheshire, 1760–1830." In W. B. Stephens (ed.), *Studies in the History of Literacy: England and North America.* Educational Administration and History Monograph, no. 13, pp. 37–53. Leeds: Museum of the History of Education.

Hoggart, Richard (1957) *The Uses of Literacy.* London: Chatto and Windus.

Justice, Steven (1994) *Writing and Rebellion: England in 1381.* Berkeley: University of California Press.

Kaestle, Carl F. (1991) *Literacy in the United States: Readers and Reading since 1880.* New Haven: Yale University Press.

Keller-Cohen, Deborah (ed.) (1994) *Literacy: Interdisciplinary Conversations.* Cresskill: Hampton.

Leiris, Michel (1991) *Rules of the Game I: Scratches,* trans. Lydia Davis. New York: Paragon.

McHenry, Elizabeth (2003) *Forgotten Readers: Recovering the Lost History of African American Literary Societies.* Durham: Duke University Press.

Mignolo, Walter D. (1995) *The Darker Side of the Renaissance: Literacy, Territoriality, and Colonization.* Ann Arbor: University of Michigan Press.

Monaghan, E. Jennifer (2005) *Learning to Read and Write in Colonial America.* Amherst: University of Massachusetts Press.

National Center for Education Statistics (available at http://nces.ed.gov/naal/defining/defining.asp; accessed May 14, 2005).

Nelson Salvino, Dana (1989) "The Word in Black and White: Ideologies of Race and Literacy in

Antebellum America." In Cathy Davidson (ed.), *Reading in America: Literature and Social History*, pp. 140–56. Baltimore: Johns Hopkins University Press.

Ong, Walter (1982) *Orality and Literacy: The Technologizing of the Word*. London: Methuen.

Pattison, Robert (1982) *On Literacy*. New York: Oxford University Press.

Price, Leah (2004) "Reading: The State of the Discipline." *Book History*, 7: 303–20.

Richardson, Alan (1994) *Literature, Education, and Romanticism: Reading as Social Practice 1780–1832*. Cambridge: Cambridge University Press.

Rose, Jonathan (2001) *The Intellectual Life of the British Working Classes*. New Haven: Yale University Press.

Siegert, Bernhard (1999) *Relays: Literature as an Epoch of the Postal System*, trans. Kevin Repp. Stanford: Stanford University Press.

Spufford, Margaret (1981) *Small Books and Pleasant Histories: Popular Fiction and its Readership in Seventeenth-century England*. Athens: University of Georgia Press.

Stone, Lawrence (1969) "Literacy and Education in England 1640–1900." *Past and Present*, 42: 69–139.

Street, Brian (1984) *Literacy in Theory and Practice*. Cambridge: Cambridge University Press.

Thompson, E. P. (1963) *The Making of the English Working Class*. London: Victor Gollancz.

Vincent, David (1989) *Literacy and Popular Culture: England 1750–1914*. Cambridge: Cambridge University Press.

— (2000) *Rise of Mass Literacy: Readers and Writing in Modern Europe*. Cambridge: Polity.

Warner, Michael (1990) *The Letters of the Republic: Publication and the Public Sphere in Eighteenth-century America*. Cambridge, MA: Harvard University Press.

Williams, Raymond (1985) *Keywords: A Vocabulary of Culture and Society*, rev. edn. New York: Oxford University Press.

Wyss, Hilary (2000) *Writing Indians: Literacy, Christianity and Native Community in Early America*. Boston: University of Massachusetts Press.

35

Some Non-textual Uses of Books

Rowan Watson

Anecdotes about the uses of books as physical objects abound. The literary historian knows that Samuel Johnson nearly brained the bookseller Thomas Osborne with a hefty tome during work on the catalogue of the Harleian collection (1743–5). Musicians know that John Cage's artwork, *Wild Edible Papers* (1990), made on the same principles as he composed his music, was his response to seeing the poor of Santiago, Chile, boiling books and newsprint to make the pulp edible. Anthropologists may be aware that a sage in Sub-Saharan Africa of the 1950s used a printed school book as part of equipment for divination. Students of Tibet learn that books were paraded unopened and used to line the tomb of a grand lama. What can stories such as these, and representations of books, tell us about the aura that surrounds books at any time? What are the messages of books when they appear in the visual iconography of any period?

Egypt, Greece, and Rome

Instances where books were paraded as marks of conspicuous consumption rather than objects transmitting texts go back very far. The Book of the Dead was a collection of charms and spells needed for protection in the afterlife: left in an Egyptian tomb, its physical characteristics were no less effective than the quality and quantity of tomb furnishings to mark the status of the departed. Produced according to established formulae after c.1500 BC, ready-made versions were made speculatively, with empty spaces for the insertion of names. When one encounters a late version, of the Ptolemaic period (200 BC), written in hieratic script rather than the more imposing hieroglyphs, it seems that we are seeing a work at the bottom end of the market, the upper reaches of which were dominated by works signifying social distinction.

Scrolls were abundant in classical Greece in the fifth century BC, but possession of them had no implications about status. Philosophers and scholars were represented with the beards of sages; scrolls denoted a trade or profession. Socrates famously mistrusted the written word as a basis for education. In Roman statuary, the holding of a scroll might represent literary interests, though portraits of retired soldiers with such scrolls may signify no more than integration into civilian life. Representations of poets before the late antique period usually show inspiration as coming from a Muse rather than a book. But by the first century, Seneca (d.65) could complain that owners accumulated scrolls with decorated knobs and colored labels for display rather than use (Kenyon 1951). A lady of the second century from Fayûm in Egypt was buried with an illustrated roll of the second book of the Iliad beneath her head, perhaps to relay to the afterworld an element of what gave her distinction in this. In the third century, a scroll with a scriptural text was carefully built into a wall in a Greco-Roman house in Egypt, perhaps an early example of a book as a talisman to protect the house at a time of persecution: the learned John Chrysostom (347–407) felt that the presence of the Scriptures in a house would save it from harm. There may have been a parallel with Jewish custom, which dictated the hanging of texts on the doorpost (the *Mezuza*) to allow those passing through to say a prayer.

The Ritual Function of Christian Bibles and Service Books

As objects of awe, the book joined the cross and crucifix as a major element in the iconography of the Roman empire's new state religion after the conversion of the emperor Constantine. The image of the codex was used to represent the word of God, the source of salvation for the individual and for society as a whole, for which the Church was uniquely responsible. Early Christian art privileged images of Christ as ruler holding a book. In the Greek regions, images of Christ Pantocrator clasping a codex dominated the east end of churches. The Evangelists identified themselves with books, held open or closed, and saints were similarly shown to indicate that sanctity derived from study of the Scriptures. It is worth noticing the *traditio clavis et legis* iconography where a Christ in Majesty hands a key to St. Peter and a book to St. Paul: Paul never met Christ, so there needed to be a visible sign of Christ handing him the law to underline his authority.

Initially, individuals rather than churchmen may have led the way in making copies of the Gospels into objects of display. In 384, St. Jerome complained that women used scriptural texts written in gold on purple vellum and decorated with jewels. In less-civilized surroundings, St. Boniface, an English missionary working in what is now Germany, asked Abbess Eadburh in 735 for a copy of the Epistles in gold letters to impress the "carnal men" he was trying to convert. Orthodox Christianity developed the image of the codex on its own. A miniature of c.880 from Byzantium shows a church council of the fourth century presided over by Emperor Theodosius who sits next to a Gospel book mounted on a throne: proceedings took place under the aegis of the Word.

Bibles and service books were given bindings that used gold, gems, and ivories to enhance their significance among believers. The earliest surviving examples date from the fifth century, and many incorporated late antique carved ivories, a visible sign of their attachment to the earliest – and purest – years of the religion. Their texts had a functional use in the liturgy, but their format had quite another function as ceremonial objects, carried in processions and displayed on altars and lecterns. In Rome, books were ceremonially carried to the altar by deacon and acolytes before the Pope entered to say mass. They were also used in rituals with secular participants. When the remains of St. Adalbert were brought to Gnesen, the archbishop and Emperor Otto III waited for the train with crosses and books to lead the saint into the city. When the same emperor visited the abbey of Farfa near Rome in c.1000, he was greeted by abbot and monks holding crosses and the Gospels: he was sprinkled with holy water, incensed, and given the Gospels to kiss. The kissing of missals, a kind of service book that emerged in the eleventh to twelfth centuries, became standard practice for priests celebrating mass.

The making of Gospel and service books was regarded as an act of piety, encouraged by the rulers and aristocracy of Carolingian and Ottonian Europe. Images in surviving works give prominence to the holy book as the source of authority. However much the theory of sacralized kingship might be expounded in the images, the control of the sacred word rested firmly with the Church: temporal power was represented by sword, orb, and crown, not by the book. Secular rulers could do no more than offer books to the Church. Thus Dietricht Count of Holland and his wife were shown handing a book to the abbey of Egmont in c.940/970, a visual reminder of their subservient position and their support for the Church's mission. The saints too were guardians of the word and recipients of books: Abbess Hitda of Meschede had herself shown presenting her Gospel book to St. Walburga in c.1000 (Mayr-Harting 1991). Images such as these can be found throughout the Middle Ages. Only at the Reformation was it possible for a ruler to show himself enthroned, distributing the Word of God to both clergy and laity – as appeared in Henry VIII's Great Bible in English of 1539.

Divination

Methods of divination in republican and imperial Rome – those using chicken's entrails are most fondly remembered today – included the random selection of passages in revered works, particularly Homer and Virgil. Hadrian, before becoming emperor in 117, is said to have opened at random a book of the Aeneid and chanced on a passage predicting his elevation. The first centuries of Christianity saw Bibles, liturgical books, and saints' lives used in this way (the practice was known as *Sortes*) for elections and other matters. St. Augustine (354–430) denounced the practice, as did a number of Church councils, from that at Vannes in 465 to Aenham in England in 1109. However, writers such as Sulpicius Severus (c.360–c.425) and Gregory of Tours (c.539–c.594) described the practice in relation to episcopal elections, while Theodore, made Archbishop of Canterbury in 668, referred to it in the process of installing canons (Leclercq 1951).

The practice evidently survived. The French writer Rabelais (c.1494–1553) has Pantagruel order copies of Homer and Virgil to be brought before him: opened three times, the texts were to reveal whether Panurge's marriage would be successful (a disquisition follows about famous instances of such divination in the past). There are incidental references to such practices at a less-educated level of society. From the late Middle Ages, we learn of the custom of using a Bible or Psalter and a key: the latter was stuffed with slips of paper bearing the names of suspects. When the book fell, the last name to be stuffed into the key was taken to be that of the guilty party. Instances of this are recorded in England as late as 1551 and 1641 (Thomas 1971). In Islamic communities outside Europe, copies of the Qur'ān and, for example, works of the fourteenth-century Sufi poet Hafiz were used to cast fortunes. The *Fal-Nāmah* was specially made as a book for divination: surviving examples from India, Iran, and Turkish lands date from the sixteenth and seventeenth centuries (Lewis 1965: 760).

Talismanic Use of Books and Texts

Books and written texts joined rings and amulets as devices to ward off evil. There are early references to the habit of wearing the Gospels around the neck, in the form of small books (*parvula evangelia* was the phrase used by St. Jerome). Small books that could be worn in this way are known to have existed at this time. Perhaps they were not unlike a tenth-century Gospel of St. John, measuring only 70 × 55 mm, which was found in 1712 in the tenth-century shrine of the veil of the Virgin Mary, said to have been given to the cathedral of Chartres by Charlemagne himself. Other works were equally effective. An enthusiast in Durham was reported by John of Salisbury to have worn a book with the life of St. Cuthbert around his neck.

The special powers of St. John's Gospel were respected for long after the Middle Ages. Shortly after 1600, copies were being sold in Nottingham as preservatives against witchcraft for the extortionate price of ten shillings. Perhaps we should see the girdle books worn as jewelry by noble ladies in Tudor times as an up-market version of this practice. The texts here were suitable for Protestant devotions: the writer John Lyly in 1580 remarked that this custom had made Englishwomen as "cunning in the scriptures as Italian women were in the works of Ariosto and Petrarch." The special powers of the Bible as an object were probably widely respected: Thomas Pennant in his *Tour of Wales* (1778) reported the use of one in an elaborate ceremony to cure the sick at the church of St. Tecla in Llandegla.

The wearing of sacred or magical texts on small pieces of paper or parchment as a defense against harm has a long history, and can be found all over the world. In Europe, Alcuin (d.804), advisor to Charlemagne, called such slips *pittaciole*. If the texts were biblical they could do little damage in the eyes of Church authorities. The interrogation of a spy in 1472 before a royal judge in Tours shows what an individual might carry: he had a series of pieces of parchment (*brevets, rouleaux*), some designed to be carried round the neck. There were texts to cure toothache, others to obtain the love of a woman; a few had been bought in a tavern, but others had been copied out for him from a book by a friar in Poitiers – the presumed spy admitted that he could not read the writing (Day 2002). A vagrant in Elizabethan England, William Wake, seems to have traded in such scraps of writing. The opening words of St. John's Gospel were especially popular. Mementoes of this kind survived into the age of printing: Joseph Hall, Bishop of Exeter from 1627 and of Norwich from 1642, denounced the habit of wearing small roundels printed with the text of St. John's Gospel to ensure freedom from danger. Soldiers from the Auvergne undertaking an attack on Geneva in 1602 were discovered with charms on paper on which the first words of St. John's Gospel were written.

"Associational Copies": The Book as Relic

Relics – parts of a saint's body or objects used during their lifetime – were venerated by Christians from the fourth century. There was a lively trade in such things, since the presence of a famous relic could bring material as well as spiritual benefits to any church. Books used by saints were regarded as having special powers. When St. Patrick's tomb was opened in 553, some 60 years after his death according to the Annals of Ulster, his Gospel book was removed as a relic and bestowed on St. Columba. Books associated with saints Canice, Cronan, Declan, and Enda of Aran were similarly prized. Perhaps the best documented book of this kind is the Stonyhurst Gospel, written in Northumbria in the late seventh century in imitation of Italian books of the fifth to sixth centuries and removed from the tomb of St. Cuthbert (d.687) in 1104 (Brown 1969). John of Salisbury reported that Cuthbert had healed the sick by the laying-on of the book; St. Augustine had reported a similar practice to cure headaches. Other venerated books had similar powers: a deluxe copy of St. Dionysius' works brought to St. Denis near Paris by legates of the Byzantine emperor in 827 performed nineteen miraculous cures the night it arrived. A copy of the *Cantigas de Santa Maria* (hymns to the Virgin) made for Alfonso X of Castile (1252–84) was placed on his chest to cure a threatening illness.

In Ireland, such works were frequently given metalwork cases to act as shrines. These shrines were used for activities as various as administering oaths, leading armies into battle, and the protection of tax gatherers. When the Normans defeated Domnall Ua Lochlainn in 1182, they took as spoil the Gospel of St. Martin, depriving the Irish of their special protection. The most celebrated book shrine is that of the Psalter of St. Colomba (521–97), known as the Cathach of Colmcille, made between 1062 and 1098 to the order of Cathbar O'Donnell. A sixteenth-century source records its function as a military trophy: carried to the right, three times around an army, it ensured victory. The power of manuscripts such as these had a long life: in 1627, the custodian of the Book of Durrow, then associated with St. Columba, was said to put water on the book and use it to cure sick cattle (Bede, d.735, had reported a similar practice with scrapings from Irish books to cure snake bites in his *Ecclesiastical History*). By the nineteenth century, books of this kind were sometimes the property of gentry families in Ireland, who hired them out for the taking of oaths (Lucas 1986).

Taking Oaths upon the Book

Medieval practice allowed a contract to be sworn in front of witnesses, upon relics or upon books. Even when recourse to properly constituted law courts was possible, details of legal transactions, especially the transfer of property to the Church, might be entered into a Gospel book or service book. The transaction was thus sanctioned by the full weight of religious authority. As late as c.1200, the administrators of St. Augustine's, Canterbury copied details of tenants, churches, and rents into a Gospel book. In late twelfth-century England, an oath taken upon a service book was challenged, it being held that kneeling before the Gospels was the correct procedure. This was certainly the case by the fifteenth century. Fear of divine retribution was a potent force against perjury.

Coronation oaths taken before the peers of the realm and parliament were not dependent upon any book, but the *Book of Oaths* of 1649 indicates that swearing "by the holy contents of this book," with a hand on the Bible, was usual practice by this date. Exceptions caused a stir. In 1657, Dr. Owen, Vice-Chancellor of Oxford, refused to be sworn as a witness by laying his right hand on the Bible and kissing it afterwards; legal opinion declared his oath invalid. When a Massachusetts colonist, Samuel Sewell, took the oath of allegiance in 1686, he held the book in his left hand, holding the right hand up to heaven, to the consternation of lawyers present. A German visitor seeking to use the Bodleian Library in 1710 was surprised to have to touch a Greek New Testament with his right hand and then kiss the book – an English postulant would perhaps have remarked only on the language of the sacred text (Spurr 2001). James Tyler's work on oaths of 1834 insisted that kissing the thumb and not the book made an oath invalid. William Congreve's play of 1700, *The Way of the World*, made use of this: when Mincing has to swear not to disclose what she has seen in the blue garret, she is clever enough to see that she is being asked to swear not on a Bible but on a book of poems. Kissing Bibles was deemed unhygienic by the end of the nineteenth century: on the advice of the medical profession, an act of 1909 discontinued the practice (Stringer 1910: 84).

Books that Boast

It is easily said that individuals invested in books by way of illustration, ornament, or binding as a matter of prestige, as an aspiration, in order to establish themselves at an elevated point in a real or imagined social hierarchy. The theme is not always easy to document. Was investment in a beautifully illuminated Book of Hours a matter of social rivalry or a recognition that the cycle of prayer supported by such books, and the contact with the Almighty involved, deserved only the most expensive materials and workmanship? In the latter case, the embellishment was an act of piety, not display.

There are certainly indications, however, that such books were intended to impress in public arenas. The fourteenth-century poet Eustache Deschamps (1346–1406) famously teased wealthy housewives of Paris for needing to appear in church with expensively decorated Books of Hours, and there are similar derogatory remarks about using prayer-books as a fashion accessory at later dates. Certainly, such books included more texts toward 1500 that were relevant for services in church rather than in private. When the covers of books used the same materials and ornament as contemporary fashions, we can assume that display was as significant as text. This was as true of the gorgeous textiles on the c.1400 binding of the Hours of the French queen, Isabel of Bavaria, as it was of the chaste black leather favored by ladies of Jansenist sympathies for similar books at Louis XIV's court.

The non-textual role of books such as these is underlined by the fact that they were kept not in libraries but as fashion accessories – as appears in the famous illuminated genealogy of the kings of Spain and Portugal by Simon Bening of 1530–34, where a Book of Hours appears in a box with rosaries and jewels as the accoutrements of a princess. From their appearance as independent texts in the thirteenth century, Books of Hours or similar devotional prayer-books became a standard sign of piety. The Virgin was commonly shown with such a book, and the clasping of books of this kind was the standard way of representing piety at a later date. In Protestant England, the descendants of Thomas More had themselves painted by Rowland Lockey in the late sixteenth century with such books in their hands as a sign of continued loyalty to the Church of Rome.

Non-textual Uses of Libraries

Discussing the later Middle Ages, Armando Petrucci (1988) made a useful distinction between libraries that were intended for the distraction of their owners and those that were built up as an adjunct of power. The most prominent example of the latter was the library of Charles V of France (reigned 1364–80) who commissioned translations of authoritative texts of the medieval and classical past as a conscious policy to legitimate the new Valois dynasty. The works underpinned the ideology of royal government, one promoted by a corps of university-trained administrators. Many of these works have illustrated frontispieces that show the translator handing over the completed work to the king, placing the intellectual capital of the past under his protection.

As an attribute of state power, libraries such as this suffered the fortunes of the state in question. When Charles VIII of France conquered Naples in 1496, his opponent, King Alfonso II, took as much of the royal library as he could to the safety of Ischia. The French king was able to send over a thousand volumes back to France. Louis XII defeated the Sforza duke of Milan in 1499: almost half of the ducal library was removed from Pavia to the royal collection in Blois, the remainder being made available for the king's companions in arms. Both kings profited from the habit of Italian princes in developing libraries as acts of magnificence to broadcast their position as the heirs of ancient Rome. The memoirs of the Florentine bookseller Vespasiano da Bisticci make clear the role of libraries as instruments of prestige and conspicuous consumption for Renaissance potentates, even if we are less clear about the social rituals associated with them. We know that Borso d'Este paraded his magnificent Bible, illuminated by the most expensive illuminators of the land, as he journeyed to Rome in 1471 to receive the title of duke of Ferrara – this and a number of other works were given special luxury bindings and covers for the purpose.

Manifest signs of mastery of the intellectual and religious worlds encapsulated in books were necessary adjuncts for an effective display of power. Angelo Decembrio, the humanist servant of the future lord of Ferrara, described preparations for a reception given by his master in 1438 in the library of one of his courtiers: the aim was to upstage Florentine guests. The floor was strewn with cut flowers and the young prince gave a disquisition upon Terence and Donatus: the books were a setting that enabled the host to display literary refinement and total mastery of classical scholarship. The library of Federico da Motefeltro, lord of Urbino, in his palace at Gubbio had a similar role: from the 1470s it was open to the public, and the magnificently bound volumes were regularly shown to guests, ambassadors, and scholars, a crucial tool in the cultural politics and political maneuverings of its creator. Similar ambition was evidenced by François I when in August 1546 he treated English ambassadors to a discourse about his Greek books, bound in the new *alla greca* fashion from Italy, even though he knew none of the language.

The self-conscious development of libraries as physical expressions of their owner's relation to the intellectual capital of the day is something that has its own history. At what time does it become normal for the palaces of princes, the stately homes of aris-tocrats, and the manors of the gentry classes to include libraries that functioned on the same basis as other apartments? It is striking that Castiglione's *Book of the Courtier* first published in 1528 asks his courtier to be learned but almost to eschew contact with books. Sixteenth-century portraiture certainly confirms that courtiers, aristocrats, and gentlemen in general signified their social position by dress: books on the whole denoted those who needed them professionally, that is to say academics, clerics, or pedants. Henry Peachman's *Compleat Gentleman* (1622) likewise advises aspirant gentlemen not to be seen reading: learning was better developed by conversing with the learned. He refers to libraries amassed for show as a substitute for learning. Books that had too much gilding "for ostentation sake," he likened to "prayer books of girls and gallants which are carried to the church but for their outsides." However, he does recommend having those books that *were* owned by a gentleman properly bound and annotated by the owner to show that they had been studied.

Books and Ornament

From the mid-fifteenth century, technological advances made decoration of run-of-the-mill books possible. Stamps, plaques, and rolls allowed covers to be decorated at little cost. From the 1470s, Italian binders imitated the Islamic practice of tooling gold onto leather, and this was taken up in northern Europe shortly before 1510. The design repertoire was largely peculiar to bindings, but the advent of strapwork and arabesque designs from the 1530s shows an effort to match ornament used for other articles: strapwork, in particular, could be found in the decoration of François I's Fontainbleau palace and on St. Porchaire ceramics, for example.

Any private library at this date was liable to be a collective resource, so that books needed to impress the friends of the owner. The French collector Jean Grolier had the words *Io. Grolierii et amicorum* impressed on his bindings; Willibald Pirkheimer (1470–1530) had a similar phrase on the bookplate Dürer designed for him. Books here appear as the physical manifestation of the cult of friendship and intellectual solidarity cultivated among humanistic scholars. Gabriel Naudé's 1627 publication about libraries assumed them to be accessible to a public beyond their owners. Lavish binding signaled that the object was worthy of respect and claimed homage from its users.

Books had always been used as gifts, though before the fifteenth century it is probably fair to say that the typical gift was from a potentate to the Church. By the Renaissance, scholars sought employment or favors by offering books to potential patrons. Deluxe books could be exchanged between rulers. Cosimo de' Medici had no qualms in sending, for example, a text of Livy corrected by Petrarch to the king of Naples in 1444. If in 1456 Francesco Sforza, duke of Milan, was advised that a horse might be a better present to the king of France than a book, later French kings were avid collectors of magnificent volumes.

In the nineteenth century, books were mass produced specifically to be offered as gifts. Companies like Alfred Mame in Tours and Martial Ardant in Limoges, from the 1850s, used the new-found ability of machines to block colorful designs onto cloth boards to create books intended as gifts at baptism, confirmation, and marriage, as well as school prizes and Christmas presents. Many surviving copies appear virtually unread. Similar books found a ready market in England, the covers broadcasting the taste and artistic culture of giver and recipient. John Ruskin was critical: of a gift book represented in Holman Hunt's *Awakening Conscience* (1854), he referred to "embossed books, vain and useless, they also [like the furniture of the house] new, marked with no happy wearing of the beloved leaves." Such books might be given singly or in sets. John Murray around 1848 marketed a set of small volumes of Byron's works in a miniature Grecian temple, covered in leather and with glass doors, which could hold its own with other ornaments on the mantelpiece (V&A, National Art Library, 802.AE.0042). In this period as much as in the fifteenth or sixteenth century, decoration gave a non-textual message: it showed investment in what the text represented (scholarship, religious orientation, literary refinement). Decorative binding was a corrective to the banality of the book as an object after the invention of printing.

Books as Interior Decoration

In the sixteenth century, books that were not of the pocket or bedside variety were stored in cupboards or on shelves. If the artistic convention was to show scholars and authors surrounded by carelessly arranged piles of tomes, more ordered settings showed volumes arranged neatly on slanting surfaces in such a way that they added to the decoration of the room or storage space: Carpaccio's *Vision of St. Augustine*, painted c.1502, is a powerful example. The increase in book production after the invention of printing created problems of storage. Some libraries can be shown to have stored books with their decorative boards showing (the eighteenth-century Jesuit library in Reims is one such, the Leistler bookcase shown at the Great Exhibition in 1851 and now at the V&A is another), but the norm was to line books up on shelves, initially with the fore-edge turned outwards, but from the latter part of the seventeenth century with the spine facing outwards.

A significant development was the free-standing bookcase, where books became furniture. Samuel Pepys famously asked his joiner to construct free-standing bookcases with glass doors, asking his binder to gild the backs of the books in them "to make them handsome." In the grand houses of the eighteenth century, books could be totally subordinated to schemes of interior design, so that, for instance, Robert Adam would rebind whole libraries on bookcases covering the larger part of the wall surface to present decorated spines as part of a scheme of interior decoration. Perhaps to relieve a potential monotony came the conceit of false spines. A letter in *The Spectator* of April 12, 1711 described such false bindings as a novelty in the library of one Lady Leonora (Joseph Addison was too discreet to give further particulars): there were "several . . . counterfeit books on the upper shelves which were carved in wood and served only to fill up the number, like faggots in the muster of a regiment" (faggots were people paid to stand in for those escaping duty in the militia). The library installed by Viscount Tyrconnel at Belton House, Lincolnshire, in 1721–37 gives us an idea of what might be achieved by lining each wall of a room with volumes that sported gold-tooled labels on the spine. The uprights of the shelving were disguised with false spines made of tooled leather, attached so that the run of spines should seem uninterrupted over the whole surface of the wall – this was strange enough to be commented upon by Simon Yorke, a visitor from Erddig, in the 1740s.

The conceit of false spines was to have a glorious future, the titles displaying the owner's wit and, when they concealed a door, providing a disguised means of escape. By the end of the eighteenth century, the door or pilaster disguised by false spines was common, the false spines having titles that could be satirical (*The Honest Lawyer*, *The Present State of Morocco*) or puzzling (*Block's Thoughts* was one at Belton). When the library at Belton was re-sited on the first floor in the 1870s, false spines disguising a door were given titles such as *Canzonetti degli asini*, *Arte of Deception*, and *Paradise Improved*; more serious titles were *Palanteonis Historia Ocrearum*, *Leatherhead's Shakespeare*, and *Epitome of the Trial of Arthur Orton*, this last being a reference to the Tichbourne case of 1874, one of the longest trials in English legal history. An original example dating from the 1770s comes from Antwerp: Francis Adrien van den Bogaert bought the house known as Den Wolsack and had the lavatory decorated entirely with false spines, doubtless to the frustration of occupants accustomed to perusing books when about their easements. In the nineteenth century, the idea was taken up on wallpaper; one of 1889 by the French manufacturer Isidore Leroy provided a variation on the theme, showing a scatter of open and closed volumes by Cervantes, Jules Verne, and Walter Scott. More conventional was a design of 1905–10, recorded at 35 Commonwealth Avenue, Boston, Massachusetts, which shows how an alcove could be converted into a fictive library.

Libraries were a discrete part of well-furbished houses in the eighteenth century, a necessary feature of the stately home in the nineteenth. At what point did contact with books become inescapable? In the early nineteenth century, the designer Humphrey Repton referred to the recent habit of using the library as "the general living room," the parlor or drawing room being reserved "to give the visitors a formal cold reception." By 1820, the novelist Maria Edgworth could describe such an environment where books were displayed next to sofas, small tables, and "other means of agreeable occupation" (Edwards 2004: 98). However, Charles Eastlake's influential work *Hints on Household Taste* (1868) still talks in terms of a separate library, the bookcases proposed (cabinets with shelves above cupboards) following medieval models.

The invasion of books into living spaces was to come later in the century. Houses had to be built in increasingly compact spaces. Collections of books were thrust into living rooms and suitable corners. The *Cabinet Maker* of 1893 proposed a "Library cosy corner" in which books could be stored and presented as part of the arrangement of a larger room. Though the encyclopedic *Book of the Home* (1900) insisted that every home "of moderate size ought to have one room set aside for literary recreation," it described how books could be stored to decorative advantage in flats. Here, a recess in the dining room, rather than the drawing room, was deemed best to house an escritoire and bookcase. Walsh's *Manual of Domestic Economy* (1879 edition) assumed that a house run on £1,500 a year had a library, evidently a social space since six chairs were recommended, one on £750 a year a "library or breakfast room," while on £350 or less books were kept in a chiffonier in a living room. Here was displayed the household's literary capital.

Just as dust-jackets with attractive colors and designs were used to sell books, so other ways were devised to encourage book buying. The great inventor of the profession of public relations manager, Edward L. Bernays (1891–1995), was commissioned in the 1920s by American publishers to get shelving spaces included in house designs used by speculative builders, so that the rooms would look incomplete unless the eventual owners dashed out to buy books to fill them (Tye 1998: 52). The 1977 play by Mike Leigh, *Abigail's Party*, shows this in action: as an antidote to his wife's vulgarity, Laurence draws attention to his set of Shakespeare, "the complete works, a lovely set, embossed in gold, really nice"; it was "part of our heritage, [but of] course not something you can actually read." A fourteenth-century equivalent is suggested by a group of nearly twenty-five illuminated manuscripts of the *Roman de la rose* decorated by a single team of illuminators in Paris: all have such monumental errors in the placement of initials and rubrics in the text as to suggest that they were never actually read – they were for display. Owners of books like this might have benefited from the service proposed by Myles na Gopaleen (Flann O'Brien) in the 1950s: for a modest sum, works in such libraries would be thumbed, dog-eared, and have inserted bits of theater tickets, tram tickets, and pamphlets as forgotten bookmarks; a "deluxe handling service" was to include underlining and annotation as evidence of actual use.

The ultimate non-textual use of books is destruction. Today, people find it difficult to get rid of their books. Each represents a memory or act which may have little to do with the text. In the past, when books went out of fashion, they tended to be destroyed. In the first century of printing, university libraries throughout Europe jettisoned manuscript books as better printed editions became available. Binders used leaves from discarded manuscript and printed books to strengthen bindings for some centuries. There are records of leaves from manuscript books being used to wrap up groceries and in the jakes in the sixteenth century (Brownrigg and Smith 2000: 22). Memory of this evidently lived on. In 1765, Thomas Gray, in his poem "William Shakespeare to Mrs. Anne," suggests that Mrs. Anne steal to a critic's closet to purloin his notes and use them as paper for baking and roasting.

Books have traditionally been burnt publicly as a gesture. Reformation Europe saw much of this as Protestants and Catholics sought to extinguish the memory of each other. The Index of the Catholic Church, first instituted in 1559, drove many zealots to pitch forbidden books on the fire. This was the fate of the copy of Eric Cross's *The Tailor and Ansty* (1942) owned by the heroes of the story in rural Ireland. Once banned as obscene by the de Valera government on publication, three priests arrived at their house to throw their copy on the fire, even though, as Ansty remarked, it was worth eight shillings and sixpence. Some cities remind us of the consequences of burning books. From 1996, Bebelplatz in Berlin has had a memorial to Nazi burnings of books. The Judenplatz in Vienna from 1997 has had a work by Rachel Whiteread as a Holocaust Memorial, a cast of spaces around books on bookshelves, to signify books not written, not read, and not loved by citizens who were Jewish. Whether the symbolic role attributed to books will change as future generations rely on electronic means to store texts remains to be seen.

References and Further Reading

Brown, T. J. (ed.) (1969) *The Stonyhurst Gospel.* Oxford: Oxford University Press for the Roxburghe Club.

Brownrigg, L. L. and Smith, M. S. (eds.) (2000) *Interpreting and Collecting Fragments of Medieval Books.* Los Altos Hills: Anderson Lovelace.

Day, V. (2002) "Portrait of a Provincial Artist: Jehan Gillemer, Poitevin Illuminator," *Gesta*, 41 (1): 39–49.

Edwards, C. (2004) *Turning Houses into Homes.* Aldershot: Ashgate.

Kenyon, F. G. (1951) *Books and Readers in Ancient Greece and Rome*, 2nd edn. Oxford: Clarendon Press.

Leclercq, H. (1951) "Sortes Sanctorum." In *Dictionnaire d'archéologie chrétienne et de liturgie*, vol. 15, pt. 2, cols. 1590–2. Paris: Letouzey & Ané, 1907–53.

Lewis, B. (ed.) (1965) *Encyclopedia of Islam*, new edn., vol. II. Leiden: E. J. Brill.

Lucas, A. T. (1986) "The Social Role of Relics and Reliquaries in Ancient Ireland," *Journal of the Royal Society of Antiquaries of Ireland*, 116: 5–37.

Mayr-Harting, H. (1991) *Ottonian Book Illumination*, 2 vols. London: Harvey Miller.

Petrucci, A. (1988) "Biblioteca di Corte e Cultura Libraria nella Napoli Aragonese." In G. Cavallo (ed.), *Le biblioteche nel mondo antico e medievale.* Bari: Editori Laterza.

Spurr, J. (2001) "A Profane History of Early Modern Oaths," *Transactions of the Royal Historical Society*, 6th series, 11: 37–63.

Stringer, F. A. (1910) *Oaths and Affirmations*, 3rd edn. London: Stevens & Sons.

Thomas, K. (1971) *Religion and the Decline of Magic*. London: Wiedenfeld and Nicolson.

Tye, L. (1998) *The Father of Spin: Edward L. Bernays and the Birth of Public Relations*. New York: Crown.

36

The Book as Art

Megan L. Benton

It has covers that open and pages that turn. It appears to be made mostly of paper, and there are words, if not exactly sentences, on many of the pages. But other pages are collaged with bits of old photographs, candy wrappers, and snippets of dried flowers; tendrils of cords and ribbons tumble from the spine; fanciful projectiles bounce from folded springs when a page is turned; and the whole thing fits snugly into an embroidered velvet pouch. Is it a book? Is it art? Is a book still a book when it conveys an artist's messages more than, or instead of, an author's?

In today's art galleries, museums, and libraries, it is not uncommon to come across these intriguing objects, known as *artists' books*, and to overhear those eagerly whispered, or sadly muttered, questions. Over the past century, and particularly since the 1960s, visual artists have embraced the book as a new medium, treating the page, the object, and the very concept of the book as a vehicle for artistic expression. Many book enthusiasts welcome this lively, often inventive, and provocative activity, believing that it has helped to re-energize interest in the physical book, especially in light of dire predictions of its eclipse by electronic successors. Others scoff, dismissing artists' books as merely art in the semblance of books' clothing, not "real" books at all.

Conflicting definitions of both *book* and *art* lurk at the heart of the debate. Some insist that a book is first and foremost a functional object, intended to convey an author's written text. They welcome books that do so in attractive or appealing ways, but only if such features do not disrupt or compete with that essential textual function. Others believe that a book can bloom into art when it is released from this traditional subservience, when its surfaces and structures reveal an artist's energies as much as or more than an author's. "Service to a text" is the sticking point: book purists rarely consider anything a book without it, while art purists tend to scorn anything that attends to it.

The difficulty stems from an old tension between two fundamental aspects of the nature of the book. The word *book* commonly refers both to the linguistic text that an author writes and to the physical object (or electronic presentation) that renders that text visible and so enables us to read it. To distinguish between these two related but neither interchangeable nor inextricable meanings, in this discussion the word *book* refers to the physical package – what we see, touch, and smell as we engage with it as a material object. The word *text* refers to the linguistic messages represented on its surfaces.

This distinction between *text* and *book* is generally clarified as one of content and form. But this is misleading because the material features of books have always been an essential part of their appeal and meaning, and in many instances they have awed, inspired, and moved readers as much as or more than their texts. Often the physical book is not merely a peripheral vehicle for textual content but is an essential element of what we perceive and interpret. Thus the book itself can be a meaningful work of art when its beauty, originality, or other striking or provocative qualities independently engage and affect readers.

This chapter is a selective historical overview (focusing on the Western world) of those books whose impact, significance, or meaning derives from their visual and physical features as much as or more than from their texts. In general, the less a book must accommodate focused, attentive reading, the more freely it may strive instead to engage us as art. Such books-as-art may even forgo conventional text altogether. Modern artists' books are clearly part of the story. But they are merely the latest development in a long tradition of books notable for the artistry of their visual elements or material form.

From the earliest forms of what we now call books, art has often been an integral part of their making. Before the fifteenth century, the power and significance of books commonly rested as much in their tactile and visual qualities as in their texts. They often held great iconic significance, in part because they were rare and costly objects, and because the ability to read their texts was even rarer. Particularly when the texts were sacred or religious in nature, as most were, those fortunate enough to see books at all often simply viewed them, perceiving them as precious objects imbued with the mysterious, sacred qualities of their texts. At times, the scribes and artists who created the pages lavished them with an extravagance of color, gilt, design, and imagery that awed and humbled those who beheld them. Such books were primarily visual objects, crafted into virtual icons of the abstract texts they bore.

By the twelfth and thirteenth centuries, books began to serve more secular purposes. While still largely sacred objects, they increasingly became the prized property of fortunate individuals, not just of religious communities, signaling the wealth, power, and piety of their owner as well as the exalted status of their texts. Among the best examples of this late medieval infusion of visual beauty and power into bookmaking are the personal devotional aids known as Books of Hours. Because they were usually made to order, Books of Hours sometimes incorporated remarkably revealing visual information about the person for whom the book was commissioned. The owner might be discreetly depicted worshiping a patron saint, for example, or witnessing a familiar biblical scene. In this way, medieval Books of Hours are early ancestors of contemporary one-of-a-kind artists' books that also embed uniquely personal content within the more public.

The fifteenth century marked a major turning point in the history of books as art, involving three related factors. First, the visual and aesthetic character of the page changed, slowly at first and then dramatically, as the new printing process pioneered by Johann Gutenberg replaced unique, hand-produced pages with more or less identical, mechanically rendered multiples. Secondly, growing humanist interests in science, philosophy, law, literature, and other secular knowledge, coupled with the increasing accessibility of books spurred by printing, stimulated the spread of literacy, though it was still limited to a small portion of the population. Thirdly, Renaissance societies came to view art as the expressive achievement of a creative individual, breaking from the medieval belief that the artist was merely an anonymous craftsman. Together, these developments shifted the predominant nature of books from visual to textual.

In the following centuries, the primacy of the text grew so pronounced that images, decoration, and other aesthetic enhancements were often scorned, for a variety of reasons that remain potent to this day. Some considered them simply superfluous, "visual aids" no longer needed and even somewhat demeaning when readers could actually read the texts. Bolstered by the new Protestant emphasis on personal Bible reading, others regarded images warily as rivals for readers' attention, distracting them or (worse) contradicting, distorting, or oversimplifying the text's message. Still others appreciated the value of occasionally illustrating or adorning a book, but balked at considering that work as art, since such embellishments were clearly subordinate to the book's text.

Despite this new resistance to art in books, there continued to be books made with exquisite artistry, although their numbers were dwarfed by the great majority of books produced with an emphasis on economy, efficiency, and utility. Books-as-art can be divided into two categories: those that feature notable artistry in their making, and those with exemplary artwork on their pages.

As the first printed books began to make their way into readers' hands, many were skeptical that they could match the beauty of manuscript books. What was gained in economy and quantity was lost, they lamented, in visual quality. Many of these fears were reasonable: the need to produce books quickly and relatively cheaply (pressures stemming from the printers' precarious finances as well as from growing market demands) quickly forced several compromises in the printers' original aims to recreate the look of manuscript books as closely as possible.

Most immediately striking was the loss of color. Because each color had to be printed separately, to replicate the traditional red and blue initials and other colorful features of manuscript pages would have dramatically multiplied production costs. The earliest printers simply printed the text and left blank spaces where the color initials would go, intending to subcontract a scribe or artist to complete the pages, just as he would have completed a manuscript page. Very shortly, however, printers dispensed with this cumbersome (and often never completed) practice, instead hiring engravers to cut relief wood blocks of the decorative initials, which could be inked and printed in black ink like type. Yet much was gained as well as lost with this shift. While manuscripts had usually been decorated on only a small number of pages, printers could use woodcuts to print intricate borders, initials, and illustrations on virtually any page – or all pages – because, like type, woodcuts could be used repeatedly. In fact, many early modern editions seem profligate in their use of woodcut images, even reusing the same cut to illustrate different subjects. One German printer, Conrad Dinckmut of Ulm, repeated a full-page depiction of "torments of the damned" more than thirty times in a profusely illustrated edition of the *Seelenwurzgarten*.

As it quickly became apparent that printing could only approximate, not truly replicate, the centuries-old bookmaking handcrafts of calligraphy and illumination, a new aesthetic of bookmaking emerged, based on the new skills required for printing: type design, typography, and woodcut or engraved imagery and decoration. At the same time, Renaissance sensibilities drove bookmaking aesthetic values in new directions. Printing had originated in Germany, where the medieval letterforms known generically as blackletter prevailed. By the 1460s, printers in Italy, eager to publish new classical and humanist texts but loath to present them in these Gothic forms tainted with "barbaric" medieval associations, pioneered new types based on the letterforms of classical Rome and the eighth-century reign of Charlemagne, and hence called *roman*. A Frenchman living in Venice, Nicholas Jenson, is usually credited with producing the first enduringly fine roman types, which he premiered in 1470 to wide acclaim. Accompanied from about 1500 by a cursive Renaissance letterform called *italic*, roman type soon became the new foundation for typographic beauty in Italy and much of Europe.

The foremost typographic master of the Renaissance was the Venetian printer Aldus Manutius. The elegance, clarity, and refinement of his roman and italic types and his typographic layout demonstrate that, within the first half-century after Gutenberg, the book had already achieved a new, essentially modern look, deemed particularly appropriate for humanist and classical texts. Although Aldus is primarily remembered for the intelligent dignity and beauty of serious works of scholarship, his most famous work is anomalous, an illustrated work of fiction: his 1499 edition of *Hypnerotomachia Poliphili* (the love-dream of Poliphilus), often touted as the most beautiful book ever printed (figure 36.1). It features the stately roman types of Francesco Griffo, sculptural arrangements of type columns, sometimes tapering to a V-shape, and liberal yet judicious use of type ornaments or fleurons (printers' flowers). The book is also generously illustrated by an unnamed artist with 170 woodcuts rich with both narrative content and classical ornament.

In the sixteenth century, the greatest achievements in bookmaking artistry came from France, where Geoffrey Tory and Claude Garamond designed graceful new Renaissance types. Premier publishers Simon de Colines and the Estienne family similarly continued and refined Aldus' pursuit of a typographic ideal grounded in the pure beauty of type and careful symmetry, proportion, and balance in the arrangement of the printed page. As in other matters of culture and the arts, the French, and to a lesser degree the Dutch, dominated European book artistry in the seventeenth and early eighteenth

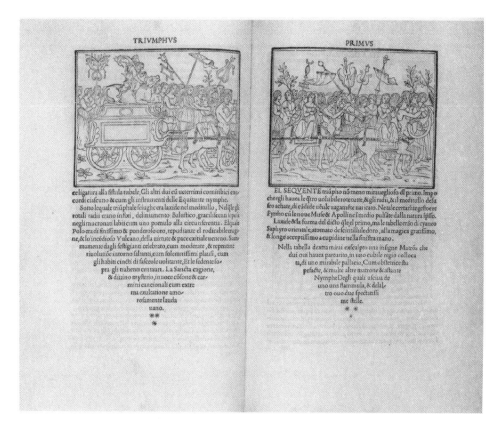

Figure 36.1   Francesco Colonna, *Hypnerotomachia Poliphili* (Venice: Aldus Manutius, 1499).

centuries. Baroque books, however, featured opulent title pages engraved in copperplate and were dense with exquisitely detailed ornamental imagery and ornate calligraphic lettering. They were followed by a lighter, more delicate rococo style in both type design and ornamentation. In the 1760s, Pierre-Simon Fournier's elegant types, fleurons, and decorative borders epitomized the highly cultivated aesthetic values of the era (figure 36.2). Between 1745 and 1772 the French book reached what many regard as its zenith with the appearance of *L'Encyclopédie*, the crowning achievement of Enlightenment scholarship and thought. It was equally impressive as a visual masterpiece: eleven of its twenty-eight folio volumes were devoted to nearly three thousand scrupulously detailed engraved illustrations, comprising an unsurpassed portrait of eighteenth-century life, especially its technology.

The first major English printers to influence Western typographic art emerged in the eighteenth century. Following William Caslon's sturdy, almost rustic type designs of the 1730s, maverick William Baskerville offered new roman and italic types that were precise and statuesque, and pages that dazzled contemporaries' eyes with radiant space around and between letters, as if the paper were a pedestal for the type alone.

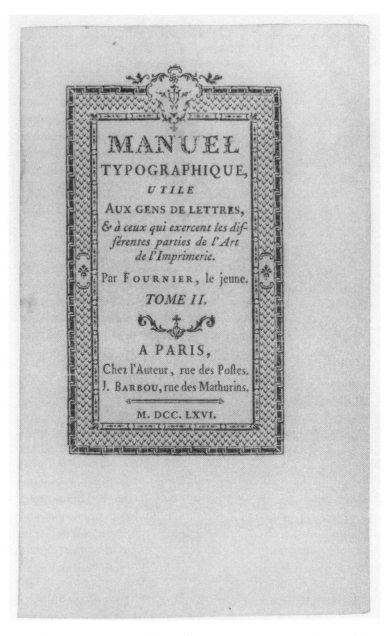

Figure 36.2   Pierre-Simon Fournier, *Manuel typographique* (Paris: Joseph Gérard Barbou, 1766).

Although too extreme for many English book connoisseurs of his own day (his editions took years to sell), Baskerville's work helped inspire the most influential design figure of the late eighteenth and early nineteenth centuries, Giambattista Bodoni of Parma. In the cool precision of his austere, supremely formal types and typography, Bodoni blended a neoclassical aristocratic arrogance with the promise and power of the dawning industrial age.

As the nineteenth century progressed, however, the bookmaking trades were swept up in the great industrial transformations of the era, particularly when steam power was harnessed to replace human labor in both papermaking and printing. The new Fourdrinier machine replaced handmade sheets of rag-based paper with far more plentiful and less costly rolls of paper made from wood pulp, while new steam-powered printing presses yielded thousands of pages per hour, far more than the two to three hundred sheets skilled printers could produce in an hour using a traditional hand press (whose design had changed little from Gutenberg's day).

Just as fifteenth-century technology had altered the aesthetics of bookmaking as well as its economics, so in the nineteenth century the new plenitude of books and other printed matter was accompanied by a marked change in their look and feel. Machine-made papers were often distinctly less durable and crisp than handmade sheets, and they lacked the latter's telltale fine irregularities and feathery deckle edges. Machine-printed books were printed from types whose letterforms had been slightly compressed to better endure the stress of the high-speed action and with inks thinned to enable the presses to run more smoothly. Moreover, new mechanical engraving technologies could achieve the elaborate, ornate typography and ornamentation that delighted Victorian book enthusiasts.

Near the end of the century, however, in the wake of the Arts and Crafts Movement in England, the nearly dormant handcrafts of bookmaking experienced a dramatic revival. Led by writer, artist, and social visionary William Morris and his private Kelmscott Press, a small but influential group of printers and publishers rekindled interest in and appreciation for preindustrial bookmaking aesthetics and techniques, which in their modern guise soon became known as *fine printing*. Morris and others vigorously denounced machine-made books as anemic and sterile, both for their typically pale, grayish texts and for the capitulation of human skill and judgment to mechanical expedience. Paying zealous attention to details of design and handcraft, the early private presses (private in that they were governed by personal values rather than commercial considerations) demonstrated the forms that they believed the "ideal book" should aspire to, turning to models from earlier golden eras of typographic mastery. The Kelmscott Press evoked the robust and decorative late medieval German style (figure 36.3), while the Ashendene and Doves presses preferred the more pristine beauty of Italian Renaissance typography. These and other influential private presses sparked an eager resurrection of historic typefaces and preindustrial design values that resonate throughout most of the great fine-printing achievements of the early twentieth century. The American master of so-called "allusive" typography, Bruce Rogers, designed books that recreated the style and spirit of earlier eras, from the Renaissance through the eighteenth century.

Turn-of-the-century artists and writers on the continent also rebelled against sterility and complacency in Victorian book design; however, they sought inspiration not from the past but from the swiftly changing political, economic, and industrial conditions

Figure 36.3   Geoffrey Chaucer, *Works* (London: Kelmscott Press, 1896). Designed and decorated by William Morris, with illustrations by Edward Burne-Jones.

of the new century. Avant-garde artists in France, Italy, Germany, and Russia linked to the Dada and Futurist movements in modern art, including Filippo Marinetti and Wassily Kandinsky, boldly championed a new aesthetic based on the streamlined precision, universality, and elemental starkness of modern technology, rejecting traditional notions of beauty as decadent and frivolous. In 1928, a young Jan Tschichold at Germany's Bauhaus school of design articulated the call for a modernist "new typography," advocating sans serif types, asymmetrical layouts, and abstract geometric visual elements for dynamic coherence. While modernist principles have profoundly influenced worldwide graphic design – governing magazine and advertising typography, signage, and other public and commercial forms of print – historicized traditional values remain predominant in most Western book typography. Tschichold himself later renounced his strident modernist stance: his redesign of the Penguin paperback in the late 1940s remains a paragon of twentieth-century traditional book typography.

Finally, bindings have long represented a particular vein of bookmaking artistry. For centuries, most books were sold unbound, their pages typically folded and gathered into temporary wrappers; purchasers hired bookbinders to house them in permanent covers, providing an opportunity to embellish a treasured book with ornamental patterns stamped into the leather and even embedded with precious metals and jewels. Legendary sixteenth-century French bibliophile Jean Grolier was one of the first to focus particular attention on bindings: he commissioned spectacular works executed with intricate designs, often in gold or silver. In the nineteenth century, as publishers began selling most books bound in machine-made covers, unique "designer" bookbinding emerged as an independent modern art form, commissioned by wealthy collectors and institutions for their most elite copies of valued books. Modern designer binders like Paul Bonet, Philip Smith, and Angela James have elevated the craft into a rarefied art form, creating bindings of fine leathers and precious materials composed in interpretive designs inspired by the book's content but expressing the binder's own creative vision.

From the earliest efforts to endow the pages with beauty and power, bookmakers often included images. Ancient Egyptians were among the first to add friezes of imagery to their books, typically a swathe of stylized human and animal figures poised above or beneath the columns of text spread across the scroll. A few scrolls feature images interjected into the text area, remarkably prefiguring modern page design that integrates text and imagery.

Medieval manuscript books were also frequently adorned with images. Added by artists after scribes had copied the text, historiated initials (for example) depicted figures or scenes within large and often elaborate capital letters. Images incorporated into decorative borders and embellishments surrounding the text brought visual messages of their own, sometimes at odds with the messages of the texts, often including human figures or fantastical creatures performing familiar activities or cavorting in outlandish behaviors. These images, part of a widely recognized symbolic vocabulary, were often more "read" than the formal Latin text.

This imagery was considered part of the larger didactic or embellishment scheme, rather than illustration in the modern sense. Even miniatures, or original small paintings included in the most extravagant of medieval manuscript books, were intended more to add beauty to the book than to provide an artist's particular interpretation of the text. Depicting not only biblical or religious scenes but also secular subjects, including landscapes, historical events, daily life, and portraits of the book's owner, miniatures were commonly included in lavish copies of Books of Hours produced for European nobles.

As discussed earlier, the nature of art in books evolved dramatically with the Renaissance and the advent of printing. On one hand, images in printed books lost much of the prestige that was accorded the artwork in manuscripts. As Walter Benjamin would famously put it nearly five hundred years later, art reproduced in multiples from woodcuts lacked the "aura" that animated original art direct from the hand of the artist (Benjamin 1969). On the other hand, print enabled a veritable explosion in the sheer number and variety of images, and gradually but significantly expanded the presence of images and art for all readers, not merely the wealthiest few.

Moreover, as humanism placed new value on the capacity of the human imagination, intellect, and talent, artists began to participate more centrally in the making of books. Although many books included some form of visual imagery on their pages, in only a few did the caliber and prominence of that imagery rise to a noteworthy level. An early example is the 1486 edition of *Peregrinations in montem Syon* (Travels in Mount Syon) printed in Mainz and illustrated with woodcuts by Erhard Reuwich. Norma Levarie credits Reuwich's work as the first to have "a truly modern spirit" (1968: 103). The woodcuts accurately depicted the contemporary natural world (Reuwich traveled with the author in order to illustrate the geography, architecture, and peoples of the lands visited) and, more importantly, the edition boldly featured Reuwich's art in its own right. For the first time, the artist was named in the edition, and the images were printed on a generous scale, including some as foldouts, extending as much as five feet.

Albrecht Dürer was among the first book illustrators also to enjoy an undisputed reputation as a major artist. At times, his work so dominated the edition that the text seemed merely an excuse for producing the art, provoking the tension between text and image that continues to trouble text-centered sensibilities today. Other sixteenth-century artists of major stature who also illustrated books include Hans Holbein, working in Basel and Lyon, and Lucas Cranach and his son Hans in Germany. They brought to books the same expressive and interpretive talents that made their paintings and other work so prized, helping to elevate the status of illustration as an art form in its own right.

In the following centuries, a few major artists similarly illustrated books as part of their repertoire. In the 1630s, Frenchman Jacques Collot was one of the first to debut the new technique of etching, exploiting its capacity to render sketch-like lines and subtle shading. When lithography was developed nearly two centuries later, Eugène Delacroix was among the first to exploit its rich, continuous-tone qualities in illustrations for an 1828 edition of Goethe's *Faust*. The prolific, romantic Gustave Doré soon followed, illustrating many editions of literary classics with dramatic wood engravings, often dark and brooding.

Particularly in France, the practice of pairing fine art illustrations with literary texts reached a grand and costly scale in the late nineteenth century. Yet a restless dissatisfaction began to stir in some quarters, especially in light of the English fine-printing revival of preindustrial bookmaking aesthetics discussed earlier. Some chafed at the usual practice of inserting plates of illustrations at intervals throughout the text (since they were printed separately, using different processes), so that text and illustration were rarely designed to work together in any meaningful way. By contrast, fine printers preached close integration of the textual and visual aspects of bookmaking, urging balance and coherence across facing pages.

In 1900, Ambroise Vollard gave those principles a distinctly French flavor when he published Paul Verlaine's *Parallèlement* with lithographs by Pierre Bonnard. This landmark work launched a new genre, the *livre d'artiste*, in which imagery was deemed as important a factor in a book's design as its text. Softly rendered and printed in pale inks, Bonnard's illustrations settled comfortably across facing pages, surrounding the elegantly simple italic poems. Visually inseparable, image and text were perfectly married. Supported mainly by elite clubs of wealthy bibliophiles, the *livre d'artiste* flourished in the early decades of the twentieth century. An all-star array of modern artists participated, including Picasso, Chagall, Matisse, Maillol, and Dufy, and the books that resulted are now often as rare and valued as their other works.

Although initially more focused on type and typography, the Anglo-American fine-printing movement soon showcased masterful illustration as well. In keeping with its revivalist spirit, most artists returned to woodcuts and wood engravings, the earliest techniques of printing images. Artists such as Rockwell Kent in the United States and Eric Gill, Blair Hughes-Stanton, and Claire Leighton in Britain produced exquisite illustrations for finely printed, deluxe limited editions. Less well-known artists in other countries offered equally fine but more accessible examples of the wood-engraving renaissance: Denmark's Jane Muus and Povl Christensen, for instance, illustrated several moderately priced editions of Danish literary works throughout the 1940s and 1950s (figure 36.4).

The practice of producing handsome editions that pair important literary texts and original artwork by leading contemporary artists has continued, albeit usually for well-heeled collectors. Andrew Hoyem's Arion Press in San Francisco has published such major works as the King James's Version of *The Apocalypse*, with woodcuts by Jim Dine (1982), and James Joyce's *Ulysses*, illustrated by Robert Motherwell (1988).

These examples all feature art that is explicitly paired with, while not strictly subordinated to, a literary text by a printer or publisher. Beginning with the extraordinary work of William Blake in the late eighteenth and early nineteenth centuries, artists themselves have turned to the book as a medium in which they could fuse visual, linguistic, and formal elements into their own coherent artistic vision. Blake's achievement was so original and all-encompassing that it nearly defies description. A skillful engraver by trade, Blake modified the process to produce copies of his own poems and illustrations. He developed a mysterious, hybrid printmaking process which he called relief etching, rendering plates from which he could print an entire page, both drawn images and handwritten text. After printing each plate in a small edition, Blake and his wife water-colored and assembled the sheets into books, one at a time by hand, as prospects of a buyer occurred. Because he controlled every aspect of the book's creation, from concept to execution, each unique book fairly bursts with artistic "aura."

Few subsequent artists have replicated Blake's feat of personally producing every element of the book, from text to images to completed final pages, but he has inspired many to undertake a much broader role than illustrators have traditionally played. In the early decades of the twentieth century, for example, François-Louis Schmied designed, illustrated, and supervised the elaborate production of several deluxe editions. The stunning decorative detail, rich colors, and sensual subject matter of his *pochoir* (stencil) illustrations, integrated through the books with Schmied's own ornaments and borders and deft typography, make his works landmark examples of the lavish art deco book in France. Even more pervasive was Henri Matisse's hand in the production of *Jazz* in

Herre«. Jo høiere de fløi med Speilet, des stærkere gri-
nede det, de kunde neppe holde fast paa det; høiere og
høiere fløi de, nærmere Gud og Englene; da zittrede Speilet saa frygteligt i sit Griin, at det foer dem ud af Hæn-
derne og styrtede ned mod Jorden, hvor det gik i hundrede
Millioner, Billioner og endnu flere Stykker, og da just
gjorde det megen større Ulykke end før; thi nogle Styk-

6

Figure 36.4   H. C. Andersen, *Sneedronningen* [*The Ice Queen*] (Copenhagen: Nordlundes Bogtrykkeri, 1959).
Designed by C. Volmer Nordlunde, with illustrations by Jane Muus.

1947. Matisse wrote the text to "interrupt" his colorful paper-cut images, reproduced
with stencils, and the text is printed from Matisse's own calligraphy. American wood
engraver Barry Moser offers a notable contemporary example: under his Pennyroyal
Press imprint, Moser has published editions of such literary classics as *Alice's Adventures
in Wonderland* (1982) and *Frankenstein* (1984), accompanied by his haunting and powerful illustrations. To the delight of thousands of book lovers, several of Moser's productions have been reproduced in affordable trade facsimile editions.

While much of the most prestigious art in books has been reserved for costly deluxe
editions, modern trade publishing also offers notable examples of books whose power
derives from art as much as or more than from text. In the 1920s and 1930s, Belgian
Franz Masereel and American Lynd Ward produced the first so-called woodcut novels,

which are entirely image-based. Through a series of 139 dramatic woodcuts without captions or narrative text, Ward's most famous work, *God's Man* (1929), tells the poignant tale of a young artist's tragic encounters with modern urban corruption. More recent examples include graphic novels such as the 1986 trade book *Maus: A Survivor's Tale*, in which Art Speigelman used the comic strip narrative model to express his father's Holocaust experience. Similarly adapting image-narrative techniques associated with children's books, Canadian writer–artist Nick Bantock created visually saturated pages and interactive reading for his novel about the mysterious relationship between *Griffin and Sabine* (1991): the texts are read through a series of exchanged postcards and letters, printed separately and inserted in envelopes on the book's pages.

As these two contemporary examples suggest, modern children's books have generally been much more visually imaginative and innovative than books for adults. Beatrix Potter and Kate Greenaway produced stories told as memorably through their illustrations as through their prose. In the twentieth century, several artists have sustained and deepened this mode of complete integration: Maurice Sendak, Chris Van Alsberg, and David Weisner immerse readers in compelling visual environments that adults often find as irresistible as children do.

The strongest evidence of an increasingly visual aesthetic in modern bookmaking is the burgeoning interest in artists' books. Although definitions are slippery and inevitably contested, Johanna Drucker, a leading critic as well as a practitioner of the genre, distinguishes an artist's book from its cousins the illustrated book and the *livre d'artiste* by its provocative challenge of our preconceptions, by the ways in which it "interrogates the conceptual or material form of the book as part of its intention, thematic interests, or production activities" (1995: 3). In *The Century of Artists' Books*, Drucker usefully surveys a broad spectrum of works functioning as an "auratic object," a "democratic multiple," and an "agent of social change."

As those categories suggest, an artist's book may be a one-of-a-kind construction, perhaps featuring original drawings or paintings and commanding a lofty price, or it could be an inexpensive photocopied pamphlet reproduced by the hundreds and distributed for little or no charge. Both extremes testify to the range of artists' attractions to the book form in the twentieth century. Some see it as an affordable means of extending art beyond the galleries and into everyday lives, often carrying powerful political and social messages. Others see the book as a supremely multilayered medium, combining opportunities for simultaneous literary, visual, sculptural, kinetic, and sequential expression. For all book artists, however, the book itself, as a whole, comprises its identity as art; each element – text (if any), imagery (if any), form, and structure – contributes to the work's meaning.

Among the first artists heralded for adopting the book as a vehicle for art was American Ed Ruscha, whose 1962 *Twenty-six Gasoline Stations* is often placed at the forefront of the new movement. The book consists of twenty-six black-and-white photographs of gasoline stations, in all their stark banality. Unlike a trade art book that features reproductions of works actually in galleries or private collections, Ruscha's book itself – its selection, sequence, and presentation of images – is the work of art.

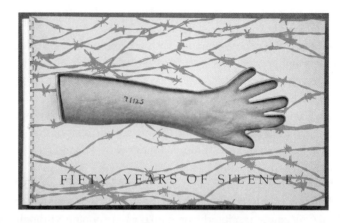

Figure 36.5   Tatana Kellner, *71125: Fifty Years of Silence* (Rosendale: Women's Studio Workshop, 1992). Designed, illustrated, and produced by Tatana Kellner.

Also in the 1960s, British artist Tom Phillips began work on another ground-breaking, highly influential artist's book, *A Humument*. By painting over large portions of the pages of the 1892 novel *A Human Document*, leaving legible only a few phrases, words, or parts of words, Phillips foregrounded a disruptive, partial, and hence "new" text embedded in fully visual fields rather than displayed in conventional blocks of print surrounded by white margins. This technique of creating "altered books" has opened up a popular and provocative new field of activity, blending at times with the interest in affixing images, texts, and objects to existing pages, scrapbook-style, in order to create a unique book expressing the subjective vision of the artist.

Artists' books offer a particularly rich venue for highly personal content; many of the most moving works are in this vein. For example, Tatana Kellner's *71125: Fifty Years of Silence* (1992) tells the story, through text printed over and wrapped around images, of her mother's reluctance or inability to speak of her experiences in a German concentration camp (figure 36.5). Each wide page is die-cut to fit around a life-size cast of a woman's forearm, stamped with a number, protruding from the book's back through its front cover. As a reader moves through the book, the arm remains as a fixed, three-dimensional presence embedded within each recto page, while each verso page is dominated by the arm-shaped hole in its center. As with all successful artists' books, one reads the material object as much as the text printed on its pages.

Other artists explore the book as a purely visual, kinetic, and sculptural medium. These books' meanings reside fully in their materials, forms, and action. Among the most famous examples is Keith Smith's *Book No. 91* (1982), commonly known as his String Book because it consists of series of strings woven through small holes in the thick paper pages of a traditional codex. The strings intersect, drape, and pull as the pages are turned, producing changing patterns of sliding sound and spokes of shadow, animating the work's tension and slippage. Fascinated with books' structural possibilities, Smith has explored dozens of historically and ethnically diverse binding styles and invented as many more. Through his prolific work, incorporating accordion folds, scrolls, containers, fans, codexes, and more, he has demonstrated the myriad ways in which form and material alone can invite thoughtful encounters.

The most important intent of this brief survey is to suggest the great scope of art in books. While only a small number of books might register as works of art *per se*, in a larger sense all books are intrinsically visual and sculptural objects, no matter how much those qualities are obscured by convention and familiarity. As we become more aware of the rich, aesthetic powers of the book itself, beyond those of its text, our experiences as readers can only grow more full and meaningful.

REFERENCES AND FURTHER READING

Benjamin, Walter (1969) "The Work of Art in the Age of Mechanical Reproduction." In *Illuminations*, ed. Hannah Arendt, trans. Harry Zohn, pp. 217–51. New York: Schocken.

Bettley, James (ed.) (2001) *The Art of the Book: From Medieval Manuscript to Graphic Novel*. London: V&A.

Bland, David (1969) *A History of Book Illustration: The Illuminated Manuscript and the Printed Book*, 2nd edn. Berkeley: University of California Press.

Camille, Michael (1992) *Image on the Edge: The Margins of Medieval Art*. Cambridge, MA: Harvard University Press.

Drucker, Johanna (1995) *The Century of Artists' Books*. New York: Granary.

de Hamel, Christopher (1994) *A History of Illuminated Manuscripts*. London: Phaidon.

Harthan, John P. (1981) *The History of the Illustrated Book: The Western Tradition*. London: Thames & Hudson.

Hogben, Carol and Watson, Rowan (eds.) (1985) *From Manet to Hockney: Modern Artists' Illustrated Books*. London: V&A.

Katz, Bill (ed.) (1994) *A History of Book Illustration: 29 Points of View*. Metuchen, NJ: Scarecrow.

Levarie, Norma (1968) *The Art and History of Books*. New York: Heinemann.

Lewis, John (1984) *The Twentieth-century Book: Its Illustration and Design*, 2nd edn. New York: Van Nostrand Reinhold.

Lewis, Roy Harley (1984) *Fine Bookbinding in the Twentieth Century*. London: David & Charles.

Viscomi, Joseph (1993) *Blake and the Idea of the Book*. Princeton: Princeton University Press.

Whalley, Joyce Irene and Chester, Tessa Rose (1988) *A History of Children's Book Illustration*. London: John Murray.

37

Obscenity, Censorship, and Modernity

Deana Heath

> This anonymous cove at the Customs,
> This storehouse for horrible stuff
> Is as venal, I'll bet
> As the rest of us, yet
> Does he whine that his job is too tough?
> No. He keeps his identity secret,
> His knowledge safe under his hat;
> And he lurks all alone
> Unsuspected, unknown
> Such as hangmen and heroes like that.
>
> ("Den," 1935)

Much like this Australian poet, we tend to regard censors (if we view censorship as more than a disembodied and anonymous process) in a derogatory light – as, at the very least, hacks who snuff out human creativity. The censor is generally typed as, first and foremost, ignorant, such as the police sergeant in charge of the 1948 New South Wales prosecution for obscenity against Lawson Glassop's *We Were the Rats* (1944), who claimed that "he didn't read very much, he hadn't heard of Byron" (nor, for that matter, of Chaucer, *Don Juan*, or *Lady Chatterley's Lover*), and who believed that the term "pornographic" meant "poor class or poor quality" (*The Sun* 1948). Given that Australia's wartime censors included individuals who had previously held such unliterary positions as grazer, pearl diver, and chemist, it should come as little surprise that they were not greatly respected (Pullan 1984: 147). Australians had, in fact, coined a term, "wowsers," to describe such regulators, or indeed any individual who seeks to "devote himself zealously to reforming the morals of his neighbours, and, in particular, to throwing obstacles in the way of their enjoyment of what they choose to regard as pleasures" (Dunstan 1972: 2). "Wowsers," according to Keith Dunstan, first appeared *en masse* in the 1880s (a product of the nonconformist, particularly Methodist, churches), and were thereafter behind the regulation of practically every form of public (and often private) behavior in Australia until the 1960s.

Every society undoubtedly has its version of the "wowser," but to make censorship the provenance of puritanical prudes is to mitigate the nature, meaning, and effects of censorship. It is, in fact, to fall prey to what Michel Foucault has termed the "repressive hypothesis," in which censorship is generally defined as "the repressive intervention of authority," and is traced most notably through the operations of law (Foucault 1990: 5). Thus, to take the example of the censorship of obscenity in Britain, according to proponents of the repressive hypothesis this emerged in conjunction with the suppression of sexuality beginning in the seventeenth century. Although the explanations for the origins of such repression vary (from socio-religious factors, such as the decline of medieval ecclesiastical jurisdiction over moral offences and the state inheritance of such jurisdiction, to economic shifts, such as the development of capitalism and the perceived incompatibility of sexuality with an intensive work imperative), most advocates of the repressive hypothesis concur that censorship remained relatively "liberal" until the passage of the portentous Obscene Publications Act of 1857. Following this, the dark days of prudery, hysteria, and repression purportedly set in, as exemplified by a series of censorship trials, such as the landmark *Queen* v. *Hicklin* in 1868, and the initiation of prosecutions against "serious" scientific and literary works with the trial of Henry Bradlaugh and Annie Besant in 1877 for republishing Henry Knowleton's *The Fruits of Philosophy*, and Henry Vizetelly in 1888 for publishing translations of Emile Zola's novels.

The late nineteenth century is a crucial period for advocates of the repressive hypothesis, for, as Norman St. John-Stevas claims, this was the period "when the Victorian synthesis was breaking down and when Forster's Education Act had created a vast new reading public" (1956: xix), a factor that instituted what many commentators on British censorship regard as a "moral panic." Once the stable door had opened on the prosecution of types of literature that had never been censored before, the horse supposedly bolted, particularly following the "banning" of D. H. Lawrence's *The Rainbow* in 1915, and the censorship of a spate of "literary" works in the 1920s such as *Ulysses* in 1923, *The Well of Loneliness* in 1928, and *Pansies, Lady Chatterley's Lover*, and *The Sleeveless Errand* in 1929. The dark days of prudery continued, the theory concludes, until the "age of enlightenment" in the 1960s, following which (barring some minor aberrations) freedom of speech reigned (see, for example, Siebert 1965; Thomas 1969; Tribe 1973; Sutherland 1982; Davenport-Hines 1990).

In this approach, censorship is inseparable from law and, as such, its "severity" or "pervasiveness" is charted through a series of "show trials" that are made to stand in for all forms of censorship activity. Such show trials were, however, few and far between in Britain, the types of work they sought to censor shifted over time, and the trials were grounded in particular historical circumstances that render it problematic to throw them all together to form a coherent history of censorship (Saunders 1992). The regulation of obscenity in Britain has not, in short, been a unified historical project: not only did the objectives and the specific targets of censorship change over time, but so did the means of censoring and the particular agents involved in carrying these out. Censorship cannot, therefore, be reduced purely to prohibition or equated simply with silencing.

What, then, is censorship, and how does it work? During the past two decades a substantial body of scholarship has emerged, inspired in part by Foucault, that challenges the "repressive hypothesis." According to Foucault:

> What sustains our eagerness to speak of sex in terms of repression is doubtless this opportunity to speak out against the powers that be, to utter truths and promise bliss, to link together enlightenment, liberation, and manifold pleasures; to pronounce a discourse that combines the fervor of knowledge, the determination to change the laws, and the longing for the garden of earthly delights. (Foucault 1990: 7).

Instead of repression, Foucault argues that what occurred in Western European culture at the end of the sixteenth century was a discursive explosion (deriving from the confessional during the course of the Counter-Reformation) about sex. By the eighteenth century, sex had become a "police matter," part of the emergence of "population" as an economic and political problem, and with it the need to monitor sexual behavior, birth rates, legitimate versus illegitimate births, and the physical and psychological effects of contraception. While an expurgation of the authorized vocabulary did occur, and new relations of discretion were formed between such social groups as parents and children and teachers and students (what Foucault refers to as a "restrictive economy"), at the level of discourse there was an incitement to speak about sex. Instead of one discourse about sex, however, what instead emerged were multiple discourses, both "institutional" (through disciplines such as medicine, psychiatry, criminal justice, and demography) and social (through a variety of social controls that emerged in the later nineteenth century). Thus, "[r]ather than a massive censorship, beginning with the verbal proprieties imported by the Age of Reason, what was involved [in the regulation of sexuality] was a regulated and polymorphous incitement to discourse" (Foucault 1990: 34).

For Foucault and his followers, censorship is therefore productive rather than (or rather than purely) repressive. It is also "*distributive* rather than repressive," since acts of restriction are not uniform in their application; they instead hinge upon access (Hunter et al. 1993: 52). Thus, terms like *obscenity* and *indecency* are socially determined concepts that, as far as those responsible for regulating them are concerned, change according to who is reading or viewing the work in question, and when and where they are doing so. We can see such thinking at work in the first British case to criminalize obscenity (and thus remove it from the purview of the church courts), the 1757 trial of Edmund Curll for publishing an obscene libel in the form of *Venus in the Cloister; or, The Nun in her Smock*. But, as Colin Manchester reveals, "the court was not concerned with penalizing obscenity in literature as *obscenity*," but with "obscenity's relationship with two other factors, religion and breach of the peace" (1991: 41). The obscenity in question threatened to breach the peace because of the widely disseminable format in which it was purveyed, namely in a printed work (Saunders 1990: 437). Obscenity law thus first emerged "in a complex technical environment formed by the overlap of a new governmental distinction between public and private spheres and the spread of a specific cultural technology and competence" (Hunter et al. 1993: 51).

Determining the "competence" of particular individuals or social groups to partake of the "cultural technology" of the printed word was a question not simply of gender, class, or age but also of practices of reading. That is, different groups were conceived of as being endangered by a variety of texts at different times based on notions of how the group in question was perceived to read or "utilize" such texts – what Ian Hunter, David Saunders, and Dugald Williamson refer to as the notion of "variable obscenity" (1993: 10). Such a notion was laid down in Britain in what became the "classic" test of obscenity, Lord Chief Justice Cockburn's 1868 ruling in *Queen* v. *Hicklin* that the obscenity of a given work was to be determined by "whether the tendency of the matter charged with as obscenity is to deprave and corrupt those whose minds are open to such immoral influences" (*The Law Reports: Court of Queen's Bench*, 1868) – namely, those deemed incapable of self-control, such as children, women, the working classes, and (since the judgment became the standard "test" of obscenity throughout the British empire) Britain's colonial subjects (Heath 2003). Hence it was common for inexpensive or translated editions of works to be censored but not expensive ones or those in their original languages.

While Foucauldian approaches to censorship have vastly enhanced our understanding of what censorship is and how it works, they have also complicated and problematized it in new ways. The chief difficulty lies in the way in which power has been conceptualized, for Foucauldian scholars have largely abandoned the focus on the legal constraints upon speech to focus on power itself as an object of study: how it is constituted, the intersections of resistance and domination through which it is exercised, and how discursive and disciplinary practices are enacted. Censorship has thus become viewed as a technique through which discursive practices are maintained; as Pierre Bourdieu argues, censorship is "constituted by the very structure of the field in which the discourse is produced and circulates" (1991: 137). In this reading, all discourse is a product of censorship, and hence censorship is the norm rather than the exception, since it is, quite literally, everywhere.

While such approaches to understanding censorship have offered important insights into its productive nature, its omnipresence poses a problem. As Frederick Schauer argues, "Once we acknowledge that our abilities to express and to communicate are so dependent on the actions of others . . . to continue to speak of some of those actions as censorship appears odd" (1998: 149). For Schauer, censorship is, in fact, "a conclusion masquerading as an analytic device," for why, he asks, do we characterize the words of Salman Rushdie as the target of censorship and the words of the Ayatollah Khomeini calling for a *fatwa* against Rushdie as censorship, even though words were the only things that he employed? Or why do we regard it as censorship when library boards seek to keep certain books out of libraries but not when librarians do (Schauer 1998: 160)? Seeing censorship as everywhere thus makes it impossible, Schauer implies, to distinguish between different types, means, and degrees of censorship: between, for example, the suppression of speech caused by state legal action, market forces, and dominant discourses, or between what we might refer to as "soft" forms of censorship (such as literary criticism or the ways in which pornography serves to "silence" women) and "hard" forms (such as imprisonment or death). These represent different mechanisms of silencing and different kinds of power, as well as different methods of constructing subjects. As Judith Butler has illustrated, "implicit" forms of censorship (namely "operations of power that rule out in unspoken ways what will remain unspeakable") may not only be more effective than "explicit" forms, such as state policy, in making certain kinds of speech unspeakable (particularly since the latter tend to proliferate the very terms that they seek to suppress), they also "make certain kinds of citizens possible and others impossible" (Butler 1998: 250, 257).

It is thus necessary to mediate between "juridical" regulation (in which power limits and constrains the object on which it operates) and "productive" regulation (in which power contributes to making the object that it also constrains), between "liberal" approaches to the study of censorship (in which censorship is viewed as the suppression of individual liberty by the state) and what Debora Shuger (1998: 89) refers to as "multicultural" approaches (in which censorship is regarded as the intimidation of marginalized groups by the dominant culture). We should preserve, in other words, the analytic force of the new scholarship without sacrificing the values and concerns of more traditional accounts. It is also necessary to broaden our historical understanding of how censorship works: to explore, for example, what particular criteria rendered certain works in need of censorship; how terms such as "blasphemy" and "obscenity" were constituted over time and in different places, and why such concepts were deemed to be such a problem in the first place and to whom; and how ideas of the "blasphemous" or "obscene" were disseminated and transformed to become part of different regulatory projects. Dozens of nations, for example, signed the 1923 International Treaty for the Suppression of the Circulation of and the Traffic in Obscene Publications, but this does not mean that they all shared the same conceptions of what constituted an obscene publication, or why such publications needed to be regulated, and how to accomplish this. While by the early twentieth century Western conceptions of obscenity would certainly have been familiar in countries as diverse as Japan, Iran, and India (all of which signed the treaty), and while similar regulatory projects were undertaken in each, not only did such projects draw upon indigenous aesthetic traditions that intersected with Western ones, but the rationales behind them were undoubtedly distinct. To understand how such regulations worked, we will briefly examine the conception of "obscenity" in Western aesthetics and explore why obscenity was deemed to be a social danger, and then consider how such conceptions of the obscene were translated, transformed, and subverted in colonial India.

Obscenity is a notably protean concept that continues to evade definition. The problem is that "such words as 'indecent,' 'lewd,' and 'obscene' can be defined only in terms of one another, producing a closed system that thwarts even the most assiduous inquiry into what any part of it might mean" (Kendrick 1987: 160). But while it may be difficult to establish a coherent or universal definition of the term, it is at least possible to ascertain a set of criteria under which texts, images, and objects have historically been rendered obscene in Western culture. One of the most basic criteria is that the obscene, as used in the "Greek sense" by Peter Michelson, is the "bringing onstage what is customarily kept offstage" (1993: xi) or, in the words of Linda Nead, is the representation of "matter that is beyond representation," or "which is beyond the accepted codes of public visibility" (Nead 1992: 90). While such a conception clearly encompasses representations of or references to sex or sexuality, it also serves to encompass other representations that have commonly been viewed as unrepresentable, such as images of or references to the excremental functions or to certain degrees or forms of violence. All pornography is thus clearly obscene (since "[p]ornography is the representation of sexuality so as to make its obscenity conspicuous, to the point of evoking its transgression of conventional taboos"; Michelson 1993: xii), but not all obscenity is pornographic. This is evident based upon our second criteria under which works have commonly been deemed obscene in the West, namely the espousal of "unconventional moral attitudes" (St. John-Stevas 1956: 2) such as free love or homosexuality. In the case of this conceptualization of the obscene, it is subject matter rather than language or imagery that is the source of contention.

The third and final criterion is mode of representation. Under this criterion, language could become the basis for rendering a work obscene, as in the case of advertisements or texts relating to medical matters (generally sexuality) that employed "colloquial" rather than "scientific" language (Sarch 1987). But by the late nineteenth century, form was often the most important consideration in classifying a work obscene in Western aesthetics, particularly in the case of art and literary works. Thus, Aubrey Beardsley's sketches and James Joyce's *Ulysses* were able to evade being labeled "obscenity" (although only after a series of trials and tribulations) by virtue of the highly stylized nature of their works (Michelson 1993; Pease 2000).

The ability to judge whether the form, language, or content of a particular work rendered it obscene was dependent on what in Western aesthetics was deemed to be the antithesis of the obscene, namely art. As Linda Nead reveals, form and framing are central to Western conceptions of both art, "defined in terms of the containing of form within limits," and of the obscene, "defined in terms of excess, as form beyond limit, beyond the frame and representation" (Nead 1992: 20). The importance of form can be traced back to Plato, for whom objects were merely the reflection of absolute forms which lie beyond the realm of the senses. The dichotomies that Plato established – between form and matter, mind and body, ideal and real – became the basis of the Enlightenment reformation of aesthetics, most notably embodied in Immanuel Kant's *Critique of Aesthetic Judgment* (1790). Kant sought to distinguish between contemplative pleasure (which was predicated upon reflection on an object) and sensory pleasures (which were not and hence were less refined). Crucial to the experience of contemplative pleasure was that the observer should remain a disinterested rather than a desiring subject during the act of contemplating an object; the object itself, in order to be labeled art, should exist for no other purpose than to be contemplated. But art was also, according to Kant, defined by form. As Nead argues, for Kant "what is bad, what is outside of or goes beyond aesthetic taste and judgement, is matter – that which is motivated, which seduces, embarrasses, or leads the viewer astray, away from the proper consideration of intrinsic form" (Nead 1992: 24–5). By the nineteenth century, such arguments had come to be used to distinguish between art and obscenity, with the latter being denied the status of art because it invited *interested* rather than disinterested contemplation. The obscene was thus what served to promote action or arousal, to create embodied viewers or readers, rather than disembodied contemplating ones.

Obscenity is not, therefore, inherently intrinsic to an object: an object becomes obscene, in part, by virtue of the response of the viewing subject. How an individual responds to a given object, as Pierre Bourdieu (1984) has argued, is dependent on the cultural capital of the viewer, which is largely contingent on class. Emerging out of the rise of industrial capitalism in the late eighteenth century, aesthetic judgment or taste became a means through which gentlemen could conceptualize themselves as apart from or outside the realm of material experience and hence capable of disinterested, socially generous behavior. "High" culture, predicated on a rational, disinterested pleasure, was seen as distinct from "low" culture, predicated on the pleasures of the appetite; elevating high over low culture thereby served to assert an individual's cultural distinction. As Alison Pease reveals, the problem with the obscene (particularly in its most iniquitous form, the pornographic) was not only that it was associated with the working classes and hence "threatened the class hierarchies upon which aesthetic theories of the eighteenth century rested by exposing common experience in bodily sensation," but that "the selfish individualism that pornography celebrated was viewed as pestilential to civility" (Pease 2000: xii). Since in an increasingly egalitarian society the acquisition of civil liberty was equated with self-control, the loss of self-control threatened, quite literally, the body politic (Bataille 1986). For conservative social theorists such as Edmund Burke, fashioning the social order through a typology of aesthetic responses was thus proof against revolutionary upheavals. While by the late nineteenth century, social theorists such as Matthew Arnold, John Ruskin, William Morris, and Oscar Wilde were attempting to inculcate a rapidly expanding reading public with a "high" cultural aesthetic, as Linda Dowling (1996) has demonstrated, they also feared that this would debase elite culture in the process. The danger was that objects, images, and words would all take on new meanings through their contamination by the masses, who had yet to cultivate disinterest.

But why was there such fierce debate over obscenity in the nineteenth and twentieth centuries, and to what particular uses has obscenity been put? In the West, the censorship of obscenity evolved in the context of social and cultural transformations such as the industrial and French revolutions, secularization, urbanization, class formation, nationalism, women's emancipation, and the professionalization of medicine. While brought under the purview of state control through criminal law, until the latter half of the nineteenth century the regulation of obscenity tended to remain largely in the hands of moral reform organizations (Bristow 1977: 40–1; Alan Hunt 1999: 57).

Although the "dissipation" of the upper classes was always a concern of such organizations, their main goal remained the moralization of the poor (Goldstein 1992: 129; Roberts 1992: 146; Alan Hunt 1999: 62). However, a new spate of purity movements emerged in the last quarter of the nineteenth century that were distinguished from their predecessors in a number of important ways: they were mass movements (in which large sections of both the middle and "respectable" working classes were mobilized); women played an important role in them; and, while they made attempts to reform the morality of the working classes, their chief target was the middle and upper classes (Foucault 1990: 123; Beisel 1993; Lynn Hunt 1993: 12–13; Alan Hunt 1999: 98). The aim of middle-class reformers was, in short, to ensure that "those who were to govern should themselves be morally regulated so as to secure cultural hegemony" and to "cement the two great modern classes into a 'new' national community under the leadership of the middle class . . ." (Alan Hunt 1999: 189, 120).

Such concerns did not only exist in the West, however. By the late nineteenth century, India, subject to the "civilizing mission" of British colonial rule for over a century, was in the process of fashioning a nationalist modernity that, while derivative, represented a distinct and decidedly anti-colonial political rationality, including its conceptions of, and attitudes toward, the obscene. While English-educated Indians were certainly well versed in Western aesthetics, they were also, along with their more traditionally trained counterparts, grounded in Indian aesthetic traditions. Since in Hinduism *kama* (the satisfaction of desire) was perceived to be one of the four elements of human activity, obscenity was viewed in a slightly different light from its general perception in the West. Although the concept of obscenity (*aslilata*) existed, for example, in Sanskrit poetry, the presence of "obscene" images in a poem was regarded not as a moral wrong but as a literary fault. What determined whether such "faults" should be considered obscene or not was whether the author's intention was to sexually excite his or her readers (Masson-Moussaieff 1971; Dwivedi 1981). Although the doctrine of original sin (which permeated Muslim as well as Christian literature) had effected some changes in Indian aesthetics by the onset of colonial rule, obscenity was still largely deemed an intellectual rather than a practical "problem" (Khosla 1976).

British rule altered Indian conceptions of obscenity by introducing both Western conceptions of obscenity and new forms and types of "obscene" literature into India. By 1895, more than five million packages of books and newspapers a year were being imported into India from Britain, a figure which jumped to more than twelve million by the early twentieth century (National Archives of India 1895, 1911). At the same time, changes in the indigenous publishing industry (in terms of the amount and type of literature being published) and the rise of new socio-religious reform and nationalist movements all fed debates over obscenity and emergent discourses about degeneracy, racial purity, and moral reform. While similar to such discourses in the West, they were also in many ways distinct (see, for example, Chatterjee 1995; Robb 1995; Gupta 2001; Sarkar 2001). Indian educators and moral reformers, for example, tended to regard much of both Western and Indian literature and popular culture as morally corrupt. Religious leaders and social reformers, on the other hand, were inclined to deem the literature of their own community as "pure" in opposition to that of the "infidels" (of both foreign and indigenous origin). Nationalists maintained that not only were the British prudes when it came to censoring their own literature, but that they were responsible for introducing the idea of obscenity into India in the first place – and, in doing so, had forced Indians to view elements of their own culture in a derogatory light. But since the damage, once done, could not be undone, nationalists tended to criticize the colonial government for failing to sufficiently regulate Indian print culture which, many of them were convinced, needed to be purified before India could obtain *swaraj* (self-rule).

These variant discourses were united, however, by one major concern, namely the depiction of Indian women as exotic and sexualized beings. Although purifying the image of women was a standard trope of anti-obscenity crusaders in the late nineteenth and early twentieth centuries, such concerns assumed particular resonance in a colonial context such as India. Since colonial rule severely limited the ability of Indian national- ists to challenge threats to their power and authority in the public sphere, they placed a distinct emphasis on "restoring" their masculinity and redeeming the Indian "race" by transforming the domestic sphere – an agenda that Pradip Kumar Bose regards in Foucauldian terms as "a change from the government *of families* to government *through the family*" (Bose 1995: 125). A key method adopted by Indian (particularly Hindu) elites to achieve this was to reform the role of Indian women. While "orthodox" Hindus regarded women as the bearers of Hinduism (since they were believed to be ruled by Scripture and to be uncorrupted by Western education or the depredations suffered by Hindu men in the colonial public sphere; Sarkar 1998), and Hindu "reformers" believed that they were the repositories of a new, reformed Hinduism (from which practices such as child marriage and enforced widowhood would be abolished), both regarded women as the embodiment of the virtues of chastity, purity, and self-sacrifice (Katrak 1992). Not only were figures of Hindu mythology, such as Sita, Savitri, and Draupadi, held up as ideals of Hindu womanhood, but the discourse of the civilizing mission was turned on its head through pitting the "pure" Indian woman against her "impure" colonial counterpart. The European woman was regarded as impure because she exhib- ited not only her face (in beauty contests reported in "respectable" journals) but also her body (in European films and cinema posters). As one nationalist critic noted, "In India . . . even women of evil fame will not consent to display their bodies in this shameless manner" (National Archives of India 1923).

The path to self-rule was thus dependent on the de-exoticization and desexualization of the Indian woman, and the creation of a new moral code. During the course of the nationalist movement, Indian elites made numerous efforts to fashion such a code. In the nineteenth century, these included attempts to replace ritual correctness with a system of personal ethics, to develop physical culture, and to uplift the "depressed" classes (Raychaudhuri 1975; Rosselli 1980; Bayly 1999). Efforts to regenerate Indian morality became more complex in the twentieth century, and they also became more intimately entwined with concerns over biological regeneration, influenced in part by the eugenics movement (Hodges 2005). It is in the context of such movements that the drive to censor "the obscene" must be placed. Hence, while the explicit aim of an organization such as the Society for the Suppression of Public Obscenity, founded in 1873, was to enforce the law against obscene publications as it stood and to improve the law if it were deemed necessary, the larger goal was distinctly nationalist. Not only did the Society contain an impressive array of Hindus, Christians, Muslims, and Brahmos ("all united in this great work by a common morality") but they all sought to promote "the progress of the country" through "the promotion of pure, and the suppression of undoubtedly vicious, literature" (*Counterpoint* 1978: 179) – to overcome, in short, the effects on Indian society of the project of colonial modernity. Yet appropriating or "translating" Western aesthetics was not, perhaps, the best way to achieve this. As the novelist, essayist, and linguistic reformer Bankim Chandra Chattopadhyay lamented, in "observing the aesthetically new Bengali literature of the modern time ascendant on the path of progress, I sometimes wonder – it may be beautiful, but perhaps it is alien, not ours. Why don't I find the pure Bengali feelings in the pure Bengali style?" (quoted in Banerjee 1989: 175). The translation of Western aesthetics into the Indian cultural milieu undermined, as Chattopadhyay was well aware, the very "pure" Indian culture that nationalists and reformers were battling to construct.

REFERENCES AND FURTHER READING

Banerjee, Sumanto (1989) "Marginalization of Women's Popular Culture in Nineteenth Century Bengal." In Kumkum Sangari and Sudesh Vaid (eds.), *Recasting Women: Essays in Colonial History*, pp. 127–79. New Delhi: Khali for Women.

Bataille, George (1986) "Sexual Plethora and Death." In *Eroticism*, pp. 94–108. San Francisco: City Lights.

Bayly, Susan (1999) "Race in Britain and India." In Peter van der Veer and Hartmut Lehmann (eds.), *Nation and Religion: Perspectives on Europe and Asia*, pp. 71–95. Princeton: Princeton University Press.

Beisel, Nicola (1993) "Morals versus Art: Censorship, the Politics of Interpretation, and the Victorian Nude." *American Sociological Review*, 58: 145–62.

Bose, Pradip Kumar (1995) "Sons of the Nation: Child Rearing in the New Family." In Partha Chatterjee (ed.), *Texts of Power: Emerging Disciplines in Colonial Bengal*, pp. 118–44. Minneapolis: University of Minnesota Press.

Bourdieu, Pierre (1984) *Distinction: A Social Critique of the Judgment of Taste*, trans. Richard Nice. London: Routledge and Kegan Paul.

— (1991) "Censorship and the Imposition of Form." In *Language and Symbolic Power*, ed. John B. Thompson, trans. Gino Raymond and Mathew Adamson, pp. 137–59. Cambridge, MA: Harvard University Press.

Bristow, Edward (1977) *Vice and Vigilance: Purity Movements in Britain since 1700*. Dublin: Gill and Macmillan.

Butler, Judith (1998) "Ruled Out: Vocabularies of the Censor." In Robert Post (ed.), *Censorship and Silencing: Practices of Cultural Regulation*, pp. 247–59. Los Angeles: Getty Research Institute for the History of Art and the Humanities.

Chatterjee, Partha (1995) "The Disciplines in Colonial Bengal." In Partha Chatterjee (ed.), *Texts of Power: Emerging Disciplines in Colonial Bengal*, pp. 1–29. Minneapolis: University of Minnesota Press.

Counterpoint (1978) "The Society for the Suppression of Public Obscenity in India." *Counterpoint*, 2: 179–211.

Das, Arjun (1935) "Display of Obscene Posters" (letter). *Tribune* [Bombay], May 17.

Davenport-Hines, Richard (1990) *Sex, Death and Punishment: Attitudes to Sex and Sexuality in Britain since the Renaissance*. London: Collins.

"Den" (1935) "The Anonymous Altruist." *The Herald* [Melbourne], August 29.

Dowling, Linda (1996) *The Vulgarization of Art: The Victorians and Aesthetic Democracy.* Charlottesville: University Press of Virginia.

Dunstan, Keith (1972) *Wowsers: Being an Account of the Prudery Exhibited by Certain Outstanding Men and Women in such Matters as Drinking, Smoking, Prostitution, Censorship and Gambling,* 2nd edn. Sydney: Angus and Robertson.

Dwivedi, R. C. (1981) "Concept of Obscenity (*Aslilata*) in Sanskrit Poetics." *Annals of the Bhandarkar Oriental Research Institute,* 62 (1–4): 67–76.

Foucault, Michel (1990) *The History of Sexuality,* vol. 1: *An Introduction,* trans. Robert Hurley. New York: Vintage.

Goldstein, Robert Justin (1992) "A Land of Relative Freedom: Censorship of the Press and the Arts in the Nineteenth Century (1815–1914)." In Paul Hyland and Neil Sammells (eds.), *Writing and Censorship in Britain,* pp. 125–40. London: Routledge.

Gupta, Charu (2001) *Sexuality, Obscenity, and Community: Women, Muslims, and the Hindu Public in Colonial India.* Delhi: Permanent Black.

Heath, Deana (2003) "Creating the Moral Colonial Subject: Censorship in India and Australia, 1880s to 1939." Unpublished PhD thesis, University of California, Berkeley.

Hodges, Sarah (2005) "Indian Eugenics in an Age of Reform." In Sarah Hodges (ed.), *Reproductive Health in India: History, Politics, Controversies.* Delhi: Orient Longman.

Hunt, Alan (1999) *Governing Morals: A Social History of Moral Regulation.* Cambridge: Cambridge University Press.

Hunt, Lynn (1993) *The Invention of Pornography: Obscenity and the Origins of Modernity.* New York: Zone.

Hunter, Ian, Saunders, David, and Williamson, Dugald (1993) *On Pornography: Literature, Sexuality and Obscenity Law.* New York: St. Martin's Press.

Katrak, Ketu H. (1992) "Indian Nationalism, Gandhian *Satyagraha,* and Representations of Female Sexuality." In Andrew Parker (ed.), *Nationalisms and Sexualities,* pp. 395–406. New York: Routledge.

Kendrick, Walter (1987) *The Secret Museum: Pornography in Modern Culture.* New York: Viking.

Khosla, G. D. (1976) *Pornography and Censorship in India.* New Delhi: Indian Book Company.

Manchester, Colin (1991) "A History of the Crime of Obscene Libel." *Journal of Legal History,* 12 (1): 37–57.

Masson-Moussaieff, J. (1971) "Obscenity in Sanskrit Literature." *Mahfil,* 7: 3–5.

Michelson, Peter (1993) *Speaking the Unspeakable: A Poetics of Obscenity.* Albany: State University of New York Press.

National Archives of India (1895) 83-83/January 1895, Separate Revenue (Post Office, General), A, Finance and Commerce Department.

— (1911) 6–10/October 1911, Post Office, A, Department of Commerce and Industry.

— (1923) 570/1923, Judicial, Home Department.

Nead, Linda (1992) *The Female Nude: Art, Obscenity and Sexuality.* London: Routledge.

Pease, Allison (2000) *Modernism, Mass Culture, and the Aesthetics of Obscenity.* Cambridge: Cambridge University Press.

Pullan, Robert (1984) *Guilty Secrets: Free Speech in Australia.* North Ryde, Australia: Methuen.

Raychaudhuri, Tapan (1975) "Norms of Family Life and Personal Morality among the Bengali Hindu Elite, 1600–1850." In Rachel Van M. Baumer (ed.), *Aspects of Bengali History and Society,* pp. 13–25. Honolulu: University Press of Hawaii.

Robb, Peter (ed.) (1995) *The Concept of Race in South Asia.* Delhi: Oxford University Press.

Roberts, M. J. D. (1992) "Blasphemy, Obscenity and the Courts: Contours of Tolerance in Nineteenth-century England." In Paul Hyland and Neil Sammells (ed.), *Writing and Censorship in Britain,* pp. 141–53. London: Routledge.

Rosselli, John (1980) "The Self-image of Effeteness: Physical Education and Nationalism in Nineteenth-century Bengal." *Past and Present,* 86: 121–48.

St. John-Stevas, Norman (1956) *Obscenity and the Law.* London: Secker and Warburg.

Sarch, Amy (1987) "Those Dirty Ads! Birth Control Advertising in the 1920s and 1930s." *Critical Studies in Mass Communication,* 14: 31–48.

Sarkar, Tanika (1998) "Orthodoxy, Cultural Nationalism, and *Hindutva* Violence: An Overview of the Gender Ideology of the Hindu Right." In Ruth Roach Pierson and Nupur Chaudhuri (eds.), *Nation, Empire, Colony: Histori-*

cizing Gender and Race, pp. 166–81. Indianapolis: Indiana University Press.

— (2001) *Hindu Wife, Hindu Nation: Community, Religion, and Cultural Nationalism*. Bloomington: Indiana University Press.

Saunders, David (1990) "Copyright, Obscenity and Literary History." *English Literary History*, 57 (2): 431–44.

— (1992) "Victorian Obscenity Law: Negative Censorship or Positive Administration." In Paul Hyland and Neil Sammells (eds.), *Writing and Censorship in Britain*, pp. 154–70. London: Routledge.

Schauer, Frederick (1998) "The Ontology of Censorship." In Robert Post (ed.), *Censorship and Silencing: Practices of Cultural Regulation*, pp. 147–68. Los Angeles: Getty Research Institute for the History of Art and the Humanities.

Shuger, Debora (1998) "Civility and Censorship in Early Modern England." In Robert Post (ed.), *Censorship and Silencing: Practices of Cultural Regulation*, pp. 89–110. Los Angeles: Getty Research Institute for the History of Art and the Humanities.

Siebert, F. S. (1965) *Freedom of the Press in England, 1476–1776*. Urbana: University of Illinois Press.

The Sun (1948) "A. I. F. Book Obscene: Firm Fined." *The Sun* [Sydney], April 24.

Sutherland, J. (1982) *Offensive Literature: Decensorship in Britain, 1960–1982*. London: Junction.

Thomas, Donald (1969) *A Long Time Burning: The History of Literary Censorship in Britain*. London: Routledge and Kegan Paul.

Tribe, D. (1973) *Questions of Censorship*. London: Allen and Unwin.

38

Copyright and the Creation of Literary Property

John Feather

Copyright is defined by the *Oxford English Dictionary* as "the exclusive right given by law for a certain term of years to an author, composer, designer, etc. (or his assignee), to print, publish, and sell copies of his original work." The first usage recorded there is in 1735, but the two words "copy" and "right" had been closely associated since at least the middle of the seventeenth century (Nichol 1990), and in the phrase "rights in copies" since before 1600. This chapter traces the development of the concept of copyright, and how its evolution has influenced both publishing and authorship.

The idea that authors "own" their books after publication is a product of European print culture and its worldwide offspring. Conceptually, it is a complex idea which might be thought to be in conflict with the whole notion of "ownership." How can we sell something and still have a claim to it? In essence, that is the question with which generations of authors, publishers, and lawyers – especially lawyers – have had to grapple. The answer that has been developed is that we can distinguish between a physical object – a book, a drawing, a photograph – and its intellectual or artistic content. Ownership of the object does not confer ownership of the content. Once that principle is established, then the purpose of copyright law is to define the extent to which the owner of the physical object may legitimately make use of the content while ensuring that the creator and owner of the content (who may not be the same person) are appropriately rewarded.

The practical application of copyright law is important to everyone who writes, publishes, sells, buys, lends, borrows, or reads books. You may have bought this book, or you may have borrowed it from the person or organization that bought it. You have the undoubted right to read it – indeed, we who wrote and edited it want you to do just that! But you are not allowed to make unlimited photocopies or to digitize large parts of the book, or to use long passages as quotations in your own published work, although in each case you can ask for permission to do so and you may get that permission if you pay for it. Who gives permission depends on who owns the content: it might be the author or the publisher, depending on the formal contractual agreements between them, and in the case of a contributed book like this one the editors might also have some standing. And this is a simple case! Consider a complicated (and more commercially valuable) example: a book which is published in hardback and paperback, sold all over the world in its original language, translated into other languages, read on the radio with the recording published commercially, dramatized for television and the stage, made into a movie which has specially commissioned music and which is issued as a DVD with the sound track on a CD. The original book has generated dozens of different forms of content and output. This whole range of "rights" (as they are now commonly called) in these formats and media is, like the humble copyright in this book, regulated by law and contract in many different legal jurisdictions and traditions throughout the world. And this case is not a fantasy – or rather it is, because it is more or less the position of *The Lord of the Rings*.

The issues, moreover, are not only legal and commercial. Once we accept the distinction between ownership of the content and ownership of the object – between book and text – there may be an impact on the attitude and behavior of the creator of the content. For Virgil, Chaucer, and almost every other ancient or medieval author, there was no serious possibility of financial reward beyond any which accrued from "selling" the "book" to a patron or a scribe. From Maecenas in the first century AD to the Earl of Leicester in the reign of Elizabeth I of England (1558–1603), the patron was the author's principal source of income. For many writers, the real rewards actually lay in preferment to profitable jobs, in prestige, or (for many Christian writers) in moral satisfaction during their lifetimes or posthumous salvation. When writing and the distribution of writing began to move into a commercial sphere, however, writers could begin to see the possibility of financial benefits to themselves. The author of a printed book who sold what he had written to a printer was rather different from an author who "worked for" a patron. The author's income, however, typically consisted only of the proceeds of that single sale. It was the author's sole gain from the book, with the possible exception of the intangible benefits of a reputation. Nevertheless, the fact that printers were paying authors for books, and sometimes indeed commissioning them, opened up new possibilities and new modes of thought.

Some authors remained aloof from such mundane considerations. Perhaps because of the growing association between authorship and money, there were writers who deliberately avoided the marketplace, publishing their work anonymously, pseudonymously, or in a limited number of copies. The majority, however, were trying to maximize financial benefits from their work long before copyright was embodied in law. In eighteenth-century England, where many of the critical developments in copyright first happened, the phrase *literary property* came to be used to describe the author's creation. Moreover, this idea soon extended beyond the written word. Graphic prints were protected before the end of the eighteenth century. During the nineteenth century, protection was extended to designs, the performance of plays and music, drawings and paintings, photographs and other derivatives of the imagination. Literary property thus evolved into copyright. In due course, copyright became part of the wider sphere of *intellectual property*, which now also encompasses the concept of patents in inventions, which have similar origins but a very different history. The second theme of this chapter is to explore how copyright evolved in practice, and the part which it plays in the history of authorship.

Copyright, as we now understand it, is essentially a product of the age of printing. The early printers soon discovered a basic fact of economic life: that printed books would only be profitable if enough copies were sold, that they would only sell if the price was acceptable, and that the right price could only be achieved by printing enough copies to keep the unit cost down to a level that could achieve a profit at a price acceptable to the market. It is a tricky and complex equation that is still a central business concern for a publisher. The first printers learned the hard way, by trial and (more often perhaps) error, and they soon came to recognize that one way to protect their investments in equipment, materials, and employees was to try to ensure that each product – each book – was unique, so that the competition was from other titles, not from other editions of the same text. The printers turned for protection to secular and ecclesiastical authorities: kings, bishops, and other rulers and churchmen in their own jurisdictions were asked to grant the right to print particular titles to named individuals. These printing privileges, as they are usually called, are first found in Venice in the later fifteenth century. The first of them was granted in 1469 to John of Speyer, the man who introduced printing to the Republic. Speyer was actually given a monopoly on printing in the city; later grants were for individual titles or groups of books and were sometimes time-limited. The Venetian example was soon followed by the kings of France. The earliest English examples date from the reign of Henry VII (1485–1509), when he appointed a king's printer who had the unique right to print certain sorts of books.

There were various motives for these early grants. Sometimes it was certainly an attempt at censorship, by controlling what could be printed and limiting the right to print to those who conformed to the requirements of the state or the Church. Sometimes it enabled the authorities to put into print essential documents that were to their own benefit (such as laws and service books) and to encourage desirable publications. This was one of the functions of the king's printer in England and the holders of similar offices in other countries. When Oxford and Cambridge universities were given the right to operate presses in the late sixteenth century, there was at least a tacit understanding that they would print and publish learned works which might not otherwise find an outlet. The link between permission to print and the right to print is perhaps best expressed in the Latin formula which is still used by the Roman Catholic Church: *nihil obstat* (nothing obstructs, i.e. there is nothing in the content to which exception can be taken) and *imprimatur* (it may be printed, i.e. permission is granted to a publisher to produce an edition). In different ways, and with very different emphases, the same distinction applies widely.

Whether intentionally or not, commercial benefits also flowed from the grants. The privileged printers had a *de facto* monopoly in terms of their grants. This was territorially limited, in the sense that it applied only in the jurisdiction in which the grant had been made, but within that territory it was absolute and the whole power of the state or the Church was available to support it and to punish any infringements. The system of printing privileges spread, in various forms, across the whole of Europe as the art of printing was disseminated between 1450 and 1550. It established the basic principle that the right to print a particular book, or category of books, could be granted to a named individual or organization.

By the middle of the sixteenth century, however, another development was beginning in England which was to have profound consequences. It arose out of the peculiar circumstances of the English book trade, which was noticeably insular. From the beginning of printing in that country, books in the English language were important and soon became predominant. Until well into the seventeenth century, learned works (still largely in Latin) were imported rather than produced domestically: the market for them was too small to sustain an independent publishing trade. The English language itself, however, was almost unknown outside the British Isles, and was by no means universal even there. But there was a vibrant national literary culture, and an increasingly strong sense of national identity which was closely related to the language and to a growing perception of its equality of status with Latin and French. The English book trade was both the beneficiary of linguistic nationalism, and one of the means for creating and sustaining it. The market, however, was limited, and competition was intense. After the middle of the sixteenth century, printing was almost entirely confined to London; the few exceptions were a handful of surreptitious presses and the university presses which were of no real commercial significance. The English book trade was therefore geographically, linguistically, and culturally very narrowly focused.

After 1557, the freemen of the Stationers' Company had an effective monopoly of English printing. There was an understanding, which soon became a formal requirement, that no more than about twenty master printers would be licensed at any one time. All books had to be licensed by the ecclesiastical or state authorities before printing; the Company was required to ensure that nothing was printed without a license. Stationers gradually evolved their own means of working together which allowed them to compete commercially in this restricted environment. The Company instituted the practice of recording licenses and licensees in its own records. It is not clear exactly when this began, but the earliest surviving documents are from 1576, and thereafter the sequence is continuous. The document itself was known to contemporaries as the "Entry Book of Copies" and to later scholars as the "Stationers' Register."

The Register records the fact that a named member of the Company had the right to print a particular book, and that, to the best of the knowledge of the Company's senior officers, he (not she until much later) had obtained the appropriate permission from the licensing authorities. From there it was but a short step to formal recognition that the permission was a negotiable commodity. Within a decade, "rights in copies" (derived from the phrase "printer's copy," meaning the manuscript used by the typesetter) were being bequeathed, inherited, bought, and sold. The transfers of ownership were duly recorded in the Register. By the turn of the seventeenth century, the concept of copy ownership was well recognized within the London book trade. It was also becoming increasingly complicated. Some copies were jointly owned by two or more booksellers. Some booksellers owned many copies. The Court of Assistants, the self-electing oligarchy which ran the Stationers' Company, spent increasing amounts of time ruling on disputes between members about copy ownership and thus began, probably unwittingly, to develop some general principles and rules to make the system work more smoothly.

The authority of the Stationers' Company as a trade guild was reinforced by the authority of the state. There is still some scholarly controversy about precisely how this relationship worked and what motivated the various parties, but the consequences of it are clear and important. It was in the interest of the crown and the Church that all books should be licensed before printing. Between 1558 and 1640, the licensers were usually the bishops or other clergymen acting on their behalf. It was therefore necessary to maintain some sort of record of what licenses had been granted and to whom: this record was the Stationer's Register. It was in the use of the Register for their own pur-poses – in which the authorities had little or no interest – that the Stationers laid the foundations for the development of the purely commercial rights which were to evolve into copyright.

These English developments were fundamentally different from what was happening on the continent, and indeed in neighboring Scotland, where licensing by the state or the Church was the sole source of rights, and continued to be essentially a mechanism for the control of content. In England, where formal censorship of content usually had a fairly light touch, the commercial aspect of rights in copies became more important. This began to raise some other issues, as early as the late sixteenth century. Most fun-damentally, there was the question of who created what everyone agreed was clearly a piece of property. The answer ultimately could only be that it was the author, and indeed we see glimmerings of the concept of authors' rights (although not the term) in the first half of the seventeenth century. In the mere act of paying an author for the copy, the bookseller (to use the normal contemporary term for what, after about 1820, was called a publisher) was acknowledging the origin of the property which was being acquired.

In the second half of the seventeenth century, these underlying questions became both more urgent and more complicated. The Stationers' Company's control of the trade broke down, along with the royal authority which had created and sustained it, from 1640 onward. Yet throughout the English Civil War (1642–6) and the republican regimes which followed the execution of Charles I (1649), the book trade continued to function. Economically, it went through bad times, but copies and shares in copies were still traded, and at least some of the transactions were recorded in the Register. When the monarchy was restored in the person of Charles II (1660), there was an understand-ing within the trade that the pre-1640 rights were intact and enforceable, and that any properly recorded transactions between 1640 and 1660 were legitimate. Indeed, the authority of the Company and its system for protecting rights was to receive an unex-pected boost by being brought into the sphere of statute law for the first time. The Printing Act (sometimes called the Licensing Act) of 1662 was primarily designed to institute a new system of prepublication censorship which was secular rather than ecclesiastical in intention and implementation. But it also required entry in the Stationers' Register of books that were licensed; this gave a new force and significance to the Register itself, which now became a statutory record. This legislation was allowed to lapse in 1672, but it was revived in 1685 and renewed again in 1688 and 1693. However, when it was next due for renewal in 1695, it seemed less attractive. The Glorious Revolution (1688) had deposed James II, and the new system of government was essentially a constitutional parliamentary monarchy with embryonic political parties. Prepublication censorship came to an end.

The problem for the trade after 1695 was how to protect a hundred years of investments in rights in copies. A group of copy-owning booksellers and their business associates petitioned for a renewal of the Printing Act, but parliament would not hear of it. In 1707, the booksellers changed their tack, and asked for what they actually wanted – protection for rights in copies. They got their way, and in "An Act for the Encouragement of Learning" rights in copies were formally recognized in statute law for the first time. The 1710 Copyright Act is a milestone, but it was also a millstone. It was imprecise and ambiguous. It appeared to give protection to all existing copies for twenty-one years, and to new copies for fourteen years with the possibility of renewal for another fourteen, but exactly what this meant was only imperfectly explained. For more than sixty years, the trade, the authors, and the courts in both England and Scotland argued about exactly what the Act meant. Eventually, in the leading case of *Donaldson* v. *Becket*, the House of Lords determined in 1774 that the Act meant what it said: rights in copies subsisted for a period of twenty-eight years, and thereafter they were in public domain. During these long and complicated legal developments, two crucial principles were identified and developed: authors' rights and public domain.

Legal protection for the rights of authors was embedded in the 1710 Act. Its title indicated that its purpose was – in the broadest sense – to encourage learning and, by implication, the learned. The clear assumption in the Act was that authors originated the rights that were being protected. Within a few years, some authors were beginning to assert those rights. Most notable among them was Alexander Pope, who used the formidable power of his popularity to manipulate his dealings with the book trade to his own advantage. Not every author could emulate Pope, but by the middle of the eighteenth century authorship in England was established as an occupation (albeit not a particularly respectable one) from which it was possible to make a living. Copyright law underpinned this, both by recognizing that an author created a piece of property at the moment of composition, and by protecting the investment of whoever bought or leased that property from the author in order to put it into printed circulation.

Public domain was, in its way, an equally important concept. Just as the recognition of authors' rights began to deal with the question of where the property embodied in copyright originated, so the development of the idea of public domain answered the question that hovered over the other end of the process: what happened to time-limited rights when the period of protection expired? Indeed, the whole English legal controversy from 1731 (when the twenty-one-year rights expired) to 1774 could be argued to have revolved around this issue. The eventual resolution, which flowed from the Lords' decision in 1774, was that these rights were owned by no one and therefore by everyone. In other words, anyone could print a book which was no longer protected by copyright. This opened up a whole new field of highly competitive publishing – the reprint series whose modern descendant is to be found in paperback editions of the classics – and forced the development of a new kind of entrepreneurial publishing in which practitioners sought new titles to replace those that they no longer controlled.

By the end of the eighteenth century, British law and practice had developed a notion of copyright that was far removed from the rights and privileges that were granted by early modern states and churches. While the early privileges were essentially mechanisms of control that happened to confer some commercial benefits, British copyright had evolved in way that enabled the operation of a purely commercial device that could be exploited by authors and publishers alike. Subsequent legislation reinforced this perception and the relationships that grew out of it. In 1814, and even more forcefully in 1842, new legislation fully acknowledged both the position of the author and the consequences of the time-limitation on copyrights. The 1842 Act even gave some protection after an author's death, for the benefit of his or her family or other copyright owner. This provision, *post mortem* copyright, was strengthened in the 1911 Copyright Act, which gave protection for fifty years after the author's death, extended in the 1990s to seventy years in line with European Union legislation.

British developments were of international importance in the longer term, but there were other approaches. In continental Europe, there were few developments of any significance until after the French Revolution (1789). Thereafter, in successive constitutions and legislation derived from them, there was protection for authors' rights, including the development of the concept of *droit moral*, the author's "moral right" to control the use made of his work even after he or she had sold it to a publisher. This principle was not to be incorporated into British law until 1988. Article I of the United States Constitution gave Congress the power to make copyright legislation "to promote the progress of science and useful arts, by securing for limited times to authors and inventors the exclusive right to their respective writings and discoveries," a power which it exercised in the first federal Copyright Act (1790). Although this was derived from the 1710 British Act, it actually took account of the later eighteenth-century developments and interpretations of the law in Britain, and had a strong focus on authors' rights. Subsequent American legislation, up to and including the 1976 Act (still in force), gradually extended the provisions, including the fifty years of protection after the author's death. In both Europe and the United States, the tendency has been to give greater emphasis to authors' rights.

An important nineteenth-century innovation was the development of international copyright law. From the mid-1830s onward, a number of European states passed domestic legislation that empowered their governments to make treaties with other states that would provide mutual copyright protection. The relevant British legislation was in 1838, and the first treaty was signed with Prussia in 1846. Gradually, a network of bilateral treaties developed between the European powers, including, in Britain's case, extensions to colonies (which were included in the provisions of the 1842 Act). In 1886, largely in response to an initiative by various groups representing authors, five of the major European powers came together in Berne to negotiate a more general treaty: the following year the first Berne Convention came into force. In brief, its effect was (and is) to give protection to copyrights owned by authors resident in any signatory state in all other signatory states as if they were resident there. Thus, if the term of protection differs between countries (as it often did until European legislation was standardized in the last quarter of the twentieth century), protection was afforded in terms of the laws of each country, regardless of the nationality or place of residence of the author.

The Berne Convention did not, however, deal with a running sore that was of particular concern to British authors and publishers. The United States was invited to Berne in 1886, but took only observer status. Not until 1891 did it have domestic legislation that gave some meaningful protection to foreign authors, and even then Congress had passed the Chace Act only reluctantly and after decades of argument. Essentially, the concern was to protect the American printing industry by requiring books copyrighted in the United States to be produced there; there were also complex rules about whether the book was first published in the US or abroad. The effect was to make it almost impossible before 1891, and difficult thereafter, for a foreign author or publisher to gain any kind of copyright protection. To the Europeans (and particularly the British), this was piracy – illegal reprinting; to the Americans, it was free trade. It was not until 1976 that the US became a full member of the international copyright family. By that time, virtually every other country in the world was a signatory of Berne and of the rather less onerous International Copyright Convention developed by UNESCO. The last major gap in the international copyright protection system was plugged by the accession of China to the Berne Convention in 1990–1.

The importance of the legal history of copyright lies in the effect that it has had – and continues to have – on the practice of authorship and publishing. The first glimmerings of the rights of authors can be found in the *de facto* recognition that they were creating marketable products. It is arguably anachronistic to speak of authors' rights in early seventeenth-century England, but there is no doubt that at least some authors considered that they had them, and sought to use whatever influence they might have for both commercial and literary ends. The early eighteenth-century authors who began to exploit their rights were building on this tradition, which was at least partly embodied in the 1710 Act. In the mid-eighteenth century, however, the English and Scottish legal controversies – which are central to the formal evolution of the law of copyright – took comparatively little account of authors. In historical retrospect, it is as if two parallel sets of developments were taking place. While the lawyers were arguing on behalf of the booksellers about the meaning of the law, the authors – or at least the more enterprising of them – were using their position as the primary producers of an increasingly popular and valuable commodity to create a better income for themselves. The normal practice was still to sell the "copy" to the bookseller who was to publish it, usually in return for a one-off payment, although by the end of the eighteenth century there are examples of authors who negotiated what we would now call reprint rights and other sources of continuing income.

The clarification of the law in 1774 was the proximate cause of revolutionary changes in the book trade in Britain. Publishers were forced to be more entrepreneurial: they had to rely less on their backlists and more on the risky business of publishing new books. The demand for such books was incessant and increasing, offering obvious openings for authors. The first generation of entrepreneurial publishers, in the 1780s and 1790s, were active commissioners of books. This was especially true at the popular end of the spectrum where, for example, the Noble Brothers and the Minerva Press published hundreds of Gothic novels for the circulating library market. For a few authors, this created real wealth; for many more, it generated a steady stream of income. These authors included many women, a significant development in itself. Anonymous or pseudonymous authorship protected the respectability of middle-class women who preferred not to bring themselves to public attention; at the same time, writing was something a woman confined by the social conventions of the period could actually take on as an intellectual occupation. Jane Austen and Fanny Burney stand out from the crowd, but there were scores of writing women in the late eighteenth century who began to gain some economic independence from their fathers, husbands, and brothers.

By the end of the second decade of the nineteenth century, the economic potential of successful authorship was very clear. Authors were identifying themselves as a community, and were beginning to press for their economic and cultural rights. An author could make a publisher's fortune, as Scott did for Constable. At the same time, a publisher could make a fortune from the work of many writers producing cheap fiction, popular nonfiction, and (increasingly so as the century wore on) articles for general interest and literary magazines. The British Copyright Act of 1814 and its successor in 1842 both acknowledged explicitly the role of the author in the process. The American Constitution had recognized authors' rights since its ratification in 1788. In continental Europe, the system of grants of privileges survived until the end of the *ancient regime*, but after 1789 authors' rights were rapidly adopted.

By the second quarter of the nineteenth century, the practice of selling copyright to a publisher was beginning to be replaced. The first stage was the system of "half-profits": author and publisher took an equal share of the profits once the costs of producing the book had been met. This was certainly more equitable from the author's perspective, although an unscrupulous publisher who was less than frank about his financial affairs could all too easily hoodwink an author with little business acumen. Half-profits and outright sale (the latter usually for commissioned work or for periodical journalism) continued in parallel throughout the middle decades of the century. In the 1880s, however, writers became more assertive. The Society of Authors, founded by the novelist Walter Besant in 1884, became a major player in the British publishing world and on the international stage. Along with its continental counterparts, especially the French Société des Gens des Lettres, it lobbied for the adoption of the Berne Convention. In the 1890s, it was a partner in negotiations with publishers and booksellers which led to the Net Book Agreement, which provided the formal framework for the operation of the British book trade for almost the whole of the twentieth century.

Most importantly, authors' societies everywhere, but particularly in the United Kingdom, campaigned for a new financial relationship between themselves and the publishers, built around a system of royalty payment rather than the sale of copyrights or half-profits agreements. The basic principle of royalties is very simple: the author takes a percentage of the revenue from every copy sold of his or her book. Thus, the author of a successful book shares with the publisher the long-term profits of his or her work. Royalty agreements gradually became the norm; by the middle of the twentieth century, authors expected at least 10 percent for most general trade books.

For almost two hundred years, authors have been in the forefront of campaigns for better and more effective copyright law, and have sought to exploit it for their own ends. This has had formal legislative consequences, both nationally and internationally, but it has also led to a fundamental change in the business relationships between authors and publishers. Nineteenth-century legislation in most countries effectively provided authors with a legal framework within which their books could generate an income for their lifetimes and to some extent for their heirs. But the framework was no more than that. In practice, the law itself is perhaps less important than the way in which the framework is used. Without a law of copyright it is unlikely that authors could have won financial recognition of their contribution to the publishing industry and the book trade. Within such a law, literary property – the strange entity created from the brain of a man or woman sitting in front of a white piece of paper (or a blank screen) – takes on the reality of a physical entity and a marketable commodity.

Contemporary copyright has become immensely complex. The multiplication of formats and media since the second half of the nineteenth century has created new markets for intellectual products. Subsidiary rights can be created in any or all of these media and forms of output, rights that can have specifically territorial applications – another source of tension between the British and American book trades through the middle decades of the twentieth century.

The most recent technological developments are beginning to raise fundamental issues about the long-term enforceability of copyright laws. Photocopying, which has been widespread since the late 1960s, opened the floodgates, and electronic document delivery may well have created the flood. Photocopying was dealt with under "fair-dealing rules" that allowed a limited amount of copying without charge for private purposes. Beginning as an informal arrangement between publishers and librarians, fair dealing was incorporated into American law in 1976 and British law in 1988. Enforcement has proved difficult, but the Publishers' Association in the UK and the Association of American Publishers in the US have mounted effective campaigns against infringement, as they have against the illegal reprinting of copyright works in certain countries in Asia. The development of the Internet, however, creates an altogether more formidable problem. Even basic issues such as payment regimes for electronic journals remain partly unresolved. The protection of copyright works that are in the public sphere in a digital format presents formidable technical, legal, and practical difficulties. Some contemporary commentators incline to the view that the long history of copyright may be coming to an end. That will be a question for the twenty-first century.

References and Further Reading

Armstrong, Elizabeth (1990) *Before Copyright: The French Book-privilege System 1498–1526*. Cambridge: Cambridge University Press.

Astbury, Raymond (1978) "The Renewal of the Licensing Act in 1693, and its Lapse in 1695," *Library*, 5th series, 33 (4): 291–322.

Bonham Carter, Victor (1978–84) *Authors by Profession*, 2 vols. London: Society of Authors/Bodley Head.

Clegg, Cyndia Susan (1997) *Press Censorship in Elizabethan England*. Cambridge: Cambridge University Press.

Collins, A. S. (1927) *Authorship in the Days of Johnson*. London: Routledge and Kegan Paul.

Crist, Timothy (1979) "Government Control of the Press after the Expiration of the Printing Act in 1679," *Publishing History*, 5: 49–77.

Deazley, Ronan (2004) *On the Origin of the Right to Copy: Charting the Movement of Copyright Law in Eighteenth-century Britain (1695–1775)*. Oxford: Hart.

Feather, John (1980) "The Book Trade in Politics: The Making of the Copyright Act of 1710," *Publishing History*, 8: 19–44.

— (1994a) "From Rights in Copies to Copyright: The Recognition of Author's Rights in English Law and Practice in the Sixteenth and Seventeenth Centuries." In Martha Woodmansee and Peter Jaszi (eds.), *The Construction of Authorship: Textual Appropriation in Law and Literature*, pp. 191–209. Durham: Duke University Press.

— (1994b) *Publishing, Piracy and Politics: An Historical Study of Copyright in Britain*. London: Mansell.

— (2005) *A History of British Publishing*, rev. edn. London: Routledge.

Foxon, David (1991) *Pope and the Early Eighteenth-century Book Trade*, rev. edn. Oxford: Clarendon Press.

Gerulaitis, L. V. (1976) *Printing and Publishing in Fifteenth-century Venice*. London: Mansell.

Hepburn, James (1968) *The Author's Empty Purse and the Rise of the Literary Agent*. London: Oxford University Press.

Nichol, D. W. (1990) "On the Use of 'Copy' and 'Copyright': A Scriblerian Coinage?" *Library*, 6th series, 12: 110–20.

Patterson, L. Ray (1968) *Copyright in Historical Perspective*. Nashville: Vanderbilt University Press.

Rose, Mark (1993) *Authors and Owners: The Invention of Copyright*. Cambridge, MA: Harvard University Press.

Woudhuysen, H. R. (1996) *Sir Philip Sidney and the Circulation of Manuscripts 1558–1640*. Oxford: Clarendon Press.

39

Libraries and the Invention
of Information

Wayne A. Wiegand

Throughout recorded history, libraries have partnered with books, and since the invention of movable type, libraries have played major roles in an evolving culture of print. Many scholars argue that for the past five thousand years libraries have been essential to the advancement of civilizations. To document their heritage, these civilizations depended upon information contained in texts. Libraries have been responsible not only for preserving these texts, but also for making them accessible by superimposing upon them systems of organization. But the texts libraries have chosen to preserve, and the methods of organization they have developed, also manifest culturally and chronologically distinctive patterns that reflect not only the role of power in the construction of heritage, but also the very definition of the word "information." While book history clearly demonstrates that the "information age" started when humans began creating texts, librarianship generally defines the "information age" as a modern phenomenon that began in the last quarter of the twentieth century. This chapter seeks to explain why.

Libraries have always been collections of texts (no matter the format), organized to facilitate access (sometimes for their administrators, more often in recent times for the libraries' publics) and maintained for the use of individuals. Because they are largely voluntary institutions (people do not have to use them), the services and collections they provide (especially in recent centuries) have been regularly influenced and modified by the public they have sought to serve. Generally, libraries have consisted of easily transported yet durable objects that have taken many forms (most often books and periodicals, but in earlier years bones, clay tablets, papyrus roles, and animal skins, and in later years magnetic tape, computer disks, and machine-readable databases) on which literate people have recorded information. Once humans developed standardized sets of signs and symbols into a written language in Mesopotamia and Egypt sometime before 3000 BC, libraries emerged.

Early library collections (often indistinguishable from what today we call "archives") consisted of a few clay tablets and papyrus rolls made accessible to the tiny literate fraction of the population. They were created to record the accomplishments and the transactions of the politically and economically powerful. Because ancient civilizations made little distinction between church and state (rulers were often considered to be gods), many early libraries were located in temples where scribes recorded information that the governing class considered important, and preserved, classified, and arranged it for future reference.

In the middle of the third millennium BC, a library at Ebla (located in what is now northwestern Syria) contained more than 15,000 clay tablets consisting of government documents, gazetteers, and linguistic and religious reference works. In the seventh century BC, Assyrian king Ashurbanipal ordered scribes to gather tablets from private houses and temples for a palace collection that he put together in Nineveh. Its holdings – accessible only to the king and his scribes – reflected his interests, and included syllabaries, horoscopes, incantations, proverbs, poetry, and omen texts, all inscribed on clay or wooden tablets, organized by physical format, and housed in labeled containers.

The Alexandrian Library, founded by Ptolemy I Soter about 300 BC, had three aims: (1) to collect every work written in Greek as well as sacred texts of contiguous civilizations; (2) to edit and authenticate Greek poets and dramatists; and (3) to create a research library for scholars to study all these materials. Famous scholars were hired as directors, among them Callimachus (d. 240 BC): he compiled the library's catalogue called the *Pinakes*, a classified shelf list of ten main classes (for example, drama, laws, history) that referenced labels attached to the ends of the papyrus rolls. Within each class, texts were first arranged alphabetically by main author, after which followed titles of his works. Estimates of the library's collection range from 40,000 to 700,000 scrolls. Destroyed in the seventh century, the Alexandrian Library nonetheless left an enduring legacy. It became the prototype of the modern national library, demonstrated that a well-organized collection was essential to scholarly study, and created precedents for bibliographical control of large collections of texts, no matter their format.

During the early centuries of the first millennium, the format of the library's standard information container changed, in part because Christianity, which was emerging as a powerful force, based itself on the examination, comparison, and discussion of the Bible. That text was made much more easily accessible when written on parchment sheets, folded and joined together along one edge. The resulting "codex" also offered ample opportunities for adornment and decoration, thus elevating the work's value (actual and perceived) to the status of "treasure." For the next ten centuries in the Western world, the Roman Church gave libraries responsibility for collecting and preserving these treasures; access to them was reserved for individuals who could be trusted to understand that the information contained therein was a part of God's grand plan. Not coincidentally, the librarians who managed them were most often church officials.

In Asia, the rise of Jainism and Buddhism around the sixth century BC led to the evolution of a canon of religious writings that libraries were established to collect, preserve, and replicate. Emperors in the Han dynasty (206 BC – AD 220) supported efforts to compile and collect Confucian writings and other texts, which were greatly expanded after the invention of paper and the use of block printing made it possible to accelerate rapidly the production of books. Followers of Confucius and Buddha carried their texts to other parts of Asia, where libraries were quickly established to collect and house them for access by people who could mine these information resources for explanations of contemporary phenomena. Three types of libraries developed during India's ancient period (3000 BC – AD 1206): some were attached to palaces and courts, others to centers of learning, still others to places of worship.

What people did to preserve and organize book collections in Latin Christendom's Middle Ages (c. 450–1450) laid the foundation for the concept and organization of contemporary libraries. Monastic libraries, advocated by Western European missionary monks and encouraged by the Benedictine Order, set up often elaborate textual copying systems, and thus preserved many of the classical manuscripts and Church writings for later generations. Nonetheless, few of these libraries contained more than several hundred volumes. In population centers, cathedral libraries developed to support newly emerging schools serving local clergy and civil servants. Universities were established in the twelfth century: because these institutions were less religious and more secular than monastic libraries, the scholarship they fostered encouraged exposure to other cultures. As Western European universities evolved, the libraries connected to them assumed larger responsibilities for collecting, preserving, and organizing information. By the sixteenth century, newer university libraries had impressive models to follow at Padua, Bologna, Paris, Oxford, and Cambridge. At each, a central library grew, albeit largely by donation.

For fresh perspectives, some scholars working in these emerging university environments looked to Muslim cultures, which, beginning in the seventh century, reversed the agenda of the extinct Alexandrian Library by translating Greek and Latin manuscripts into Arabic. They also opened large libraries to members of the elite classes in population centers such as Baghdad and Cairo. In tenth-century Cordoba (Spain), Caliph al-Hakim II constructed in a mosque an impressive library of 400,000 volumes which required a forty-four volume catalogue just to list them all. Scholars from the East and the more secular West frequented the library, where for the first time the latter were introduced to a new carrier of information – paper – which Muslims had brought with them from China centuries earlier.

When Johann Gutenberg developed movable type in Mainz in the middle of the fifteenth century, he set in motion forces that had a profound and irreversible impact on libraries. Within half a century, printing presses spread throughout Europe and expanded book production from hundreds to hundreds of thousands per year. This increase accelerated at the beginning of the sixteenth century, when Reformation leaders used mass-produced pamphlets and books to promote religious education and Bible reading not only as a public good, but also as an effective check to what they perceived as control of the masses by the Catholic Church. Many Protestant zealots showed their contempt for this control by sacking monastery libraries. In turn, the Roman Church created an *Index librorum prohibitorum* to exercise more influence over lay Catholic reading.

For a while, elite collectors continued to favor the manuscript form of the book, in part to distinguish themselves from newer collectors whose capacity to acquire was made possible by the press's ability to reproduce text at less cost. Eventually, elite collectors shifted their habits to printed texts as the expanding audience for all printed materials began to fractionalize. The wealthy collected unique and often sumptuously bound texts of literary works considered worthy of preservation. The emerging middle classes, prospering through commerce and manufacturing, collected informational texts that helped them advance and documented their social, economic, and cultural achievements. The poor passed amongst themselves cheaply printed materials (at least some of them could read) that captured the folklore they had previously communicated orally. All used these information resources to help make sense of the world around them.

Because libraries identified with power, the information resources of the most powerful consistently found their way onto library shelves, middle-class texts increasingly so (especially after civic institutions emerged to educate and inform the bourgeoisie), and lower-class texts hardly at all. Library collections, services, and access were marked by gender as well as class, since they existed in a milieu of information creation, production, and dissemination that was deliberately designed to bolster existing patriarchies. Some libraries existed on the margins of these power structures, however. People connected to minority creeds, or people secretly collecting materials considered offensive to elite cultural norms, often developed their own libraries (personal and institutional) of information resources. As long as they remained hidden away, or as long as those libraries were not perceived by those in power to be threats to their social order, they were generally safe from harm. In addition, wives and daughters of "gentlemen" who boasted impressive private libraries (acquired in part to demonstrate their wealth) frequently had access to these books, which they often read differently from the way in which their mostly male authors and owners intended. Increasingly, libraries began to function as places where multiple interpretations and appropriations of texts were made possible, since no external authority could mandate a uniform interpretation of any text read in solitude.

Just as religious groups sought to propagandize readers through the distribution of texts (many of which found their way into libraries supported by those same groups), so those in political power realized that texts could create a new sense of community by persuading people they were part of a unique "nation." To make manifest the uniqueness of nations, each eventually combined what previously had been the libraries of local social, political, and economic elites with the collections of royalty to create a government-supported national library whose primary responsibility was to identify, collect, record, and organize the information resources that documented the nation's cultural heritage, however narrowly that heritage was defined. So began national libraries in Prussia (later Germany), France, Austria, Spain, Great Britain, and Sweden in the eighteenth century, the US Library of Congress in the nineteenth century, and the Russian State Library and the National Library of China in the twentieth century.

Nations also recognized that they could expand their power by confronting other nations of equal or lesser strength. Colonialism represented a joint effort by national political and religious elites to spread their influence and exploit resources and people beyond their home territories. Portugal, Spain, France, and Great Britain (among others) conquered millions of people on the continents of Africa, Australia, South America, and North America (and thousands of islands in between). Many of those people (especially Africans) were forcibly relocated and/or enslaved. Always the colonizers took with them the cultural institutions they had developed over the centuries, including libraries. Jesuit missionaries who accompanied military forces sent out by national governments quickly established schools and libraries in Asia and South America to hasten the process of converting the indigenous peoples they subjugated. In the colonies of North America, the established Anglican Church of Great Britain worked through the Society for Promoting Christian Knowledge and the Society for the Propagation of the Gospel in Foreign Parts to establish several kinds of libraries for the use of clergy and laity, some to help steel the faithful against temptation, others to help convert Native Americans.

In the seventeenth century, a new order we now call "modernity" emerged that separated people's daily life experiences into work and leisure. Over time, those who established and ran libraries came to regard as most important the kinds of information that addressed questions related to work, or helped readers become intelligent consumers, educated people, and better-behaved citizens. In their collecting practices, librarians clearly favored the kinds of information they and others labeled "useful knowledge."

As the Enlightenment secularized Western societies and cultures in the eighteenth and nineteenth centuries, it led to the emergence of new institutions that gradually evolved a "public sphere" designed to voice a "public interest" that neither governments nor marketplaces could safely ignore. Because institutions created by this movement (for example, newspapers, periodicals, political parties, and professions) insisted on participating in public life, they effectively forced the expansion of access to existing libraries for larger numbers of the citizenry, and even created several new types of libraries. Besides national libraries, private libraries, and university libraries, many individuals began to pool resources to create social libraries. Membership was restricted to those who paid dues, and those invited to membership generally had to meet certain qualifications. As a result, social libraries were run by a fairly homogeneous socioeconomic group with a clear idea of what constituted "useful knowledge." The first order of books that Benjamin Franklin sent to London in 1731 to begin the Library Company of Philadelphia contained no novels, but instead concentrated on dictionaries, grammars, atlases, histories, and works on science and agriculture "suited to the tastes and purposes of young tradesmen." Some social libraries evolved into athenaeums (socially exclusive reading institutions); others eventually made the transition to public libraries.

To satisfy a different kind of information need, many entrepreneurs challenged convention by purchasing whole collections called "circulating libraries," which largely consisted of "leisure reading," and then for a subscription fee rented access to these books to anyone who could pay. Often these libraries were located in or near coffeehouses which functioned as popular, social gathering places; sometimes they were located near millinery shops frequented by women. Over time, circulating libraries increasingly specialized in novels, though such books were widely considered a waste of time, if not genuinely harmful. Increasingly, circulating libraries served women, whose literacy rate was catching up with men in the late eighteenth and early nineteenth centuries. Most complaints about novel reading came from men who little understood how women used this activity to challenge contemporary conventions on female social behavior, and construct a sense of community that patriarchy continued to deny them in public life.

About the middle of the nineteenth century, tax-supported libraries serving the general public began to appear in the Western world. After the British Public Libraries Act of 1850 authorized municipalities to collect taxes for the support of libraries, Liverpool, Manchester, and Birmingham quickly established these civic institutions. In the United States, individual states passed similar enabling legislation in the last half of the century. The Boston Public Library, which opened its doors in 1854, became a prototype for many public libraries that followed (for example, Cleveland, Pittsburgh, Atlanta, Los Angeles). Each trumpeted the provision of, and access to, "useful knowledge" as the public library's primary community role; each defined itself as an educational institution which, along with schools and churches, constituted one of the three pillars of civilization. But while public library officials worked hard to identify and make accessible "useful knowledge," they constantly met resistance from their publics, who instead mostly wanted novels. This put public libraries in an awkward position: they claimed a right to public funding as educational institutions, yet they had to satisfy popular desires for leisure reading or risk losing their clientele. That frustration is evident in a poem one anonymous librarian wrote to mime the lyrical construction of "Titwillow," a song in Gilbert and Sullivan's *Mikado*:

> At a library desk stood some readers one day,
> Crying "Novels, oh, novels, oh, novels!"
> And I said to them, "People, oh, why do you say
>   Give us novels, oh, novels, oh, novels?
> Is it weakness of intellect, people," I cried,
> "Or simply a space where the brains should abide?"
> They answered me not, or they only replied,
>   "Give us novels, oh, novels, oh novels!"

> A librarian may talk till he's black in the face
>   About novels, oh, novels, oh, novels!
> And may think that with patience he may raise the taste
>   Above novels, oh, novels, oh, novels!
> He may talk till with age his round shoulders are bent
> And the white hairs of time 'mid the black ones are sent,
> When he hands his report in, still seventy per cent
>   Will be novels, oh, novels, oh, novels!
>   ("Fiction Song," 1890)

For generations thereafter, public librarians engaged in a war of subtle persuasion. The American Library Association (ALA), established by white, Anglo-Saxon, educated, middle-class men in 1876, three years later adopted as a motto: "the best reading for the greatest number at the least cost." By the end of the century, the ALA had published standards that recommended that novels ought to total no more than 15 percent of a library collection, though novels consistently accounted for 65–75 percent of circulation across the nation. Many public libraries instituted limits: users could check out up to two books per visit, but only one could be a novel.

Ironically, in the late nineteenth century American librarians abdicated authority to define "the best reading" to a Northeastern literary establishment and to academics on campuses across the country, who were just then organizing into formal disciplines and departments. Because librarians trusted this new hierarchy of experts to identify "the best reading," the ALA and the Library Association (a sister organization in the United Kingdom established in 1877) instead devoted their energies primarily to providing for "the greatest number at the least cost" by improving access systems and institutional management. These priorities effectively drew parameters around the discourse of librarianship, and quickly established its professional jurisdiction. Eventually, the practice of librarianship in most of the rest of the world followed this model.

Reinforcing these jurisdictional claims was a professional curriculum that originated with Melvil Dewey's bootleg School of Library Service, which (against the wishes of trustees who wanted to protect their all-male campus) opened in an off-campus Columbia College (later University) storeroom in January 1887. Its first class of twenty included seventeen women, thus signaling to women who aspired to professional careers that they would be welcome in librarianship. Dewey's students concentrated on learning the most efficient modern methods of library practice (developing collections, cataloguing and classification, retrieving information, and managing the physical plant and bureaucracy), and on developing a "library faith" – a conviction that the "best reading" which libraries made accessible was essential for democracy and an informed citizenry. Two years later, Dewey took his library school to Albany when he became New York State Library Director. The Albany curriculum became a model for most library schools established in subsequent years, each graduating new professionals intensely loyal to Dewey's methods. Many of these graduates initially became itinerant cataloguers and classifiers, hired temporarily by municipalities to systematize book collections inherited from local social libraries being converted into public libraries. In many cases, local officials were reacting to pressure brought by elite women's clubs that embraced the library faith and took responsibility for establishing local public libraries as a project of civic improvement.

All were players in a "public library movement" largely stimulated by steel magnate Andrew Carnegie, who between 1881 and 1917 spent $56,136,430.97 constructing a total of 2,507 library buildings in the United States (1,681 buildings), Canada (125), Great Britain and Ireland (660), New Zealand (17), South Africa (12), the West Indies (5), Australia and Tasmania (4), the Seychelles (1), Mauritius (1), and Fiji (1). His philanthropy doubled the size of the American public library system, greatly expanded the market for booksellers, and cemented into municipal budgets a sense of obligation to support an institution that constituted yet another effective mechanism for book distribution. By combining Carnegie's largesse with Dewey's library science, the public library became a ubiquitous, efficiently managed (if relatively low-profile) cultural institution. Any day of the week a stranger could walk into one of thousands of these institutions to see retired men pouring over newspapers in the reading room, children listening to someone reading aloud in the children's room, or women checking out the latest popular novel over the circulation desk. During periods of high unemployment and cold weather, or late afternoons (after schools closed and before parents returned home from work), the number of visitors swelled; so did circulation. But throughout the twentieth century, library users continued to demand "novels, oh, novels, oh, novels," and librarians had to supply them or lose valuable public support.

Collections and services in US academic libraries also mushroomed in the late nineteenth century. Many colleges across the country were transforming themselves from undergraduate institutions with well-defined classical curricula to universities that offered elective courses, supported graduate education, and gave research high priority. Academia also institutionalized and legitimated a literary canon, and then claimed authority to identify what fiction people ought to read. Dutifully, academic libraries collected these canonical titles and the published research that analyzed them. To support an elective system of courses and the research conducted by faculty and graduate students, college libraries greatly expanded their collections and services, including hours of opening. At Columbia, for example, between 1883 and 1886 nine departmental libraries were consolidated into one large, central facility, whose collections were identified in an elaborate public card catalogue and classified by the new Dewey Decimal system. Hours of opening were extended from four hours a day, three days a week to 8.00 a.m. to midnight, seven days a week.

Thereafter, Columbia (like most other institutions making the transition from classical college to research university) allocated a greater share of its budget to expanding collections, acquiring unique items that either attracted other donated collections or directly served the university's curricular strengths and research needs. By the middle of the twentieth century, many university library systems had grown to include scores of departmental libraries scattered across campuses, each of which served particular clienteles. Academic libraries became primary markets for the scholarly books faculty research produced. And when returning World War II veterans and their children multiplied enrollments even more, academic library collections expanded along with them.

American school libraries experienced substantial growth in the wake of late nineteenth-century compulsory education laws. Many school boards, desiring to stretch state appropriations for library books, worked out cooperative agreements with public libraries which promised to make their books accessible to local schoolchildren. By the end of World War I, however, the National Education Association (NEA) began pressing for direct control over school library collections. It advocated the creation of separate libraries to be acquired, staffed, and organized by the school system specifically for teachers and students, and specifically in support of the school curriculum. In the 1920s, the NEA developed standards for elementary and secondary school libraries, and shortly thereafter some state and local governments started funding school library supervisors, issuing school library handbooks, and publishing recommended reading lists. The Depression interrupted growth, but in postwar America school libraries expanded their collections to include non-print texts. As a result, many transformed into "instructional media centers." Then came the Great Society legislation of the mid-1960s, including the Library Services and Construction Acts, the Higher Education Act, and (particularly important to school libraries) the Elementary and Secondary Education Act. Assisted by this funding, the percentage of public schools with libraries increased from 50 in 1958 (40,000) to 93 in 1985 (74,000), while the average size of their book collections increased from 2,972 to 8,466. School libraries across the globe emulated the American model.

Modern librarians have generally divided the world of libraries into four types: public, academic, school, and special. This last category constitutes a miscellany, into which are placed libraries of many kinds (including national libraries) that have had significant influence on the history of books. Examples in the US include research libraries like the American Antiquarian Society, the Huntington Library in San Marino, California, the Folger Shakespeare Library of Washington, DC, and the Newberry Library of Chicago; state library agencies (some of which, as in New York, function like national libraries for their states); law libraries; information centers for business and industry; and libraries attached to cultural institutions like art museums, music halls, and opera houses.

By the last quarter of the twentieth century, librarianship had sedimented into a set of traditional services carried out in tens of thousands of libraries in the Western world, hundreds of thousands across the globe. All wanted to provide "the best reading for the greatest number at the least cost," but by this time systems to identify "the best reading" had established themselves outside the jurisdiction of librarianship. Generations of librarians had come to regard print largely as an object to be handled, and library practice focused much more on information access than information content. As a result, the profession concentrated on harnessing the latest technologies to improve service.

Meanwhile, influential intellectuals began arguing that economies in Western world countries were shifting from industry to services, and one of the most important services in this new economic order was the provision of information. In his *The Gutenberg Galaxy* (1962), Marshall McLuhan predicted "a paperless society." In his *Understanding Media* (1964), he said the book was "like a dinosaur just before he disappeared." These influential books were followed by Daniel Bell's *The Coming of the Post-industrial Society* (1973) and Alvin Toffler's *Future Shock* (1970) and *The Third Wave* (1980). All these arguments were grounded on the perceived potential of the computer, which had a tremendous capacity to process rapidly what in the nineteenth century had been called "useful information."

For librarians, the catalyst that linked "best reading" to the kinds of "information" computers could handle best was F. Wilfrid Lancaster, a University of Illinois library educator who in 1978 published *Toward Paperless Information Systems*, one of the most cited works of library literature in recent times. That Lancaster made this prediction should not be surprising. His professional experience in science and technology libraries led him to value most the kinds of "information" his professional forebears often called "useful knowledge," and because librarianship for the most part shared these values, librarians were easily persuaded that newer information technologies held the secret to the future of the profession.

Librarianship quickly turned from an "education" profession to an "information" profession (some even argued "*the* information profession"), and attempted to position itself as a major player in the "age of information," in which "information" was redefined – one might even say "invented" – by the technology. In the absence of an adequate historical understanding of how terms like "useful knowledge" and "best reading" had morphed into "information," many librarians dreaded predictions by information-technology evangelists that books and libraries would not survive the twentieth century. They also worried as they watched one of the library's traditional user and support groups – middle-class professionals – begin to use computers for some of their information needs and thus bypass libraries more and more. The subtext to all this was a narrowed definition of "information," one driven by technology and invented by powerful people with substantial self-interest in defining the parameters of "the information age."

Just at the time when librarianship transformed itself into an "information profession" focused on technologies, however, scholars in the humanities (and some "softer" social sciences) began to question the historical traditions surrounding cultural definitions of "best reading." Where previously humanities scholars had concentrated mostly on "culture as text," they now began to explore questions addressing "culture as agency" and "culture as practice." Although elements of "culture as text" remained in the practice of librarianship (for example, rare books and children's librarianship), the profession manifested little interest in or knowledge of culture as agency or culture as practice – an approach that would have repositioned the physical book as an essential element in library service. And largely because the profession's perspective had been "user in the life of the library" rather than "library in the life of the user," library and information studies discourse in the last quarter of the twentieth century focused hardly at all on information content, but almost entirely on information access made possible by new technologies.

In 1967, for example, the Ohio College Association founded the Ohio College Library Center (OCLC). For the first four years, the Center developed a systems architecture, and provided catalogue card production services. In 1971, it began online operation with its Cataloguing Subsystem. Because OCLC had also adopted MARC records (a standard format for machine-readable bibliographic records developed by the Library of Congress) on which many libraries depended, by 2000 thousands of libraries around the world were using its database for cooperative cataloguing and author/title verification.

Meanwhile, the US Defense Department's Advanced Research Projects Agency established a computer network. When the federal government sponsored a program to establish communication protocols to integrate multiple networks, the Internet was born. By the turn of the century, thousands of libraries of all types had also developed online public access catalogues accessible through the Internet, adopted packaged automated circulation systems, and incorporated the use of CD-ROM products and Internet-accessible databases into the provision of traditional library services. Among billions of other library users, students and scholars of book history have benefited substantially from the searching capacities that these systems provide. Libraries and their information technologies deserve much credit for the quality and quantity of recent book history research (print and electronic).

In the past decade, a small group of library historians have begun analyzing culture as agency and practice from a "library in the life of the user" perspective, and thus located the historical study of libraries and librarianship in the broader context of book history. For example, in a 1998 *American Quarterly* article entitled "The Business of Reading in Nineteenth-century America," Thomas Augst demonstrated how users of the New York Mercantile Library commodified their reading into categorizations like "useful knowledge" and "rational amusements," and how the library's middle-class, male patrons then used the act of reading as an agent to demonstrate their "character." In the process of adapting to these interests, library managers articulated a new rationale for understanding these new dynamics for reading to justify it as a civic enterprise worthy of private and public support.

Other studies took similar approaches, including Abigail Van Slyck's *Free to All: Carnegie Libraries and American Culture, 1890–1920* (1995), Alistair Black's *The Public Library in Britain, 1914–2000* (2000), and, in part, my own *Irrepressible Reformer: A Biography of Melvil Dewey* (1996). Perhaps the best example of this kind of scholarship is Christine Pawley's *Reading on the Middle Border: The Culture of Print in Late Nineteenth-century Osage, Iowa* (2001), which harnesses census and extant library circulation records to identify who read what from the collections of a small town library in northern Iowa between 1890 and 1895. From her research, Pawley constructed a reading profile for an entire community, and located the multiple roles the public library played in facilitating its individual and collective reading experiences.

Over the past century and a half, the priorities of librarianship have been reflected in the ALA motto: "the best reading for the greatest number at the least cost." During that time, libraries worldwide have done three things very well: (1) made information on many subjects accessible to billions of people; (2) provided tens of thousands of places where patrons have been able to meet formally, as clubs or groups, or informally as citizens and students utilizing a civic institution and a cultural agency; and (3) furnished billions of reading materials to billions of patrons. In the past half-century, library statistics on book circulation and visits around the globe demonstrate mostly steady growth. For students and scholars of book history, libraries have always been valuable research sites. Today, library historians are harnessing theoretical constructs that deepen our understanding of the multiple roles these ubiquitous institutions have played in their host communities over many generations.

REFERENCES AND FURTHER READING

Augst, Thomas (1998) "The Business of Reading in Nineteenth-century America: The New York Mercantile Library." *American Quarterly*, 50: 267–305.

Battle, Matthew (2003) *Library: An Unquiet History.* New York: Norton.

Bell, Daniel (1973) *The Coming of the Post-industrial Society: A Venture in Social Forecasting.* New York: Basic.

Black, Alistair (1996) *A New History of the English Public Library: Social and Intellectual Contexts, 1850–1914.* London: Leicester University Press.

— (2000) *The Public Library in Britain, 1914–2000.* London: British Library.

Casson, Lionel (2001) *Libraries in the Ancient World.* New Haven: Yale University Press.

Christ, Karl (1984) *The Handbook of Medieval Library History.* Metuchen, NJ: Scarecrow.

Cole, John Y. and Aikin, Jane (eds.) (2005) *Encyclopedia of the Library of Congress: For Congress, the Nation, and the World.* Lanham: Bernan.

"Fiction Song" (1890) *Library Journal*, 15: 325.

Fyfe, Janet (1992) *Book Behind Bars: The Role of Books, Reading, and Libraries in British Prison Reform, 1701–1911.* Westport, CT: Greenwood.

Garrison, Dee (2003) *Apostles of Culture: The Public Librarian and American Society, 1876–1920*, 2nd edn. Madison: University of Wisconsin Press.

Gilmore, William J. (1989) *Reading Becomes a Necessity of Life: Material and Cultural Life in Rural New England, 1780–1835.* Knoxville: University of Tennessee Press.

Harris, Michael H. (1995) *History of Libraries in the Western World.* Metuchen, NJ: Scarecrow.

Harris, P. R. (ed.) (1991) *The Library of the British Museum.* London: British Library.

Knuth, Rebecca (2003) *Libricide: The Regime-sponsored Destruction of Books and Libraries in the Twentieth Century.* Westport, CT: Praeger.

Lancaster, F. Wilfrid (1978) *Toward Paperless Information Systems.* New York: Academic.

Lerner, Fred (1998) *The Story of Libraries: From the Invention of Writing to the Computer.* New York: Continuum.

McHenry, Elizabeth (2002) *Forgotten Readers: Recovering the Lost History of African American Literary Societies.* Durham: Duke University Press.

MacLeod, Roy (ed.) (2000) *The Library of Alexandria: Centre of Learning in the Ancient World.* London: I. B. Tauris.

McLuhan, Marshall (1962) *The Gutenberg Galaxy: The Making of Typographic Man.* Toronto: University of Toronto Press.

— (1964) *Understanding Media: The Extension of Man.* New York: McGraw-Hill.

Marshall, D. N. (1983) *History of Libraries: Ancient and Medieval.* New Delhi: Oxford University Press.

Pawley, Christine (2001) *Reading on the Middle Border: The Culture of Print in Late Nineteenth-century Osage, Iowa.* Amherst: University of Massachusetts Press.

Robbins, Louise (2000) *The Dismissal of Miss Ruth Brown: Civil Rights, Censorship, and the American Library.* Norman: University of Oklahoma Press.

Rose, Jonathan (ed.) (2001) *The Holocaust and the Book: Destruction and Preservation.* Amherst: University of Massachusetts Press.

Rubin, Richard (2004) *Foundations of Library and Information Science.* New York: Neal-Schuman.

Sherman, William H. (1995) *John Dee: The Politics of Reading and Writing in the English Renaissance.* Amherst: University of Massachusetts Press.

Staikos, Konstantinos Sp. (2000) *The Great Libraries: From Antiquity to the Renaissance*, trans. Timothy Cullen. New Castle: Oak Knoll.

Stam, David H. (ed.) (2001) *International Dictionary of Library Histories.* Chicago: Fitzroy Dearborn.

Thompson, James (1977) *A History of the Principles of Librarianship.* Hamden: Linnet.

Toffler, Alvin (1970) *Future Shock.* New York: Random House.

— (1980) *The Third Wave.* New York: William Morrow.

Van Slyck, Abigail (1995) *Free to All: Carnegie Libraries and American Culture, 1890–1920.* Chicago: University of Chicago Press.

Wiegand, Wayne A. (1996) *Irrepressible Reformer: A Biography of Melvil Dewey.* Chicago: American Library Association.

— and Davis, Donald G., Jr. (eds.) (1994) *Encyclopedia of Library History.* New York: Garland.

Coda

40
Does the Book Have a Future?

Angus Phillips

Old media don't die; they just have to grow old gracefully.
(Douglas Adams, *The Hitchhiker's Guide to the Future*)

From the beginnings of the digital revolution, commentators have examined the prospects for the book and wondered whether it can survive alongside new technologies. In an age when text can be accessed all over the world through a variety of devices, and when the book competes with many other forms of entertainment, does it seem a dated and outmoded technology or a reliable and robust companion? What sort of future can we see for the book?

If the book has had its day, what would be the test? When readers are avid followers of fiction on their mobile phones? When children study using laptops and are leaving behind the use of print resources? When less than half of all adults in the world's largest economy read literature? When a successful publisher sells off its print program to concentrate on electronic resources and services? When dictionary users consult electronic pens for a definition or a translation?

This is the world now, and if some of these trends continue, the future of the book in its traditional sense is certainly under question. Yet if we apply other tests – for example, the number of books published each year or the success of individual writers such as J. K. Rowling – the book remains resilient in the face of changes in technology, culture, and society. Paradoxically, the world going digital is helping to keep the book alive, with the possibility that books may remain in print indefinitely while being available to buy anywhere in the world.

The Digital Revolution

Industries are going through major upheavals as a result of the "digital revolution." This can be defined as: "The effects of the rapid drop in cost and rapid expansion of power of digital devices such as computers and telecommunications. It includes changes in technology and society, and is often specifically used to refer to the controversies that occur as these technologies are widely adopted" (*Wikipedia*, accessed May 3, 2005). Two examples of industries that have been affected are photography and music. The switch from film to digital photography has impacted on the processing industry, the manu- facture and sales of traditional film cameras, and the way in which people share and store their holiday snaps and family memories. What began as a switch from film to digital cameras has taken another turn with the development of high-resolution camera phones.

The music industry transferred from analog to digital (Negroponte 1995), with compact discs (CDs) replacing vinyl records. Subsequently, the resistance to music downloads and file sharing has broken down, and the music charts now take account of downloaded music. Most artists openly support the changes. The concept of owning music is under question; for some consumers, it may be enough to listen on demand without having a personal copy of a particular track. "With ubiquitous broadband, both wired and wireless, more consumers will turn to the celestial jukebox of music services that offer every track ever made, playable on demand" (Anderson 2004).

If we turn to book production, the *process* of publishing books has gone thoroughly digital – from the delivery of text from authors on disk or by e-mail through to page design on computer and the electronic delivery of files to the printer. The concept of "create once/publish many" has led to print being only one of the formats employed by publishers, alongside Web delivery and CD-ROMs. Educational, reference, and professional publishing have adopted electronic publishing as a central part of their activities.

In scholarly publishing, online access is the dominant mode of delivery for many journals. There is also a trend toward digital publication of academic monographs. Oxford Scholarship Online, launched in 2003, is a service for delivering monographs to libraries, using titles published by Oxford University Press. With search facilities and cross-referencing, the service replicates "the kind of system that academics already use in the online environment of scholarly journals" (Thompson 2005: 363). Lynne Brindley, Chief Executive of the British Library, predicts that by the year 2020, 40 percent of UK research monographs will be available in electronic format only, while a further 50 percent will be produced in both print and digital formats (British Library 2005). This development will require a major cultural shift in academic communities, as print publication (with peer review) for book-length works is still a requirement for career advancement in many disciplines.

Educational publishing in many parts of the world is moving further toward the development of electronic resources. In the United Kingdom, the government has directed monies toward e-learning resources and high-speed broadband connections in schools. In China, there is government support for educational resources with online delivery, especially for the teaching of English. The CD-ROM was once seen as a uni- versal means of electronic delivery for educational and reference material, and in the early 1990s publishers invested heavily in multimedia versions of print products. With poor sales and the rapid expansion of the Web, investment soon switched to online developments. As home users increasingly adopt broadband, there are renewed opportunities for publishers to produce multimedia content and reduce emphasis on print.

A decade ago, the novelist E. Annie Proulx said that the information highway was meant for "bulletin boards on esoteric subjects, reference works, lists and news – timely, utilitarian information, efficiently pulled through the wires. Nobody is going to sit down and read a novel on a twitchy little screen. Ever" (*New York Times*, May 26, 1994). Today, e-books of novels are certainly available to read on computers and handheld devices, and versions of classic novels can be downloaded for free. There are people who read novels on handhelds, but the numbers remain tiny in comparison with traditional print readers. Could this position change? If the iPod and other music players have revolutionized the way in which people engage with music, could an equivalent highly portable device work for print? Could there be added value in e-books, in a similar manner to the extra features found on DVDs? Will readers browse texts using a randomizing facility? Audio book companies are already seeing the potential for downloads of their products, replacing tapes and CDs.

The Japanese book industry is mature, with negative sales growth over a number of years, and commentators view the market as saturated. Madoka Hanajiri sees that "Customers' behaviour has been and is continuing to change. More than twenty years ago, it was cool and fashionable for college students to carry around philosophy books even if they didn't actually read them. Now college students pay more attention to their mobile phones" (Hanajiri 2003: 55). As elsewhere in the world, phones are being used for e-mail, surfing the Web, games, and photography; e-book sales are growing fast, and new titles are being written for readers on mobile phones. One reader commented: "My eyes sometimes get tired but I like the idea of being able to read on trains when they are so packed there isn't even space to open a book . . . I also like dipping in and out of books, rather than always reading straight narratives" (McCurry 2005). The author Yoshi wrote *Deep Love* (2002), the story of a 17-year-old girl who finds romance, in installments for reading on mobile phones:

> Instalments of the novel started receiving millions of hits, mainly from teenage girls, many of whom wouldn't touch an ordinary book . . . Unlike authors of traditional novels, Yoshi knows immediately when his readers are getting bored: they either stop visiting his site or e-mail him directly. Because he writes in instalments, he can meddle with the storyline at any time. (McCurry 2005)

Dedicated electronic devices – e-book readers specifically designed to store and display books with the clarity of the printed page – have not yet achieved a mass sale. In 2006, Sony launched a new lightweight reader with a memory that could support up to eighty titles. Echoing the development of Apple's iTunes music store, agreements were reached with major publishers to sell digital books via an online store. Victoria Barnsley, Chief Executive of HarperCollins UK, commented: "Whether it is the Sony Reader that proves successful or the next generation of reading devices, this could be a big market and provide opportunities for publishers" (Andrews 2006). Meanwhile, work has been progressing on the development of electronic paper. Just as vinyl records, CDs, videos, and DVDs can all disappear into a hard disk in your living room, so could your library of books. When you want to read your chosen title, you would be able to download and display it within a book-like object with flexible pages similar to paper. The book would be highly portable and you could take several titles on holiday with you using a small memory device. Using wireless technology, you could stream in whatever title you chose. The costs of electronic paper remain too high for mass production, but development work continues.

The linking of mobile and GPS (global positioning system) technologies offers further opportunities; for example, to revolutionize travel publishing. Although guidebooks are available as e-books, they are not yet linked to the user's location, offering local cultural or restaurant tips. There is the potential to offer a range of novels or travel literature suitable to the reader's destination: for example, the tourist in Paris could have a downloadable copy of Victor Hugo's *The Hunchback of Notre-Dame*, Hemingway's *The Sun Also Rises*, or Dan Brown's *The Da Vinci Code* with the relevant text highlighted.

Society and Culture

The book competes with a variety of other entertainments, and the current younger generation is accustomed to alternative ways of acquiring information. The newspaper industry has had to adapt to competition from television and the Web. In 2004, *The Times* of London went tabloid. The editor, Robert Thomson, quoted the Web as an influence on the paper's new design: "The traditional broadsheet involves what you might call scanning skills, but for an increasing number of people, especially young people who are used to internet presentation, they have developed scrolling skills. Interestingly enough, those scrolling skills work a lot better in the compact format than they do in a broadsheet" (Greenslade 2004).

The primacy of print is under question, undermined by the ease of access to the Internet and a new generation brought up without the same unequivocal respect for the book. For many, Google is the first port of call in the search for facts, replacing the reference shelf by the desk. Schoolchildren are encouraged by their teachers to surf for background information for their homework rather than use an encyclopedia. Universities struggle to teach the virtues of citing sources correctly, but students see little wrong in adapting or copying the words of others. In pilot projects in schools in the UK and the US, schoolchildren are being given laptops or PDAs to use at home and school, replacing the heavy rucksack of schoolbooks. Interactive whiteboards are changing the style of teaching and offer opportunities for new classroom activities.

For adults, reading for pleasure has to be fitted into busy lifestyles. Reasons for not reading books (given by non-readers in the UK) include: preferring newspapers or magazines; having insufficient time; preferring a more relaxing activity; not enjoying reading (Bury 2005: 13). In Ian McEwan's novel *Saturday*, Henry Perowne, a busy and highly intelligent neurosurgeon, persists with fiction recommended by his daughter, but remains cautious of this other world:

> Henry never imagined he would end up living in the sort of house that had a library. It's an ambition of his to spend whole weekends in there, stretched out on one of the Knole sofas, pot of coffee at his side, reading some world-rank masterpiece or other, perhaps in translation . . . But his free time is always fragmented, not only by errands and family obligations and sports, but by the restlessness that comes with these weekly islands of freedom. He doesn't want to spend his days off lying, or even sitting, down. (McEwan 2005: 66)

We could never catch up with our reading in any case. The Mexican writer Gabriel Zaid, in his playful treatise on reading, *So Many Books*, points out that a new book is published every thirty seconds: "Books are published at such a rapid rate that they make us exponentially more ignorant. If a person read a book every day, he would be neglecting to read four thousand others, published the same day" (Zaid 2003: 22).

In the UK, around half of all leisure time is spent watching television (National Statistics 2005: 174). Only one in five adults is classified as a heavy book-buyer, while a third of adults surveyed had not bought a single book in the past year. "Broadly speaking, the richer and more educated a person, the more books they buy" (Bury 2005: 4), yet growth in the UK economy and a higher proportion of the population entering higher education have not led to a boom in the sale of books. Between 1993 and 2003, the number of books borrowed from UK libraries declined by 36 percent and the active lending stock fell by 17 percent (LISU 2004: 19). Yet the use of audiovisual and electronic media in libraries grew over this period.

In the United States, considerable concern was created by the appearance of the National Endowment for the Arts report on *Reading at Risk* (2004). Between 1982 and 2002, the proportion of the US adult population reading literature (novels, short stories, plays, and poetry) fell by 10 percentage points, from 56.9 percent to 46.7 percent. The proportion reading any kind of book fell by 7 percentage points. In 2002, while 55 percent of women read literature, the figure for men was only 37.6 percent. In the preface, Dana Gioia, Chairman of the National Endowment for the Arts, wrote:

> This comprehensive survey of American literary reading presents a detailed but bleak assessment of the decline of reading's role in the nation's culture. For the first time in modern history, less than half of the adult population now reads literature . . . *Reading at Risk* merely documents and quantifies a huge cultural transformation that most Americans have already noted – our society's massive shift towards electronic media for information and entertainment. (National Endowment for the Arts 2004: vii)

To those horrified by these statistics, it is important to consider what went before. As Umberto Eco wrote, "We can complain that a lot of people spend their day watching

TV and never read a book or a newspaper, and this is certainly a social and educational problem, but frequently we forget that the same people, a few centuries ago, were watching at most a few standard images and were totally illiterate" (Eco 1996: 297).

If newspapers have to consider competition from other media, then the book industry is also likely to continue to see erosion of their base readership. In highly developed nations, as more television is watched, as the Internet is more frequently surfed, and as more electronic games are played, is there not an inevitability about the decline in time spent reading books? The US analyst Barrie Rappaport commented in 2004:

> The problem is that you can only grow by attracting new customers, but the industry is not attracting new customers; in fact it's losing customers . . . That means it's relying more and more on the heavier book-buyer – the more affluent, higher-educated customer – but we're seeing some slack in that area as well. There's only so many books that those people can buy. (quoted in Nance and Thomas 2004)

This is at the heart of the present debate in the mature industries in the US and the UK. How can they reach out to a new audience? What kind of books do light-buyers and non-buyers want? Boyd Tonkin writes: "The book market certainly needs to expand. What it requires is creative innovation, not mad downmarket plunges. For a start, publishers have to think harder about how to reach the hordes of critical consumers of film, TV, internet and pop culture who should be reading books as sharp and savvy as all the shows, sites and bands they adore" (Tonkin 2005).

To stimulate a wider sector of the population to read, is it possible for the publishing industry to be less elitist in its approach and more imaginative in its workings with other media? Publishing recruits the same personnel as make up its readership, as the publisher John Blake highlighted: "Publishing is dominated by middle-class publishers, publishing books for middle-class people to read" (Bury 2005: 12). Could representatives of a wider cross-section of the population produce books that more people want to read, with content more appropriate to their interests? The success of *manga* (Japanese comic books) is an example of more visual material that can encourage reading amongst young people who are attracted to DVDs and games rather than books. Does it in the end matter what type of books people read? The debate echoes concerns from an earlier age, as Edward Tenner notes: "Even in the golden age of print culture from the 1880s to the 1930s, literary men and women were appalled by most Americans' indifference to book buying and by what they saw as the masses' preference for trashy and sensational reading" (Tenner 2004).

Aside from the Harry Potter phenomenon, a great stimulus to sales of books has been the involvement of television shows. Recommendations by Oprah in the US and Richard and Judy in the UK have led to big sales increases for the books concerned, suggesting there is a market for quality literature and nonfiction. However, especially in the UK, the increasing reliance of chain booksellers on sales figures to drive their stock decisions means that a new book has very little time to make its mark in the market. The concentration of bookselling has made it much more difficult for independent publishers to place their books in front of potential readers. Smaller bookshops have given up trying to compete against the discounting of the chains and the supermarkets, either ceasing to trade or becoming more specialist in the type of stock they offer.

The concentration of production in the publishing industry looks certain to continue. An Arts Council report into independent publishing in England concluded that the industry is becoming increasingly polarized "between a small number of very large corporate publishers, mainly divisions of multinational media and publishing groups, and a large number of small and very small operators" (Hampson and Richardson 2004: 14). The larger publishing houses strive to maintain branding and innovation by keeping smaller imprints alive within the larger business, but there are questions over the diversity of publishing if the industry is dominated by the larger players in both publishing and bookselling.

Free Culture

Lawrence Lessig's book *Free Culture* (2004) is subtitled "How big media uses technology and the law to lock down culture and control creativity." Lessig argues that "A free culture supports and protects creators and innovators. It does this directly by granting intellectual property rights. But it does so indirectly by limiting the reach of those rights, to guarantee that follow-on creators and innovators remain as free as possible from the control of the past" (Lessig 2004: xiv).

The development of the Internet has led to new ways of thinking about intellectual property and the rights of copyright holders and users. The Web provides tremendous opportunities for collaborators to develop software, create multimedia projects, and write stories together. One example is *Wikipedia*, the free online encyclopedia whose entries anyone can edit. Yet the rules surrounding intellectual property remain rigid. When readers share a book – a novel passed round a family or set of friends – they are not penalized for those further uses, and copies can be bought and sold second-hand without royalties being payable to the copyright holder. By contrast, passing on the digital file of an e-book is rarely allowed by the terms of purchase, and controls in the software would most likely prevent this.

If the music industry has become more relaxed about music downloads, should not the publishing industry be more open to new ways of thinking about the copyright environment? In the area of academic journal publishing, there is a debate about whether the Internet changes the rules. Without the costs of print, journal publishing potentially becomes more profitable. Publishers would argue that they still have the editorial and quality assurance costs (articles are normally peer reviewed), but challenges from the Open Access movement have led to some journals becoming freely available to users (Worlock 2004). Some would also argue that publishers ought not to profit from information whose creation has been paid for by the government and research institutions. Should not critical research in medicine be available gratis to anybody? There is no clear indication of how great a hold Open Access will have on the journal industry, but experimentation continues and increasingly authors are allowed to post the final versions of their papers on personal websites. If monographs were also to go online, publishers would have to work ever harder to justify their existence (Phillips 2004).

Another initiative is the Creative Commons, based at Stanford Law School, which provides a set of intellectual property (IP) licenses for authors to use. For example, a photographer could publish a photo on the Web and allow others to use it on their websites as long as it is properly attributed. Creative Commons was founded on the notion that not everybody wants to exercise all their IP rights:

> Many people have long since concluded that all-out copyright doesn't help them gain the exposure and widespread distribution they want. Many entrepreneurs and artists have come to prefer relying on innovative business models rather than full-fledged copyright to secure a return on their creative investment. Still others get fulfilment from contributing to and participating in an intellectual commons. For whatever reasons, it is clear that many citizens of the Internet want to share their work – and the power to reuse, modify, and distribute their work – with others on generous terms. (Creative Commons 2005)

The content of the Internet is often criticized, but over time its quality will improve as more resources are digitized. Moves to digitize library holdings are underway, and Google is driving a project to digitize some major collections, including the New York Public Library and the Bodleian in Oxford. Google Print is also digitizing, for free, books in print from a variety of publishers, so that searches in Google will lead to the insides of the books. (Amazon has a similar scheme.) Links then offer ways of purchasing either the printed book or online access. Such developments have divided the publishing industry between those who welcome a new way of marketing their books and those fearful of the "Napsterization" of book publishing. If the digital files of books are readily available, will they start to be shared like music files?

This also presents a concern for those authors who need to make a living out of their writing. They are already questioning their share of the proceeds from digital delivery (Adams 2001). The instinct of publishers is to apply the same thinking as with print, i.e., a basic percentage of the proceeds goes to the author. But if the print cost disappears, authors will wonder why they cannot receive a larger share, perhaps equal to the publisher's income.

The Book's Digital Future

Advances in technology are producing a range of devices on which text can be read, and the possibility is that a dominant format will emerge. Digital technology has also revolutionized the production of printed books. Digital printing, as opposed to traditional offset printing, has changed the economics of book production, enabling genuine print on demand (single copies to order) as well as short runs (say, fifty copies). This facility has little relevance to the world of mass-market paperbacks, where large print-runs mean that the benefits of offset printing still apply, but it is of great interest to academic publishers and those who want to self-publish. John Thompson calls this a "fundamental change in the life cycle of the book" (2005: 436). Some publishers are bringing out-of-print works back into print, while others are keeping books going with sales of only a few copies a year (Taylor 2003). As an example, the whole Virago backlist of women's fiction is now available again in decent editions, whereas previously books had to achieve a minimum sale to stay in print. Publishers are no longer forced to put books that are selling only a few hundred copies a year out of print; they can build up orders and reprint, or use systems at wholesalers and the digital printers to supply copies on demand within a few days. Digital printing is also encouraging self-publishing. The author of a memoir unlikely to be taken on by a mainstream publisher can at low cost have it published by a third-party press or publish it him- or herself.

Chris Anderson (2004) writes of the "Long Tail," an effect apparent in the music and publishing industries. Usually retailers will carry only stock that can generate enough profit: the major book chains will return books that are not selling through in sufficient numbers within a certain period. Yet there are many more titles out there and the Internet provides a means of displaying and accessing them. Previous thinking has been dominated by the Pareto rule: 80 percent of sales come from 20 percent of the output. A few books are bestsellers; most are not. But what if that tail of misses extends a long way along the graph?

> Combine enough nonhits on the Long Tail and you've got a market bigger than hits . . . The average Barnes and Noble carries 130,000 titles. Yet more than half of Amazon's book sales come from outside its top 130,000 titles. Consider the implication: if the Amazon statistics are any guide, the market for books that are not even sold in the average book-store is larger than the market for those that are. (Anderson 2004)

The "Long Tail" could be supplied by delivery of online files or by books printed on demand. Anderson argues for everything to be made available – books should not go out of print – and for prices to be lowered to encourage consumers to visit the tapering end of the tail. Online delivery and print-on-demand could be especially useful in semi-developed nations like India or China, where books with a limited market (particularly academic books) are difficult to publish and distribute (Xin 2005).

A logical extension of print-on-demand at large production facilities would be the development of cheap point-of-sale machines. Jason Epstein sees a new order in which books will be printed and bound on demand by machines that "within minutes will inexpensively make single copies that are indistinguishable from books made in factories" (Epstein 2002: 178). These machines could be placed anywhere in the world, in bookshops, libraries, and universities, with access to an unlimited catalogue of titles over the Internet. An example of this technology is the Espresso Book Machine, which went on trial in 2006 at the World Bank's InfoShop in Washington. The machine can print and bind a 300-page paperback in three minutes.

The Resilience of Print

In the early 1990s, the printed word appeared to be facing a terminal crisis, viewed as "a noble anachronism crushed between televised entertainment and burgeoning electronic information sources" (Tenner 2004). Subsequently, the book has proved to be resilient in the face of challenges from other media, confounding the predictions of those who saw its replacement, while digital technology is providing mechanisms that enhance our ability to produce and distribute printed books (Staley 2003).

Some publishers have switched to other modes of delivering texts. Lexis-Nexis, part of Reed Elsevier, sold off its print operation in the area of law, and delivers a fast and reliable service to its customers online. Large reference works such as the *Oxford English Dictionary* and the *Dictionary of National Biography* (DNB) have moved online, offering superior search facilities and regular updating, giving access to an evolving title rather than a static edition. The *Encyclopaedia Britannica* abandoned door-to-door selling of print volumes in favor of offering a free service over the Web, trusting that advertising revenues would support its operations. This was in turn replaced by the current online subscription service. Yet the *Britannica* has revitalized its print offerings with a new print set as well as other reference works. The new edition of the *DNB* (2005) came out in print as well.

The number of new print titles published continues to grow in many countries around the world. In China, between 1992 and 2002, title output grew from around 90,000 to 170,000; in Brazil, between 1990 and 2000, the total rose from 13,000 to 45,000.

Print remains resilient because there is a continuing demand from consumers and it offers a model of publishing that publishers understand and know how to make work. They are comfortable with the book: the sale of a physical item yields a return against a predictable cost. A digital product can be highly creative but since there are no set boundaries, there are uncertainties over the costs involved and profitability is more difficult to control. Publishers remain fearful of digital piracy and copyright infringement.

There are anxious debates over the long-term decline in reading. How can this trend be reversed? Is it right to head downmarket? Should the industry reduce the number of titles published and reduce the clutter in the consumer's mind? As UK literary agent Caroline Michel has commented, "a Dickensian mix of wild optimism and gloomy despair does seem to characterise much of what is written and said about publishing nowadays" (Michel 2005).

Does the book have a future? As a portable and durable item of technology, it remains in good shape. It can be taken most places, read in bed or in the bath, and passed around friends with ease. The production standards of the average paperback are not high, but it can be sold at a highly competitive price. As a simple storage device, the book remains highly functional. You may not have the equipment to play a vinyl record from the 1960s or an 8-track from the 1970s, but you can still pick up Shakespeare's First Folio and read it. Print solves the archiving problem of the modern age, when formats change with great rapidity, and the pages of websites alter or disappear overnight.

For an author, appearing in print remains better than being published on the Web. There is an affirmation of one's worth as a writer, and receiving a beautifully printed hardback of one's work is an undeniable pleasure. For readers, print still holds out the prospect of disappearing into another world, away from computers, into a rich landscape of discovery and imagination. The book remains for some a status item, to be displayed prominently at home or carried around in public. The marketing campaign "Good Booking," run in the UK by Penguin Books in 2004, was based on research that men seen reading a book are more attractive to the opposite sex. The success of reading groups – one estimate is that there are 50,000 groups in the UK alone (Michel 2005) – reveals reading to be a social activity: we like to read, share, and discuss. The distinction can be drawn between "lean forward" technologies like the Internet, which are becoming the primary means to access information for work and education, and the "lean back" technology of the book, still important for enjoyment and relaxation (Adams 2001).

The book can also work with and alongside other media; for example, through cooperation with television shows that recommend titles. In virtual reading groups, readers discuss authors online and offer up new plot directions for their favorite titles. Published books may have their origins in blogs; textbooks offer added value on associated websites; a travel guide can include a mini-CD; and authors offer extra content on their own websites.

If the digital revolution poses new challenges to the book, it also offers fresh opportunities. The choice available on Amazon dwarfs that in any terrestrial bookshop, and new features on the Web enable browsing inside books as well as among the selection of titles available. The Web has stimulated the second-hand market in books, and shops that could not make a profit as physical entities have found a new lease of life online. Digital printing means that books no longer need go out of print. Genuine print-on-demand produces a single-copy reprint to each customer order. It could also enable customization to the customer's specification. Presently, it can provide large-print editions at economic prices – why not have your copy of *Pride and Prejudice* in the fount, type size, or binding of your choice? In the 1990s, Umberto Eco looked forward to a time when people could communicate directly without the intermediation of publishing houses:

A great many people do not want to publish; they simply want to communicate with each other. The fact that in the future they will do it by E-mail or over the Internet will be a great boon for books and for the culture and the market of the book. Look at a bookstore. There are too many books. I receive too many books every week. If the computer network succeeds in reducing the quantity of published books, this would be a paramount cultural improvement. (Eco 1996: 301)

In fact, more books are published than ever before, and the feasibility of short print-runs is stimulating self-publishing. For those with a novel or memoir bursting to be written, there is now a mechanism – and a publisher – who will help you to get into print. As Gabriel Zaid muses, if "our passion for writing goes unchecked, in the near future there will be more people writing books than reading them" (Zaid 2003: 9).

REFERENCES AND FURTHER READING

Adams, Douglas (2001) *The Hitchhiker's Guide to the Future*. BBC Radio 4, April 21 (available at www.bbc.co.uk/radio4/hhgttf).

Anderson, Chris (2004) "The Long Tail." *Wired*, 12.10 (October).

— (2006) *The Long Tail: Why the Future of Business is Selling Less of More*. New York: Hyperion.

Andrews, Amanda (2006) "Will Readers Do for Books what iPod Did for Music?" *The Times*, February 4.

British Library (2005) "British Library Predicts 'Switch to Digital by 2020.'" Press release, June 29 (available at http://www.bl.uk/news/pressreleases.html; accessed October 31, 2006).

Bury, Liz (2005) "Expanding the Book Market." Supplement to the *Bookseller*, March 11.

Cope, Bill and Phillips, Angus (2006) *The Future of the Book in the Digital Age*. Oxford: Chandos.

Creative Commons (2005) http://creativecommons. org (accessed October 31, 2006).

Eco, Umberto (1996) "Afterword." In Geoffrey Nurnberg (ed.), *The Future of the Book*, pp. 295–306. Berkeley: University of California Press.

Epstein, Jason (2002) *Book Business: Publishing Past, Present, and Future*. New York: W. W. Norton.

Feather, John (2003) *Communicating Knowledge: Publishing in the 21st Century*. Munich: Saur.

Greenslade, Roy (2004) "Why We Went Tabloid." *Guardian*, November 8.

Hampson, John and Richardson, Paul (2004) *Kitchen Table to Laptop: Independent Publishing in England*. London: Arts Council.

Hanajiri, Madoka (2003) "The Challenge of a Saturated Book Market in Japan." *Publishing Research Quarterly*, 19 (3): 52–9.

Institute for the Future of the Book website (available at www.futureofthebook.org/).

Kasdorf, William E. (2003) *The Columbia Guide to Digital Publishing*. New York: Columbia University Press.

Lessig, Lawrence (2004) *Free Culture*. New York: Penguin.

LISU (Library and Information Statistics Unit) (2004) *Annual Library Statistics 2004*. Loughborough: LISU.

McCurry, Justin (2005) "Mobiles Turn over a New Leaf among Japan's Youth." *Guardian*, March 25.

McEwan, Ian (2005) *Saturday*. London: Jonathan Cape.

Michel, Caroline (2005) "Follow Mr. Colman's Recipe". *Guardian*, March 5.

Nance, Kevin and Thomas, Mike (2004) "The End of Books?" *Chicago Sun–Times*, July 22.

National Endowment for the Arts (2004) *Reading at Risk: A Survey of Literary Reading in America*. Washington: National Endowment for the Arts.

National Statistics (2005) *Social Trends*. Basingstoke: Palgrave Macmillan.

Negroponte, Nicholas (1995) *Being Digital*. London: Hodder and Stoughton.

Phillips, Angus (2004) "Where is the Value in Publishing? The Internet and the Publishing Value Chain." *International Journal of the Book*, 2: 241–5.

Staley, David J. (2003) "The Future of the Book in a Digital Age." *Futurist*, September–October.

Taylor, David (2003) "Biggles and the Black Hole". *Bookseller*, June 13: 22–3.

Tenner, Edward (2004) "Rebound." *Boston Globe*, April 25.

Thompson, John B. (2005) *Books in the Digital Age*. Cambridge: Polity.

Tonkin, Boyd (2005) "A Week in Books." *Independent*, April 22.

Worlock, Kate (2004) "The Pros and Cons of Open Access" (available at www.nature.com/ nature/focus/accessdebate; accessed October 31, 2006).

Xin, Guangwei (2005) *Publishing in China*. Singapore: Thomson Asia.

Zaid, Gabriel (2003) *So Many Books*. London: Sort of Books.

Index

Page numbers in italic denote illustrations